Mathematics for Christian Living Series

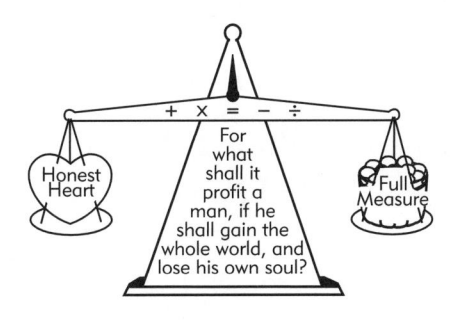

Honest Heart · Full Measure

For what shall it profit a man, if he shall gain the whole world, and lose his own soul?

Mathematics for Christian Living Series

Progressing With Arithmetic

Grade 4

Teacher's Manual

Part 1

Rod and Staff Publishers, Inc.
P.O. Box 3, Crockett, Kentucky 41413
Telephone: (606) 522-4348

Acknowledgments

We are indebted to God for the vision of the need for a *Mathematics for Christian Living Series* and for His enabling grace. Charitable contributions from many churches have helped to cover the expenses for research and development.

This revision was written by Sister Sandra Bauman. The brethren Marvin Eicher, Jerry Kreider, and Luke Sensenig served as editors. Brother Lester Miller and Brother Timothy Conley drew the illustrations. The work was evaluated by a panel of reviewers and tested by teachers in the classroom. Much effort was devoted to the production of the book. We are grateful for all who helped to make this book possible.

–The Publishers

Copyright, 1995

by

Rod and Staff Publishers, Inc.

P.O. Box 3, Crockett, Kentucky 41413

Printed in U.S.A.

ISBN 978-07399-0469-5

Catalog no. 13491.3

Materials for This Course

Books and Worksheets
- Pupil's textbook
- 2 Teacher's Manuals
- Speed Drills
- Tests
- 8 1/2" X 11" tablet, wide ruled

Teaching Aids
- Addition and Subtraction flash cards 0–18
- Multiplication and Division flash cards 0–12
- Real or play money
- Yardstick
- Meter stick
- Foot ruler for each child
- Metric ruler for each child
- Colored chalk
- Cardboard thermometer (with moveable mercury)

To The Teacher

God has called you to teach children about the orderly world He created. One evidence of His order is the field of arithmetic.

By Grade 4, students should have mastered the basic addition and subtraction facts and terminology. They should know how to carry in addition and how to borrow in subtraction. They should know the multiplication and division facts through the 9's, although they may not have complete mastery of them. Also, Grade 4 students should have been introduced to multiplication and division by one-digit numbers.

This Grade 4 course continues to review the basic facts and teaches the 10's, 11's, and 12's multiplication and division facts. It reviews carrying in addition, borrowing in subtraction, and multiplying and dividing by one-digit numbers. Other important areas of study are the introduction of two-digit multipliers, the long division process, and increased work with fractions and measures.

Mathematics is an orderly study. One fact leads to another. For example, understanding the basic addition facts leads one to understand more difficult addition as well as subtraction and multiplication. Use every opportunity you can to link a new mathematical concept to a fact that was learned before. Only as you do this will the pupils find mathematics to be the orderly and logical study it ought to be. "Precept must be [built] upon precept, . . . here a little, and there a little."

Mathematics is also an exact study. Part of its beauty and simplicity is that a number problem has only one correct answer. Number facts with their single, correct answers must be memorized exactly, in order to gain mastery of more difficult processes. Require your students to learn those facts thoroughly if they have not done so before Grade 4. Teach them to work accurately and carefully to the best of their ability. In requiring accuracy, you are doing more than teaching mathematics. You are helping to form a base from which a child gains a proper concept of a God who pays attention to exactness and detail.

Our goal is that mathematics would be a tool to help our children serve a holy God and become useful citizens of the world in which we live.

The Daily Lesson Plans

The lesson plans in the Teacher's Manual are provided as a base to teach the lessons effectively. They are an important part of this math course, especially in the review pattern. It is recommended that beginning teachers follow the plan as closely as their schedules allow.

Boldface type in the teacher's guide indicates words the teacher can say.

The daily lesson plans include the following parts.

Objectives are the primary goals of the lesson. If a concept is introduced for the first time in this math series, it is marked with a star.

Preparation lists what the teacher should prepare for class in addition to studying the lesson.

Oral Drill reviews and reinforces material that has already been taught, and it prepares students for learning new concepts. The time allowed for oral drill should be no more than 10 minutes.

Speed Drill is a short exercise that emphasizes speed and accuracy. Every second lesson includes a speed drill, which is found in a separate tablet. (Speed drill numbers agree with the lesson numbers.) Students are timed for two minutes, or three if the score is being recorded. Total class time for doing the speed drills and checking them should not exceed 5 minutes.

Teaching Guide is the core of the lesson. This part gives a step-by-step plan for meeting the lesson objectives; there is generally one point for each objective. This class-time work should prepare the pupils to do the lesson in the book with a minimum of teacher help. Plan to spend about 15 to 20 minutes on this part.

Chapter Review lessons do not have a separate *Oral Drill* section. *Teaching Guide* in those lessons reviews both mental and written skills. The parts that can be reviewed mentally are listed first, and the more time-consuming reviews are listed later.

Extra Review is optional practice included in some lessons for those teachers who need it. The concepts reviewed usually relate to some of the review exercises in the pupil's book.

Supplementary Drills for extra practice are provided in the back of the pupil's book. They are arranged according to skills to make it easy for the teacher to find material for special assignments. The teacher's manual lists suggested drills with the daily lessons for those who need additional work. Drills that exercise a new concept of the lesson are marked with an asterisk. Those marked with the symbols of the four processes (+ − × ÷) provide a steady diet of drill on the basic facts. Drills with no mark are review. The pages of multiplication and division facts with answers are for reference in studying the tables.

Generally, the written work to be assigned is all the numbered parts of the pupil's lesson. An occasional note to the teacher calls attention to possible snags.

Fitting the Lesson Plans to Your Classroom

These Grade 4 math lessons are designed for about 30 minutes of class time and 30 to 45 minutes of assigned work. Because of a broad range of teaching situations, teachers may find it necessary to alter the lesson plans.

Teachers of three or more grades may

need to decrease the half hour of class time and increase the amount of study time. In making such a reduction, the teacher must be careful to allow enough time to teach new material, but he must also be careful not to neglect the oral drill. Instead of cutting out parts of the oral work, keep each part brief. A well-organized drill can review many different areas of mathematics in only a few minutes.

A teacher of only fourth grade will probably want to spend more than half an hour in actual class time, taking more time with class drills and chalkboard exercises. Some of the pupil's lesson can be done in class, and the out-of-class assignment can be smaller.

In this math series, the multiplication facts through the 9's are taught in Grade 3 and are treated as review material in Grade 4. If you want to progress one lesson per day when you reach the lessons on multiplication, have your pupils begin studying the multiplication facts near the beginning of the year.

Flash Cards for the Course

To teach this course effectively, you should have a set of flash cards for each of the four operations of math (called math processes at this level). Buy flash cards from a school supplier, or make your own. Rod and Staff Publishers, Inc., has these cards available including the 10's, 11's, and 12's facts in multiplication and division. If your present sets do not have these, make them.

Other teacher-made flash cards can also be used for drill in this course. A very helpful set of four flash cards could be used to drill the terminology of the four processes (such as *addend, subtrahend,* and *factor*). Write a math problem on one side and the same problem with labels on the other side.

Make flash cards true to their name—*flash* cards. Show the card only briefly. Children should answer quickly and accurately.

Checking Student Assignments

Many teachers usually check arithmetic in class. The definite advantage of checking in class is that the pupil and teacher can both see what mistakes were made before beginning another assignment. The teaching plan of this book designates no time for checking the pupils' lessons, but a good time for checking is just before teaching the main points of the lesson (found in *Teaching Guide*). To cut down on checking time, have pupils always exchange papers in the same order. Say the answers clearly and not too fast. Do not repeat answers until you have finished reading them all.

Some teachers only "spot check" in class. They check only the first two examples in each row, only the new part of the last lesson, or only the parts they know pupils found difficult before. In this way they avoid using too much class time to check papers, and they still detect trouble spots in good time.

Fourth graders should be able to check each other's arithmetic papers accurately, but it is often a time-consuming process. For that reason, some teachers prefer collecting the papers and checking them after class to allow enough time for *teaching* in class, particularly if the lesson for the day is new or difficult. Other teachers assign arithmetic at the beginning of the day, collect the papers at the end of the day, and check them *before* the next arithmetic class. If you have many grades with only a few pupils in each one, you will probably want to do most of the checking out of class.

Even if lessons are checked in class, the teacher ought to collect the papers at least twice a week and look them over for accuracy. Grades need not be recorded on the other days.

Check each review lesson before the test period to ascertain needs for last-minute review and to allow maximum time for the test.

Scoring

In the daily lessons, some problems should count for more value than others. For example, reading problems and column addition or subtraction should carry more value than single-digit number facts. It is suggested that you assign one point each to the simple facts and two points to computation and reading problems. Long practice drills or very new material that is done largely in class should not be counted in the score at all.

For the speed drills, a certain number of points is assigned to each answer. The score is obtained by multiplying that number by the number wrong and subtracting from 100. This is done because many drills have just a few problems, and a strict percentage score would be unfair. In Speed Drill 6, for example, six points are assigned to each problem. If a pupil has 3 wrong, his score is 82 (3 × 6 = 18, and 100 - 18 = 82); whereas the score as a percent would be only 73 (8 correct out of 11). In this case, a pupil could get all the answers wrong and still have a score of 34—but that is obviously a failing score.

The speed drills should always be checked, but it is not necessary to record more than one speed drill grade per week. **On days when you record the grades, time the drills for three minutes instead of two,** unless everyone is finished before the time is up.

The chapter tests, like the speed drills, have a certain number of points assigned to each answer. Tests are arranged in the order of difficulty, beginning with simpler items valued at 1 point each and ending with more difficult items valued at 3 or 4 points each. To obtain the test score, multiply those points by the number wrong and subtract from 100.

At least two homework scores and one speed drill score should be recorded each week. These scores should be valued equally and counted as half of the final grade for a marking period. The test scores should count as the other half of the final grade.

Table of Contents

Numbers given first are pupil page numbers.
Numbers at the far right are actual manual page numbers printed at the bottom of the pages.

Chapter 1

Addition and Subtraction

1. Reviewing Addition 12 12
2. Carrying in Addition 14 16
3. More Carrying in Addition 16 20
4. Carrying in Column Addition 18 24
5. Reviewing Subtraction 20 28
6. Addition and Subtraction Families 22 32
7. Place Value to Ten Thousands 24 36
8. Reading and Writing Large Numbers 26 40
9. Chapter 1 Review 28 44
10. Chapter 1 Test (in test booklet) 437

Chapter 2

Subtraction With Borrowing

11. Borrowing in Subtraction 32 52
12. More Borrowing 34 56
13. Borrowing Twice 36 60
14. Subtracting From Zero 38 64
15. Working With Money 40 68
16. Adding and Subtracting Money 42 72

	17. Telling Time	44	76
	18. More About Time	46	80
	19. More Large Numbers	48	84
	20. Chapter 2 Review	50	88
	21. Chapter 2 Test (in test booklet)		439
Chapter 3 Multiplication Facts: 1–6	22. Regrouping in Addition	54	96
	23. Multiplication Facts: 1's, 2's, 3's	56	100
	24. Multiplying Two-Digit and Three-Digit Numbers	58	104
	25. Changing Units of Measure; Multiplication: 4's and 5's	60	108
	26. Carrying in Multiplication	62	112
	27. Multiplication Facts: 6's	64	116
	28. Roman Numerals	66	120
	29. More Roman Numerals	68	124
	30. Chapter 3 Review	70	128
	31. Chapter 3 Test (in test booklet)		441
Chapter 4 Division Facts: 1–6	32. Division Facts: 1's, 2's, 3's	74	136
	33. Introduction to Fractions	76	140
	34. Division Facts: 4's and 5's	78	144
	35. Units of Length	80	148
	36. Multiplication and Division Facts: 6's	82	152
	37. The Parts of a Division Problem	84	156
	38. The Steps in Division	86	160
	39. More Division With Remainders	88	164
	40. First Quarter Review	90	168
	41. Chapter 4 Test (in test booklet)		443
	Puzzle Page 1	94	176
Chapter 5 Multiplication and Division Facts: 7–9	42. Multiplication and Division Facts: 7's	96	180
	43. Dividing by 6 and 7	98	184
	44. Multiplication and Division Facts: 8's	100	188
	45. Changing Units of Measure	102	192
	46. Multiplication and Division Facts: 9's	104	196
	47. Multiplying Numbers by 10 or 100	106	200
	48. Multiplication With Zero in Ones' Place	108	204
	49. Multiplication With Zero in Tens' Place	110	208
	50. Chapter 5 Review	112	212
	51. Chapter 5 Test (in test booklet)		445
Chapter 6 Division With Two-Digit Quotients	52. Division With Two-Digit Quotients	116	220
	53. Two-Digit and Three-Digit Quotients	118	224
	54. Dividing to Get a Fraction	120	228
	55. Expressing Remainders as Fractions	122	232
	56. Checking Your Work	124	236
	57. Zeroes in Four-Digit Subtraction	126	240
	58. More Work With Money	128	244
	59. Chapter 6 Review	130	248
	60. Chapter 6 Test (in test booklet)		447

Chapter 7	61. More About Fractions......................134......256
More Fractions and Measures	62. Fractional Parts in a Whole................136......260
	63. Finding Equivalent Fractions by Multiplying...138......264
	64. Fractions on a Ruler........................140......268
	65. Measuring With Eighths on a Ruler..........142......272
	66. Finding Equivalent Fractions by Dividing....144......276
	67. Fractions in Changing Units of Measure.....146......280
	68. Helps for Solving a Reading Problem........148......284
	69. Chapter 7 Review..........................150......288
	70. Chapter 7 Test (in test booklet)..................449

Chapter 8	71. Another Kind of Long Division..............154......296
Long Division	72. More Long Division.........................156......300
	73. Two-Step Reading Problems.................158......304
	74. Long Division With Remainders in the Quotient...160......308
	75. Reducing Fractions to Lowest Terms.........162......312
	76. Remainders as Fractions in Lowest Terms...164......316
	77. Learning About Multiples....................166......320
	78. Learning More About Factors................168......324
	79. Midyear Review............................170......328
	80. Chapter 8 Test (in test booklet)..................451
	Puzzle Page 2..............................174......336

Supplementary Drills.................................359......339

Speed Drills 2–104...................................410

Tests 1–8..437

Handbook..431......455

Index...438......462

Contents of Book 2

Chapter 9   Large Numbers and Money

Chapter 10   Adding and Subtracting Measures

Chapter 11   Multiplication With Two-Digit Multipliers

Chapter 12   Adding and Subtracting Fractions

Chapter 13   Larger Quotients in Division

Chapter 14   Introduction to Decimals

Chapter 15   Bible and Metric Measures

Chapter 16   Division Facts: 10–12

Chapter 17   Dividing by Two-Digit Divisors and Year-End Review

                Supplementary Drills

                Speed Drills 48–168

                Tests 9–17

Chapter 1

Addition and Subtraction

Whatsoever thy hand findeth to do, do it with thy might.
(Ecclesiastes 9:10)

1. Reviewing Addition

Numbers are part of the orderly world that God created. We use numbers to count, to measure, and to tell time. Can you imagine going through a day without using numbers?

In fourth grade you will learn more about addition, subtraction, multiplication, and division—the four basic arithmetic processes. Here are some facts you should know about addition.

---

1. **Addition** is the mathematical process of putting numbers together.
2. The numbers added together are the **addends**, and the answer is the **sum**.
3. The **plus sign** tells you to add.
4. **Plus** means "added to" or "increased by."

$$\begin{array}{r} 27 \text{ addend} \\ \text{plus sign } + 12 \text{ addend} \\ \hline 39 \text{ sum} \end{array}$$

A. Do this exercise.

1. Turn to Drill 1 on page 362, and write the answers to the addition facts there. You should be able to write the answers in 4 minutes or less.
   If you have trouble with a fact, write it ten times on another paper.

B. *Copy these problems and add. Check by adding up.*

2.
13	10	23	33	54	64
+ 6	+ 9	+12	+36	+75	+43
19	19	35	69	129	107

3.
421	264	986	243	550	634
+ 68	+735	+ 12	+350	+327	+142
489	999	998	593	877	776

4.
184	235	382	637	965	642
+605	+451	+716	+501	+224	+605
789	686	1,098	1,138	1,189	1,247

LESSON 1

Objectives

- To review the terms related to addition.
- To drill the basic addition facts.
- To teach *horizontal addition of three addends (without carrying).
- To review addition of two- and three-digit numbers without carrying.

Preparation

1. Arithmetic textbooks
2. Addition flash cards
3. Chalkboard:

   a. 58   300   245   107   679   460

   b. 27   addend   c.   254
      +32   addend   +641
       59   sum   (895)

(Do not write answers given in parentheses.)

Oral Drill

1. Count by 2's, 5's, 10's, and 100's.
2. Read the numbers *(a)* on the board. **The names of the places are ones, tens, hundreds.** Point as you say the place names.

   Point to some of the numbers on the board, and ask how many ones, tens, or hundreds are in the number.

3. Drill the pupils' understanding of numbers. Ask questions such as the following: **What is 1 more than 58? What comes right after 300? right before? Which is more, 245 or 425? 170 or 107?**

4. Review telling time. **Look at the clock and tell what time it is. What time will it be in one hour? How long is it since 9:00?**

5. Give some simple story problems. Have students pick out the words which tell that the answer is found by adding. Do not stress the key words (italicized) when you read the problems.

   a. You have 2 cookies and your sister has 2. How many do you have *altogether*? (4 cookies)
   b. If 5 rabbits are in one pen and 6 are in another, what is the *total* number of rabbits? (11 rabbits)
   c. There are 3 girls and 4 boys in fourth grade. How many children *in all* are in fourth grade? (7 children)
   d. What is the *sum* of 6 and 3? (9)

T–13   Chapter 1   Addition and Subtraction

Teaching Guide

Pass out the books, and have pupils look through them briefly. Point out that each lesson covers two pages. Items within boxes are important directions or things to remember. Fact drills are at the back of the book.

1. *Addition terminology.*
   Point to addition problem *b* on the board. **The numbers added together are called** (addends), **and the answer is the** (sum). **The process of putting things together is called** (addition).

2. *Addition facts.*
   a. Drill addition flash cards in mixed order.
   b. Exercise 1 could be done in class. Help the pupils to find Drill 1 in the back of the book. Have them try to write the answers to the hundred addition facts in 4 minutes or less. You may want to teach them how to use folded paper on fact pages like this.

3. *Horizontal addition of three addends.*
   a. Say three numbers and have students add them mentally. Give only problems in which the sum of the first two addends is less than 10.
      3 + 6 + 8 (17)   1 + 7 + 6 (14)
      4 + 5 + 2 (11)   6 + 2 + 5 (13)
   b. **The addition facts can help us do harder problems than these. How much is 2 + 3? If 2 + 3 is 5, then how much is 12 + 3? 12 + 3 ends with 5 because 2 + 3 is 5. What is 22 + 3?** Emphasize *twenty* as you say it. **32 + 3? 42 + 3? How much is 4 + 4? 14 + 4? 34 + 4?...**

      If the pupils have difficulty answering, write the numbers *horizontally* on the board as you say them. Watch for pupils who catch the pattern of 10's, 20's, 30's, and so on, without thinking what numbers you say. Skip some numbers in the sequence to avoid this problem.
      24 + 3 (27)   16 + 2 (18)
      41 + 5 (46)   32 + 7 (39)

4. *Adding two- and three-digit numbers.*
   a. Point to addition problem *c* on the board. **How do we find the answer to this problem? Add ones to ones, tens to tens, . . .**
   b. Together work through problem *c* on the board. **Always begin adding at the right side of a problem. Always add ones to ones, . . .**
   c. The following problems may be used for individual practice at the board or on paper.

14	52	82
+ 65	+ 31	+ 47
(79)	(83)	(129)

626	842	947
+ 302	+ 315	+ 521
(928)	(1,157)	(1,468)

   Note: If you have a half day of school on the first day, you could have the pupils do only exercise 1 for the day's assignment.

Supplementary Drill

Drill 1 +

Lesson 1

C. *Copy these addition problems, and find the answers. Beside each part write* addend *or* sum.

5.   43 addend   361 addend   23 addend
   + 26 addend   + 325 addend   42 addend
     69 sum   686 sum   + 53 addend
                                              118 sum

D. *Add these numbers down. Check by adding up. Write only the answers on your paper.*

6.   3   6   4   2   4   5   7   3
     4   3   2   7   3   4   2   5
   + 2   + 5   + 6   + 1   + 5   + 4   + 6   + 4
     9   14   12   10   12   13   15   12

E. *Write only the answers. Use the addition facts to help you.*

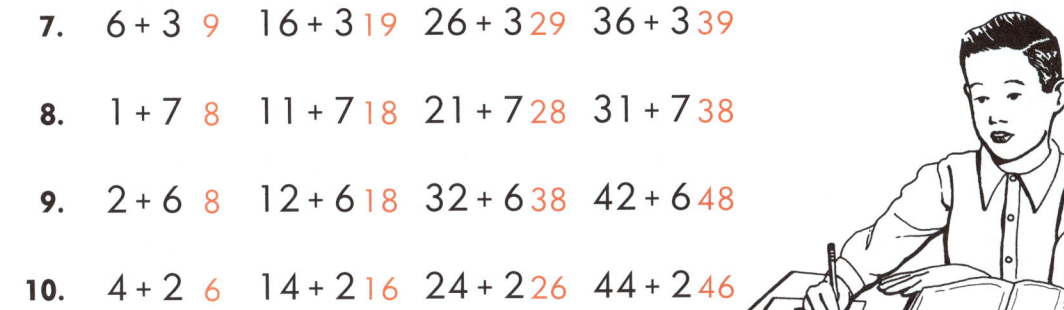

7. 6 + 3 9   16 + 3 19   26 + 3 29   36 + 3 39

8. 1 + 7 8   11 + 7 18   21 + 7 28   31 + 7 38

9. 2 + 6 8   12 + 6 18   32 + 6 38   42 + 6 48

10. 4 + 2 6   14 + 2 16   24 + 2 26   44 + 2 46

11. 11 + 5 16   12 + 3 15   15 + 3 18   13 + 5 18

F. *Solve these reading problems. Write the arithmetic problem and the answer neatly on your paper. Be careful! They are not all addition problems.*

12. One day Jeremy read 26 verses in his Bible. The next day he read 31 verses. How many verses did he read altogether?   57 verses

13. On the first day of school there were 12 boys and 14 girls in Maria's classroom. How many children were there in all?   26 children

14. Fourteen girls is how many more children than 12 boys?   2 children

14　Chapter 1　Addition and Subtraction

2. Carrying in Addition

If an addition problem has more than two addends, use the basic facts to find the answers.

> To add:　7
> 　　　　　6
> 　　　　+ 5
>
> Think:　7 + 6 = 13
> 　　　　13 + 5 = 18
>
> The answer is 18.

A. *Write only the answers.*

1.
5	6	4	3	5	8	7	9
8	7	4	8	4	9	3	7
+ 3	+ 2	+ 9	+ 6	+ 8	+ 2	+ 6	+ 1
16	15	17	17	17	19	16	17

2.
8	2	4	9	8	6	3	7
8	9	6	3	7	9	3	7
+ 3	+ 5	+ 5	+ 6	+ 4	+ 2	+ 7	+ 4
19	16	15	18	19	17	13	18

Remember that you start at the right side to add larger numbers. Sometimes the answer for the ones' column is more than 9. Then you must carry the tens' part of the answer to the tens' column and add it to the tens. If the tens' column is more than 9, you must carry to the hundreds' column.

> 　1
> 　47
> + 25
> ――――
> 　72
>
> Carry 1 ten to the tens' column.
>
> 　1
> 　463
> + 381
> ――――
> 　844
>
> Carry 1 hundred to the hundreds' column.
>
> Can you tell all the steps to solve the problems?

B. *Copy and add down. Check by adding up.*

3.
57	25	19	65	76	39
+ 26	+ 49	+ 58	+ 29	+ 48	+ 69
83	74	77	94	124	108

LESSON 2

Objectives

- To review the carrying process in addition.
- To review the use of key facts in horizontal addition.
- To introduce *column addition in which a one-digit number is mentally added to a two-digit number.

Preparation

1. Addition flash cards
2. Speed Drill 2
3. Chalkboard:

   a. 200   2,000   2,001   2,010   2,211
       306   8,634   5,967   6,000   3,674
       2,560 4,695 6,701 1,246

   b. 68   c. 47   d. 284
      +25   + 66   +523
      ─────   ─────   ─────
       93   (113)   (807)

(Do not write answers given in parentheses.)

Oral Drill

1. Flash addition facts in mixed order.
2. Count by 10's to 200; by 100's to 2,000; by 1's from 990 to 1,010.
3. Have pupils read the numbers (a) on the board. **What does the 6 stand for in each number in the second row?**
4. Review telling time. **What time is it now? What time was it an hour ago? How long will it be until recess? Until lunch?**

   Do not labor over the concept of time now if the children have difficulty. At this point you are finding out what they know. Later, time will be taught in the main part of the lesson.

5. Drill oral addition.

4 + 5 + 3 (12)	6 + 1 + 9 (16)
3 + 4 + 7 (14)	7 + 2 + 9 (18)
3 + 2 + 8 (13)	4 + 4 + 9 (17)
3 + 5 + 6 (14)	2 + 5 + 6 (13)

6. Review addition terminology. Have the children identify the addends and sum of addition problem b on the board. *Then erase the sum.*

7. Review pairs of addition facts. **Addition facts are in pairs. If you know the answer to 6 + 5, you know the answer to 5 + 6.**
   a. **If 9 + 3 is 12, what is 3 + 9?**
   b. **What fact pairs with 3 + 7 = 10?**
   c. **What two addition facts can be made from the numbers 4, 7, and 11?**

Speed Drill

Pass out Speed Drill 2 (addition facts). All students should look at you and raise their hands with their pencils until you give the signal to begin. After two minutes say: **Stop. Exchange papers and check.**

T–15   Chapter 1   Addition and Subtraction

Teaching Guide

1. *Carrying in addition.*
   a. Point to addition problem *b* on the board. **How many tens and ones are in 68 and 25?**
   b. **When we add, we add the ones first. How much is 8 plus 5?** Point to the digits, and have pupils respond.
   c. **The answer 13 has more than one digit.** Write 13 beside the problem. **It has how many tens and ones? We do not write 13 below the 8 and 5. We write only the ones part of 13—the 3.** Write 3. **We carry the tens part—the 1—to the tens' column.** Write 1 above the tens' digits. **Now we add 1, 6, and 2. The answer for the tens' column is 9.** Write 9. **How much is 68 plus 25?** (93)

      If the sum in any column is more than 9, we must carry to the next column.
   d. Point to problems *c* and *d* on the board, and have two volunteers solve them. Note that the sums of both problems have three digits.
   e. Dictate some of the problems below for pupils to solve at the board. If your class is large, have some work on paper at their seats while others work at the board.

   ```
    49    53    89    363   274
   +25   +17   +27  +628  +364
   ────  ────  ────  ────  ────
   (74)  (70) (116) (991) (638)

    78    46    99
    24    38    15
   +43   +27   +56
   ────  ────  ────
  (145) (111) (170)
   ```

   f. Turn to Lesson 2 in the book, and read the text above Part B together. Have someone explain the steps in solving the problems in the following box.

2. *Key facts in horizontal addition.*
   Give students these numbers to add mentally. Ask what key facts help them find the answers.

   12 + 3 (15)   12 + 6 (18)
   12 + 4 (16)   12 + 7 (19)
   14 + 5 (19)   16 + 1 (17)
   11 + 6 (17)   13 + 5 (18)

3. *Harder column addition.*
   Call attention to the first box in the lesson, and discuss the information given. Give some three-addend problems for pupils to do mentally. Give two addends, pause, then give the third. If pupils have trouble adding the third number mentally, prompt them to think of the basic fact involved.

   Example: What is 2 + 5? Then what is 12 + 5?

   4 + 8 + 5 (17)   8 + 2 + 4 (14)
   6 + 5 + 4 (15)   7 + 3 + 6 (16)
   8 + 3 + 3 (14)   8 + 7 + 4 (19)

Supplementary Drills

Drill 55*

Drill 57*

4.	33	69	76	24	14	15
	42	10	12	43	82	22
	+ 27	+ 41	+ 46	+ 15	+ 31	+ 66
	102	120	134	82	127	103
5.	685	746	965	324	515	
	+ 374	+ 139	+ 27	+ 184	+ 366	
	1,059	885	992	508	881	
6.	325	307	267	342	475	
	+ 68	+ 463	+ 329	+ 397	+ 19	
	393	770	596	739	494	

Review Exercises

C. *Write only the answers.*

7. 7 + 2   9   17 + 2   19   37 + 2   39   47 + 2   49

8. 15 + 3 18   13 + 4   17   12 + 6   18   11 + 4   15

9. 15 + 4 19   21 + 3   24   15 + 2   17   10 + 7   17

10. 20 + 5 25   11 + 8   19   30 + 6   36   21 + 5   26

D. *Copy and solve these addition problems. Beside each number write* **addend** *or* **sum.**

11.   46   addend   368   addend
      13   addend   + 218   addend
    + 17   addend   586   sum
      76   sum

E. *Addition facts go in pairs. If 9 + 4 = 13, then 4 + 9 = 13. What are the missing numbers?*

12. a. 8 + 9 = 17, so 9 + 8 = __17__   b. 7 + 6 = __13__, so 6 + 7 = __13__

13. a. 16 + 5 = __21__, so 5 + 16 = __21__   b. 27 + 43 = 70, so 43 + 27 = __70__

F. *Using the rule given in Part E write two addition facts for each set of numbers.*

14. a. 6, 5, 11   b. 7, 8, 15   c. 4, 6, 10   d. 3, 9, 12

     6   5   7   8   4   6   3   9
   +5 +6   +8 +7   +6 +4   +9 +3
   11   11   15   15   10   10   12   12

16   Chapter 1   Addition and Subtraction

3. More Carrying in Addition

Sometimes you need to carry twice in the same addition problem. Study the example in the box.

> ```
>   1 1
>   345      Think:  5 + 9 = 14.  Write 4 and carry 1.
> + 289             1 + 4 + 8 = 13.  Write 3 and carry 1.
> -----             1 + 3 + 2 = 6.  Write 6.
>   634
> ```

A. *Copy and add. You may need to carry twice.*

1. 738   574   807   951   425
   +473   +693   +285   +957   +984
   ----   ----   ----   ----   ----
   1,211   1,267   1,092   1,908   1,409

2. 685   912   369   933   126
   +717   +869   +874   + 28   +589
   ----   ----   ----   ----   ----
   1,402   1,781   1,243   961   715

3. 480   393   209   335   776
   +142   +871   +874   +987   + 88
   ----   ----   ----   ----   ----
    622   1,264   1,083   1,322   864

4. 246   445   162   431   52
    321   213   27   245   426
   +325   + 46   +532   +274   +198
   ----   ----   ----   ----   ----
    892   704   721   950   676

B. *Write the answers only. Add the columns in your head.*

5.   6   9   7   4   3   8   8   5
     5   4   3   5   8   7   6   7
    +7   +5   +6   +8   +4   +2   +5   +4
    --   --   --   --   --   --   --   --
    18   18   16   17   15   17   19   16

LESSON 3

Objectives

- To review carrying twice in addition.
- To teach carrying mentally in more difficult column addition and *in horizontal addition.

Preparation

1. Addition and subtraction flash cards
2. Chalkboard:

   a. 3,042   6,250   4,006
      5,101   2,070   8,099

   b.   589   c.   487
      +624   +356
     (1,213)   (843)

   d. 7 + 2   17 + 2   27 + 2
        7 + 3   17 + 3   27 + 3
        7 + 4   17 + 4   27 + 4

Oral Drill

1. Drill addition flash cards in mixed order. Concentrate on the facts that the children do not know as well.

2. Drill subtraction flash cards in mixed order. **Subtraction is the opposite of addition. Knowing the addition facts well helps you with subtraction.** If your pupils seem very "rusty," concentrate on the easier facts with minuends of 10 or less.

3. Give mental drill with addition and subtraction.

   9 + 3   9 – 3
   10 + 4   10 – 4
   12 + 5   12 – 5
   3 + 5 + 9 (17) 7 + 2 + 4 (13)
   6 + 1 + 5 (12) 6 + 4 + 7 (17)
   5 + 8 + 4 (17) 6 + 6 + 3 (15)
   7 + 8 + 5 (20) 9 + 7 + 6 (22)

4. Discuss pairs of addition facts. Show one flash card, such as 4 + 8. Ask for the other addition fact in that pair.

5. **In an addition problem, the numbers being added are called** (addends). **The answer is the** (sum).

6. Have the children read the numbers (a) on the board. **What do the zeroes stand for in each number? If zero means "none," why must the numbers have zeroes?** (Zeroes are written to show that there are *none* in those places. The zeroes keep the other digits in their places.)

Chapter 1 Addition and Subtraction

Teaching Guide

1. *Carrying twice in addition.*
   a. Have pupils open their books to Lesson 3 and look at the example in the first box. **How many understand how to solve this kind of problem?**
   b. Point to problem *b* on the board. Ask the children to tell you one step at a time how to find the answer. Do what they tell you in the order they say. Then ask how many agree that the answer is right. If you do something wrong and no one catches the mistake by the time you finish writing the answer, be sure to point it out before going on.
   c. Solve problem *c* on the board. Give the following reminders.
      (1) Always start adding in the ones' place.
      (2) Write the ones' digit of the answer in each column.
      (3) If there is a tens' digit, carry it to the next place.
      (4) Be sure to add correctly.
      (5) Do not carry unless it is necessary.

2. *Carrying mentally.*
   a. Point to the horizontal addition problems (*d*) on the board. **What is 7 + 2? 17 + 2? 27 + 2? How does the key fact, 7 + 2, help us find the other answers?** (The others end with the same digit.)
   b. Now look at the next row. **What is 7 + 3? Then 17 + 3 ends with 0, but the tens' place is one more than 10. What is 17 + 3? 27 + 3? How is this row different from the first row?** (The tens' place changes also; we need to carry.) **The answer to the key fact is more than 9, so we need to carry for the answer.**
   c. **What is 7 + 4? 7 + 4 is 11, so 17 + 4 ends with 1. The tens' place is one more than the tens' place in 11. How much is 17 + 4? 27 + 4? How does the key fact help you to find the other answers?** (They all end with the same digit.)
   d. Give more oral problems such as the ones below. Encourage children to use key facts to find answers rather than counting to add the second addend. Expect that it will take some pupils a little while to do this well. If any pupils have trouble, let them write the problems vertically and carry without writing the carried digit.

      16 + 5 (21)   18 + 4 (22)
      17 + 6 (23)   16 + 8 (24)
      25 + 7 (32)   24 + 6 (30)
      28 + 5 (33)   26 + 6 (32)

   e. Have pupils go to the board for some practice with addition. Include some problems with three addends.

      ```
        268      542      767
       +899     +379     +668
      (1,167)   (921)   (1,435)
      ```

      ```
                725      369
        593     446      283
       +775    +263     +125
      (1,368) (1,434)   (777)
      ```

Supplementary Drills

Drill 54*

Drill 60*

Can you carry in your head? Knowing the basic facts will help you. Study this example.

> 17 + 4 = ?
>
> Think: 7 + 4 = 11.
> 7 + 4 ends with 1.
> 17 + 4 must also end with 1.
> You must carry 1 to the tens' place.
> 17 + 4 = 21

C. *Write the answers only. The first one in each row is a key fact to help you find the others.*

6. 2 + 8 **10**   12 + 8 **20**   22 + 8 **30**   32 + 8 **40**
7. 5 + 7 **12**   15 + 7 **22**   25 + 7 **32**   35 + 7 **42**
8. 9 + 6 **15**   19 + 6 **25**   29 + 6 **35**   39 + 6 **45**
9. 8 + 4 **12**   18 + 4 **22**   38 + 4 **42**   58 + 4 **62**
10. 9 + 2 **11**   29 + 2 **31**   39 + 2 **41**   49 + 2 **51**

D. *Follow the directions.*

11. Write the key fact that will help you find each answer.

    a. 27 + 5   b. 33 + 7   c. 16 + 6   d. 28 + 3
       7 + 5 = 12   **3 + 7 = 10**   **6 + 6 = 12**   **8 + 3 = 11**

12. Add 3 to each number below. Write only the answers.

    8 **11**   12 **15**   17 **20**   9 **12**   18 **21**   14 **17**   20 **23**   29 **32**

13. Add 4 to each number. Write only the answers.

    6 **10**   14 **18**   20 **24**   18 **22**   9 **13**   19 **23**   16 **20**   11 **15**

E. *Solve these reading problems.*

14. The Graber family went on a trip to visit their cousins in Texas. They traveled 578 miles on Monday and 423 miles on Tuesday. How many miles did they travel altogether on the two days?   **1,001 miles**

15. How many more miles did the Graber family travel on Monday than on Tuesday? (See number 14.)   **155 miles**

16. On the first day, Darvin and Janell counted license plates on cars. They counted 65 from Ohio, 39 from Pennsylvania, and 12 from Indiana. How many was that in all?   **116 plates**

18 Chapter 1 Addition and Subtraction

4. Carrying in Column Addition

In column addition, you must sometimes carry in your head. Knowing the basic facts will help you. Study this example.

```
   2
  26     Think: 6 + 7 = 13; 13 + 8 = ?
  37            3 + 8 ends with 1.
+ 18            13 + 8 must also end with 1.
 ———           13 + 8 = 21
  81            You must carry 2 to the tens' place.
                2 + 2 = 4;  4 + 3 = 7;  7 + 1 = 8
```

A. *Write the answers only. See how quickly and accurately you can do this.*

1. 8   5   9   3   7   9   6   8
   +7   +9   +9   +8   +9   +6   +7   +5
   ——   ——   ——   ——   ——   ——   ——   ——
   15   14   18   11   16   15   13   13

2. 12 + 3 **15**   15 + 5 **20**   14 + 5 **19**   16 + 7 **23**   13 + 8 **21**

3. 16 + 5 **21**   18 + 4 **22**   17 + 3 **20**   14 + 6 **20**   15 + 7 **22**

B. *Some of these problems are harder than those in Lesson 3. You may need to carry in your head. Write the answers only.*

4. 8   4   9   3   6   8   7   5
    4   6   3   7   6   7   5   9
   +3   +8   +7   +6   +9   +5   +4   +8
   ——   ——   ——   ——   ——   ——   ——   ——
   15   18   19   16   21   20   16   22

5. 8   5   9   6   7   9   8   5
    6   7   9   9   8   5   4   8
   +7   +8   +4   +7   +9   +6   +7   +6
   ——   ——   ——   ——   ——   ——   ——   ——
   21   20   22   22   24   20   19   19

C. *Copy and find the answers. You will need to carry once or twice.*

6. 357   542   767   593   725
  + 429   + 379   + 668   + 775   + 964
   ———   ———   ———   ———   ———
   786   921   1,435   1,368   1,689

7. 777   258   346   748   369
    436   846   785   383   746
  + 245   + 104   + 23   + 458   + 322
  ————   ————   ————   ————   ————
  1,458   1,208   1,154   1,589   1,437

LESSON 4

Objectives

- To introduce *carrying within columns in column addition.
- To teach the recognition of key words in reading problems solved by addition.

Preparation

1. Addition and subtraction flash cards
2. Speed Drill 4
3. Chalkboard:

   a. 7 + 5   17 + 5   27 + 5
      7 + 6   17 + 6   37 + 6

   b.

4	5	3	7	9
4	8	7	6	8
+6	+6	+9	+8	+5
(14)	(19)	(19)	(21)	(22)

   c. James and Michael are collecting stamps. James has 359 and Michael has 425.

Oral Drill

1. Drill subtraction flash cards.
2. Review *addend* and *sum*.
3. Give mental drill with addition and subtraction.

8 + 7	8 − 7	11 + 6
11 − 6	13 + 5	13 − 5
12 + 6	12 + 8	13 + 4
13 + 7	16 + 6	14 + 6
14 + 7	19 + 6	16 + 8
18 + 4	17 + 3	15 + 8

4. Drill the more difficult addition flash cards.
5. Review using key facts to carry mentally. Use the horizontal problems *(a)* on the board to drill this concept as in Lesson 3.

Speed Drill

Give Speed Drill 4 (addition facts).

T–19 Chapter 1 Addition and Subtraction

Teaching Guide

1. *Carrying within columns in column addition.*
   a. Add the columns *(b)* on the board. Quite often column addition requires carrying mentally, as in the last several columns. Horizontal addition, as in the *a* problems, helps to prepare students for this kind of column addition.
   b. Use the following problems for more mental practice. You could do the work at the board, but have pupils write answers only. Give extra help to those who need it. Allow them to *write* what they think (such as 11 + 5).

4 + 7 + 5 (16)	8 + 7 + 6 (21)
5 + 7 + 8 (20)	9 + 9 + 5 (23)
7 + 7 + 7 (21)	6 + 5 + 9 (20)
8 + 8 + 7 (23)	6 + 9 + 7 (22)
6 + 7 + 4 (17)	8 + 6 + 6 (20)
7 + 9 + 6 (22)	9 + 8 + 7 (24)

   c. If the pupils are at the board already, give them a few problems, such as these, to review carrying in addition.

   ```
     684      386      515
   + 69     +475     +366
   (753)    (861)    (881)


              276      364
    267      159      287
   +329     +382     +983
   (596)    (817)   (1,634)
   ```

2. *Key words in reading problems solved by addition.*
   a. Point to the "reading problem" *(c)* on the board. **Is this really a problem?** (No, it does not ask a question.) Now add this question: How many stamps did they have together? **What do we need to do to find the answer? What are some other ways of asking the same question?**
   b. Turn to the second page of Lesson 4 and read the questions in the box, noting the key words. **The words *altogether, both, total, in all,* and *sum* in reading problems usually mean addition is needed.**
   c. Give a few simple problems, such as the ones below. Have pupils say the answers and tell how they got each one.
      • Janet has 1 doll and Julia has 2. How many do they have when they play together? (3 dolls; add)
      • If you pay 20¢ for a comb and 30¢ for a ball, how much do you spend in all? (50¢; add)
      • What is the total number of pupils in a Sunday school class of 4 boys and 5 girls? (9 pupils; add)
   d. If you have not already done so, show the pupils how you want them to set up reading problems on their papers. You should insist that they write the whole problems, not just the answers, and that they label their answers.

Note: If your slower students have difficulty obtaining correct answers for numbers 4 and 5, allow them to write the mental carrying step on scrap paper. (Encourage them to carry without writing the carried digit.) At this point it is more important to be accurate than to do all the work mentally.

Supplementary Drills

Drill 62*

Drill 61

Key Words in Reading Problems

One Sunday Marsha put 25 cents in the offering. The next Sunday she put 50 cents in the offering.

How much did Marsha give **altogether**?
How much did she give on **both** Sundays?
What was the **total** that Marsha gave?
How much did she give **in all**?
What was the **sum** of her offerings?

All the questions above ask the same thing. To find the answers, you **add**. The words in bold print are **key words** that help you know that you should add. Watch for these key words when you solve reading problems.

D. *Solve these problems. Write both the problem and the answer on your paper. Label your answers. Be ready to tell what key words helped you to know that you should add.*

8. David and Daniel helped Father hoe the tomato rows. Father hoed 16 rows, Daniel hoed 13 rows, and David hoed 7. How many rows did they hoe altogether?   36 rows

9. The Groves had 325 chickens in one house and 565 in another house. What was the total number of chickens?   890 chickens

10. After dinner Ruby washed 14 cups, 39 pieces of silverware, and 11 plates. How many pieces did Ruby wash in all?   64 pieces

11. Find the sum of 784 and 529.   1,313

12. Last week Donald picked 75 baskets of apples. This week he picked 150 baskets. How many baskets did he pick in both weeks?   225 baskets

13. Karl has a job mowing lawns. One day he earned $2.25, another day he earned $1.25, and the third day he earned $3.00. How much did he earn in all? $6.50

14. Father said Karl may use his earnings to buy a present for his neighbor boy. Karl wants to buy a baseball glove for $5.75 and a ball for $1.50. How much will it take to pay for them both? $7.25

Review Exercises

E. *Write two addition facts for each set of numbers.*

15. a. 12, 5, 7   b. 6, 8, 14   c. 6, 15, 9

$$\begin{array}{r} 5 \\ +7 \\ \hline 12 \end{array} \quad \begin{array}{r} 7 \\ +5 \\ \hline 12 \end{array} \qquad \begin{array}{r} 6 \\ +8 \\ \hline 14 \end{array} \quad \begin{array}{r} 8 \\ +6 \\ \hline 14 \end{array} \qquad \begin{array}{r} 6 \\ +9 \\ \hline 15 \end{array} \quad \begin{array}{r} 9 \\ +6 \\ \hline 15 \end{array}$$

Chapter 1 Addition and Subtraction

5. Reviewing Subtraction

Subtraction is the second of the four basic processes of arithmetic. Subtraction is the opposite of addition. Add 3 + 4. You get 7. Now subtract 7 − 4. You are back to the first number—3.

Here are some important facts you should know about subtraction.

> 1. **Subtraction** is the mathematical process of taking one number away from another.
>
> 2. The number you subtract from is the **minuend**. The number you take away is the **subtrahend**. The answer is the **difference**.
>
> $$\begin{array}{r} 14 \\ -\ 6 \\ \hline 8 \end{array}$$ minuend
>   subtrahend
>   difference
>
>   (minus sign points to −6)
>
> 3. The **minus sign** tells you to subtract. **Minus** means "take away."

A. *Do this exercise.*

1. Turn to Drill 3 in the back of the book, and write the answers to the subtraction facts there, You should be able to write the answers in 4 minutes or less.

    If you have trouble with a fact, write it ten times on another paper.

B. *Copy these problems, and find the answers. Subtract ones from ones, tens from tens, and hundreds from hundreds.*

2.
18	14	28	68	53	49
− 6	− 12	− 14	− 27	− 21	− 5
12	2	14	41	32	44

3.
580	695	398	629	497	508
− 360	− 444	− 75	− 506	− 375	− 203
220	251	323	123	122	305

4.
996	485	734	582	659	741
− 632	− 143	− 413	− 411	− 328	− 721
364	342	321	171	331	20

LESSON 5

Objectives

- To drill the subtraction facts, especially those with minuends of 10 or less.
- To show the relationship between addition and subtraction.
- To review the terms related to subtraction.
- To review subtraction of two- and three-digit numbers without borrowing.

Preparation

1. Addition and Subtraction facts
   Separate the Addition facts and Subtraction facts into two sets for each process. Have facts with sums (or minuends) of 10 or less in one set, and those with sums (minuends) of more than 10 in another.

2. Chalkboard:

   a. 8,000   8,001   8,100   8,010
       8,101   8,011   8,111

   b. 26 minuend (sum)
       −14 subtrahend (addend)
       12 difference or remainder (addend)

Oral Drill

1. Drill the harder addition facts.
2. Count by 2's to 40; by 5's to 100. Count by 1's from 990 to 1,010.
3. Review place value. Read the numbers *(a)* on the board.
4. Give mental drill with addition.

3 + 7 + 8 (18)	4 + 8 + 5 (17)
6 + 8 + 7 (21)	5 + 6 + 8 (19)
3 + 9 + 7 (19)	8 + 7 + 5 (20)
6 + 9 + 7 (22)	9 + 8 + 4 (21)
8 + 5 + 9 (22)	9 + 7 + 4 (20)
5 + 4 + 8 (17)	7 + 4 + 9 (20)

5. **In these reading problems, which words tell you to add?**
   a. If Mary baked 100 cookies and Sue baked 85 cookies, how many cookies did they both bake? (both)
   b. What is the sum of 16 and 4? (sum)
   c. One village has a population of 320. A neighboring village has a population of 450. What is the total population of the two towns? (total)

Chapter 1 Addition and Subtraction

Teaching Guide

1. *Subtraction facts.*
   a. Drill with flash cards, concentrating on those with minuends of 10 or less, unless pupils seem to know those very well.
   b. Exercise 1 could be done in class. Have pupils try to answer the hundred subtraction facts in 4 minutes or less. If they have any facts wrong, tell them to write those facts with the answers at least ten times.

2. *Relationship between addition and subtraction.*
   Subtraction is the opposite of (addition). **If 2 + 3 = 5, what is 5 − 3? What is 4 + 3? 7 − 3? 8 + 4? 12 − 4? Subtraction "undoes" what addition does. It takes away what addition puts on.**

3. *Subtraction terminology.*
   a. **In addition, the numbers added are called** (addends). **The answer is the** (sum).
   b. **In a subtraction problem, the *first* number is the sum of the other two. So it could be called the sum. But the numbers have different names.** Call attention to the terms that go with the subtraction problem *(b)* on the board. Then erase the difference.
   c. Have the pupils open their books to Lesson 5. Read the information in the box. Then have them name the various parts of the problems in row 2 of the exercises. **(Which is the minuend? Which is the subtrahend? . . .)**

4. *Subtracting two- and three-digit numbers.*
   a. Discuss the problem on the board. Start with the ones' place. Subtract ones from ones. **The bottom number is *always* subtracted *from* the top number.**
   b. After subtracting the ones, subtract tens from tens, and then hundreds from hundreds. Keep columns straight.
   c. Use the following problems for individual practice. The problems in this lesson do not involve borrowing, so they are not difficult for most beginning fourth graders.

```
   75      84      59
 −  3    −42     −24
 (72)    (42)    (35)

  491    872     548
 − 81   −610    −517
 (410)  (262)    (31)
```

Supplementary Drills

Drill 68*

Drill 3 −

Lesson 5   21

C. *Copy these subtraction problems, and find the answers. Then write the correct label beside each part.*

5.   85 minuend   930 minuend   567 minuend
   − 13 subtrahend   − 520 subtrahend   − 40 subtrahend
     72 difference   410 difference   527 difference

Because subtraction is the opposite of addition, addition facts help you to know subtraction facts. If 5 + 5 = 10, then 10 − 5 = 5. If 7 + 9 = 16, then 16 − 9 = 7.

D. *Use the addition problems to find the answers to the following subtraction problems. Write the answers on your paper.*

6. a. 7 + 4 = 11; so 11 − 4 = __7__   b. 8 + 6 = 14; 14 − 6 = __8__
7. a. 23 + 15 = 38; 38 − 15 = __23__   b. 65 + 45 = 110; 110 − 45 = __65__

Review Exercises

E. *Write the answers to these column additions.*

8.   3   6   4   7   8   8   9   7
     8   6   9   8   6   8   7   7
   + 9   + 9   + 7   + 6   + 8   + 8   + 9   + 8
    20   21   20   21   22   24   25   22

9.   7   6   5   8   9   4   7   9
     7   5   9   8   6   8   5   8
   + 6   + 9   + 5   + 7   + 5   + 9   + 8   + 6
    20   20   19   23   20   21   20   23

F. *Solve these reading problems.*

10. If Stanley has 34 butterflies in his collection and Vivian has 19, how many do they have together?
    53 butterflies

11. What is the total of 450, 147, and 289?   **886**

12. At Valley View Christian School there are 12 pupils in Room 1, 23 pupils in Room 2, and 19 pupils in Room 3. How many pupils in all are in the three rooms?   **54 pupils**

22 Chapter 1 Addition and Subtraction

6. Addition and Subtraction Families

Do you remember how addition facts work together? They are in pairs. If 6 + 4 = 10, then 4 + 6 = 10.

Subtraction is the opposite of addition. Every addition fact has a subtraction fact that matches it. **If 6 + 4 = 10, then 10 − 4 = 6.**

Look again at the facts above. See how they all use 10, 6, and 4.

> You can make two addition and two subtraction facts that use the same numbers. These four facts are called a **number family.** The four facts below are a number family. They belong to the 9, 6, 3 family.
>
> 6 + 3 = 9   3 + 6 = 9   9 − 3 = 6   9 − 6 = 3

A. Do these exercises.

1. Write the other addition facts that match those below.

   a. 6 + 9 = 15   9 + 6 = 15   b. 4 + 7 = 11   7 + 4 = 11   c. 5 + 8 = 13   8 + 5 = 13

2. Write the subtraction facts that match these addition facts.

   a. 5 + 3 = 8   8 − 5 = 3   b. 8 + 8 = 16   16 − 8 = 8   c. 7 + 5 = 12   12 − 7 = 5
               8 − 3 = 5   12 − 5 = 7

B. Write the two addition and two subtraction facts that belong to each number family below.

3. a. 4, 9, 13   b. 9, 8, 17   c. 9, 2, 7   d. 14, 8, 6

      4   9 13 13   9   8 17 17   2   7   9   9   8   6 14 14
    +9 +4 −4 −9   +8 +9 −9 −8   +7 +2 −2 −7   +6 +8 −8 −6
    13 13   9   4   17 17   8   9   9   9   7   2   14 14   6   8

How do you do the subtraction at the right? First subtract the ones. Then think: 11 − 8 = 3. Remember that you **cannot** subtract 8 from 1.

  116
− 84
───
  32

C. Copy and subtract.

4. 112   154   165   134   108   116
   − 60   − 82   − 81   − 44   − 35   − 25
     52   72   84   90   73   91

LESSON 6

Objectives

- To review addition and subtraction families (number families).
- To review checking subtraction with addition.
- To review subtracting two-digit numbers from three-digit numbers.

Preparation

1. Addition and Subtraction flash cards
    Use only the most difficult addition facts or those with which pupils were having trouble.
2. Speed Drill 6
3. Chalkboard:

    a. 158
        - 64
        ─────
         94

    b.   800   450   320   1,000
       3,499 2,460   899   1,010

    c. 3, 7, 10   12, 8, 4

    d. 749   426
       −323   +323
       ─────   ─────
       (426)   (749)

Oral Drill

1. Drill the addition facts.
2. Drill the subtraction facts. Separate the pack into well-known facts and less familiar ones. Drill more on the harder facts.
3. Read the numbers *(b)* on the board. Have the students tell what number comes right before and right after each number. Then have them arrange the numbers by size.
4. Ask what time it is.
5. Review subtraction terminology. **In subtraction, the first number is the** (minuend), **the second number is the** (subtrahend), **and the answer is the** (difference).
    Point to problem *a* on the board. **What number is the subtrahend? the minuend? the difference? the number that is being subtracted? the number that is being subtracted *from?* the remainder?**
    Erase the difference.
6. Give mental drill with addition. Say each number one at a time and pause before you give the next one.
    2 + 8 + 4 + 5 (19)   3 + 4 + 5 + 3 (15)
    5 + 6 + 4 + 8 (23)   5 + 3 + 5 + 6 (19)
    7 + 8 + 5 + 2 (22)   6 + 7 + 4 + 5 (22)

Speed Drill

Give Speed Drill 6 (addition practice).

T–23   Chapter 1   Addition and Subtraction

Teaching Guide

1. *Addition and subtraction families.*
   a. **What other addition fact pairs with 4 + 7 = 11? with 6 + 3 = 9?**
   b. Point to row *c* on the board. **Who can write two addition facts with the numbers 3, 7, and 10? with 12, 8, and 4?** Have someone write the addition facts on the board.
   c. **You know that addition facts come in pairs. You also know that subtraction "undoes" addition. If 6 + 5 = 11, what is 11 – 5?**
   d. Again point to row *c*. **What *subtraction* facts can you make with the numbers 3, 7, and 10? with 12, 8, and 4?** Have someone write these facts below the addition facts.
      Four facts that are written with the same three numbers make a *number family*. What four facts are in the 2, 8, 10 number family?

2. *Checking subtraction with addition.*
   a. **Because addition and subtraction are opposite, we can use addition to see if the answers to our subtractions are right. We add the difference to the subtrahend, and the answer should be the minuend.**
   b. Point to problem *d* on the board, and ask for a volunteer to solve it. Then work out the check beside it. Do another example if necessary.

3. *Subtracting two-digit numbers from three-digit numbers.*
   a. Point to problem *a* on the board. **Let's see if you know how to subtract in this problem.** Have the pupils tell you what number goes in the ones' place. Then see if someone can tell what number goes in the tens' place. **You must think 15 – 6 and not 5 – 6. We cannot subtract a larger number like 6 from a smaller number like 5. We must subtract 6 from the 15.**
   b. Use the following problems for individual practice. Have pupils write the addition check beside each one.

   ```
    114      137      158
   – 62     – 46     – 75
   ────     ────     ────
   (52)     (91)     (83)

    126      782      429
   – 61     –520     –315
   ────     ────     ────
   (65)    (262)    (114)
   ```

   Note: Consider the Number Riddles as extra credit. Add 1 percentage point to the pupil's score for each correct answer.

Supplementary Drills

Drill 4 –

Drill 71

Lesson 6

Because addition and subtraction are opposite, you can use addition to check subtraction. Study the example in the box.

	Subtraction	Check
To check a subtraction problem, add the **difference** to the **subtrahend**. The **sum** should be the same as the **minuend**.	74 − 53 ――― 21	21 + 53 ――― 74

D. *Copy and subtract. Check the answers by addition.*

5. a. 873   251   b. 145   91   c. 98   70   d. 123   63
       − 622 + 622   − 54 + 54   − 28 + 28   − 60 + 60
       ―――   ―――   ――― ―――   ――― ―――   ――― ―――
        251   873   91   145   70   98   63   123

6. a. 168   84   b. 594   533   c. 115   82   d. 106   43
       − 84 + 84   − 61 + 61   − 33 + 33   − 63 + 63
       ―――   ―――   ――― ―――   ――― ―――   ――― ―――
        84   168   533   594   82   115   43   106

Review Exercises

E. *Write the answers to these column additions.*

7.   6   7   4   6   2   9   6   5
     9   5   4   6   8   3   7   9
    + 6   + 4   + 9   + 5   + 7   + 8   + 5   + 8
    ―――   ―――   ―――   ―――   ―――   ―――   ―――   ―――
    21   16   17   17   17   20   18   22

F. *Copy and add.*

8.   584   493   529   408   487   926
    + 86   + 854   + 198   + 562   + 724   + 645
    ―――   ―――――   ―――――   ―――――   ―――――   ―――――
    670   1,347   727   970   1,211   1,571

Number Riddles

G. *Can you give the answers?*

9. If you add 7 to me, I become 12. What am I?   5

10. If you subtract 4 from me, I will be 5. What am I?   9

11. I am 3 less than the sum of 7 and 6. What am I?   10

24 Chapter 1 Addition and Subtraction

7. Place Value to Ten Thousand

How do you read the **numeral** 42,357? Study the diagram at the right for help. It shows the values of **digits** up to the ten thousands' place.

The comma helps to make 42,357 easier to read. First say the part before the comma: "forty-two thousand." Then say the part after the comma: "three hundred fifty-seven."

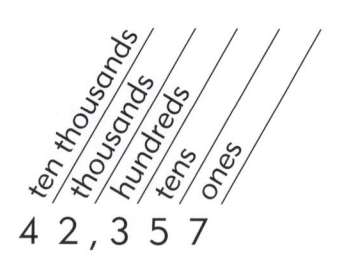

Each digit of 42,357 has a certain value because of **what** it is (digital value) and **where** it is (place value). For example, the 4 stands for 4 ten thousands (40,000). The 2 stands for 2 thousands (2,000).

ten thousands / thousands / hundreds / tens / ones

4 2 , 3 5 7

A. *Read these numerals in class.*

1. 10,000   50,000   62,000   36,000   75,600
2. 45,307   12,007   34,080   29,100   40,521
3. 13,040   60,702   12,345   98,764   99,999

B. *Write numerals for these number words.*

4. two thousand, eight hundred fifty 2,850
5. thirty-nine thousand, four hundred 39,400
6. eight thousand, one hundred twelve 8,112
7. ninety thousand 90,000
8. fifteen thousand, six hundred nine 15,609
9. seventy-seven thousand, seven hundred seventy-seven 77,777

C. *Copy these numbers and place commas correctly. Start at the right and say "1, 2, 3, comma."*

10. 49601   61883   71765   96032   30265
    49,601 61,883 71,765 96,032 30,265

LESSON 7

Objectives

- To review place value up to the ten thousands' place.
- To practice reading and writing numbers to the ten thousands.

Preparation

1. Subtraction flash cards
2. Chalkboard:
   a. 15, 9, 6   16, 8, 8
   b. A simple place value chart as in the pupil's lesson
   c. 3,007   8,703   6,014   1,780   3,901
   d. 40,000   64,950   20,911
       71,048   99,900

Oral Drill

1. Drill subtraction facts. Encourage speed.
2. Review subtraction terms, checking subtraction with addition, and subtraction problems such as 135 − 83.
3. Give mental drill with addition and subtraction.

12 + 6	14 + 5	11 + 6	12 − 6
14 − 5	11 − 6	15 + 7	15 − 7

   8 + 8 + 6 (22)   3 + 8 + 7 (18)
   6 + 8 + 9 (23)   9 + 5 + 4 (18)
   4 + 6 + 6 (16)   2 + 7 + 9 (18)

4. Count by 10's to 200; by 2's from 30 to 50; by 1's from 395 to 410.
5. Ask questions about time, such as what time it is now, what time it was an hour ago, and how long it has been since 8:00.
6. Review number families. Have students tell the four facts that can be made with the first set of numbers in row *a* on the board.

   Some number families have only two facts. Illustrate with 16, 8, 8. See if pupils can tell why there are only two members in this family.

Chapter 1 Addition and Subtraction

Teaching Guide

1. *Place value up to ten thousands.*
   a. Use the place value chart *(b)* on the board. Label the ones', tens', and hundreds' places on the chart as students give the names.
   b. **What is the largest number we can write with only three digits?** (999) **What is 1 more than that?** (1,000) Point to the thousands' place and write *thousands*.
   c. **One thousand is how many times 100? Each place in our number system is 10 times the place to its right.** Point to ten thousands' place. **This place is how many times 1,000? This place is called ten thousands.** Write *ten thousands*.
   d. Have the students recite all the places, starting at the right. Then erase the labels. Point to places at random and have students name the places.

2. *Reading and writing large numbers.*
   a. Have the students read the numbers in row *c* on the board. Arrange the numbers in order from smallest to largest.
   b. Write 12,345 on the board. **To make it easy to read large numbers, the numbers are separated into periods by commas. This is the ones' period, and this is the thousands' period.** Point to the respective periods. **To know where to place the commas, count three digits from the right, and put a comma there. There *must* be three digits to the *right* of a comma, but there may be one, two, or three digits to the *left* of a comma.**
   c. **Read the thousands' places first, like this: twelve thousand; then say the rest: three hundred forty-five.**
   d. Have pupils read the numbers in row *d* on the board. Point to digits, and have students tell the value of that digit in the number. Have them say "6 ten thousands" (or "60 thousand"), not simply "ten thousands." (Do not labor over the terms *digital value* and *place value*.)
   e. Have students take turns reading the numbers in Part A of the lesson.
   f. Dictate numbers for the students to write. There must be three digits *after* each comma, but there may be only one or two digits *before* the comma.

40,600	52,029	78,080
12,305	70,004	6,009

Supplementary Drills

Drill 2 +

Drill 43

D. *Do these exercises.*

11. Write what the 8 stands for in each number below.

    a. 38,210   b. 6,508   c. 85,462   d. 1,689
       8 thousands   8 ones   8 ten thousands   8 tens

12. Figure out the patterns. Copy and fill in the missing numbers.

    a. 146, 147, 148, <u>149</u>, <u>150</u>, <u>151</u>, 152, <u>153</u>

    b. 100, <u>200</u>, 300, 400, 500, <u>600</u>, <u>700</u>, <u>800</u>

    c. 35, 40, <u>45</u>, 50, <u>55</u>, <u>60</u>, 65, 70

    d. 996; 997; <u>998</u>; <u>999</u>; <u>1,000</u>; <u>1,001</u>; 1,002; <u>1,003</u>

13. Write the numbers in each row in order of size, beginning with the smallest.

    a. 998   989   988   9,898   899
       899, 988, 989, 998, 9,898

    b. 100   1,000   1,010   101   1,001
       100, 101, 1,000, 1,001, 1,010

    c. 426   642   462   246   624
       246, 426, 462, 624, 642

Review Exercises

E. *Write the answers to these column additions.*

14.

5	6	2	9	1	7	2	3
6	4	3	6	5	3	2	5
+9	+5	+8	+7	+9	+7	+8	+8
20	15	13	22	15	17	12	16

F. *Write two addition and two subtraction facts that belong to the number families below.*

15. a. 15, 8, 7

       8   7   15 15
     +7 +8 −8 −7
     15 15   7   8

b. 7, 5, 2

       5   2   7   7
     +2 +5 −5 −2
      7   7   2   5

c. 16, 7, 9

      7   9   16 16
    +9 +7 −7 −9
    16 16   9   7

G. *Copy and subtract. Check your answers by addition. Write the check beside each subtraction problem.*

16.

a. 149	87	b. 865	414	c. 136	90
− 62	+ 62	− 451	+ 451	− 46	+ 46
87	149	414	865	90	136

17.

a. 590	350	b. 118	23	c. 107	54
− 240	+ 240	− 95	+ 95	− 53	+ 53
350	590	23	118	54	107

8. Reading and Writing Large Numbers

Look at the place value chart on the right. One new place, hundred thousands, has been added. Now you know the names of six numeral places.

Read the numeral 333,333. Tell the place value of each 3. Our number system is based on tens. Each 3 stands for **ten times** as much as the 3 to its right.

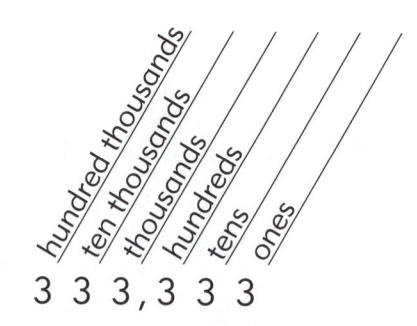

hundred thousands / ten thousands / thousands / hundreds / tens / ones

3 3 3, 3 3 3

A. *Do these exercises.*

1. Write numerals for these number words.
   a. twenty-nine thousand, six hundred   29,600
   b. eight hundred three thousand, four hundred fifteen   803,415
   c. seven hundred thousand, ten   700,010
   d. three hundred twenty-four thousand, one hundred forty   324,140
   e. two hundred six thousand, nine hundred eighteen   206,918

2. Write the value of each underlined digit below. (See Lesson 7.)
   a. 9,7<u>6</u>2   b. <u>4</u>,803   c. 15,<u>9</u>64   d. <u>5</u>80,719   e. 1<u>4</u>8,230
   6 tens   4 thousands   9 hundreds   5 hundred thousands   4 ten thousands

3. Write these numbers with words. Watch your spelling.
   a. 27,004   (See facing page.)   b. 450,095   c. 348,126

The symbol < means "is less than."
The symbol > means "is greater than."

17 < 71   Read it like this: 17 is less than 71.
530 > 350   Read it like this: 530 is greater than 350.

B. *Do these exercises.*

4. Copy the two numbers in each pair. Write < or > between the numbers to show which is more.

   a. 1,000 < 10,000   d. 60,000 > 59,998
   b. 7,681 > 7,618   e. 520,000 < 529,999
   c. 42,009 < 42,090   f. 709,999 < 710,000

LESSON 8

Objectives

- To practice place value *up to the hundred thousands' place.
- To introduce *the symbols < and >.
- To review key words in reading problems solved by subtraction.

Preparation

1. The more difficult addition and subtraction flash cards
2. Speed Drill 8
3. Chalkboard:
   a. Place value chart to hundred thousands. (Do not write the names in the places.)

   b. 12,568   31,098   54,680
      79,006   18,200   50,074

   c. 123,456   760,981   109,870
      300,895   407,300   560,008

Oral Drill

1. Drill the more difficult addition and subtraction facts.
2. Review *addend, sum, minuend, subtrahend,* and *difference.*
3. Give mental drill with three addends.

   8 + 7 + 6 (21)   4 + 7 + 9 (20)
   5 + 8 + 7 (20)   2 + 8 + 4 (14)
   9 + 5 + 5 (19)   6 + 7 + 5 (18)
   8 + 8 + 7 (23)   7 + 9 + 4 (20)

4. Count by 1's from 1,997 to 2,005; by 10's from 1,000 to 1,100; by 1,000's from 26,000 to 30,000.
5. Have pupils read the numbers in the first two rows *(b)* on the board.
6. Review key words in reading problems solved by addition. **The word *sum* in a reading problem usually means that ___ is needed.** (addition) **What other words usually mean addition is needed?** (altogether, both, total, in all)

Speed Drill

Give Speed Drill 8 (column addition practice).

Answers for exercise 3

a. twenty-seven thousand, four

b. four hundred fifty thousand, ninety-five

c. three hundred forty-eight thousand, one hundred twenty-six

Teaching Guide

1. *Place value to hundred thousands.*
   a. Point to the places on the chart *(a)* and have the pupils give the names to 10,000.
   b. Write the number 44,444 below the place value chart. Point to each 4 and have pupils tell what it means. **Each 4 is ten times as much as the 4 just to the right of it. That is because our number system is based on *tens*.**
   c. Introduce the new place—100,000. It is the third place in the thousands' period. Have the pupils read the numbers in the other two rows *(c)* on the board.
   d. Point to digits in the numbers, and have pupils tell the values.
   e. Dictate numbers for pupils to write. *This kind of exercise is important.*

100,000	100,001	300,005
459,724	350,000	408,100

2. *Symbols < and >.*
   a. Ask questions such as the following: **Which is more, 10,000 or 9,999? 78,000 or 78,010?**
   b. Write the numbers 999 and 1,000 on the board beside each other. **Is the first number more or less than the second?** (less) **This symbol (<) can be placed between the numbers to show this. We read the symbol "is less than."**
   c. Write the numbers 4,050 and 4,005 on the board. **Is the first number more or less than the second?** (more) **This symbol (>) can be placed between the numbers to show this. We read the symbol "is greater than."**
   d. **To remember which symbol is which, always make the smaller end (the "arrow") point to the *smaller* number.**

   Drill with several easy pairs of numbers so pupils can concentrate on the two signs. Then do some harder number pairs. Be sure the children realize that a greater *place* always means more than a large *digit*. For example, 100,000 is more than 9,998, even though the first number is mostly zeroes.

3. *Key words in reading problems solved by subtraction.*
   a. Have the pupils turn to Lesson 8 in their books. Have someone read problem 1 in the box *Key Words in Reading Problems*. Discuss the three different ways of asking the same question. Note the words in bold print. These are some key words for this kind of problem.
   b. Have someone read problem 2, and again note the key words. Caution the children that not every reading problem will have these key words in them. But whenever they know two numbers and want to find how much is between the two, they must subtract. And whenever they know the total and one part, and they want to find the other part, they must subtract.
   c. Read the following questions to the pupils. Have them tell whether they would **add** or **subtract** to answer each one.
      How many more? (s)
      What is the difference? (s)
      What is the sum? (a)
      How many altogether? (a)
      How many in all? (a)
      How much younger? (s)
      How many are left? (s)
      What is the total? (a)
      How much older? (s)
      How much less? (s)

Supplementary Drills

Drill 136*

Drill 137*

5. Copy each number on your paper. Then write the next three numbers that come after it.

   a. 2,000   b. 17,888   c. 329,077   d. 806,998

   a. 2,000
   2,001
   2,002
   2,003

   b. 17,888
   17,889
   17,890
   17,891

   c. 329,077
   329,078
   329,079
   329,080

   d. 806,998
   806,999
   807,000
   807,001

> **Key Words in Reading Problems**
>
> **Problem 1:** There were 8 boys and 4 girls in a van.
> What is the **difference** between 8 and 4?
> There were how many **more** boys than girls?
> There were how many **fewer** girls than boys?
>
> $$\begin{array}{r} 8 \\ -4 \\ \hline ? \end{array}$$
>
> You know two numbers, and you want to find the difference between them. You must subtract to find the answer.
>
> **Problem 2:** There were 12 children in a van, and 5 got out.
> How many children were **left?** $12 - 5 = ?$
> You know the total number and one part. You must subtract to find the answer.

C. *Write whether you must* add *or* subtract *to solve each problem below. Then find the answers.*

6. Aunt May brought 68 cookies to school for a treat. There are only 5 cookies left. How many cookies did the children eat?   subtract   63 cookies

7. Gerald is 6 years old, and Michael is 11. How much older is Michael than Gerald?   subtract   5 years

8. Uncle Peter paid $14.49 for gasoline and $1.10 for a quart of oil. How much did he spend in all?   add $15.59

9. One month Rod and Staff Publishers sent out 2,106 copies of the *Christian School Builder*, 2,950 copies of the *Christian Contender*, and 10,330 copies of the *Christian Example*. What was the total number of these papers sent out that month?   add   15,386 papers

10. Sharon sewed 24 quilt patches, and Melissa sewed 14. Sharon sewed how many more patches than Melissa did?   subtract   10 patches

Review Exercises

D. *Copy and add. Keep the columns straight.*

11.
```
  2,314      3,152      6,248      3,157      3,051
  4,152      1,263        174        825      2,837
+   260     +   53     +2,752     +1,946     +3,162
  ─────      ─────      ─────      ─────      ─────
  6,726      4,468      9,174      5,928      9,050
```

9. Chapter 1 Review

A. *Write the answers to these facts. Watch the signs!*

1. 9 + 5 = 14   12 − 7 = 5   5 − 3 = 2   9 − 6 = 3   6 + 7 = 13   18 − 9 = 9   11 − 8 = 3   16 − 7 = 9   10 − 4 = 6

2. 8 + 4 = 12   17 − 9 = 8   7 + 3 = 10   4 + 5 = 9   10 − 9 = 1   7 − 7 = 0   15 − 8 = 7   12 − 6 = 6   5 + 8 = 13

B. *Do these exercises.*

3. Copy and solve the problems below. Then label each number.

   387   addend
   + 27 addend
   414   sum

   682   minuend
   − 262 subtrahend
   420   difference

4. Add 4 to each number below.

   6 → 10   9 → 13   4 → 8   11 → 15   15 → 19   17 → 21   13 → 17   18 → 22   12 → 16

5. Write the addition and subtraction facts that belong in these number families.

   a. 5, 8, 13
      5 + 8 = 13   8 + 5 = 13   13 − 5 = 8   13 − 8 = 5

   b. 6, 6, 12
      6 + 6 = 12   12 − 6 = 6

C. *Add, and write only the answers.*

6. 12 + 4 = 16   15 + 5 = 20   13 + 7 = 20   17 + 7 = 24   19 + 4 = 23

7. 11 + 6 = 17   12 + 5 = 17   17 + 4 = 21   18 + 6 = 24   16 + 5 = 21

8. 8 + 6 + 6 = 20   2 + 5 + 8 = 15   6 + 8 + 5 = 19   8 + 4 + 9 = 21   1 + 8 + 6 = 15   5 + 5 + 6 = 16   7 + 7 + 8 = 22   9 + 4 + 7 = 20

LESSON 9

Objective

- To review the concepts taught in Chapter 1 (listed below).
  - Addition and subtraction facts
  - Addition of 2- and 3-digit numbers with or without carrying
  - Subtraction of 2- and 3-digit numbers
  - Mental addition of a 1-digit number to a 2-digit number
  - Column addition

Note: The test focuses on what was taught in the first six lessons. Place value and large numbers are not included.

Preparation

1. Addition and subtraction flash cards
2. Chalkboard:
   a. Simple place value chart
   b. 879034   402851   98765
      12004   560306
   c.   875   982   115
       +792   -351   -44
      (1,667)   (631)   (71)

Teaching Guide

1. Review the addition and subtraction facts.
2. Review mental addition.
   13 + 5   17 + 8   11 + 4   16 + 5   13 + 7
   3 + 6 + 7 (16)   6 + 6 + 8 (20)
   8 + 8 + 5 (21)   9 + 3 + 5 (17)
   8 + 2 + 6 (16)   7 + 5 + 5 (17)
   7 + 3 + 4 + 6 (20)   2 + 5 + 4 + 8 (19)
3. Review the parts of addition and subtraction problems.
4. Review addition and subtraction families.
5. Review large numbers.
   a. Review place value, using the chart (a) on the board.
   b. Have pupils insert commas in the numbers (b) on the board. You could also do exercises 11 and 12 in class.
   c. Have pupils read the numbers used in b. Let them tell what certain digits mean.
6. Review the symbols < and >. You could do exercise 13 in class.
7. Review addition and subtraction.
   a. Together solve the three problems (c) on the board.
   b. Have pupils work some problems individually.
8. Review key words in reading problems. Read the following problems and ask: **Do we need to add or subtract to find the answers?** Have pupils find the answers if there is time.
   a. Harry had $3.50 in his bank. He earned $1.00 more. How much does he have *altogether* now? (add; $4.50)

   Note the word *more* in the problem. But the answer is found by

T–29   Chapter 1   Addition and Subtraction

  addition because the question has *altogether*.
  b. A small tree is 12 feet tall, and a big tree is 65 feet tall. The big tree is *how much taller* than the small tree? (subtract; 53 ft.)
  c. Mother made 3 dozen cupcakes. The family ate 15 for supper. *How many are left?* (subtract; 21 cupcakes)
  d. One week Samuel had 5 words wrong in spelling. The next week he tried harder and had only 1 word wrong. *How many fewer* words did Samuel have wrong the second week? (subtract; 4 words)
9. Tell students that they will have a test in the next class.

Note: Assign as much of Lesson 9 as you think your students need and can handle. You could assign exercises 1–10 and 14–23, especially if you did 11–13 in class. That will prepare them for the test since place value is not tested. Do not omit the reading problems.

Lesson 9 29

D. *Copy and work carefully. Follow the signs.*

9.
```
              57      29     383     577
  297   438   25      41     837     655
 +548  +783  +42     +35    +231    +546
  ───   ───   ──      ──    ────    ────
  845 1,221  124     105   1,451   1,778
```

10.
```
   85    73   117    854    965    137
  -44   -23   -65   -150   -652    -43
  ───   ───   ───   ────   ────   ────
   41    50    52    704    313     94
```

E. *Follow the directions.*

11. Write numerals for these number words.
    a. two thousand, three hundred seven   2,307
    b. sixty-nine thousand, forty-eight   69,048
    c. one hundred thirty thousand, five hundred   130,500
    d. seven hundred eighty-four thousand, two   784,002

12. Copy the numbers below and insert commas properly. Then write what the underlined digit stands for in each number. Be ready to read the numbers.

    a. 8<u>5</u>,702   b. 1<u>2</u>6,000   c. 790,1<u>7</u>8   d. 54,<u>8</u>10   e. <u>8</u>70,336
    5 thousands   2 ten thousands   7 tens   8 hundreds   8 hundred thousands

13. Copy the numbers in each pair, and write < or > between them.
    a. 1,003 < 3,001   d. 11,111 > 9,999
    b. 8,999 < 9,888   e. 30,789 > 20,789
    c. 12,999 > 12,899   f. 91,988 > 90,999

F. *Solve these reading problems.*

14. There were 27 children on a school bus. At one stop 6 children got off. How many were left on the bus?   **21 children**

15. Mother bought a gallon of milk for $1.95, a box of cereal for $2.25, and a loaf of bread for $0.89. How much did she pay in all?   **$5.09**

16. Grandma gave Ray 25 cents for his birthday. Ray put 10 cents in the offering and the rest in his piggy bank. How much did he put in his bank?   **15¢**

17. Sue has a collection of 15 butterflies and 10 moths. How many more butterflies than moths does she have?   **5 butterflies**

(continued on next page)

47

30   Chapter 1   Addition and Subtraction

18. One Sunday all the Smith family went to Uncle Marvin's. The number of cousins was 13 girls and 17 boys. How many cousins was that altogether?
30 cousins

19. How many more boy cousins than girl cousins were in the Smith family? (See number 18.)
4 cousins

20. The oldest cousin was 16 years old and the youngest cousin was 2. What was the difference in their ages?
14 years

21. Aunt Ella brought 36 doughnuts to serve at dinnertime, and Aunt Lois brought 48. How many doughnuts did they both bring?
84 doughnuts

22. The family sang in the afternoon. They sang 7 songs from the *Life Songs* and 6 songs from the *Church Hymnal*. How many more songs did they sing from the *Life Songs*?
1 song

23. How many songs did the family sing in all? (See number 22.)
13 songs

Number Strings

G. *See if you can find the number that belongs at the end of each number string.*

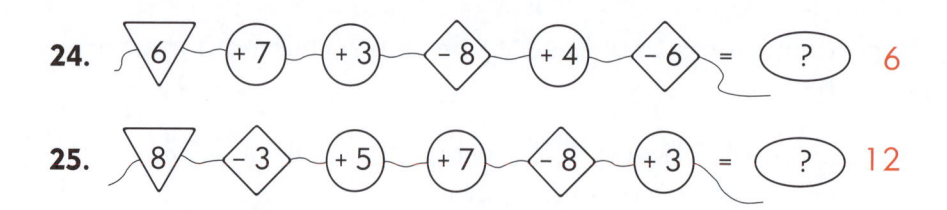

24.   6 +7 +3 −8 +4 −6 = ?   6

25.   8 −3 +5 +7 −8 +3 = ?   12

10. Chapter 1 Test

LESSON 10

Objective

- To test the pupils' mastery of the concepts taught in Chapter 1.

Teaching Guide

1. Give Speed Drill 10 (addition practice).

Note: Speed Drills are optional on test days.

2. Give any last-minute review that you feel is necessary.

3. Administer the test. Arrange pupils to minimize the possibility of cheating, and encourage them to do their best.

Note: Chapter 1 Test is found in the test section in the back of this manual.

Chapter 2

Subtraction With Borrowing

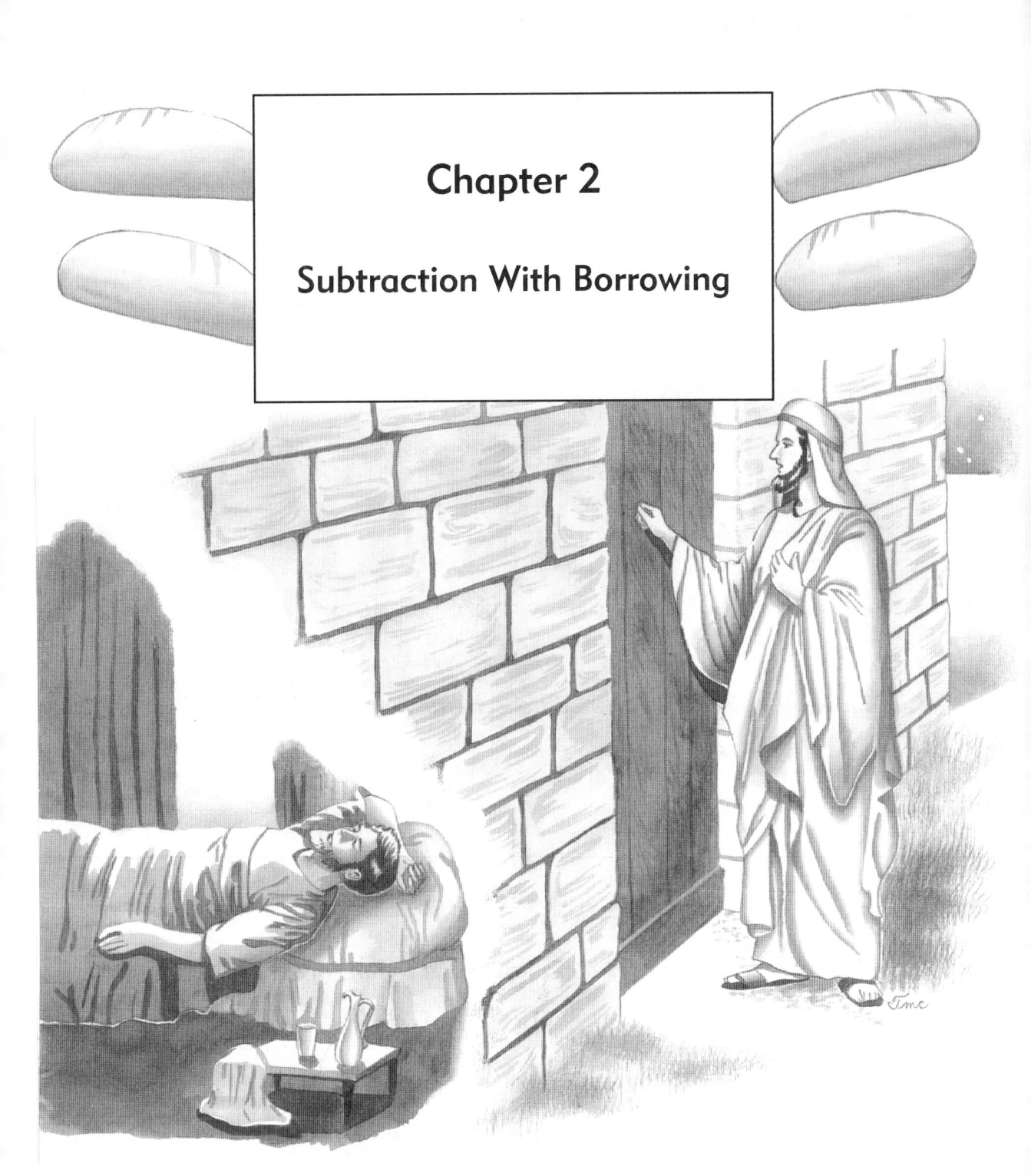

"Friend, lend me three loaves."
He will rise and give him as many as he needeth.
(Luke 11:5, 8)

11. Borrowing in Subtraction

Sometimes you need to **borrow** in a subtraction problem. If there are not enough ones in the minuend, you need to borrow from tens. The example and the steps in the box show how to borrow.

> **Think:** 42 = 4 tens 2 ones = 3 tens 12 ones
> − 15 = 1 ten 5 ones = 1 ten   5 ones
> ─────────────────────
>   2 tens 7 ones
>
> **Do:** $\overset{3}{\cancel{4}}12$
>   − 1 5
>   ─────
>   2 7
>
> 1. Subtract ones: 2 − 5 cannot be done.
> 2. Borrow 1 ten from the tens' column. Cross out 4 tens and write 3 above it.
> 3. The 1 borrowed ten changes to 10 ones. Write 1 before the 2 ones to add the borrowed ones.
> 4. Subtract 12 ones − 5 ones = 7 ones. Write 7.
> 5. Subtract 3 tens − 1 ten = 2 tens. Write 2.

You do not need to borrow in all subtraction problems. Borrow only when the upper digit in a column is **less than** the lower digit.

A. Copy and subtract. You will need to borrow.

1. | 31 − 18 = 13 | 50 − 35 = 15 | 92 − 84 = 8 | 90 − 36 = 54 | 55 − 29 = 26 |
2. | 21 − 16 = 5 | 94 − 56 = 38 | 77 − 69 = 8 | 43 − 25 = 18 | 82 − 46 = 36 |

B. Write *yes* or *no* to tell if you would need to borrow.

3. a. 46 − 18 **yes**
    b. 17 − 11 **no**
    c. 43 − 23 **no**
    d. 80 − 61 **yes**
    e. 51 − 27 **yes**
    f. 38 − 15 **no**

C. Copy and subtract. Borrowing is not needed in this row.

4. | 138 − 95 = 43 | 119 − 26 = 93 | 120 − 50 = 70 | 148 − 93 = 55 | 115 − 62 = 53 |

LESSON 11

Objectives

- To review borrowing from the tens' column.
- To introduce column addition *with four addends.

Preparation

1. Subtraction flash cards
2. Pennies and dimes or bundles of sticks or straws (optional)
3. Chalkboard:

   a. 600,4<u>2</u>0   2<u>3</u>0,008   <u>6</u>54,000
   401,<u>7</u>00   550,<u>0</u>19

   b. 126   117   105   134
       −62   −45   −73   −24
       (64) (72) (32) (110)

   c. 5 + 7 + 6 + 9 (27)
      8 + 7 + 4 + 5 (24)

Oral Drill

1. Have the pupils read the numbers *(a)* on the board. Also drill the six places they have studied so far. Ask the value of the underlined digits.
2. Review the symbols < and >.
3. Ask what time it is.
4. Drill subtraction flash cards, especially those your students find more difficult.
5. Give drill with mental addition.
   4 + 3 + 8 (15)   5 + 6 + 3 (14)
   8 + 9 + 5 (22)   3 + 7 + 9 (19)

T–33   Chapter 2   Subtraction With Borrowing

Teaching Guide

1. *Borrowing from the tens' column.*
   a. Review the kind of subtraction used to solve the problems *(b)* on the board. These problems do not involve actual borrowing, but they prepare the child for borrowing because he must think of the next place to the left. See if pupils recognize that the last problem is a bit different from the rest.
   b. **Have you ever borrowed anything? We borrow money if we do not have enough ourselves. In subtraction we borrow from tens if we do not have enough ones.**
   c. Have the children turn to Lesson 11 in their books and study what is in the box. Then put the same example on the board and see if the pupils can explain what to do. Stress: **We can never take a larger number away from a smaller one.** We must borrow from its "neighbor."
   d. Use pennies and dimes or bundles of sticks or straws to give a visual illustration of borrowing. **A dime can be changed to ten pennies. A bundle of ten straws can be opened and changed to ten single straws. This is the same thing that happens when we borrow, even though we do not always think about it.**
   e. Put some problems on the board and have pupils tell if they would need to borrow in each one. Here are some examples.

65	97	14	36
−17	−45	−11	−19
(48)	(52)	(3)	(17)

50	72	21
−28	−43	−10
(22)	(29)	(11)

   f. Work through a few of the problems step by step.
   g. Have pupils solve the following problems at the board or in their seats. Allow them to cross out the number they are borrowing and write the smaller number above it. They need this crutch until the process is firmly established in their minds.

60	42	55	31
−17	−25	−42	−19
(43)	(17)	(13)	(12)

27	128	113
−18	−44	−85
(9)	(84)	(28)

2. *Column addition with four addends.*
   a. Point to the horizontal problems *(c)* on the board. Tell the children that adding four numbers is much like adding three numbers. Show how to add one number at a time.
   b. Give practice with the following problems.

   4 + 9 + 7 + 2 (22)
   5 + 4 + 3 + 5 (17)
   8 + 3 + 5 + 6 (22)
   1 + 4 + 5 + 7 (17)
   8 + 6 + 4 + 7 (25)

Supplementary Drills

Drill 56*

Drill 69*

D. Copy and subtract. Borrow only when you need to.

5.
```
  24      87      40      71      89
- 17    - 67    - 28    - 39    - 52
----    ----    ----    ----    ----
   7      20      12      32      37
```

E. Copy and subtract. Check your answers by adding.

6. a.
```
  43     27        b.  125     30       c.  92     24
- 16   + 16          -  95   + 95         - 68   + 68
----   ----          -----   -----        ----   ----
  27     43             30    125           24     92
```

To add four addends, add one number at a time.

4 + 9 + 7 + 2   Think: 4 + 9 = 13, + 7 = 20, + 2 = 22

F. Add. Write the answers only.

7.
```
  5     4     1     8     4     6     8     3
  4     8     4     2     9     4     3     4
  3     6     4     6     3     5     0     6
+ 6   + 5   + 7   + 5   + 7   + 2   + 6   + 0
---   ---   ---   ---   ---   ---   ---   ---
 18    23    16    21    23    17    17    13
```

Review Exercises

G. Find the answers.

8. A checkers game has 12 black checkers and 12 red ones. How many checkers is that altogether?
   24 checkers

9. Dennis has a game with 25 pieces, but he can find only 21. How many pieces are lost?
   4 pieces

10. Write these numbers, using numerals.
    a. sixty-five thousand, eight hundred fifty-nine
       65,859
    b. four hundred twenty thousand, thirty-five
       420,035
    c. nine hundred thousand, one
       900,001
    d. two hundred eighty-one thousand, fourteen
       281,014

11. Copy the two numbers in each pair, and write < or > between them.

    a. 6,100 __>__ 1,600   b. 3,999 __<__ 4,001   c. 27,899 __<__ 28,899

34 Chapter 2 Subtraction With Borrowing

12. More Borrowing

In subtraction you borrow from tens when there are not enough ones. You borrow from hundreds when there are not enough tens.

$$\begin{array}{r} 381 \\ -168 \\ \hline \end{array} \text{ not enough ones } \begin{array}{r} 3\,\overset{7}{\cancel{8}}\,{}_1 1 \\ -1\,6\,8 \\ \hline 2\,1\,3 \end{array} \qquad \begin{array}{r} 425 \\ -261 \\ \hline \end{array} \text{ not enough tens } \begin{array}{r} \overset{3}{\cancel{4}}\,{}_1 2\,5 \\ -2\,6\,1 \\ \hline 1\,6\,4 \end{array}$$

You **must not** borrow unless you need more in order to subtract. But when there are not enough, you **must** borrow to get the right answer.

A. *Follow the directions.*

1. Copy and subtract. There are not enough ones, so you will need to borrow from tens.

   $\begin{array}{r} 720 \\ -519 \\ \hline 201 \end{array}$ $\quad$ $\begin{array}{r} 634 \\ -17 \\ \hline 617 \end{array}$ $\quad$ $\begin{array}{r} 547 \\ -429 \\ \hline 118 \end{array}$ $\quad$ $\begin{array}{r} 376 \\ -247 \\ \hline 129 \end{array}$

2. Copy and subtract. There are not enough tens, so you will need to borrow from hundreds.

   $\begin{array}{r} 246 \\ -164 \\ \hline 82 \end{array}$ $\quad$ $\begin{array}{r} 704 \\ -134 \\ \hline 570 \end{array}$ $\quad$ $\begin{array}{r} 251 \\ -90 \\ \hline 161 \end{array}$ $\quad$ $\begin{array}{r} 953 \\ -682 \\ \hline 271 \end{array}$

3. Copy and subtract. You must decide if you need to borrow from tens or from hundreds.

   $\begin{array}{r} 713 \\ -581 \\ \hline 132 \end{array}$ $\quad$ $\begin{array}{r} 940 \\ -537 \\ \hline 403 \end{array}$ $\quad$ $\begin{array}{r} 862 \\ -745 \\ \hline 117 \end{array}$ $\quad$ $\begin{array}{r} 155 \\ -39 \\ \hline 116 \end{array}$

4. Copy and subtract. You must decide if you will need to borrow at all.

   $\begin{array}{r} 376 \\ -144 \\ \hline 232 \end{array}$ $\quad$ $\begin{array}{r} 688 \\ -593 \\ \hline 95 \end{array}$ $\quad$ $\begin{array}{r} 820 \\ -490 \\ \hline 330 \end{array}$ $\quad$ $\begin{array}{r} 116 \\ -52 \\ \hline 64 \end{array}$

LESSON 12

Objectives
- To review borrowing from the hundreds column.
- To review key words in reading problems.

Preparation
1. Subtraction flash cards
2. Samples of coins and a dollar bill (optional)
3. Speed Drill 12
4. Chalkboard:

    a. 398   4,000   16,009
        329,999   245,998

    b. 861   450   937
        −230   −234   −756
        (631)   (216)   (181)

Oral Drill
1. Give mental drill of addition.

    $4 + 5 + 9 + 2$ (20) $8 + 3 + 4 + 6$ (21)
    $7 + 3 + 5 + 8$ (23) $6 + 2 + 5 + 6$ (19)
    $4 + 6 + 3 + 7$ (20) $9 + 4 + 3 + 6$ (22)
    $5 + 7 + 5 + 8$ (25) $7 + 7 + 5 + 4$ (23)
    $8 + 4 + 2 + 9$ (23)

2. Ask what time it is to the nearest five minutes. Ask what time it was five minutes ago; what time it will be in five more minutes.

3. Ask: **What piece of money is worth 10 cents? 5 cents? 25 cents? 1 cent? 100 cents? 50 cents?** You could also ask the children to point out each piece of money as it is named.

4. Drill the subtraction facts.

5. Review *minuend, subtrahend,* and *difference*.

6. Have pupils read the numbers *(a)* on the board. Then have them count by ones from those numbers until you tell them to stop.

Speed Drill
Give Speed Drill 12 (subtraction facts).

T–35   Chapter 2   Subtraction With Borrowing

Teaching Guide

1. *Borrowing from the hundreds' column.*
   a. Look at the first subtraction problem *(b)* on the board. Together find the answer step by step. The pupils should notice that no borrowing is needed. Borrowing must not be done unless more is needed to make subtraction possible.
   b. **In the second problem there are not enough ones in the minuend, so we must borrow from the tens. There are enough tens, so we do not need to borrow from the hundreds.**
   c. **In the third problem there are enough ones so that we can subtract. But there are not enough tens, so we must borrow from the hundreds.**
   d. Use the following problems for individual practice. If your pupils seem unsure about when to borrow, have them turn to Lesson 12, row 4, in their textbooks. Ask: **Are there enough ones? Are there enough tens?**

   ```
     658     310     843     904
    -264    -105    -261    -462
    (394)   (205)   (582)   (442)

     116    572     191
     -83   -528     -33
     (33)   (44)   (158)
   ```

   Watch for trouble spots. Do some pupils strike out digits before thinking whether they need to borrow? Are they writing an unnecessary 0 in the place at the far left?

2. *Key words in reading problems.*
   a. Read these questions, and ask if they tell the pupils to add or subtract.
      How many in all? (a)
      What is the difference? (s)
      How many are left? (s)
      How many altogether? (a)
      What is the sum? (a)
      What is the total? (a)
      How many less? (s)
      What is the remainder? (s)
      How many more? (s)
      How much younger or older? (s)
   b. Caution the pupils: **The key words are not always in a problem. You must *think* whether you need to put numbers together or whether you are finding a part of a total.**
      Here are some reading problems with the key words more hidden. See if you can tell whether you should add or subtract to find the answers.
      • I am 8 and my father is 32. How old was my father when I was born? (subtract; 24)
      • My sister is 12 and my brother is 4 years older. How old is my brother? (add; 16)
      • We gave our dog 5 bones. He ate 2 and buried the rest. How many did he bury? (subtract; 3)
      • Mother had $50.00 when she went to the store. She had $9.34 when she came back. How much did she spend? (subtract; $40.66)

   Note: Consider the Riddles About Age as extra credit. Add 1 percentage point to the pupil's score for each correct answer.

Supplementary Drill
Drill 63

Review Exercises

B. *Write answers only.*

5.
6	7	1	3	8	9	0
2	3	8	5	2	3	5
6	4	6	7	9	6	7
+3	+5	+5	+7	+5	+1	+8
17	19	20	22	24	19	20

6.
11	11	14	11	12	13	10	12	10	15
−4	−9	−8	−3	−6	−7	−8	−9	−4	−8
7	2	6	8	6	6	2	3	6	7

C. *Do these exercises.*

7. Write what each underlined digit stands for in these numbers.

   a. 6<u>9</u>,024   b. 59,0<u>2</u>8   c. 2<u>1</u>9,045   d. <u>6</u>70,273

   9 thousands   2 tens   1 ten thousand   6 hundred thousands

8. Copy each number. Then write the next three numbers that come after it if you were counting by ones.

   a. 989   989, 990, 991, 992
   b. 2,000   2,000, 2,001, 2,002, 2,003
   c. 6,798   6,798, 6,799, 6,800, 6,801
   d. 17,999   17,999, 18,000, 18,001, 18,002

9. Write two addition and two subtraction problems with each set of numbers.

   a. 8, 12, 20
   8 + 12 = 20
   12 + 8 = 20
   20 − 12 = 8
   20 − 8 = 12

   b. 17, 6, 23
   17 + 6 = 23
   6 + 17 = 23
   23 − 17 = 6
   23 − 6 = 17

Riddles About Age

D. *Solve these riddles.*

10. Sara said, "My grandfather is 70 years old, and my father is 36. What is the difference in their ages?"   34 years

11. Louise said, "My brother was 6 when I was born. Now I am 9 years old. How old is my brother?"   15 years

12. Norman said, "My oldest sister is 20 and my youngest sister is 5. My little sister is how much younger than my big sister?"   15 years

13. Grace said, "My mother is 35 and my father is 41. How much older is my father than my mother?"   6 years

14. David said, "My great-grandfather died 6 years ago. He was 85 when he died. How old would he be if he were still living?"   91 years

36 Chapter 2 Subtraction With Borrowing

13. Borrowing Twice

In some subtraction problems there are not enough ones **or** tens. Then you need to borrow twice in the same problem. The example in the box shows how to borrow twice.

```
      2                                  3 12
    4 3̸11      There are not           4 3̸11      There are not
  - 2 9 5      enough ones, so        - 2 9 5      enough tens, so
  ———————      we borrow from         ———————      we also borrow
        6      the tens.                1 3 6      from the hundreds.
```

A. *Copy and subtract. You will need to borrow twice in each problem.*

1.   942   836   523   724   916
     - 253   - 488   - 264   - 237   - 48
       689   348   259   487   868

2.   755   420   617   846   711
     - 78   - 349   - 358   - 469   - 324
       677   71   259   377   387

B. *Copy and subtract. You will need to borrow once or twice.*

3.   713   825   444   376   940
     - 365   - 285   - 396   - 158   - 637
       348   540   48   218   303

C. *Copy and subtract. Check each problem by addition.*

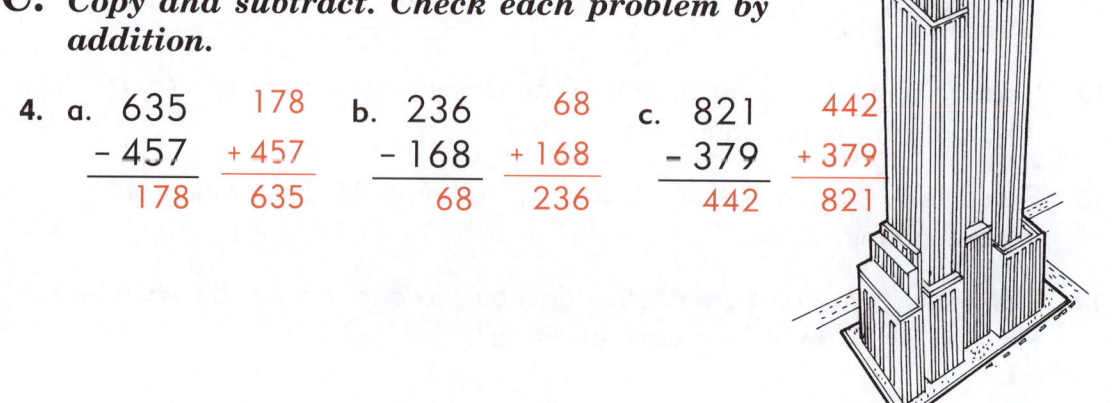

4. a. 635   178   b. 236   68   c. 821   442
       - 457   + 457   - 168   + 168   - 379   + 379
         178   635   68   236   442   821

LESSON 13

Objectives
- To review borrowing twice in subtraction.
- To review key words such as *longer*, *older*, and *taller* in reading problems.

Preparation
1. Subtraction flash cards
2. Multiplication flash cards: 1's–3's
3. Chalkboard:

    | 652 | 437 | 820 |
    | −347 | −153 | −561 |
    | (305) | (284) | (259) |

Oral Drill
1. Drill the subtraction facts quickly.
2. Drill the 1's–3's facts of multiplication. This is the first time this year that your pupils are being exposed to multiplication, so don't expect too much.
3. Give mental drill of addition.

    7 + 3 + 4 + 5 (19)   6 + 7 + 5 + 6 (24)
    3 + 2 + 8 + 7 (20)   8 + 6 + 4 + 7 (25)
    5 + 7 + 4 + 8 (24)   9 + 2 + 6 + 8 (25)
    4 + 3 + 6 + 2 (15)   8 + 2 + 8 + 4 (22)

4. Ask what time it is to the nearest 5 minutes. Ask if anyone knows whether that is A.M. or P.M. time.

T-37   Chapter 2   Subtraction With Borrowing

Teaching Guide

1. *Borrowing twice in subtraction.*
   a. Review borrowing by doing together the first two problems on the board.
   b. Point to the third problem. Ask: **Are there enough ones for us to subtract, or must we borrow from the tens?** Show the borrowing, and write 9 in the ones' place. **Can we subtract 6 from 1? No, we must borrow again.** Show how to borrow from the hundreds' place. **Our answer is 259.**
   c. Use these problems for further practice.

   ```
    823    631    825    716
   -275   -492   -439   - 47
   (548)  (139)  (386)  (669)

    555    836    940
   - 27   -156   -268
   (528)  (680)  (672)
   ```

2. *Key words in reading problems.*
   a. Tell the pupils that some words are used in making comparisons. If we say James is *taller* than Matthew, we are comparing the two boys. Other comparing words are *longer, shorter,* and *farther*. See if the pupils can think of more such words.
   b. **Numbers can be compared by subtraction. We subtract to find the difference between two numbers.**
   c. Call attention to the second box in the lesson. Read the information in the box together. Emphasize: If a question asks things like **how much more, how much smaller,** or **how much shorter,** we subtract to find the difference.
   d. If you feel that your pupils are ready for it, caution them that some problems with these comparison words are solved by addition.
      Example: I am 11 years old. My brother is 6 years older than I am. How old is my brother? (17)
      Note, however, that there is still a difference in the question. It asks "how old," not "how much older."
      Addition is not used to solve any reading problem in today's lesson.

Supplementary Drills

Drill 70*

Drill 3 –

> **Key Words in Reading Problems**
> If reading problems ask questions like the ones below, you must usually **subtract**.
>   How much younger? How much farther?
>   How much older?   How much longer?

D. Solve these reading problems.

5. Susan said, "Grandma Jones lives 12 miles from us, but Grandma Martin lives 80 miles from us." How much farther is it to Grandma Martin's house than to Grandma Jones's house?   68 miles

6. John is 49 inches tall and Harold is 53 inches tall. John is how much shorter than Harold?   4 inches

7. Loren is 14 and Larry is 9. Larry is how many years younger than Loren?   5 years

8. Geraldine's mother usually buys flour in 25-pound bags. Lois's mother bakes bread to sell, and she buys flour in 100-pound bags. A 100-pound bag is how much heavier than a 25-pound bag?   75 pounds

9. For 40 years the Empire State Building in New York was the tallest building in the world. It has 102 stories. Now several other buildings are taller. One is the Sears Tower in Chicago. It has 110 stories. It is how much taller than the Empire State Building?   8 stories

Review Exercises

E. Write the answers only.

10. 13 + 4 17   14 + 5 19   17 + 9 26   19 + 4 23

11. 10 + 6 16   17 + 5 22   13 + 8 21   11 + 6 17

F. Write only the answers. Watch the signs!

12. 12   13   8   14   9   10   11   10   7   6
     − 3 − 4 + 5 − 7 + 2 − 8 − 7 − 3 + 4 + 3
      9   9   13   7   11   2   4   7   11   9

13.   5   2   13   15   6   3   8   18   14   7
     + 7 + 5 − 8 − 9 + 5 + 7 − 6 − 9 − 5 + 2
     12   7   5   6   11   10   2   9   9   9

14. Subtracting From Zero

Study the problem in the box. You must borrow because there are not enough ones. Can you borrow from zero tens? No, you cannot borrow if nothing is there. You must borrow from the hundreds' place.

Think of 3 hundreds as 30 tens. Borrow 1 from 30. That makes 29 tens and 10 ones. Now you can subtract.

Think: $300 = 29$ tens 10 ones	**Do:** $\overset{29}{\cancel{3}}\,0\,10$	**Check:** $\overset{11}{}124$
$\underline{-176 = 17\text{ tens }6\text{ ones}}$	$\underline{-1\,7\,6}$	$\underline{+176}$
12 tens 4 ones	$1\,2\,4$	300

A. Copy and subtract. Check your answers by addition.

1. a. 800   341   b. 600   424   c. 500   126
      −459 +459   −176 +176   −374 +374
       341   800   424   600   126   500

2. a. 605   248   b. 801   317   c. 403   168
      −357 +357   −484 +484   −235 +235
       248   605   317   801   168   403

3. a. 600   154   b. 406   173   c. 730   595
      −446 +446   −233 +233   −135 +135
       154   600   173   406   595   730

4. a. 825   183   b. 700   435   c. 593   534
      −642 +642   −265 +265   − 59 + 59
       183   825   435   700   534   593

Review Exercises

B. Write the answers as quickly as you can. Watch the signs.

5. 9   11   13   5   3   8   10   2   15   11
   +7   − 3   − 6   +3   +9   −6   − 7   +5   − 7   −9
   ──   ───   ───   ──   ──   ──   ───   ──   ───   ──
   16   8   7   8   12   2   3   7   8   2

6. 10   16   8   6   9   18   14   4   9   10
   −4   −8   +6   +5   +4   − 9   − 7   +7   −6   −9
   ──   ──   ──   ──   ──   ───   ───   ──   ──   ──
    6   8   14   11   13   9   7   11   3   1

LESSON 14

Objective

- To introduce borrowing from hundreds *when zero is in tens' place.

Preparation

1. Subtraction flash cards
2. Multiplication flash cards: 2's–4's
3. Speed Drill 14
4. Chalkboard:

   a. 3,700 ___ 3,699
       4,080 ___ 4,800
       7,575 ___ 7,557

   b. 532   c. 500   d. 502
      −265   −265   −265
      (267)   (235)   (237)

Oral Drill

1. Drill the 2's and 3's multiplication facts. Go on to the 4's if your pupils are ready.
2. Review < and > by using the pairs of numbers *(a)* on the board.
3. Give drill with mental addition. Your pupils should be growing more proficient in this.

   8 + 3 + 5 + 4 (20)   7 + 1 + 8 + 6 (22)
   5 + 7 + 8 + 4 (24)   7 + 3 + 5 + 9 (24)
   6 + 2 + 5 + 7 (20)   4 + 3 + 6 + 5 (18)

4. Drill the more difficult subtraction facts.

Speed Drill

Give Speed Drill 14 (subtraction facts).

T–39   Chapter 2   Subtraction With Borrowing

Teaching Guide

Borrowing from hundreds when zero is in tens' place.

a. Together work through subtraction problem *b* on the board. Go through it one step at a time. Note that borrowing needs to be done twice.

b. Point to problem *c* on the board. Ask: **Can we subtract the ones without borrowing? Can we borrow from the tens' place? Why not? If we cannot borrow from the tens, where can we borrow from?** (hundreds)

c. **Think of 500 as 50 tens. We can borrow 1 ten from the 50 tens.** Cross out the 50 and write 49 above it. **Now we'll change that ten to 10 *ones* so that we can subtract.** Write 1 before the 0 in the ones' place.

Note: When 1 hundred is borrowed from 5 hundreds, the 1 hundred is actually changed to 10 tens, and then 1 of those tens is changed to 10 ones. Most children have less difficulty, however, if they think of the 5 hundreds as 50 tens and then change 50 tens to 49 tens and 10 ones. This course teaches the simpler concept.

d. Work through problem *d* on the board. It needs to be done the same way as problem *c*, even if there is no zero in the ones' place.

e. Use the following problems for board work or seatwork. (A few of these are not of exactly the same type.) Have the pupils show their addition checks.

```
  700      800      426      502
 -321     -458     - 87     -375
 (379)    (342)    (339)    (127)

  604      503      572
 -456     -493     -378
 (148)    (10)     (194)
```

Note: Consider number 13 as extra credit. Add 1 percentage point to the pupil's score for a correct answer.

Answers for exercise 8

a. one thousand, eighty-three
b. twenty-nine thousand, four hundred
c. three hundred two thousand
d. eight hundred sixty-five thousand, seven

Supplementary Drill

Drill 72*

C. Follow the directions.

7. Add. Write answers only.

4	7	9	0	5	3	8	2
6	5	2	8	4	9	2	6
3	5	4	8	9	7	6	1
+8	+2	+5	+6	+3	+6	+0	+8
21	19	20	22	21	25	16	17

8. Write the words for these numerals.

    a. 1,083   b. 29,400   c. 302,000   d. 865,007

    (See facing page.)

9. Write numerals for these number words.

    a. two hundred six thousand, four hundred twelve   206,412

    b. fifty-nine thousand, eighty-one   59,081

    c. six hundred ninety thousand, three hundred   690,300

    d. seventy thousand, one hundred forty-five   70,145

10. Copy the pairs of numbers, and put < or > between them.

    a. 320 _>_ 203   b. 4,090 _>_ 4,089   c. 1,035 _<_ 1,300

Number Strings

D. Can you find the answers?

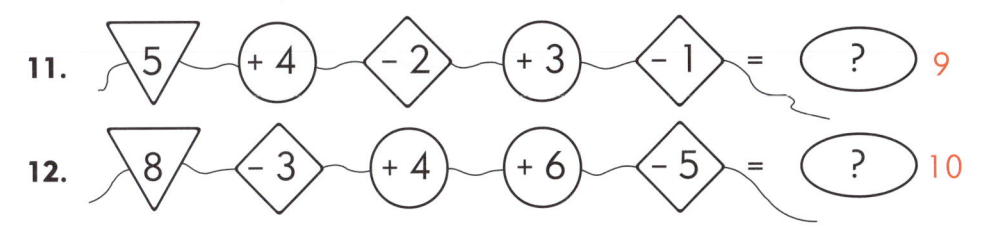

11. 5 → +4 → −2 → +3 → −1 = ?   9

12. 8 → −3 → +4 → +6 → −5 = ?   10

13. Mark's story is like a number string. Can you answer his question correctly? Mark said, "One day I was looking for pretty stones. I had two in my pocket when I started. Soon I found 3 more in the field lane. Then I found another one, but I threw it at a hole in a tree. In the woods I found six more stones along the creek. When I got home, I realized I had a hole in my pocket and I had lost four stones. How many stones were still in my pocket?"   7 stones

40   Chapter 2 Subtraction With Borrowing

15. Working With Money

Most people are interested in money. Money is used to buy things that people need or want. Money can also be given to others.

God wants us to use wisely the money He allows us to have. We learn about money in arithmetic so that we can make wise use of this gift from God.

Pictured below are some of the most common pieces of United States money. Can you name them all?

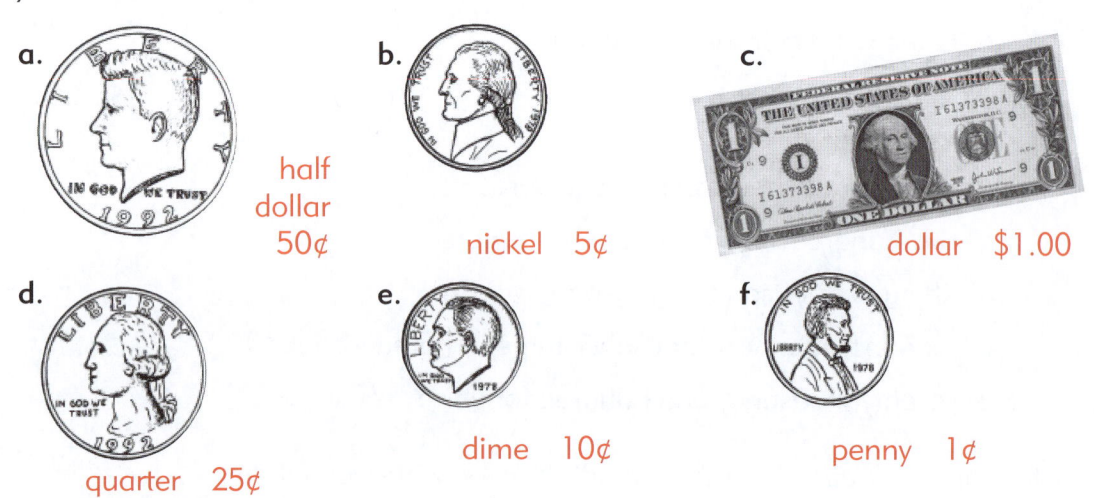

a. half dollar 50¢

b. nickel 5¢

c. dollar $1.00

d. quarter 25¢

e. dime 10¢

f. penny 1¢

A. *Follow the directions.*

1. Write the letters **a** through **f**. After each letter write the **name** and **value** of each piece of money shown above. Choose names from the box at the right.

dime	quarter
dollar	half dollar
nickel	penny

The examples in the box show how to write money amounts correctly.

Writing Prices
five cents: 5¢ or $0.05
twenty-five cents: 25¢ or $0.25
one dollar: $1.00 or $1
   (One dollar = 100¢, but it is not usually written that way.)
two dollars and fifty-nine cents: $2.59

2. Write each amount in two ways, as shown in the box.
   a. 65 cents 65¢ $0.65
   b. 50 cents 50¢ $0.50
   c. 17 cents 17¢ $0.17
   d. 1 cent 1¢ $0.01
   e. 9 cents 9¢ $0.09
   f. 1 dollar $1 $1.00

LESSON 15

Objectives

- To teach the identity and value of the penny, nickel, dime, quarter, half dollar, and dollar bill.
- To teach various ways of writing money amounts.
- To teach counting money by beginning with coins of larger values.

Preparation

1. Subtraction flash cards with minuends of 10 or less
2. Multiplication flash cards: 2's–4's
3. A supply of coins, either real or play money (If you have a dollar coin, bring it to class.)
4. Chalkboard:

   a. $\begin{array}{r} 500 \\ -159 \\ \hline (341) \end{array}$ $\begin{array}{r} 402 \\ -386 \\ \hline (16) \end{array}$

   b. 5¢   65¢ $0.65 $0.09

   $2.00 $4.98 $7.03

Oral Drill

1. Briefly drill the subtraction and multiplication facts.
2. Drill mental addition.

   5 + 5 + 3 + 9 (22)   6 + 8 + 2 + 7 (23)
   3 + 9 + 2 + 5 (19)   4 + 3 + 8 + 2 (17)
   9 + 1 + 7 + 3 (20)   8 + 7 + 6 + 4 (25)

3. Say a number, and have someone tell what number comes next.

   1,000   399   458   779
   2,899   40,000   2,010   6,009

4. Ask someone what time it is to the nearest five minutes.
5. Review subtraction from zero by doing the problems (a) on the board together.

T–41   Chapter 2   Subtraction With Borrowing

Teaching Guide

1. *Identity and value of coins and the dollar bill.*

   Show the pupils a penny, and ask what it is called and how much it is worth. Do the same with a nickel, dime, quarter, half dollar, and dollar, but not necessarily in that order.

2. *Writing money amounts.*
   a. **There are two ways to write prices less than a dollar. We can use the cents sign like this: 5¢, or the dollar sign like this: $0.05. There are always *two places* to the right of the the dot (decimal point). So *five cents* written with the dollar sign needs a 0 to the left of the 5.**
   b. **The dollar sign means whole dollars. For an amount less than one dollar, a zero is needed to the left of the dot to show that there is no whole dollar. $0.58, $0.79, $0.04**
   c. **Whole dollar amounts can also be written in two ways; like this: $2.00 or like this: $2.**
   d. **One dollar and twenty-nine cents is written like this: $1.29. The cents sign is seldom used for amounts more than 99¢** (like 129¢).
   e. Have pupils read the prices *(b)* on the board.
   f. Dictate these prices for pupils to write (in two ways for the first three).
   48 cents   3 cents   4 dollars
   7 dollars and 28 cents
   30 dollars and 7 cents

3. *Counting money.*
   a. If you have a small class, have them gather around your desk and count money together. Give each child several coins to count. With a larger class, draw coins on the board or have a few children come to your desk at a time.
   b. Teach pupils to count the larger denominations first and continue with the smaller ones.
   c. Emphasize quarters rather than half dollars. Half dollars are not in common use in the United States.
   d. Some children have a problem with quarters. Practice counting by 25's: 25, 50, 75, $1.00.
   e. Ask questions such as the following: **How many nickels does it take to equal a dime? a quarter? a half dollar? a dollar? How many dimes are in a half dollar? a dollar?**

      If you have a quarter and nickel, how much do you have? (30¢) **a quarter and a dime?** (35¢) **a quarter and three pennies?** (28¢) **two quarters and a dime?** (60¢) **three dimes and a nickel?** (35¢)
   f. The amount of time you need to spend with money concepts depends on the pupils' experience in other years. Even if your pupils lack the background, do not despair. The subject of money will appear in other lessons throughout the year.

Extra Review

Write prices on the board, and have pupils tell what pieces of money could be used to equal those amounts. Encourage them to use as few coins as possible. Allow pupils to use play money to help them.

Supplementary Drills

Drill 1 +

Drill 58

3. Write these prices with dollar signs.
   a. six dollars and forty cents $6.40
   b. eleven dollars and fifteen cents $11.15
   c. twenty dollars and five cents $20.05
   d. five dollars and ninety-eight cents $5.98

4. Write the numbers that fit in the blanks.
   a. one dollar = 100 pennies
   b. one dime = 2 nickels
   c. one dollar = 10 dimes
   d. one dollar = 4 quarters
   e. one quarter = 5 nickels
   f. one half dollar = 5 dimes
   g. one quarter = 25 pennies
   h. one half dollar = 10 nickels

5. Write the value of each **group** of coins.
   a. 2 dimes, 1 penny   21¢
   b. 1 dollar, 2 pennies $1.02
   c. 1 half dollar, 1 dime, 1 penny   61¢
   d. 3 quarters, 1 dime   85¢
   e. 2 quarters, 3 nickels   65¢

Review Exercises

B. *Write the answers only.*

6. 13 + 7   20   25 + 5   30   15 + 4   19   50 + 5   55   20 + 6   26
7. 15 + 8   23   18 + 9   27   24 + 4   28   22 + 6   28   21 + 8   29

C. *Copy and subtract. Check by addition.*

8. a. 700 − 147 = 553; +147 = 700
   b. 402 − 285 = 117; +285 = 402
   c. 900 − 702 = 198; +702 = 900
   d. 760 − 465 = 295; +465 = 760
   e. 706 − 196 = 510; +196 = 706

9. a. 558 − 269 = 289; +269 = 558
   b. 673 − 186 = 487; +186 = 673
   c. 428 − 195 = 233; +195 = 428
   d. 896 − 477 = 419; +477 = 896
   e. 127 − 62 = 65; +62 = 127

D. *Solve these problems.*

10. Anne had 51¢ in her pocket when she began weeding the flower bed. After the flower bed was finished, she found that she had only 26¢. What piece of money had she lost?   quarter

11. Bill has a dollar and 26 cents. If he spends a half dollar, how much will he have left?   76¢

42   Chapter 2   Subtraction With Borrowing

16. Adding and Subtracting Money

Money amounts can be added or subtracted like other numbers. The columns must be kept straight, and the **decimal points** must be kept in line with each other.

Remember that exact dollar amounts can be written in two ways. Six dollars can be written $6 or $6.00. Write $6.00 to add or subtract.

> Add or subtract the following amounts of money.
>
> $4 + $1.39 $6 − $2.78
>
> | $2.36 | $8.25 | $4.00 | $6.00 |
> |-------|-------|-------|-------|
> | + 3.57 | − 4.79 | + 1.39 | − 2.78 |
> | $5.93 | $3.46 | $5.39 | $3.22 |

A. *Copy and add or subtract. Be sure to put a dollar sign and decimal point in each answer.*

1.
$5.63	$8.97	$4.25	$7.89	$5.75
8.24	4.36	0.20	3.46	2.80
+ 3.00	+ 8.25	+ 9.60	+ 2.45	+ 0.75
$16.87	$21.58	$14.05	$13.80	$9.30

2.
$6.00	$8.00	$9.00	$3.05	$4.02
− 0.95	− 3.79	− 1.92	− 0.63	− 2.98
$5.05	$4.21	$7.08	$2.42	$1.04

B. *Copy in straight columns, and follow the signs. Change amounts like $3 to $3.00.*

3. a. $2.75 + $3.28 $6.03   b. $4.35 + $6.00 $10.35   c. $9.25 + $0.75 $10.00
4. a. $0.45 + $0.98 + $1.20 $2.63   b. $6.34 + $0.06 + $6 $12.40
5. a. $3 + $0.75 + $1.54 $5.29   b. $0.87 + $0.69 + $5 $6.56
6. a. $4.72 − $3.41 $1.31   b. $7.95 − $6.78 $1.17   c. $5.00 − $0.75 $4.25
7. a. $5.75 − $2.95 $2.80   b. $5 − $0.56 $4.44   c. $8 − $3.25 $4.75

Review Exercises

C. *Write these amounts in two ways.*

8. a. fifty-nine cents   b. six cents   6¢ $0.06   c. two dollars $2 $2.00
        59¢ $0.59
9. a. eleven cents   b. ten dollars   c. four cents 4¢ $0.04
       11¢ $0.11 $10 $10.00

LESSON 16

Objectives

- To give more drill with the money concepts taught in Lesson 15.
- To review addition and subtraction of money.

Preparation

1. Multiplication flash cards: 3's–5's
2. Pieces of money as in Lesson 15
3. Speed Drill 16
4. Chalkboard:

   a. 37¢   59¢ $0.85 $0.03
   $5.09 $19.95 $4.00 $4

   b. 500   603
      −185   −207
      (315)   (396)

   $5.00 $6.03 $2.45
   − 1.85   − 2.07   5.63
   ($3.15)   ($3.96)   + 1.36
                      ($9.44)

Oral Drill

1. Have the pupils count by 2's to 24, by 3's to 36, by 4's to 48, and by 5's to 60. If they have trouble counting by 3's and 4's, tell them to add 3 or 4 each time.

2. Drill the multiplication facts.

3. Drill mental addition and subtraction.

12 + 6	22 + 6	42 + 6
15 + 7	35 + 7	17 + 4
18 + 8	25 + 5	30 + 6
22 + 4	12 − 5	14 − 8
18 − 9	13 − 7	16 − 9

4. Have the children read the money amounts *(a)* on the board. Point out that the last two amounts are the same.

5. Drill addition and subtraction in random order, with problems such as the following:
   7 + 4 − 2 = (9)   8 − 4 + 9 + 5 = (18)
   6 − 3 + 8 − 1 = (10) 5 + 7 − 6 + 8 = (14)

Speed Drill

Give Speed Drill 16 (practice with numerals).

T–43 Chapter 2 Subtraction With Borrowing

Teaching Guide

1. *Money concepts.*
   a. Count money in class again, especially if the pupils had difficulty in Lesson 15.
   b. Ask questions such as these: **How many cents is 3 dimes and 3 nickels?** (45¢) **2 quarters and a nickel?** (55¢) **a quarter, a dime, and a nickel?** (40¢) **5 nickels and 4 pennies?** (29¢) Allow children to count the 5's and 10's on their fingers.
   c. Practice reading and writing prices. Be sure to include some like $3 as well as $0.03. (See part *a* on chalkboard.) Emphasize: **There must be two numbers after the decimal point.**
      Dictate prices for pupils to write on the board.

2. *Addition and subtraction of money.*
   a. Point to the subtraction problems *(b)* on the board. Do the first two together. Then ask: **How are the next two like the first two? How are they different?** Show that the money problems are solved in the same way as the other problems. **When the subtraction is finished, remember to put a dollar sign and decimal point in the answer.**
   b. **Adding money is similar to ordinary addition.** Together do the money addition problem on the board.
   c. **To add or subtract correctly, always write whole dollar amounts with two zeroes. Keep the columns straight, and keep the decimal points in line with each other.** Write these problems horizontally. Have volunteers set up the problems vertically and compute.
      $6 – $2.87 ($3.13)
      $3.25 + $0.57 + $4 ($7.82)
   d. Use the following problems for further practice. Pupils should solve each problem in column form.

   $$\begin{array}{r} \$8.02 \\ -\ 4.95 \\ \hline (\$3.07) \end{array} \qquad \begin{array}{r} \$2.59 \\ 0.57 \\ +\ 5.44 \\ \hline (\$8.60) \end{array}$$

   $7 – $4.50 ($2.50)
   $6.89 – $2 ($4.89)
   $8.40 + $6 + $0.75 ($15.15)

Note: In Part E of the review exercises, allow pupils to count by 5's, 10's, and 25's on their fingers if they need to. Keeping track of 5's on the fingers is not the same as counting on fingers to add.

Have all the children try to do the number strings (21–23). If they do very poorly, do not record grades for that part.

Supplementary Drills

Drill 66*

Drill 4 –

D. *Write these amounts with dollar signs.*

10. a. 3 dollars and 85 cents $3.85   b. 15 dollars and 9 cents $15.09

E. *Write the value of each group of money. Use play money if you have trouble.*

Example: 1 quarter, 1 nickel, 3 pennies   Answer: 33¢

11. a. 4 nickels 20¢   b. 3 quarters 75¢   c. 4 dimes, 6 pennies 46¢
12. a. 7 dimes 70¢   b. 6 half dollars $3.00   c. 2 quarters, 3 dimes 80¢
13. a. 5 quarters $1.25   b. 9 nickels 45¢   c. 3 dimes, 3 nickels, 1 penny 46¢
14. a. 17 pennies 17¢   b. 1 dime, 1 nickel 15¢   c. 1 quarter, 2 dimes, 1 nickel 50¢

*15. (extra) all the money in the set below 94¢

F. *Copy and fill in the missing numbers.*

16. 596, 597, 598, __599__, __600__, __601__, __602__, __603__

17. 120, 125, 130, __135__, __140__, __145__, 150, __155__

18. 700; __800__; 900; __1,000__; __1,100__; 1,200; 1,300; __1,400__

19. 2,995; 2,996; __2,997__; __2,998__; 2,999; __3,000__; __3,001__; __3,002__

G. *Write the answers.*

20.
6	14	8	5	11	10	7	5	13	3
+9	−5	−7	+8	−6	−8	+3	+9	−7	+9
15	9	1	13	5	2	10	14	6	12

Number Strings

H. *Can you figure out these number strings? Watch the signs!*

21. a. 5 + 8 + 4 + 2 = ? 19   b. 6 + 3 + 5 + 7 = ? 21   c. 9 + 4 + 5 + 6 = ? 24
22. a. 6 + 5 − 4 − 1 = ? 6   b. 5 − 2 + 6 + 4 = ? 13   c. 7 + 2 − 6 + 3 = ? 6
23. a. 8 − 3 + 8 − 5 = ? 8   b. 4 + 6 − 5 − 5 = ? 0   c. 9 − 7 + 8 + 6 = ? 16

44 Chapter 2 Subtraction With Borrowing

17. Telling Time

What time is it?

Probably you look at a clock many times in a day. You know that the short hand on the clock is the **hour hand**, and the long hand is the **minute hand**. The hour hand shows the hour, and the minute hand shows how many minutes before or after the hour.

It takes one hour for the hour hand to move from one number to the next. In that time, the minute hand moves all the way around the clock. Five minutes pass each time the minute hand moves from one number to the next.

A. *Write the answers.*

1. How many minutes does it take the minute hand to travel from

    a. 12 to 1? 5   c. 12 to 6? 30   e. 12 to 5? 25   g. 12 to 7? 35

    b. 12 to 3? 15   d. 12 to 9? 45   f. 12 to 10? 50   h. 12 to 11? 55

2. How many hours are between

    a. 1 o'clock and 5 o'clock? 4 hours   c. 12 o'clock and 3 o'clock? 3 hours

    b. 6 o'clock and 8 o'clock? 2 hours   d. 2 o'clock and 10 o'clock? 8 hours

3. Write the matching times beside each other. You will not use all the times from the row below.

    a. six o'clock   6:00   c. quarter till seven   6:45   e. ten after six   6:10

    b. half past six   6:30   d. quarter after seven   7:15   f. ten till seven   6:50

    6:00   6:10   6:15   6:30   6:45   6:50   7:00   7:10   7:15

4. Tell what time each clock shows.

    a. 4:00   b. 11:30   c. 8:15   d. 6:55   e. 3:20   f. 1:40

5. Draw clocks to show the following times.

    a. 9:15   b. half past 4:00   c. quarter till 11:00   d. 1:25

LESSON 17

Objectives
- To review telling time.
- To teach reading time in two ways.

Preparation
1. Subtraction flash cards
2. Multiplication flash cards: 3's–5's
3. A clock with movable hands (If you do not have an actual clock, you can easily make a suitable one with a paper plate.)
4. A dollar, half dollar, quarter, dime, nickel, penny
5. Chalkboard:

   5<u>4</u>,090   <u>9</u>81,000   400,0<u>0</u>8
   <u>2</u>0,600   705,3<u>8</u>0

Oral Drill
1. Drill subtraction facts quickly.
2. Drill multiplication facts: 3's–5's.
3. Review reading large numbers. Have the pupils read the numbers on the board and tell what the underlined digits stand for. They should say *4 thousands* or *4,000*, not merely *thousands*.
4. Review money concepts.
   a. Have pupils identify the pieces of money, one at a time if necessary. Then put several pieces together and have pupils tell the value.
   b. Ask questions such as these: **How much is 3 quarters?** (75¢) **2 dimes and a nickel?** (25¢) **6 nickels?** (30¢)

      How many nickels would make 40¢? (8) **How many quarters would make $1.50?** (6) **$2.00?** (8)

      What coins would you use to make 35¢? 75¢? 70¢? 90¢? Accept two quarters for 50¢. In the United States, quarters are used much more than half dollars.

T–45   Chapter 2   Subtraction With Borrowing

Teaching Guide

1. *Telling time.*
   a. Many fourth graders already have a good understanding of time. Ask questions such as these: **What time is it now? What time will it be in 20 minutes? in a half hour?** Such questions will let you know where the children are in their understanding. Do they count by fives on the clock to tell what time it will be in 20 minutes, or are they confused?
   b. **What are the names of the two hands of the clock? How long does it take the minute hand to go around the clock? How far does the hour hand travel in that time? How long does it take the minute hand to travel from one number to the next? How many minutes does it take the minute hand to go all the way around the clock?**
2. *Reading time in two ways.*
   a. Using your clock, move the hands to the following times and have pupils read those times.

      5:00   5:30   5:45   5:50
      8:30   8:15   8:05   8:45

      Have the pupils say the times in two ways: "quarter till 6" and "5:45," "quarter after 8" and "8:15," "half past 8" and "8:30."
   b. Have the pupils show times by moving the hands of the clock. If they have trouble, show them how to set the hour hand first, then count by fives from the 12 to set the minutes. To read times like "quarter till 6," they must count *back* from the 12.
   c. Show a time such as 9:10. Have someone move the hands to the time 15 minutes later, a half hour later, and so on. They should count by fives for this also. Ask questions such as this one: **If you start working on your math at 10:15 and it takes you 45 minutes to do it, when will you be finished?**
   d. Use the following exercises for further practice.
      Read each time in another way.
         7:45   4:30   8:55
      Tell what time it will be twenty minutes after 2:25 . . . 6:30 . . . 3:40 . . . 10:05

Extra Review

$6.00 $8.25 $7 − $3.29 ($3.71)
−4.75   −2.50
($1.25)   ($5.75)

Review addition and subtraction of money.
a. Use the above problems on the board to review subtraction, and check them to review addition.
b. Give further practice if necessary.

$4.98 $6.00 $3.06
−2.89   −3.99   − 2.50
($2.09)   ($2.01)   ($0.56)

$5.10 $7.25
− 3.75   − 4.98
($1.35)   ($2.27)

Note: The last exercise of Teaching Guide should prepare the pupils for exercises 6–8. If they have difficulty, let them use the toy clock to find the answers. Have them start at the time stated in the problem, and count ahead the indicated number of minutes. Ask, "What time would that be?" Do not confuse them by showing addition or subtraction of time on paper.
   Let the pupils use their fingers for exercise 10.

Supplementary Drills

Drill 2 +

Drill 73

Lesson 17   45

B. *Use a clock to help you solve these reading problems.*

6. A bus leaves the city every twenty minutes. The last bus left at ten minutes after 8:00. When will the next bus leave?   **8:30**

7. Sister Sylvia told the fourth graders, "I want you to study at least a half hour for your science test." Kevin glanced at the clock. It was 1:15. When may Kevin put his science book away?   **1:45**

8. School starts at 8:30. Devotions lasts for 25 minutes, and arithmetic class is next. When does arithmetic class begin?   **8:55**

Review Exercises

C. *Follow the directions.*

9. Write these amounts in two ways.

    a. sixty cents **60¢ $0.60**   b. three dollars **$3 $3.00**   c. eight cents **8¢ $0.08**

10. How many coins does it take to equal the amount of money shown?

    a. __8__ dimes = 80¢   f. __3__ half dollars = $1.50
    b. __7__ nickels = 35¢   g. __5__ quarters = $1.25
    c. __43__ pennies = 43¢   h. __10__ dimes = $1.00
    d. __9__ nickels = 45¢   i. __7__ quarters = $1.75
    e. __3__ quarters = 75¢   j. __10__ nickels = 50¢

11. Tell what coins equal these amounts. Use as few coins as possible without using half dollars, since half dollars are not commonly used.

    a. $0.46 **1 quarter, 2 dimes, 1 penny**
    b. $0.78 **3 quarters, 3 pennies**
    c. 92¢ **3 quarters, 1 dime, 1 nickel, 2 pennies**
    d. 31¢ **1 quarter, 1 nickel, 1 penny**

12. Subtract. Check by addition.

    a. $4.00 $1.45   b. $7.98 $2.39   c. $2.05 $0.57   d. $1.00 $0.63   e. $9.00 $2.02
       − 2.55 + 2.55   − 5.59 + 5.59   − 1.48 + 1.48   − 0.37 + 0.37   − 6.98 + 6.98
       $1.45 $4.00 $2.39 $7.98 $0.57 $2.05 $0.63 $1.00 $2.02 $9.00

13. Copy in straight columns. Follow the signs.

    a. $5.75 − $0.08 **$5.67**   c. $9.03 − $2.60 **$6.43**   e. $8.57 + $7.84 **$16.41**
    b. $8 − $7.35 **$0.65**   d. $6.47 + $3.89 **$10.36**   f. $5.90 + $2 + $0.67 **$8.57**

46 Chapter 2 Subtraction With Borrowing

18. More About Time

The boxes in this lesson teach several more facts about time.

> **Midnight** is 12:00 at night. **Noon** is 12:00 in the day.
> Time from 12:00 midnight to 12:00 noon is **A.M.**
> **A.M.** means "before noon."
> Time from 12:00 noon to 12:00 midnight is **P.M.**
> **P.M.** means "after noon."

A. *Follow the directions.*

1. Write **A.M.** or **P.M.** for each blank.
   a. The school day begins at 8:30 __A.M.__ and ends at 3:00 __P.M.__ .
   b. On Sunday morning we go to church at 9:00 __A.M.__ .
   c. Some children go to bed at 8:30 __P.M.__ and get up at 6:30 __A.M.__ .
   d. 2:00 in the afternoon is 2:00 __P.M.__ ; 2:00 at night is 2:00 __A.M.__ .
   e. You could have a dentist appointment at 11:00 __A.M.__ or 4:00 __P.M.__ .

2. How many hours is it from
   a. 12:00 noon to 4:00 P.M.?   4
   b. 10:00 A.M. to 12:00 noon? 2
   c. 6:00 P.M. to midnight?   6
   d. 7:00 A.M. to 11:00 A.M.?   4
   e. 8:00 A.M. to 1:00 P.M.?   5
   f. 10:00 P.M. to 4:00 A.M.?   6
   g. 6:00 A.M. to 6:00 P.M.?   12
   h. 3:00 P.M. today to 3:00 P.M. tomorrow? 24

> 60 seconds (sec.) = 1 minute (min.)
> 60 minutes = 1 hour (hr.)
> 24 hours = 1 day

3. Copy and fill in the missing numbers.
   a. 2 min. = __120__ sec.
   b. 2 hr. = __120__ min.
   c. 2 days = __48__ hr.
   d. 3 hr. = __180__ min.
   e. $\frac{1}{2}$ hr. = __30__ min.
   f. $\frac{1}{2}$ min. = __30__ sec.

4. Write the time that each clock shows. 
   a. 4:45
   b. 10:00
   c. 12:30
   d. 7:15
   e. 1:50
   f. 4:20

LESSON 18

Objectives

- To give more practice with telling time.
- To teach *the meaning of A.M. and P.M.
- To teach units of time.

Preparation

1. Mixed addition and subtraction flash cards
2. Multiplication flash cards: 2's–5's
3. Clock with moveable hands
4. Speed Drill 18
5. Chalkboard:

    32,005   400,630   65,020
    980,267   406,019

Oral Drill

1. Drill addition and subtraction facts in mixed order.
2. Drill the multiplication facts studied so far.
3. Drill mental addition.

    4 + 8 + 5 + 5 (22)   3 + 7 + 6 + 9 (25)
    6 + 7 + 2 + 8 (23)   8 + 3 + 4 + 6 (21)
    5 + 3 + 6 + 8 (22)   9 + 4 + 5 + 7 (25)

4. Review large numbers. Read the numbers on the board. Point to various digits and ask what their value is.
5. Review money by asking the following questions.
    a. **What is the value of 1 quarter?** (25¢) **2 quarters?** (50¢) **3 quarters?** (75¢) **2 quarters and 2 dimes?** (70¢) **4 dimes and 6 pennies?** (46¢) **3 nickels and 10 pennies?** (25¢)
    b. **What coins could you use to equal 25¢? 50¢? $1.00? 40¢? 35¢?** Accept all correct answers.

Speed Drill

Give Speed Drill 18 (subtraction practice).

Teaching Guide

1. *Further practice with time.*
    a. Show 7:30 on the toy clock, and have someone tell the time. Have someone move the hands to 15 minutes from then; an hour from then.
    b. Show another time such as quarter after 2. Have someone else show the time 20 minutes later; a half hour later.
    c. Ask: **What time is it now? What time will it be 2 hours from now? 5 hours from now? 12 hours from now?** Have pupils use the clock as a type of number line to figure out the

T–47   Chapter 2   Subtraction With Borrowing

answers if they do not know. Then use other times on the toy clock for similar practice.

d. Pupils should soon realize that twelve hours from any time is read with the same numbers. Ask: **When it is 9:30 twelve hours from now, is it really the same time of day as 9:30 now?** (No; now it is daytime, and in twelve hours it will be night.)

2. *A.M. and P.M.*
   a. **Midnight is 12:00 at night. Noon is 12:00 in the day. Any time from 12:00 midnight until 12:00 noon is A.M. time. From 12:00 noon to 12:00 midnight is P.M. time. If you want to be sure someone understands what time of day you mean, use A.M. or P.M.**

   If someone asks, you could tell the pupils that 12:00 noon is 12:00 M. (M. stands for *meridiem*, the Latin word for "midday.") 12:00 midnight is 12:00 A.M. But it is less confusing to use *noon* or *midnight* with 12:00.

   b. Ask: **Is 3:00 P.M. in the night or the afternoon? At 6:00 A.M., would someone more likely be getting out of bed or eating supper? At 2:00 A.M., would you probably be sleeping or studying? at 2:00 P.M.? What time does church start on Sunday morning? on Sunday evening?**

   c. Here are several more questions.
   • Is 7:00 A.M. in the morning or in the evening?
   • Is 8:00 P.M. in the morning or in the evening?
   • Is 1:00 A.M. 1 hour after noon or after midnight?
   • Is 2:00 P.M. 2 hours after noon or after midnight?

3. *Units of time.*
   a. Call the pupils' attention to the units of time in the box in Lesson 18. These are probably not new to them. You could count around the clock by fives to show that there are 60 minutes in 1 hour.

   b. If your classroom clock has a second hand, point out that it takes the second hand one minute to go around the clock. It takes the second hand five seconds to go from one number to another. Ask: **If there are five seconds between each number, how many seconds are there in a whole trip around the clock?**

   c. Ask: **How long is it from 12:00 noon until 12:00 midnight? How long is it from 12:00 midnight to 12:00 noon? So how long is it from 12:00 noon one day until 12:00 noon the next day?**

   From any time one day until the same time the next day is 24 hours. There are 24 hours in 1 day.

   d. Have pupils find how long it is between the following times by using a clock and counting ahead from the earlier time. This will help to prepare them for exercise 2.
   2:00 P.M. to 8:00 P.M. (6 hr.)
   12:00 midnight to 3:00 A.M. (3 hr.)
   9:00 A.M. to 4:00 P.M. (7 hr.)
   7:00 A.M. to 12:00 noon (5 hr.)

   Most children will probably realize that they can subtract to find the answers above, but do not labor over showing subtraction on paper. That is especially hard to do when one time is A.M. and the other is P.M. Have the children use a clock and count ahead from the first time.

Note: Many children enjoy the challenge of counting a mixture of money. You could, however, consider exercise 8e as extra credit. This lesson is not as long as some. You may want to supplement it with extra work.

Supplementary Drills

Drill 3 –

Drill 44

B. *Solve these reading problems.*

5. If you start studying your Bible memory at 4:05 and study for 15 minutes, when will you finish?   4:20

6. The Graham family begins family worship at 7:15. If their worship usually takes 20 minutes, about what time do they finish?   7:35

7. It takes the Horsts 10 minutes to drive to school. If they leave home at 8:10, what time do they arrive at school?   8:20

Review Exercises

C. *Do these exercises.*

8. What is the value of each set of money below?

   a. 1 dollar, 2 quarters, 3 dimes $1.80

   b. 4 quarters, 4 nickels $1.20

   c. 1 half dollar, 1 dime, 3 nickels   75¢

   d. 3 quarters, 1 dime, 6 pennies   91¢

   e. The money pictured at the bottom of the page $1.09

9. Name the coins that equal these amounts. Use as few coins as possible, without using half dollars.

   a. 35¢ — 1 quarter, 1 dime

   b. 42¢ — 1 quarter, 1 dime, 1 nickel, 2 pennies

   c. $0.85 — 3 quarters, 1 dime

   d. $0.69 — 2 quarters, 1 dime, 1 nickel, 4 pennies

10. Copy, subtract, and check by addition.

   a. $5.69 − 2.99 = $2.70 ; + 2.99 = $5.69

   b. $8.00 − 6.35 = $1.65 ; + 6.35 = $8.00

   c. $3.50 − 2.69 = $0.81 ; + 2.69 = $3.50

   d. $10.00 − 5.70 = $4.30 ; + 5.70 = $10.00

   e. $7.15 − 3.37 = $3.78 ; + 3.37 = $7.15

48 Chapter 2 Subtraction With Borrowing

19. More Large Numbers

Each digit in a number has a digital value and a place value. The **digital value** of 5 is 5, no matter where it is found in a number. The digital value of 8 is 8.

The **place value** of a digit depends on its **place** in a number—ones, tens, hundreds, and so on. In 350 the place value of 3 is hundreds. In 13,500 the place value of 3 is thousands.

When you say the 3 in 350 has a **value** of 3 hundreds or 300, you are giving its **combined** digital and place value.

A. Read these numerals in class.

1. 780,000   504,090   28,003   50,700   218,050

2. 21,038   487,200   190,061   903,006   329,457

B. Write the answers.

3. What is the place value of the 6 in each number below?

   a. 2<u>6</u>0,784   b. 893,<u>6</u>70   c. <u>6</u>85,041   d. 5<u>6</u>,790   e. 98,13<u>6</u>
   ten thousands   hundreds   hundred thousands   thousands   ones

4. What is the digital value of the underlined digits?

   a. 6<u>9</u>0,439   b. 31,0<u>5</u>8   c. 43<u>7</u>,566   d. <u>2</u>94,107   e. 502,<u>8</u>51
   nine   five   seven   two   eight

5. What is the combined value of the underlined digits?

   a. 47<u>5</u>,039   b. 20,<u>9</u>61   c. 310,8<u>4</u>6   d. <u>7</u>38,250   e. <u>3</u>5,008
   5 thousands   9 hundreds   4 tens   7 hundred thousands   3 ten thousands

6. Write numerals for these number words.

   a. three thousand, one hundred eighty-two   3,182

   b. twelve thousand, eighteen   12,018

   c. sixty-two thousand, seven hundred seven   62,707

   d. five hundred fourteen thousand, ninety-five   514,095

   e. four hundred two thousand, one hundred fifty-two   402,152

   f. two hundred thirty thousand, nine   230,009

LESSON 19

Objectives

- To review place value to hundred thousands.
- To introduce *finding change by subtraction, including *two-step problems.

Preparation

1. Multiplication facts: 1's–5's
2. Clock with movable hands
3. A variety of coins and bills (optional)
4. Chalkboard:

   a. Simple place value chart

   b. 5<u>4</u>,090   380,<u>2</u>30   400,06<u>5</u>
       32,00<u>9</u>   <u>6</u>93,210   5<u>0</u>8,017

   c. $5.00 $2.00 $7.00 $10.00
       −2.69   −1.85   −3.70   −5.98
       ($2.31)   ($0.15)   ($3.30)   ($4.02)

Oral Drill

1. Drill the multiplication facts 1's–5's. If your pupils are doing well with these, you could go on to the 6's.

2. Give mental drill of addition and subtraction.
   6 + 5 − 8 + 3 (6)   7 − 4 + 6 + 7 (16)
   9 − 6 + 3 + 8 (14)   14 − 4 − 3 − 2 (5)
   11 − 5 + 4 + 3 − 6 (7) 8 + 7 − 2 − 5 − 4 (4)

3. Review money. **How much is a dime and a nickel?** (15¢) **a quarter and a nickel?** (30¢) **two quarters and a nickel?** (55¢) **two dimes and two nickels?** (30¢)
   What are two ways to write 16 cents? 9 dollars?

4. Review time.
   a. Show the following times on the toy clock, and have pupils read them.
      quarter after 2:00   4:20
      quarter till 11:00   9:30
   b. Ask: **Is 3:00 P.M. in the morning or afternoon? Is 2:00 A.M. a good time to go shopping? What are you usually doing at 10:00 P.M.?**

5. Review < and >. If pupils have trouble remembering which is which, remind them that the arrow always points to the smaller number.

T–49   Chapter 2   Subtraction With Borrowing

Teaching Guide

1. *Place value and large numbers.*
   a. Review place value, using the chart *(a)* on the board. Say the places in unison, beginning at the right. **Each place is worth how many times as much as the place to its right?** (10)

      Point to each place and say: *10 is 10 times 1; 100 is 10 times 10; 1,000 is 10 times 100; 10,000 is 10 times 1,000; 100,000 is 10 times 10,000.* Then have the pupils say it with you.

   b. Have the pupils read the numbers *(b)* on the board and tell the value of the underlined digits. Discuss the difference between digital value and place value as explained in the pupil's lesson. Ask: **What is the digital value of this digit? What is its place value? What is its combined value?**

      If a question does not specify *place* value, the answer should be the combined value. Pupils have already been doing this kind of exercise without talking about "digital value."

   c. Dictate numbers for the pupils to write at the board. When you say *thousand*, they should place a comma. There are always three digits after the comma, even if those digits are only zeroes.

      20,758   340,600   988,000
      207,045   162,007   39,018

   d. If time permits, do the following drills on number values.

      Dictate a number, such as 540,328, and have someone write it on the board. Have someone else change the number to make it 1 more. (The 8 should be erased and changed to 9.) **Change it to 100 more; 1,000 more; 10,000 more . . .** Each time only one digit needs to be erased to make the change.

      Of course, if a 9 is in a given place, adding 1 will require changing more than one digit. Avoid giving directions that have this effect.

2. *Finding change by subtraction.*
   a. **In reading problems we are sometimes asked how much change someone receives when he buys something. To find change, we must subtract. Asking "how much change" is like asking "how much is left." We subtract to find how much is left.**
   b. Work through the problems *(c)* on the board to review subtracting from 0 and borrowing twice. Many "change problems" involve these procedures.
   c. Here are several more problems for practice.
      • Allen had $2.00. He bought a gallon of milk for $1.89. How much change did Allen receive? ($0.11)
      • Mother's bill was $8.58. She gave the clerk a $10.00 bill. What was her change? ($1.42)
      • Suppose you buy batteries for $2.69 and light bulbs for $1.89. If you pay with a $5.00 bill, what will be your change? ($0.42)

      The last problem requires addition before subtraction can be done. This is the first kind of two-step problem the pupils have had this year.

   Note: This is another shorter lesson than usual, which may need to be supplemented.

Supplementary Drills

Drill 1 +

Drill 64

Lesson 19   49

> **Finding Change**
> To find how much change you should get when you buy something, subtract the **amount you spent** from the **amount you gave** to the clerk.
>
> $$\begin{array}{r}\$5.00\\ -\ 3.48\\ \hline \$1.52\end{array}$$
>
> Example: You spent $3.48. You gave the clerk a $5.00 bill. Your change is $1.52.

C. *Solve these reading problems.*

7. Father spent $6.95 for a roll of wire. He handed the clerk $7.00. How much change should Father get? $0.05

8. Darla bought a bunch of bananas for $1.39 and a head of lettuce for $0.69. What was her change from a $5.00 bill? (First find the amount that Darla spent.) $2.92

9. If Merle spent $8.50 for gasoline, what was his change from $10.00? $1.50

10. Grandma bought a dozen oranges for $1.25, and a pound of peaches for $0.89. What was her change if she gave the clerk $3.00? $0.86

11. Matthew and Frank pick strawberries for Brother Wilmer. They earn 25¢ for every box they pick. One day Matthew earned $7.50 and Frank earned $6.75. How much more did Matthew earn than Frank? $0.75

Review Exercises

D. *Write each pair of numbers and put < or > between them.*

12. a. 5,004 _>_ 4,005   b. 15,120 _<_ 15,220   c. 6,989 _>_ 6,898

E. *Write A.M. or P.M. for each blank.*

13. 10:00 at night is 10:00 _P.M._ . 10:00 in the morning is 10:00 _A.M._ .

14. You might be in school at 9:00 _A.M._ .

15. Prayer meeting begins at 7:30 _P.M._ .

F. *Write the time that each clock shows.*

16. a. 9:15   b. 12:00   c. 3:30   d. 3:55   e. 6:45   f. 6:25

50 Chapter 2 Subtraction With Borrowing

20. Chapter 2 Review

A. *Write the answers to these facts. Watch the signs!*

1.
8	13	5	7	10	16	11	4	12	9
+4	−6	+9	+3	−4	−7	−5	+3	−9	+6
12	7	14	10	6	9	6	7	3	15

2.
10	14	7	6	9	11	15	17	3	8
−2	−8	+7	+3	−5	−8	−7	−9	+8	−6
8	6	14	9	4	3	8	8	11	2

B. *Write only the answers to these column additions.*

3.
4	6	9	3	5	1	8
6	7	5	4	6	7	8
5	3	5	6	7	4	4
+3	+5	+4	+6	+8	+5	+3
18	21	23	19	26	17	23

C. *Copy and subtract.*

4.
71	93	80	36	98
−63	−35	−48	−24	−88
8	58	32	12	10

5.
997	432	568	360	325
−469	−165	−79	−179	−64
528	267	489	181	261

6.
$5.35	$5.00	$3.01	$7.00	$9.50
−2.65	−2.45	−0.79	−3.50	−6.75
$2.70	$2.55	$2.22	$3.50	$2.75

D. *Subtract. Show the check by addition.*

7. a. 503 228   b. 800 541   c. 300 265   d. 701 202
   −275 +275   −349 +349   −35 +35   −499 +499
   228   503   451   800   265   300   202   701

LESSON 20

Objective

♦ To review the concepts taught in Chapter 2 (listed below).
  - Addition and subtraction facts
  - Column addition
  - Subtraction with or without borrowing
  - Checking subtraction by addition
  - Money concepts
  - Time (not included on test)
  - Place value and reading larger numbers
  - Reading problems with words like *longer* or *older* and *change*

Preparation

1. Addition and subtraction flash cards
2. Speed Drill 20
3. Chalkboard:

   560,050   39,500   802,004
   70,123   456,039

Speed Drill

Give Speed Drill 20 (mixed addition and subtraction).

Teaching Guide

1. Drill the addition and subtraction facts.
2. Drill mental addition.
   5 + 4 + 7 + 6 (22)   3 + 7 + 9 + 5 (24)
   7 + 8 + 4 + 3 (22)   4 + 2 + 9 + 5 (20)
   8 + 6 + 4 + 8 (26)   4 + 7 + 5 + 5 (21)
3. Review time.
   a. **What time is it? Is it A.M. or P.M.? When is A.M. time? P.M. time? When is noon?**
   b. **How many seconds are in a minute? How many hours in a day? How many minutes in an hour?**
4. Review money concepts: identifying bills and coins, counting money, writing prices, and making change.
5. Review large numbers, place value, and digital value. (These two terms are not on the test.)

   Read the numbers on the board. Point to various digits, and have pupils identify the value (such as 6 ten thousands or 5 tens).
6. Review the borrowing process. Have the pupils solve a variety of problems at the board or in their seats.

45	800	376	116	129
−28	−387	−129	−58	−73
(17)	(413)	(247)	(58)	(56)

70	502	$4.00	$7.25
−15	−95	− 0.79	− 6.85
(55)	(407)	($3.21)	($0.40)

T–51   Chapter 2   Subtraction With Borrowing

7. Review checking subtraction by addition. *Make sure pupils are actually checking* and not just doing another problem.
8. Review reading problems.
    a. Subtracting to find the amount of change.
    b. Subtracting to find how much older, longer, heavier, and so forth.
    c. Subtracting to find how much more, how much less, or how many left.
9. Tell students that they will have a test in the next class.

Note: This is a rather long lesson. Pick out the parts you feel your students need. To reduce the amount of work, you could assign only the first three problems in each row of Part C. Or you could do the reading problems in class.

E. *Write the answers.*

8. Write each price in two ways.
   a. six cents   6¢   b. seventy-nine cents   79¢   c. eight dollars $8
              $0.06 $0.79 $8.00

9. Write the value of each set of money below.
   a. 1 quarter, 3 nickels   40¢
   b. 3 dimes, 2 nickels, 2 pennies   42¢
   c. 2 quarters, 2 dimes, 4 pennies   74¢
   d. 1 half dollar, 1 quarter, 2 dimes, 1 nickel $1.00
   e. the coins pictured at the right   61¢

10. Write numerals for these number words.
    a. sixty-five thousand   65,000
    b. three thousand, one hundred twenty   3,120
    c. four hundred seventeen thousand, thirty-eight   417,038
    d. nine hundred ninety thousand, nine hundred nine   990,909

11. Write the combined value of the underlined digits.
    a. 6<u>7</u>,034   b. <u>4</u>9,201   c. 948,7<u>2</u>5   d. <u>8</u>50,000   e. 398,<u>6</u>40
       7 thousands   4 ten thousands   2 tens   8 hundred thousands   6 hundreds

12. Write the correct answers.
    a. 12:00 in the day is called 12:00 (midnight, <u>noon</u>).
    b. A good time to eat supper is 5:30 (A.M., <u>P.M.</u>).
    c. You are usually sleeping at 2:00 (<u>A.M.</u>, P.M.).
    d. 1 hr. = __60__ min.
    e. 1 day = __24__ hr.
    f. 1 min. = __60__ sec.

13. What times do these clocks show?
    a. 8:30   b. 11:05   c. 6:10   d. 2:35   e. 8:15

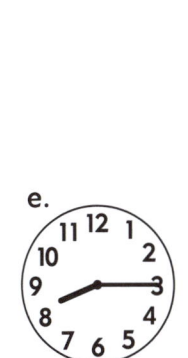

(continued on next page)

Chapter 2 Subtraction With Borrowing

F. Solve these reading problems.

14. Helen bought tablet paper for $0.69 and gave the clerk $1.00. How much change did she receive? $0.31

15. Noah lived to be 950 years old. Abraham died at 175. How much longer did Noah live than Abraham? 775 years

16. How much feed has been used from a 100-pound bag if 64 pounds are left? 36 pounds

17. Mother bought butter for $1.59, cheese for $2.69, and bread for $1.25. What was her total bill? $5.53

18. Father gave $40.00 for a pair of shoes priced at $37.95. What was his change? $2.05

19. Christine said, "My grandfather is 83 and my grandmother is 72. How much older is my grandfather than my grandmother?" 11 years

20. If you start your homework at 6:30 and it takes 45 minutes to do it, when will you be finished? 7:15

21. Mother was buying a new shirt for Philip. One shirt cost $7.98 and another cost $9.25. What was the difference in price? $1.27

22. Jesse can carry 40 pounds, and his big brother can carry 125 pounds. How much more weight can Jesse's brother carry? 85 pounds

23. In second grade Barbara learned 72 Bible verses. In third grade she learned 150 verses. How many more verses did Barbara learn in third grade? 78 verses

21. Chapter 2 Test

LESSON 21

Objective

♦ To test the pupils' mastery of the concepts taught in Chapter 2.

Teaching Guide

1. Give any last-minute review that you feel is necessary.
2. Administer the test.

Note: Chapter 2 Test is found in the test section in the back of this manual.

Chapter 3

Multiplication Facts: 1–6

And the Lord thy God will make thee plenteous
in every work of thine hand . . . and in the fruit of thy land.
(Deuteronomy 30:9)

54 Chapter 3 Multiplication Facts: 1–6

22. Regrouping in Addition

See if you can do these horizontal addition problems. You should find the first two easier than the other two.

      10 + 4   20 + 6   13 + 5   17 + 8

Here is a different kind of horizontal addition. Can you give the answers? For **14 + 15**, think: **14 + 10 + 5 = 29**.

A. *Write the answers.*

1. 10 + 6 **16**   20 + 4 **24**   10 + 8 **18**   30 + 7 **37**   20 + 9 **29**
2. 12 + 5 **17**   15 + 8 **23**   14 + 6 **20**   18 + 7 **25**   13 + 8 **21**
3. 12 + 14 **26**   13 + 10 **23**   15 + 11 **26**   16 + 13 **29**   14 + 14 **28**
4. 12 + 16 **28**   11 + 14 **25**   13 + 15 **28**   17 + 12 **29**   14 + 13 **27**

Column addition is sometimes easier if you regroup the numbers. Study the following examples.

| 5
3
5
+ 7 | Think: 5 + 5 = 10

3 + 7 = 10

10 + 10 = 20 | 4
9
8
+ 6 | Think: 4 + 6 = 10

9 + 8 = 17

10 + 17 = 27 |

Finding groups of ten makes the problems easier. **You can regroup addends in any way and still get the same answer.**

B. *Write the answer to each addition, grouping the numbers as shown. For the first problem in row 5, think: 10 + 10 = 20.*

5.   1   7   3   4   4   3   8   6
    9   3   5   6   1   4   2   7
    3   2   2   5   5   9   8   4
  + 7   + 5   + 6   + 3   + 9   + 7   + 6   + 5
   20   **17**   **16**   **18**   **19**   **23**   **24**   **22**

6.   4   6   7   5   8   6   2   3
    9   6   6   5   3   8   8   9
    3   5   8   7   9   4   7   4
  + 7   + 8   + 3   + 7   + 5   + 9   + 8   + 8
   23   **25**   **24**   **24**   **25**   **27**   **25**   **24**

LESSON 22

Objectives
- To teach *regrouping of numbers in column addition.
- To teach *horizontal addition of two-digit numbers (without carrying).

Preparation
1. Subtraction flash cards
2. Multiplication flash cards: 4's–6's
3. Speed Drill 22
4. Chalkboard:

    a. 150,800   405,189
        700,036   289,998

    b.
    ```
         5              6              4
         5  10 + 7      4  10 + 12     8  12 + 13
         4              7              6
       + 3            + 5            + 7
       ─────          ─────          ─────
        (17)           (22)           (25)
    ```

Oral Drill
1. Drill subtraction facts.
2. Drill multiplication facts, emphasizing the 6's.
3. Use the numbers *(a)* on the board to review place value, digital value, and reading large numbers.
4. Have the pupils tell the next three numbers that come after the ones on the board.
5. Review time. Ask: **What time is it now? What time will it be in 15 minutes? in half an hour? in 20 minutes? in an hour?**

Speed Drill
Give Speed Drill 22 (addition and subtraction).

T–55   Chapter 3   Multiplication Facts: 1–6

Teaching Guide

1. *Regrouping in column addition.*
    a. Point to each column addition *(b)* on the board. Show how the addends can be grouped to make the same numbers as in the horizontal additions beside them. **Sometimes in column addition it is easier to add groups of numbers, instead of adding each number one at a time in the order it comes. This is especially easy when we can group tens. It does not matter in what order we group the addends as long as we are sure to add them all.**
    b. Use the following problems for individual practice. You could copy them on the board and draw curved lines to show which addends to group together, as in Part B in the pupil's book.

    ```
      6        5        8        9
      4        5        2        3
      2        6        9        7
    + 8      + 7      + 3      + 2
    (20)     (23)     (22)     (21)

      3        1        7        6
      6        7        8        5
      5        9        6        8
    + 4      + 8      + 8      + 6
    (18)     (25)     (29)     (25)
    ```

2. *Horizontal addition.*
    a. Point to the three horizontal addition problems *(b)* on the board. **Which ones are easiest? It is easier to add numbers to ten than to other numbers, because our number system is based on tens.**
    b. Use the following problems for individual practice. For 10 + 14, pupils should think 10 + 10 + 4. For 13 + 14 they should think 13 + 10 + 4.

    10 + 8   (18)   10 + 14 (24)
    12 + 10 (22)   20 + 6   (26)
    13 + 14 (27)   12 + 12 (24)
    15 + 11 (26)   14 + 12 (26)

Supplementary Drills

Drill 59*

Drill 2 +

C. *Copy and add, grouping by tens when you can.*

7.   56   87   97   77   38   46
       83   96   23   60   55   84
   + 75   + 24   + 58   + 57   + 46   + 92
    214   207   178   194   139   222

Review Exercises

D. *Copy in straight columns and follow the signs.*

8. a. $4.05 + $2.26 + $1.60 $7.91   b. $0.85 + $1.74 + $3 $5.59
9. a. $7.29 + $0.48 + $3.25 $11.02   b. $10 + $2.85 + $3.65 $16.50
10. a. $9.10 − $4.25 $4.85   b. $5 − $3.69 $1.31
11. a. $8.05 − $0.79 $7.26   b. $7.61 − $4.25 $3.36

E. *Write the answers.*

12. a. Before noon is (<u>A.M.</u>, P.M.).   b. After noon is (A.M., <u>P.M.</u>).
13. a. 1 day = <u> 24 </u> hours   b. 1 hour = <u> 60 </u> minutes
14. 1 quarter, 2 dimes, 1 nickel = <u> 50 </u> cents
15. 3 quarters, 1 dime, 3 nickels = <u> 100 </u> cents
16. a. In 16,700 the 6 means <u>6 thousands</u>.   b. In 348,065 the 6 means <u>6 tens</u>.
17. 3,077; 3,078; <u>3,079</u>; <u>3,080</u>; <u>3,081</u>; <u>3,082</u>
18. 6,198; 6,199; <u>6,200</u>; <u>6,201</u>; <u>6,202</u>; <u>6,203</u>
19. 18,997; 18,998; <u>18,999</u>; <u>19,000</u>; <u>19,001</u>; <u>19,002</u>
20. 12,000; 13,000; 14,000; <u>15,000</u>; <u>16,000</u>; <u>17,000</u>; <u>18,000</u>

F. *Solve these reading problems.*

21. David got up at 6:15. Breakfast was ready 35 minutes later. What time was David's breakfast?   6:50

22. Timothy has $12.38 in a savings account and $5.75 in his bank at home. How much does he have in all? $18.13

*23. Miriam bought apples for $1.89, bread for $0.95, and carrots for $0.59. She gave the clerk $5.00. What was her change? $1.57

56 Chapter 3 Multiplication Facts: 1–6

23. Multiplication Facts: 1's, 2's, 3's

How many are three 5's? Count by 5's to find the answer. When you say, "Three 5's are 15" or "3 times 5 is 15," you are multiplying.

Two ways of writing multiplication are shown in the box. Both mean "3 times 5 is 15."

$$3 \times 5 = 15$$

The times sign (×) tells you to multiply.

```
    5   factor
  × 3   factor
   15   product
```

Multiplication is a fast way of adding **when the addends are all the same.** Multiplying 4 × 3 is a quick way of adding 3 + 3 + 3 + 3.

A. *Write the answers to these multiplication facts. Study any that you do not know well.*

1. 3 × 1 = 3   2 × 5 = 10   2 × 7 = 14   3 × 4 = 12   2 × 3 = 6   1 × 5 = 5
2. 2 × 6 = 12 3 × 8 = 24   1 × 6 = 6   3 × 5 = 15   3 × 10 = 30 3 × 7 = 21
3. 1 × 4 = 4   1 × 9 = 9   0 × 6 = 0   3 × 7 = 21   3 × 2 = 6   3 × 6 = 18
4. 2 × 9 = 18 3 × 3 = 9   3 × 9 = 27   2 × 4 = 8   2 × 10 = 20 0 × 5 = 0

5. 10   11   12   9   11   5   8   2   12
   × 3 × 3 × 3 × 1 × 1 × 3 × 2 × 3 × 0
    30   33   36   9   11   15   16   6   0

6. 4   7   10   8   9   12   6   8   3
   × 3 × 2 × 2 × 1 × 3 × 1 × 2 × 3 × 3
    12   14   20   8   27   12   12   24   9

7. 6   11   9   12   4   10   7   5   5
   × 3 × 0 × 2 × 2 × 2 × 1 × 3 × 1 × 2
    18   0   18   24   8   10   21   5   10

B. *Do these exercises.*

8. Write multiplications that mean the same as these additions.

   a. 2 + 2 + 2   3 × 2   b. 0 + 0   2 × 0   c. 4 + 4 + 4   3 × 4

9. Write additions that mean the same as these multiplications.

   a. 2 × 6   6 + 6   b. 2 × 4   4 + 4   c. 3 × 3   3 + 3 + 3

LESSON 23

Objectives

- To drill the 1's–3's multiplication facts.
- To review some basic concepts of multiplication.
- To teach measures of capacity.

Preparation

1. Multiplication flash cards (See *Teaching Guide*, number 1.)
2. Various measures: a cup, pint, quart, gallon (optional)
3. Chalkboard:

    a. I   II   III IV   V
        VI   VII VIII IX   X

    b. 1,029   40,080   56,998   35,289
        761,348

    c.   3   8   5
         4   3   9
         5   7   5
       + 6   + 6   + 3
       ────   ────   ────
       (18)   (24)   (22)

Oral Drill

1. Review the number of hours in a day, minutes in an hour, and seconds in a minute.
2. Review A.M. and P.M.
3. Have the children read the Roman numerals *(a)* on the board.
4. Review place value by using the large numbers *(b)* on the board. Have children tell what two numbers come next.
5. Count by 2's, by 3's, by 4's, by 5's. (Each time add on 3, 4, and so forth.)
6. Review grouping by tens in column addition. Pick out the tens in the additions *(c)* on the board. (Remember that not all problems have groups of ten.)

T–57 Chapter 3 Multiplication Facts: 1–6

Teaching Guide

1. *Multiplication facts.*
   Give flash card drill on the multiplication facts. Your pupils should have mastered the 1's–3's by this time if you have been reviewing them in earlier drills. Briefly review the 0's if you have not yet. Concentrate on the 4's–6's. If your pupils are ready, go on to the 7's.

2. *Multiplication concepts.*
   a. Have the pupils look at Lesson 23 in their books. Note the two ways in the box to write multiplication problems. Also note the parts of a multiplication problem: *factors* and *product*. If you introduce the terms *multiplicand* and *multiplier*, make only brief mention of them.
   b. In a vertical problem, the bottom factor should be read first. (See box.) Many pupils (and teachers) read vertical problems incorrectly. There is a reason for "reading from the bottom," but do not make an issue of it now. This fact is of minor importance in these first few lessons on multiplication.
   c. Show that 4 × 3 = 3 × 4 by dot drawings on the board. **Four groups of 3 is not the same as 3 groups of 4, but the two questions are "twins"—they have the same answer.**
   d. Show the relationship between addition and multiplication.
      The Mast family planted four rows of fruit trees with five trees in each row. How many trees did they plant in all?
      How do you find the answer to this problem? You usually add to find how many in all. You can add to find the answer to this problem too. But you need to add 5 + 5 + 5 + 5, because there are *four* rows with *five* in each row. That makes four 5's.
      A quicker way to find the answer is to multiply 4 × 5. Multiplication is a fast way of combining addends when the addends are the same.
      Illustrate with 3 + 3 + 3 + 3. Add the numbers one at a time. **How many 3's did we add? If there were four 3's, we can say 4 × 3 instead. The answer is 12.**

3. *Liquid measures.*
   a. Refer to the Liquid Measure box in the pupil's lesson. If you have cup, pint, and quart measures, display them as you discuss the equivalents. If pupils have not studied this before, use water to *show* that 2 cups = 1 pint, and so on.
   b. Ask the following questions.
      How many cups are in a pint? in a quart?
      How many cups are in a half pint? in a half quart?
      A half quart is the same as 1 (pint).
      A half pint is the same as 1 (cup).
      A half gallon is (2) quarts.
      Which is more: a quart or a pint? 2 quarts or a gallon?

Note: If your pupils do not know the multiplication facts very well, assign them to make sets of individual study cards for the more difficult facts. Also make use of the drills in the back of the book.

Supplementary Drills

Drill 5*

Drill 4 –

Learn the units of liquid measure in the box.

Liquid Measure
2 cups = 1 pint (pt.)   4 cups = 1 quart
2 pints = 1 quart (qt.)   4 quarts = 1 gallon (gal.)

C. *Answer these questions about liquid measure.*

10. Is a quart 2 times a pint? **yes**

11. Is a gallon 2 times a quart? **no**

12. Are 4 cups equal to a quart? **yes**

13. Is a half gallon the same as two quarts? **yes**

14. Can you empty a kettle of water sooner with a quart measure or with a pint measure? **quart**

D. *Write* more *or* fewer *for each blank.*

15. To can a large kettle of tomato juice, you would need

    a. **fewer** quart jars than pint jars.   c. **more** quart jars than gallon jars.

    b. **fewer** gallon jars than pint jars.   d. **more** half-pint jars than pint jars.

E. *Solve these problems.*

16. The Ramer family uses 2 gallons of milk a day. How much milk do they use in a week? (Hint: Think how many days are in a week.) **14 gallons**

17. Anna uses 3 cups of milk in a recipe for hot chocolate. How much milk will she use if she triples the recipe? (**Triple** means 3 times.) **9 cups**

Review Exercises

F. *Write only the answers. Regroup by tens when you can.*

18.
5	7	4	8	9	2	5	3
6	3	5	2	3	6	3	8
5	6	5	8	4	9	8	4
+3	+8	+3	+4	+7	+8	+7	+5
19	**24**	**17**	**22**	**23**	**25**	**23**	**20**

G. *Copy and add.*

19.
243	418	57	127	624	395
536	271	424	53	157	206
65	38	132	746	285	574
+210	+327	+48	+142	+63	+523
1,054	**1,054**	**661**	**1,068**	**1,129**	**1,698**

Chapter 3 Multiplication Facts: 1–6

24. Multiplying Two-Digit and Three-Digit Numbers

Multiplication facts go in pairs. If 8 × 2 = 16, then 2 × 8 = 16.

A. Write the products to these pairs.

1. a. 7 × 3 and 3 × 7 21   b. 4 × 3 and 3 × 4 12   c. 2 × 9 and 9 × 2 18
2. a. 5 × 3 and 3 × 5 15   b. 2 × 6 and 6 × 2 12   c. 8 × 3 and 3 × 8 24

To multiply two-digit and three-digit numbers, study the problems in the box.

```
  32    Think: 4 × 2 ones. Write 8.        213    3 × 3 ones (9)
×  4    Think: 4 × 3 tens. Write 12.       ×  3   3 × 1 ten (3)
 128    The answer is 128.                        3 × 2 hundreds (6)
                                           639    The answer is 639.
```

B. Copy and multiply.

3.
```
  91      52      13      32      83      70
×  3    ×  3    ×  2    ×  4    ×  3    ×  3
 273     156      26     128     249     210
```

4.
```
  84      31      54      73      20      23
×  2    ×  6    ×  2    ×  3    ×  9    ×  3
 168     186     108     219     180      69
```

5.
```
 221     642     324     930     800     742
×  4    ×  2    ×  2    ×  3    ×  2    ×  2
 884   1,284     648   2,790   1,600   1,484
```

Look at the numbers in the following row. They are the numbers you say when you count by 2's. They are also the answers to the 2's multiplication facts. These are called **even numbers**.

0, 2, 4, 6, 8, 10, 12, 14, 16, 18, 20, 22, 24

All numbers that are not even numbers are **odd numbers**. The odd numbers are 1, 3, 5, 7, 9, 11, and so on.

C. Do these exercises.

6. Write all the even numbers in the row below.

   23   (54)   (40)   (8)   (32)   (76)   19   25

7. Write by 3's from 0 to 36. These numbers are the answers to the 3's multiplication facts.

   0, 3, 6, 9, 12, 15, 18, 21, 24, 27, 30, 33, 36

LESSON 24

Objectives

- To give further review of basic multiplication concepts.
- To teach *multiplying a two- or three-digit number by a one-digit number (without carrying).
- To review odd and even numbers.

Preparation

1. Multiplication flash cards: 0's–6's
2. Speed Drill 24
3. Chalkboard:

   a. 20,399   469,000   280,999
      58,998   99,999

   b. I   II   III   IV   V   VI
      VII   VIII   IX   X

   c.
   ```
        12
        12              43
        12      12      43      43
       +12     × 4     +43     × 3
                      (129)   (129)
   ```

Oral Drill

1. Review large numbers and place value with the numbers (a) on the board.
2. Count by 3's, by 4's, by 5's, and by 6's.
3. Drill mental addition.
   4 + 6 + 9 + 2 (21)   5 + 8 + 4 + 6 (23)
   7 + 2 + 9 + 3 (21)   8 + 7 + 3 + 4 (22)
   7 + 4 + 5 + 5 (21)   2 + 8 + 8 + 9 (27)
4. Review Roman numerals with *b* on the board.
5. Drill the multiplication facts. Include the 4's–6's.

Speed Drill

Give Speed Drill 24 (addition facts).

Chapter 3   Multiplication Facts: 1–6

Teaching Guide

1. *Multiplication concepts.*
   a. Review *factor* and *product*.
   b. Review the relationship of addition and multiplication. Give a child a problem like 6 + 6 or 2 + 2 + 2 + 2, and have him give the corresponding multiplication fact. (2 × 6, 4 × 2)
   c. Note that multiplication facts go in pairs as addition facts do. **If we know one fact in a pair, we know the other one. If 4 × 6 = 24, how much is 6 × 4?**
   d. Ask pupils to give the matching fact for each of these.
      4 × 9   (9 × 4)
      2 × 7   (7 × 2)
      3 × 6   (6 × 3)

2. *Multiplying 2- or 3-digit numbers.*
   a. Point to the first addition problem *(c)* on the board. **How do we add a column of numbers?** (Add the ones first, then the tens.)
   b. Point to the corresponding multiplication problem. **We do the same in multiplication. We multiply the ones first, then the tens.** Do the problem together. Teach pupils to multiply the bottom factor (the multiplier) times the top factor.

Note: In the phrase "multiply 3 *times* 2," 2 is the *multiplicand*. This is written $\begin{array}{r}2\\ \times 3\end{array}$ or 3 × 2. In the phrase "multiply 3 *by* 2," 2 is the *multiplier*. This is written $\begin{array}{r}3\\ \times 2\end{array}$ or 2 × 3. In vertical multiplication, the top factor is always multiplied *by* the bottom factor.

c. Use the following problems for individual practice.

$\begin{array}{r}33\\ \times 3\\ \hline (99)\end{array}$ $\begin{array}{r}62\\ \times 3\\ \hline (186)\end{array}$ $\begin{array}{r}80\\ \times 3\\ \hline (240)\end{array}$ $\begin{array}{r}32\\ \times 4\\ \hline (128)\end{array}$

$\begin{array}{r}712\\ \times 3\\ \hline (2{,}136)\end{array}$ $\begin{array}{r}623\\ \times 2\\ \hline (1{,}246)\end{array}$ $\begin{array}{r}502\\ \times 3\\ \hline (1{,}506)\end{array}$

3. *Odd and even numbers.*
   a. Count by 2's. **All the numbers you said are *even numbers*. All even numbers end with 0, 2, 4, 6, or 8. Any of those numbers can be divided evenly into two parts.**
   b. **Now start with 1 and count by 2's from there. You will not say any of the numbers you said the first time. These numbers are *odd numbers*. All odd numbers end with 1, 3, 5, 7, or 9. They cannot be divided evenly into two equal parts.**

Supplementary Drill
Drill 80*

Review Exercises

D. *Write the answers to these facts.*

8.
2	12	5	4	9	9	7	5	8
×3	×3	×1	×2	×1	×3	×3	×2	×3
6	36	5	8	9	27	21	10	24

9.
7	8	5	3	11	0	6	10	12
×2	×1	×3	×3	×2	×2	×3	×3	×2
14	8	15	9	22	0	18	30	24

10.
4	9	9	4	11	2	6	11	3
×0	×3	×2	×3	×1	×2	×2	×3	×1
0	27	18	12	11	4	12	33	3

E. *Copy and add or subtract.*

11.
$4.00 − 1.95 = $2.05
$5.12 − 0.87 = $4.25
$9.03 − 2.78 = $6.25
$8.25 − 4.17 = $4.08
$3.69 − 1.82 = $1.87

12.
$14.95 + 25.39 = $40.34
$25.38 + 34.36 = $59.74
$40.76 + 52.59 = $93.35
$29.30 + 3.88 = $33.18
$78.25 + 21.75 = $100.00

F. *Write the numbers that belong in the blanks.*

13. 1 quart = __2__ pints   1 pint = __2__ cups

14. 1 gallon = __4__ quarts   1 quart = __4__ cups

15. ½ gallon = __2__ quarts   ½ pint = __1__ cup

16. 1 minute = __60__ seconds   1 day = __24__ hours

17. 3 quarters, 1 dime, 1 nickel = __90__ cents

18. 1 quarter, 3 dimes, 4 pennies = __59__ cents

G. *Write what time each clock shows.*

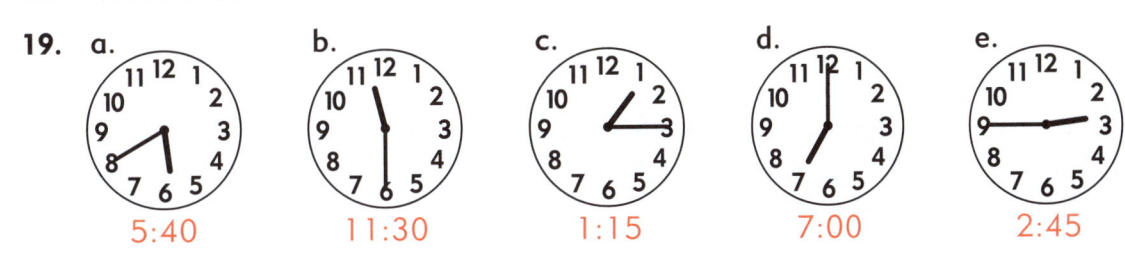

19. a. 5:40   b. 11:30   c. 1:15   d. 7:00   e. 2:45

25. Changing Units of Measure; Multiplication: 4's and 5's

To change from a larger unit of measure to a smaller unit, you must **multiply**. The **key number** for multiplying is the number of smaller units in the larger unit.

> **Changing Larger Units to Smaller Units**
> 3 gallons = ____ quarts   Think: 1 gallon = 4 quarts
> The key number is 4.
> $3 \times 4 = 12$
> 3 gallons = 12 quarts

A. *Write the missing numbers. Find the answers by multiplying.*

1. 3 quarts = __6__ pints   7 gallons = __28__ quarts
2. 3 hours = __180__ minutes   2 days = __48__ hours
3. 5 quarts = __20__ cups   8 pints = __16__ cups

B. *Write the answers to the multiplication facts below. Study any that you do not know well.*

4. $4 \times 4 = 16$ $4 \times 8 = 32$ $5 \times 5 = 25$ $4 \times 3 = 12$
5. $5 \times 7 = 35$ $5 \times 3 = 15$ $5 \times 6 = 30$ $4 \times 7 = 28$
6. $4 \times 5 = 20$ $5 \times 4 = 20$ $5 \times 8 = 40$ $5 \times 2 = 10$
7. $4 \times 6 = 24$ $5 \times 1 = 5$ $5 \times 9 = 45$ $4 \times 2 = 8$
8. $4 \times 11 = 44$ $4 \times 12 = 48$ $5 \times 11 = 55$ $5 \times 12 = 60$
9. $5 \times 10 = 50$ $4 \times 10 = 40$ $4 \times 9 = 36$ $4 \times 7 = 28$

10. 11×4=44   8×3=24   5×5=25   9×5=45   6×3=18   12×4=48   7×4=28   5×4=20   4×3=12

11. 12×5=60   8×4=32   7×5=35   4×4=16   6×5=30   9×4=36   6×4=24   8×5=40   10×4=40

Look at the following problem. Can you find the answer? $2 \times 4 + 3$

The example may be called a "times-and" problem. You must multiply and add to find the answer: $2 \times 4 = 8$, and $8 + 3 = 11$. Solving "times-and" problems will help you to get ready for carrying in multiplication.

LESSON 25

Objectives

- To introduce *changing from a larger unit to a smaller unit by multiplying.
- To drill the 4's and 5's multiplication facts.
- To review "times-and" problems.
- To give practice with reading problems solved by multiplication.

Preparation

1. Multiplication flash cards: 4's–6's
2. Chalkboard:

   a. 43   65   81   90
       32   58   49   74

   b. 1 qt. = ___ pt.   1 qt. = ___ cups
       2 qt. = ___ pt.   8 qt. = ___ cups
       1 gal. = ___ qt.   1 hr. = ___ min.
       4 gal. = ___ qt.   3 hr. = ___ min.

Oral Drill

1. Review *product* and *factors*.
2. Review odd and even numbers. Use the numbers *(a)* on the board.
3. Count by 3's from 2, by 4's from 1, and by 5's from 3.
4. Review units of time and liquid measure.

Teaching Guide

1. *Changing from a larger unit of measure to a smaller.*

   a. Ask: **Which is bigger, a quart or a pint? A quart equals how many pints? If you were dipping juice out of a big kettle, would you have to dip longer with a quart measure or a pint measure? Would you get more pints or more quarts out of the kettle of juice?** Generalize the idea that it takes more pints than quarts for any amount because the pint is smaller.

   b. **If you are measuring milk, would you get more quarts or gallons out of a container? more cups or pints? more pints or quarts? Are there more hours or more minutes in a day? more minutes or more seconds?** *There are always more of the smaller unit.*

   c. Point to the equivalents *(b)* on the board. **How many pints are in 1 quart? Then how many pints are in 2 quarts? Because there are more pints than quarts, we multiply the number of quarts (2) by the number of pints in 1 quart (2).**

T–61   Chapter 3   Multiplication Facts: 1–6

Some children have trouble with this concept; for since quarts are larger, it is natural to think division is needed. Help them to see that because the pint is *smaller*, it takes *more* pints than quarts; therefore, they must multiply.

   d. Give other equivalents such as the following.

3 qt. = (6) pt.	1 hr.= (60) min.
4 qt. = (8) pt.	2 hr. = (120) min.
5 qt. = (10) pt.	3 hr. = (180) min.
2 gal. = (8) qt.	4 hr. = (240) min.
3 gal. = (12) qt.	1 day = (24) hr.
4 gal. = (16) qt.	2 days = (48) hr.
2 qt. = (8) cups	3 qt. = (12) cups

2. *Multiplication facts.*
   Give flash card drill of the multiplication facts.

Note: If your pupils do not know the 4's and 5's multiplications, let them look at the multiplication facts with answers on page 360 of their books. As pupils look for answers several times, they will be learning. If they write the wrong answer without looking back, they are not learning.

3. *"Times-and" problems.*
   Discuss the procedure for solving "times-and" problems. Use the following problems for practice.

    6 × 4 + 4 (28)   3 × 5 + 2 (17)
    7 × 5 + 3 (38)   6 × 3 + 4 (22)
    9 × 3 + 5 (32)   8 × 4 + 3 (35)
    8 × 5 + 6 (46)   2 × 9 + 3 (21)

4. *Multiplication in reading problems.*
   a. Review the concept that multiplication is a fast way to add if the addends are the same. Because of that, *the key addition words may also be found in problems that are solved by multiplication.* These include words like *in all*, *total*, and *together*.
   b. Discuss the two reading problems in the box. The first problem is solved by multiplying because the price of each loaf is the same. The second problem is solved by multiplying because the number of flowers in each row is the same.
   c. Give these sample reading problems. **Would you add, subtract, or multiply to find the answers?**
   • Jessica did 2 pages of problems with 6 on each page. How many problems did she do? (multiply)
   • Jeremy did 3 pages of problems with 5 problems on each page How many problems did he do? (multiply)
   • Who did more problems, Jessica or Jeremy? How many more? (subtract)
   • Mother bought 4 boxes of pudding for 23¢ a box. How much did she pay in all? (multiply)
   • Mother bought 2 boxes of cereal, one for $1.98 and one for $2.79. How much did Mother pay? (add)
   • How much change did Mother get from a $5.00 bill? (subtract)

Extra Review

Review multiplying 2- or 3-digit numbers.

43	50	62
× 3	× 4	× 4
(129)	(200)	(248)

701	622	513
× 5	× 3	× 3
(3,505)	(1,866)	(1,539)

Supplementary Drills

Drill 131*

Drill 6*

C. *Write the answers only to these "times-and" problems.*

12.   4 × 6 + 3   27   5 × 4 + 4   24   3 × 7 + 2   23   8 × 5 + 3   43
13.   5 × 5 + 4   29   9 × 3 + 4   31   6 × 3 + 3   21   9 × 4 + 3   39
14.   8 × 4 + 2   34   9 × 5 + 5   50   7 × 5 + 3   38   9 × 2 + 4   22

Multiplication is a fast way to add, but **only if the addends are the same.** Study the problems in the box.

Multiplying in Reading Problems

Problem 1: Bread is $0.73 a loaf. You buy 3 loaves of bread. What is the total cost?
Answer: 3 × $0.73 = $2.19

Problem 2: Geraldine planted 4 rows of flowers, with 5 flowers in each row. How many flowers did she plant in all?
Answer: 4 × 5 = 20 flowers

D. *Solve these reading problems. You will need to multiply for some answers but not all.*

15. If you have 3 rows of subtraction problems with 7 in each row, how many problems do you have in all?   21 problems

16. In Tina's classroom there are 4 rows of pupils with 6 in each row. How many pupils are in Tina's class?   24 pupils

17. The Blue Ridge Church has 4 Sunday school classes with 12 children in each one. How many children are in the Sunday school?   48 children

18. A dozen eggs costs $0.83. How much would you pay for 2 dozen? $1.66

19. A flat of eggs has 5 rows of eggs with 6 in each row. How many eggs are on a flat?   30 eggs

20. How much would you pay for a tablet that costs $0.62 and a pen that costs $0.79? $1.41

21. The pen costs how much more than the tablet? (See number 20.) $0.17

22. Is $2.00 enough to pay for three tablets? (See number 20.)   yes

Review Exercises

E. *Copy and multiply.*

23.
62	43	81	910	524	803
× 4	× 3	× 4	× 5	× 2	× 3
248	129	324	4,550	1,048	2,409

26. Carrying in Multiplication

Carrying in multiplication is done in much the same way as in addition. Study the following problem.

> Mr. Reed bought 4 cases of canned corn for his grocery store. There were 24 cans in each case. How many cans of corn did Mr. Reed buy?
>
> $\begin{array}{r} \overset{1}{}24 \\ \times\ 4 \\ \hline 96 \text{ cans} \end{array}$
>
> Think: Multiply the ones: 4 × 4 = 16.
> Write the 6 (ones) and carry the 1 (ten).
> Multiply the tens: 4 × 2 = 8. Add the carried 1.
> The tens' digit is 9. The whole product is 96.

A. *Write the answers to these "times-and" problems.*

1. 5 × 5 + 4 29   8 × 4 + 6 38   12 × 4 + 4 52   6 × 5 + 2 32
2. 6 × 3 + 5 23   7 × 2 + 8 22   9 × 3 + 5 32   9 × 4 + 5 41
3. 7 × 3 + 4 25   7 × 5 + 3 38   10 × 5 + 3 53   11 × 4 + 3 47

B. *Copy and multiply. Remember to add the carried numbers.*

4. 95   59   78   24   48   76
   × 4   × 3   × 2   × 3   × 4   × 5
   ───   ───   ───   ──   ───   ───
   380   177   156   72   192   380

5. 45   68   65   17   12   74
   × 3   × 3   × 4   × 3   × 6   × 4
   ───   ───   ───   ──   ──   ───
   135   204   260   51   72   296

6. 24   18   35   92
   × 7   × 2   × 5   × 3
   ───   ──   ───   ───
   168   36   175   276

7. 83   15   42   19
   × 3   × 7   × 5   × 3
   ───   ───   ───   ──
   249   105   210   57

LESSON 26

Objective

- To teach multiplying a two-digit number by a one-digit number, *with carrying.

Preparation

1. Multiplication flash cards: 4's–7's
2. Clock with movable hands
3. Speed Drill 26
4. Chalkboard:

   a. 450,006   701,000   30,090
      12,700   918,024

   b. I II III IV V VI
      VII VIII IX X

   c. 8 gal. = ___ qt. (32)
      6 qt. = ___ cups (24)
      5 pt. = ___ cups (10)
      3 min. = ___ sec. (180)

   d. 45   63
      × 4   × 6
      (180)   (378)

Oral Drill

1. Drill the multiplication facts: 4's–7's.
2. Review place value and reading large numbers, using *a* on the board.
3. Review Roman numerals, using *b* on the board.
4. Show these times on the clock: 3:15, 3:30, 3:45, 3:50. Ask: **What would a person probably be doing at 1:00 A.M.?**
5. Review changing units of measure.
   a. Ask questions like the following: **Which is larger, a quart or a gallon? a quart or a pint? a quart or a cup? Are there more gallons or quarts in a container? more pints or quarts? more cups or quarts?**
   b. **If we want to change a unit like quarts to a smaller unit like pints, we multiply. How many pints are in *1* quart? We multiply by *2*.**
   c. Use *c* on the board for extra practice.

Speed Drill

Give Speed Drill 26 (value of coins).

T-63   Chapter 3   Multiplication Facts: 1–6

Teaching Guide

Carrying in multiplication.

a. Turn to the first page of the lesson, and discuss the problem and explanation in the box.
b. Together work through the problems *(d)* on the board. Be sure pupils multiply *first,* and then add the carried digit.

   Another caution: Make sure the ones' part of the answer is put down first and the tens' part is carried. In addition, the carried digit is usually 1. In multiplication, the carried digit is often more than 1. In both, the tens' part is carried to the next column.

   Encourage children to *not* write carried figures.
c. Use these problems for further practice.

```
   54        38        92        53
 ×  4      ×  3      ×  5      ×  4
 (216)    (114)    (460)    (212)


   67        70        16        25
 ×  3      ×  5      ×  4      ×  6
 (201)    (350)     (64)    (150)
```

Note: Number 11 in the pupil's lesson could be counted as extra credit (2 percentage points).

Supplementary Drill
Drill 81*

C. Solve these reading problems.

8. Mr. Reed buys groceries in large cases for his grocery store. There are 36 cans in a case of tuna fish. How many cans are in three cases?   **108 cans**

9. Toothpaste comes in cases of 48. How many tubes of toothpaste are in 2 cases?   **96 tubes**

10. There are 12 boxes of corn flakes in a case. How many boxes are in 7 cases?   **84 boxes**

*11. Large boxes of corn flakes come in cases of 12. Smaller boxes come in cases of 18. How many boxes of corn flakes would be in 2 cases of large boxes **and** 2 cases of small boxes?   **60 boxes**

Review Exercises

D. Write the answers only.

12.
| 10 × 5 = **50** | 7 × 4 = **28** | 9 × 3 = **27** | 2 × 5 = **10** | 4 × 4 = **16** | 5 × 5 = **25** | 8 × 5 = **40** | 12 × 3 = **36** |

13.
| 11 × 3 = **33** | 8 × 1 = **8** | 9 × 4 = **36** | 5 × 4 = **20** | 6 × 4 = **24** | 8 × 3 = **24** | 12 × 2 = **24** | 3 × 3 = **9** |

14.
| 6 × 2 = **12** | 7 × 3 = **21** | 9 × 5 = **45** | 8 × 4 = **32** | 6 × 0 = **0** | 5 × 3 = **15** | 6 × 3 = **18** | 12 × 4 = **48** |

15.
| 4 + 3 + 2 + 7 = **16** | 6 + 4 + 7 + 3 = **20** | 3 + 8 + 7 + 6 = **24** | 2 + 8 + 9 + 5 = **24** | 8 + 4 + 5 + 9 = **26** | 3 + 9 + 4 + 4 = **20** | 1 + 8 + 9 + 4 = **22** | 7 + 5 + 7 + 8 = **27** |

E. Find the missing numbers. Write out the problem if you cannot figure the answer in your head.

16. 3 pt. = __6__ cups   6 gal. = __24__ qt.

17. 4 hr. = __240__ min.   3 days = __72__ hr.

18. 5 qt. = __10__ pt.   5 qt. = __20__ cups

19. 5 days = __120__ hr.   5 min. = __300__ sec.

64   Chapter 3   Multiplication Facts: 1–6

27. Multiplication Facts: 6's

Here are the 6's multiplication facts. Learn them.

0	1	2	3	4	5	6	7	8	9	10	11	12
×6	×6	×6	×6	×6	×6	×6	×6	×6	×6	×6	×6	×6
0	6	12	18	24	30	36	42	48	54	60	66	72

A. Write the answers to the facts below.

1. 6 × 3 = 18   6 × 6 = 36   6 × 10 = 60   6 × 5 = 30
2. 6 × 4 = 24   6 × 11 = 66   6 × 12 = 72   6 × 2 = 12
3. 6 × 1 = 6   6 × 8 = 48   6 × 7 = 42   6 × 9 = 54
4. 3 × 8 = 24   5 × 9 = 45   4 × 4 = 16   4 × 12 = 48
5. 6 × 6 = 36   6 × 9 = 54   5 × 7 = 35   6 × 11 = 66
6. 4 × 7 = 28   3 × 9 = 27   6 × 9 = 54   6 × 12 = 72

7.
7	6	11	9	2	12	10	8	4
×6	×6	×6	×6	×6	×6	×6	×6	×6
42	36	66	54	12	72	60	48	24

8.
5	7	9	8	5	6	9	12	11
×4	×6	×4	×3	×6	×6	×6	×6	×4
20	42	36	24	30	36	54	72	44

9.
8	8	7	0	5	6	4	6	7
×6	×5	×2	×4	×5	×3	×6	×5	×3
48	40	14	0	25	18	24	30	21

B. Write the answers to these "times-and" problems.

10. 6 × 8 + 3 51   4 × 8 + 2 34   6 × 9 + 3 57   6 × 4 + 4 28
11. 6 × 12 + 2 74   6 × 11 + 4 70   6 × 7 + 5 47   4 × 12 + 2 50

Sometimes you need to carry twice in multiplication. Study the example in the box.

$$\begin{array}{r} \overset{1\ 2}{325} \\ \times\quad 5 \\ \hline 1{,}625 \end{array}$$

Think: 5 × 5 = 25 (Write 5 and carry 2.)
5 × 2 + 2 = 12 (Write 2 and carry 1.)
5 × 3 + 1 = 16 (Write 16.)
The answer is 1,625.

LESSON 27

Objectives

- To drill the 6's multiplication facts.
- To introduce *carrying twice in multiplication.

Preparation

1. Multiplication flash cards, at least up to the 7's
2. Division flash cards—1's to 3's
3. Chalkboard:

   a. Roman numerals from I to XX (Write I–X in one row and XI–XX in another row directly beneath.)

   b. 2 gal. = ___ qt. (8)
   3 pt. = ___ cups (6)
   4 qt. = ___ cups (16)

   c. 50<u>8</u>,444

   d. 24   214   124   624
      × 6   × 6   × 6   × 6
      (144) (1,284) (744)   (3,744)

Oral Drill

1. Drill division facts 1's to 3's. Encourage pupils to think of the related multiplication fact if they are not sure of an answer.

2. Review odd and even numbers. Say the following numbers, and have pupils identify them as odd or even.

   36 17 58 29 50 64 83 12

3. Review Roman numerals, using *a* on the board.

4. Review units of measure.
   a. 1 pt. = (2) cups   1 qt. = (4) cups
      1 qt. = (2) pt.   1 gal. = (4) qt.
      1 hr. = (60) min.   1 day = (24) hr.
   b. Review changing units of measure, using *b* on the board.

5. **Review concepts of multiplication. Multiplication is a fast way to** (add) **numbers that are alike. The numbers multiplied are the** (factors)**, and the answer is the** (product).
   What fact pairs with 6 × 4 = 24? with 3 × 5 = 15? What multiplication means the same as 5 + 5 + 5 + 5? (4 × 5) **What addition means the same as 5 × 6 = 30?** (6 + 6 + 6 + 6 + 6)

6. Look at the large number *(c)* on the board. **What is the *digital* value of the underlined digit? What is its *place* value? What is its *combined* value?**
   Point to the 4's in the tens' and ones' places. **This 4 has how many times the value of this 4?** (10 times)

T–65   Chapter 3   Multiplication Facts: 1–6

Teaching Guide

1. *Multiplication facts.*
   Give flash card drill of the multiplication facts, emphasizing the 6's.

2. *Carrying twice in multiplication.*
   a. Work together through the problems *(d)* on the board. The first one is just like the ones in Lesson 26. The second one is also like those except that the top factor is a three-digit number. There is no carrying to the hundreds' place.
   b. The third problem requires carrying twice. Caution the pupils again: **Always *multiply first,* and then *add the carried digit.***
   c. The fourth problem again requires carrying twice. It has four digits in the answer.
   d. Use the following problems for individual practice.

65	19	254	623
× 5	× 4	× 5	× 6
(325)	(76)	(1,270)	(3,738)

750	326	$1.29
× 6	× 3	× 3
(4,500)	(978)	($3.87)

Supplementary Drills
Drill 1 +

Drill 82

C. Copy and multiply. Remember to add the carried digits.

12.	72 × 6 **432**	69 × 3 **207**	64 × 6 **384**	37 × 4 **148**	83 × 6 **498**	16 × 6 **96**
13.	162 × 4 **648**	835 × 3 **2,505**	916 × 5 **4,580**	483 × 4 **1,932**	276 × 3 **828**	824 × 6 **4,944**
14.	257 × 4 **1,028**	931 × 6 **5,586**	154 × 6 **924**	953 × 4 **3,812**	521 × 8 **4,168**	735 × 5 **3,675**

Review Exercises

D. Copy in straight columns, and follow the signs.

15. a. $4.25 + $6 + $0.79 **$11.04**   b. $8 + $1.78 + $5.32 **$15.10**   c. $6.45 + $0.85 + $2 **$9.30**

16. a. $8.17 − $5.99 **$2.18**   b. $5 − $2.35 **$2.65**   c. $9.05 − $6.88 **$2.17**

E. Examine this number and answer the questions about it.
6**2**5,014

17. a. What is the **digital value** of the underlined digit? **2**

   b. What is the **place value** of the underlined digit? **ten thousands**

   c. What is the **combined value** of the digit in bold print? **5 thousands**

   d. Write the number with words. **six hundred twenty-five thousand, fourteen**

F. Solve these reading problems.

18. Jason got up promptly when Mother called him at 6:30. Twenty minutes later he was ready for school. What time was he ready? **6:50**

19. Mother, Loretta, and Judy canned 15 full canners of peaches. A full canner holds 7 jars. How many jars of peaches were canned? **105 jars**

20. They also canned 6 full canners of pears. If a full canner holds 7 jars, how many jars of pears was that? **42 jars**

21. How many full canners of fruit did they can altogether? (See numbers 19 and 20.) **21 canners**

28. Roman Numerals

The number system we use most is called the **Arabic** (ar′ə·bik) **numeral system**. Each digit in a numeral has a place value and a digital value.

The **Roman numeral system** was used in Jesus' time. In a Roman numeral, each letter has a digital value but not a place value. A letter has the same value no matter where it is in the numeral.

Here are the Roman numerals from 1 to 30.

I	II	III	IV	V	VI	VII	VIII	IX	X
XI	XII	XIII	XIV	XV	XVI	XVII	XVIII	XIX	XX
XXI	XXII	XXIII	XXIV	XXV	XXVI	XXVII	XXVIII	XXIX	XXX

Read the following rules. They will help you understand Roman numerals better.

1. If a letter is **followed** by an **equal or smaller** value, **add** the two values.
   Example: XXII = X + X + I + I = 10 + 10 + 1 + 1 = 22
2. If a smaller letter comes **before** a larger letter, **subtract** the smaller value from the larger.
   Example: IX = X − I = 10 − 1 = 9
3. If a smaller letter comes **between** two larger letters, first **subtract** the small value from the one after it. Then **add**.
   Example: XIV = ?
   First subtract: 5 − 1 = 4. Then add: 10 + 4 = 14.
4. Do not use the same letter more than three times in a row.
   Example: Nine is written as IX, not VIIII.

A. *Do these exercises.*

1. Write Roman numerals for these Arabic numerals.
   a. 17 XVII   b. 22 XXII   c. 30 XXX   d. 8 VIII   e. 15 XV   f. 29 XXIX
2. Write Arabic numerals for these Roman numerals.
   a. XIX 19   b. XXX 30   c. IV 4   d. VII 7   e. XXVI 26   f. XV 15

B. *Write the missing numbers.*

3. X means __10__ ; VI means __6__ ; so XVI means 10 + 6 or __16__ .
4. V means __5__ ; I means __1__ ; so IV means __5__ − __1__ or __4__ .
5. X means __10__ ; IX means __9__ ; so XIX means __10__ + __9__ or __19__ .
6. XX means __20__ ; VIII means __8__ ; so XXVIII means __28__ .

LESSON 28

Objective

- To teach the Roman numerals from 1 *to 30.

Preparation

1. Multiplication flash cards (at least through the 7's)
2. Division flash cards: 1's–5's
3. Speed Drill 28
4. Chalkboard:

   Roman numerals from I to XXX

Oral Drill

1. Drill multiplication and division facts. Multiplication and division facts are related in the same way as addition and subtraction facts. Division "undoes" multiplication.

2. Drill mental arithmetic. Say the numbers slowly, allowing the pupils to compute one step at a time.
   $4 + 5 \times 6 - 1$ (53) $6 - 3 + 5 \times 6$ (48)
   $11 + 5 - 9 \times 6$ (42) $12 - 6 \times 6 + 3$ (39)
   $3 \times 6 - 9 + 5$ (14) $7 + 8 - 3 \times 6$ (72)

3. Review key words in reading problems. Say the following key words, and have pupils decide if they indicate addition, subtraction, or multiplication.
   sum (a)
   difference (s)
   product (m)
   total (a *or* m)
   altogether (a *or* m)
   how many left (s)
   how many more (s)
   how many in all (a *or* m)
   how many less (s)
   how much change (s)
   how much older (s)
   cost at 15¢ each (m)
   twice as many (m)

4. Review place value and digital value. Remind pupils that the *total value* is a combination of both.

5. Review odd and even numbers. It is the *ones'* digit that determines whether the number is odd or even.

Speed Drill

Give Speed Drill 28 (subtraction facts).

T-67   Chapter 3   Multiplication Facts: 1–6

Teaching Guide

Roman numerals.

a. **Our number system is called the Arabic numeral system. Each digit in a numeral has a digital value and a place value.** Write 333 on the board to illustrate. The value of 3 changes as its location changes.

b. **There are other number systems, and one that we still use sometimes is the Roman numeral system. Here are the first 30 Roman numerals.** Have the pupils recite the Roman numerals 1 to 30 as you point. Then point to numerals at random and have pupils identify them.

c. Point to I, II, III, IV, and VI. Ask: **Does I mean "one" no matter where it is placed?** (Yes; Roman numerals do not have place value as Arabic numerals do.)

d. Discuss the rules in the pupil's book. In brief, they state that if one value *follows* another that is equal or larger, the values are added. If a smaller value *precedes* a larger one, the smaller value is subtracted. If a smaller value is *between* two larger ones, it is *subtracted* from the value after it and the result is *added* to the value before it.

Example: XXIV = XX + (V − I)
= 20 + (5 − 1)
= 20 + 4 = 24

e. Give oral practice with Roman numerals whose values are found by adding (XV, VI, XX, XXVII). Then discuss some whose values are found by subtracting (IV, IX).

f. Explain that the same letter is not used more than three times in a row. Teacher: There is one exception. On some clocks with Roman numerals, the number 4 is shown as IIII.

Note: The letter V never precedes a larger value. The only values subtracted are I and X (and C of the higher values).

You may want to do exercises 3–6 in class.

Extra Review

Review multiplication. Use these problems for practice.

34	75	451	350
× 5	× 6	× 5	× 7
(170)	(450)	(2,255)	(2,450)

824	532	900
× 6	× 8	× 6
(4,944)	(4,256)	(5,400)

Supplementary Drill

Drill 83

Lesson 28

Review Exercises

C. *Write the answers quickly.*

7. | 5 × 6 = 30 | 12 × 5 = 60 | 8 × 4 = 32 | 6 × 6 = 36 | 7 × 0 = 0 | 9 × 3 = 27 | 5 × 5 = 25 | 9 × 6 = 54 | 8 × 5 = 40 |

8. | 12 × 6 = 72 | 8 × 3 = 24 | 11 × 6 = 66 | 6 × 4 = 24 | 9 × 5 = 45 | 4 × 5 = 20 | 7 × 6 = 42 | 3 × 6 = 18 | 8 × 6 = 48 |

9. | 9 × 6 = 54 | 5 × 3 = 15 | 9 × 4 = 36 | 7 × 3 = 21 | 8 × 2 = 16 | 8 × 6 = 48 | 10 × 6 = 60 | 12 × 4 = 48 | 7 × 6 = 42 |

D. *Copy and multiply.*

10. | 77 × 4 = 308 | 23 × 6 = 138 | 63 × 8 = 504 | 73 × 5 = 365 | 86 × 4 = 344 | 29 × 3 = 87 |

11. | 364 × 5 = 1,820 | 652 × 6 = 3,912 | 412 × 8 = 3,296 | 670 × 5 = 3,350 | 843 × 6 = 5,058 | 632 × 7 = 4,424 |

E. *Follow the directions.*

12. Write the value of each set of money.

   a. 31¢

   b. 57¢

13. Fill in the blanks.

   a. 1 hr. = __60__ min.
   b. 1 gal. = __4__ qt.
   c. 1 day = __24__ hr.
   d. 3 hr. = __180__ min.
   e. 3 gal. = __12__ qt.
   f. 3 days = __72__ hr.
   g. 5 pt. = __10__ cups
   h. 2 min. = __120__ sec.
   i. 4 qt. = __16__ cups
   j. 3 qt. = __6__ pt.
   k. 3 qt. = __12__ cups
   l. 2 gal. = __8__ qt.

14. Copy all the even numbers.

   (60) (52) (38) 63 21 (40) 89 (74) 17

15. Solve these number strings.

   a. 6 + 5 − 4 × 6 = 42 = ?

   b. 8 × 6 + 3 = 51 = ?

29. More Roman Numerals

Here are the first four letters in the Roman numeral system.

I = 1   V = 5   X = 10   L = 50

If you know the values of these four letters and the rules from Lesson 28, you can write the Roman numerals up to 89.

Here are the Roman numerals for counting by **tens**. Learn them well.

X   XX   XXX   XL   L   LX   LXX   LXXX

A. Write the missing numbers.

1. L means _50_ ; X means _10_ ; LX means _50_ + _10_ , or _60_ .
2. LXXX means _50_ + _10_ + _10_ + _10_ , or _80_ .
3. LXVII means _50_ + _10_ + _5_ + _1_ + _1_ , or _67_ .
4. XL means _50_ − _10_ , or _40_ . IX means _10_ − _1_ , or _9_ .

B. Write the Arabic numerals for these Roman numerals.

5. a. XXVII _27_   b. XIX _19_   c. IX _9_   d. XXXVI _36_   e. XIII _13_
6. a. XL _40_   b. LIII _53_   c. LXV _65_   d. LXXX _80_   e. XLII _42_
7. a. LXIV _64_   b. LXXIX _79_   c. XLIV _44_   d. LVII _57_   e. LXVI _66_
8. a. LXXXIII _83_   b. LXVIII _68_   c. XLIX _49_   d. LI _51_   e. LXXXVI _86_

C. Write Roman numerals for these Arabic numerals.

9. a. 28 _XXVIII_   b. 82 _LXXXII_   c. 53 _LIII_   d. 61 _LXI_   e. 46 _XLVI_   f. 34 _XXXIV_
10. a. 75 _LXXV_   b. 60 _LX_   c. 15 _XV_   d. 38 _XXXVIII_   e. 89 _LXXXIX_   f. 73 _LXXIII_

Review Exercises

D. Copy and add.

11.
```
  542        929        526        285        264
  216        542        471        125         37
   38        125         62        736        214
+ 124       + 60       + 528      + 443      + 529
-----      -----      -----      -----      -----
  920      1,656      1,587      1,589      1,044
```

LESSON 29

Objectives

- To introduce the Roman numerals *from 31–89.
- To review reading problems.

Preparation

1. Multiplication flash cards: 4's–7's
2. Division flash cards: 1's–5's
3. More difficult addition and subtraction flash cards
4. Chalkboard:
   a. Roman numerals in two rows: I to X and XI to XX.
   b. X XX XXX XL L
      LX LXX LXXX

Oral Drill

1. Drill multiplication and division facts separately.
2. Drill addition and subtraction facts in mixed order.
3. Review measures of time and liquid measures.
4. Review A.M. and P.M.
5. Review time, using a toy clock if you wish. **What time will it be in 15 minutes? in 20 minutes? in 30 minutes? in 45 minutes?**
6. Give mixed mental drill.
   $7 + 4 - 8 \times 5 - 2$ (13)
   $16 - 7 \times 6 + 4$ (58)
   $12 + 5 - 9 \times 6$ (48)
   $10 - 5 \times 6 + 4 - 2$ (32)
   $3 \times 6 - 4 - 7 \times 6$ (42)
   $4 + 9 - 7 \times 6 - 1$ (35)

Chapter 3 Multiplication Facts: 1–6

Teaching Guide

1. *Roman numerals.*
   a. Review the value of I, V, and X, and the rules in Lesson 28.
   b. Review the numerals from I to XX, using (a) on the board. Have pupils give the Roman numerals from 21 to 30.
   c. Introduce the new letter: L = 50.
   d. Have the pupils try to figure out the value of the third row of Roman numerals (b) by using their knowledge of the rules. Especially note XL = 40. X *before* L means L *minus* X. Pupils should soon recognize XL as a unit, without having to subtract 50 – 10 each time. The same applies to IV and IX.
   e. Have pupils give Roman numerals for the following Arabic numerals. Encourage them to look at the numbers on the board or in their books if they have trouble.
      52 (LII)   35 (XXXV)   84 (LXXXIV)
      60 (LX)   71 (LXXI)   49 (XLIX)
   f. Have pupils give Arabic numerals for the following Roman numerals.
      IV (4)   VI (6)   IX (9)   XI (11)
      XIV (14)   XL (40)   LXIII (63)
      LI (51)   XLV (45)   XXX (30)
      XXVIII (28)   XIX (19)
      LXXXVIII (88)   LXXVII (77)
      XXII (22)

2. *Reading problems.*
   a. Give some problems without numbers, and have pupils tell whether they would add, subtract, or multiply.
      • You know the price for one can of soup. You want to find the cost of five cans. (multiply)
      • You know how much your grocery bill is and how much money you gave the clerk. You want to find how much change. (subtract)
      • You know how old Adam and Methuselah were when they died. You want to find how much longer Methuselah lived than Adam. (subtract)
      • You know how high the two highest mountains are. You want to find how much higher the one is than the other. (subtract)
      • You know the cost of each item on a grocery bill. You want to find the total bill. (add)
      • You know two numbers, and you want to find out how much less the smaller one is than the larger. (subtract)
      • You know two numbers, and you want to find their sum. (add)
      • You know two numbers, and you want to find their product. (multiply)
      • You want to find the difference between two numbers. (subtract)
   b. For extra practice, choose problems from the pupil's text or Teaching Guide of lessons 4, 8, 13, 19, and 25. Especially review the two-step problems of adding to find the total and then subtracting to find change, as in Lesson 19, problems 8 and 10 and Teaching Guide 2c.

Supplementary Drills

Drill 143*

Drill 144*

E. Solve these reading problems.

12. The first man, Adam, lived to be 930 years old. Methuselah, the oldest man, lived to be 969. How much older was Methuselah than Adam?   **39 years**

13. Joyce said, "My great-grandfather lived to be 98." Methuselah lived how many more years than Joyce's great-grandfather?   **871 years**

14. Noah lived 600 years before the Flood came and 350 years after the Flood. How many years did Noah live altogether?   **950 years**

15. There are 12 things in one dozen. How many eggs are in 5 dozen?   **60 eggs**

16. Larry gathers eggs each morning and evening. One evening he gathered 75 eggs. Is that more or less than 6 dozen? (First find how many eggs are in 6 dozen.)   **more**

17. When Larry worked diligently, he could gather the eggs and feed the chickens in half an hour. If he started his chores at 4:45, at what time would he be finished?   **5:15**

18. Larry gives the chickens feed from a hundred-pound sack. After he has used 73 pounds of feed from the sack, how many pounds are left?   **27 pounds**

19. Mother sold the eggs for 65¢ a dozen. What will Mrs. Greene pay for 4 dozen eggs?   **$2.60**

*20. Mrs. Miller bought a dozen eggs for $0.65 and a gallon of milk for $1.25. How much change did Mother give her from $2.00?   **$0.10**

F. Follow the number trails. What number should be at the end?

21. a. start 8, +7, −9, ×6, +3, = ?   **39**

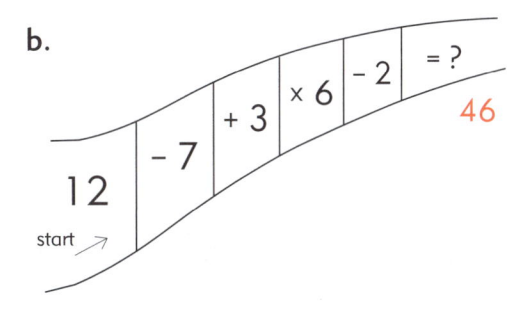

b. start 12, −7, +3, ×6, −2, = ?   **46**

30. Chapter 3 Review

A. *Write the answers to these facts.*

1. | 6 | 5 | 8 | 2 | 6 | 5 | 8 | 9 | 8 |
    |---|---|---|---|---|---|---|---|---|
    | × 5 | × 3 | × 4 | × 6 | × 6 | × 5 | × 5 | × 6 | × 3 |
    | 30 | 15 | 32 | 12 | 36 | 25 | 40 | 54 | 24 |

2. | 7 | 0 | 9 | 9 | 12 | 8 | 7 | 7 | 8 |
    |---|---|---|---|---|---|---|---|---|
    | × 6 | × 5 | × 4 | × 3 | × 6 | × 1 | × 3 | × 5 | × 6 |
    | 42 | 0 | 36 | 27 | 72 | 8 | 21 | 35 | 48 |

3. | 5 | 7 | 6 | 11 | 9 | 12 | 10 | 6 | 4 |
    |---|---|---|---|---|---|---|---|---|
    | × 4 | × 4 | × 4 | × 6 | × 5 | × 3 | × 2 | × 3 | × 4 |
    | 20 | 28 | 24 | 66 | 45 | 36 | 20 | 18 | 16 |

B. *Write the answers to these "times-and" problems.*

4. 4 × 6 + 4 28   7 × 4 + 3 31   8 × 6 + 2 50

5. 3 × 9 + 4 31   8 × 5 + 6 46   4 × 8 + 3 35

C. *Write the answers only.*

6. 10 + 13 23   12 + 11 23   10 + 16 26   14 + 13 27   13 + 16 29

7. | 5 | 7 | 2 | 8 | 3 | 8 | 6 |
    |---|---|---|---|---|---|---|
    | 7 | 4 | 3 | 8 | 6 | 7 | 4 |
    | 2 | 8 | 5 | 4 | 7 | 5 | 7 |
    | + 8 | + 2 | + 6 | + 3 | + 5 | + 6 | + 6 |
    | 22 | 21 | 16 | 23 | 21 | 26 | 23 |

D. *Copy and add.*

8. | | 79 | | | 761 | 903 |
    |---|---|---|---|---|---|
    | 64 | 54 | 386 | 824 | 39 | 612 |
    | 28 | 72 | 728 | 236 | 542 | 895 |
    | + 46 | + 56 | + 255 | + 79 | + 326 | 244 |
    | 138 | 261 | 1,369 | 1,139 | 1,668 | 2,654 |

LESSON 30

Objective

- To review the concepts taught in Chapter 3 (listed below).
  - Multiplication facts: 1's–6's
  - Multiplying two- or three-digit numbers by one-digit numbers
  - Units of capacity
  - Multiplying to change from larger units to smaller units
  - Column addition
  - "Times-and" problems
  - Roman numerals (not included on test)
  - Telling time
  - Reading problems

Preparation

1. Flash cards for multiplication facts: 3's–7's
2. Speed Drill 30
3. Chalkboard:

   I   V   X   L   IV   LI
   LXX   XLIX   XXIII

Speed Drill

Give Speed Drill 30 (mixed facts)

Teaching Guide

1. Drill multiplication facts.
2. Drill Roman numerals. Have pupils read the numerals on the board. Review the rules for reading and writing Roman numerals.

   Ask: **What does the X mean in LXX? in XL? in IX? in XXIII? How is this different from Arabic numerals?**

3. Review units of measure.
   a. 1 pt. = (2) cups   1 hr. = (60) min.
       1 qt. = (4) cups   1 min. = (60) sec.
       1 gal. = (4) qt.   1 day = (24) hr.
       1 qt. = (2) pt.   1 doz. = (12) things
   b. Ask questions like these: **If you know the number of things in 1 dozen, how can you find the number in 8 dozen? If you know the number of minutes in 1 hour, how can you find the number in 6 hours?**

4. Review "times-and" facts.
   $5 \times 6 + 3$ (33) $4 \times 4 + 2$ (18)
   $7 \times 4 + 3$ (31) $5 \times 5 + 4$ (29)

5. Review *factors* and *product*. See if pupils can tell you some factors of 12, of 21, and of 24.

6. Review computation skills.
   a. Column addition and regrouping of numbers.

5	7	6	3	9
6	3	8	9	4
7	8	4	5	7
+5	+8	+6	+3	+2
(23)	(26)	(24)	(20)	(22)

T–71   Chapter 3   Multiplication Facts: 1–6

b. Column addition with two- or three-digit numbers.

```
           29
  75    83   47    492
  26    74   84     29
 +65   +27  +32   +365
 ────   ───  ───   ────
(166) (184)(192)  (886)
```

```
         251   377
  967    286   824
  361    603    63
 +473   +747  +261
 ─────  ─────  ─────
(1,801)(1,887)(1,525)
```

c. Subtraction.

```
  116    624    800    503
 - 44   -265   -389   - 87
 ────   ────   ────   ────
 (72)  (359)  (411)  (416)
```

```
  911   $4.00   $8.25
 -250   - 1.75  - 5.88
 ────   ──────  ──────
(661)  ($2.25) ($2.37)
```

d. Multiplication.

```
   23    412     56     87
 ×  3   ×  4   ×  4   ×  3
 ────   ─────  ────   ────
 (69) (1,648) (224)  (261)
```

```
   352    816    934
 ×   5   ×  5   ×  3
 ─────   ─────  ─────
(1,760)(4,080)(2,802)
```

7. Review key words in reading problems. Here is a summary of the key words studied so far.

Addition: total, in all, sum, altogether, both

Subtraction: difference, how many more, how many less (fewer), how many left, change, comparative forms such as *older* and *longer*

Multiplication: total cost when each price is the same, (3) *times* as many, how many in (3) groups, how many quarts in (3) gallons

Note: Multiplication concepts have not been drilled as much as the others. It would be good to spend extra time here.

Note: This is another three-page review lesson. Assign your students the parts they need most. **Be sure not to omit the third page.**

E. Copy and multiply.

9.
35	21	46	45	82
× 9	× 7	× 3	× 6	× 6
315	147	138	270	492

10.
731	642	813	412	534
× 5	× 2	× 5	× 7	× 8
3,655	1,284	4,065	2,884	4,272

F. Write the correct answers.

11. 12:00 noon is during the (<u>day</u>, night).

12. Before noon is (<u>A.M.</u>, P.M.) time.

13. You might eat supper at 6:00 (A.M., <u>P.M.</u>).

14. To change pints to cups you (subtract, <u>multiply</u>, divide).

15. 1 day = __24__ hours   1 hr. = __60__ min.   1 min. = __60__ sec.

16. 1 pint = __2__ cups   1 gal. = __4__ qt.   1 qt. = __2__ pt.

17. 3 pints = __6__ cups   5 qt. = __20__ cups   4 qt. = __8__ pt.

18. 5 days = __120__ hours   6 gal. = __24__ qt.   4 doz. = __48__ things

19.
a. 9:15   b. 4:00   c. 5:40   d. 11:05   e. 4:45

G. Write Roman numerals for Arabic numerals, and Arabic numerals for Roman numerals.

20. a. 6 **VI**   b. 17 **XVII**   c. 32 **XXXII**   d. 25 **XXV**   e. 49 **XLIX**   f. 50 **L**

21. a. IX **9**   b. XIII **13**   c. XL **40**   d. LIV **54**   e. LXXX **80**

22. a. XXXV **35**   b. XLVII **47**   c. LXXVIII **78**   d. XXVI **26**   e. LXIX **69**

(continued on next page)

72   Chapter 3   Multiplication Facts: 1–6

H. *Do exercise 23. Then solve the reading problems after it.*

23. For each question write **add**, **subtract**, or **multiply**.
    a. How many are left? subtract
    b. What is four times as many? multiply
    c. What is the total? add
    d. How much less? subtract
    e. What is the product? multiply
    f. How many in all? add
    g. What is the sum? add
    h. How much change? subtract
    i. How many quarts in 6 gallons? multiply
    j. What is the total cost at 5 cents each? multiply
    k. How much older? subtract
    l. How much more? subtract

24. Grandpa bought a calf for $63.00 and a bushel of corn for $5.30. How much did Grandpa pay? $68.30

25. At the feed store Grandpa bought a bag of calf starter for $8.49 and a bag of feed for $7.75. How much more did the calf starter cost than the feed? $0.74

26. The calf starter Grandpa bought was on special. How much did he save if the regular price was $9.35 a bag? (See number 25.) $0.86

27. Grandpa paid $63.00 for the calf, $5.30 for corn, $8.49 for calf starter, and $7.75 for feed. What were Grandpa's total expenses? $84.54

28. Ronald had 8 rows of math problems to do. Each row had 6 problems. Ronald completed them quickly and checked each problem. How many problems did Ronald do?   48 problems

29. One day when Ronald did not check his work, he had three wrong in a lesson with 42 problems. How many problems did he have right?   39 problems

30. When Grandma had a birthday, Jerry asked her how old she was. Grandma said, "I'm six times as old as you." Jerry was twelve. How old was Grandma?   72 years

31. Jerry's father is 40. How many years younger is Jerry than his father? (See number 30.)   28 years

31. Chapter 3 Test

LESSON 31

Objective

- To test the pupils' mastery of the concepts taught in Chapter 3.

Teaching Guide

1. Give any last-minute review that you feel is necessary.
2. Administer the test.

Note: Chapter 3 Test is found in the test section in the back of this manual.

Chapter 4

Division Facts: 1–6

The same LORD over all
is rich unto all that call upon him.
(Romans 10:12)

32. Division Facts: 1's, 2's, 3's

Addition and subtraction are opposites. Addition puts on, and subtraction takes away.

Multiplication and division are also opposites. Multiplication is a fast way of adding the same number again and again. **Division is a fast way of subtracting the same number again and again.** When you ask, "How many 2's are in 8?" you are dividing.

Two ways of writing division are shown in the box. Both mean "8 divided by 2 is 4."

$$8 \div 2 = 4 \qquad 2\overline{)8}^{\,4} \qquad \text{The division sign} \div \text{ or } \overline{)} \text{ tells you to divide.}$$

A. *Write the answers to these division facts. Study any that you do not know well.*

1. $6 \div 1 = 6$ $8 \div 1 = 8$ $11 \div 1 = 11$ $3 \div 1 = 3$
2. $4 \div 2 = 2$ $10 \div 2 = 5$ $18 \div 2 = 9$ $20 \div 2 = 10$
3. $9 \div 3 = 3$ $18 \div 3 = 6$ $24 \div 3 = 8$ $33 \div 3 = 11$
4. $6 \div 2 = 3$ $27 \div 3 = 9$ $36 \div 3 = 12$ $14 \div 2 = 7$
5. $1\overline{)7}^{\,7}$ $2\overline{)12}^{\,6}$ $2\overline{)22}^{\,11}$ $3\overline{)3}^{\,1}$ $3\overline{)12}^{\,4}$ $1\overline{)10}^{\,10}$
6. $2\overline{)16}^{\,8}$ $1\overline{)1}^{\,1}$ $1\overline{)9}^{\,9}$ $2\overline{)10}^{\,5}$ $3\overline{)21}^{\,7}$ $3\overline{)15}^{\,5}$
7. $3\overline{)0}^{\,0}$ $2\overline{)24}^{\,12}$ $3\overline{)6}^{\,2}$ $2\overline{)2}^{\,1}$ $1\overline{)5}^{\,5}$ $3\overline{)27}^{\,9}$

You know that addition and subtraction facts form number families of four facts each. The four facts below form another kind of number family. **Two multiplication and two division facts with the same numbers make a number family.**

$2 \times 6 = 12 \qquad 6 \times 2 = 12 \qquad 12 \div 2 = 6 \qquad 12 \div 6 = 2$

B. *Do these exercises.*

8. Use each set of numbers to write the four facts in an addition–subtraction family. Look at Lesson 6 if you need help.

    a. 6, 5, 11
    $6 + 5 = 11$
    $5 + 6 = 11$
    $11 - 6 = 5$
    $11 - 5 = 6$

    b. 6, 8, 14
    $6 + 8 = 14$
    $8 + 6 = 14$
    $14 - 6 = 8$
    $14 - 8 = 6$

    c. 9, 7, 16
    $9 + 7 = 16$
    $7 + 9 = 16$
    $16 - 9 = 7$
    $16 - 7 = 9$

    d. 3, 7, 10
    $3 + 7 = 10$
    $7 + 3 = 10$
    $10 - 3 = 7$
    $10 - 7 = 3$

9. Use each set of numbers to write the four facts in a multiplication–division family.

    a. 4, 6, 24
    $4 \times 6 = 24$
    $6 \times 4 = 24$
    $24 \div 4 = 6$
    $24 \div 6 = 4$

    b. 9, 3, 27
    $9 \times 3 = 27$
    $3 \times 9 = 27$
    $27 \div 9 = 3$
    $27 \div 3 = 9$

    c. 2, 8, 16
    $2 \times 8 = 16$
    $8 \times 2 = 16$
    $16 \div 2 = 8$
    $16 \div 8 = 2$

    d. 6, 1, 6
    $6 \times 1 = 6$
    $1 \times 6 = 6$
    $6 \div 6 = 1$
    $6 \div 1 = 6$

LESSON 32

Objectives

- To drill the 1's–3's division facts.
- To review some basic concepts of division.
- To introduce *multiplication–division families.

Preparation

1. Multiplication flash cards through the 7's
2. Division flash cards 1's–3's
3. Speed Drill 32
4. Chalkboard:

    a. I   V   X   L   IV   XI
        XL   LXXX   LXIX

    b. $8 \div 2 = 4$ $2\overline{)8}^{\,4}$

    c. 6,   9,   15

Oral Drill

1. Drill multiplication facts in mixed order.
2. Give mental drill. Say the numbers one at a time.
   $6 + 5 - 4 \times 5$ (35) $3 \times 8 - 2 + 4$ (26)
   $6 - 4 \times 6 + 5$ (17) $7 + 8 - 3 \div 2$ (6)
   $4 \times 4 \div 2 - 7$ (1) $12 - 7 \times 3 + 6$ (21)
3. Review Roman numerals. Use the numerals (a) on the board.
4. Review measures. Ask: **How do we change a large unit like quarts to a smaller unit like cups?** (We take the number of smaller units in one of the larger units, and multiply the number of units by that.) Pupils may not be able to express this idea in that way, but they should know by now that multiplication is used to change a large unit to a small one.

Speed Drill

Give Speed Drill 32 (multiplication facts).

T–75   Chapter 4   Division Facts: 1–6

Teaching Guide

1. *Division facts.*
   Give mixed drill of the 1's, 2's, and 3's division facts.

2. *Division concepts.*
   a. Draw 8 sticks or X's on the board. Ask: **How many 2's are in 8?** Have someone draw rings around groups of 2. **To find how many 2's are in 8, we divide 8 into groups of 2. There are 4 groups of 2. There are four 2's in 8.**
   b. **We could also subtract to find how many 2's are in 8. How many are 8 – 2** (hold up 1 finger), **– 2** (2 fingers), **– 2** (3 fingers), **– 2** (4 fingers)? **If we subtract 2 four times, we are at zero. So there are four 2's in 8. Division is a quick way to subtract the same number again and again, just as multiplication is a quick way to add the same number again and again.**
   c. Point to the divisions *(b)* on the board. **These are two ways to write the division problem for "how many 2's are in 8?" We read both of them "8 divided by 2 is 4."**

   Note: Many children develop the habit of saying "2 into 8" rather than "8 divided by 2." Teach them the correct way. The larger number is read first in a division problem the same as in a subtraction problem.

   d. Practice reading division problems. You could use some in the pupil's book.

3. *Multiplication–division families.*
   a. **What process is the opposite of addition? Addition puts on while subtraction takes away. Because addition and subtraction are opposites, we can use the same numbers to make a family of facts.** Refresh the pupils' minds on addition-subtraction families *(c)*.
   b. **Multiplication also has an opposite. Its opposite is division. Division and multiplication facts work together the same as addition and subtraction facts. If 6 × 2 = 12, then 12 ÷ 2 = 6.**
   c. Have pupils use each of the following sets to write the four facts in a multiplication–division family.

   4, 1, 4   4, 5, 20   8, 3, 24

Supplementary Drills

Drill 25*

Drill 2 +

Review Exercises

C. Copy and multiply.

10.
25	32	64	83	42	36
× 7	× 7	× 9	× 4	× 5	× 3
175	224	576	332	210	108

11.
256	398	324	125	336	287
× 5	× 2	× 4	× 4	× 3	× 3
1,280	796	1,296	500	1,008	861

D. Write Arabic numerals for the Roman numerals, and Roman numerals for the Arabic numerals.

12. a. XIII **13**   b. XLV **45**   c. LXX **70**   d. XXVIII **28**   e. XXXIX **39**

13. a. LXI **61**   b. LVI **56**   c. IX **9**   d. LXXXIV **84**   e. XLVII **47**

14. a. 40 **XL**   b. 24 **XXIV**   c. 19 **XIX**   d. 38 **XXXVIII**   e. 52 **LII**   f. 79 **LXXIX**

E. Follow these directions.

15. Copy and solve these problems. Then label each part.

```
  659   addend           802   minuend          354   factor (multiplicand)
+ 725   addend         - 269   subtrahend      ×  4   factor (multiplier)
1,384   sum              533   difference     1,416   product
```

16. Write **add**, **subtract**, or **multiply**.

   a. How many more? **subtract**
   b. What is the amount of change? **subtract**
   c. How many pints in 6 quarts? **multiply**
   d. How many in 5 equal rows? **multiply**
   e. What is the sum? **add**
   f. What is the total in 3 groups that size? **multiply**

F. Solve these reading problems.

17. Judy planted two rows of tulips along the house. There were 18 tulips in each row. How many tulips did Judy plant? **36 tulips**

18. Mother and Mabel baked cupcakes for the all-day meeting at church. A small recipe called for 1 cup of milk. Mabel said, "We have two quarts of milk." How many batches of cupcakes can they make with 2 quarts of milk? (Hint: They can make one batch with each cup. How many cups are in two quarts?) **8 batches**

76 Chapter 4 Division Facts: 1–6

33. Introduction to Fractions

Mother gave Jessica and Jeremy a candy bar to share. "Oh, thank you, Mother," they said. Jeremy carefully cut the candy bar into two equal pieces. He let Jessica choose the first piece. "You could have picked first," she said. "The pieces are exactly the same size."

If the two pieces are the same size, Jeremy has cut the candy bar in **half**. Numbers like one-half are fractions.

A fraction is a part of a whole. Some important facts about $\frac{1}{2}$ are given in the box. These facts relate to other fractions also.

- **One half** is written $\frac{1}{2}$.
- The bottom number (2) means that the whole is divided into 2 equal parts.
- The bottom number is called the **denominator**.
- The top number (1) means 1 of the two parts.
- The top number is called the **numerator**.
- **One half** means "1 part out of 2."

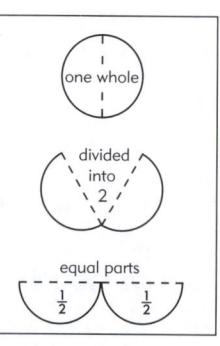

A. Follow the directions.

1. Write the fraction to name **one** part if a whole is divided into
   a. 2 equal parts. $\frac{1}{2}$
   b. 3 equal parts $\frac{1}{3}$
   c. 4 equal parts $\frac{1}{4}$

2. Write the numbers that fit in the blanks.
   a. 1 whole = __2__ halves, __3__ thirds, __4__ fourths, or __5__ fifths.
   b. One-third means __1__ part out of __3__ parts.
   c. One-fifth means __1__ part out of __5__ parts.
   d. Three-fourths means __3__ parts out of __4__ parts.

3. Write these fractions with numbers.
   a. one-fourth $\frac{1}{4}$
   b. one-sixth $\frac{1}{6}$
   c. two-fifths $\frac{2}{5}$
   d. two-thirds $\frac{2}{3}$
   e. three-fourths $\frac{3}{4}$
   f. three-fifths $\frac{3}{5}$

4. Write a fraction to tell what part of each figure is shaded.
   a. 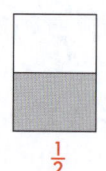 $\frac{1}{2}$
   b. 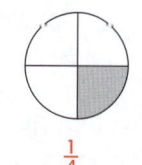 $\frac{1}{4}$
   c. 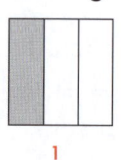 $\frac{1}{3}$
   d. 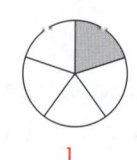 $\frac{1}{5}$
   e. 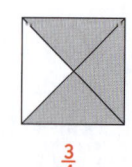 $\frac{3}{4}$

LESSON 33

Objectives
- To teach that a fraction is a part of a whole.
- To teach finding a fractional part of a number, using the fractions 1/2 and 1/3.

Preparation
1. Addition and subtraction flash cards
2. Multiplication flash cards
3. Division flash cards up to 3's
4. Visual aid to show meaning of fractions, either a flannel board or actual items such as apples or soft cookies (at least 4 whole items)
5. Chalkboard:

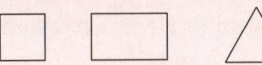

   □ ▭ △ ○

Oral Drill
1. Drill addition and subtraction facts in mixed order.
2. Drill the multiplication flash cards up to the 8's if your pupils can handle them.
3. Drill the division flash cards up to the 3's.
4. Drill the shapes on the board. Note the number of corners in each one, and the fact that a circle has no corners. Also note that a square is really a rectangle with equal sides.
5. Give mixed mental practice.
   $5 + 7 \div 3 - 2 \times 12$ (24)
   $3 \times 7 - 1 \div 2 + 4$ (14)
   $14 - 7 \times 6 - 2 + 5$ (45)
   $8 \times 4 + 1 \div 3 + 5$ (16)
6. Review Roman numerals, especially those with 4, 9, or 40.
7. Review multiplication–division number families.

Chapter 4 Division Facts: 1–6

Teaching Guide

1. *A fraction as a part of a whole.*
   a. Show the pupils an apple (or some other visual aid). **If I cut this apple in half, how many parts will there be?** When the answer 2 is given, cut the apple into two *unequal* parts. **Did I cut it into two parts? Did I cut it in half? No, it is not cut in half unless it is divided into two *equal* parts.** Illustrate by cutting another apple exactly in half.
   b. Have a volunteer write the fraction $\frac{1}{2}$ on the board.
   c. Take another apple and call for pupil response about thirds. Cut the apple into thirds. Pick up one piece. **What is this part of the apple called?** Have someone write $\frac{1}{3}$ on the board. Pick up two pieces. **What are two parts of the apple called?** Have $\frac{2}{3}$ written on the board. Refer to $\frac{3}{3}$, and have it written on the board. Note that $\frac{3}{3}$ is the same as one whole.
   d. In a similar way, cut another apple into fourths. Have pupils identify $\frac{1}{4}$, $\frac{2}{4}$, $\frac{3}{4}$, and $\frac{4}{4}$. **How many fourths are in a whole apple? How many thirds? How many halves?**
   e. **If I cut an apple into five parts, what would each part be called? What would two parts be? three parts? four parts? five parts? How many fifths are in a whole?**
   f. Have the pupils turn to Lesson 33 in their books. Discuss the information in the first box. **In any fraction, the bottom number tells how many parts are in the whole. The top number tells how many of those parts the fraction is naming. The top number is called the *numerator*, and the bottom number is called the *denominator*.**
   g. Have pupils go to the board. Give them instructions such as the following.
      • Draw a circle. Divide it into fourths. Shade one part. Write the fractional name for that part.
      • Draw a triangle. Divide it into 2 equal parts. Write the name of each part on the part.
      • Draw a rectangle. Divide it into 3 equal parts. Shade 2 out of 3 parts. Write the fraction for 2 out of 3.

2. *Finding a fractional part of a number.*
   a. Draw 4 circles on the board. **If we divide this group of cookies in half, how many are in each half?** Draw a box around two circles. **Half of 4 is 2. To find half of a number, divide the number into two equal groups. Divide the number by 2.**
   b. Have a similar demonstration with one-half of 12 and then with one-third of 12. **To find one-third of a number, divide the number by 3.**
   c. Use the following problems for oral practice.
      1/2 of 10   1/2 of 18   1/3 of 18
      1/2 of 24   1/3 of 24

Note: This lesson will probably not take as long to complete as most lessons. Supplement it with work on Roman numerals, multiplication, or reading problems.

Supplementary Drill

Drill 7 ×

Lesson 33 77

5. Draw a circle and divide it into two equal parts. Write the name of each part on the part.

6. Draw a square and divide it into four equal parts. Color $\frac{1}{4}$ blue and $\frac{3}{4}$ yellow.

7. Draw a rectangle and divide it into thirds. Color $\frac{2}{3}$ red.

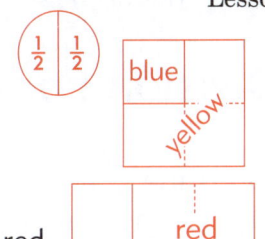

To divide a candy bar in half, Jeremy cut it into two equal parts. You can find $\frac{1}{2}$ of a **group** of things in the same way. **Divide the number of things by 2.** That divides it into 2 equal parts.

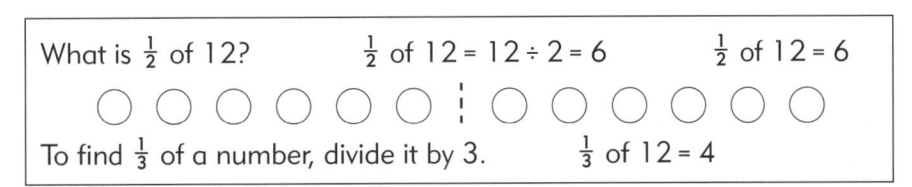

> What is $\frac{1}{2}$ of 12? $\frac{1}{2}$ of 12 = 12 ÷ 2 = 6 $\frac{1}{2}$ of 12 = 6
>
> To find $\frac{1}{3}$ of a number, divide it by 3. $\frac{1}{3}$ of 12 = 4

8. Find one-half of each number: 6 *3* 10 *5* 18 *9* 20 *10* 4 *2* 14 *7* 16 *8*

9. Find one-third of each number: 9 *3* 33 *11* 21 *7* 36 *12* 6 *2* 18 *6* 15 *5*

10. Find these one-half measures.

    a. $\frac{1}{2}$ gal. = __2__ qt.
    b. $\frac{1}{2}$ day = __12__ hr.
    c. $\frac{1}{2}$ qt. = __1__ pt.
    d. $\frac{1}{2}$ hr. = __30__ min.
    e. $\frac{1}{2}$ qt. = __2__ cups
    f. $\frac{1}{2}$ pt. = __1__ cup

Review Exercises

B. *Write the answers.*

11. 7×6=42   9×6=54   12×5=60   11×4=44   8×3=24   12×6=72   9×5=45   4×6=24   2×6=12

12. 8×5=40   6×6=36   9×3=27   8×4=32   8×6=48   5×6=30   9×4=36   12×2=24   7×4=28

C. *Copy and multiply.*

13. 840 × 5 = 4,200   567 × 3 = 1,701   429 × 4 = 1,716   753 × 6 = 4,518   742 × 6 = 4,452   916 × 6 = 5,496

D. *Write the four facts in each multiplication–division family.*

14. a. 5, 7, 35
    5 × 7 = 35
    7 × 5 = 35
    35 ÷ 5 = 7
    35 ÷ 7 = 5

    b. 9, 6, 54
    9 × 6 = 54
    6 × 9 = 54
    54 ÷ 9 = 6
    54 ÷ 6 = 9

    c. 7, 3, 21
    7 × 3 = 21
    3 × 7 = 21
    21 ÷ 7 = 3
    21 ÷ 3 = 7

    d. 4, 12, 48
    4 × 12 = 48
    12 × 4 = 48
    48 ÷ 4 = 12
    48 ÷ 12 = 4

78   Chapter 4   Division Facts: 1–6

34. Division Facts: 4's and 5's

Division is the opposite of multiplication. If you know the multiplication facts well, the division facts are not hard.

A. *Write the answers as quickly and accurately as you can.*

1. 12 ÷ 4 = 3   20 ÷ 4 = 5   36 ÷ 4 = 9   48 ÷ 4 = 12
2. 4 ÷ 4 = 1   16 ÷ 4 = 4   24 ÷ 4 = 6   32 ÷ 4 = 8
3. 28 ÷ 4 = 7   8 ÷ 4 = 2   40 ÷ 4 = 10   44 ÷ 4 = 11
4. 10 ÷ 5 = 2   25 ÷ 5 = 5   45 ÷ 5 = 9   30 ÷ 5 = 6
5. 40 ÷ 5 = 8   15 ÷ 5 = 3   5 ÷ 5 = 1   60 ÷ 5 = 12
6. 55 ÷ 5 = 11   20 ÷ 5 = 4   35 ÷ 5 = 7   45 ÷ 5 = 9

7. 4)$\overline{24}$ = 6   4)$\overline{48}$ = 12   5)$\overline{25}$ = 5   5)$\overline{40}$ = 8   4)$\overline{32}$ = 8   3)$\overline{27}$ = 9
8. 3)$\overline{0}$ = 0   5)$\overline{60}$ = 12   4)$\overline{16}$ = 4   4)$\overline{28}$ = 7   4)$\overline{20}$ = 5   5)$\overline{45}$ = 9
9. 4)$\overline{48}$ = 12   2)$\overline{12}$ = 6   3)$\overline{24}$ = 8   5)$\overline{30}$ = 6   4)$\overline{40}$ = 10   4)$\overline{8}$ = 2
10. 5)$\overline{35}$ = 7   5)$\overline{55}$ = 11   4)$\overline{12}$ = 3   3)$\overline{18}$ = 6   5)$\overline{5}$ = 1   1)$\overline{6}$ = 6
11. 3)$\overline{21}$ = 7   4)$\overline{36}$ = 9   2)$\overline{2}$ = 1   3)$\overline{15}$ = 5   1)$\overline{7}$ = 7   5)$\overline{0}$ = 0
12. 3)$\overline{36}$ = 12 5)$\overline{15}$ = 3   4)$\overline{40}$ = 10   4)$\overline{4}$ = 1   5)$\overline{30}$ = 6   4)$\overline{32}$ = 8

> To find $\frac{1}{2}$ of a number, divide by 2.
> To find $\frac{1}{3}$ of a number, divide by 3.
> To find $\frac{1}{4}$ of a number, divide by 4.
> To find $\frac{1}{5}$ of a number, divide by 5.

B. *Find these fractional parts.*

13. $\frac{1}{2}$ of 6 = 3 $\frac{1}{4}$ of 12 = 3 $\frac{1}{3}$ of 18 = 6 $\frac{1}{2}$ of 16 = 8
14. $\frac{1}{5}$ of 20 = 4 $\frac{1}{3}$ of 24 = 8 $\frac{1}{5}$ of 35 = 7 $\frac{1}{4}$ of 8 = 2
15. $\frac{1}{5}$ of 45 = 9 $\frac{1}{2}$ of 10 = 5 $\frac{1}{4}$ of 4 = 1 $\frac{1}{3}$ of 27 = 9

LESSON 34

Objectives

- To drill the 4's and 5's division facts.
- To review fraction concepts.

Preparation

1. Multiplication flash cards up to 8's
2. Division flash cards up to 5's
3. Speed Drill 34
4. Chalkboard:

   a. IV VI IX XI LX XL
      XLIII LXXXVIII XXIV LIX

   b. $\frac{1}{2}$ $\frac{1}{3}$ $\frac{1}{4}$ $\frac{1}{5}$ $\frac{2}{2}$ $\frac{2}{3}$
      $\frac{3}{3}$ $\frac{3}{4}$ $\frac{3}{5}$ $\frac{4}{4}$ $\frac{5}{5}$

Oral Drill

1. Drill the multiplication facts. Remove the ones that pupils know well, if you have not already done so.

2. Review key words in reading problems. Ask the following questions, and have pupils tell whether they would add, subtract, or multiply.

   a. You know the price for one loaf of bread. How much do 3 loaves cost? (multiply)
   b. You know how many apple trees and how many peach trees Brother Seth planted. How many trees did he plant in all? (add)
   c. How many more peach trees than apple trees did Brother Seth plant? (subtract)
   d. You know how many trees are in one row and how many rows were planted. How many trees is that altogether? (multiply)
   e. You know how much each item costs. What is the total bill? (add or multiply)
   f. How much change from $10.00? (subtract)
   g. What is the cost at 15¢ each? (multiply)
   h. You know how many gallons. How many quarts is that amount? (multiply)

   If your pupils are slow with the last problem, review multiplying to change from a larger unit to a smaller one.

3. Review Roman numerals with the examples *(a)* on the board.

4. Review place value in Arabic numerals. Write the number 666,666 on the board. Name the places, beginning at the right.
   Have someone read the number.

T-79 Chapter 4 Division Facts: 1–6

Each 6 is worth ten times as much as the 6 to its right.

5. Review multiplying to change a larger unit of measure to a smaller unit.

Speed Drill

Give Speed Drill 34 (multiplication facts).

Teaching Guide

1. *Division facts.*
   Drill the division facts. Concentrate on the 4's and 5's.
2. *Fraction concepts.*
   a. Read and discuss the fractions *(b)* on the board. Ask questions such as these: **Which fraction means 2 parts out of 3? 1 part out of 4? Which fractions are equal to one whole? Which fractions mean only 1 part out of a whole? Which numbers are numerators? Which are denominators? Which is smaller, 1/2 or 1/3?** This last question tests the pupils' former knowledge of fractions.
   b. Have pupils draw simple shapes and divide them into halves, thirds, or fourths. This will review the shape names as well as the fractions.
   c. Review the fact that fractions refer to a number of *equal* parts.
   d. Ask if anyone remembers how to find 1/2 of a number and 1/3 of a number. Extend that concept to include fourths and fifths. We divide by 4 to find 1/4 of a number. We divide by 5 to find 1/5 of a number.
   e. Review briefly the concept of multiplying to change from a larger unit of measure to a smaller one, if you did not cover it in the oral drill.
   f. Have pupils give answers to these reading problems.

• Mother baked 35 cookies. Mary put 1/5 of them into the school lunches. How many were used in the lunches? (7 cookies)
• Sister Joyce has 16 children in her class. If 1/4 of the children missed school one day, how many children were absent? (4 children)
• Luke had 24 subtraction problems to do, and now he has finished half of them. How many problems has he done? (12 problems)

Extra Review

Give multiplication practice.

573	635	214	543
× 4	× 5	× 9	× 8
(2,292)	(3,175)	(1,926)	(4,344)

842	930	765
× 6	× 6	× 6
(5,052)	(5,580)	(4,590)

Answers for exercise 16

a. 8 × 5 = 40   40 ÷ 8 = 5
   5 × 8 = 40   40 ÷ 5 = 8
b. 3 × 1 = 3   3 ÷ 3 = 1
   1 × 3 = 3   3 ÷ 1 = 3
c. 4 × 7 = 28   28 ÷ 4 = 7
   7 × 4 = 28   28 ÷ 7 = 4
d. 5 × 12 = 60 60 ÷ 5 = 12
   12 × 5 = 60 60 ÷ 12 = 5

Supplementary Drill

Drill 26*

Lesson 34   79

Review Exercises

C. Do these exercises.

16. Write the four facts in each multiplication–division family.
  a. 8, 5, 40   **b.** 3, 1, 3   **c.** 4, 7, 28   **d.** 5, 12, 60
  (See facing page.)

17. Two-thirds means __2__ parts out of __3__ .

18. Tell what part of each figure below is shaded.
  a. $\frac{1}{4}$ **b.** $\frac{1}{3}$ **c.** $\frac{1}{2}$ **d.** $\frac{2}{4}$ **e.** $\frac{3}{4}$

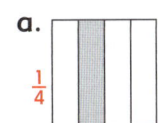

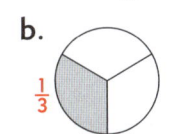

19. Draw a circle and divide it into four equal parts. Color one part green and two parts yellow.

20. Write a fraction for **a.** the total part that is colored in number 19. $\frac{3}{4}$
  b. the part that is **not** colored. $\frac{1}{4}$

D. Write which is larger.

21. a cup or a **pint**   a **day** or an hour
22. a **gallon** or a quart   a second or a **minute**
23. a **quart** or a pint   an **hour** or a minute

E. Write the missing numbers. Remember that to change from a large unit of measure to a smaller unit, you must multiply.

Example: 3 qt. = _____ cups.   Think: A quart is larger than a cup.
                                 1 qt. = 4 cups
                                 3 qt. = 3 × 4 cups = 12 cups

24. 6 qt. = __12__ pt.   3 hr. = __180__ min.
25. 5 days = __120__ hr.   4 min. = __240__ sec.
26. 5 gal. = __20__ qt.   3 pt. = __6__ cups

F. Copy and multiply.

27.
  731 × 6 = 4,386
  642 × 4 = 2,568
  813 × 6 = 4,878
  415 × 7 = 2,905
  834 × 5 = 4,170
  782 × 4 = 3,128

28.
  765 × 5 = 3,825
  825 × 6 = 4,950
  617 × 2 = 1,234
  284 × 3 = 852
  926 × 6 = 5,556
  634 × 9 = 5,706

80 Chapter 4 Division Facts: 1–6

35. Units of Length

Learn the facts in this box.

Units of Length
1 foot (ft.) = 12 inches (in.)   1 yard (yd.) = 3 feet (ft.)
1 yard (yd.) = 36 inches (in.)

A. Follow the directions.

1. Write whether you would use a **foot ruler** or a **yardstick** to measure the following things.

    a. your schoolroom   yardstick
    b. your pencil   foot ruler
    c. your paper   foot ruler
    d. a living room rug   yardstick
    e. your own height   yardstick

2. Write **yes** or **no** to tell whether each measure is sensible.

    a. The little boy was 71 inches tall.   no
    b. Our classroom floor is 6 feet wide.   no
    c. The tall man was 2 yards tall.   yes
    d. My finger is 8 inches long.   no
    e. The living room floor was 14 feet wide.   yes
    f. The hall door is 36 inches wide.   yes

To change from a smaller unit of measure to a larger unit, you must **divide**. Study the example in the box.

Changing Smaller Units to Larger Units
6 feet = ___ yards   Think: 1 yard = 3 feet. The key number is 3.
Divide by 3.
6 ÷ 3 = 2
6 feet = 2 yards

B. Write the missing numbers. You will need to *divide*.

3. 12 ft. = __4__ yd.   12 qt. = __3__ gal.

4. 10 pt. = __5__ qt.   16 cups = __4__ qt.

5. 24 ft. = __8__ yd.   8 cups = __4__ pt.

LESSON 35

Objectives
- To teach English units of length.
- To teach *changing from a smaller unit to a larger one by dividing.

Preparation
1. Flash cards of the four processes
2. A foot ruler and a yardstick

Oral Drill
1. Drill addition and subtraction facts in mixed order.
2. Drill multiplication facts through the 8's.
3. Drill the division facts through the 6's.
4. Drill mental math. If some pupils always "get lost," have them say the answers aloud through the whole string.
   $4 + 5 \times 6 - 2$ (52)
   $11 - 6 + 3 \times 6$ (48)
   $3 \times 8 \div 4 + 7$ (13)
   $2 \times 6 \div 4 + 2 \times 3$ (15)
   $6 \times 5 \div 3 - 3 \times 4$ (28)
5. Review fractions.
   a. **What fraction means 2 out of 3? 3 out of 5? 1 out of 4? Which number is the numerator? the denominator?**
   b. **What is 1/2 of 12? 1/3 of 21? 1/4 of 32? 1/5 of 5?**
   c. **There were 15 cookies on a plate. Fred ate 1/5 of them. How many did he eat?** (3 cookies)
   d. **There are 6 chapters in 1 Timothy. Alice read 1/2 of the chapters. How many chapters did she read?** (3 chapters)

T–81   Chapter 4   Division Facts: 1–6

Teaching Guide

1. *Units of length.*
   a. Ask the pupils to hold their fingers about an inch apart to check their understanding of the size of an inch. Then show them a foot ruler. Tell them to hold their hands about a foot apart. Show them the yardstick. Have them hold their hands about a yard apart.
   b. With the ruler and the yardstick visible, ask questions like these: **Might a boy your age be 2 feet tall? Would a tall man be closer to 1 yard or 2 yards tall? Would you measure across your desk in inches or yards? Would you measure the playground in feet or yards? Is your math paper closer to 1 inch or 1 foot long?**
   c. Discuss the units in the first box on the pupil's page. Show with the ruler and the yardstick that 3 feet equals 1 yard. Ask: **How many feet are in 2 yards? 3 yards? 4 yards? How many inches are in 2 feet? 3 feet? 4 feet? How could we find how many *inches* are in 3 yards?** (multiply by 36)

2. *Changing from a smaller unit of measure to a larger one.*
   a. **Which is smaller, a foot or a yard? a foot or an inch? an inch or a yard? an hour or a day? a quart or a pint? a quart or a cup? a quart or a gallon? If** [supply student's name] **measures the classroom in feet and** [supply student's name] **measures the room in yards, who will have the smaller number?** (There will be fewer *yards* because a yard is larger than a foot.)
   b. **In changing measures so far, we have always changed from a larger unit to a smaller one.** Then we had to *multiply* to find the correct number of the smaller units. Sometimes we change from a *small* unit, like feet, to a *larger* one, like yards. There are *fewer* of the larger unit, so we *divide* to find the number of larger units. Have pupils compare the rules for changing units in lessons 25 and 35 of their books.
   c. Use the following exercises for practice with changing from smaller to larger units.

   6 ft. = (2) yd.   10 cups = (5) pt.
   12 ft. = (4) yd.   8 cups = (4) pt.
   15 ft. = (5) yd.   8 pt. = (4) qt.
   12 qt. = (3) gal.   8 cups = (2) qt.

Extra Review

Review column addition, subtraction, and multiplication.

```
   7        4        5       35
   5        8        4       28
   6        5        6       24
  +6       +9       +7      +43
 (24)     (26)     (22)    (130)
```

```
                764
   893      327     8,026    5,493
   490      836     3,841    6,758
  + 57    + 146    +6,585   +2,437
 (1,440)  (2,073) (18,452) (14,688)
```

```
   900      403      830      521
  -285     -139     -762     -419
  (615)    (264)    (68)    (102)
```

```
   534      679      513      756
  × 8      × 4      × 5      × 6
 (4,272)  (2,716)  (2,565)  (4,536)
```

Supplementary Drills

Drill 132*

Drill 8 ×

Lesson 35

Review Exercises

C. *Write the missing numbers. You will need to* multiply.

6. 4 yd. = __12__ ft.   3 ft. = __36__ in.   2 yd. = __72__ in.

7. 4 yd. = __144__ in.   10 yd. = __30__ ft.   6 ft. = __72__ in.

D. *Write the answers to these facts as quickly as you can.*

8.
8	6	11	3	14	7	5	12	17
+4	+9	−8	+6	−5	+9	+6	−9	−8
12	15	3	9	9	16	11	3	9

9.
7	9	8	8	0	9	9	5	7
×6	×4	×5	×6	×4	×3	×6	×6	×4
42	36	40	48	0	27	54	30	28

10. 5)25 = 5   4)32 = 8   1)12 = 12   3)24 = 8   4)20 = 5   3)3 = 1

11. 6)60 = 10   5)35 = 7   3)18 = 6   4)16 = 4   5)55 = 11   4)0 = 0

12. $\frac{1}{5}$ of 15   3 $\frac{1}{3}$ of 27   9 $\frac{1}{4}$ of 24   6 $\frac{1}{2}$ of 14   7

E. *Write the answers only.*

13.
6	5	4	8	2	9	3
5	5	7	4	5	1	9
6	7	8	5	6	7	4
+4	+6	+8	+7	+8	+5	+8
21	23	27	24	21	22	24

F. *Copy and work carefully. Be sure to follow the signs.*

14.
6,246	3,592	7,126	4,388	1,502
485	4,217	5,093	164	2,857
+1,735	+6,430	+875	+3,827	+5,674
8,466	14,239	13,094	8,379	10,033

15.
117	800	392	815	925	743
−65	−279	−156	×5	×6	×6
52	521	236	4,075	5,550	4,458

G. *Write Roman numerals for these Arabic numerals.*

16. a. 70 LXX   b. 15 XV   c. 39 XXXIX   d. 43 XLIII   e. 81 LXXXI

17. a. 12 XII   b. 27 XXVII   c. 58 LVIII   d. 66 LXVI   e. 44 XLIV

82   Chapter 4   Division Facts: 1–6

36. Multiplication and Division Facts: 6's

Learn the division facts in this box.

$\overset{0}{6\overline{)0}}$	$\overset{1}{6\overline{)6}}$	$\overset{2}{6\overline{)12}}$	$\overset{3}{6\overline{)18}}$	$\overset{4}{6\overline{)24}}$	$\overset{5}{6\overline{)30}}$	$\overset{6}{6\overline{)36}}$
$\overset{7}{6\overline{)42}}$	$\overset{8}{6\overline{)48}}$	$\overset{9}{6\overline{)54}}$	$\overset{10}{6\overline{)60}}$	$\overset{11}{6\overline{)66}}$	$\overset{12}{6\overline{)72}}$	

Multiplication and division are opposite. If you know the multiplication facts well, the division facts are not hard.

If 6 × 3 = 18, then 18 ÷ 3 = 6.

A. Write the answers to these multiplication–division sets.

1. a. 6 × 6 = **36**   36 ÷ 6 = **6**   b. 6 × 8 = **48**   48 ÷ 6 = **8**
2. a. 6 × 4 = **24**   24 ÷ 6 = **4**   b. 6 × 11 = **66**   66 ÷ 6 = **11**
3. a. 6 × 3 = **18**   18 ÷ 6 = **3**   b. 6 × 5 = **30**   30 ÷ 6 = **5**
4. a. 6 × 2 = **12**   12 ÷ 6 = **2**   b. 6 × 7 = **42**   42 ÷ 6 = **7**
5. a. 6 × 9 = **54**   54 ÷ 6 = **9**   b. 6 × 12 = **72**   72 ÷ 6 = **12**

B. Write the answers to these division facts as quickly as you can.

6. $6\overline{)42}$ = **7** $6\overline{)48}$ = **8** $6\overline{)18}$ = **3** $6\overline{)54}$ = **9** $6\overline{)72}$ = **12** $6\overline{)30}$ = **5**
7. $6\overline{)24}$ = **4** $6\overline{)36}$ = **6** $5\overline{)40}$ = **8** $4\overline{)36}$ = **9** $6\overline{)66}$ = **11** $5\overline{)20}$ = **4**
8. $2\overline{)22}$ = **11** $1\overline{)6}$ = **6** $4\overline{)32}$ = **8** $6\overline{)60}$ = **10** $5\overline{)60}$ = **12** $3\overline{)24}$ = **8**
9. $5\overline{)25}$ = **5** $4\overline{)16}$ = **4** $5\overline{)15}$ = **3** $2\overline{)18}$ = **9** $6\overline{)6}$ = **1** $2\overline{)14}$ = **7**

C. Multiply to find the answers.

10. 3 yd. = **9** ft.   4 ft. = **48** in.   4 yd. = **144** in.
11. 2 hr. = **120** min.   5 days = **120** hr.   6 gal. = **24** qt.
12. 5 qt. = **10** pt.   6 ft. = **72** in.   5 qt. = **20** cups

LESSON 36

Objectives

- To drill the 6's multiplication and division facts.
- To teach *the use of division in reading problems.

Preparation

1. Multiplication and division flash cards
2. Toy clock
3. Speed Drill 36
4. Chalkboard:

   a. IV VIII IX XV XXXII
      XLVI LIV LXXVII LXXXIX

   b. 980,647   593,200   48,003
      600,058   240,111

Oral Drill

1. Review *factor* and *product*. **If 2 and 5 are the factors, what is the product? If one factor is 4 and the product is 20, what is the other factor?**
2. Review finding a part of a number. Remind pupils to find the answers by dividing. Give some oral questions. **What is 1/2 of 10? 1/3 of 24? 1/3 of 15? 1/4 of 16? 1/5 of 20? 1/4 of 20? 1/2 of 20?**
3. Review Roman numerals. Use the numbers *(a)* on the board.
4. Review place value and reading large numbers. Use the numbers *(b)* on the board.
5. Show these times on the toy clock, and have pupils read them.
   6:45   8:05   4:15   10:30
   12:10   2:50   3:25   11:40
6. Review measures.
   1 ft. = 12 in.   1 yd. = 3 ft.
   1 yd. = 36 in.
   a. Ask: **When we change a larger unit, like feet, to a smaller unit, like inches, do we <u>multiply</u> or divide? When we change a smaller unit to a larger one, do we multiply or <u>divide</u>?**
   b. Give two units of measure and have pupils respond with *multiply* or *divide*.
      inches to feet (divide)
      yards to inches (multiply)
      yards to feet (multiply)
      feet to yards (divide)
      pints to cups (multiply)
      gallons to quarts (multiply)
      quarts to gallons (divide)
      cups to quarts (divide)

Speed Drill

Give Speed Drill 36 (multiplication facts).

Teaching Guide

1. *Division facts.*
   Drill the multiplication and division facts. Concentrate on the 6's.

2. *Division in reading problems.*
   a. Review key words in reading problems. (See Lesson 30 for a list.) Give the sample reading problems below, and have pupils tell whether they would add, subtract, multiply, or divide. If there is time, they could solve the problems in their seats or at the board.

   • There are 28 chapters in Matthew and 16 chapters in Mark. How many chapters are in both books? (add; 44 chapters)

   • The Book of Matthew has how many more chapters than the Book of Mark? (subtract; 12 chapters)

   • Mark, Romans, and 1 Corinthians have 16 chapters each. How many chapters are in the 3 books? (multiply; 48 chapters)

   • I have 2 brothers. My cousin has 4 times as many brothers as I have. How many brothers does my cousin have? (multiply; 8 brothers)

   • I have how many fewer brothers than my cousin? (subtract; 6 brothers)

   • If Mother buys milk for $2.15, bread for $1.29, and cereal for $3.25, what does she spend altogether? (add; $6.69)

   • How much change does Mother get from $7.00? (subtract; $0.31)

   • The price of orange juice is $0.89 a can. What is the cost of 3 cans? (multiply; $2.67)

   b. Point out that some reading problems are solved by division. **Sometimes we have a number, and we want to find a part of it. We divide to find a part of a number. What is 1/2 of 18? We divide by 2 to find the answer. We divide by 3 to find 1/3 of a number.** Do not go beyond fractions with a numerator of 1.

   c. **Sometimes we have a number, and we want to find how many groups of a certain size are in the number. We divide to find how many groups. How many 3's are in 15?**

   d. **Sometimes we have a number, and we know how many groups we want to make from it. We divide to find how many are in each group. If there are 18 children to divide into 2 groups for a spelling bee, how many children will be in each group?**

   e. Discuss the three problems in the second box in Lesson 36. Encourage the pupils to think: Is it sensible to get a smaller number of equal groups? Then we divide.

   f. Use these reading problems for further practice.

   • David, Daniel, and Daryl shared 15 pieces of candy equally. How many pieces did each boy get? (5 pieces)

   • Kevin has 14 marbles. Luke has 1/2 as many. How many marbles does Luke have? (7 marbles)

   • Mother needs 3 eggs to make a batch of cookies. How many batches can she make if she has a dozen eggs? (4 batches)

Supplementary Drill

Drill 27*

> **Dividing to Solve Reading Problems**
>
> Here are some reading problems where you need to divide.
>
> **Problem 1:** You want to find a **part of a number**.
>   Example: Sarah has 6 brothers. Elaine has $\frac{1}{3}$ as many. How many brothers does Elaine have?
>   Answer: 6 ÷ 3 = 2 brothers
>
> **Problem 2:** You want to find **how many groups** of a certain size are in a number.
>   Example: How many songbooks are needed for 12 children if 2 children share each book?
>   Answer: 12 ÷ 2 = 6 songbooks
>
> **Problem 3:** You know how many groups are in a number, and you want to find **how many are in each group**.
>   Example: There are 16 children in Room 3. When they play ball, how many children are on each team?
>   Answer: 16 ÷ 2 = 8 children

D. *Solve these reading problems. Show your work.*

13. If Ruby hangs 2 socks with each clothespin, how many clothespins does she need to hang up 14 socks? *7 clothespins*

14. Father bought 28 calves at a farm sale. Rodney helped Father put the calves into 4 pens. How many calves were in each pen? *7 calves*

15. Arlene made 24 brownies. The family ate $\frac{1}{2}$ of them for supper. How many brownies did they eat? *12 brownies*

16. Mother had 12 brownies for school lunches. If she uses 3 brownies each day, how many days will the brownies last? *4 days*

E. *Write* add, subtract, *or* multiply. *Then solve the problems.*

17. Martha learned Psalm 19, Psalm 27, and John 1:1–14. Each passage has 14 verses. How many verses did Martha learn in all? *multiply   42 verses*

18. Psalm 119 has 176 verses. Jonathan has learned 32 of them. If he wants to learn the whole psalm, how many more verses must he learn? *subtract   144 verses*

19. The verses in Psalm 119 are grouped in sets of 8. How many verses will Jonathan know when he has learned six sets? *multiply   48 verses*

20. How many verses are in Psalm 19, Psalm 27, and Psalm 119 together? (See numbers 17 and 18.) *add   204 verses*

37. The Parts of a Division Problem

In a division problem, the number being divided is the **dividend**. It is divided by the **divisor**, and the answer is the **quotient**.

$$\text{divisor} \rightarrow 3\overline{)15} \leftarrow \text{dividend} \quad\quad \underset{\uparrow}{15} \div \underset{\uparrow}{3} = \underset{\uparrow}{5}$$
$$\text{quotient above 5} \quad\quad \text{dividend} \quad \text{divisor} \quad \text{quotient}$$

A. *Write the words that belong in the blanks.*

1. $\quad$ 7 ← b. <u>quotient</u>
    a. <u>divisor</u> → 4)28 ← c. <u>dividend</u>

2. In 42 ÷ 6 = 7, 42 is the <u>dividend</u>, 6 is the <u>divisor</u>, and 7 is the <u>quotient</u>.

3. In multiplication you know two factors and find the <u>product</u>.

4. In division you know the product (dividend) and one factor (divisor). You must find the other factor (called the <u>quotient</u>).

B. *Make two division facts from each set. Label each number.*

5. a. 18, 3, 6 $\quad$ b. 5, 7, 35

    divisor 3)18 dividend (6 quotient) $\quad$ divisor 6)18 dividend (3 quotient)

    divisor 5)35 dividend (7 quotient) $\quad$ divisor 7)35 dividend (5 quotient)

Amanda was folding the wash. There were 12 socks in the clothes basket. Since there are two socks in a pair, Amanda could fold 12 socks into 6 pairs.

$$12 \div 2 = 6$$

Another time when Amanda was folding the wash, she found only 9 socks in the basket. "Mother," she called, "I can make four pairs of socks, but here is a sock without a partner."

The number 9 is an **odd number**. An **even number** can be divided evenly by 2, but an odd number cannot. There is always 1 left over. The 1 left over is called a **remainder**.

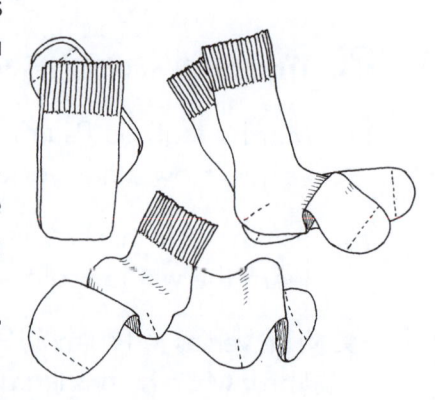

Lesson 37   T–84

LESSON 37

Objectives

- To teach the parts of the division problem.
- To teach that some numbers divide evenly by 2, 3, and 4, and that others have remainders.

Preparation

1. Multiplication and division flash cards
2. Counters, coins, or buttons
3. Chalkboard:

   a. $\frac{1}{2}$ $\frac{1}{4}$ $\frac{1}{3}$ $\frac{2}{2}$ $\frac{2}{3}$ $\frac{3}{3}$
      $\frac{3}{4}$ $\frac{1}{5}$ $\frac{2}{5}$ $\frac{3}{5}$

   b.
1	2	1	2	3
3	4	4	5	6
5	6	7	8	9
7	8	10	11	12
9	10	13	14	15
11	12	16	17	18
13	14	19	20	21
15	16	22	23	24
17	18	25	26	27
19	20	28	29	30

   Use colored chalk to write the numbers in the last columns (2, 4, 6 . . . and 3, 6, 9 . . .). *These numbers will also be needed in Lesson 38.*

Oral Drill

1. Drill the multiplication and division facts.
2. Review fractions. Have pupils read the fractions *(a)* on the board and tell what they mean (1 part out of 2, etc.).
3. Review finding a part of a number by dividing.

   1/3 of 12   1/2 of 14   1/4 of 8

   1/2 of 20   1/3 of 18

4. a. Count by 2's. **These numbers are even numbers.** Then start at 1 and count by 2's. **These numbers are odd numbers.**

   b. Count by 3's, by 4's, by 5's, and by 6's. **These numbers can be divided evenly by 3, by 4 . . .**

5. Review the two rules for changing units of measure.

T–85   Chapter 4   Division Facts: 1–6

Teaching Guide

1. *Parts of a division problem.*
   a. Review the relationship between division and multiplication. Give three numbers such as 7, 4, and 28. Have pupils volunteer the four facts that can be made with those numbers. Write the facts on the board.
   b. Review factors and products. Label each part of one of the multiplication facts. Note that the corresponding numbers in the division facts could also be called *factors* and *product*. (The product comes first.)
   c. **The numbers in a division problem have other names besides** *factors* **and** *product*. **The number that is divided is called the** *dividend*. **The number we divide by is called the** *divisor*, **and the answer is called the** *quotient*. Label each part as you say it, and have pupils repeat the names after you.
   d. Write several division facts on the board, using both forms of the division sign, and have pupils identify the dividends, divisors, and quotients.

2. *Division with remainders.*

Note: Division with remainders is difficult for many children. This is only an introduction to it. Allow children to use small objects at first if necessary.

   a. Review odd and even numbers. **Tell if these numbers are odd or even. Even numbers divide evenly by 2. They always end with 0, 2, 4, 6, or 8.**   23   54   80   31   94   69   76   17
   b. **Mittens come in pairs. How many pairs are in 6 mittens? Pairs are 2's. Asking "how many pairs" is the same as asking "how many 2's." Divide by 2 to find the answer.**
   c. **How many pairs are in 7 mittens, 3 pairs or 4 pairs? How many mittens are in 4 pairs?** (8 mittens)
   There are not enough for 4 pairs, so 7 mittens make only 3 complete pairs, with 1 mitten left over. The 1 left over is called the *remainder*. **7 is an odd number. Odd numbers always have remainders when divided by 2.** If pupils have difficulty understanding the concept, use counters or buttons and have pupils count out 7 buttons and separate them into groups of 2. They will *see* that there is one left over.
   d. Use counters or buttons to show other numbers that divide unevenly by 2. Have pupils state the answers in the form "6 remainder 1."
   e. Point to the lists of numbers *(b)* on the board. Both lists are made by writing the numbers in order. Note that the arrangement of the first list places odd numbers in the first column and even numbers in the second. The numbers in the second column are the answers to the 2's multiplication facts.
   f. In the other list, the numbers in the last column are numbers that divide evenly by 3. All the numbers in the first two columns have remainders when divided by 3. Note that the numbers in the last column are the answers to the 3's multiplication facts.
   g. Have pupils tell whether these numbers can be divided evenly by 2; by 3.
   10   6   23   14   18
   24   13   30   15   9

Note: Today's lesson may require more class time than usual. If you spend that time in class, the written exercises should not be difficult.

Supplementary Drills

Drill 6 ×

Drill 45

C. Do these exercises.

6. Write numbers by 2's from 2 to 20. (You will write even numbers.)   2, 4, 6, 8, 10, 12, 14, 16, 18, 20

7. Write numbers by 2's from 1 to 19. (You will write odd numbers.)   1, 3, 5, 7, 9, 11, 13, 15, 17, 19

8. Divide these even numbers by 2.

    8   **4**   12   **6**   20 **10**   6 **3**   14 **7**   18 **9**   10 **5**

9. Write the numbers by 3's from 3 to 30. These numbers divide by 3 with no remainder.   3, 6, 9, 12, 15, 18, 21, 24, 27, 30

10. Write the numbers that divide by 3 with no remainder.

    (6)   10   (12)   17   (21)   (30)   26   (18)   (9)   (24)

11. Write the numbers that divide by 4 with no remainder.

    6   9   10   (12)   (20)   22   27   (24)   (32)   34

Review Exercises

D. Write the quotients of these division facts.

12. $25 \div 5 = $ **5** $36 \div 4 = $ **9** $16 \div 2 = $ **8** $54 \div 6 = $ **9**

13. $16 \div 4 = $ **4** $66 \div 6 = $ **11** $27 \div 3 = $ **9** $28 \div 4 = $ **7**

14. $10 \div 5 = $ **2** $4 \div 4 = $ **1** $32 \div 4 = $ **8** $20 \div 5 = $ **4**

15. $5 \div 1 = $ **5** $18 \div 3 = $ **6** $48 \div 6 = $ **8** $30 \div 3 = $ **10**

16. 5)40 = **8**   4)12 = **3**   6)36 = **6**   5)35 = **7**   6)72 = **12**   6)6 = **1**

17. 6)24 = **4**   4)48 = **12**   3)24 = **8**   6)18 = **3**   5)15 = **3**   4)24 = **6**

18. 6)42 = **7**   5)45 = **9**   4)0 = **0**   5)60 = **12**   4)44 = **11**   3)21 = **7**

E. Solve these reading problems.

19. Brother Timothy has a chair shop. His boys help put the chairs together. How many chairs can be made with 28 legs? (Think: How many legs does one chair have?)   **7 chairs**

20. The back of each chair has 7 spindles. How many spindles are needed to make 53 chairs?   **371 spindles**

21. One kind of chair costs $49 unfinished. If it is finished, it costs $95. The finished chair costs how much more than the unfinished one?   **$46**

38. The Steps in Division

How many groups of 4 pennies are in 14 pennies? The picture shows that there are 3 groups of 4 with 2 left over.

The answers to the multiplication facts help us to divide. To find how many 4's are in 14, think: 4, 8, 12, 16 . . . The 4's number just below 14 is 12. There are three 4's in 14, but there is a **remainder** of 2.

Steps for Solving Division Problems

1. **Divide.** Think: How many 4's are in 14?
   3 groups of 4 fit in 14.
   Write 3 above the 4 in 14.

   $$4\overline{)14} 3$$

2. **Multiply.** Think: Three 4's is 12.
   Write 12 below the 14.

   $$\begin{array}{r} 3 \\ 4\overline{)14} \\ 12 \end{array}$$

3. **Compare.** Think: Is 12 less than 14? Yes.

4. **Subtract.** Draw a line under the 12.
   Think: 14 − 12 = 2. Write 2 below the line. It is the remainder.

   $$\begin{array}{r} 3 \\ 4\overline{)14} \\ \underline{12} \\ 2 \end{array}$$

5. **Compare.** Think: Is the remainder less than the divisor? Yes.
   Write **R 2** beside the 3 in the quotient.

   $$\begin{array}{r} 3\text{ R }2 \\ 4\overline{)14} \\ \underline{12} \\ 2 \end{array}$$

A. *Solve these division problems by following the five steps in the lesson. Remember to write the remainders in the answers.*

1. $3\overline{)7}$ = 2 R 1 $3\overline{)16}$ = 5 R 1 $2\overline{)11}$ = 5 R 1 $3\overline{)20}$ = 6 R 2 $4\overline{)9}$ = 2 R 1

2. $4\overline{)6}$ = 1 R 2 $2\overline{)15}$ = 7 R 1 $4\overline{)23}$ = 5 R 3 $4\overline{)21}$ = 5 R 1 $3\overline{)25}$ = 8 R 1

3. $2\overline{)5}$ = 2 R 1 $4\overline{)17}$ = 4 R 1 $4\overline{)29}$ = 7 R 1 $3\overline{)19}$ = 6 R 1 $4\overline{)33}$ = 8 R 1

LESSON 38

Objectives
- To review division with remainders.
- To teach the steps in the division process.

Preparation
1. Multiplication and division flash cards
2. Subtraction flash cards
3. Speed Drill 38
4. Chalkboard:

   a. L   IX   VI   LXXXV
      XIV   XLIII   XXVIII

   b. Number lists as in Lesson 37

   c. $3\overline{)16}\,^{(5\ R\ 1)}$

Oral Drill
1. Drill the multiplication and division facts.
2. Drill the subtraction facts. (Long division uses multiplication and subtraction facts as well as division.)
3. Count by 2's; by 3's; by 4's; by 5's.
4. Review *factor, product, dividend, divisor, quotient,* and *remainder.*
5. Review Roman numerals by reading the numerals *(a)* on the board.
6. Give mixed mental drill. Do not copy these on the board in this form. Give the numbers orally, one by one.

   $2 + 4 \times 5 \div 3 - 2$ (8)
   $6 + 8 \div 2 - 5 \times 8$ (16)
   $10 \div 5 + 4 \times 6 - 1$ (35)
   $11 - 5 \times 4 \div 3 + 5$ (13)
   $8 - 4 \times 5 \div 2 + 7$ (17)
   $5 \times 12 \div 6 - 4 \times 7$ (42)

Speed Drill
Give Speed Drill 38 (subtraction, addition, multiplication).

Teaching Guide

1. *Division with remainders.*
   a. Refer to the numbers *(b)* on the board. Begin with 2 and divide by 2, using the lists.
   $2 \div 2 = 1$; $3 \div 2 = 1$ R 1;
   $4 \div 2 = 2$; $5 \div 2 = 2$ R 1 ...
   b. Follow a similar pattern with the 3's. $3 \div 3 = 1$; $4 \div 3 = 1$ R 1; $5 \div 3 = 1$ R 2 ... Help the pupils to see the pattern of even and uneven divisions. **The answers (products) to the multiplication facts divide evenly. Numbers that are not answers to multiplication facts do not divide evenly.**
   c. Read the following problems and ask: **Will these numbers divide evenly or not? Use the page of multiplication facts in the back of the book if you are not sure.**

$8 \div 3$ (no)	$9 \div 2$ (no)
$14 \div 2$ (yes)	$14 \div 3$ (no)
$18 \div 3$ (yes)	$15 \div 2$ (no)
$27 \div 3$ (yes)	$7 \div 2$ (no)
$26 \div 3$ (no)	$10 \div 3$ (no)
$16 \div 3$ (no)	$16 \div 2$ (yes)

2. *Steps in the division process.*
   a. **If we know the multiplication facts well, we can find answers to all divisions, whether or not there are remainders.** Point to the problem *(c)* on the board. **To solve this division problem, think of the 3's facts: $3 \times 3 = 9$, $4 \times 3 = 12$, $5 \times 3 = 15$, $6 \times 3 = 18$.**
   b. **How many 3's are in 16?** Write 5 as the quotient. **Dividing is step 1 in finding the answer.**
   c. **Step 2 is multiplying.** Point to the quotient and the divisor. **5 times 3 is what?** Write 15 below 16.
   d. **Step 3 is comparing.** Point to 15 and 16 respectively. **This number must be less than this number. Is 15 less than 16?**
   e. **Step 4 is subtracting. That is how we find the remainder.** Draw a line under 15. **What is 16 − 15?** Write 1 below the 5.
   f. **Step 5 is comparing again.** Point to 1 and 3 respectively. **The remainder must be smaller than the divisor. Is it? Then we are finished with this division except for one important thing. We must write the remainder up beside the quotient.** Write R 1 beside the 5.

   Writing the remainder where it belongs is not considered a separate step. There is a sixth step in long division—*Bring down*—but it is not taught at this point.
   g. Do several more problems together, such as $17 \div 4$ and $25 \div 3$. You may want to have one of the children write the correct numbers on the board while you prompt responses and record the five steps in a column. When you are finished, your list should look like the list in the pupil's book.
   h. Use the following problems for individual practice.

   $4\overline{)6}$ (1 R 2) $4\overline{)21}$ (5 R 1) $3\overline{)17}$ (5 R 2)

   $2\overline{)19}$ (9 R 1) $3\overline{)5}$ (1 R 2) $4\overline{)10}$ (2 R 2)

   $4\overline{)19}$ (4 R 3) $3\overline{)20}$ (6 R 2)

Supplementary Drill

Drill 99*

Review Exercises

B. *Write the answers quickly.*

4.
8	9	4	5	8	9	7	8	7
×3	×6	×6	×5	×4	×4	×5	×5	×6
24	54	24	25	32	36	35	40	42

5.
10	11	9	10	13	18	8	12	7
−3	−4	−5	−6	−8	−9	−3	−9	−5
7	7	4	4	5	9	5	3	2

C. *Divide to find the parts.*

6. ½ of 14 **7**   ¼ of 36 **9**   ⅓ of 18 **6**   ⅕ of 20 **4**

7. ¼ of 24 **6**   ½ of 24 **12**   ⅕ of 30 **6**   ⅓ of 12 **4**

D. *Do these exercises.*

8. Write the Roman numerals for these Arabic numerals.
   a. 42 **XLII**   b. 16 **XVI**   c. 85 **LXXXV**   d. 29 **XXIX**   e. 57 **LVII**   f. 74 **LXXIV**

9. Write the Arabic numerals for these Roman numerals.
   a. XVIII **18**   b. XLV **45**   c. LXX **70**   d. XXXIV **34**   e. LIX **59**   f. LXI **61**

10. Tell what part of each figure is shaded.
    a. ¼   b. ⅕   c. ¾   d. ⅔   e. ½

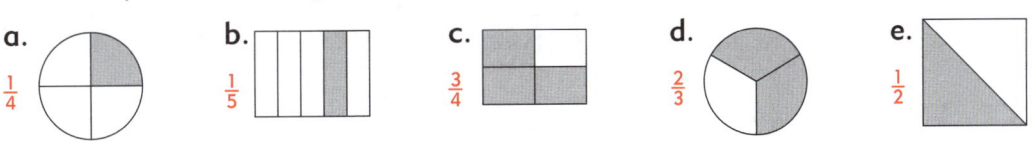

E. *Change these measures to smaller units. You need to multiply.*

11. 3 yd. = __9__ ft.   4 gal. = __16__ qt.   4 ft. = __48__ in.

12. 2 hr. = __120__ min.   3 days = __72__ hr.   3 yd. = __108__ in.

F. *Change these measures to larger units. You need to divide.*

13. 8 pt. = __4__ qt.   12 qt. = __3__ gal.   9 ft. = __3__ yd.

88 Chapter 4 Division Facts: 1–6

39. More Division With Remainders

Do you remember the steps for solving division problems? Study the five steps in Lesson 38 until you can say them without looking.

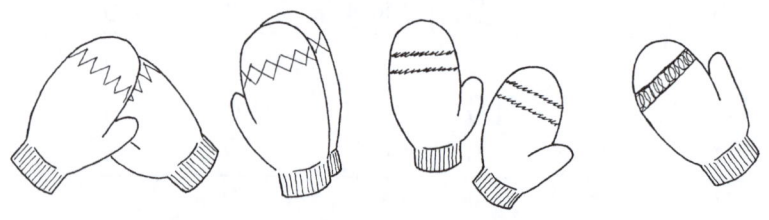

A. *Copy and solve these problems. The numbers do not divide evenly.*

1. 5)17̄ = 3 R 2   3)19̄ = 6 R 1   4)17̄ = 4 R 1   2)9̄ = 4 R 1   5)8̄ = 1 R 3

2. 3)22̄ = 7 R 1   5)28̄ = 5 R 3   5)13̄ = 2 R 3   3)20̄ = 6 R 2   4)23̄ = 5 R 3

3. 4)11̄ = 2 R 3   3)7̄ = 2 R 1   2)15̄ = 7 R 1   2)5̄ = 2 R 1   5)36̄ = 7 R 1

4. 3)13̄ = 4 R 1   5)24̄ = 4 R 4   3)11̄ = 3 R 2   4)30̄ = 7 R 2   4)10̄ = 2 R 2

Review Exercises

B. *Write the answers as quickly as you can. Watch the signs!*

5. 5)25̄ = 5   3)15̄ = 5   4)28̄ = 7   6)42̄ = 7   6)48̄ = 8   4)36̄ = 9

6. 3)9̄ = 3   4)12̄ = 3   5)10̄ = 2   2)8̄ = 4   2)18̄ = 9   3)24̄ = 8

7. 7 × 4 = 28   6 × 6 = 36   9 × 5 = 45   7 × 2 = 14   9 × 3 = 27   7 × 5 = 35   9 × 6 = 54   8 × 4 = 32   7 × 3 = 21

8. 15 − 9 = 6   11 − 6 = 5   9 − 3 = 6   8 − 5 = 3   10 − 9 = 1   13 − 4 = 9   12 − 7 = 5   9 − 7 = 2   10 − 6 = 4

9. Copy these division problems, and label each number.

quotient ⟶ 6 R 1 ← remainder
divisor ⟶ 4)25 ← dividend

quotient ⟶ 3 R 4 ← remainder
divisor ⟶ 5)19 ← dividend

LESSON 39

Objectives

- To give further practice with the steps in the division process.
- To review reading problems that are solved by the four processes.

Preparation

1. Subtraction flash cards
2. Multiplication and division flash cards
3. Chalkboard:

   $3\overline{)17}$ (5 R 2) $4\overline{)27}$ (6 R 3)

   $2\overline{)5}$ (2 R 1) $5\overline{)28}$ (5 R 3)

Oral Drill

1. Drill the subtraction facts.
2. Drill the multiplication and division facts.
3. Review the relationship between multiplication and division. Have someone write number families using three numbers such as 3, 8, and 24.
4. Give mixed mental drill.
   - $6 + 4 \div 2 \times 4 - 2$ (18)
   - $11 - 5 \times 3 \div 2 \times 5$ (45)
   - $3 \times 7 + 3 \div 3 - 3$ (5)
   - $30 \div 6 + 2 \times 6 - 2$ (40)
   - $10 - 6 \times 4 \div 2 \times 4$ (32)
   - $5 + 7 \div 3 \times 6 - 3$ (21)
5. Review the parts of a division problem.

Teaching Guide

1. *Division with remainders.*
   a. Even though this is not totally new, you should spend enough class time to thoroughly cover the subject again. Do some sample problems together, such as those on the board. See if the pupils can recall the five steps. If they cannot, have them turn to Lesson 38 and refresh their memories.
   b. Today's work involves dividing by 5, as well as by 2, 3, and 4. Note that the larger the divisor, the larger the remainder can be. Ask: **What is the largest remainder we can have if we divide by 2? by 4? by 3? by 5?**
   c. Use the following problems for individual practice.

   $$4\overline{)19}^{(4\,\text{R}\,3)} \quad 5\overline{)32}^{(6\,\text{R}\,2)} \quad 2\overline{)11}^{(5\,\text{R}\,1)}$$

   $$4\overline{)30}^{(7\,\text{R}\,2)} \quad 5\overline{)46}^{(9\,\text{R}\,1)} \quad 5\overline{)39}^{(7\,\text{R}\,4)}$$

2. *Reading problems solved by the four processes.*
   a. Summarize the key words presented so far.
   Addition: total, altogether, in all, both, sum
   Subtraction: left, how many (much) more, how many less (fewer), difference, change, older, younger, longer, farther
   Multiplication: (4) times as many, how much at (14¢) each, how many in (5) groups that size, changing a larger unit to a smaller one
   Division: (1/3) of a number, how many groups in, how many in each group, changing a smaller unit to a larger one
   b. Have pupils tell how to solve each problem; then have them find the answer.

- If 14 children make 2 teams, how many are on each team? (divide; 7 children)
- There were 12 cookies on a plate. Daryl ate 1/4 of them. How many did he eat? (divide; 3 cookies)
- On the Byler farm there are 37 cows, 15 heifers, 22 steers, and 8 calves. How many head of cattle do the Bylers have? (add; 82 head)
- One Sunday 87 people came to church. The next Sunday 140 people came. How many more people were in church the second Sunday? (subtract; 53 people)
- How many eggs are in 6 dozen? (multiply; 72 eggs)
- Jana is making small balls of dough to help Mother make cloverleaf rolls. Mother uses 3 little balls to make 1 roll. Jana has made 27 small balls. How many rolls will that make? (divide; 9 rolls)

Supplementary Drill

Drill 7 ×

C. *Write* **add, subtract, multiply,** *or* **divide** *for each question.*

10. How much change? subtract
11. What is 5 times as much? multiply
12. What is $\frac{1}{4}$ of a number? divide
13. What is the total? add
14. How many in 3 groups that size? multiply
15. How many more? subtract
16. How many in each group? divide
17. How many are left? subtract
18. What is the sum? add
19. How many groups of 3? divide

D. *Solve these reading problems. Look for key words. Be careful!*

20. Mother bought material to make dresses. The material for Mother's dress cost $7.69; the material for Alta's dress cost $5.35; and the material for little Susan's dress cost $2.27. What was the total cost of the material? $15.31

21. Aunt Mary gave Melinda $5.00 for her birthday. Melinda wants to buy the book *Mary Jones and Her Bible*, but it costs $7.65. How much more does Melinda need to buy the book? $2.65

22. Mother picked 6 bushels of peas. Regina picked only one-third as many. How many bushels did Regina pick? 2 bushels

23. Altogether the Myer family picked 12 bushels of peas. Each bushel yielded 8 quarts of peas for the freezer. How many quarts of peas were put in the freezer? 96 quarts

24. Jesus sent out His twelve disciples two by two. How many groups of two disciples were sent? 6 groups

Number Strings

E. *Find the answers to these number strings.*

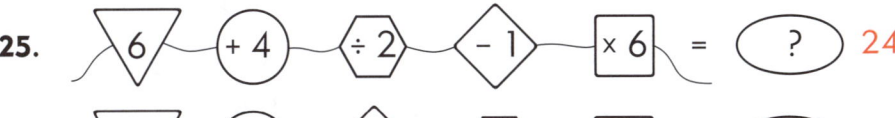

25. 6, +4, ÷2, −1, ×6 = ? 24
26. 5, +9, −2, ÷3, ×4 = ? 16
27. 3, ×4, +3, ÷5, −2 = ? 1

90   Chapter 4   Division Facts: 1–6

40. First Quarter Review

A. *Write the answers quickly.*

1.
   10   5   11   18   3   7   12   9   8
   −7   +7   −8   −9   +6   +8   −4   −8   +9
   --- --- ---   --- --- --- --- --- ---
    3   12   3   9   9   15   8   1   17

2.
    8   13   10   9   6   4   11   15   6
   +5   −7   −5   +5   −2   +5   −6   −9   +8
   --- ---   --- --- --- ---   --- --- ---
   13   6   5   14   4   9   5   6   14

3.
    8   4   7   8   12   1   7   8   0
   ×5   ×5   ×3   ×6   ×6   ×5   ×4   ×2   ×3
   --- --- --- ---   --- --- --- --- ---
   40   20   21   48   72   5   28   16   0

4.
    6   2   5   9   8   9   7   1   12
   ×6   ×4   ×5   ×5   ×4   ×3   ×6   ×6   ×3
   --- --- --- --- --- --- --- ---   ---
   36   8   25   45   32   27   42   6   36

5. 3)12 = 4   4)16 = 4   3)24 = 8   5)40 = 8   2)18 = 9   4)36 = 9

6. 1)7 = 7   6)54 = 9   4)4 = 1   6)60 = 10   3)9 = 3   5)30 = 6

B. *Do these exercises.*   (See facing page.)

7. Write the four facts in each addition–subtraction family.
   a. 6, 3, 9   b. 8, 7, 15   c. 4, 5, 1

8. Write the four facts in each multiplication–division family.
   a. 4, 5, 20   b. 3, 27, 9   c. 1, 5, 5

9. Copy these problems and label the parts.

   45 addend   60 minuend   38 factor (multiplicand)
   +29 addend   −14 subtrahend   × 5 factor (multiplier)
   ---   ---   ---
   74 sum   46   difference   190 product

   quotient ⟶ 3 R 2 ⟵ remainder
   divisor ⟶ 4)14 ⟵ dividend

LESSON 40

Objective

- To give a cumulative review of the things taught in the first four chapters (listed below).
  - Basic facts
  - Computational skills (division with remainders not included in test)
  - Secondary skills, including money, time, place value, Roman numerals, measures, and fractions
  - Reading problems

Preparation

1. Flash cards for addition, subtraction, multiplication, and division
2. Optional materials: toy clock, coins for counting, visual aids to review fractions
3. Speed Drill 40

Note: Decide before class which areas of review your children need most. You will probably not be able to cover everything in class.

Answers for exercises 7 and 8

7. a. 6 + 3 = 9   9 − 6 = 3
      3 + 6 = 9   9 − 3 = 6
   b. 8 + 7 = 15 15 − 8 = 7
      7 + 8 = 15 15 − 7 = 8
   c. 4 + 1 = 5   5 − 4 = 1
      1 + 4 = 5   5 − 1 = 4

8. a. 4 × 5 = 20 20 ÷ 4 = 5
      5 × 4 = 20 20 ÷ 5 = 4
   b. 3 × 9 = 27 27 ÷ 3 = 9
      9 × 3 = 27 27 ÷ 9 = 3
   c. 1 × 5 = 5   5 ÷ 1 = 5
      5 × 1 = 5   5 ÷ 5 = 1

Speed Drill

Give speed Drill 40 (vertical multiplication).

Teaching Guide

1. Drill the basic facts in the four processes.
2. Review addition–subtraction number families and multiplication–division number families.
3. Review the terminology of the four processes: addend, sum, and so forth.
4. Review time. Show or have pupils show times on the toy clock.
      3:15   4:05   7:30
     11:45   9:55   1:35
5. Review money. Have some actual coins for pupils to count. Or have them turn to Lessons such as 15, 16, 18, 20 where there are pictures of coins that can be counted.
   How many nickels equal a quarter? How many dimes equal a dollar? What coins would you use to pay 45¢? 80¢?
6. Review measures.
   1 ft. = (12) in.   1 pt. = (2) cups
   1 yd. = (3) ft.   1 qt. = (4) cups
   1 yd. = (36) in.   1 qt. = (2) pt.
   1 hr. = (60) min. 1 gal.= (4) qt.
   1 min. = (60) sec. 1 doz. = (12) things
   1 day = (24) hr.
   To change from a larger unit to a smaller one, we (multiply).
   To change from a smaller unit to a larger one, we (divide).
7. Give mixed mental practice.
      2 + 7 ÷ 3 + 4 × 5 (35)
      4 + 7 − 1 ÷ 2 × 6 (30)
      4 ÷ 2 × 7 + 4 ÷ 3 (6)
      8 − 5 × 4 ÷ 6 + 9 (11)

8. Review place value and large numbers. Have the pupils do this and the remaining exercises on the board where you can *see* what they are doing.
   a. **Write the number 409,000. Underline the digit that is in ten thousands' place. Circle the digit that has a place value of hundred thousands.**
   b. **Write the number 33,333. Circle the 3 that means 3,000.**
9. Review the symbols < and >.
10. Review Roman numerals.
    a. **Write the Roman numerals for 40** (XL), **29** (XXIX), **86** (LXXXVI), **17** (XVII), **and 64** (LXIV).
    b. **Write the Arabic numerals for IV** (4), **LXX** (70), **XLII** (42), **XXXV** (35), **and LIX** (59).
11. Review prices.
    a. **Write each price in two ways: $0.40, $0.05, $1.00, $5.00.**
    b. **Write these prices correctly: $2.63, $4.09.**
12. Review fractions.
    a. **Write the fraction that means 1 part out of 3; 1 part out of 5; 2 parts out of 4.**
    b. **Draw a circle. Divide it into 2 equal parts. Write the fraction for each part. Divide it into 4 equal parts. Write the fraction.**
    c. **What is 1/3 of 15? 1/2 of 8? 1/5 of 20?**
13. Review computation.
    a. Addition.

$3.24	5	7	4	
1.92	8	3	7	62
+4.61	6	8	3	28
	+5	+8	+9	+16
($9.77)	(24)	(26)	(23)	(106)

75	604		438
19	47	872	644
76	946	395	16
+23	+352	+238	+591
(193)	(1,949)	(1,505)	(1,689)

   b. Subtraction.

118	136	524	381
−46	−55	−94	−259
(72)	(81)	(430)	(122)

500	407	$6.10
−346	−125	−3.85
(154)	(282)	($2.25)

   c. Multiplication.

23	95	37	142
×3	×4	×3	×6
(69)	(380)	(111)	(852)

713	837	650	671
×6	×4	×6	×5
(4,278)	(3,348)	(3,900)	(3,355)

   d. Division.

   3)11 (3 R 2)   5)36 (7 R 1)   4)9 (2 R 1)

   5)17 (3 R 2)   2)13 (6 R 1)   4)27 (6 R 3)

14. Review reading problems. See Lesson 39 Teaching Guide for some sample problems and a review of key words used in reading problems.
15. Tell students that they will have a major test in the next class.

Note: It is recommended that you do *not* assign this whole review lesson on one day. If you want to cover it in a day, pick out the parts your pupils need. For two-day coverage, assign the first, third, and fourth pages on one day; and the second page (computation practice) on another day.

C. *Write the answers only.*

10. 14 + 4   18   16 + 6   22   18 + 9   27   15 + 5   20   12 + 6   18
11. 29 + 5   34   17 + 3   20   24 + 6   30   27 + 8   35   35 + 6   41
12. 11 + 12 23   13 + 14 27   10 + 15 25   16 + 12 28   17 + 10 27

13.
6	4	3	7	9	3	5
5	4	5	3	2	6	8
5	8	9	6	4	8	6
+7	+5	+8	+7	+5	+2	+7
23	21	25	23	20	19	26

D. *Copy and work carefully. Follow the signs.*

14.
		87	98	761
76	278	25	79	652
88	346	95	5	249
+64	+975	+32	+67	+436
228	1,599	239	249	2,098

15.
115	724	600	403	582
− 44	− 146	− 387	− 368	− 46
71	578	213	35	536

16.
34	69	98	72	93
× 4	× 4	× 3	× 6	× 5
136	276	294	432	465

17.
231	526	647	814	874
× 6	× 5	× 3	× 6	× 4
1,386	2,630	1,941	4,884	3,496

18. a. $3.45 + $4.57   b. $2.49 + $0.37 + $0.65   c. $7 + $0.85 + $2.69
       $8.02 $3.51 $10.54

19. a. $5.93 − $2.28   b. $7.00 − $0.83   c. $9 − $1.43
       $3.65 $6.17 $7.57

20. 4)25 6 R 1   3)20 6 R 2   2)9 4 R 1   3)11 3 R 2   5)19 3 R 4

21. 2)17 8 R 1   5)7 1 R 2   4)15 3 R 3   5)32 6 R 2   3)26 8 R 2

(continued on next page)

92 Chapter 4 Division Facts: 1–6

E. *Write the answers.*

22. Look at this number: 850,417   Which digit is in the ten thousands' place? **5**

23. Write numerals for these number words.
    a. two hundred thousand, sixty-five   **200,065**
    b. fifty-seven thousand, nine hundred   **57,900**
    c. eight hundred four thousand, one   **804,001**

24. Copy the numbers, and write < or > between them.
    a. 4,300 __>__ 3,400   b. 19,999 __<__ 20,001   c. 16,748 __>__ 16,479

25. Write these Roman numerals as Arabic numerals.
    a. XVIII **18**   b. LIX **59**   c. XLV **45**   d. XXIV **24**   e. LXXVI **76**

26. Write each price in two ways.
    a. five cents **5¢ / $0.05**   b. forty-nine cents **49¢ / $0.49**   c. eight dollars **$8 / $8.00**

27. What is the value of each set of money?
    a. **45¢**   b. **21¢**   c. **42¢**

28. A.M. time is (<u>before</u>, after) noon.

29. Tell what time each clock shows.
    a. **11:30**   b. **2:35**   c. **8:15**   d. **1:50**

30. a. Find $\frac{1}{4}$ of 16. **4**   b. Find $\frac{1}{3}$ of 24. **8**   c. Find $\frac{1}{5}$ of 35. **7**

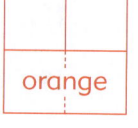

31. Draw a square. Divide it into fourths. Color $\frac{2}{4}$ orange.

32. 1 min. = __60__ sec.   1 ft. = __12__ in.   1 qt. = __4__ cups

33. 1 yd. = __3__ ft.   1 day = __24__ hr.   1 yd. = __36__ in.

34. Which is the larger unit,
    a. second or <u>minute</u>?   b. <u>gallon</u> or quart?   c. foot or <u>yard</u>?

35. To change a larger unit to a smaller one, you __multiply__ .

T–93   Chapter 4   Division Facts: 1–6

LESSON 41

Objective

- To test the pupils' mastery of the concepts taught in the first quarter of this course.

Teaching Guide

1. Give any last-minute review that you feel is necessary.
2. Administer the test.

Note: Chapter 4 Test is found in the test section in the back of this manual.

36. Multiply to find the answers.

5 gal. = __20__ qt.   4 yd. = __144__ in.   3 doz. = __36__ things

37. Divide to find the answers.

8 qt. = __2__ gal.   6 cups = __3__ pt.   12 ft. = __4__ yd.

F. Write *add, subtract, multiply,* or *divide.*

38. a. How many groups?   divide   d. How much is half as much?   divide

b. How many altogether?   add   e. How much farther?   subtract

c. How much at 15¢ each?   multiply   f. How many in each group?   divide

G. Solve these problems.

39. When Joseph was ruler of Egypt during the seven years of plenty, he collected $\frac{1}{5}$ of all the crops grown. If someone raised 40 bushels of wheat, how many bushels did he give to Joseph?   **8 bushels**

40. Brother Marvin put up tract racks in some business places near his home. In one month people took 265 tracts from the rack at the grocery store, 381 tracts from the rack at the Laundromat, and 248 tracts at the diner. How many tracts were taken altogether?   **894 tracts**

41. How many more tracts were taken from the Laundromat than from the grocery store? (See problem 40.)   **116 tracts**

42. One month Brother Marvin received 8 notes from people who had read the tracts. At that rate, how many notes would Brother Marvin receive in a year?   **96 notes**

43. Brother Marvin puts different tracts in the rack each week. If he uses 3 kinds of tracts each week, in how many weeks would he use 12 kinds of tracts?   **4 weeks**

44. What is the cost of 6 dozen tracts at $0.65 a dozen?   **$3.90**

41. Chapter 4 Test

Puzzle Page 1

A rectangle has four sides and four square corners. **Opposite** sides are equal.

Rectangles

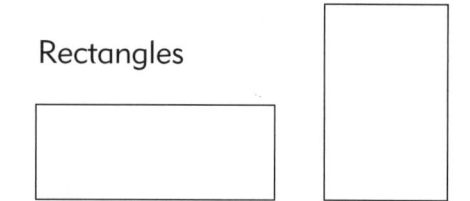

A square has four sides and four square corners. **All** sides are equal.

Squares

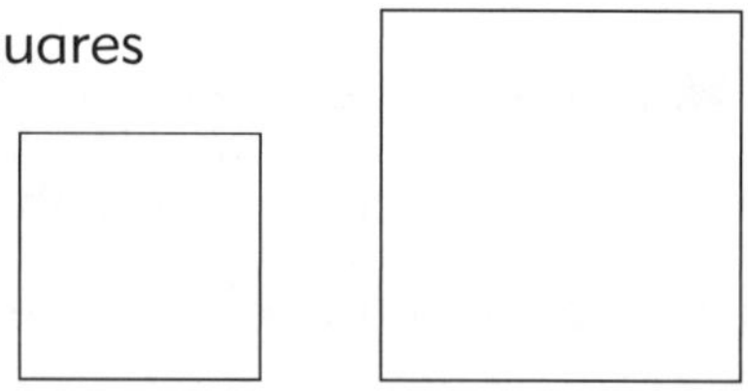

A triangle has three sides and three corners. The sides may be equal, but they do not have to be.

Triangles

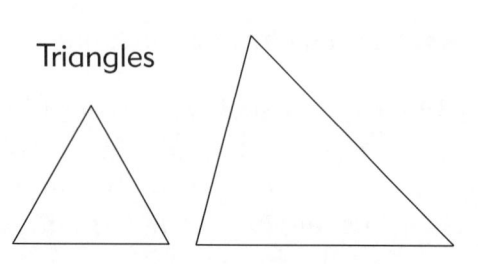

Can you do this?

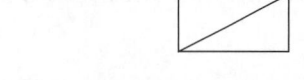

1. Find 5 triangles in Figure A.
2. Find 5 squares in Figure B.
3. Find 8 triangles in Figure C.
4. Draw a rectangle. Divide it into two triangles like this:
5. How many triangles do you see in Figure D? If you find them all, you will find 8 different triangles.
6. Arrange toothpicks to form a figure like this: 
   Now see if you can take two toothpicks away and have two complete squares left. Ask your teacher for help if you need it.

A.

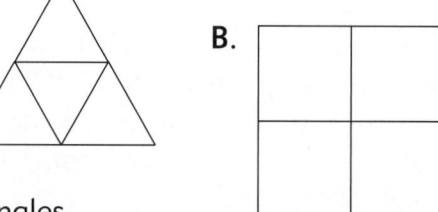

B.

C.

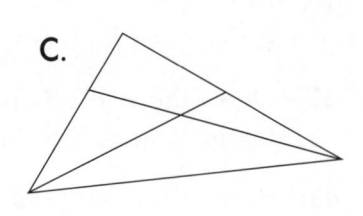

D.

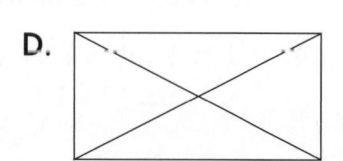

PUZZLE PAGE 1

To the Teacher

This page is the first of four optional puzzle pages in the book. The purpose of the these pages is twofold:

1. To spark the children's interest with some variety in arithmetic.
2. To provide an enjoyable challenge for faster students.

Remember that the puzzle pages are optional. Do not spend valuable class time on these pages at the expense of more necessary things. Also, do not assign the pages for scoring.

Allow pupils to work on their own before discussing the information on the pages. Do take time to discuss the page with interested pupils. One idea is to use the puzzle pages for lunchtime topics.

If pupils cannot grasp numbers 1–5 on Puzzle Page 1, help them understand that the triangles and squares overlap.

The answer to number 6 is to remove two perpendicular toothpicks within the larger square. That leaves only two squares: the large square and a small one in a corner.

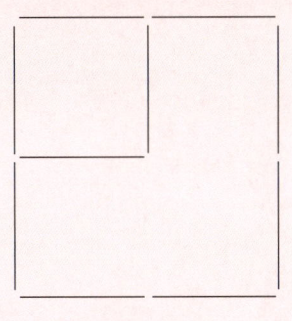

Chapter 5

Multiplication and Division Facts: 7–9

And he divided unto them his living.
(Luke 15:12)

42. Multiplication and Division Facts: 7's

Learn the multiplication and division facts in this box.

0 × 7 = 0	1 × 7 = 7	2 × 7 = 14	3 × 7 = 21	4 × 7 = 28	5 × 7 = 35	6 × 7 = 42	7 × 7 = 49	8 × 7 = 56	9 × 7 = 63	10 × 7 = 70	11 × 7 = 77	12 × 7 = 84
0 ÷ 7 = 0	7 ÷ 7 = 1	14 ÷ 7 = 2	21 ÷ 7 = 3	28 ÷ 7 = 4	35 ÷ 7 = 5	42 ÷ 7 = 6	49 ÷ 7 = 7	56 ÷ 7 = 8	63 ÷ 7 = 9	70 ÷ 7 = 10	77 ÷ 7 = 11	84 ÷ 7 = 12

A. *Write the answers to these multiplication–division sets.*

1. a. 7 × 6 = **42**   42 ÷ 7 = **6**   b. 7 × 9 = **63**   63 ÷ 7 = **9**
2. a. 7 × 7 = **49**   49 ÷ 7 = **7**   b. 7 × 12 = **84**   84 ÷ 7 = **12**
3. a. 7 × 4 = **28**   28 ÷ 7 = **4**   b. 7 × 11 = **77**   77 ÷ 7 = **11**
4. a. 7 × 8 = **56**   56 ÷ 7 = **8**   b. 7 × 5 = **35**   35 ÷ 7 = **5**

B. *Write the answers to these multiplication facts.*

5. 8 × 7 = **56**; 4 × 7 = **28**; 9 × 7 = **63**; 11 × 7 = **77**; 6 × 7 = **42**; 7 × 7 = **49**; 12 × 7 = **84**; 10 × 7 = **70**; 1 × 7 = **7**
6. 5 × 7 = **35**; 8 × 6 = **48**; 9 × 4 = **36**; 3 × 7 = **21**; 9 × 6 = **54**; 5 × 5 = **25**; 11 × 6 = **66**; 7 × 7 = **49**; 9 × 3 = **27**
7. 8 × 4 = **32**; 8 × 5 = **40**; 1 × 7 = **7**; 8 × 7 = **56**; 9 × 7 = **63**; 12 × 4 = **48**; 6 × 3 = **18**; 12 × 2 = **24**; 6 × 1 = **6**
8. 7 × 7 = **49**; 5 × 7 = **35**; 12 × 7 = **84**; 12 × 3 = **36**; 0 × 3 = **0**; 6 × 2 = **12**; 7 × 2 = **14**; 5 × 3 = **15**; 8 × 7 = **56**

C. *Write the answers to these division facts.*

9. 49 ÷ 7 = **7**; 56 ÷ 7 = **8**; 84 ÷ 7 = **12**; 21 ÷ 7 = **3**; 7 ÷ 7 = **1**; 42 ÷ 7 = **6**
10. 70 ÷ 7 = **10**; 0 ÷ 7 = **0**; 63 ÷ 7 = **9**; 14 ÷ 7 = **2**; 35 ÷ 7 = **5**; 28 ÷ 7 = **4**
11. 72 ÷ 6 = **12**; 24 ÷ 6 = **4**; 45 ÷ 5 = **9**; 20 ÷ 4 = **5**; 42 ÷ 6 = **7**; 56 ÷ 7 = **8**
12. 54 ÷ 6 = **9**; 24 ÷ 3 = **8**; 30 ÷ 5 = **6**; 36 ÷ 6 = **6**; 28 ÷ 4 = **7**; 32 ÷ 4 = **8**

LESSON 42

Objectives

♦ To drill the 7's multiplication and division facts.

♦ To teach more facts about time.

♦ To review long division.

Preparation

1. Multiplication and division flash cards
2. A large calendar with all the pages
3. Speed Drill 42
4. Chalkboard:

   $2\overline{)11}$ $3\overline{)8}$ $4\overline{)19}$

   $5\overline{)34}$ $3\overline{)29}$ $5\overline{)27}$

Oral Drill

1. Drill the multiplication and division facts up to the 6's.
2. Give mixed mental practice.
   $6 + 4 \div 5 \times 6 - 4$ (8)
   $8 - 3 \times 7 - 5 \div 6$ (5)
   $4 + 5 \div 3 - 1 \times 9$ (18)
   $6 \times 9 + 1 \div 5 - 2$ (9)
   $3 \times 8 \div 4 - 1 \times 5$ (25)
   $5 + 9 - 2 \div 3 - 4$ (0)
3. Count by 2's, by 3's, by 4's, by 5's, by 6's, and by 7's.
4. a. **Which of these numbers divide evenly by 3?**
      5   9   11   24   32
      30   27   21   20   23
   b. **Which of these numbers divide evenly by 4?**
      8   5   12   14   24
      32   18   20   28   36
5. **How many hours are in a day? How many seconds in a minute? How many minutes in an hour? How many inches in a foot? in a yard? How many feet in a yard? How many inches in a half foot?**

   Note: If pupils do not know these equivalents by this time, be sure to drill them again later.

Speed Drill

Give Speed Drill 42 (mixed computation).

T-97   Chapter 5   Multiplication and Division Facts: 7–9

Teaching Guide

1. *Multiplication and division facts.*
   a. Drill the 7's multiplication and division facts. Allow the pupils to find the answers in Lesson 42 of their books if they are unsure of some.
   b. **If something is divided in half, it is divided into how many parts? How do we find half of a number?** (divide by 2) **How do we find 1/3 of a number? 1/4? 1/5? 1/6?**
   c. **How do you think we would find 1/7 of a number?** (divide by 7)
   d. **Find these parts in your head.**

1/2 of 16	1/5 of 25	1/4 of 24
1/6 of 36	1/3 of 24	1/4 of 20
1/3 of 18	1/6 of 54	1/5 of 35
1/2 of 18	1/7 of 49	1/7 of 35
1/7 of 54	1/7 of 28	1/7 of 42

2. *More facts about time.*
   a. Have the pupils recite the days of the week and the months of the year in unison.
   b. Using a month on the calendar, show that the numbers in the first column are Sundays, in the second column are Mondays, and so on. Say a date, and have pupils tell what day of the week that date is on.
   c. Teach the pupils the rhyme in the box ("Thirty days have September..."). Recite it in unison.
   d. Give the names of months at random, and have pupils tell how many days are in each one.
   e. Introduce the new equivalents: 1 week = 7 days; 1 year = 12 months. **How many days are in 2 weeks? in 3 weeks? in 4? How many months are in 2 years? 3 years? 4?... Did we multiply or divide to find the answers? Why do we multiply?** (We are changing from a larger unit to a smaller one.)

3. *Reviewing long division.*
   a. Review the parts of division problems.
   b. Review the five steps in Lesson 38. Work through the problems on the board with the class, and give some to pupils to solve individually. Encourage them to think of the "helper numbers": numbers that divide evenly by 3, by 4, and so on.

   $4\overline{)11}$ (2 R 3) $5\overline{)37}$ (7 R 2) $2\overline{)9}$ (4 R 1)

   $4\overline{)29}$ (7 R 1) $3\overline{)23}$ (7 R 2) $5\overline{)28}$ (5 R 3)

Supplementary Drill

Drill 9*

Learn these facts about time. The rhyme will help you remember the days in each month.

> 7 days = 1 week (wk.)   12 months (mo.) = 1 year (yr.)
>
> Thirty days have September, April, June, and November.
> All the rest have 31, except February alone;
> It has 28 most times; every leap year, 29.

D. Follow the directions.

13. Change these units to smaller ones. You will need to multiply.
   a. 1 wk. = __7__ days   c. 1 yr. = __12__ mo.   e. 7 wk. = __49__ days
   b. 1 day = __24__ hr.   d. 3 yr. = __36__ mo.   f. 2 min. = __120__ sec.

14. Find the parts of these units. Remember to divide to find a part.
   a. $\frac{1}{2}$ yr. = __6__ mo.   c. $\frac{1}{4}$ yr. = __3__ mo.
   b. $\frac{1}{3}$ yr. = __4__ mo.   d. $\frac{1}{2}$ day = __12__ hr.

E. Do these exercises. Use the calendar pages at the right for help with numbers 15 and 16.

15. On what day of the week is October 27? November 13?
   Sunday   Wednesday

16. What date is one week after November 2?
   November 9

17. To find $\frac{1}{7}$ of a number, divide by 7.

God rested one day in seven. He rested $\frac{1}{7}$ of the days in the week. Find $\frac{1}{7}$ of the numbers below.

42 __6__   49 __7__   14 __2__   56 __8__   35 __5__   63 __9__   70 __10__   84 __12__

October
S M T W T F S
1 2 3 4 5
6 7 8 9 10 11 12
13 14 15 16 17 18 19
20 21 22 23 24 25 26
27 28 29 30 31

November
S M T W T F S
1 2
3 4 5 6 7 8 9
10 11 12 13 14 15 16
17 18 19 20 21 22 23
24 25 26 27 28 29 30

Review Exercises

F. Write the answers only.

18. 15 + 8   23   37 + 6   43   43 + 9   52   27 + 4   31

19. 5 × 9 + 4   49   6 × 7 + 5   47   4 × 7 + 5   33   7 × 7 + 4   53

G. Review the division steps in Lesson 38. Then copy and divide.

20. 5)24 = 4 R 4   3)11 = 3 R 2   4)9 = 2 R 1   2)13 = 6 R 1   4)35 = 8 R 3   5)22 = 4 R 2

21. 4)17 = 4 R 1   3)20 = 6 R 2   2)7 = 3 R 1   3)26 = 8 R 2   5)18 = 3 R 3   4)6 = 1 R 2

98 Chapter 5 Multiplication and Division Facts: 7–9

43. Dividing by 6 and 7

Count by 5's from 5 to 60. Count by 6's from 6 to 72. Count by 7's from 7 to 84.

The numbers you said are the products of the 5's, 6's, and 7's multiplication facts. They will help you to divide larger numbers.

A. *Copy and solve these divisions. Follow the steps in Lesson 38. You will have remainders.*

1. 6)13̄ 2 R 1   6)25̄ 4 R 1   6)40̄ 6 R 4   6)32̄ 5 R 2   6)9̄ 1 R 3
2. 7)12̄ 1 R 5   7)8̄ 1 R 1   7)26̄ 3 R 5   7)50̄ 7 R 1   7)33̄ 4 R 5
3. 6)20̄ 3 R 2   6)15̄ 2 R 3   7)27̄ 3 R 6   6)19̄ 3 R 1   7)40̄ 5 R 5

When you add, you usually carry a small digit such as 1 or 2. But when you multiply, you must often carry 3, 4, 5, or an even larger digit. Be especially careful with adding on these large, carried digits.

```
   4              5 4
  47             598
 × 7            ×  6
 ───            ─────
 329           3,588
```

B. *Write the answers.*

4. 6 × 5 + 4   34   7 × 6 + 5   47   8 × 7 + 4   60
5. 7 × 5 + 3   38   7 × 7 + 4   53   9 × 7 + 5   68
6. 7 × 3 + 4   25   3 × 9 + 5   32   4 × 7 + 3   31

C. *Copy and multiply.*

7. 46   89   57   19   42
   × 7   × 5   × 7   × 6   × 8
   ───   ───   ───   ───   ───
   322   445   399   114   336

8. 364   718   953   547   563
   × 7   × 7   × 7   × 6   × 8
   ────   ────   ────   ────   ────
   2,548 5,026 6,671 3,282 4,504

9. 645   936   287   315   879
   × 6   × 7   × 5   × 8   × 6
   ────   ────   ────   ────   ────
   3,870 6,552 1,435 2,520 5,274

LESSON 43

Objectives

- To teach division by 6 and 7 with remainders.
- To teach multiplication with carrying of the digits *4 and 5.

Preparation

1. More difficult addition and subtraction flash cards
2. Multiplication and division flash cards: 4's–7's
3. Chalkboard:

   XVIII   LXIV   LIX   XLIII   XXXVI

Oral Drill

1. Drill addition and subtraction facts.
2. Drill multiplication and division facts, especially the 6's and 7's.
3. Review parts of a division problem: dividend, divisor, quotient, remainder.
4. Have pupils read the Roman numerals on the board.
5. **How do you find 1/7 of a number? 1/4? 1/6? 1/3?**
6. Review the rules for changing larger units of measure to smaller units, and vice versa.
7. **How many days are in one week? How many months are in one year? Which months have 30 days? How many days are in February?**

Teaching Guide

1. *Division by 6 and by 7.*
   a. Review the steps of division from Lesson 38. Do some examples together with divisors of 2, 3, 4, and 5. Remind pupils that if the divisor is 3, for example, they should think of "helper numbers" that divide evenly by 3.
   b. Put this division on the board: $6\overline{)15}$. Ask: **How many 6's are in 15?** If pupils hesitate, count by 6's. **Which "helper number" is just smaller than 15? How many 6's are in 12?** Continue, and finish the problem.
   c. **What is the largest remainder we can have if we divide by 6? if we divide by 7? by 5?** (The remainder must always be smaller than the divisor, so the largest possible remainder is one less than the divisor.)
   d. Caution pupils to be careful with their subtraction. Use these problems to review subtraction with borrowing.

   $\quad\ 20 \qquad\ 30 \qquad\ 40$
   $\underline{-14} \qquad \underline{-28} \qquad \underline{-36}$
   $\ \ (6) \qquad\ \ (2) \qquad\ \ (4)$

   $\quad\ 31 \qquad\ 21 \qquad\ 41$
   $\underline{-28} \qquad \underline{-18} \qquad \underline{-36}$
   $\ \ (3) \qquad\ \ (3) \qquad\ \ (5)$

   e. Use the following problems for individual practice.

   $\quad (2\text{ R }4) \qquad (3\text{ R }4) \qquad (4\text{ R }4)$
   $6\overline{)16} \qquad\ \ 7\overline{)25} \qquad\ \ 6\overline{)28}$

   $\quad (4\text{ R }5) \qquad (7\text{ R }3)$
   $7\overline{)33} \qquad\ \ 7\overline{)52}$

   If the pupils have the division process firmly in their minds, they will probably not have much trouble with dividing larger numbers. However, the remainders in this lesson are larger, and subtraction in the division problems involves more borrowing. Pupils must be careful to subtract correctly.

2. *Multiplication involving carried digits up to 5.*
   a. Give some oral "times-and" problems.
      $6 \times 5 + 4\ (34) \qquad 8 \times 6 + 5\ (53)$
      $7 \times 7 + 3\ (52) \qquad 4 \times 7 + 5\ (33)$
      $6 \times 7 + 4\ (46) \qquad 9 \times 7 + 5\ (68)$
   b. **When we multiply, we often need to carry larger digits than when we add. We must be especially careful with adding on a larger carried digit.**
   c. Use the following as sample problems.

   $\quad\ 75 \qquad\ \ 67 \qquad\ 296$
   $\underline{\times\ 7} \qquad \underline{\times\ 7} \qquad \underline{\times\ 6}$
   $(525) \qquad (469) \qquad (1{,}776)$

   $\quad 965 \qquad 367$
   $\underline{\times\ 7} \qquad \underline{\times\ 8}$
   $(6{,}755) \qquad (2{,}936)$

   This is the first lesson in which the pupils are carrying digits greater than 3. The process is the same as before; however, more mistakes are usually made with problems involving larger carried digits. The pupils often do not know the higher multiplication facts as well, and they are more likely to make mistakes with "carrying in their heads." Encourage them to think carefully and work slowly enough to be accurate. When they finish a problem, they should go over it again to be sure they made no mistakes.

Note: It may take longer than usual to do the whole lesson, especially if pupils are slow in both division and multiplication. You may want to have your pupils omit some of the problems. Stress accuracy rather than speed.

Supplementary Drills

Drill 100*

Drill 28 ÷

Review Exercises

D. *Write the answers to these facts quickly.*

10. 7×7=49   7×5=35   8×6=48   9×4=36   8×7=56   9×5=45   9×6=54   9×7=63   7×4=28

11. 7×6=42   11×7=77   9×7=63   11×5=55   6×6=36   9×2=18   7×7=49   3×6=18   8×4=32

12. 8×7=56   10×4=40   12×5=60   12×7=84   9×3=27   1×7=7   7×5=35   12×6=72   9×7=63

13. 42÷7=6   20÷4=5   48÷6=8   63÷7=9   56÷7=8   54÷6=9

14. 24÷3=8   7÷1=7   7÷7=1   21÷7=3   84÷7=12   35÷5=7

15. 70÷7=10   14÷7=2   54÷6=9   40÷5=8   27÷3=9   36÷4=9

E. *Solve these problems.*

16. When Sister Mary was in the hospital, the four girls in grade 4 weeded her garden. If each girl weeded 15 tomato plants, how many plants were weeded?   **60 plants**

17. Altogether Sister Mary had 20 rows of vegetables in her garden. If each of the 4 girls weeded the same amount, how many rows did each girl do?   **5 rows**

18. When the tomatoes were ripe, Sister Mary picked 28 tomatoes from the first row. If all 3 rows yielded the same amount, how many tomatoes did she pick?   **84 tomatoes**

F. *Change these units to smaller ones. You will need to multiply.*

19. 6 yr. = __72__ mo.   4 wk. = __28__ days   3 days = __72__ hr.

20. 7 wk. = __49__ days   7 yr. = __84__ mo.   6 yd. = __18__ ft.

21. 5 gal. = __20__ qt.   4 yd. = __144__ in.   7 ft. = __84__ in.

44. Multiplication and Division Facts: 8's

Learn the multiplication and division facts in this box.

0	1	2	3	4	5	6	7	8	9	10	11	12
×8	×8	×8	×8	×8	×8	×8	×8	×8	×8	×8	×8	×8
0	8	16	24	32	40	48	56	64	72	80	88	96

| 8)0̄ 0 | 8)8̄ 1 | 8)1̄6̄ 2 | 8)2̄4̄ 3 | 8)3̄2̄ 4 | 8)4̄0̄ 5 | 8)4̄8̄ 6 | 8)5̄6̄ 7 | 8)6̄4̄ 8 | 8)7̄2̄ 9 | 8)8̄0̄ 10 | 8)8̄8̄ 11 | 8)9̄6̄ 12 |

A. *Write the answers to these multiplication–division sets.*

1. a. 8 × 7 = 56   56 ÷ 8 = 7   b. 8 × 8 = 64   64 ÷ 8 = 8
2. a. 8 × 5 = 40   40 ÷ 5 = 8   b. 8 × 9 = 72   72 ÷ 8 = 9
3. a. 8 × 11 = 88   88 ÷ 8 = 11   b. 8 × 12 = 96   96 ÷ 8 = 12
4. a. 8 × 6 = 48   48 ÷ 8 = 6   b. 7 × 7 = 49   49 ÷ 7 = 7

B. *Write the answers to these facts.*

5. 8×8=64   7×8=56   4×8=32   9×8=72   6×8=48   8×8=64   11×8=88   12×8=96   9×8=72

6. 5×8=40   3×8=24   9×8=72   7×8=56   6×7=42   6×8=48   9×5=45   9×7=63   12×8=96

7. 7×7=49   4×7=28   11×1=11 10×8=80 12×7=84 12×5=60 9×3=27   8×8=64   8×7=56

8. 8)5̄6̄=7   8)7̄2̄=9   8)6̄4̄=8   8)4̄8̄=6   8)9̄6̄=12   8)8̄0̄=10

9. 8)2̄4̄=3   8)4̄0̄=5   8)5̄6̄=7   8)3̄2̄=4   8)8̄=1   8)1̄6̄=2

10. 7)5̄6̄=8   7)8̄4̄=12 7)4̄9̄=7   7)2̄8̄=4   7)4̄2̄=6   7)7̄7̄=11

LESSON 44

Objective

- To drill the 8's multiplication and division facts.
- To review changing units of measure.
- To review computation, especially multiplication and division.

Preparation

1. Multiplication and division flash cards up to 8's
2. Speed Drill 44
3. Chalkboard:

   3 ft. = ___ yd. 14 days = ___ wk.
   6 cups = ___ pt. 20 qt. = ___ gal.
   12 mo. = ___ yr. 4 pt. = ___ qt.

Oral Drill

1. Review parts of a division problem, including the remainder.
2. Count by 4's, by 5's, by 6's, by 7's, and by 8's.
3. **Which of these numbers divide evenly by 3?**
   5 3 6 8 12 30 25 15 24 28
   Which of these divide evenly by 4?
   8 16 24 27 35 12
   Which of these divide evenly by 5?
   10 15 24 12 30 45
   Which of these divide evenly by 6?
   24 15 30 40 36 18
   Which of these divide evenly by 7?
   21 49 64 56 18 28
4. Drill "times-and" problems.
   $6 \times 8 + 4$ (52) $6 \times 9 + 3$ (57)
   $4 \times 7 + 5$ (33) $8 \times 8 + 4$ (68)
   $7 \times 7 + 5$ (54) $7 \times 8 + 4$ (60)
   $6 \times 7 + 4$ (46) $9 \times 4 + 4$ (40)

Speed Drill

Give Speed Drill 44 (addition–subtraction chains).

Chapter 5 Multiplication and Division Facts: 7–9

Teaching Guide

1. *Multiplication and division facts.*
   a. Drill multiplication and division facts through the 7's.
   b. Drill the 8's multiplication and division facts. Allow the pupils to find the answers in Lesson 44 of their books if they are unsure of some.
   c. **If something is divided in half, it is divided into how many parts? How do we find half of a number?** (divide by 2) **How do we find 1/3 of a number? 1/4? 1/5? 1/6? 1/7?**
   d. **How do you think we would find 1/8 of a number?** (divide by 8)
   e. **Find these parts in your head.**

1/2 of 14	1/5 of 30	1/4 of 24
1/6 of 36	1/7 of 21	1/6 of 18
1/4 of 20	1/7 of 56	1/6 of 54
1/5 of 40	1/8 of 16	1/8 of 64
1/8 of 48	1/8 of 96	1/8 of 56

2. *Changing measures.*
   a. **How many feet are in a yard? inches in a foot? inches in a yard? days in a week? months in a year? hours in a day? seconds in a minute? minutes in an hour? pints in a quart? cups in a quart? quarts in a gallon? cups in a pint?**
   b. **Which is the *smaller* unit: inch or foot? yard or foot? second or minute? hour or day? week or day? month or year? pint or cup? quart or cup? quart or gallon?**
   c. **How do we change a smaller unit to a larger one?** (We *divide* because there are fewer of the larger unit.) **How do we change a larger unit to a smaller one?** (We *multiply* because there are more of the smaller unit.)
   d. Together work the equivalents on the board. They are all changing from smaller units to larger, but question the pupils anyway about which unit is smaller. In the next lesson they will need to decide which operation to use.

3. *Mixed computation practice.*
   If time permits, have pupils do a variety of exercises on the board. Here are some samples.

   ```
     65        79       458        394
    × 8       × 6      ×  7       ×  5
   (520)    (474)   (3,206)   (1,970)
   ```

   ```
       (2 R 4)      (6 R 4)      (7 R 1)
    6)16         5)34         7)50
   ```

   ```
     6       7       4                 463
     5       6       3      289        458
     4       5       8      492        318
    +8      +7      +5     +344       +732
   (23)   (25)   (20)  (1,125)    (1,971)
   ```

   ```
    900     503     285
   -127    -381    -169
   (773)  (122)   (116)
   ```

Supplementary Drill

Drill 11*

Lesson 44

> To find $\frac{1}{8}$ of a number, divide by 8.

C. *Find $\frac{1}{8}$ of these numbers.*

11. 64 8   56 7   80 10   24 3   72 9   96 12   40 5   88 11

Review Exercises

D. *Change these units to larger ones. You will need to divide.*

12. 7 days = __1__ wk.   12 mo. = __1__ yr.   12 in. = __1__ ft.
13. 42 days = __6__ wk.   36 mo. = __3__ yr.   8 pt. = __4__ qt.
14. 21 ft. = __7__ yd.   12 qt. = __3__ gal.   12 cups = __6__ pt.
15. 8 cups = __2__ qt.   9 ft. = __3__ yd.   49 days = __7__ wk.

E. *Write the answers only.*

16. 6 × 7 + 5   47   8 × 8 + 4   68   7 × 8 + 5   61
17. 7 × 7 + 4   53   4 × 7 + 5   33   9 × 8 + 3   75
18. 8 × 6 + 2   50   5 × 7 + 5   40   9 × 7 + 4   67

F. *Copy and find the answers. Check by going over your work.*

19. 47   89   93   28   76
    × 7   × 5   × 7   × 6   × 7
    ---   ---   ---   ---   ---
    329   445   651   168   532

20. 354   948   826   946   945
    × 8   × 7   × 8   × 6   × 8
    ---   ---   ---   ---   ---
    2,832   6,636   6,608   5,676   7,560

21. 6 R 2   4 R 4   7 R 2   6 R 3   8 R 2
    6)38   5)24   7)51   7)45   6)50

22. 2 R 3   8 R 2   5 R 4   2 R 6   1 R 3
    5)13   3)26   7)39   7)20   6)9

G. *Study these division problems. Then copy each number and write what part of the division problem it is.*

23. 56 ÷ 8 = 7   56 _dividend_   5 R 4   7 _divisor_
                  8 _divisor_   7)39   39 _dividend_
                  7 _quotient_   5 _quotient_
                                                      4 _remainder_

45. Changing Units of Measure

Do you remember the two rules for changing units of measure?

> To change from a **larger** unit to a **smaller** unit, **multiply**.
> To change from a **smaller** unit to a **larger** unit, **divide**.

In today's lesson you will need to multiply to change some measures, and divide to change others. You can solve problems like these by following the three steps in the box.

1. Decide whether you will multiply or divide.
2. Find the key number.
3. Multiply or divide the number in the problem by the key number.

Example A: 9 yd. = ___ ft.
Changing from larger to smaller unit. Multiply.
1 yd. = 3 ft. Key number is 3.
9 × 3 = 27   9 yd. = 27 ft.

Example B: 8 pt. = ___ qt.
Changing from smaller to larger unit. Divide.
1 qt. = 2 pt. Key number is 2.
8 ÷ 2 = 4   8 pt. = 4 qt.

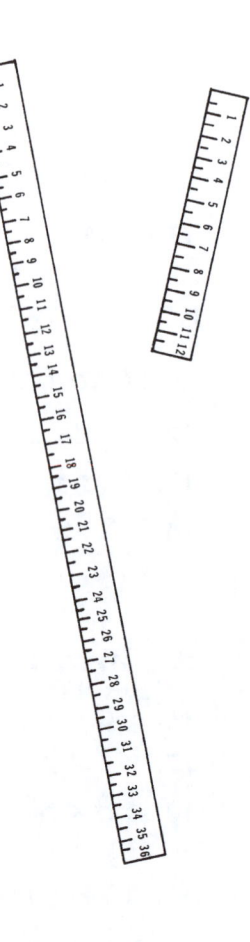

A. *Write how many of the smaller units are in* one *of the larger unit. These are the* key numbers *that you need for changing units.*

1. 1 ft. = __12__ in.   1 yd. = __3__ ft.   1 wk. = __7__ days
2. 1 hr. = __60__ min.   1 pt. = __2__ cups   1 day = __24__ hr.
3. 1 yr. = __12__ mo.   1 gal. = __4__ qt.   1 yd. = __36__ in.
4. 1 qt. = __4__ cups   1 qt. = __2__ pt.   1 min. = __60__ sec.

B. *Change these units of measure. You must multiply or divide.*

5. 3 ft. = __36__ in.   4 hr. = __240__ min.   4 pt. = __2__ qt.
6. 4 pt. = __8__ cups   12 qt. = __3__ gal.   10 qt. = __20__ pt.
7. 9 ft. = __3__ yd.   28 days = __4__ wk.   10 pt. = __5__ qt.
8. 12 gal. = __48__ qt. 3 days = __72__ hr.   14 days = __2__ wk.

The key number is also used to find a **part** of a measure. Study the following example.

$\frac{1}{3}$ day = _____ hours

Think: 1 day = 24 hours
$\frac{1}{3}$ day = $\frac{1}{3}$ of 24 hours
$\frac{1}{3}$ of 24 hours = 24 ÷ 3 = 8 hours

LESSON 45

Objectives

- To teach *when to multiply or divide in changing units of measure.
- To teach finding part of a measure.
- To drill division with larger divisors (up to 8).

Preparation

1. Multiplication and division flash cards. Take the easier facts out of the pack.
2. Subtraction flash cards
3. Chalkboard:

    555,555   120,308   704,019

Oral Drill

1. Drill multiplication and division flash cards, concentrating on the more difficult 6's, 7's, and 8's.
2. Drill subtraction facts.
3. Review "times-and" problems.

9 × 7 + 4 (67)	8 × 6 + 3 (51)
6 × 6 + 4 (40)	7 × 7 + 2 (51)
8 × 7 + 5 (61)	9 × 6 + 4 (58)
4 × 7 + 3 (31)	9 × 5 + 5 (50)

4. Review place value and large numbers.
    a. Name the number places from right to left in the first number on the board. Review that each 5 stands for 10 times as much as the 5 to its right.
    b. Read and discuss the other two numbers.

T–103 Chapter 5 Multiplication and Division Facts: 7–9

Teaching Guide

1. *Deciding when to multiply or divide in changing units of measure.*
   This is the first lesson in which pupils are not told when to multiply or divide.
   a. Use the first box in Lesson 45 to review the rules for changing units of measure.
   b. **How many inches are in one foot? Then 12 is the number that we use for changing inches to feet, or feet to inches. We call 12 the *key number*.**
      What key number do we use to change pints to quarts? quarts to gallons? yards to inches? days to weeks?
   c. **In today's lesson you will need to multiply to change some units, and divide to change others. What is the rule for changing from larger to smaller units? What is the rule for changing from smaller to larger units?** Repeat the rules in the box.
   d. Discuss the steps in the second box. Then have pupils use the three steps to do these exercises.
      2 wk. = (14) days   9 ft. = (3) yd.
      16 qt. = (4) gal.   8 yd. = (24) ft.
      35 days = (5) wk.   7 ft. = (84) in.
2. *Finding part of a measure.*
   a. Review finding part of a number. **What is 1/3 of 12? 1/4 of 8? 1/2 of 24?**
   b. **How many inches are in 1/2 foot?** (Think: 1/2 foot = 1/2 of 12 inches; 1/2 of 12 inches = 12 ÷ 2 = 6 inches.) **How many inches are in 1/3 foot? in 1/4 foot? How many hours are in half a day? How many quarts are in half a gallon?**
   c. Give practice with the following problems.
      1/3 yr. = (4) mo.   1/4 qt. = (1) cup
      1/6 ft. = (2) in.   1/6 day = (4) hr.
      1/3 doz. = (4) things   1/4 yd. = (9) in.
      Pupils should *divide* to find the answers as they have been doing to find a *part*, rather than try to follow the three steps. The three steps do apply to these problems as well as to whole-number problems, but fourth graders have not yet learned to multiply fractions.
3. *Division with larger divisors.*
   This is not new material except that the divisors are larger. Extra caution is needed in the multiplying and subtracting steps. Give practice with several problems on the board.

   $6\overline{)43}$ (7 R 1) $7\overline{)38}$ (5 R 3) $8\overline{)50}$ (6 R 2)
   $7\overline{)60}$ (8 R 4) $8\overline{)29}$ (3 R 5) $8\overline{)71}$ (8 R 7)

Supplementary Drills

Drill 133*

Drill 29 ÷

C. *Divide to find the parts of these measures. Use the key numbers.*

9. $\frac{1}{3}$ ft. = __4__ in. $\quad$ $\frac{1}{4}$ doz. = __3__ things $\quad$ $\frac{1}{2}$ doz. = __6__ things
10. $\frac{1}{2}$ yr. = __6__ mo. $\quad$ $\frac{1}{4}$ day = __6__ hr. $\quad$ $\frac{1}{4}$ gal. = __1__ qt.
11. $\frac{1}{2}$ qt. = __2__ cups $\quad$ $\frac{1}{6}$ hr. = __10__ min. $\quad$ $\frac{1}{2}$ pt. = __1__ cup

D. *Do these exercises.*

12. Write numbers by 6's from 6 to 72. 6, 12, 18, 24, 30, 36, 42, 48, 54, 60, 66, 72
13. Write numbers by 7's from 7 to 84. 7, 14, 21, 28, 35, 42, 49, 56, 63, 70, 77, 84
14. Write numbers by 8's from 8 to 96. 8, 16, 24, 32, 40, 48, 56, 64, 72, 80, 88, 96

E. *Copy and divide. Your answers in Part D will help you. Be especially careful with the larger divisors in these problems.*

15. 6)21 = 3 R 3 $\quad$ 7)17 = 2 R 3 $\quad$ 8)18 = 2 R 2 $\quad$ 5)14 = 2 R 4 $\quad$ 8)25 = 3 R 1 $\quad$ 8)36 = 4 R 4
16. 6)50 = 8 R 2 $\quad$ 8)49 = 6 R 1 $\quad$ 5)29 = 5 R 4 $\quad$ 7)51 = 7 R 2 $\quad$ 6)56 = 9 R 2 $\quad$ 7)30 = 4 R 2
17. 8)10 = 1 R 2 $\quad$ 7)25 = 3 R 4 $\quad$ 5)18 = 3 R 3 $\quad$ 8)67 = 8 R 3 $\quad$ 7)60 = 8 R 4 $\quad$ 6)32 = 5 R 2

Review Exercises

F. *Follow the directions.*

18. Answer **yes** or **no**.
    a. Does $\frac{2}{3}$ mean 2 parts out of 3? yes
    b. Do 67 and LXVII mean the same thing? yes
    c. Does 12 ÷ 4 mean 4 ÷ 12? no
    d. Are there 3 yards in 1 foot? no
    e. In the problem 24 − 17 = 7, are 24 and 17 called addends? no
    f. In the problem 24 ÷ 6 = 4, is 6 the divisor? yes
    g. In the fraction $\frac{1}{4}$, is 4 the denominator? yes
    h. In the number 34,570,912, is 7 in the thousands' place? no
    i. Could someone have a birthday on December 31? yes
    j. Do five quarters equal $1.50? no

19. Write the four facts in each family.
    a. the 13, 6, 7 addition–subtraction family $\quad$ 6 + 7 = 13 $\quad$ 13 − 6 = 7
    $\qquad\qquad\qquad\qquad\qquad\qquad\qquad\qquad$ 7 + 6 = 13 $\quad$ 13 − 7 = 6
    b. the 42, 6, 7 multiplication–division family
    $\qquad\qquad\qquad$ 6 × 7 = 42 $\quad$ 7 × 6 = 42 $\quad$ 42 ÷ 6 = 7 $\quad$ 42 ÷ 7 = 6

Chapter 5 Multiplication and Division Facts: 7–9

46. Multiplication and Division Facts: 9's

Learn the multiplication and division facts in this box.

0	1	2	3	4	5	6	7	8	9	10	11	12
×9	×9	×9	×9	×9	×9	×9	×9	×9	×9	×9	×9	×9
0	9	18	27	36	45	54	63	72	81	90	99	108

$9\overline{)0}=0$ $9\overline{)9}=1$ $9\overline{)18}=2$ $9\overline{)27}=3$ $9\overline{)36}=4$ $9\overline{)45}=5$ $9\overline{)54}=6$ $9\overline{)63}=7$ $9\overline{)72}=8$ $9\overline{)81}=9$ $9\overline{)90}=10$ $9\overline{)99}=11$ $9\overline{)108}=12$

A. Write the answers to these multiplication–division sets.

1. a. 9 × 8 = **72**   72 ÷ 9 = **8**   b. 9 × 9 = **81**   81 ÷ 9 = **9**
2. a. 9 × 6 = **54**   54 ÷ 9 = **6**   b. 9 × 11 = **99**   99 ÷ 9 = **11**
3. a. 9 × 7 = **63**   63 ÷ 9 = **7**   b. 9 × 12 = **108**   108 ÷ 9 = **12**
4. a. 8 × 8 = **64**   64 ÷ 8 = **8**   b. 9 × 4 = **36**   36 ÷ 9 = **4**

B. Write the answers to these facts.

5.   7×9=**63**   5×9=**45**   0×9=**0**   9×9=**81**   10×9=**90**   6×9=**54**   8×9=**72**   3×9=**27**   12×9=**108**

6.   7×8=**56**   8×9=**72**   7×9=**63**   4×9=**36**   7×7=**49**   6×5=**30**   9×8=**72**   9×9=**81**   8×6=**48**

7.   7×6=**42**   8×8=**64**   2×9=**18**   3×8=**24**   9×6=**54**   8×5=**40**   7×4=**28**   12×9=**108**   12×4=**48**

8.   9)90 = **10**   9)72 = **8**   9)81 = **9**   9)45 = **5**   9)9 = **1**   9)54 = **6**

9.   9)36 = **4**   9)27 = **3**   9)63 = **7**   9)18 = **2**   9)108 = **12**   9)99 = **11**

10.   7)49 = **7**   8)56 = **7**   7)42 = **6**   7)63 = **9**   8)64 = **8**   8)96 = **12**

> To find $\frac{1}{9}$ of a number, divide by 9.

C. Find $\frac{1}{9}$ of each number.

11.   81 **9**   36 **4**   45 **5**   9 **1**   90 **10**   63 **7**   72 **8**   27 **3**

LESSON 46

Objectives

- To drill the 9's multiplication and division facts.
- To review reading problems.

Preparation

1. Multiplication and division flash cards: 6's–9's
2. Speed Drill 46
3. Chalkboard:

   777,777   119,045   860,002

Oral Drill

1. Drill multiplication flash cards 6's–8's.
2. Drill division flash cards 6's–8's.
3. Review the number of days in each month.
4. Review place value and large numbers.
   a. Say the number places in the first number on the board. **Each 7 is worth 10 times as much as the 7 to its right.**
   b. Read the other two numbers.
5. Review changing units of measure. Write problems on the board, and work through them together. Have pupils supply the three steps.

   12 ft. = (4) yd.   8 gal. = (32) qt.
   12 yd. = (36) ft.   8 qt. = (2) gal.
   3 yd. = (108) in.   6 wk. = (42) days

Speed Drill

Give Speed Drill 46 (converting measures).

T–105　Chapter 5　Multiplication and Division Facts: 7–9

Teaching Guide

1. *Multiplication and division facts.*
   Introduce and drill the 9's facts. The only really new ones are 9 × 9, 9 × 10, 9 × 11, and 9 × 12.

2. *Reading problems.*
   a. Review the key words taught to this point. See Lesson 39 for a list.
   b. Discuss the key word *share*. This word has been used before but not specifically pointed out.

   　Stanley and Vernon have six cookies. They want to share the cookies equally. How many cookies will each boy have?

   　If two boys *share* the cookies, they are dividing the cookies into two groups. You *divide* to find the answer.

   c. Give more reading problems.
   • Three girls want to share six apples. How many apples will each girl have? (2 apples)
   • James, Nathan, and Rebecca hoed 15 rows of potatoes. If they shared the work evenly, how many rows did each hoe? (5 rows)
   • If five boys share 50 stamps, how many stamps will each boy have? (10 stamps)
   • If Raymond has 32 stamps, Delbert has 45 stamps, and Joshua has 39 stamps, how many stamps do they have together? (116 stamps)
   • Delbert has how many more stamps than Raymond? (13 stamps)
   • Mother needs 1 quart of water to make oatmeal for breakfast. Doris can find only a pint measure. How many pints of water should they use? (2 pints)

Supplementary Drills

Drill 13*

Drill 30 ÷

> The word **share** in a problem usually means you should divide.

D. Solve these reading problems.

12. Four boys are sharing 12 plums. How many plums will each boy have? **3 plums**

13. Three vans arrive at school at the same time. Each van has 9 children. How many children are in the three vans? **27 children**

14. The third, fourth, and fifth grades went on a nature hike. Sister Rhoda told the children to gather one leaf each of as many different kinds as they could. Third grade found 19 different kinds, fourth grade found 26 kinds, and fifth grade found 23 kinds. How many leaves did the children collect altogether? **68 leaves**

15. Fourth grade found how many more different leaves than third grade? (See number 14.) **7 leaves**

16. If 3 girls share 36 leaves equally, how many leaves should each girl have? **12 leaves**

17. Rachel washes the breakfast dishes. Mother says she should finish in 20 minutes. Rachel starts at 7:45. When should she finish? (Look at a clock for help.) **8:05**

18. There are 18 children in Room 3. Two children share each songbook during devotions. How many songbooks are needed? **9 songbooks**

19. Each morning Room 3 sings 4 songs. How many songs would they sing in one school week (five days)? **20 songs**

Review Exercises

E. Copy and divide.

20. 4)25 **6 R 1**   3)17 **5 R 2**   5)43 **8 R 3**   4)39 **9 R 3**   2)11 **5 R 1**

21. 6)39 **6 R 3**   8)54 **6 R 6**   7)30 **4 R 2**   8)60 **7 R 4**   6)35 **5 R 5**

22. 5)27 **5 R 2**   8)20 **2 R 4**   6)26 **4 R 2**   8)52 **6 R 4**   7)45 **6 R 3**

F. Follow the steps in Lesson 45 to find the answers.

23. 9 yd. = **27** ft.   9 ft. = **3** yd.   3 hr. = **180** min.

24. 16 qt. = **4** gal.   16 gal. = **64** qt.   7 wk. = **49** days

47. Multiplying Numbers by 10 or 100

It is easy to multiply by 10 or 100. Follow these rules.

| To multiply a number by 10, write 0 after it. | 10 × 8 = 80 |
| To multiply a number by 100, write 00 after it. | 100 × 8 = 800 |

A. Do these exercises.

1. Multiply these numbers by 10. Write only the answers.

   4 40   9 90   27 270   35 350   71 710   86 860

2. Multiply these numbers by 100. Write only the answers.

   5 500   2 200   32 3,200   69 6,900   47 4,700   10 1,000

You can use the rules above to do some multiplication problems in your head. Follow the steps in the box.

| 20 × 7 = ___ | 1. Think: 20 is 2 times 10.
2. Multiply 2 × 7.
3. Write 0 after the answer. | 2 × 7 = 14
20 × 7 = 140 |

B. Write the answers. Do the work in your head.

3. 30 × 3 90   60 × 2 120   50 × 5 250   40 × 6 240   20 × 5 100
4. 40 × 4 160   70 × 3 210   60 × 7 420   90 × 5 450   80 × 9 720

C. Copy and solve. You may need to borrow from thousands' place.

5.
```
  8,392      4,650      3,672      7,803      4,721      8,614
- 1,467    - 2,389    - 3,498    -   297    - 3,592    - 6,817
  6,925      2,261        174      7,506      1,129      1,797
```

Review Exercises

D. Write the answers.

6. Write numerals for these number words.
   a. six hundred seventy-five thousand, forty-two   675,042
   b. eight hundred four thousand, one hundred   804,100
   c. three hundred thousand, three   300,003
   d. ninety-two thousand, three hundred sixty-five   92,365
   e. five hundred two thousand, eighteen   502,018

7. Write the place value of the 5 in each number.
   a. 45,903   b. 568,302   c. 471,058   d. 350,421   e. 92,576
      thousands   hundred thousands   tens   ten thousands   hundreds

LESSON 47

Objectives

- To teach *annexing zeroes to multiply numbers by 10 or 100.
- To teach *mental multiplication by multiples of 10.
- To teach *subtracting four-digit numbers.

Preparation

1. Multiplication and division flash cards: 7's–9's
2. More difficult addition and subtraction flash cards
3. Chalkboard:
   a. 8 qt. = ___ pt. (16)
      8 qt. = ___ gal. (2)
      8 qt. = ___ cups-(32)
      9 ft. = ___ yd. (3)
      14 days = ___ wk. (2)
      14 wk. = ___ days (98)
   b. 222,222   320,006   47,019

Oral Drill

1. Drill multiplication and division facts.
2. Drill harder addition and subtraction facts.
3. Review *factors, product, dividend, divisor, quotient, minuend,* and *subtrahend*.
4. **Tell if these numbers divide evenly**
   by 3: 3, 13, 23, 33, 12, 21
   by 4: 16, 14, 24, 30, 28, 36
   by 6: 16, 12, 20, 24, 30, 40, 44, 48
   by 7: 17, 27, 36, 49, 28, 35, 56, 42, 63
   by 8: 8, 18, 28, 24, 32, 36, 40, 56, 64, 72
5. Give mixed mental drill.
   $5 - 3 \times 9 + 2 \div 4$ (5)
   $5 + 3 \times 5 \div 4 - 3$ (7)
   $6 \times 8 - 3 \div 5 + 7$ (16)
   $8 + 7 \div 3 \times 7 - 2$ (33)
   $4 \div 2 \times 9 - 9 \times 9$ (81)
   $9 \div 3 \times 7 + 4 \div 5$ (5)
6. Review changing units of measure, using the problems (a) on the board.

T–107   Chapter 5   Multiplication and Division Facts: 7–9

Teaching Guide

1. *Multiplying a number by 10 or 100.*
   a. Use the first number on the board *(b)* to review the names of the number places. **Each 2 in this number is equal to *10 times* the 2 to its right.** Read the other numbers on the board.
   b. **Because our number system is based on ten, it is easy to multiply by 10. How many are 10 × 6? 10 × 8? 10 × 3? The 10's facts are easy. We just put a 0 after the other number.**
   c. **Let's multiply some bigger numbers by 10. Remember, just put 0 at the end.**   10 × 64   10 × 15   10 × 26   10 × 40
   d. **100 is 10 times 10. To multiply a number by 100, put *two* 0's after it. Multiply these numbers by 100.**
      26   74   18   39   50   67

2. *Mental multiplication by multiples of 10.*
   a. **Knowing how to multiply by 10 helps us do some multiplication problems in our heads. If 10 × 4 is 40, what is 20 × 4? Multiply 2 × 4 and put 0 after it. The answer is 80.**
   b. **What is 20 × 7? 20 × 9? How did you get the answers?**
   c. **Multiply in your head, and give only the answers.**
      40 × 3   50 × 6   70 × 7
      60 × 8   80 × 9

3. *Subtracting four-digit numbers.*
   Review the borrowing process, and extend it to include four-digit numbers. Caution pupils to borrow only when necessary.
   Note that the problems in today's lesson have no zeroes in the hundreds' place.

4,830	5,142	7,613	9,635
−1,275	−4,658	− 591	−5,837
(3,555)	(484)	(7,022)	(3,798)

Extra Review

Briefly review the steps of division.

$\overset{(6\ \text{R}\ 3)}{4\overline{)27}}$ $\overset{(5\ \text{R}\ 1)}{6\overline{)31}}$ $\overset{(8\ \text{R}\ 4)}{8\overline{)68}}$

$\overset{(8\ \text{R}\ 4)}{7\overline{)60}}$ $\overset{(7\ \text{R}\ 2)}{5\overline{)37}}$

Supplementary Drills

Drill 31 ÷

Drill 46

E. *Write the answers to these facts quickly.*

8.
9	12	8	9	10	7	8	9	8
×9	×9	×9	×7	×9	×8	×8	×6	×7
81	108	72	63	90	56	64	54	56

9.
8	7	7	6	5	4	8	3	12
×6	×9	×7	×7	×8	×9	×9	×9	×8
48	63	49	42	40	36	72	27	96

F. *Write the answers to these number strings.*

10. a. 5 +3 ÷4 ×9 ÷3 = ? **6** b. 7 −4 ×8 ÷4 ×9 = ? **54**

11. a. 4 ×4 +5 ÷3 −6 = ? **1** b. 11 −4 ×7 +1 ÷5 = ? **10**

12. a. 9 ÷3 +6 ×7 −3 = ? **60** b. 6 +8 ÷7 +4 ×0 = ? **0**

G. *Write the letters of the terms below. After each letter write the correct numbers from the problems at the right.*

13.
- a. addend (2) **23, 37**
- b. difference **17**
- c. divisor **4**
- d. dividend **26**
- e. factor (2) **19, 3**
- f. minuend **51**
- g. product **57**
- h. quotient **6**
- i. remainder **2**
- j. subtrahend **34**
- k. sum **60**

```
  23        51        19
+ 37      − 34        × 3
  60        17        57

      6 R 2
  4)26
```

H. *Copy and solve.*

14.
5,830	5,932	1,982	3,084	2,904	7,383
			8,461	9,463	9,270
1,294	284	3,092	935	1,575	3,846
+5,648	+6,339	+5,863	+7,346	+4,756	+437
12,772	12,555	10,937	19,826	18,698	20,936

15.
384	859	783	692	987	854
×6	×5	×7	×6	×6	×8
2,304	4,295	5,481	4,152	5,922	6,832

16.
6 R 2	8 R 2	8 R 2	5 R 5	4 R 3	7 R 3
4)26	5)42	6)50	7)40	8)35	7)52

48. Multiplication With Zero in Ones' Place

Whenever a **factor** in a multiplication problem has a zero in the ones' place, the **product** will also have a zero in ones' place. Remember, any number times 0 is 0.

$$\begin{array}{r} 570 \\ \times\ 7 \\ \hline 3{,}990 \end{array} \text{zeroes} \qquad \begin{array}{r} \$3.80 \\ \times\ 6 \\ \hline \$22.80 \end{array} \text{zeroes}$$

A. *Copy these problems and multiply. Do not forget dollar signs and decimal points in your answers to money problems.*

1. | 560 × 7 = **3,920** | 490 × 6 = **2,940** | 830 × 8 = **6,640** | 970 × 7 = **6,790** | 520 × 8 = **4,160** |

2. | 940 × 9 = **8,460** | 590 × 5 = **2,950** | 318 × 4 = **1,272** | 835 × 9 = **7,515** | 750 × 3 = **2,250** |

3. | $4.73 × 4 = **$18.92** | $6.00 × 9 = **$54.00** | $8.50 × 4 = **$34.00** | $8.30 × 6 = **$49.80** | $7.25 × 5 = **$36.25** |

4. | $5.00 × 8 = **$40.00** | $9.13 × 9 = **$82.17** | $8.20 × 8 = **$65.60** | $6.35 × 7 = **$44.45** | $7.40 × 9 = **$66.60** |

> If you understand place value, you can easily add 10, 100, 1,000, 10,000, or 100,000 to a number, or subtract them from a number. Look at the following problems. Only one digit changes in each one.
>
> 11,570 + 100 = 11,670   264,725 − 10,000 = 254,725
> 53,289 − 1,000 = 52,289   723,452 + 100,000 = 823,452

B. *Do these exercises.*

5. Add 100 to each number. Only the hundreds' place will change.
   a. 23,504 **23,604**
   b. 982,740 **982,840**
   c. 34,006 **34,106**
   d. 375,400 **375,500**
   e. 418,123 **418,223**

6. Subtract 1,000 from each number. Only the thousands' place will change.
   a. 43,981 **42,981**
   b. 409,327 **408,327**
   c. 511,200 **510,200**
   d. 674,079 **673,079**
   e. 82,000 **81,000**

LESSON 48

Objectives

- To teach multiplying factors with zero in ones' place, including money figures.
- To teach *adding or subtracting numbers such as 100 and 1,000, without writing the problem.

Preparation

1. Multiplication and division facts: 6's–9's
2. Calendar to review months
3. Speed Drill 48
4. Chalkboard:
   a. 888,888
   b. 24 qt. = __ gal. (6)
      24 gal. = __ qt. (96)
   c.
   $$\begin{array}{ccc} 340 & 760 & \$4.00 \\ \times\ 7 & \times\ 7 & \times\ 6 \\ \hline (2{,}380) & (5{,}320) & (\$24.00) \end{array}$$

   $$\begin{array}{cc} \$8.50 & \$9.70 \\ \times\ 8 & \times\ 6 \\ \hline (\$68.00) & (\$58.20) \end{array}$$

Oral Drill

1. Drill harder multiplication and division facts.
2. Read the number (a) on the board. Say the place names together.
3. Review mental multiplication.

   10 × 7   10 × 43   10 × 19   10 × 85

   100 × 9   100 × 58   100 × 20   100 × 14

   30 × 6   50 × 4   20 × 7

   80 × 7   90 × 9   40 × 8

4. Say the months in order. Review the number of days in each month, using a calendar. Review the little rhyme, *Thirty days have September* . . . (See Lesson 42.)

5. a. Review units of measure. **How many days are in one week? How many months in a year? inches in a foot? inches in a yard? quarts in a gallon? cups in a pint?**

   b. Review the rules for changing measures. Work through the two problems (b) on the board. Division is required for the first one, and multiplication for the second.

6. **How do you find 1/3 of a number? 1/7 of a number? 1/9? What is 1/9 of 72? 1/8 of 56? 1/6 of 48? 1/9 of 81?**

Speed Drill

Give Speed Drill 48 (division facts).

Teaching Guide

1. *Multiplying factors with zero in ones' place.*
   Note that this concept is not new. The purpose is simply to focus on multiplication with zero in the ones' place.
   a. Together do some of the multiplication problems *(c)* on the board. Remind pupils of this fact: **Any number times zero is always zero.** If there is a zero in the ones' place of either factor, the product will also have a zero in ones' place. There may be more than one zero, but there is always one.
   b. Remind pupils to put dollar signs and decimal points in money answers.
   c. Use the following problems for individual practice.

790	840	460	$9.00
× 6	× 9	× 8	× 5
(4,740)	(7,560)	(3,680)	($45.00)

$4.50	$7.80	$5.25
× 7	× 7	× 8
($31.50)	($54.60)	($42.00)

2. *Mental addition and subtraction of numbers such as 100 and 1,000.*
   a. Point to the number *(a)* on the board. **What number is 1,000 more than this number?** (889,888) **Only the thousands' place changes. What number is 100 less than this number?** (888,788) **Only the hundreds' place changes.**
   b. **What number is 100,000 less than this number?** (788,888) **What is the only place that changes?** (hundred thousands)
   c. Write 320,006 on the board. **What number is 10 more? Only the tens' place changes because 10 is *1 ten*.** Write 320,016.
   d. **What number is 10,000 more than 320,006? What number is 100,000 more? What number is 1 less?** Each time only one place changes.
   e. Work similarly with 47,019. **What number is 1,000 less? 10,000 less? 100 more? . . .**
   f. **When you find the number that is 100 more, you are adding 100. When you find the number that is 1,000 less, you are subtracting 1,000.**
   g. A good board exercise is to have the pupils write a number, such as 340,528. Then give a series of directions and have pupils erase only the digit necessary to perform the needed step. *Example:* Add 100. Subtract 10,000. Now add 10.

   Avoid giving directions that require changing more than one digit at a time, such as adding 100 to 2,945.

Supplementary Drill

Drill 14 ×

7. Write the number that is
   a. 10 less than 451 441
   b. 1,000 more than 27,000 28,000
   c. 100,000 more than 238,190 338,190
   d. 10,000 less than 45,982 35,982

Review Exercises

C. *Write only the answers to these facts.*

8.
8	6	8	7	6	9	4	2	9
×9	×9	×8	×9	×6	×9	×8	×7	×5
72	54	64	63	36	81	32	14	45

9. 9)81 = 9   9)54 = 6   9)18 = 2   8)64 = 8   7)70 = 10   9)108 = 12

10. 7)49 = 7   8)40 = 5   9)90 = 10   8)72 = 9   7)63 = 9   4)36 = 9

D. *Do these exercises.*

11. Multiply each number by 10. Write answers only.
    5 50   7 70   40 400   29 290   83 830   18 180

12. Multiply each number by 100. Write answers only.
    8 800   2 200   85 8,500   24 2,400   50 5,000   61 6,100

13. Write only the answers to these problems.
    60 × 3 180   40 × 5 200   80 × 8 640   70 × 4 280   90 × 6 540

14. Copy and solve these divisions.
    6)34 = 5 R 4   7)40 = 5 R 5   5)14 = 2 R 4   8)30 = 3 R 6   7)25 = 3 R 4   6)44 = 7 R 2

15. Write the number of days in each month.
    a. January 31   b. August 31   c. June 30   d. November 30   e. February 28 or 29

E. *Multiply or divide to change these units of measure.*

16. 6 ft. = __2__ yd.   6 yd. = __18__ ft.   3 ft. = __36__ in.

17. 16 gal. = __64__ qt.   16 qt. = __4__ gal.   8 pt. = __16__ cups

49. Multiplication With Zero in Tens' Place

When a factor in a multiplication problem has a zero in the tens' place, the answer is easy to find. In the first example below, 7 × 8 = 56 and 7 × 5 = 35. The answer is 3,556.

```
   508          $7.06
 ×   7          ×   6
 -----          ------
 3,556          $42.36
```

A. *Write the answers to these "times-and" problems. Notice that row 4 is especially easy.*

1. 8 × 4 + 5 **37**   6 × 9 + 4 **58**   8 × 9 + 5 **77**   6 × 7 + 4 **46**
2. 8 × 7 + 4 **60**   9 × 9 + 3 **84**   7 × 7 + 7 **56**   8 × 8 + 3 **67**
3. 4 × 1 + 5 **9**   6 × 1 + 4 **10**   9 × 1 + 3 **12**   7 × 1 + 2 **9**
4. 6 × 0 + 5 **5**   7 × 0 + 4 **4**   8 × 0 + 3 **3**   5 × 0 + 4 **4**

B. *Copy and solve these multiplication problems.*

5. 107×7 = **749**   804×6 = **4,824**   907×8 = **7,256**   406×5 = **2,030**   708×4 = **2,832**

6. 904×7 = **6,328**   709×5 = **3,545**   709×3 = **2,127**   308×8 = **2,464**   806×9 = **7,254**

7. 480×5 = **2,400**   760×6 = **4,560**   602×9 = **5,418**   702×5 = **3,510**   560×2 = **1,120**

8. $4.03×8 = **$32.24** $8.05×7 = **$56.35** $6.30×3 = **$18.90** $9.40×9 = **$84.60** $5.28×7 = **$36.96**

Sometimes when you solve a reading problem by dividing, the division does not come out even.

> Example: How many 5-cent pencils can Mildred buy for 27¢?
> Answer: You must find how many 5's are in 27. Divide 27 by 5.
>
> ```
>      5 R 2 ¢
>   5)27¢
> ```
> Mildred can buy **5 pencils**, with **2¢ left over**.

Notice that the labels for the quotient and the remainder are different.

LESSON 49

Objectives

- To introduce *multiplication with zero in the tens' place.
- To introduce *reading problems involving division that does not come out even.

Preparation

1. Multiplication and division flash cards
2. Chalkboard:

   a. 44,444   760,329   186,005

   b. 807   805   906   450
      × 7   × 5   × 8   × 6
      ─────   ─────   ─────   ─────
     (5,649) (4,025) (7,248) (2,700)

Oral Drill

1. Drill the harder multiplication and division facts.

2. Read the numbers (a) on the board. **What number is 100 more than 760,329? 10,000 less? ...**

3. Drill mental multiplication.
   10 × 45   10 × 29   10 × 67   10 × 30
   100 × 34 100 × 70 30 × 8   40 × 6
   50 × 7   80 × 5   90 × 8   50 × 5

4. Give mixed mental drill.
   5 + 4 × 5 + 3 ÷ 6 (8)
   8 ÷ 4 × 8 + 4 ÷ 4 (5)
   7 × 3 + 4 ÷ 5 × 8 (40)
   12 − 5 × 7 − 4 ÷ 5 (9)
   11 − 3 × 9 − 2 ÷ 7 (10)
   4 × 9 − 1 ÷ 7 + 3 (8)

5. **What is 1/3 of 21? 1/9 of 63? 1/8 of 48? 1/6 of 54?**

6. Drill number terminology, such as *addend, sum,* and *minuend.*

Teaching Guide

1. *Multiplication with zero in tens' place.*

   a. **Give the answers to these "times-and" problems.**
      7 × 9 + 0 (63)   3 × 9 + 5 (32)
      7 × 7 + 3 (52)   8 × 1 + 4 (12)
      6 × 0 + 3 (3)   8 × 0 + 5 (5)
      4 × 0 + 6 (6)   9 × 0 + 4 (4)

      Why were the last problems so easy? (It is easy to multiply by 0; the answer is always 0. It is also easy to add a number to 0.) Emphasize: **Any number times zero is zero.** Take note if anyone confuses 6 × 0 with 6 × 1 (6) or with 6 + 0 (6). 6 × 0 is 0, not 6.

T–111   Chapter 5   Multiplication and Division Facts: 7–9

b. Point to the problems *(b)* on the board. **Here are some multiplications with "times-and" problems like the ones we just did.** Work through the problems together. When pupils realize how this type of problem is done, they usually find it easier than problems without zeroes. Be sure they think of 7 × 0 as 0 and not as 7.

c. Here are some extra problems. Note that the first and last ones do not require carrying to the tens' place. If your pupils have trouble with that, give them more practice.

$$\begin{array}{cccc} 903 & 408 & 506 & 750 \\ \times\ 3 & \times\ 6 & \times\ 4 & \times\ 8 \\ \hline (2{,}709) & (2{,}448) & (2{,}024) & (6{,}000) \end{array}$$

$$\begin{array}{ccc} 340 & 912 & 802 \\ \times\ 7 & \times\ 5 & \times\ 3 \\ \hline (2{,}380) & (4{,}560) & (2{,}406) \end{array}$$

2. *Reading problems requiring uneven division.*

   a. Review the key words in reading problems. **Which process is usually needed to solve a problem with these key words?**
   How much less? (s)
   How much at 15¢ each? (m)
   How much change? (s)
   How much is 1/6 of a number? (d)
   How many in all? (a)
   What is the difference? (s)
   How much more? (s)
   How many groups of 4 in 12? (d)
   What is the total? (a)
   How many in 5 groups of 15 each? (m)
   Make 3 equal groups from 18; how many in each group? (d)

   b. Introduce reading problems with uneven division. Discuss the problem in the lesson, or use the ones below.
   • Jane is making gingerbread cookies. She needs 3 small cinnamon candies for each cookie. How many cookies can Jane make if she has 26 candies? Will she have any candies left over?
   • Bertha has 25¢. A small eraser costs 7¢. How many erasers can Bertha buy? How much money will she have left?

   In all these reading problems, note that the quotient is the main answer and the remainder is the leftover part. Also note that the quotient part and the remainder part must be labeled differently, such as *8 cookies* with *3 candies left over*.

   If you give additional reading problems, be sure the remainder is always something "left over." Avoid any that require the next higher number for the correct answer, such as "How many cars are needed to take 21 people if 6 people fit in a car?"

Note: In the exercises, the first four reading problems involve unequal division. Pupils should use the following pattern to answer the two questions.

3 stamps, 3¢ left over
2 erasers, 4¢ left

Supplementary Drills

Drill 88*

Drill 32 ÷

C. Solve these reading problems.

9. How many 5¢ stamps can Melvin buy for 18¢? How much money will be left over?
3 stamps, 3¢

10. How many 8¢ erasers can Trudy buy for 20¢? How many cents will be left?
2 erasers, 4¢

11. Kenneth wants to cut a 15-foot pole into 2-foot pieces to burn in the wood stove. How many 2-foot pieces can Kenneth get out of the pole? How many feet will be left over?
7 pieces, 1 foot

12. Kenneth can put 3 pieces of wood into the stove at one time. If there are 20 pieces of wood cut now, how many times can Kenneth fill the stove? How many pieces will be left over?
6 times, 2 pieces

13. Mother bought shoe polish for $1.19 and a shoe brush for $2.59. How much change did she get from $5.00? (Be careful! This is a two-step problem.) $1.22

14. Flashlight batteries cost $0.89 each. How much do four batteries cost? $3.56

Review Exercises

D. Write the answers quickly.

15. 9×8=72   7×9=63   12×8=96   12×9=108   9×9=81   12×6=72   8×7=56   6×9=54   7×7=49

16. 64÷8=8   90÷9=10   42÷7=6   72÷9=8   48÷8=6   56÷7=8

E. For each question write add, subtract, multiply, or divide.

17. How many groups of 3 are in 21? divide
18. 857 is how many more than 25? subtract
19. How much change? subtract
20. What is the total bill? add
21. How many in 4 groups of 8 each? multiply
22. What is the difference? subtract
23. If you make 4 equal groups out of 20, how many are in each group? divide
24. How much for 5 at 30¢ each? multiply
25. What is $\frac{1}{5}$ of the number? divide
26. How much longer did Adam live than Abraham? subtract

50. Chapter 5 Review

A. *Write the answers to these number facts.*

1.
| 9 × 6 = 54 | 9 × 8 = 72 | 6 × 7 = 42 | 8 × 8 = 64 | 7 × 5 = 35 | 12 × 9 = 108 | 5 × 7 = 35 | 3 × 9 = 27 | 8 × 7 = 56 |

2.
| 7 × 7 = 49 | 12 × 8 = 96 | 11 × 4 = 44 | 9 × 9 = 81 | 5 × 9 = 45 | 8 × 9 = 72 | 12 × 8 = 96 | 12 × 7 = 84 | 4 × 9 = 36 |

3.
| 6 × 6 = 36 | 12 × 3 = 36 | 2 × 9 = 18 | 8 × 4 = 32 | 2 × 6 = 12 | 7 × 8 = 56 | 6 × 9 = 54 | 7 × 9 = 63 | 7 × 4 = 28 |

4. 48 ÷ 8 = 6 ; 60 ÷ 5 = 12 ; 81 ÷ 9 = 9 ; 63 ÷ 7 = 9 ; 54 ÷ 9 = 6 ; 56 ÷ 8 = 7

5. 49 ÷ 7 = 7 ; 42 ÷ 6 = 7 ; 63 ÷ 9 = 7 ; 40 ÷ 8 = 5 ; 36 ÷ 6 = 6 ; 72 ÷ 8 = 9

6. 108 ÷ 9 = 12 ; 64 ÷ 8 = 8 ; 96 ÷ 8 = 12 ; 70 ÷ 7 = 10 ; 9 ÷ 9 = 1 ; 56 ÷ 7 = 8

B. *Copy and solve the problems.*

7.
| 685 × 6 = 4,110 | 937 × 7 = 6,559 | 429 × 6 = 2,574 | $7.35 × 3 = $22.05 |

8.
| 740 × 6 = 4,440 | 950 × 9 = 8,550 | 705 × 8 = 5,640 | $6.09 × 4 = $24.36 |

9.
| 7,403 − 3,742 = 3,661 | 3,894 − 2,649 = 1,245 | 8,320 − 7,485 = 835 | 9,102 − 646 = 8,456 |

10. 36 ÷ 7 = 5 R 1 ; 27 ÷ 8 = 3 R 3 ; 45 ÷ 8 = 5 R 5 ; 49 ÷ 6 = 8 R 1 ; 20 ÷ 6 = 3 R 2

LESSON 50

Objective

♦ To review the concepts taught in Chapter 5 (listed below).
  - Multiplication and division facts: 7's–9's
  - Multiplying mentally by 10 or 100
  - Multiplying mentally by multiples of 10
  - Finding a part of a number
  - Changing from one unit of measure to another
  - Mentally finding 1,000 more, 10,000 less, and so on
  - Division with one-digit quotients and with remainders
  - Subtraction of four-digit numbers
  - Multiplication of two- and three-digit numbers, with carried digits up to 5
  - Multiplication of money
  - Multiplication of 3-digit numbers with zeroes in ones' or tens' place

Preparation

1. Multiplication flash cards: 7's–9's
2. Speed Drill 50
3. Chalkboard:

   6 yd. = ___ ft. (18)   6 ft. = ___ yd. (2)

Speed Drill

Give Speed Drill 50 (division facts).

Teaching Guide

1. Drill multiplication facts.
2. Review measures.
   a. 1 week = (7) days
      1 year = (12) months
      Number of days in each month
   b. **To change a larger unit to a smaller unit, we** (multiply). **To change a small unit to a larger one, we** (divide).
   c. Point to the two problems on the board. **Which one requires multiplication?** Find the answers in class. Note the difference between the answers, even though the two problems seem similar.
3. Review the parts of a division problem.
4. Review mental multiplication.

10 × 5	10 × 50	10 × 54
10 × 87	10 × 41	100 × 7
100 × 70	100 × 73	100 × 18
100 × 49	40 × 7	30 × 2
60 × 8	20 × 5	80 × 9

5. Give mixed mental practice.
   4 × 5 − 2 ÷ 9 + 4 (6)
   8 + 9 − 2 ÷ 5 − 3 (0)
   10 − 3 × 7 − 1 ÷ 6 (8)
   12 ÷ 3 × 9 + 4 ÷ 5 (8)

6. Review place value and larger numbers.
   a. Have pupils write the numbers you dictate. Here are samples:
      300,500   35,000   654,001
      708,062   690,328
   b. Ask pupils to circle the number in the hundreds' place, ten thousands' place, and so on.
   c. Have pupils write the number that is 100 more, 1,000 less, and so on.

T–113   Chapter 5   Multiplication and Division Facts: 7–9

7. Review computation skills. *This is a major part of the test.*

   a.   804   750   763
        × 5   × 7   × 9
       (4,020)   (5,250)   (6,867)

       $4.00 $8.05 $9.45
       ×   6   ×   7   ×   9
      ($24.00)   ($56.35)   ($85.05)

   b.   8,705   4,893   7,621
       −3,784   −3,955   −4,853
       (4,921)   (938)   (2,768)

       9,340   7,102
       − 625   −5,847
       (8,715)   (1,255)

   c.   (5 R 5)   (4 R 2)   (5 R 3)
        7)40   8)34   5)28

        (8 R 2)   (7 R 3)   (5 R 5)
        8)66   7)52   6)35

8. Tell students that they will have a test in the next class.

Note: This is another three-page review lesson. If it is too much for the pupils, do some parts orally in class. Do not omit the reading problems, for most children *need* that practice.

C. Do these exercises.

11. Multiply each number by 10:   7   35   50   88   24
                                    70 350 500 880 240

12. Multiply each number by 100:   9   14   93   61   70
                                     900 1,400 9,300 6,100 7,000

13. Multiply and write answers only.
   60 × 3 180   90 × 6 540   70 × 4 280   40 × 5 200

14. Write these with numerals.
   a. two hundred twelve thousand, six hundred four   212,604
   b. ninty-five thousand, twenty-nine   95,029
   c. three hundred eighty-four thousand, one hundred fifty 384,150
   d. six hundred thousand, seven   600,007

15. Copy this number: 888888. Place the comma correctly. Then circle the digit that means 8 ten thousands (80,000).   8⑧8,888

16. Write the number that is
   a. 1,000 more than 45,321 46,321   c. 10,000 less than 943,026 933,026
   b. 100,000 more than 390,218 490,218 d. 100 less than 75,167 75,067

17. Write the answers only.
   $\frac{1}{4}$ of 36 9 $\frac{1}{7}$ of 42 6 $\frac{1}{9}$ of 72 8 $\frac{1}{8}$ of 56 7

18. How many days are in the months below?
   a. March   b. September   c. July   d. February   e. June
      31   30   31   28 or 29   30

D. Multiply or divide to change these measures.

19. 3 qt. = __6__ pt.   3 wk. = __21__ days   27 ft. = __9__ yd.
20. 21 days = __3__ wk.   10 cups = __5__ pt.   4 gal. = __16__ qt.
21. 6 ft. = __72__ in.   7 wk. = __49__ days   6 days = __144__ hr.

E. Figure out these number strings.

22. a. 5 × 4 − 2 ÷ 6 + 6 = ?   9

   b. 12 − 4 × 6 + 1 ÷ 7 = ?   7

(continued on next page)

F. For each question write add, subtract, multiply, or divide.

23. 6 equal groups in 42. How many in each group? divide
24. How many altogether? add
25. What is $\frac{1}{7}$ of a number? divide
26. How many fewer? subtract
27. How many left? subtract
28. How many in 6 groups of 24? multiply
29. How many groups of 8 in 48? divide
30. What is the sum? add
31. How many in 3 groups if 9 are in each group? multiply

G. Solve these problems.

32. How many groups of 3 are in 24? 8 groups
33. What is the total of $4.85, $3.29, and $8.15? $16.29
34. How many 5¢ clips can be bought for 27¢? How many cents will be left over? 5 clips, 2¢
35. Merlin goes to school 5 days a week. This year he has gone to school 45 days without missing a day. How many weeks has Merlin gone to school? 9 weeks
36. Jacob in the Bible lived to be 147 years old. His father Isaac lived to be 180 years old. Isaac lived how many years longer than Jacob? 33 years
37. The longest book in the Old Testament is Psalms, with 2,461 verses. The longest New Testament book is Luke, with 1,151 verses. How many verses are in both books? 3,612 verses
38. Rosalie baked 6 trays of cookies with 18 on each tray. How many cookies did she bake? 108 cookies
39. Four boys want to share 17 marbles. How many will each boy get? How many marbles will be left over? 4 marbles, 1 marble
40. Mother bought 5 bushels of peaches priced at $13.00 a bushel. How much did the peaches cost? $65.00

51. Chapter 5 Test

LESSON 51

Objective

- To test the pupils' mastery of the concepts taught in Chapter 5.

Teaching Guide

1. Give any last-minute review that you feel is necessary.
2. Administer the test.

Note: Chapter 5 Test is found in the test section in the back of this manual.

Chapter 6

Division With Two-Digit Quotients

To him that soweth righteousness shall be a sure reward.
(Proverbs 11:18)

Chapter 6 Division With Two-Digit Quotients

52. Division With Two-Digit Quotients

Do you remember the five steps for simple division? When larger numbers are divided, a sixth step is needed: **Bring down.** Each time we **bring down,** we must go through the other five steps again.

The Six Steps of Division

1. **Divide.** Think: There are no 3's in 1. How many 3's are in 12? Write 4 above the 2 in 12.

$$\begin{array}{r} 4 \\ 3\overline{)129} \end{array}$$

2. **Multiply.** Think: 4 × 3 = 12. Write 12 below the 12 of the dividend.

$$\begin{array}{r} 4 \\ 3\overline{)129} \\ 12 \end{array}$$

3. **Compare.** Think: Is 12 more than 12? No.

4. **Subtract.** Think: 12 − 12 = 0. Write 0 below the 2 in 12.

$$\begin{array}{r} 4 \\ 3\overline{)129} \\ 12 \\ \hline 0 \end{array}$$

5. **Compare.** Think: Is 0 more than the divisor? No.

6. **Bring down.** Bring down the 9 from the dividend, and write it beside the remainder. (The digits 09 mean the same as 9.)

$$\begin{array}{r} 4 \\ 3\overline{)129} \\ 12 \\ \hline 09 \end{array}$$

Now go through the steps again, using 9 as the dividend. Subtracting 9 − 9 gives 0; there is no remainder. There are no more digits in the dividend to bring down, so the division is finished.

$$\begin{array}{r} 43 \\ 3\overline{)129} \\ 12 \\ \hline 09 \\ 9 \\ \hline 0 \end{array}$$

A. Copy and divide. Follow the six steps in the lesson.

1. $2\overline{)48} = 24$ $3\overline{)96} = 32$ $4\overline{)84} = 21$ $3\overline{)36} = 12$ $2\overline{)82} = 41$

2. $4\overline{)128} = 32$ $5\overline{)155} = 31$ $6\overline{)126} = 21$ $2\overline{)148} = 74$ $8\overline{)168} = 21$

3. $3\overline{)126} = 42$ $4\overline{)208} = 52$ $2\overline{)184} = 92$ $5\overline{)255} = 51$ $3\overline{)219} = 73$

To check the answer to a division problem, multiply the quotient by the divisor. The answer is the dividend.

$$3\overline{)129}^{\,43} \longleftarrow \begin{array}{r} 43 \\ \times\ 3 \\ \hline 129 \end{array}$$

LESSON 52

Objectives

♦ To introduce *the "bringing down" step in long division.

♦ To teach checking division by multiplication.

Preparation

1. Division and multiplication flash cards: 7's–9's
2. Subtraction flash cards with minuends of 10 or more
3. Speed Drill 52
4. Chalkboard:

   a. 405
       −164
       (241)

   b. (3 R 1) (4 R 1)
       3)10   4)17

       (3) (4)
       3)9   4)16

       (32) (42) (54)
       3)96   4)168 2)108

Oral Drill

1. Drill the 7's–9's multiplication and division facts.
2. Drill the subtraction facts.
3. Review *dividend, divisor, quotient,* and *remainder*.
4. Review multiplication-division families. Have pupils make families of four facts with these sets: 7, 9, 63; and 6, 8, 48.
5. Review checking subtraction with addition. Solve the subtraction problem *(a)* on the board. Write the addition check beside it.
6. Drill mental multiplication.

   10 × 78   100 × 43   30 × 8
   50 × 9   80 × 7

Speed Drill

Give Speed Drill 52 (multiplication facts).

T–117   Chapter 6   Division With Two-Digit Quotients

Teaching Guide

1. *"Bringing down" in division.*
   a. Review the five steps of division from Lesson 38. Do the first two problems *(b)* on the board.
   b. Do the next two problems on the board the long way also. These are basic facts, but go through all the division steps to show the regular procedure. Show that the remainder is zero, so it should not be written as a remainder after the quotient. A remainder of zero is *no* remainder.
   c. **In longer division problems, there is another step: the "bring down" step. If the dividend is large, we do not divide the whole dividend at once. We divide it one part at a time. That is why we need to bring down. Let's see how it works.**
   d. Proceed to the next problem on the board. **Are there any 3's in 9?** Go through the five division steps, ending with a remainder of 0. **Is the problem finished?** (No, we have divided only the 9, not 96.) **The next step is to bring down the 6.** Write the 6. **Now think of 6 as the new dividend, and go through the five steps of division again. How many 3's are in 6?** Go through the steps and complete the problem. Notice that the remainder is 0, so it does not need to be written.
   e. Do the other two problems on the board. **Are there any 4's in 1? No, so we must think: How many 4's in 16?**
   f. Emphasize: **Each digit in the quotient must be written above the correct digit in the dividend. The 4 in this problem belongs above the 6, not above the 1.**

2. *Checking division by multiplication.*
   a. **What arithmetic process is the opposite of addition?** (subtraction) **How can we check the answer to a subtraction problem?** (with addition)
   b. **What arithmetic process is the opposite of multiplication?** (division) **We can check the answer to a division problem by using the opposite process—multiplication.** Show the check for the last three division problems. **We take the quotient and multiply it by the divisor. What is 3 times 32? The answer to that problem is the same as the dividend in the division problem.**
   c. Give board practice with division and checking.

   $$\begin{array}{cccc} (32) & (31) & (12) & (42) \\ 2\overline{)64} & 3\overline{)93} & 4\overline{)48} & 3\overline{)126} \end{array}$$

   $$\begin{array}{ccc} (52) & (94) & (41) \\ 4\overline{)208} & 2\overline{)188} & 6\overline{)246} \end{array}$$

   Note: The division problems in this lesson are easy and could be done the "short way," without writing any work below. However, following the steps in these easy problems will acquaint the pupils with the "bring down" procedure and prepare them for more difficult problems. Later, as they gain skill in division, the pupils will learn the shorter method (short division).

Supplementary Drill

Drill 33 ÷

B. *Do these divisions. Check each problem with multiplication.*

4. a. $2\overline{)64}$ = 32 $32 \times 2 = 64$ b. $3\overline{)159}$ = 53 $53 \times 3 = 159$ c. $7\overline{)357}$ = 51 $51 \times 7 = 357$

Review Exercises

C. *Write the answers only.*

5.
| 9 × 8 = 72 | 8 × 6 = 48 | 5 × 7 = 35 | 4 × 8 = 32 | 9 × 9 = 81 | 8 × 8 = 64 | 7 × 7 = 49 | 6 × 4 = 24 | 2 × 8 = 16 |

6.
| 8 × 7 = 56 | 5 × 9 = 45 | 4 × 4 = 16 | 3 × 6 = 18 | 12 × 9 = 108 | 7 × 4 = 28 | 12 × 6 = 72 | 10 × 5 = 50 | 11 × 8 = 88 |

7. $7\overline{)35}=5$ $8\overline{)72}=9$ $8\overline{)64}=8$ $7\overline{)63}=9$ $5\overline{)40}=8$ $3\overline{)27}=9$

8. $8\overline{)96}=12$ $9\overline{)63}=7$ $7\overline{)56}=8$ $9\overline{)54}=6$ $6\overline{)36}=6$ $7\overline{)70}=10$

D. *Copy and solve. The divisions have remainders.*

9. $4\overline{)17} = 4\text{ R }1$ $6\overline{)21} = 3\text{ R }3$ $5\overline{)32} = 6\text{ R }2$ $2\overline{)19} = 9\text{ R }1$ $3\overline{)26} = 8\text{ R }2$

10. $594 \times 5 = 2{,}970$ $903 \times 6 = 5{,}418$ $578 \times 6 = 3{,}468$ $296 \times 4 = 1{,}184$ $804 \times 8 = 6{,}432$

E. *Multiply in your head. Write the answers.*

11. $10 \times 61 = 610$ $10 \times 78 = 780$ $10 \times 90 = 900$ $100 \times 5 = 500$ $100 \times 47 = 4{,}700$

12. $40 \times 9 = 360$ $60 \times 5 = 300$ $80 \times 7 = 560$ $70 \times 5 = 350$ $50 \times 3 = 150$

F. *Do these exercises.*

13. Tell how many days are in each of the months below.
    a. March — 31   b. October — 31   c. May — 31   d. February — 28 or 29   e. November — 30

14. Write the Roman numerals for these Arabic numerals. (See Lesson 29.)
    a. 48 — XLVIII   b. 17 — XVII   c. 60 — LX   d. 39 — XXXIX   e. 54 — LIV   f. 83 — LXXXIII   g. 25 — XXV

15. 1 yd. = __36__ in.   1 gal. = __4__ qt.   1 doz. = __12__ things

16. 6 ft. = __2__ yd.   6 yd. = __18__ ft.   6 ft. = __72__ in.

118   Chapter 6   Division With Two-Digit Quotients

53. Two-Digit and Three-Digit Quotients

Study the division problems at the right. They are solved by following the same six steps that you learned in Lesson 52. But in the second problem, it is necessary to go through the steps **three times**, and write **three quotient figures**. Also, the divisions do not come out even. Both have remainders.

```
    34 R 1          210 R 3
 2)69            4)843
    6               8
    ──              ──
    09              04
     8               4
    ──              ──
     1              03
                     0
                    ──
                     3
```

A. *Solve these divisions. They are just like the ones in Lesson 52.*

1. 3)39̄ = 13   2)68̄ = 34   3)216̄ = 72   4)364̄ = 91   5)405̄ = 81

B. *Solve these divisions. The quotients have three digits.*

2. 4)484̄ = 121   2)468̄ = 234   3)693̄ = 231   3)939̄ = 313   2)824̄ = 412

C. *Divide, and check your answers with multiplication.*

3. a. 4)288̄ = 72   72 × 4 = 288
   b. 3)96̄ = 32   32 × 3 = 96
   c. 8)648̄ = 81   81 × 8 = 648

4. a. 5)250̄ = 50   50 × 5 = 250
   b. 3)249̄ = 83   83 × 3 = 249
   c. 2)68̄ = 34   34 × 2 = 68

D. *Solve these divisions. The answers have remainders.*

5. 3)95̄ = 31 R 2   4)86̄ = 21 R 2   2)125̄ = 62 R 1   3)151̄ = 50 R 1

6. 7)79̄ = 11 R 2   4)49̄ = 12 R 1   7)359̄ = 51 R 2   5)258̄ = 51 R 3

Review Exercises

E. *Write answers only to these division facts.*

7. 6)48̄ = 8   9)81̄ = 9   7)56̄ = 8   8)64̄ = 8   9)63̄ = 7   7)7̄ = 1

8. 8)56̄ = 7   9)108̄ = 12   8)72̄ = 9   7)63̄ = 9   5)45̄ = 9   6)36̄ = 6

9. 7)49̄ = 7   8)88̄ = 11   7)84̄ = 12   9)90̄ = 10   8)96̄ = 12   7)21̄ = 3

10. 9)54̄ = 6   9)27̄ = 3   9)36̄ = 4   8)32̄ = 4   7)42̄ = 6   8)40̄ = 5

224

LESSON 53

Objectives

♦ To introduce division *with three-digit quotients.

♦ To introduce division *with two-digit quotients and with remainders.

Preparation

1. More difficult division flash cards
2. Chalkboard:

   $\quad\;(24)\qquad(53)\qquad(73)$
   $2\overline{)48}\quad\;\;2\overline{)106}\quad3\overline{)219}$

   $\quad\;(22)\qquad(31)\qquad(92)$
   $4\overline{)88}\quad\;\;6\overline{)186}\quad3\overline{)276}$

Oral Drill

1. Give mixed mental drill.
   10 − 4 × 6 ÷ 4 × 7 (63)
   3 + 5 × 6 + 1 ÷ 7 (7)
   15 − 7 × 8 − 1 ÷ 7 (9)
   6 × 4 + 1 ÷ 5 + 8 (13)
   9 + 7 ÷ 8 − 2 × 7 (0)
   9 × 8 ÷ 6 + 2 ÷ 7 (2)

2. Review measures.
   1 yr. = (12) mo.   1 yd. = (3) ft.
   1 wk. = (7) days   1 yd. = (36) in.
   1 day = (24) hr.   1 ft. = (12) in.
   1 hr. = (60) min.   1 gal. = (4) qt.
   1 min. = (60) sec. 1 qt. = (2) pt.
   June = (30) days   1 qt.= (4) cups
   July = (31) days   1 pt. = (2) cups
   April = (30) days

3. Count by 6's, by 7's, by 8's, and by 9's.

4. Drill the more difficult division facts.

5. **Which of the following are even numbers?**
   40   53   98   47   19   36   74   62

6. **Which numbers divide evenly by 3?**
   16   24   30   4   9
   by 6? 16   6   18   35   48   54   24
   by 7? 14   21   30   40   49   72   63

Teaching Guide

1. *Division with three-digit quotients.*
   a. Use the problems on the board to review the "bring down" step in division. Show the multiplication check for a few problems.
   b. Introduce problems with three-digit quotients. **A division problem is not complete until *all* the digits in the dividend have been divided. Bring down one digit at a time. Sometimes you must go through the steps three times or more.**

   $\quad\;(241)\qquad(101)\qquad(320)$
   $2\overline{)482}\quad\;5\overline{)505}\quad\;3\overline{)960}$

   $\quad\;(212)\qquad(334)\qquad(123)$
   $4\overline{)848}\quad\;2\overline{)668}\quad\;3\overline{)369}$

   c. Show the children how to tell whether the quotient will have two digits or three. First they must decide where the first quotient figure will go. They must think: Is the first digit of the dividend large enough to contain the divisor? If so, the first quotient figure will go above that digit. If not, they must ask: Are the first *two* digits of the dividend large enough to contain the divisor? If so, the first quotient figure will go above the second digit in the dividend.

   Now it is possible to tell how many places the quotient will have. After the first quotient figure is written, a quotient figure *must* be written above every digit in the dividend, even if it is 0.

2. *Two-digit quotients with remainders.*
   Have the pupils follow the division steps to solve the following problems. In the last place of the quotient, the subtracted number is *not* 0; so the remainder must

T–119   Chapter 6   Division With Two-Digit Quotients

be written after the quotient as in one-digit answers with remainders.

$$2\overline{)107}\;\;(53\text{ R }1)\qquad 3\overline{)188}\;\;(62\text{ R }2)\qquad 3\overline{)37}\;\;(12\text{ R }1)$$

$$4\overline{)285}\;\;(71\text{ R }1)\qquad 2\overline{)163}\;\;(81\text{ R }1)$$

Extra Review

Review reading problems.

a. **Do we add, subtract, multiply, or divide to answer these?**
   How many are left? (s)
   How many in each group? (d)
   How much less? (s)
   How much change? (s)
   What is the sum? (a)
   How much at 30¢ each? (m)
   How many more? (s)
   How many groups of 5 in 40? (d)
   How much longer? (s)
   How many altogether? (a *or* m)
   How many in 4 groups the same size? (m)
   How many in four groups of different sizes? (m)
   How much is 1/5 of a number? (d)
   What is the total? (a *or* m)
   What is the difference? (s)
   Three are sharing; how many for each? (d)

b. Give some simple problems.
   • What is one-fourth of 20? (5)
   • Four girls share 8 cookies. How many for each? (2 cookies)
   • Mary had 50¢. She spent 25¢. How much was left? (25¢)
   • What is the total of 4 groups with 6 in each? (24)
   • Carl is 60 inches tall. Curvin is 55 inches tall. Carl is how much taller? (5 in.)
   • How much for 3 pounds of bananas at 33¢ a pound? (99¢)
   • How many teams of 4 can be made with 18 people? How many people would be left over? (4 teams, 2 left over)
   • What is the total of 3, 6, 4, and 5? (18)
   • If 21 is separated into 3 equal groups, how many are in each group? (7)

Note: If your pupils are having difficulty with the "bring down" step of division, you may want to delay division with remainders for another day. However, if they have mastered the former work with remainders and the steps in the division process, they will probably have little trouble with this.

The reading problems in today's lesson are longer than usual. The actual numbers in the problems are simple, but the extra words may cause trouble for slower pupils. Encourage them to think what the question is asking and how they can solve it. If they cannot find key words, they should think whether a smaller number or a larger one would make sense. You may want to do number 18 in class.

Supplementary Drills

Drill 15 ×

Drill 47

F. *Do these exercises.*

11. Copy the numbers that divide evenly by 4.
    42   6   18   (16)   (24)   (32)   (40)   35   (36)

12. Copy the numbers that divide evenly by 6.
    (18)   (42)   27   (30)   56   (48)   (72)   (36)   28

13. Copy the numbers that divide evenly by 7.
    17   (42)   48   (49)   (63)   (14)   (28)   (56)   32

14. Write **add**, **subtract**, **multiply**, or **divide**.

    a. How much change?   subtract
    b. How much at $1.29 each?   multiply
    c. How many are left?   subtract
    d. What is $\frac{1}{6}$ as many?   divide
    e. How much older?   subtract
    f. How many groups of 2 in 10?   divide
    g. What is the total?   add
    h. What is the cost of both items?   add
    i. 4 equal groups made from 16. How many in each group?   divide
    j. How many marbles in 4 groups of 8 each?   multiply
    k. 3 boys share 6 apples. How many does each get?   divide

G. *Solve these problems. Think: Is my answer sensible?*

15. God told Moses that the tabernacle was to be 45 feet long and 15 feet wide. The tabernacle was how much longer than it was wide?   30 feet

16. Ten curtains each 6 feet wide were joined into a large curtain to cover the tabernacle. How many feet wide was the large curtain?   60 feet

17. Another large curtain was made of goat's hair and spread over the first curtain. The goat's-hair curtain was 66 feet wide, and it was made of smaller curtains each 6 feet wide. How many smaller curtains were used to make the large curtain?   11 curtains

18. Around the tabernacle was a court or fence that was 150 feet long on the two sides that faced north and south. On the west side the court was 75 feet long. How long were the **three** sides of the court? (Use the drawing for help.)   375 feet

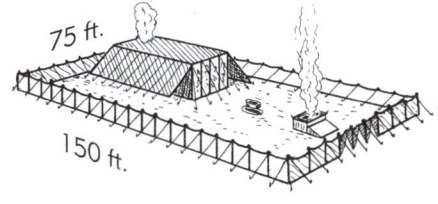

19. On the east side of the court, part of the 75-foot space was used for a gate. If the gate was 30 feet wide, how much was left for fence on that side?   45 feet

20. There were two rooms in the tabernacle. The smaller room had one piece of furniture, and the larger room had three pieces. Outside the tabernacle in the courtyard were two more pieces of furniture. How many pieces of furniture were there altogether?   6 pieces

21. Priests offered many sacrifices to God on the altar of burnt offering. If they offered 750 sacrifices each day, how many sacrifices did they offer in a week? (Think: How many days are in a week?)   5,250 sacrifices

54. Dividing to Get a Fraction

Shirley and Sylvia had two bananas. Then Janelle came to visit them. They wanted to share their bananas with her, but how could 2 bananas be divided equally among 3 girls? How could a small number be divided by a larger one? They knew each girl could get only part of a banana, but what part?

"I know," said Sylvia. "I'll cut my banana into thirds. You cut your banana into thirds too. Then each of us can have 2 thirds of a whole banana."

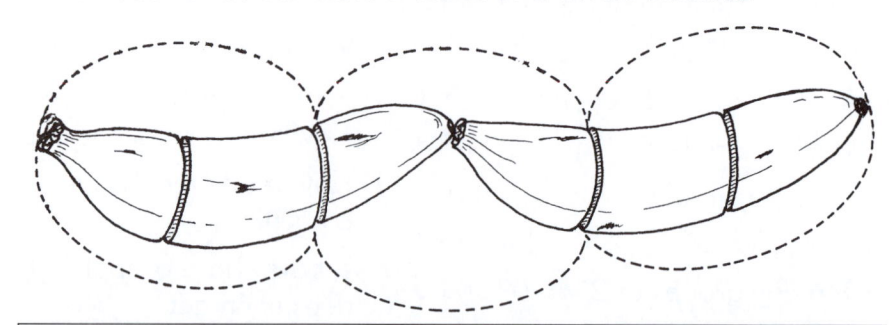

> When a smaller number like 2 is divided by a larger number like 3, the answer is a fraction. The number being divided is the **numerator** of the fraction, and the number it is divided by is the **denominator**.
>
> $2 \div 3 = \frac{2}{3}$ $1 \div 4 = \frac{1}{4}$ $3 \div 4 = \frac{3}{4}$

The following questions ask much the same thing. Both are answered in the same way.   Questions: What is 2 divided by 5? 2 is what part of 5?
            Answer: $2 \div 5 = \frac{2}{5}$

A. *Solve these problems. Write the answers as fractions.*

1. $2 \div 5$ $\frac{2}{5}$ $1 \div 3$ $\frac{1}{3}$ $4 \div 5$ $\frac{4}{5}$ $1 \div 8$ $\frac{1}{8}$ $3 \div 7$ $\frac{3}{7}$ $5 \div 6$ $\frac{5}{6}$

2. a. 3 is what part of 4? $\frac{3}{4}$ d. 2 is what part of 3? $\frac{2}{3}$

    b. 5 is what part of 7? $\frac{5}{7}$ e. 1 is what part of 4? $\frac{1}{4}$

    c. 1 is what part of 6? $\frac{1}{6}$ f. 3 is what part of 8? $\frac{3}{8}$

B. *Solve these reading problems.*

3. Nelson has a board that is 6 feet long. Is the board long enough to make a 65-inch shelf?   yes

4. Nelson needs four metal braces for the shelf. How much will they cost at $2.39 each? $9.56

5. Each metal brace will be fastened to the wall with three screws. How many screws does Nelson need? (See number 4.)   12 screws

LESSON 54

Objectives

- To introduce *dividing a small number by a larger number to get a fraction.
- To teach *the divisibility rules for 2 and 5.

Preparation

1. Multiplication and division flash cards
2. Apples, bananas, cookies, or flannelgraph pieces to illustrate fractions
3. Speed Drill 54
4. Chalkboard:
   $\frac{2}{3}$ $\frac{3}{4}$ $\frac{5}{8}$ $\frac{3}{7}$ $\frac{2}{5}$
   $\frac{6}{7}$ $\frac{1}{8}$ $\frac{5}{6}$ $\frac{1}{6}$ $\frac{4}{5}$

Oral Drill

1. Drill the more difficult multiplication and division facts.
2. Review changing units of measure.
3. Review the parts of multiplication and division problems.
4. Review multiplication–division number families.
5. Review place value up to 100,000.
6. Look at the clock and tell what time it is. **Is it A.M. or P.M.?**

Speed Drill

Give Speed Drill 54 (horizontal computation).

Teaching Guide

1. *Dividing a small number by a larger one*.
   a. Have the pupils read the fractions on the board. Have them tell how many parts are in the whole thing and how many parts the fraction is naming. (2/3 means 2 parts out of 3.)
   b. Review how to find 1/4 of a number; 1/7 of a number; ... **To find 1/4 of a number we divide by 4, because 1/4 means** *1 part out of 4,* **or** *1 divided by 4.*
   c. Hold up four items such as apples. **If** (Name two pupils) **share these apples, how many would each one have? How did you get the answer?** (We must *divide* 4 into 2 parts. Or we could think: Half of 4 is 2. Either way, we divide.)
   d. Hold up two apples. **If** (Name two pupils) **share these apples, how many would each one have?** (Each would have one apple; half of 2 is 1.)

T–121   Chapter 6   Division With Two-Digit Quotients

e. Now hold up one apple. **If** (Name two pupils) **share just this one apple, how much would each one get? Would they each get a whole apple? Do you think sharing one apple shows division in the same way as sharing 4 apples or 2 apples?** (Yes, it also shows division.)
f. **Dividing a small number like 1 by a larger number like 2 always makes a fraction. One-half means 1 divided by 2.** Write the fraction on the board, and point to 1 and 2 respectively. **What fraction means 2 divided by 3? 4 divided by 5?**
g. Hold up two bananas or read the story in the pupil's book. **If 2 bananas are divided among 3 girls, can each of them have a whole banana?** No, each girl will have only a part. **Dividing a small number by a large one always results in a fraction.** If you have real bananas, cut each one into three pieces and *show* that each of the three girls will get 2 thirds if the bananas are shared equally.
h. **Another way to express this idea is to say that 2 is 2/3 of 3. 3 is what part of 4? 5 is what part of 8? 1 is what part of 5? The number being divided is the *numerator* of the fraction, and the number of parts is the *denominator*.**

2. *Divisibility rules.*
   a. **Tell which of these numbers divide evenly by 8.**
      18   28   16   32   36
      80   48   60   64   56
   b. **Tell whether these numbers are odd or even.**
      4   7   10   30   85   64
      73   96   18   50   72   15
      How can you tell if a number is odd or even?

c. **Tell which of these numbers divide evenly by 5.**
   57   85   40   38   20
   95   15   12   5   8
   How can you tell if a number divides evenly by 5?
d. **It is easier to tell if a number is divisible by 2 or 5 than by 8. The rules of divisibility help us.** Call attention to the rules in the box.
e. **Which of the following numbers are divisible by 2? Which are divisible by 5?**
   12   25   40   57   65   90
   104   120   137   146   170

Extra Review

1. Together do a variety of division problems, some having one-digit quotients with remainders, and some having two- or three-digit quotients with or without remainders. Have pupils determine the number of quotient figures before a problem is started. For the one-digit quotients, pupils should also be able to tell whether the answer will have a remainder.

   4)30̄ (7 R 2)   7)69̄ (9 R 6)   3)129̄ (43)

   3)127̄ (42 R 1)   4)840̄ (210)   4)326̄ (81 R 2)

   5)308̄ (61 R 3)   6)45̄ (7 R 3)   6)423̄ (70 R 3)

   2)286̄ (143)   3)97̄ (32 R 1)   4)249̄ (62 R 1)

2. If time permits, have the pupils go to the board and do some problems themselves. Note their areas of difficulty. Do they have trouble with problems involving zero?

Supplementary Drill

Drill 34 ÷

Lesson 54

It is easy to tell which numbers are divisible (divide evenly) by 2 or by 5. Perhaps you already know the following rules.

> **Divisibility Rules for 2 and 5**
>
> **Rule for 2:** Any number that ends with 0, 2, 4, 6, or 8 divides evenly by 2. A number that divides evenly by 2 is an even number. A number that does not divide evenly by 2 is an odd number.
>
> **Rule for 5:** Any number that ends with 5 or 0 divides evenly by 5.

C. Write the answers.

6. Which numbers are divisible by 2?   (4) (12) (18)   13   9   (16) (10)
7. Which numbers are divisible by 5?   (15) (5) (40)   64   32   (35) (50)
8. Which numbers are divisible by 3?   (6) (15)   20   (24) (30) (36)   28
9. Which numbers are divisible by 8?   (16)   18   (24)   30   (48) (56) (72)

D. These numbers are bigger than those in Part C. Use the rules.

10. Which numbers are divisible by 2?   213   49   (56) (78) (500) (384)
11. Which numbers are divisible by 5?   (80) (125) (470)   556   307   (95)

Review Exercises

E. Copy and divide.

12. 6)21 = 3 R 3   7)54 = 7 R 5   4)31 = 7 R 3   8)60 = 7 R 4

13. 4)84 = 21   3)369 = 123   5)355 = 71   2)168 = 84

14. 5)156 = 31 R 1   4)487 = 121 R 3   2)69 = 34 R 1   4)163 = 40 R 3

15. 2)420 = 210   3)397 = 132 R 1   7)40 = 5 R 5   3)219 = 73

F. Divide. Then multiply to check.

16. a. 6)486 = 81   81 × 6 = 486
     b. 7)490 = 70   70 × 7 = 490
     c. 3)996 = 332   332 × 3 = 996

122   Chapter 6 Division With Two-Digit Quotients

55. Expressing Remainders as Fractions

Susan and Linda have 5 pieces of colored paper. If they share it equally, how many pieces will each girl have?

Each girl will have 2 pieces of paper. 1 piece is left over. Susan and Linda could share the extra piece. Then they would each have another half. 5 divided by 2 can be expressed as $2\frac{1}{2}$.

$$2\overline{)5} \quad \text{R } 1 \qquad 2\frac{1}{2}\,\overline{)5}$$

> To express a remainder as a fraction, divide it by the divisor. The remainder is the numerator of the fraction, and the divisor is the denominator.

A. *Copy and divide. Express remainders as fractions.*

1. $2\overline{)17} = 8\frac{1}{2}$ $4\overline{)21} = 5\frac{1}{4}$ $5\overline{)37} = 7\frac{2}{5}$ $8\overline{)59} = 7\frac{3}{8}$ $7\overline{)45} = 6\frac{3}{7}$

2. $4\overline{)35} = 8\frac{3}{4}$ $2\overline{)11} = 5\frac{1}{2}$ $6\overline{)43} = 7\frac{1}{6}$ $3\overline{)23} = 7\frac{2}{3}$ $3\overline{)13} = 4\frac{1}{3}$

3. $6\overline{)17} = 2\frac{5}{6}$ $5\overline{)24} = 4\frac{4}{5}$ $3\overline{)20} = 6\frac{2}{3}$ $7\overline{)38} = 5\frac{3}{7}$ $8\overline{)45} = 5\frac{5}{8}$

4. $7\overline{)53} = 7\frac{4}{7}$ $8\overline{)37} = 4\frac{5}{8}$ $2\overline{)13} = 6\frac{1}{2}$ $6\overline{)52} = 8\frac{4}{6}$ $4\overline{)27} = 6\frac{3}{4}$

B. *Divide to find the fractional parts in these reading problems.*

5. If Richard and Jason share 3 doughnuts equally, how many doughnuts will each boy have? $1\frac{1}{2}$ doughnuts

6. If four girls share 5 apples equally, how many apples will each girl have? $1\frac{1}{4}$ apples

7. Twila, Darlene, and Faye want to share 4 sheets of blue paper equally. How many sheets of paper should each girl have? $1\frac{1}{3}$ sheets

Review Exercises

C. *Give these answers as fractions.*

8. $5 \div 7\ \frac{5}{7}$ $1 \div 4\ \frac{1}{4}$ $2 \div 3\ \frac{2}{3}$ $1 \div 2\ \frac{1}{2}$ $4 \div 5\ \frac{4}{5}$ $3 \div 8\ \frac{3}{8}$

LESSON 55

Objectives

- To review dividing a small number by a larger one.
- To teach *expressing remainders as fractions in division.

Preparation

1. Subtraction flash cards
2. Division flash cards
3. Money for Oral Drill, number 5 (optional)
4. Chalkboard:

   (Write Roman numerals only.)

   VIII (8)   XIX (19)   XXXIV (34)
   XL (40)   LX (60)   LXXXIII (83)
   LXXVII (77)

Oral Drill

1. Drill harder subtraction facts.
2. Drill harder division facts.
3. Count by 6's, 7's, and 8's.
4. Give practice with "times-and" problems.

6 × 8 + 5 (53)	7 × 7 + 4 (53)
8 × 8 + 3 (67)	9 × 8 + 4 (76)
5 × 9 + 5 (50)	8 × 7 + 5 (61)
9 × 9 + 4 (85)	7 × 9 + 3 (66)

5. **Give the value of the following coins.** Let pupils use fingers to count the fives and tens.
   2 quarters (50¢)   12 nickels (60¢)
   3 quarters (75¢)   5 dimes (50¢)
   8 nickels (40¢)   12 dimes ($1.20)
   a quarter and a dime (35¢)
   a quarter and a nickel (30¢)
   4 dimes and 5 nickels (65¢)
   a quarter, a dime, and a nickel (40¢)

6. **How much is 1/3 of 15? 1/4 of 24? 1/8 of 32?**

7. **Give the values of the Roman numerals on the board.**

T–123 Chapter 6 Division With Two-Digit Quotients

Teaching Guide

1. *Dividing a small number by a larger one.*

   a. **What is 1 divided by 3? 1 ÷ 4? 3 ÷ 5? 2 ÷ 4?** (Fraction answers do not need to be reduced at this point.)

   b. **2 is what part of 3? 2 is what part of 7? 2 is what part of 8? 2 is what part of 9? 2 is what part of 5?**

   c. **1 quart is what part of a gallon? 1 pint is what part of a quart? 1 foot is what part of a yard? 1 day is what part of a week? 1 thing is what part of a dozen?**

   d. **If 4 boys share 3 doughnuts, each boy should get what part of a doughnut? If 3 girls share 1 piece of paper, each gets what part?**

2. *Expressing remainders as fractions.*

   a. Use the little story in the pupil's book to introduce remainders as fractions. Pupils should see that the division does not come out evenly. If the girls share the 5 sheets of paper, each will have 2 sheets with 1 left over. That one sheet can also be divided between the two girls, with each girl having half the sheet.

   b. **Instead of writing this answer as 2 R 1, we can write it as 2 1/2. The remainder *1* is divided by the divisor *2* to get the fraction 1/2. A remainder can be expressed as a fraction by dividing it by the divisor.**

   In the previous lesson, the pupils learned that a smaller number divided by a larger one results in a fraction. You could show how this works out in the long division form, with the following illustration for 2 ÷ 3.

$$3\overline{)2} \;\; 0\text{ R }2 = 0\tfrac{2}{3} = \tfrac{2}{3}$$
$$\underline{0}$$
$$2$$

   c. Solve several more problems with remainders, and express the remainders as fractions. Note that R is not used when a remainder is written as a fraction.

   • Bethany and Grace shared 3 cookies equally. How many cookies did each girl have? (1 1/2 cookies)

   • Three boys divided 4 boards equally among themselves. How many boards did each boy get? (1 1/3 boards)

   • Three girls equally shared 8 sheets of paper. How many sheets did each girl get? (2 2/3 sheets)

   Note: Caution pupils to divide the right numbers. In the first problem above, the dividend is 3 because 3 *cookies* are being divided—not 2 girls. The answer is 1 1/2, not 2/3. It is also helpful to think, "Will the answer be more or less than 1?" If more, divide the larger number by the smaller: 3 ÷ 2 = 1 1/2. If less, divide the smaller number by the larger: 2 ÷ 3 = 2/3.

Supplementary Drills

Drill 16 ×

Drill 74

D. *Write fractions for these parts.*

9. a. 1 is what part of 4? $\frac{1}{4}$
    b. 1 is what part of 3? $\frac{1}{3}$
    c. 2 is what part of 7? $\frac{2}{7}$
    d. 3 is what part of 5? $\frac{3}{5}$
    e. 5 is what part of 8? $\frac{5}{8}$
    f. 1 is what part of 6? $\frac{1}{6}$

E. *Write the answers only.*

10. 6 × 8 = 48   8 × 9 = 72   9 × 7 = 63   8 × 7 = 56   12 × 7 = 84   6 × 9 = 54   9 × 9 = 81   12 × 8 = 96   7 × 7 = 49

11. 8 × 4 = 32   5 × 8 = 40   11 × 4 = 44   8 × 8 = 64   12 × 9 = 108   7 × 6 = 42   10 × 6 = 60   9 × 4 = 36   7 × 4 = 28

12. $\frac{1}{9}$ of 81 9 $\frac{1}{9}$ of 72 8 $\frac{1}{7}$ of 63 9 $\frac{1}{7}$ of 84 12

F. *Write the answers only. Watch the signs!*

13. 10 × 65 = 650   10 × 37 = 370   100 × 24 = 2,400   100 × 30 = 3,000
14. 20 × 8 = 160   40 × 9 = 360   50 × 7 = 350   80 × 6 = 480
15. 4 × 9 + 5 = 41   7 × 8 + 4 = 60   9 × 9 + 3 = 84   5 × 8 + 7 = 47
16. 16 − 9 = 7   14 − 6 = 8   11 − 7 = 4   15 − 8 = 7
17. 8 + 5 + 4 = 17   9 + 6 + 5 = 20   7 + 5 + 4 = 16   6 + 8 + 5 = 19

18. a. ▽6 ◯+4 ⬡÷2 □×8 ◇−3 = ? **37**
    b. ▽8 □×8 ◇−1 ⬡÷9 ◯+4 = ? **11**

G. *Write Arabic numerals for these Roman numerals.*

19. a. XXIII 23   b. LXXV 75   c. XLVII 47   d. XV 15   e. LIX 59   f. LXXXIV 84

H. *Write the missing numbers. Two answers will be fractions.*

20. 3 gal. = __12__ qt.   12 ft. = __4__ yd.   10 pt. = __5__ qt.
21. 1 qt. = __$\frac{1}{4}$__ gal.   5 wk. = __35__ days   2 yd. = __72__ in.
22. 4 qt. = __16__ cups   1 ft. = __$\frac{1}{3}$__ yd.   4 yr. = __48__ mo.

56. Checking Your Work

The Bible says, "Let all things be done decently and in order." Doing arithmetic "decently and in order" means doing it carefully and accurately. Checking the work helps to make it accurate.

	Problem	Check
	76 R 5	76
	7)537	× 7
	49	532
	47	+ 5
	42	537
	5	

Check division by multiplying the quotient and the divisor. Then add any remainder. See if the sum is equal to the dividend.

A. Copy, divide, and check as shown above.

1. a. 5)33, quotient 6 R 3; check: 6 × 5 = 30, + 3 = 33
   b. 6)40, quotient 6 R 4; check: 6 × 6 = 36, + 4 = 40
   c. 7)54, quotient 7 R 5; check: 7 × 7 = 49, + 5 = 54

2. a. 3)22, quotient 7 R 1; check: 7 × 3 = 21, + 1 = 22
   b. 2)864, quotient 432; check: 432 × 2 = 864
   c. 3)247, quotient 82 R 1; check: 82 × 3 = 246, + 1 = 247

Check addition by adding the addends in a different order.

```
  8   Think: 8 + 5 = 13,      8   This time start at the bottom.
  5          + 7 = 20,        5   Think: 6 + 7 = 13,
  7          + 6 = 26.        7          + 5 = 18,
+ 6   Are you right? Check! + 6          + 8 = 26.   Right!
```

B. Copy and add. Check by adding each column in a different order.

3.
5	4	9	6	3	8	7
7	8	5	3	8	6	9
5	7	4	8	4	5	4
+ 6	+ 5	+ 7	+ 4	+ 9	+ 8	+ 3
23	24	25	21	24	27	23

4.
	73	49		843	125
57	44	52	274	329	943
25	59	17	188	726	678
+ 64	+ 27	+ 31	+ 325	+ 152	+ 385
146	203	149	787	2,050	2,131

LESSON 56

Objectives

- To introduce *checking divisions that have remainders.
- To review the other three processes and how to check them.

Preparation

1. Addition, subtraction, multiplication, and division flash cards
2. Money (optional)
3. Speed Drill 56
4. Chalkboard:

    $$6\overline{)39}^{(6\,R\,3)} \quad 4\overline{)29}^{(7\,R\,1)}$$

    $$\begin{array}{r} 5 \\ 8 \\ +7 \\ \hline (20) \end{array} \qquad \begin{array}{r} 320 \\ -185 \\ \hline (135) \end{array} \qquad \begin{array}{r} 476 \\ \times\ \ 6 \\ \hline (2{,}856) \end{array}$$

Oral Drill

1. Give rapid drill of the basic facts in the four processes.
2. Review the parts of the problems on the board.
3. Give mixed mental drill.
   $5 + 4 \times 6 + 2 \div 7$ (8)
   $14 \div 2 + 1 \times 9 \div 6$ (12)
   $8 \times 5 \div 4 - 7 \times 4$ (12)
   $12 - 4 \div 2 \times 8 + 3$ (35)
   $6 \times 8 + 2 \div 5 - 4$ (6)
   $7 + 6 - 5 \times 8 - 1 \div 7$ (9)
4. Review dividing a small number by a larger one.
   What is 2 divided by 3? $4 \div 5$? $1 \div 2$? $5 \div 8$?
5. Review finding a part of a number.
   What is 1/4 of 28? 1/7 of 56? 1/9 of 63?
6. Review money values.
   a. **What is the value of 1 nickel? 3 nickels? 5 nickels? 8 nickels? 12 nickels?**
   b. **What is the value of 1 dime? 3 dimes? 3 dimes and a nickel?**
   c. **What is the value of 1 quarter? 2 quarters? 3 quarters? 4 quarters? 5 quarters?**
7. Review multiplying by 10, 100, and multiples of 10.
   a. **What is 10×4? 10×56? 10×30?**
   b. **What is 100×6? 100×18? 100×50? 100×73**
   c. **What is 20×4? 50×5? 70×3? 90×8?**

Speed Drill

Give Speed Drill 56 (terminology in the four operations). Allow at least 3 minutes.

Chapter 6 Division With Two-Digit Quotients

Teaching Guide

1. *Checking divisions that have remainders.*
   a. Work through the two problems on the board.
   b. Show how to check the answer by multiplying the quotient and the divisor, and adding on the remainder. The sum matches the dividend of the division problem.
   c. Note that the lesson exercises do not ask pupils to write the multiplication check for problems that have remainders written as fractions.
   d. Use the following problems for further practice.

   $7\overline{)54}$ (7 R 5) $8\overline{)43}$ (5 R 3) $3\overline{)639}$ (213)

   $2\overline{)168}$ (84) $6\overline{)68}$ (11 R 2) $4\overline{)489}$ (122 R 1)

2. *Checking in the other three processes.*
   a. Point to the addition problem on the board. **Let's add these three numbers.** (5 + 8 = 13; 13 + 7 = 20) **Are we right? A good way to check column addition is to add the addends in a different order. Let's check by adding the numbers again, starting at the bottom.** (7 + 8 = 15; 15 + 5 = 20) **We got the same answer both times, so we can be fairly sure the answer is right.**
   b. Do the subtraction problem together. Turn back to Lesson 6 if pupils do not remember how to check subtraction problems with addition.
   c. Do the multiplication problem, and check it by going over the work again. It is not practical to check this kind of problem by reversing the factors. Neither should you show checking by division at this point.

   d. Use these problems for further practice.

   ```
     9
     7        253
     5        758       806
   + 6       +637      -387
   ────      ────      ────
   (27)     (1,648)    (419)
   ```

   ```
     345
   ×   7        8)659  (82 R 3)
   ─────
   (2,415)
   ```

Extra Review

Review expressing remainders as fractions.
   a. Do several problems together. Instead of writing the remainder with R, write it as a fraction.

   $2\overline{)15}$ (7 1/2) $3\overline{)14}$ (4 2/3) $4\overline{)19}$ (4 3/4)

   $5\overline{)31}$ (6 1/5) $6\overline{)17}$ (2 5/6) $8\overline{)35}$ (4 3/8)

   b. State some of the problems as "find 1/2 of 15" or "find 1/3 of 14." Pupils know the rule for finding a part of a number, if the number divides evenly. The same rule applies for numbers that do not divide evenly. **If a question asks for a part of a number, the remainder is changed to a fraction.**

Note: Because the required checks make two problems out of one in the subtraction and division sections, there are not many problems in those rows. Most pupils will be able to handle the whole lesson.

Supplementary Drills

Drill 35 ÷

Drill 48

Lesson 56

> Check subtraction by adding the difference to the subtrahend.

```
Problem      Check
  851         375
- 476       + 476
  375         851
```

C. *Copy and subtract. Check by addition.*

5. a. 451   125   b. 800   432   c. 7,139   666
      -326   +326   -368   +368   -6,473   +6,473
       125   451   432   800   666   7,139

6. a. $5.04 $3.65   b. $9.17 $6.37   c. $48.25 $30.58
      -1.39   +1.39   -2.80   +2.80   -17.67   +17.67
      $3.65 $5.04 $6.37 $9.17 $30.58 $48.25

> Check multiplication by going over your work again.

```
Problem      Check
  634       (Go over
x   8       the work
5,072        again.)
```

D. *Copy and multiply. Check by going over your work.*

7.   385   927   158   863
    x 6   x 7   x 5   x 9
    2,310   6,489   790   7,767

8. $5.27 $3.98 $7.18 $8.60
    x   4   x   4   x   3   x   7
   $21.08 $15.92 $21.54 $60.20

Review Exercises

E. *Write the answers as fractions.*

9. $4 \div 7 \; \frac{4}{7}$ $3 \div 4 \; \frac{3}{4}$ $1 \div 2 \; \frac{1}{2}$ $2 \div 3 \; \frac{2}{3}$ $1 \div 4 \; \frac{1}{4}$ $5 \div 8 \; \frac{5}{8}$

10. a. 3 is what part of 5? $\frac{3}{5}$ b. 1 is what part of 6? $\frac{1}{6}$

F. *Copy and divide. Write remainders as fractions.*

11. $5\overline{)24} \;\; 4\frac{4}{5}$ $2\overline{)13} \;\; 6\frac{1}{2}$ $4\overline{)17} \;\; 4\frac{1}{4}$ $3\overline{)26} \;\; 8\frac{2}{3}$ $8\overline{)35} \;\; 4\frac{3}{8}$

126   Chapter 6 Division With Two-Digit Quotients

57. Zeroes in Four-Digit Subtraction

Sometimes before you can subtract, you must borrow from the thousands' place. Study the problem in the box.

```
   3 9 9                                          Check
  4,0̷0̷10    There are no tens and no hundreds.    1,165
 -2,835    Borrow from the thousands' place.     +2,835
  1,165                                           4,000
```

When borrowing is needed, always go to the nearest place first. If that place is empty, go to the next place. And of course, never borrow unless the top digit is **less** than the bottom digit.

A. *Copy and subtract. Check the answers by addition.*

1. a.   6,000   4,753   b.   8,002   4,157   c.   7,001   2,177
      − 1,247 + 1,247   − 3,845 + 3,845   − 4,824 + 4,824
        4,753   6,000   4,157   8,002   2,177   7,001

2. a.   5,010   411   b.   4,060   339   c.   9,072   4,092
      − 4,599 + 4,599   − 3,721 + 3,721   − 4,980 + 4,980
          411   5,010   339   4,060   4,092   9,072

3. a.   7,300   1,808   b.   4,000   2,602   c.   6,020   2,602
      − 5,492 + 5,492   − 1,398 + 1,398   − 3,418 + 3,418
        1,808   7,300   2,602   4,000   2,602   6,020

4. a. $10.00 $6.33   b. $41.03 $15.53   c. $50.20 $32.35
      − 3.67 + 3.67   − 25.50 + 25.50   − 17.85 + 17.85
        $6.33 $10.00 $15.53 $41.03 $32.35 $50.20

Review Exercises

B. *Write the answers only.*

5.   8   9   5   4   8   7   9   6   12
    ×8   ×7   ×9   ×6   ×9   ×7   ×4   ×7   ×8
    64   63   45   24   72   49   36   42   96

6.   7   8   12   12   9   7   3   12   7
    ×8   ×4   ×5   ×9   ×9   ×6   ×8   ×6   ×5
    56   32   60   108   81   42   24   72   35

LESSON 57

Objective

♦ To introduce *subtraction with zero in the hundreds' place of the minuend.

Preparation

1. Subtraction flash cards
2. Division flash cards
3. Toy clock
4. Chalkboard:

   a. 500   602
       −176   −489
       (324)   (113)

   b. 4,000   4,059   7,030 $60.50
       −1,846   −3,894   −4,567   −14.39
       (2,154) (165)   (2,463) ($46.11)

Oral Drill

1. Drill the subtraction facts.
2. Drill the division facts.
3. Review time.
   a. Have pupils show or read times on the clock.
   b. Review A.M. and P.M. **Is breakfast at 7:00 A.M. or 7:00 P.M.?**
   c. Show a time such as 8:15. **What time is 20 minutes later than this? A half hour later? An hour later?**
4. Review money.
   a. **What is the value of 3 quarters? 4 quarters? 6 quarters? 5 dimes? 6 nickels?**
   b. **What is the value of 2 quarters and 5 dimes?** ($1.00)
      3 quarters and 2 dimes? (95¢)
      1 quarter and 5 nickels? (50¢)
      2 quarters and 3 nickels? (65¢)
      1 quarter, 1 dime, 1 nickel? (40¢)
5. a. Review some of the key words and phrases in reading problems.
   b. Give some simple problems to be solved mentally.
      • Melvin had 15 butterflies and 6 moths in his collection. How many butterflies and moths did he have together? (21 butterflies and moths)
      • Joyce had 2 cats, and each cat had 4 kittens. How many kittens were there? How many more kittens were there than mother cats? (8 kittens; 6 more kittens)
      • Three boys shared 6 apples. How many apples could each boy have? (2 apples)
      • Three boys shared 1 apple. What part of the apple could each boy have? (1/3)

Chapter 6 Division With Two-Digit Quotients

Teaching Guide

Subtraction with zero in the hundreds' place of the minuend.

a. Do the first two of the subtraction problems *(a)* on the board together. Stress: **We cannot borrow from zero.**

b. Go to the second row *(b)*. **Can we subtract the 6 ones without borrowing? Can we borrow from the tens? Can we borrow from the hundreds? Why not? We must go all the way to the thousands to borrow, because all the places in between are empty.**

c. **Think of this as 400 tens.** Point to the left three digits. **We will borrow 1 from 400.** Cross out the 400. **What is 1 less than 400?** Write 399 above. **We will add the 1 borrowed ten to the ones.** Write 1 before the 0 in the ones' place. **Now we can subtract.** Finish the problem.

d. Do the other problems on the board. Caution pupils to borrow *only when necessary*. Do not allow them to cross out all the numbers before they start subtracting, except in the case of "all zeroes on the top." For example, in the third problem in row *b* on the board, borrow from the 3 and subtract 10 - 7 before borrowing from the next place (70 in this case).

e. Have pupils go to the board for practice with similar problems.

```
  5,000      3,010      4,002
 -1,832     -2,684     -2,589
 ───────   ───────    ───────
 (3,168)    (326)     (1,413)


 $20.00    $42.09     $70.25
 -17.36    -25.50     -47.94
 ───────   ───────    ───────
 ($2.64)   ($16.59)   ($22.31)
```

Supplementary Drills

Drill 75*

Drill 3 –

C. Do these exercises.

7. Add 1,000 to each number. Write the answers only.
   a. 51,036   b. 502,893   c. 620,755   d. 46,123   e. 945,000
      52,036   503,893   621,755   47,123   946,000

8. Subtract 100 from each number. Write the answers only.
   a. 49,640   b. 327,901   c. 888,888   d. 54,395   e. 280,133
      49,540   327,801   888,788   54,295   280,033

9. Write **add**, **subtract**, **multiply**, or **divide**.
   a. How much more? — subtract
   b. How much if shared equally? — divide
   c. How many less? — subtract
   d. What is the total? — add
   e. How much change? — subtract
   f. How much at 27¢ each? — multiply
   g. What is one-fourth of a number? — divide
   h. How many groups of 3 in a number? — divide
   i. How much in 5 groups the same size? — multiply
   j. 4 equal groups in a number. How many in each group? — divide

D. Solve these reading problems.

10. There are 39 books in the Old Testament and 27 in the New Testament. How many books are in the whole Bible? — 66 books

11. How many more books are in the Old Testament than in the New Testament? (See number 10.) — 12 books

12. Edward wants to read the Bible through this year. He reads 4 chapters each day. How many chapters does Edward read in a week? — 28 chapters

13. Louise has 12 gumdrops to share with her friends, Sara and Teresa. How many gumdrops will each girl have if they are shared equally among the **three** girls? Will there be any left over? — 4 gumdrops, no

14. If 5 boys share one pie, what part of the pie can each boy have? — $\frac{1}{5}$ pie

15. If a jet plane flies 575 miles an hour, how many miles will it fly in 3 hours? — 1,725 miles

16. Father bought a staple gun for $14.98 and a box of staples for $1.59. What was his total bill? — $16.57

17. Mother bought some fresh peaches for $2.35. How much change did she get from $5.00? — $2.65

18. Three boys shared 4 peaches. How many peaches did each boy get? (Express the remainder as a fraction.) — $1\frac{1}{3}$ peaches

128   Chapter 6   Division With Two-Digit Quotients

58. More Work With Money

Below are illustrations of the fronts and backs of the four most common United States bills.

one-dollar bill

five-dollar bill

ten-dollar bill

twenty-dollar bill

A. *Write the value of the following sets of bills.*

1. a. 6 one-dollar bills $6   b. 1 five-dollar bill and 3 one-dollar bills $8
2. a. 5 five-dollar bills $25   b. 3 ten-dollar bills and 1 five-dollar bill $35
3. a. 8 ten-dollar bills $80   b. 1 twenty-dollar bill and 3 five-dollar bills $35
4. a. 4 twenty-dollar bills $80   b. 2 twenty-dollar bills and 3 ten-dollar bills $70

B. *Write the value of the following sets of money.*

5. 3 one-dollar bills, 2 quarters, 1 dime, 6 pennies $3.66
6. 1 five-dollar bill, 2 one-dollar bills, 3 quarters, 2 nickels $7.85
7. 2 ten-dollar bills, 4 one-dollar bills, 1 quarter, 3 dimes $24.55
8. 1 ten-dollar bill, 2 half dollars, 2 quarters, 4 pennies $11.54
9. 3 twenty-dollar bills, 1 quarter, 3 nickels, 4 dimes $60.80

LESSON 58

Objectives

- To study *the most common denominations of United States bills.
- To teach *division of money amounts.
- To introduce *counting out change (optional—in teacher's guide only).

Preparation

1. Subtraction flash cards
2. Three each of one-dollar, two-dollar (optional), five-dollar, ten-dollar, and twenty-dollar bills; and a variety of coins.
3. Speed Drill 58
4. Chalkboard:

   a. XVII   LXIII   XLVI
      LXXXIV   XXXI   XII   LIX
   b.   361,580

Oral Drill

1. Drill subtraction facts.
2. **What is 1/8 of 24? 1/4 of 16? 1/7 of 56? 1/9 of 63?**
3. Drill mental multiplication.
   10 × 24   10 × 600   100 × 12
   30 × 5   60 × 7
4. Read the Roman numerals (a) on the board.
5. **Which of these numbers divide evenly by 8?**
   18   24   48   56   36
   28   72   63   64   88
   Which of these numbers divide evenly by 9?
   9   19   18   32   27
   28   64   72   81   54
6. Review place value. Read the number (b) on the board. Have someone change one digit to make it 100 less; 100,000 less; 10,000 more; 10 more; 1,000 less.
7. Review finding change by subtraction.

Speed Drill

Give Speed Drill 58 (number strings).

T–129   Chapter 6   Division With Two-Digit Quotients

Teaching Guide

1. *Denominations of United States bills.*
   a. Briefly show the fronts and backs of the various bills, and let pupils identify them. Pupils have studied all except the two- and twenty-dollar bills in third grade.
   Note: The two-dollar bill is an authentic United States bill but is rarely used. For this reason it is not included in the pupil's lesson at this point. The teacher may choose to introduce it in class.
   b. Put several bills together and have pupils tell the value.
   3 fives   3 tens   3 twenties   3 twos
   1 ten, 1 five, 1 one ($16.00)
   1 twenty, 1 ten, 1 five ($35.00)
   1 five, 3 ones ($8.00)
   1 twenty, 2 tens, 2 fives ($50.00)
   c. Gather the pupils around a table to practice counting sets of bills and coins. Teach them to always begin with the largest bill, "count on" all of that kind, go to the next smaller bill, and continue to the smallest coins. Give each child a turn if possible.

2. *Dividing money amounts.*
   a. Review addition, subtraction, and multiplication with money. Add the dollar sign and decimal point after the computation is finished.

   ```
     $3.00       $16.38
      5.79         4.46       $6.00
   +12.45       + 9.24       -4.95
   ($21.24)    ($30.08)     ($1.05)

    $10.00       $3.48       $9.73
   -  6.29       ×   6       ×   7
   ($3.71)    ($20.88)    ($68.11)
   ```

   b. Introduce division with money. It is done just as if the money symbols were not there. As with other operations, the dollar sign and decimal point are added after the computation is complete.

   ```
      ($0.32)       ($0.51)      ($0.94)
   4)$1.28       6)$3.06      2)$1.88

      ($3.13)       ($2.43)
   3)$9.39       2)$4.86
   ```

3. *Counting out change* (optional).
   a. If you have time, briefly introduce another way to find change. **We can find change by counting it out rather than by subtracting. This is how to count out change for a quarter if the bill is 22¢.** Begin with 22¢ and count out (add on) pennies until 25¢ is reached: 22¢, 23¢, 24¢, 25¢. The change is 3¢.
   b. **Count out the change for a quarter if the bill is 18¢.** Begin with 18¢, and count pennies until the nearest 5¢ or 10¢ is reached (18¢, 19¢, 20¢). Then use nickels and dimes until the nearest quarter is reached.
   c. **Count out the change for a quarter if the bill is 15¢, if the bill is 12¢, 10¢, 21¢, 8¢, 19¢, 14¢, 23¢.** Note that after 15¢ is reached, one arrives at 25¢ by using a dime (15¢, 25¢) rather than two nickels (15¢, 20¢, 25¢).

Supplementary Drill

Drill 76

Lesson 58 129

C. Do these exercises.

10. Name the bills that equal these amounts. Use as few as possible.

a. $17.00
 1 ten
 1 five
 2 dollars

b. $45.00
 2 twenties
 1 five

c. $36.00
 1 twenty
 1 ten
 1 five
 1 dollar

d. $75.00
 3 twenties
 1 ten
 1 five

e. $29.00
 1 twenty
 1 five
 4 dollars

11. Name the bills and coins that equal these amounts. Use as few as possible, not including half dollars.

a. $1.60
 1 dollar
 2 quarters
 1 dime

b. $9.45
 1 five
 4 dollars
 1 quarter
 2 dimes

c. $4.32
 4 dollars
 1 quarter
 1 nickel
 2 pennies

d. $6.77
 1 five
 1 dollar
 3 quarters
 2 pennies

e. $0.98
 3 quarters
 2 dimes
 3 pennies

12. Suppose you bought things that cost the amounts in number 11, and you paid for each one with a ten-dollar bill. How much change would you receive each time? Do five subtraction problems to find out. Write them on your paper like this:

```
  $10.00      $10.00      $10.00      $10.00      $10.00
-  1.60     -  9.45     -  4.32     -  6.77     -  0.98
  -----       -----       -----       -----       -----
  $8.40       $0.55       $5.68       $3.23       $9.02
```

D. Copy in straight columns, and add or subtract. Remember that $4 means $4.00.

13. a. $4.35 + $3.65 $8.00   b. $79.90 + $16.32 $96.22   c. $4.82 + $6 + $10.49 $21.31

14. a. $6.71 + $5 $11.71   b. $35.09 + $6.81 $41.90   c. $5.25 + $2.68 + $3 $10.93

15. a. $14.95 − $3.48 $11.47   b. $5 − $2.79 $2.21   c. $20 − $13.75 $6.25

E. Copy and multiply.

16.
```
  $5.30      $9.65      $4.89      $5.72      $8.46
×    7     ×    6     ×    6     ×    8     ×    7
------     ------     ------     ------     ------
$37.10     $57.90     $29.34     $45.76     $59.22
```

> To divide **money** into parts, place the decimal point in the quotient directly above the decimal point in the dividend.
>
> $1.32 $0.82
> 3)$3.96   4)$3.28

F. Copy and divide carefully.

17.
```
   $0.41        $2.14        $3.23        $0.31        $0.82
5)$2.05      2)$4.28      3)$9.69      6)$1.86      3)$2.46
```

G. Figure out these number strings.

18. a. ▽6 ◇+4 ○×5 □−2 ○÷8 = ? 6

b. ▽5 □×6 ◇÷3 ◇−7 □×9 = ? 27

59. Chapter 6 Review

A. *Write the answers quickly.*

1.
8	9	7	5	9	8	6	7	6
×6	×7	×8	×7	×9	×9	×9	×7	×7
48	63	56	35	81	72	54	49	42

2. 6)36 = 6, 8)64 = 8, 9)63 = 7, 7)49 = 7, 8)96 = 12, 5)40 = 8

3. 9)72 = 8, 8)56 = 7, 4)32 = 8, 2)4 = 2, 5)60 = 12, 6)72 = 12

B. *Follow the directions.*

4. Copy and multiply. Check by going over your work.

608	904	$3.90	$8.35	$7.56
× 5	× 9	× 6	× 7	× 6
3,040	8,136	$23.40	$58.45	$45.36

5. Copy and subtract.

6,043	8,000	5,400	5,010	8,030
− 5,493	− 1,574	− 2,961	− 3,285	− 6,536
550	6,426	2,439	1,725	1,494

6. Copy and subtract. Check by addition.

a.
713	354
− 359	+ 359
354	713

b.
$9.00	$2.18
− 6.82	+ 6.82
$2.18	$9.00

c.
$20.30	$3.71
− 16.59	+ 16.59
$3.71	$20.30

7. Add down, and check by adding up.

	83	295	164
65	49	62	747
17	32	853	568
+ 84	+ 16	+ 144	+ 352
166	180	1,354	1,831

LESSON 59

Objective

♦ To review the concepts taught in Chapter 6 (listed below).

Computation skills
- Multiplication with 0 in tens' place
- Subtraction of 4-digit numbers with 0's in the minuend
- Division with two- or three-digit quotients
- Finding a part of a number
- Dividing a small number by a larger to get a fraction
- Expressing remainders as fractions
- Money in the four operations
- Checking the four operations

Secondary skills
- Odd and even numbers
- Numbers divisible by 2, 4, 5, . . .
- Divisibility rules for 2 and 5
- Reading problems
- Identifying and counting money (not included on test)

Preparation

Real or play money

Teaching Guide

1. Review odd and even numbers. Review divisibility rules for 2 and 5.

2. a. **Tell which numbers divide evenly by 7.**
   16   21   36   42   48   49
   56   66   63   81   28
   b. **Tell which numbers divide evenly by 4.**
   14   16   24   32   42
   28   21   8   10

3. **Find the parts of these numbers.**
   1/4 of 32   1/6 of 60
   1/8 of 64   1/3 of 27

4. Review dividing a small number by a large.
   a. **What is 3 divided into 4 parts? 1 ÷ 5? 3 ÷ 7?**
   b. **1 is what part of 3? 5 is what part of 8?**

5. Count combinations of bills and coins as in Lesson 58.

6. Review computation. Have pupils solve problems on the board.
   a. Review division with two- or three-digit quotients.
   Without remainders:

   $3\overline{)159}$ (53) $2\overline{)488}$ (244) $7\overline{)217}$ (31)

   $4\overline{)480}$ (120) $5\overline{)255}$ (51)

   With remainders:

   $4\overline{)166}$ (41 R 2) $3\overline{)962}$ (320 R 2) $6\overline{)368}$ (61 R 2)

   $2\overline{)485}$ (242 R 1) $3\overline{)278}$ (92 R 2)

   b. **What is 1/2 of 13?** (6 1/2) **1/3 of 14?** (4 2/3) **1/4 of 17?** (4 1/4) Have pupils divide and express remainders as fractions.

Chapter 6 Division With Two-Digit Quotients

c. Review checking in the four operations
Addition: Add in different order.
Subtraction: Add difference to subtrahend.
Multiplication: Check over work again.
Division: Multiply quotient by divisor and add remainder.

```
   4        65
   7        72
   8        47      7,453        396
  +6       +35     -2,559        × 4
 (25)    (219)    (4,894)     (1,584)
```

```
         (32)        (31 R 2)      (423 R 1)
      4)128         3)95          2)847
```

d. Review money calculations in the four processes.

```
 $43.92      $19.06
  17.46       37.54       $7.00
 +25.36     +52.70       -3.79
($86.74)  ($109.30)    ($3.21)
```

```
  $8.56       $3.08             ($0.62)
  ×  6        ×  7           3)$1.86
($51.36)   ($21.56)
```

7. Review reading problems.
   a. **Tell if you would add, subtract, multiply, or divide to find the answers.**
      How many are left? (s)
      What is the total? (a *or* m)
      How much older? (s)
      What is 1/3 as much? (d)
      How many in one part? (d)
      How many altogether? (a *or* m)
      How much change? (s)
      How many times as much? (d)
      How much less? (s)
      How many in 5 equal groups? (m)
      How many in all? (a *or* m)
      How many more? (s)
      How much shorter? (s)
      How much for three at 4¢ each? (m)
      How many equal groups of 3 in a number? (d)
      4 equal groups in a number; how many in each group? (d)
   b. **Find the answers to these problems.**
      • Timothy ate 3 candies and Helen ate 4. Helen ate how many more? (1 candy)
      • Timothy's candy was what part of Helen's? (3/4)
      • Three boys shared 6 cookies. How many did each get? (2 cookies)
      • Three boys shared 2 cookies. Could each boy have a whole cookie? What part could each boy have? (no; 2/3 cookie)
      • What is the total of 4 butterflies, 6 butterflies, and 8 butterflies? (18 butterflies)
      • How much change does Mother receive from $10.00 if her bill is $8.00? ($2.00)
      • Karen has 2 brothers. Janice has 6 brothers. Janice has how many times as many brothers as Karen has? (3 times)

8. Tell students that they will have a test in the next class.

Note: This review lesson has three pages, as usual. Assign your students what they need.

C. Copy and divide. Check by multiplication.

8. a. 4)168 → 42; 42 × 4 = 168 b. 2)69 → 34 R 1; 34 × 2 = 68, +1 = 69 c. 3)396 → 132; 132 × 3 = 396

9. a. 2)147 → 73 R 1; 73 × 2 = 146, +1 = 147 b. 4)286 → 71 R 2; 71 × 4 = 284, +2 = 286 c. 5)$2.55 → $0.51; $0.51 × 5 = $2.55

D. Divide. Express remainders as fractions.

10. 3)124 = $41\frac{1}{3}$ 2)485 = $242\frac{1}{2}$ 5)12 = $2\frac{2}{5}$ 4)27 = $6\frac{3}{4}$

E. Write the answers.

11. Multiply these numbers by 10.
    57 **570**   13 **130**   80 **800**   5 **50**   24 **240**

12. Multiply these numbers by 100.
    12 **1,200**   20 **2,000**   48 **4,800**   99 **9,900**   7 **700**

13. Multiply. Write the answers only.
    50 × 4 **200**   30 × 9 **270**   80 × 8 **640**   60 × 9 **540**   40 × 7 **280**

14. Copy all the odd numbers in this row.
    (15)   64   38   92   50   26   (61)   (89)

15. Copy all the numbers that divide evenly by 5.
    (25)   (40)   36   (80)   (420)   (355)   552   708

16. Copy all the numbers that divide evenly by 2.
    (6)   17   (52)   (40)   29   841   (372)   (508)

17. Copy all the numbers that divide evenly by 6.
    15   (18)   (42)   (72)   52   (36)   (48)   28

18. Find the parts of these numbers.
    $\frac{1}{2}$ of 24 **12** $\frac{1}{6}$ of 48 **8** $\frac{1}{5}$ of 45 **9** $\frac{1}{3}$ of 18 **6**

F. Answer with fractions.

19. 1 ÷ 3 $\frac{1}{3}$ 4 ÷ 5 $\frac{4}{5}$ 3 ÷ 4 $\frac{3}{4}$ 2 ÷ 7 $\frac{2}{7}$

20. a. 1 is what part of 4? $\frac{1}{4}$ b. 2 is what part of 5? $\frac{2}{5}$

(continued on next page)

Chapter 6 Division With Two-Digit Quotients

G. *Do these exercises with money.*

21. Write the value of the following sets of money.
    a. 2 one-dollar bills, 3 quarters, 1 dime, 4 pennies $2.89
    b. 1 five-dollar bill, 3 one-dollar bills, 2 quarters, 2 dimes $8.70
    c. 1 ten-dollar bill, 1 five-dollar bill, 3 dimes, 2 nickels $15.40
    d. 2 twenty-dollar bills, 2 ten-dollar bills, 1 five-dollar bill $65.00
    e. 3 ten-dollar bills, 4 one-dollar bills, 4 quarters, 2 pennies $35.02

22. Write what bills and coins equal these amounts. Use the smallest possible number.
    a. 45¢   1 quarter, 2 dimes
    b. $7.00   1 five, 2 dollars
    c. $1.75   1 dollar, 3 quarters
    d. $4.33   4 dollars, 1 quarter, 1 nickel, 3 pennies

23. Find the amount of change in each case.
    a. Total bill—$8.32; amount given—$10.00 $1.68
    b. Total bill—$9.49; amount given—$20.00 $10.51

H. *Solve these reading problems.*

24. David was 30 years old when he became king. He reigned for 40 years. How old was King David then?   70 years

25. David reigned 7 years in Hebron and 33 years in Jerusalem. How many more years did he reign in Jerusalem than in Hebron?   26 years

26. David showed kindness to Jonathan's son Mephibosheth, who was lame. He told Ziba and Ziba's 15 sons and 20 servants to care for Mephibosheth's property. How many helpers did Ziba have altogether?   35 helpers

27. Ziba had 15 sons. Noah had 3 sons. Ziba had how many times as many sons as Noah had?   5 times

28. If each of Ziba's 15 sons worked for 8 hours in Mephibosheth's fields, how many hours of work were done in the fields?   120 hours

60. Chapter 6 Test

LESSON 60

Objective

- To test the pupils' mastery of the concepts taught in Chapter 6.

Teaching Guide

1. Give Speed Drill 60 (division practice).

   Note: Speed Drills are optional on test days.

2. Give any last-minute review that you feel is necessary.

3. Administer the test.

   Note: Chapter 6 Test is found in the test section in the back of this manual.

Chapter 7

More Fractions and Measures

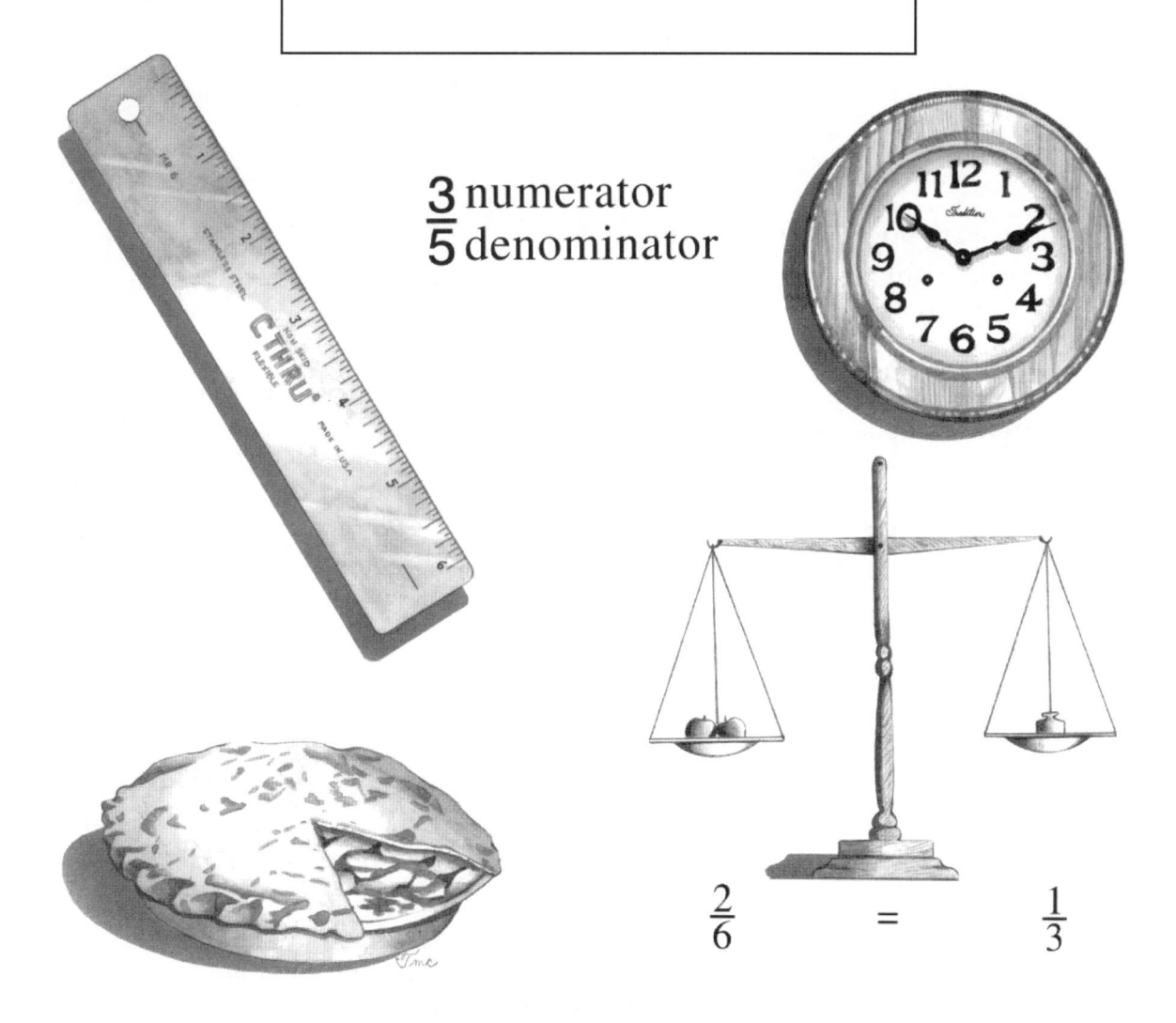

$\frac{3}{5}$ numerator
denominator

$\frac{2}{6} = \frac{1}{3}$

A just weight and balance are the LORD's.
(Proverbs 16:11)

61. More About Fractions

Here are some important facts you should know about fractions.

> 1. Every fraction is a part of a whole.
> 2. The **denominator** is the bottom number of a fraction. It tells into how many parts the whole thing is divided.
> 3. The **numerator** is the top number of a fraction. It tells how many parts the fraction names.
> 4. **Like fractions** are fractions with the same denominator.

A. Do these exercises.

1. Name the part that is shaded in each picture.
   a. $\frac{3}{4}$ b. $\frac{1}{2}$ c. $\frac{3}{6}$ d. $\frac{5}{8}$ e. $\frac{2}{5}$

2. Copy these fractions and label the parts.

   $\frac{1}{4}$ numerator / denominator

   $\frac{3}{8}$ numerator / denominator

3. Write three fractions with a denominator of 5.
   (any three) $\frac{1}{5}$ $\frac{2}{5}$ $\frac{3}{5}$ $\frac{4}{5}$ $\frac{5}{5}$

4. Write three fractions with a numerator of 1.
   (sample answers) $\frac{1}{2}$ $\frac{1}{3}$ $\frac{1}{4}$

5. A pie was cut into 5 equal pieces. Two pieces were eaten.
   a. How many pieces were in the whole pie? 5 pieces
   b. What fraction shows what one piece of the pie is called? $\frac{1}{5}$
   c. What part of the pie was eaten? $\frac{2}{5}$
   d. Count the pieces of pie by fifths. Write $\frac{1}{5}, \frac{2}{5}$ ... $\frac{1}{5}, \frac{2}{5}, \frac{3}{5}, \frac{4}{5}, \frac{5}{5}$

This row of fractions shows how to count by eighths.

$\frac{1}{8}$ $\frac{2}{8}$ $\frac{3}{8}$ $\frac{4}{8}$ $\frac{5}{8}$ $\frac{6}{8}$ $\frac{7}{8}$ $\frac{8}{8}$

The fractions in this row are **like fractions**. The denominators are the same, but the numerators are different. As the numerators become larger, the fractions also become larger.

> If two fractions have the same denominator but different numerators, the fraction with the **larger numerator** is larger.
>
> $\frac{2}{3} > \frac{1}{3}$ $\frac{4}{5} > \frac{2}{5}$ $\frac{5}{8} > \frac{3}{8}$

LESSON 61

Objectives

- To review fraction concepts and terms.
- To introduce *like fractions.
- To teach *comparing the size of fractions.

Preparation

1. Division flash cards
2. Flannel or rubber fraction cutouts (optional)
3. Bills and coins for counting money
    Prepare an envelope for each kind of bill. Cut a "window" in the envelope so that only the picture on the bill can be seen.

Oral Drill

1. Drill division flash cards.
2. Drill mental arithmetic.

10 × 45	100 × 32	40 × 6	80 × 5
20 + 8	50 + 4	63 + 4	27 + 5
12 − 6	22 − 3	30 − 2	36 − 4

3. Review measures.
   1 ft. = (12) in.   1 yd. = (36) in.
   1 yd. = (3) ft.   1 hr. = (60) min.
   1 day = (24) hr.   1 yr. = (12) mo.
   1 pt. = (2) cups   1 qt. = (2) pt.
   1 gal. = (4) qt.

4. Review finding parts of numbers.
   1/2 ft. = (6) in.   1/2 yr. = (6) mo.
   1/2 gal. = (2) qt.   1/2 qt. = (1) pt.
   1/4 yd. = (9) in.   1/3 doz. = (4) things
   1/4 qt. = (1) cup   1/4 doz. = (3) things
   1 day = (1/7) wk.   1 cup = (1/2) pt.
   1 mo. = (1/12) yr.   1 ft. = (1/3) yd.

5. Show $1.00, $5.00, $10.00, and $20.00 bills, and have pupils identify them. Point out the pictures on the fronts and backs, not just the identifying numbers. Slip each bill into a prepared "window envelope" and see if pupils can identify the bills by their pictures only.

6. Give practice with counting money.

T–135   Chapter 7   More Fractions and Measures

Teaching Guide

1. *Review of fractions.*
   Use flannelgraph or rubber pieces if you have them. If not, draw the shapes and fractions on the board.
   a. Show a circle. Show one-half of the circle. Have pupils identify and write the fraction for the part you showed.
   b. **Into how many parts is the circle divided? What is the name of one part? of two parts?**
   c. **Finish: One-half means** (one) **part out of** (two).
   d. In a similar way review 1/3, 1/4, 1/5, and 1/8. You will also use the shapes or drawings for part 2 below.
   e. Review the terms *numerator* and *denominator*. If pupils have trouble remembering which is which, tell them that the *denominator* is *down*. *Down* and *denominator* both begin with *d*.
   f. Give practice with numerators and denominators.
      • **Name fractions with denominators of 3, of 5.**
      • **Name fractions with numerators of 1, of 2, 3.**
      • **Name the fraction with a numerator of 2 and a denominator of 5, a denominator of 4 and a numerator of 1, a denominator of 8 and a numerator of 5.**

2. *Like fractions.*
   a. Point to the thirds used in part 1. Count, pointing to one part at a time.
   b. **1/3, 2/3, and 3/3 all have the same denominator. All show fractions for a whole divided into 3 parts. Fractions with the same denominator are called *like fractions*.**
   c. Count the fourths used in part 1. **All the fourths are *like fractions*.** Continue with fifths, sixths, and eighths.

3. *Comparison of fractions.*
   a. **Which is larger: 1/2 or 1/4? 2/5 or 2/3? 3/5 or 3/8?** Note that the denominator shows the number of parts in the whole. When this number increases, the fraction becomes *smaller*.
   b. **Which is larger: 1/4 or 3/4? 3/5 or 2/5? 2/7 or 5/7?** Note that the numerator shows the number of parts named by the fraction. When this number increases, the fraction becomes *larger*.
   c. **Which pairs of fractions are like fractions?**
1/2 1/4	1/4 3/4	2/5 2/3
3/5 3/8	3/5 2/5	2/7 5/7

Extra Review

Review divisions with remainders.
To express a remainder as a fraction, write the remainder as the numerator and the divisor as the denominator.

$3\overline{)13}$ (4 1/3) $5\overline{)28}$ (5 3/5) $4\overline{)39}$ (9 3/4)

$3\overline{)95}$ (31 2/3) $4\overline{)129}$ (32 1/4) $2\overline{)487}$ (243 1/2)

Note: This lesson does not have as much written work as most lessons. The teacher may want to supplement it with extra review work.

Supplementary Drills

Drill 10 ×

Drill 49

B. Write the answers.

6. Which pairs of fractions below are **like fractions**?
   a. $\frac{1}{3}$ $\frac{1}{4}$ b. ($\frac{2}{3}$ $\frac{1}{3}$)   c. ($\frac{3}{5}$ $\frac{4}{5}$)   d. $\frac{2}{3}$ $\frac{2}{4}$

7. Copy the larger fraction in each pair.
   a. ($\frac{3}{4}$) $\frac{1}{4}$ b. $\frac{2}{7}$ ($\frac{5}{7}$)   c. $\frac{1}{6}$ ($\frac{5}{6}$)   d. ($\frac{7}{8}$) $\frac{3}{8}$

Now look at the circles below.

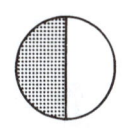

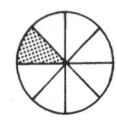

The numerators of these fractions are the same, but the denominators are different. As the denominators become **larger**, the fractions become **smaller**. This happens because the more parts there are, the smaller each part becomes.

> If two fractions have the same numerator but different denominators, the fraction with the **smaller denominator** is larger.
>
> $\frac{1}{3} > \frac{1}{4}$ $\frac{3}{5} > \frac{3}{8}$ $\frac{5}{6} > \frac{5}{8}$

C. Copy the larger fraction in these pairs.

8. a. $\frac{1}{4}$ ($\frac{1}{2}$)   b. ($\frac{3}{4}$) $\frac{3}{5}$ c. $\frac{2}{5}$ ($\frac{2}{3}$)   d. ($\frac{4}{5}$) $\frac{4}{7}$

Review Exercises

D. Follow the directions.

9. Divide. Check by multiplying.

   a. $2\overline{)48}$ 24 $\frac{\times 2}{48}$ b. $6\overline{)35}$ 5 R 5 $\begin{array}{r}5\\ \times 6\\ \hline 30\\ +5\\ \hline 35\end{array}$ c. $4\overline{)246}$ 61 R 2 $\begin{array}{r}61\\ \times 4\\ \hline 244\\ +2\\ \hline 246\end{array}$ d. $3\overline{)695}$ 231 R 2 $\begin{array}{r}231\\ \times 3\\ \hline 693\\ +2\\ \hline 695\end{array}$

10. Divide. Express remainders as fractions.

    $3\overline{)17}$ = $5\frac{2}{3}$ $7\overline{)52}$ = $7\frac{3}{7}$ $5\overline{)408}$ = $81\frac{3}{5}$ $2\overline{)687}$ = $343\frac{1}{2}$

11. Write the value of the money in each set.
    a. 3 one-dollar bills, 1 half-dollar, 2 quarters $4.00
    b. 2 five-dollar bills, 4 dimes, 3 nickels, 5 pennies $10.60
    c. 3 ten-dollar bills, 2 one-dollar bills, 3 quarters, 2 dimes $32.95
    d. 1 twenty-dollar bill, 2 ten-dollar bills, 4 quarters $41.00

12. Write Roman numerals for these Arabic numerals.
    a. 17   b. 28   c. 74   d. 59   e. 45   f. 86
    XVII   XXVIII   LXXIV   LIX   XLV   LXXXVI

62. Fractional Parts in a Whole

Marcia is preparing grapefruit for breakfast. She will cut each grapefruit in half to serve two people. How many halves will she get from 3 grapefruits?

First think: How many halves are in **one** grapefruit?

Two halves are in each whole grapefruit. So **3 × 2 halves**, or **6 halves** are in 3 grapefruits.

> To find how many halves are in a number, multiply by 2.

A. *Write the missing numbers.*

1. a. $1 = \frac{2}{2}$ b. $2 = \frac{4}{2}$ c. $3 = \frac{6}{2}$ d. $4 = \frac{8}{2}$ e. $5 = \frac{10}{2}$

B. *Do these exercises.*

2. Look at the ruler above. How many halves are in 5 inches? **10**

3. Use the ruler and write by halves to $\frac{10}{2}$. Begin: $\frac{1}{2}, \frac{2}{2}, \frac{3}{2}$ . . .
$\frac{1}{2}, \frac{2}{2}, \frac{3}{2}, \frac{4}{2}, \frac{5}{2}, \frac{6}{2}, \frac{7}{2}, \frac{8}{2}, \frac{9}{2}, \frac{10}{2}$

To show whole things and a part, write the number of whole things and then a fraction for the part.

Example: Write **one and one-half** like this: $1\frac{1}{2}$

> A number like $1\frac{1}{2}$ is called a **mixed number.**

4. Write by halves to 5 like this: $\frac{1}{2}$, 1, $1\frac{1}{2}$, 2, $2\frac{1}{2}$ . . .
$\frac{1}{2}, 1, 1\frac{1}{2}, 2, 2\frac{1}{2}, 3, 3\frac{1}{2}, 4, 4\frac{1}{2}, 5$

5. Write these words as mixed numbers.

   a. two and one-fourth $2\frac{1}{4}$ d. three and two-thirds $3\frac{2}{3}$
   b. one and one-third $1\frac{1}{3}$ e. five and one-half $5\frac{1}{2}$
   c. one and three-fourths $1\frac{3}{4}$ f. four and five-eighths $4\frac{5}{8}$

C. *Fill in the blanks. Use the ruler to help you.*

6. a. 1 inch = __2__ half inches   c. 3 inches = __6__ half inches
   b. 2 inches = __4__ half inches   d. 4 inches = __8__ half inches

7. a. $1\frac{1}{2} = \frac{3}{2}$ b. $2\frac{1}{2} = \frac{5}{2}$ c. $3\frac{1}{2} = \frac{7}{2}$ d. $4\frac{1}{2} = \frac{9}{2}$

LESSON 62

Objectives
- To introduce finding the number of fractional parts in a whole.
- To teach how to write mixed numbers.
- To introduce *equivalent fractions.

Preparation
1. Multiplication flash cards
2. A variety of bills and coins
3. Flannel or rubber fraction set (optional)
4. Oranges or grapefruits (optional)
5. Speed Drill 62
6. Chalkboard:

    $\frac{1}{2}$ $\frac{1}{3}$ $\frac{1}{5}$ $\frac{1}{4}$ $\frac{2}{3}$ $\frac{3}{5}$ $\frac{3}{7}$ $\frac{5}{7}$ $\frac{7}{8}$ $\frac{5}{8}$

Oral Drill
1. Drill the multiplication facts.
2. Review dividing a small number by a larger one. **What is 3 ÷ 4? 2 ÷ 3? 1 ÷ 5? 1 ÷ 2? 4 ÷ 7? 1 is what part of 8? 3 is what part of 5?**
3. Read the fractions on the board. Identify the numerators and denominators. Find some like fractions.
4. Compare fractions. **Which fraction in each pair is the larger? How do you know?**
5. Review counting money. Review the denominations of bills.

Speed Drill
Give Speed Drill 62 (addition facts).

T–137   Chapter 7   More Fractions and Measures

Teaching Guide

1. *Fractional parts in a whole.*
   a. **How many halves are in one whole?** Write $\frac{2}{2}$. **How many thirds are in one whole?** Write $\frac{3}{3}$. Continue with a few more numbers.
   b. **If the numerator and the denominator are the same, the fraction equals one whole. Which of these fractions equal one whole?**

3/4	5/5	7/6	8/8
4/4	7/7	3/5	6/6

   c. Read the little story at the beginning of the pupil's lesson. **If two halves are in *one* grapefruit, how many halves are in *two* whole grapefruits? in three wholes? How can we find how many halves are in any number of whole grapefruits?** (Multiply by 2.)
   d. **How many thirds are in one whole thing? in two whole things? in three wholes? How can we find how many thirds are in any number of wholes?** (Multiply by 3.)

2. *Mixed numbers.*
   a. Show a whole circle and a half. **How many circles do you see?** (one and one-half) **Who knows how to write "one and one-half" with numbers?** Write $1\frac{1}{2}$.
   b. Write $2\frac{1}{4}$. Call on someone to read the number. **The 2 means 2 whole things, and the 1/4 means one-fourth more.** Call on pupils to write the following expressions on the board.

      1 1/3   2 3/4   3 2/5

      Numbers that show a whole number and a fraction are called *mixed numbers*.
   c. **How many halves are in 1 1/2? Could we write that fraction as 3/2? Is 3/2 equal to 1 1/2?** (yes)
   d. Practice counting halves two ways. First: 1/2, 2/2, 3/2, 4/2, 5/2 . . . , then: 1/2, 1, 1 1/2, 2, 2 1/2 . . .
   e. Show a whole circle and a third. **How many thirds are in 1 1/3? Is 4/3 equal to 1 1/3?** Count by thirds.

   Note: Do not give pupils a rule for changing mixed numbers to improper fractions. Simply introduce the idea, and have them use pictures to answer questions like "How many halves are in 1 1/2?"

3. *Equivalent fractions.*
   a. Draw a square and divide it into two equal parts. **What is each part called?**
   b. Draw a similar square beside the first square, and divide it into 4 equal parts. **What is each part called? What are two parts called?** (2/4) **Are these two parts the same size as half of the first square?** (yes) **Is 1/2 equal to 2/4?** (yes) **1/2 and 2/4 are the same size; they are called *equivalent* (equal) fractions.**
   c. Draw a third square and divide it into eighths. Have pupils count by eighths as you point to the parts. **What other fraction is equivalent to 2/8?** (1/4) **to 4/8?** (1/2 or 2/4) **to 6/8?** (3/4)
   d. Show more equivalent fractions with thirds and sixths.

   Note: As in Lesson 61, this lesson does not have as much written work as most lessons. Supplement it if necessary.

Supplementary Drill

Drill 84

Lesson 62   137

Equivalent Fractions

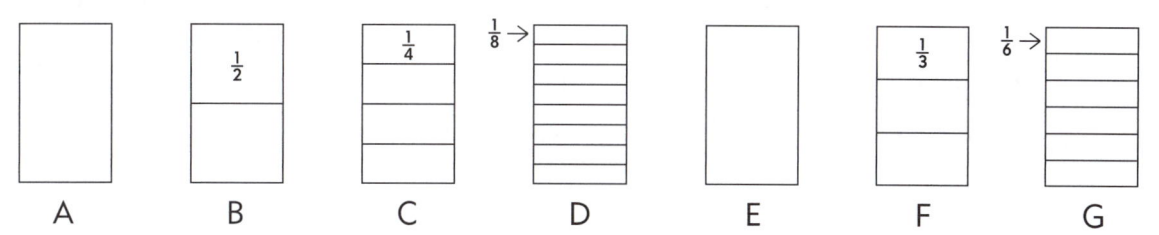

A B ($\frac{1}{2}$) C ($\frac{1}{4}$) D ($\frac{1}{8}$) E F ($\frac{1}{3}$) G ($\frac{1}{6}$)

D. *Write the missing numbers.*

8. Rectangles A, B, C, and D show that 1 whole equals __2__ halves, __4__ fourths, or __8__ eighths.

9. Rectangles E, F, and G show that 1 whole equals __3__ thirds or __6__ sixths.

10. Rectangles B and C show that 1 half is the same as __2__ fourths.

11. Rectangles C and D show that 1 fourth is the same as __2__ eighths. They also show that 2 fourths are equal to __4__ eighths.

> Fractions of equal size are called **equivalent fractions.**

E. *Write* yes *or* no *to tell if these are equivalent fractions. Use the rectangles above to help you.*

12. a. $\frac{1}{3}$ $\frac{2}{6}$ yes   b. $\frac{1}{2}$ $\frac{4}{8}$ yes   c. $\frac{1}{2}$ $\frac{2}{3}$ no   d. $\frac{3}{4}$ $\frac{5}{8}$ no

13. a. $\frac{1}{2}$ $\frac{2}{4}$ yes   b. $\frac{2}{3}$ $\frac{4}{6}$ yes   c. $\frac{1}{4}$ $\frac{3}{8}$ no   d. $\frac{1}{4}$ $\frac{2}{8}$ yes

Review Exercises

F. *Follow the directions.*

14. Write a fraction with a numerator of 2 and a denominator of 5.

15. Subtract, and check by adding.

a. $14.00 − 6.75 = $7.25; $7.25 + 6.75 = $14.00
b. $25.00 − 12.59 = $12.41; $12.41 + 12.59 = $25.00
c. $30.20 − 14.87 = $15.33; $15.33 + 14.87 = $30.20
d. $50.00 − 23.15 = $26.85; $26.85 + 23.15 = $50.00
e. $60.50 − 42.98 = $17.52; $17.52 + 42.98 = $60.50

16. Divide, and check by multiplying.

a. 4)125 = 31 R 1; 31 × 4 = 124, + 1 = 125
b. 3)64 = 21 R 1; 21 × 3 = 63, + 1 = 64
c. 2)805 = 402 R 1; 402 × 2 = 804, + 1 = 805
d. 5)455 = 91; 91 × 5 = 455
e. 8)249 = 31 R 1; 31 × 8 = 248, + 1 = 249

138 Chapter 7 More Fractions and Measures

63. Finding Equivalent Fractions by Multiplying

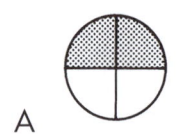

A B C D

Look at the circles above. What part of circle A is shaded? You could answer by saying that $\frac{1}{2}$ or $\frac{2}{4}$ is shaded. Remember, $\frac{1}{2}$ and $\frac{2}{4}$ are equivalent fractions.

The rule below can be used to find other fractions equal to $\frac{1}{2}$.

> To find an equivalent fraction, multiply the numerator and the denominator by the same number.
>
> $\frac{1 \times 2}{2 \times 2} = \frac{2}{4}$ $\frac{1 \times 3}{2 \times 3} = \frac{3}{6}$ $\frac{1}{2}, \frac{2}{4}$, and $\frac{3}{6}$ are equivalent fractions.

A. *Do these exercises.*

1. Write **yes** or **no** to tell whether each pair of fractions is equivalent. Use the circles in the lesson to help you.

   a. $\frac{1}{2}$ $\frac{4}{8}$ yes   b. $\frac{2}{4}$ $\frac{4}{8}$ yes   c. $\frac{1}{3}$ $\frac{2}{6}$ yes   d. $\frac{2}{3}$ $\frac{5}{6}$ no

2. Count by fourths. Copy, and fill in the missing numbers. Use mixed numbers after you reach 1.

   $\frac{1}{4}, \frac{2}{4}, \frac{3}{4}, 1, 1\frac{1}{4}, 1\frac{2}{4}, 1\frac{3}{4}, 2, 2\frac{1}{4}, 2\frac{2}{4}, 2\frac{3}{4}, 3$

3. Count by eighths. Copy, and fill in the missing numbers as you did for number 2.

   $\frac{1}{8}, \frac{2}{8}, \frac{3}{8}, \frac{4}{8}, \frac{5}{8}, \frac{6}{8}, \frac{7}{8}, 1, 1\frac{1}{8}, 1\frac{2}{8}, 1\frac{3}{8}, 1\frac{4}{8}, 1\frac{5}{8}, 1\frac{6}{8}, 1\frac{7}{8}, 2$

4. Write five fractions that are equivalent to $\frac{1}{3}$. $\frac{2}{6}$ $\frac{3}{9}$ $\frac{4}{12}$ $\frac{5}{15}$ $\frac{6}{18}$

B. *Copy these fractions, and fill in the missing parts to make equivalent fractions. For the first one, think: 1 times what number is 3? The answer is 3. So for the denominator, 2 × 3 = ____ .*

5. a. $\frac{1}{2} = \frac{3}{?}$ 6   b. $\frac{1}{2} = \frac{4}{?}$ 8   c. $\frac{1}{4} = \frac{2}{?}$ 8   d. $\frac{2}{3} = \frac{4}{?}$ 6

6. a. $\frac{1}{4} = \frac{?}{16}$ 4   b. $\frac{3}{4} = \frac{?}{8}$ 6   c. $\frac{1}{3} = \frac{?}{9}$ 3   d. $\frac{2}{3} = \frac{?}{12}$ 8

Lesson 62 states: To find how many halves are in a number, multiply by 2. A similar rule can be made about any part.

> To find how many of any part are in a whole number, multiply by the number of parts in one whole thing. For thirds, multiply by 3. For fourths, multiply by 4, and so on.

LESSON 63

Objectives
- To give more practice with fractional concepts introduced before.
- To teach *finding equivalent fractions by multiplying.

Preparation
1. Multiplication flash cards
2. A ruler for each child
3. Fraction visual aid such as flannel-graph or rubber fraction pieces (optional)
4. A variety of bills and coins
5. Chalkboard:
   a. $\frac{1}{3}$ $\frac{1}{5}$ $\frac{1}{2}$ $\frac{1}{8}$ $\frac{1}{4}$
   b. $\frac{2}{5}$ $\frac{4}{5}$ $\frac{1}{5}$ $\frac{5}{5}$ $\frac{3}{5}$

Oral Drill
1. Review multiplication facts.
2. Give mixed mental drill.
   $5 + 4 \times 7 + 1 \div 8 - 2$ (6)
   $7 \times 6 + 3 \div 5 \div 3 - 3$ (0)

   $10 + 6$ $20 + 9$ 10×8 10×74
   100×43 30×7 50×4
   80×7 $11 - 6$ $8 \times 7 + 5$ (61)
3. Count by halves to 6 (1/2, 1, 1 1/2, 2 . . .). Have children find whole and half inches on their rulers.
4. Give practice with counting money.
5. Review rules for changing units of measure (Lesson 45).

Chapter 7 More Fractions and Measures

Teaching Guide

1. *Practice with fractional concepts.*
   a. Review fraction terms: *numerator, denominator, like fractions*. **Which fractions on the board are like fractions, *a* or *b*?**
   b. Review comparing fractions. Arrange each set of fractions on the board in order of size, beginning with the smallest.
   c. **Which fraction on the board is the same as one whole? How do you know?**
   d. Dictate mixed numbers for pupils to write.
      1 1/2   2 3/4   5 2/3
   e. Count by eighths from 1/8 to 8/8.
   f. Count by thirds from 1/3 to 3, using whole and mixed numbers.
   g. **Fractions that are the same size are** (equivalent) **fractions.**
   h. *Fractional parts in a whole.*
      (1) **How many halves are in a whole? how many thirds? how many fifths? how many sevenths?**
      (2) **How many halves are two whole things? How could you find the number of halves in any number of whole things?** (Multiply by 2.)
      (3) **How can we find the number of fourths in two whole things?** (Multiply 2 by 4.)
      (4) **To find how many of a certain part are in a number of whole things, multiply the number of whole things by the number of parts in *one* whole.**
      (5) **How many thirds are in 3 whole pies? How many fourths are in 5 whole things?**
2. *Finding equivalent fractions by multiplying.*

   Note: Be sure to allow enough class time for this part.

   a. Draw two circles. Divide one circle into halves and the other into fourths. Have pupils tell what number of fourths is equivalent to 1/2.
   b. Draw another circle and divide it into sixths. **How many sixths are equal to 1/2?**
   c. Show that if the numerator and denominator of 1/2 are both multiplied by 2, the result is 2/4, an equivalent fraction. If the numerator and the denominator of 1/2 are both multiplied by 3, the result is 3/6, another equivalent fraction.
   d. **What new fraction do we get if we multiply the numerator and the denominator of 1/2 by 4? Write $\frac{1}{2} = \frac{?}{?}$.**
   e. Give the rule: **To change a fraction to an equivalent fraction, multiply both the numerator and the denominator by the same number.** Illustrate with 1/3. Multiply the numerator and the denominator by 2, then by 3, 4, and so on, to make a string of equivalent fractions.

Supplementary Drill

Drill 27 ÷

C. Write the answers.

7. One whole equals __2__ halves, __3__ thirds, or __4__ fourths.
8. How many fourths are in 1 whole pie? __4__ in 2 pies? __8__ in 3 pies? __12__
9. If each pie is cut into sixths, how many sixths are in 3 pies? __18__
10. If each pie is cut into eighths, how many pieces are in 3 pies? __24__

Review Exercises

D. Follow the directions.

11. Write numerals for these number words.
    a. one and two-thirds $1\frac{2}{3}$ c. three and one-fifth $3\frac{1}{5}$
    b. five and three-fourths $5\frac{3}{4}$ d. four and five-eighths $4\frac{5}{8}$

12. Copy and add.

490	3,728	6,041	4,837	9,432
915	402	7,486	5,519	3,851
834	5,741	385	1,073	4,764
+ 374	+ 1,255	+ 3,726	+ 2,836	+ 1,504
2,613	11,126	17,638	14,265	19,551

E. Write add, subtract, multiply, or divide. Then solve the problems.

13. Three boys are sharing 4 oranges. How many oranges can each boy have? (Your answer should have a fraction.)   divide $1\frac{1}{3}$ oranges

14. Jeffrey had 72 marbles. He lost 6. How many does he have left?   subtract   66 marbles

15. Elsie had 48 buttons. She separated them into groups of 8. How many groups did she have?   divide   6 groups

16. Carl memorized three Bible verses one week. Later he learned 6 times as many. How many verses did he learn later?   multiply   18 verses

17. The Book of Matthew has 28 chapters. The Book of Mark has 16 chapters. Matthew has how many more chapters than Mark?   subtract   12 chapters

18. At the Riverside Church, 15 children are in the preschool Sunday school class, 12 are in the primary class, and 14 are in the junior class. How many children are in these three classes?   add   41 children

140   Chapter 7   More Fractions and Measures

64. Fractions on a Ruler

Learn the facts in this box.

> 1. A number without a fraction is a **whole number.** The whole numbers are 0, 1, 2, 3, and so on.
> 2. A whole number and a fraction together form a **mixed number.** Mixed numbers include $1\frac{1}{2}$ and $2\frac{1}{4}$.
> 3. When you read or write measurements of one inch or greater, use whole numbers or mixed numbers. Use 1 instead of $\frac{2}{2}$.

A. *Do these exercises.*

1. Count by half inches on this ruler. Write the numbers: $\frac{1}{2}$, 1, $1\frac{1}{2}$ . . .

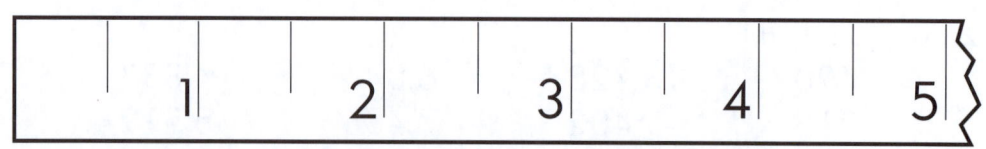

   $\frac{1}{2}$, 1, $1\frac{1}{2}$, 2, $2\frac{1}{2}$, 3, $3\frac{1}{2}$, 4, $4\frac{1}{2}$, 5

2. Look at the ruler above to measure each line. Write the lengths.

   a. ———————————————— $2\frac{1}{2}$ inches

   b. ———————————————————— 4 inches

   c. ———————— $1\frac{1}{2}$ inches

   d. ——————————————————————— $4\frac{1}{2}$ inches

B. *This ruler is divided into quarter inches. (A quarter inch is a fourth inch.) Point to each quarter inch and say its name. Notice that $\frac{2}{4}$ is read $\frac{1}{2}$.*

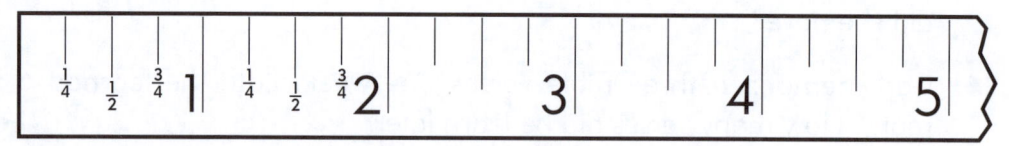

3. Count by fourths from $\frac{1}{4}$ to 5. Write the numbers.

   $\frac{1}{4}$, $\frac{1}{2}$, $\frac{3}{4}$, 1, $1\frac{1}{4}$, $1\frac{1}{2}$, $1\frac{3}{4}$, 2, $2\frac{1}{4}$, $2\frac{1}{2}$, $2\frac{3}{4}$, 3, $3\frac{1}{4}$, $3\frac{1}{2}$, $3\frac{3}{4}$, 4, $4\frac{1}{4}$, $4\frac{1}{2}$, $4\frac{3}{4}$, 5

4. Use your own ruler to measure these lines. Write the lengths.

   a. ——————————————— $3\frac{1}{4}$ inches

   b. ——————————————————— $4\frac{1}{2}$ inches

   c. ———————————— $2\frac{3}{4}$ inches

   d. ———— $1\frac{1}{4}$ inches

   e. ———————————————————— $4\frac{3}{4}$ inches

LESSON 64

Objectives

- To review finding equivalent fractions by multiplying.
- To introduce reading *quarter inches on a ruler.
- To give practice with using a ruler to measure.

Preparation

1. Division flash cards
2. A ruler for each child, preferably one with only quarter-inch markings
3. Speed Drill 64
4. Chalkboard:

   a. 205,084

   b. Large drawing of a ruler
   Divide the ruler into "quarter inches." Label it as in the pupil's book. *(This drawing will also be used in Lesson 65.)*

Oral Drill

1. Drill division facts.
2. Review < and >.
3. Review place value and large numbers. Discuss the number *(a)* on the board.
4. Review the terms *numerator, denominator, like fractions,* and *equivalent fractions.*
5. Review comparing fractions with equal numerators or denominators. Write pairs of fractions on the board, and have children write < or > between them.
6. Count by halves to 10: 1/2, 1, 1 1/2, 2, 2 1/2 . . .
7. Review units of measure, especially linear units.
   1 ft. = (12) in.
   1 yd. = (36) in.
   1 yd. = (3) ft.

Speed Drill

Give Speed Drill 64 (column addition practice).

Chapter 7 More Fractions and Measures

Teaching Guide

1. *Multiplying to find equivalent fractions.*
    a. Write 1/4 on the board. Ask: **What other fractions are equivalent to 1/4?** If pupils are slow in responding, prompt them to multiply the numerator and the denominator by the same number. Write several responses on the board.
    b. Write several pairs of fractions, and have pupils find the missing numbers.
    $\frac{1}{2} = \frac{3}{?}$ (6) $\frac{3}{4} = \frac{9}{?}$ (12)
    $\frac{2}{5} = \frac{?}{10}$ (4) $\frac{1}{4} = \frac{?}{16}$ (4)

2. *Reading quarter inches on a ruler.*
    a. Point to the drawing of a ruler (b) on the board. **This ruler is bigger than a real ruler, but it can help us to read a real ruler. The numbers 1, 2, 3, and so on, stand for inches. Each inch is divided into 4 parts, so each part is called a** (fourth or quarter).
    b. **Two parts is 2 fourths, but 2/4 is the same as 1/2. We say 1/2 instead of 2/4.**
    c. Point to each quarter inch on the ruler, and have the class read the quarter inches in unison. Say: 1/4, 1/2, 3/4, 1, 1 1/4, 1 1/2 . . .
    d. Point randomly to marks on the ruler. Have pupils read those points.
    e. Have the pupils turn to Lesson 64 in their books and lay their own rulers over the second ruler pictured in the book. Count by fourths in unison as each pupil points to the correct spot on his own ruler.
    f. Give the measurements below, and have pupils find those points on their rulers. If the rulers have eighth- and sixteenth-inch markings as well as fourths, show pupils that the *longer* marks stand for halves and fourths.
    1 1/2   2 1/4   4 1/2
    3 3/4   3/4   5 1/4

3. *Measuring with a ruler.*
    a. Instruct pupils to measure the length of their finger, the width of their book, the distance across their hand.

Supplementary Drill

Drill 11 ×

Lesson 64

Review Exercises

C. Write the answers.

5. Copy these fraction pairs. Write < or > to show which is larger.
   a. $\frac{1}{3} < \frac{1}{2}$ b. $\frac{2}{3} > \frac{2}{5}$ c. $\frac{3}{8} < \frac{5}{8}$ d. $\frac{1}{4} > \frac{1}{6}$

6. Write five other fractions that are equal to $\frac{1}{4}$. Multiply both the numerator and the denominator by the same number. (sample answers)

   Think: $\frac{1 \times 2 = ?}{4 \times 2 = ?}$ $\frac{1 \times 3 = ?}{4 \times 3 = ?}$ $\frac{2}{8}$ $\frac{3}{12}$ $\frac{4}{16}$ $\frac{5}{20}$ $\frac{6}{24}$

D. Copy the fractions below. Multiply, and fill in the missing parts to make equivalent fractions.

7. a. $\frac{1}{3} = \frac{3}{?}$ 9   b. $\frac{1}{2} = \frac{4}{?}$ 8   c. $\frac{2}{3} = \frac{4}{?}$ 6   d. $\frac{3}{4} = \frac{6}{?}$ 8

8. a. $\frac{1}{2} = \frac{?}{6}$ 3   b. $\frac{1}{4} = \frac{?}{12}$ 3   c. $\frac{3}{5} = \frac{?}{10}$ 6   d. $\frac{2}{3} = \frac{?}{12}$ 8

9. a. $\frac{1}{2} = \frac{?}{16}$ 8   b. $\frac{1}{3} = \frac{4}{?}$ 12   c. $\frac{1}{2} = \frac{5}{?}$ 10   d. $\frac{3}{4} = \frac{?}{16}$ 12

E. Solve these problems.

10. Copy and divide. Check by multiplying.

    a. 4)129   32 R 1   32 × 4 = 128 + 1 = 129
    b. 5)208   41 R 3   41 × 5 = 205 + 3 = 208
    c. 2)684   342   342 × 2 = 684

11. Write the answers quickly.

8×4	9×8	12×6	8×7	12×7	9×9	4×7	7×9	8×8
32	72	72	56	84	81	28	63	64

12. Copy and multiply.

609 × 6	658 × 7	$4.50 × 9	$8.37 × 5	$6.08 × 8
3,654	4,606	$40.50	$41.85	$48.64

13. If Allen spends $12.89, what is his change from $20.00? $7.11

14. If 2 boys share 3 sandwiches, how many will each boy get? $1\frac{1}{2}$ sandwiches

15. If 3 boys share 2 sandwiches, how much will each boy get? $\frac{2}{3}$ sandwich

    (Be careful! The answers to numbers 14 and 15 both have fractions, but they are not the same. For each problem, think: Will each boy get **more** or **less** than a whole sandwich?

142 Chapter 7 More Fractions and Measures

65. Measuring With Eighths on a Ruler

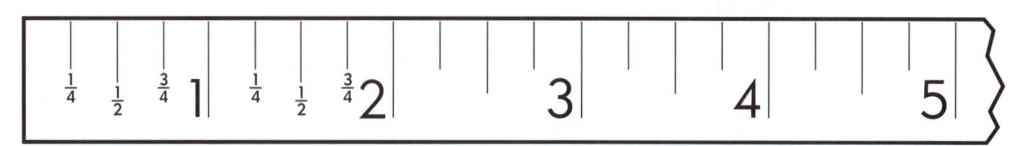

The ruler above is divided into quarter inches. Point to each quarter inch and count: $\frac{1}{4}, \frac{1}{2}, \frac{3}{4}, 1, 1\frac{1}{4} \ldots$

A. Do these exercises.

1. Use the ruler above or your own ruler to measure these lines. Write the measurements. (Include **inches** in your answer.)

    a. ———————————————— $3\frac{1}{4}$ inches

    b. ————————————————————————— 5 inches

    c. ———————— $1\frac{3}{4}$ inches

    d. —————————————————————— $4\frac{1}{2}$ inches

On the ruler below, inches are divided into **eighths**. Notice that **two eighths** equals **one quarter** inch. **Four eighths** equals **one half**. **Six eighths** equals **three quarters**.

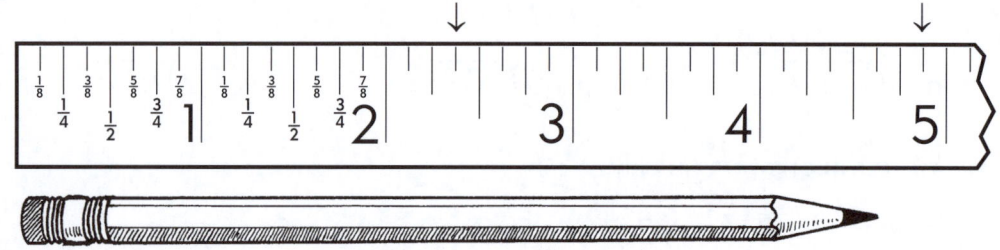

2. To what measurement does the first arrow point? $2\frac{3}{8}$ inches

3. To what measurement does the second arrow point? $4\frac{7}{8}$ inches

4. How long is the pencil below the ruler? $4\frac{5}{8}$ inches

5. Use your own ruler to measure these lines. Write the lengths.

    a. ———————————————————— $4\frac{1}{8}$ inches

    b. ——————— $1\frac{7}{8}$ inches

    c. ————————————————— $3\frac{3}{4}$ inches

    d. ————————— $2\frac{5}{8}$ inches

6. Draw lines of the following lengths.

    a. $1\frac{1}{4}$ inches   b. $3\frac{5}{8}$ inches   c. $2\frac{7}{8}$ inches

    a. ————
    b. ————————————
    c. ——————————

LESSON 65

Objective

- To review finding equivalent fractions by multiplying.
- To introduce *eighth inches on a ruler.

Preparation

1. Multiplication flash cards
2. A ruler with eighth-inch markings for each child
3. Chalkboard:

   a. 390,471

   b. Large drawing of a ruler, showing "quarter inches" (Eighth-inch markings will be added during class.)

Oral Drill

1. Drill the multiplication facts.
2. Count by halves to 10; by fourths to 5.
3. Review the terms *numerator, denominator, like fractions,* and *equivalent fractions.*
4. Have a pupil read the number *(a)* on the board. **What number is 10,000 less than this number? 100 more? 100,000 more? 1,000 more? 10 less?**
5. Review the following measures.
   a. second, minute, hour, day, week, month, year
   b. number of days in each month
   c. cup, pint, quart, gallon

Chapter 7   More Fractions and Measures

Teaching Guide

1. *Finding equivalent fractions by multiplying.*
   a. **Let's think of fractions equal to 1/2, to 1/3, to 3/4. Multiply to find equivalent fractions.**
   b. Write pairs of fractions on the board, and have pupils find the missing numbers by multiplying. Let pupils tell how they think to find the missing numbers.

2. *Eighth inches on a ruler.*
   a. Review quarter-inch markings on a ruler. Indicate points on the chalkboard drawing, and have pupils read those points.
   b. Draw a long, narrow rectangle horizontally across the board. Draw vertical lines to divide it into fourths. **Into how many parts is this rectangle divided? What is each part called?** Write 1/4, 1/2, 3/4, 1 below the dividing lines.
   c. With dotted lines divide each fourth in half. **How many parts is the rectangle divided into now? What is each part called?**
   d. Count by eighths, beginning at the left end. Write 1/8 below the first dotted line. **Two-eighths is already marked. What fraction is equivalent to two-eighths?** (1/4) **We will not change 1/4.** Continue until the fractions 1/8, 1/4, 3/8, 1/2, 5/8, 3/4, 7/8 are written below the rectangle.
   e. Point to the large ruler *(b)*. Draw eighth-inch markings between the marks already there. Make the marks shorter as on a real ruler. **Now each "inch" of this ruler is divided into eight parts like the rectangle.** Point to the first mark. **What part of an inch is this?** Write 1/8. Continue at least to the two-inch mark. **If the number of eighths is equal to a quarter or a half, we say the quarter or half. The fractions 1/4, 1/2, and 3/4 are simpler than 2/8, 4/8, and 6/8.**
   f. Count by eighths from 1/8 to 3, using quarters and halves where possible.

Supplementary Drills

Drill 1 +

Drill 85

Review Exercises

B. *Follow the directions.*

7. Write fractions that express these values.
   a. 2 parts out of 3 $\frac{2}{3}$
   b. 5 parts out of 8 $\frac{5}{8}$
   c. 1 part out of 4 $\frac{1}{4}$

8. Write as mixed numbers.
   a. two and three-fourths $2\frac{3}{4}$
   b. one and one-sixth $1\frac{1}{6}$
   c. five and seven-eighths $5\frac{7}{8}$
   d. eleven and two-thirds $11\frac{2}{3}$

9. Write a fraction with a denominator of 6 and a numerator of 2. $\frac{2}{6}$

10. Are $\frac{3}{4}$ and $\frac{3}{5}$ like fractions? **no** Are $\frac{3}{5}$ and $\frac{4}{5}$ like fractions? **yes**

11. Copy the larger fraction in each pair.
    a. $(\frac{1}{3})$ $\frac{1}{4}$
    b. $\frac{3}{8}$ $(\frac{5}{8})$
    c. $\frac{1}{8}$ $(\frac{1}{4})$
    d. $(\frac{4}{5})$ $\frac{1}{5}$

12. How many halves are in 3 whole grapefruits? **6**

13. How many fourths are in 2 whole pies? **8**

14. Are these fractions equivalent? Write **yes** or **no**.
    a. $\frac{2}{3}$ $\frac{4}{6}$ **yes**
    b. $\frac{1}{2}$ $\frac{5}{10}$ **yes**
    c. $\frac{1}{4}$ $\frac{3}{8}$ **no**
    d. $\frac{3}{4}$ $\frac{9}{12}$ **yes**

C. *Use multiplication to fill in the missing numbers.*

15. a. $\frac{1}{4} = \frac{2}{?}$ **8**
    b. $\frac{3}{4} = \frac{?}{8}$ **6**
    c. $\frac{2}{3} = \frac{?}{9}$ **6**
    d. $\frac{1}{3} = \frac{4}{?}$ **12**

16. a. $\frac{1}{3} = \frac{?}{9}$ **3**
    b. $\frac{1}{8} = \frac{2}{?}$ **16**
    c. $\frac{1}{2} = \frac{?}{12}$ **6**
    d. $\frac{2}{5} = \frac{4}{?}$ **10**

D. *Write the answers.*

17. Which of these numbers divide evenly by 2?
    (46) 85 93 (102) (170) 629 (418) 747

18. Which of these numbers divide evenly by 5?
    (25) (80) 36 (100) (265) 954 207 428

19. Which of these numbers divide evenly by 4?
    14 (28) 42 (48) (32) 30 (40) (24)

20. Copy and add.

8,503	3,219	3,047	596	1,865	3,274
387	4,856	1,845	3,652	8,104	595
3,926	1,648	5,366	7,148	497	6,327
+ 2,844	+ 5,340	+ 1,824	+ 5,821	+ 6,653	+ 8,746
15,660	15,063	12,082	17,217	17,119	18,942

66. Finding Equivalent Fractions by Dividing

You have learned that equivalent fractions can be found by multiplying both the numerator and the denominator of a fraction by the same number. Another way to find equivalent fractions is to **divide** both the numerator and the denominator by the same number.

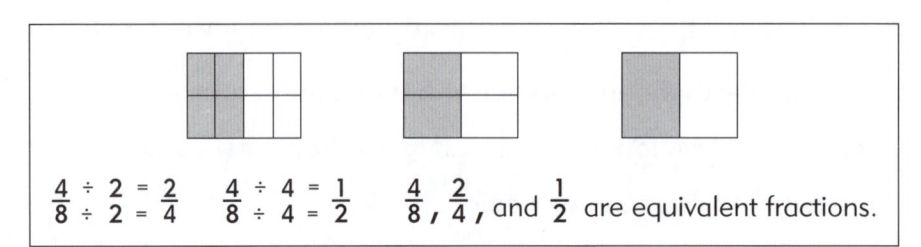

$$\frac{4 \div 2}{8 \div 2} = \frac{2}{4} \qquad \frac{4 \div 4}{8 \div 4} = \frac{1}{2}$$

$\frac{4}{8}, \frac{2}{4},$ and $\frac{1}{2}$ are equivalent fractions.

A. *Copy the fractions below. Divide to find the missing parts and make equivalent fractions.*

1. a. $\frac{3}{6} = \frac{1}{2}$ b. $\frac{2}{6} = \frac{1}{3}$ c. $\frac{5}{10} = \frac{1}{2}$ d. $\frac{2}{8} = \frac{1}{4}$
2. a. $\frac{4}{10} = \frac{2}{5}$ b. $\frac{6}{9} = \frac{2}{3}$ c. $\frac{4}{16} = \frac{1}{4}$ d. $\frac{6}{12} = \frac{2}{4}$
3. a. $\frac{4}{6} = \frac{2}{3}$ b. $\frac{3}{12} = \frac{1}{4}$ c. $\frac{8}{16} = \frac{2}{4}$ d. $\frac{4}{8} = \frac{2}{4}$

> Dividing a numerator and denominator by the same number is called **reducing the fraction**. It is called reducing because the new fraction has fewer parts than the first fraction.

B. *Reduce these fractions. Try to use the largest number that will divide both the numerator and denominator evenly.*

4. a. $\frac{4}{6}$ $\frac{2}{3}$ b. $\frac{5}{15}$ $\frac{1}{3}$ c. $\frac{2}{12}$ $\frac{1}{6}$ d. $\frac{6}{16}$ $\frac{3}{8}$ e. $\frac{3}{6}$ $\frac{1}{2}$ f. $\frac{8}{10}$ $\frac{4}{5}$ g. $\frac{6}{8}$ $\frac{3}{4}$ h. $\frac{8}{16}$ $\frac{1}{2}$

Review Exercises

C. *Follow the directions.*

5. Find the missing numbers by multiplying.
   a. $\frac{1}{5} = \frac{2}{10}$ b. $\frac{3}{8} = \frac{6}{16}$ c. $\frac{2}{5} = \frac{6}{15}$ d. $\frac{3}{4} = \frac{9}{12}$

6. Write five fractions that are equivalent to $\frac{1}{4}$. $\frac{2}{8}$ $\frac{3}{12}$ $\frac{4}{16}$ $\frac{5}{20}$ $\frac{6}{24}$

7. Write a fraction with a denominator of 7. (sample answer) $\frac{1}{7}$

LESSON 66

Objectives

- To introduce *finding equivalent fractions by dividing.
- To introduce *the reducing of fractions.

Preparation

1. Division flash cards
2. A ruler for each child, preferably with only 1/8" markings
3. Speed Drill 66

Oral Drill

1. Drill the division facts.
2. Give mixed mental drill.
   $6 + 8 - 5 \div 3$ (3) $4 \times 5 \div 2 - 8$ (2)
   $7 + 4 \times 4 - 4$ (40) $6 \div 3 + 9 + 6$ (17)
   $7 \times 8 - 2 \div 6$ (9) $3 + 7 - 5 \times 7$ (35)
   $6 \times 5 - 2 \div 4 \times 7$ (49)
   $16 \div 2 \times 6 \div 4 \div 3$ (4)
3. a. Count by eighths to 3: 1/8, 1/4, 3/8 . . . Allow pupils to look at their rulers as they count.
   b. Have pupils find the following points on their rulers and tell what measure is 1/8 inch after each.
   1/2"   1/8"   1/4"   5/8"
   3/8"   3/4"   7/8"
4. Briefly review the units of time and liquid measure.
5. Review the rules for changing units of measure:
   To change from a larger unit to a smaller unit, multiply.
   To change from a smaller unit to a larger unit, divide.
6. Review the rhyme: Thirty days have September . . .

Speed Drill

Give Speed Drill 66 (Roman numerals).

T–145 Chapter 7 More Fractions and Measures

Teaching Guide

1. *Finding equivalent fractions by dividing.*
   a. Write 1/2 and 2/4 on the board. **Are these fractions equivalent? If 1/2 is equal to 2/4, is 2/4 also equal to 1/2?**
   b. Write: $\frac{2}{4} = \frac{1}{?}$. **How can we find the missing number?** Explain that the numerator 2 divided by 2 is 1, so the denominator 4 must also be divided by 2: $4 \div 2 = 2$.
   c. **This is the second way to find equivalent fractions: Divide both the numerator and the denominator by the same number.**
   d. Write the following pairs of fractions on the board. These involve division to find the missing part—though in a way, the pupils can still think of them as multiplications.

   Look at the first pair. 2 divided by what number is 1? (2) Divide 6 by 2 to find the missing number; $6 \div 2 = 3$. Look at the second pair. . . .

   $\frac{2}{6} = \frac{1}{?}$ (3) $\frac{5}{10} = \frac{1}{?}$ (2) $\frac{3}{9} = \frac{1}{?}$ (3)

   $\frac{8}{16} = \frac{?}{4}$ (2) $\frac{10}{15} = \frac{?}{3}$ (2) $\frac{9}{12} = \frac{?}{4}$ (3)

   With the background of lessons 62–65, pupils will probably not find this lesson as difficult as those.

2. *Reducing fractions.*
   a. **Did you notice that when we divide to find an equivalent fraction, the number of parts in the new fraction is smaller than in the old one? It is easier to work with a smaller number of parts, so fraction answers are usually divided in this way. This process is called** *reducing the fraction.*
   b. **If we use the largest divisor possible to divide both the numerator and the denominator, the fraction is** *reduced to lowest terms.* **That means there is no equivalent fraction with smaller numbers.**
   c. Write the following fractions on the board and have pupils reduce them. This is essentially the same exercise as part 1 above, except that pupils must decide what number to use in dividing the numerator *and* the denominator.

   $\frac{6}{9}$ $(\frac{2}{3})$ $\frac{2}{10}$ $(\frac{1}{5})$ $\frac{4}{12}$ $(\frac{1}{3})$ $\frac{10}{16}$ $(\frac{5}{8})$

   $\frac{9}{15}$ $(\frac{3}{5})$ $\frac{10}{12}$ $(\frac{5}{6})$ $\frac{12}{16}$ $(\frac{3}{4})$ $\frac{6}{15}$ $(\frac{2}{5})$

Note: In this lesson the emphasis is on "reducing the fraction," not on "lowest terms." Encourage pupils to divide by the largest numbers possible, but do not expect too much at this point.

Supplementary Drill

Drill 14 ×

8. Write the measurement that each arrow points to on ruler A. Label your answers in **inches**. 1¼ in.   2½ in. 3 in.   3¾ in. 4¼ in.
   a. b. c. d. e.

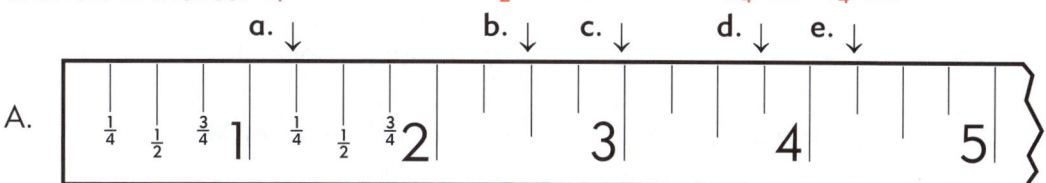

A. [ruler showing markings ¼, ½, ¾, 1, ¼, ½, ¾, 2, 3, 4, 5]

9. Write the measurement that each arrow points to on ruler B. Label your answers in **inches**. 1½ in.   2⅝ in. 3⅛ in.   4⅞ in.
   a. ⅝ in. b. c. d. e.

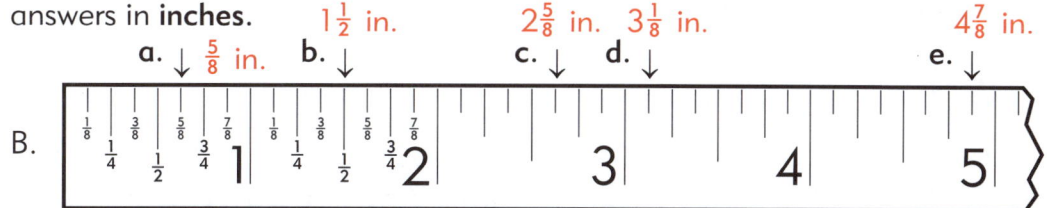

B. [ruler showing eighth-inch markings up to 5]

D. Write the answers. If you do not remember the rules for changing units, look back at Lesson 45.

10. To change from a small unit to a larger one, you <u>divide</u>.

11. To change from a large unit to a smaller one, you <u>multiply</u>.

12. Name the larger unit in each pair.
    a. cup, <u>pint</u>   b. <u>foot</u>, inch   c. month, <u>year</u>   d. pint, <u>quart</u>

13. Write whether you would **multiply** or **divide** to make each change.
    a. feet to inches   b. pints to quarts   c. hours to days
       multiply   divide   divide

E. Write the key numbers that fit in the blanks.

14. 1 min. = <u>60</u> sec.   1 day = <u>24</u> hr.   1 yr. = <u>12</u> mo.
15. 1 qt. = <u>2</u> pt.   1 qt. = <u>4</u> cups   1 gal. = <u>4</u> qt.
16. 1 hr. = <u>60</u> min.   1 pt. = <u>2</u> cups   1 wk. = <u>7</u> days
17. 1 yd. = <u>3</u> ft.   1 ft. = <u>12</u> in.   1 yd. = <u>36</u> in.

F. Answer the questions.

18. How many days are in each month?
    a. November   b. February   c. March   d. August   e. June
       30   28 or 29   31   31   30

19. Mother has two quarts of milk in the refrigerator. How many cups of milk is that?
    8 cups

20. Mother's recipe for pudding asks for 3 cups of milk. How much will she use if she makes two batches of pudding?
    6 cups

146 Chapter 7 More Fractions and Measures

67. Fractions in Changing Units of Measure

Here are the rules you have been using to change units of measure.

> To change from a large unit to a smaller one, multiply.
> To change from a small unit to a larger one, divide.

A. Write the answers.

1. Write the key numbers for these units. (The key number is the number of smaller units in the larger unit.)

   a. foot, yard **3** b. week, day **7** c. gallon, quart **4** d. inch, foot **12**

2. Write whether you would **multiply** or **divide** to make each change.

   a. gallons to quarts — multiply
   b. days to weeks — divide
   c. feet to yards — divide

B. Use the correct rule to find the missing numbers.

3. 21 days = **3** wk.   8 qt. = **2** gal.   6 qt. = **12** pt.
4. 2 yr. = **24** mo.   12 cups = **6** pt.   12 cups = **3** qt.
5. 12 qt. = **48** cups   12 qt. = **24** pt.   2 min. = **120** sec.
6. 36 mo. = **3** yr.   4 gal. = **16** qt.   2 days = **48** hr.
7. 6 yd. = **18** ft.   24 ft. = **8** yd.   3 doz. = **36** things
8. 6 wk. = **42** days   10 cups = **5** pt.   48 in. = **4** ft.

When you change units by dividing, the answer does not always come out even. Then you should divide as usual and express the remainder as a fraction. The answer will be a mixed number.

> Example: 7 ft. = ___ yd.
> Think: Key number is 3 (3 ft. = 1 yd.).
> Divide 7 by 3.
> Answer: 7 ft. = $2\frac{1}{3}$ yd.
>
> $$\begin{array}{r} 2\frac{1}{3} \\ 3\overline{)7} \\ \underline{6} \\ 1 \end{array}$$

C. These answers do not come out even. Find each missing number by dividing and expressing the remainder as a fraction.

9. 5 cups = **$2\frac{1}{2}$** pt.   5 cups = **$1\frac{1}{4}$** qt.   10 qt. = **$2\frac{1}{2}$** gal.
10. 8 ft. = **$2\frac{2}{3}$** yd.   18 days = **$2\frac{4}{7}$** wk.   13 pt. = **$6\frac{1}{2}$** qt.

LESSON 67

Objectives

- To introduce *changing units of measure when the answer is a mixed number.
- To teach *the English units of weight.
- To teach *reducing fractions to lowest terms (in teacher's guide only).

Preparation

1. Addition flash cards
2. Nine pennies

Oral Drill

1. Drill the addition facts.
2. Review key numbers in units of measure. **What is the key number for changing inches to feet? inches to yards? feet to yards? weeks to days? hours to minutes? quarts to gallons?**
3. Review finding a part of a number.
   1/4 of 20   1/6 of 36
   1/2 of 16   1/8 of 56
   1/2 year = (6) months
   1/4 dozen = (3) things
   1/3 foot = (4) inches
4. Count by fourths to 3; by eighths to 2.
5. Give mixed mental drill.
   100×64 40×9 $21 - 3$
   $30 - 2$ $49 - 4$
   $4 \times 5 \div 2 - 7 \times 9 + 5$ (32)
   $6 + 5 \times 4 + 5 \div 7 - 2$ (5)
   $8 - 5 \times 7 + 3 \div 6 - 4$ (0)
   $5 \times 6 \div 10 + 6 \times 9 - 2$ (79)

T–147 Chapter 7 More Fractions and Measures

Teaching Guide

1. *Changing units of measure when the answer is a mixed number.*
   a. Review the two rules for changing units of measure, and do some together.
      6 ft. = (2) yd. 8 gal. = (32) qt.
      6 yd. = (18) ft. 8 qt. = (2) gal.
   b. Review finding a part of a measure.
      1/2 qt. = (1) pt.
      1/4 ft. = (3) in.
      1/2 hr. = (30) min.
      1/3 yd. = (12) in.
   c. **Sometimes when you change units by dividing, the answer does not come out even. Express the remainder as a fraction. The answer will be a mixed number.**
      6 qt. = (1 1/2) gal.
      5 cups = (2 1/2) pt.
      5 cups = (1 1/4) qt.
      8 ft. = (2 2/3) yd.

2. *English units of weight.*
   a. **An ounce is a very small unit of weight. Nine pennies weigh an ounce.** Let pupils hold nine pennies to see how light an ounce is.
   b. **A pound is a larger unit of weight. It takes 16 ounces to make 1 pound. A carton of butter weighs a pound. Do you know your weight in pounds?** *Note:* The unusual spelling of the abbreviation for *pound* stands for the Latin word *libra*.
   c. **A ton is a very large unit of weight. It takes 2,000 pounds to make 1 ton. Very heavy things like feed or coal are weighed by the ton.**
   d. **Do these things weigh closer to 1 ounce, 1 pound, or 1 ton?**
      book   automobile   pencil
      boulder   spoon   eraser
      box of cornstarch   pint of water

3. *Reducing fractions to lowest terms.*
   a. Write some fractions on the board, and have pupils reduce them.
      $\frac{10}{15}$ $\frac{4}{6}$ $\frac{2}{12}$ $\frac{4}{12}$ $\frac{2}{8}$ $\frac{8}{16}$ $\frac{6}{8}$ $\frac{12}{20}$
   b. **The numerator and the denominator of a fraction are the *terms* of the fraction. A fraction is in *lowest terms* when it cannot be reduced to an equivalent fraction with smaller numbers (terms).**
      Are these fractions in lowest terms? Can both the numerator and the denominator be divided by another number? Write the following fractions on the board one at a time.
      $\frac{1}{6}$ $\frac{5}{8}$ $\frac{4}{8}$ ($\frac{1}{2}$) $\frac{3}{5}$ $\frac{8}{12}$ ($\frac{2}{3}$)
      $\frac{2}{16}$ ($\frac{1}{8}$) $\frac{3}{9}$ ($\frac{1}{3}$) $\frac{4}{9}$ $\frac{12}{16}$ ($\frac{3}{4}$)
   c. Reduce to lowest terms the fractions on the board that are not already in lowest terms. Ask: **What is the *largest* number by which both terms can be divided?** Note especially 4/8, 8/12, and 12/16.

Note: Since the concept of lowest terms is not taught in the pupil's lesson, do not require answers in lowest terms at this point. Accept any correct reduced fractions in pupils' work until they have had more practice with lowest terms.

Allow pupils to write out the problems for numbers 9–13. Tell them whether you want them to show all their work, or if you will let them do the work on scratch paper.

For number 17, accept any reduced fractions that are correct. Number 18 may be considered optional if pupils need too much help with it.

Supplementary Drills

Drill 134*

Drill 28 ÷

Learn the facts in this box.

Units of Weight
16 ounces (oz.) = 1 pound (lb.)   2,000 pounds = 1 ton

D. *Find the missing numbers. Remember to use division to find part of a number.*

11. 3 lb. = __48__ oz.   2 lb. = __32__ oz.   5 lb. = __80__ oz.
12. $\frac{1}{2}$ lb. = __8__ oz. $\frac{1}{4}$ lb. = __4__ oz. $\frac{1}{8}$ lb. = __2__ oz.
13. 2 tons = __4,000__ lb. $\frac{1}{2}$ ton = __1,000__ lb. $\frac{1}{4}$ ton = __500__ lb.

Review Exercises

E. *Follow the directions.*

14. Write the measurement that each arrow points to. Be sure to label the answers.

a. $2\frac{1}{8}$ in.   b. $2\frac{7}{8}$ in.   c. $3\frac{1}{4}$ in.   d. $3\frac{5}{8}$ in.   e. $4\frac{3}{4}$ in.

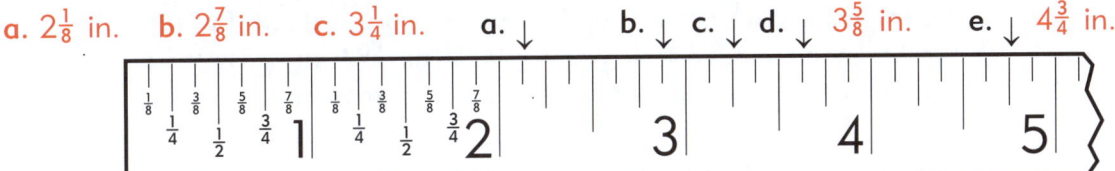

15. Find the missing numbers by multiplying.
    a. $\frac{2}{3} = \frac{10}{?}$ 15   b. $\frac{1}{5} = \frac{?}{10}$ 2   c. $\frac{1}{3} = \frac{6}{?}$ 18   d. $\frac{3}{4} = \frac{?}{16}$ 12

16. Find the missing numbers by dividing.
    a. $\frac{9}{12} = \frac{?}{4}$ 3   b. $\frac{4}{8} = \frac{1}{?}$ 2   c. $\frac{6}{10} = \frac{?}{5}$ 3   d. $\frac{4}{16} = \frac{?}{8}$ 2

17. Reduce these fractions to equivalent fractions by dividing.
    a. $\frac{3}{12}$ $\frac{1}{4}$ b. $\frac{4}{10}$ $\frac{2}{5}$ c. $\frac{8}{16}$ $\frac{1}{2}$ d. $\frac{5}{10}$ $\frac{1}{2}$ e. $\frac{6}{8}$ $\frac{3}{4}$

18. Write the missing numbers. Use the rectangles in Lesson 62 and the ruler on this page if you need help.
    a. 1 = __4__ fourths   c. 3 = __6__ halves   e. $1\frac{1}{4}$ = __5__ fourths
    b. 2 = __6__ thirds   d. $1\frac{1}{2}$ = __3__ halves   f. $2\frac{1}{4}$ = __9__ fourths

19. Tell what part is shaded in each diagram.
    a. 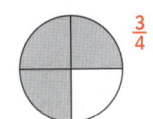 $\frac{3}{4}$ b. 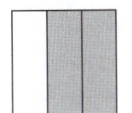 $\frac{2}{3}$ c.  $\frac{1}{6}$ d. 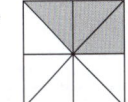 $\frac{3}{8}$

68. Helps for Solving Reading Problems

Can you solve this problem?

One bushel of potatoes weighs 60 pounds. If you have 5 bushels of potatoes, how many pounds of potatoes do you have?

Some children know arithmetic facts very well, but they have trouble with reading problems. To do well with reading problems, read the problem carefully and think what the question is asking.

These steps should help you to solve reading problems more easily.

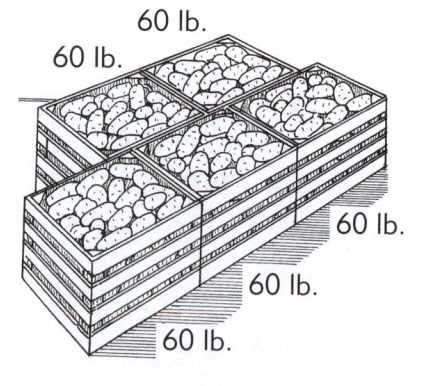

$5 \times 60 = 300$

---

1. Read the problem carefully. Think: **What am I to find out?**
2. Read the problem again. Think: **Which of the four number processes must I use to solve the problem?**
   Look for key words such as *how much more* or *total*. But not every problem has simple key words. Think: **Will the answer be larger or smaller than the numbers in the problem?**
3. Set up a number problem on your paper. Read the word problem again. Think: **Does my number problem fit the word problem?**
4. Solve the number problem carefully and check your work. Think: **Does my answer make sense?**

A. *Use the steps in the box to solve these reading problems.*

1. Sister Rhoda was baking cookies for the Bible school. She made 154 chocolate chip cookies, 119 peanut butter cookies, and 123 raisin cookies. How many cookies did she make? **396 cookies**

2. Four boys have 10 cookies. If they share the cookies equally, how many cookies can each boy have? **2½ cookies**

3. Joan is reading a book with 371 pages. She has already read 285 pages. How many pages does Joan have left to read? **86 pages**

4. Mother bought 8 bags of sugar for $1.76 a bag. What did Mother pay for the sugar? **$14.08**

5. Mother's total bill was $43.29. How much change did she receive from $50.00? **$6.71**

LESSON 68

Objectives

- To study the thinking process used to solve reading problems.
- To teach that *1 year = 365 days or 52 weeks.
- To review changing units of measure.

Preparation

1. Subtraction flash cards
2. Speed Drill 68
3. Chalkboard:

   a. $\frac{1}{2}$ $\frac{1}{5}$ $\frac{1}{3}$ $\frac{2}{5}$ $\frac{3}{5}$ $\frac{5}{5}$
   $\frac{2}{3}$ $\frac{2}{6}$ $\frac{2}{2}$ $\frac{5}{9}$ $\frac{8}{9}$ $\frac{1}{9}$

   b. $\frac{6}{9}$ $\frac{4}{16}$ $\frac{9}{12}$

Oral Drill

1. Drill the subtraction facts.
2. a. Have pupils identify the largest and smallest fractions in each set *(a)* on the board.
   Which fractions are like fractions?
   Which fractions are equal to one whole?
   b. **What are some fractions equal to 1/2? to 1/4?**
   How many sixths are equivalent to 1/3?
   c. **Reduce the fractions in set *b* on the board.**
3. **Would the following items be weighed by the ounce, by the pound, or by the ton?**
   a bag of dog food
   you
   a carton of butter
   a load of coal
   a bottle of vanilla
   a truckload of cattle feed
   a letter that you mail
   a bushel of apples
   a box of cinnamon

Speed Drill

Give Speed Drill 68 (subtraction facts).

T–149 Chapter 7 More Fractions and Measures

Teaching Guide

1. *Practice with reading problems.*
   a. **Do these key words and questions signal you to add, subtract, multiply, or divide?**
   total (a *or* m)
   altogether (a *or* m)
   share (d)
   both (a *or* m)
   sum (a)
   in all (a *or* m)
   How many more? (s)
   What is 4 times as many? (m)
   How many equal groups? (d)
   How much less? (s)
   How much longer? (s)
   How much change? (s)
   How much left? (s)
   How much farther? (s)
   How many in each group? (d)
   What is the difference? (s)
   What is the total cost at 40¢ each? (m)
   How many in 3 groups that size? (m)

   b. **Not all reading problems have key words. Many times you must simply think which process makes sense.**
      Which two arithmetic processes give larger answers than the numbers in the problem? (a and m) **Which two give smaller answers?** (s and d) **Which processes work with several groups of the same size?** (m and d) **Which usually work with unequal amounts?** (a and s)

   c. Have pupils turn to Lesson 68. Discuss the steps for solving problems; then lead the pupils through the steps to solve the problem at the beginning of the lesson. Use the following problems for further practice.
      • Rachel can put 5 rows of 4 cookies on a cookie sheet. How many cookies fit on the sheet? (20 cookies)
      • Sylvia picked out 32 apples to make pies. She plans to make 4 pies. How many apples will she use for each pie? (8 apples)
      • Doris swept for 12 minutes in the kitchen, 9 minutes in the living room, and 8 minutes in her bedroom. How long did she sweep? (29 minutes)
      • After sweeping her bedroom for 8 minutes, Doris spent 18 minutes tidying the room. How much less time did she spend sweeping than tidying her room? (10 minutes)

2. *Units of time.*
   a. Review the number of days in each month. Add the number of days in the months to show the total number in a year.
   b. Introduce: **365 days = 1 year.**
      52 weeks = 1 year.
   c. The pupils may know that there are 13 lessons in most Sunday school quarterlies and that they get 4 new Sunday school books each year. If so, you can use multiplication (4 × 13) or division (52 ÷ 4) to show that there are 52 weeks in a year.

3. *Practice changing units of measure.*
   a. Review the two rules for changing units.
   b. Change various units by using both rules.
      4 tons = (8,000) lb.   6 pt. = (3) qt.
      4 lb. = (64) oz.   6 qt. = (12) pt.
      4 oz. = (1/4) lb.   9 ft. = (3) yd.
   c. Change various units that do not divide evenly.
      9 qt. = (2 1/4) gal.
      11 ft. = (3 2/3) yd.
      6 cups = (1 1/2) qt.
      7 pt. = (3 1/2) qt.
      10 qt. = (2 1/2) gal.

Supplementary Drill

Drill 135

Lesson 68   149

Learn the facts in this box. Only the last two are new.

Units of Time

1 minute = 60 seconds	1 month = about 30 days
1 hour = 60 minutes	1 year = 12 months
1 day = 24 hours	**1 year = 52 weeks**
1 week = 7 days	**1 year = 365 days**

B. *Write the answers.*

6. To change from a large unit to a small one, you <u>multiply</u>

7. Write the key numbers for these measures.
   a. cup, quart 4   b. pound, ounce 16   c. inch, yard 36   d. hour, day 24

C. *Change these units of measure. A few answers have fractions.*

8. 2 yr. = <u>730</u> days   3 yr. = <u>156</u> wk.   3 tons = <u>6,000</u> lb.
9. 4 lb. = <u>64</u> oz.   8 qt. = <u>16</u> pt.   7 cups = <u>$1\frac{3}{4}$</u> qt.
10. 8 ft. = <u>$2\frac{2}{3}$</u> yd.   8 yd. = <u>24</u> ft.   6 cups = <u>3</u> pt.
11. 15 days = <u>$2\frac{1}{7}$</u> wk.   24 in. = <u>2</u> ft.   4 days = <u>96</u> hr.

Review Exercises

D. *Follow the directions.*

12. Write the measurement that each arrow points to.
    a. $1\frac{3}{8}$ in.   b. $2\frac{1}{4}$ in.   c. $2\frac{7}{8}$ in.   d. $3\frac{3}{4}$ in.   e. $4\frac{1}{2}$ in.

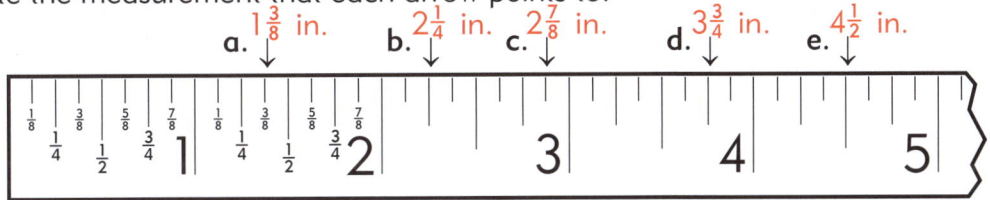

13. Find the missing numbers by multiplying.
    a. $\frac{1}{2} = \frac{4}{?}$ 8   b. $\frac{2}{3} = \frac{6}{?}$ 9   c. $\frac{1}{3} = \frac{?}{12}$ 4   d. $\frac{3}{5} = \frac{?}{10}$ 6

14. Reduce these fractions to equivalent fractions by dividing.
    a. $\frac{2}{6}$ $\frac{1}{3}$ b. $\frac{2}{8}$ $\frac{1}{4}$ c. $\frac{8}{16}$ $\frac{1}{2}$ d. $\frac{4}{12}$ $\frac{1}{3}$ e. $\frac{6}{12}$ $\frac{1}{2}$ f. $\frac{4}{6}$ $\frac{2}{3}$ g. $\frac{5}{10}$ $\frac{1}{2}$ h. $\frac{6}{8}$ $\frac{3}{4}$

15. How many halves are in 3 grapefruits? 6   in 5 grapefruits? 10   in 4? 8

16. How many fourths are in 3 inches? 12   in 4 inches? 16   in 2 inches? 8

150 Chapter 7 More Fractions and Measures

69. Chapter 7 Review

A. *Do these exercises.*

1. Write a fraction to tell what part of each example is shaded.
   a. 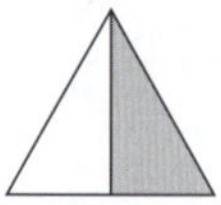 $\frac{1}{2}$ b.  $\frac{3}{4}$ c. 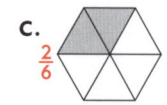 $\frac{2}{6}$ d. 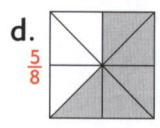 $\frac{5}{8}$ e. 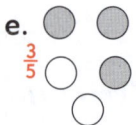 $\frac{3}{5}$

2. Count by halves to 6. Begin: $\frac{1}{2}$, 1 . . .
   $\frac{1}{2}, 1, 1\frac{1}{2}, 2, 2\frac{1}{2}, 3, 3\frac{1}{2}, 4, 4\frac{1}{2}, 5, 5\frac{1}{2}, 6$

3. Count by fourths to 3 as you would on a ruler. Begin: $\frac{1}{4}, \frac{1}{2}, \frac{3}{4}$, 1 . . .
   $\frac{1}{4}, \frac{1}{2}, \frac{3}{4}, 1, 1\frac{1}{4}, 1\frac{1}{2}, 1\frac{3}{4}, 2, 2\frac{1}{4}, 2\frac{1}{2}, 2\frac{3}{4}, 3$

4. Count by eighths to 2. Begin: $\frac{1}{8}, \frac{1}{4}, \frac{3}{8}$ . . .
   $\frac{1}{8}, \frac{1}{4}, \frac{3}{8}, \frac{1}{2}, \frac{5}{8}, \frac{3}{4}, \frac{7}{8}, 1, 1\frac{1}{8}, 1\frac{1}{4}, 1\frac{3}{8}, 1\frac{1}{2}, 1\frac{5}{8}, 1\frac{3}{4}, 1\frac{7}{8}, 2$

5. Write the words with numbers.
   a. two and three-fourths $2\frac{3}{4}$
   b. six and two-thirds $6\frac{2}{3}$

6. Write a fraction with a denominator of 5 and a numerator of 2. $\frac{2}{5}$

7. Choose the correct word.
   If two fractions have the same numerator, the larger fraction has the (<u>smaller</u>, larger) denominator.

8. Copy each pair of fractions, and write < or > between them.
   a. $\frac{1}{3} > \frac{1}{4}$ b. $\frac{2}{4} < \frac{3}{4}$ c. $\frac{3}{5} > \frac{1}{5}$ d. $\frac{2}{5} < \frac{2}{3}$

9. Write a like fraction for each of these.
   $\frac{1}{3}$ $\frac{2}{3}$ $\frac{1}{4}$ $\frac{3}{4}$ (sample answers)

B. *Write the missing numbers.*

10. 1 whole = <u>2</u> halves   3 wholes = <u>6</u> halves   5 = <u>10</u> halves
11. 1 whole = <u>3</u> thirds   2 wholes = <u>6</u> thirds   4 = <u>12</u> thirds
12. 1 whole = <u>4</u> fourths   4 wholes = <u>16</u> fourths   3 = <u>12</u> fourths
13. $1\frac{1}{2}$ = <u>3</u> halves $3\frac{1}{2}$ = <u>7</u> halves $1\frac{1}{4}$ = <u>5</u> fourths

LESSON 69

Objective

♦ To review the concepts taught in Chapter 7 (listed below).
  - Meaning of fractions
  - Number of fractional parts in a whole
  - Meaning of fraction terms: numerator, denominator, like fractions, whole numbers, mixed numbers, equivalent fractions
  - Comparing fractions with like numerators or denominators
  - Multiplying or dividing to find equivalent fractions
  - Reducing fractions
  - Dividing and expressing remainders as fractions
  - Reading and measuring lengths to the nearest 1/8 inch
  - Units of weight and time
  - Changing from a small to a large unit when the answer is a mixed number
  - Finding a fractional part of a unit

Preparation

A ruler with eighth-inch markings for each child

Teaching Guide

1. Review numerators and denominators. Review like fractions.

2. Review comparing fractions with equal numerators or denominators. Also review the signs < and >.

3. a. **How many thirds are in 1 whole thing? in 2?**
      How many halves are in 1 whole?
      in 3? in 5?
   b. Let pupils use their rulers to answer these questions.
      How many fourths are in 1 inch? in 4 inches? in 2? in 3?
      How many halves are in 1 1/2 inches? in 3 1/2 inches? in 2 1/2?
      How many fourths are in 1 1/4? in 1 3/4? in 2 1/2?

4. Review writing mixed numbers. **Write "two and three fifths."** Give other examples.

5. Count by halves, by fourths, and by eighths.

6. a. Review units of measure
      1 yr. = (365) days
      1 yr. = (52) wk.
      1 lb. = (16) oz.
      1 ton = (2,000) lb.
   b. Review the rules for changing from one unit to another.

7. Review ruler measurement.
   a. Have the pupils point to measurements on their rulers. Stick with halves, fourths, and eighths.
   b. You may want to do numbers 14 and 15 in class, especially if this kind of exercise has been difficult for your pupils.

T–151   Chapter 7   More Fractions and Measures

8. Review various fraction exercises. The following drills are suitable for practice at the board.
   a. Review finding equivalent fractions by multiplying. Make sure pupils are multiplying *both terms* by the *same number*. If some have difficulty, have them tell you how they think to find the missing numbers.
   $\frac{1}{3} = \frac{2}{?}$ (6) $\frac{2}{3} = \frac{6}{?}$ (9) $\frac{1}{2} = \frac{?}{10}$ (5)
   $\frac{3}{4} = \frac{?}{8}$ (6) $\frac{1}{4} = \frac{?}{12}$ (3)
   b. Review finding equivalent fractions by dividing.
   $\frac{4}{8} = \frac{2}{?}$ (4) $\frac{3}{6} = \frac{?}{2}$ (1) $\frac{5}{10} = \frac{1}{?}$ (2)
   $\frac{8}{16} = \frac{2}{?}$ (4) $\frac{6}{8} = \frac{?}{4}$ (3)
   c. Have pupils reduce these fractions. Encourage them to reduce to lowest terms.
   $\frac{3}{9}$ ($\frac{1}{3}$) $\frac{4}{8}$ ($\frac{1}{2}$) $\frac{2}{6}$ ($\frac{1}{3}$)
   $\frac{4}{12}$ ($\frac{1}{3}$) $\frac{8}{10}$ ($\frac{4}{5}$) $\frac{6}{16}$ ($\frac{3}{8}$)
   $\frac{4}{10}$ ($\frac{2}{5}$) $\frac{3}{12}$ ($\frac{1}{4}$) $\frac{2}{16}$ ($\frac{1}{8}$)
   d. Review changing units of measure.
   (1) Multiplying to change from a larger unit to a smaller.
       5 lb. = (80) oz.
       4 tons = (8,000) lb.
       3 min. = (180) sec.
       5 gal. = (20) qt.
   (2) Dividing to change from a smaller unit to a larger one; sometimes these involve fractions.
       6 cups = (3) pt.
       4 cups = (1) qt.
       6 qt. = (1 1/2) gal.
       7 ft. = (2 1/3) yd.
       12 pt. = (6) qt.
       9 cups = (4 1/2) pt.
       11 days = (1 4/7) wk.
       6 ft. = (2) yd.
   (3) Dividing by the denominator to find a part of a measure.
       1/2 ft. = (6) in.   1/4 lb. = (4) oz.
   e. Review dividing and expressing remainders as fractions.

9. Review reading problems. Unless your pupils have much difficulty with reading, these oral problems will provide a fairly accurate check of the pupils' competence.
   a. If a train travels 65 miles an hour, how far can it travel in 3 hours? (195 mi.)
   b. If Marlene uses 9 small quilt patches to make one large block for her quilt, how many large squares can she make with 72 small patches? (8 squares)
   c. If Christopher read 96 pages of *Safe in His Care* one week and 98 pages the next week, how many pages did he read? (194 pages)
   d. The book has 329 pages altogether. How many pages does Christopher still have to read? (135 pages)
   e. If 3 boys share 5 apples, how many apples can each boy have? (1 2/3 apples)
   f. If 5 boys share 3 apples, how much can each boy have? (3/5 apple)

   Remind pupils that the dividend is always the number being divided. In both *e* and *f*, the *apples* are divided.

10. Tell students that they will have a test in the next class.

Note: Pupils should be able to handle all three pages of this review lesson.

C. Write the answers.

14. Write the measurement that each arrow points to.

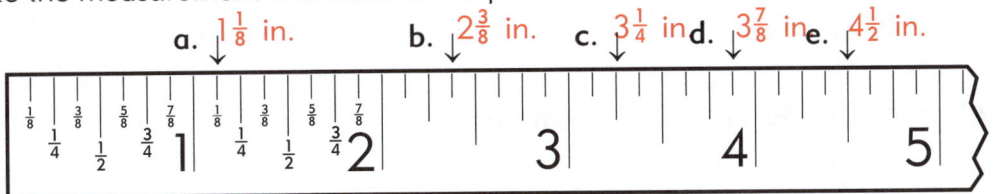

a. $1\frac{1}{8}$ in. b. $2\frac{3}{8}$ in. c. $3\frac{1}{4}$ in. d. $3\frac{7}{8}$ in. e. $4\frac{1}{2}$ in.

15. Measure each line carefully, and write the measurement.

a. ————————— $2\frac{1}{2}$ in.

b. ———————————— $3\frac{5}{8}$ in.

c. ———— $1\frac{7}{8}$ in.

d. ————————————— $4\frac{1}{4}$ in.

16. Multiply to find the missing numbers in these pairs of equivalent fractions.

a. $\frac{1}{2} = \frac{3}{6}$ b. $\frac{2}{4} = \frac{4}{8}$ c. $\frac{1}{3} = \frac{4}{12}$ d. $\frac{3}{4} = \frac{6}{8}$

17. Divide to find the missing numbers in these fraction pairs.

a. $\frac{3}{9} = \frac{1}{3}$ b. $\frac{4}{8} = \frac{1}{2}$ c. $\frac{2}{4} = \frac{1}{2}$ d. $\frac{6}{10} = \frac{3}{5}$

18. Reduce these fractions by dividing. Be sure to divide both numerator and denominator by the same number.

a. $\frac{4}{6}$ $\frac{2}{3}$ b. $\frac{2}{10}$ $\frac{1}{5}$ c. $\frac{6}{12}$ $\frac{1}{2}$ d. $\frac{2}{8}$ $\frac{1}{4}$ e. $\frac{8}{10}$ $\frac{4}{5}$ f. $\frac{4}{16}$ $\frac{1}{4}$ g. $\frac{6}{9}$ $\frac{2}{3}$

19. Are these things usually measured by ounces, pounds, or tons?

a. coal — tons   b. meat — pounds   c. cinnamon — ounces   d. sugar — pounds   e. a ship — tons

D. Write the missing numbers.

20. 1 pound = __16__ ounces   1 ton = __2,000__ pounds   1 year = __365__ days

21. 1 year = __52__ weeks   1 hour = __60__ minutes   1 yard = __36__ inches

22. 4 lb. = __64__ oz.   3 tons = __6,000__ lb.   2 yr. = __104__ wk.

23. 1 oz. = $\frac{1}{16}$ lb.   1 in. = $\frac{1}{12}$ ft.   2 ft. = $\frac{2}{3}$ yd.

24. 5 qt. = $1\frac{1}{4}$ gal.   14 days = __2__ wk.   7 pt. = $3\frac{1}{2}$ qt.

(continued on next page)

152 Chapter 7 More Fractions and Measures

E. *Copy and divide. Express the remainders as fractions.*

25. $3\overline{)127} = 42\frac{1}{3}$ $4\overline{)847} = 211\frac{3}{4}$ $2\overline{)149} = 74\frac{1}{2}$ $8\overline{)329} = 41\frac{1}{8}$ $6\overline{)31} = 5\frac{1}{6}$

F. *Solve these reading problems.*

26. If Joseph was sold into Egypt when he was 17 years old and lived there until he died at the age of 110, how many years did he live in Egypt? **93 years**

27. Judith worked carefully and got all 37 arithmetic problems correct. The next day she got all 48 problems correct. How many problems did she get correct in the two days? **85 problems**

28. Robert gathers eggs every evening after he gets home from school. One evening he gathered 348 eggs, the next evening 325 eggs, and the next evening 336 eggs. How many eggs was that altogether? **1,009 eggs**

29. A bushel of potatoes weighs 60 pounds. How many pounds would eight bushels of potatoes weigh? **480 pounds**

30. Harold helps pick up potatoes. He has already picked up 48 pounds of potatoes. How many more pounds must he pick up to have a bushel? (See number 29.) **12 pounds**

31. If Harold picks up 4 bushels of potatoes each day for 8 days, how many bushels will he pick up? **32 bushels**

32. How many 10-pound bags of potatoes can be filled with one bushel of potatoes? **6 bags**

33. A bushel of apples weighs 50 pounds. How much less does a bushel of apples weigh than a bushel of potatoes? **10 pounds**

34. How many pounds of apples are in $\frac{1}{5}$ of a bushel? (See number 33.) **10 pounds**

70. Chapter 7 Test

LESSON 70

Objective

- To test the pupils' mastery of concepts taught in Chapter 7.

Teaching Guide

1. Give Speed Drill 70 (writing numerals).

Note: Speed Drills are optional on test days.

2. Give any last-minute review that you feel is necessary.

3. Administer the test.

Note: Chapter 7 Test is found in the test section in the back of this manual.

Chapter 8

Long Division

A shepherd divideth his sheep from the goats.
(Matthew 25:32)

154 Chapter 8 Long Division

71. Another Kind of Long Division

If you know well the six division steps in Lesson 52, you already know all you need to do this lesson. Solving longer divisions is like doing several smaller division problems at one time.

Example A
In this problem:

```
   2 R 2
3)8
   6
   2
```

1. **Divide.**
2. **Multiply.**
3. **Compare.**
4. **Subtract.**
5. **Compare.**

There are no digits to **bring down**. The remainder is 2.

Example B
In this problem:

```
    28
3)84
   6
   24
   24
```

Go through the five steps.
Then **bring down** the 4.
Write 4 beside the 2.
Start over with the first step.
Think: 24 ÷ 3 = 8.
There is no remainder.

A. *Copy these problems and divide carefully. You will have remainders within the problems, but no remainders in the answers.*

1. 4)72 = 18   3)81 = 27   3)48 = 16   2)58 = 29   2)36 = 18
2. 3)54 = 18   4)64 = 16   2)70 = 35   4)56 = 14   3)42 = 14
3. 4)76 = 19   2)78 = 39   3)51 = 17   4)52 = 13   3)87 = 29

Review Exercises

B. *Write the answers to these facts quickly.*

4. 14 − 6 = 8   11 − 8 = 3   10 − 7 = 3   17 − 9 = 8   13 − 4 = 9   9 − 6 = 3   12 − 5 = 7   11 − 4 = 7   12 − 9 = 3

C. *Copy and subtract.*

5. 6,048 − 2,965 = 3,083   9,020 − 3,752 = 5,268   8,000 − 5,073 = 2,927   5,012 − 2,896 = 2,116 $52.00 − $17.56 = $34.44

LESSON 71

Objectives

- To review the steps of long division.
- To introduce long division *having remainders within problems (but no remainders in quotients).

Preparation

1. Subtraction and division flash cards
2. Chalkboard:

    $4\overline{)9}$ (2 R 1) $3\overline{)20}$ (6 R 2)

    $3\overline{)246}$ (82) $2\overline{)842}$ (421) $4\overline{)326}$ (81 R 2)

Oral Drill

1. Briefly review the subtraction and division facts.
2. Review units of weight and time.
   1 lb. = (16) oz.   1 yr. = (52) wk.
   1 ton = (2,000) lb.   1 yr. = (365) days
3. Count by fourths as you would say the numbers on a ruler.
4. a. **How many halves are in one whole? in 3 whole things?**
   b. **How many thirds are in one whole? in 5 whole things?**
   c. **If a pie is cut into eighths, how many pieces are in 1 pie? in 2 pies? in 4 pies?**
5. **Are 1/4 and 3/4 like fractions? Are they equivalent fractions?**
6. **Name some fractions equivalent to 1/2.**
7. a. **To change from a smaller unit to a larger, we** (divide).
      To change from a larger unit to a smaller, we (multiply).
   b. Give practice with at least one each of the following kinds.
      Multiply to change: 4 lb. = (64) oz.
      Divide to change; whole number answers: 21 da. = (3) wk.
      Mixed number answers: 5 pt. = (2 1/2) qt.
      Divide by denominator to find a part: 1/3 yr. = (4) mo.

T–155   Chapter 8   Long Division

Teaching Guide

1. *Review of long division.*
   a. Review the *five* division steps used in examples such as the first one on the board. The sixth step (bring down) is not needed because there are no digits to bring down. Do at least one such problem together (as the first two examples on the board).
   b. Do several problems that have more than one quotient figure, such as the last three on the board.
   c. Remind the children to write each quotient figure above the correct figure in the dividend. In the second example on the board, the 6 should be written above the 0, not above the 2, because 20 is being divided—not 2. After the first quotient figure is written, there *must* be one quotient figure for each digit in the dividend.

   Remind the pupils often: **Every time you bring a digit down, you must put a digit up.**

2. *Long division with something new.*
   a. **So far you have been solving long division problems having no remainders except in the last place. The divisions in today's lesson will have remainders *within* the problem.**
   b. Erase all the division problems on the board except the first one: $4\overline{)9}$. Beside it write: $4\overline{)92}$. Hold your hand over the 2. **If the 2 were not here, this problem would be just like the first one. Let's begin in the same way. How many 4's are in 9?** Continue with the next four steps.
   c. **We are not finished with the problem, so we will not write the remainder in the answer. The next step is "bring down." We bring down the 2 and write it beside the remainder of 1.**
   d. **Now we go through the division steps again. Think: How many 4's are in 12?** Go through the steps again. **This time there is no remainder. The answer is 23. This is the kind of problem in today's lesson.**
   e. Give some practice at the board. Stick with problems that have no remainders in the quotient.

   $2\overline{)54}^{(27)}$ $4\overline{)76}^{(19)}$ $3\overline{)81}^{(27)}$

   $2\overline{)70}^{(35)}$ $3\overline{)48}^{(16)}$ $4\overline{)64}^{(16)}$

Supplementary Drills

Drill 101*

Drill 15 ×

D. Write the missing numbers.

6. 1 yr. = __52__ wk.   1 yr. = __12__ mo.   1 yr. = __365__ days
7. 1 ton = __2,000__ lb.   1 lb. = __16__ oz.   1 day = __24__ hr.
8. 4 tons = __8,000__ lb.   2 min. = __120__ sec.   3 gal. = __12__ qt.
9. $\frac{1}{2}$ pt. = __1__ cup   4 cups = __2__ pt.   5 cups = __$2\frac{1}{2}$__ pt.

E. Do these exercises with fractions.

10. Multiply to find the missing numbers in these pairs of equivalent fractions.

    a. $\frac{2}{3} = \frac{?}{9}$ 6   b. $\frac{1}{2} = \frac{4}{?}$ 8   c. $\frac{1}{3} = \frac{?}{6}$ 2   d. $\frac{2}{4} = \frac{6}{?}$ 12

11. Divide to find the missing numbers in these pairs.

    a. $\frac{4}{12} = \frac{?}{3}$ 1   b. $\frac{2}{8} = \frac{1}{?}$ 4   c. $\frac{3}{6} = \frac{1}{?}$ 2   d. $\frac{8}{16} = \frac{?}{4}$ 2

12. How many halves are in 2 sandwiches? 4   in 5 sandwiches? 10

13. How many thirds are in 1 candy bar? 3   in 4 candy bars? 12

14. If a pie is cut into fifths, how many pieces are in one pie? 5

15. How many fifths are in 2 pies? 10 in 3 pies? 15

F. Solve these problems.

16. Mother plans to make lemon pies for Sunday dinner. If one pie serves 6 people, how many people can Mother serve with 4 pies? **24 people**

17. A carton of ice cream is enough for 10 people. Would 2 cartons of ice cream be enough to serve 25 people? **no**

18. One quart of milk contains 4 cups. How many cups are in a **gallon** of milk? (Think: How many quarts are in a gallon?) **16 cups**

19. Solve the puzzle.

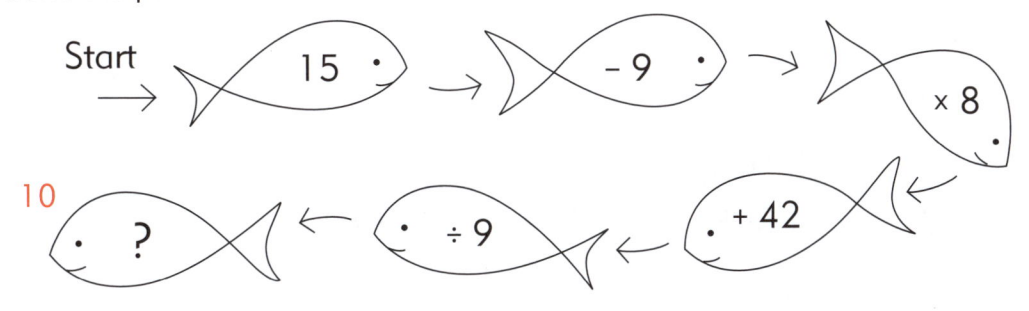

    Start → 15 · → −9 · → ×8 → +42 → ÷9 → ? **10**

156　Chapter 8　Long Division

72. More Long Division

In Lesson 71 you worked with division problems having two digits in the dividend. Some of the problems in today's lesson have three digits in the dividend. But they all have only two digits in the quotient, the same as in Lesson 71.

A. *Copy and divide.*

1. $3\overline{)57} = 19$ $5\overline{)65} = 13$ $2\overline{)76} = 38$ $4\overline{)96} = 24$ $3\overline{)45} = 15$

2. $5\overline{)285} = 57$ $4\overline{)176} = 44$ $3\overline{)234} = 78$ $5\overline{)160} = 32$ $4\overline{)380} = 95$

B. *Copy and divide. Check your work by multiplication.*

3. a. $2\overline{)156} = 78$ $78 \times 2 = 156$
   b. $5\overline{)270} = 54$ $54 \times 5 = 270$
   c. $3\overline{)255} = 85$ $85 \times 3 = 255$

4. a. $3\overline{)198} = 66$ $66 \times 3 = 198$
   b. $2\overline{)134} = 67$ $67 \times 2 = 134$
   c. $5\overline{)125} = 25$ $25 \times 5 = 125$

Review Exercises

C. *Follow the directions.*

5. Write the answers to these facts quickly.

6	8	12	5	7	9	8	6	7
×7	×9	×9	×8	×7	×9	×6	×9	×9
42	72	108	40	49	81	48	54	63

6. Write the answers only. Regroup when you can.

4	6	3	2	8	5	4
6	3	9	3	6	8	6
3	5	4	8	2	4	5
7	3	8	6	5	1	9
+5	+7	+5	+9	+9	+5	+6
25	24	29	28	30	23	30

7. Copy and multiply.

487	309	614	897	563
× 7	× 5	× 5	× 4	× 3
3,409	1,545	3,070	3,588	1,689

LESSON 72

Objectives

- To reinforce the long division process and the checking of division by multiplication.
- To review work with fractions.

Preparation

1. Division flash cards
2. A variety of coins and bills
3. Speed Drill 72

Oral Drill

1. Drill the division facts.
2. Review money. Pupils should be able to identify the penny, nickel, dime, quarter, half dollar, dollar bill, five-dollar bill, ten-dollar bill, and twenty-dollar bill. Make various combinations, and have pupils tell the value of each.
3. Count by fourths and by eighths as a ruler should be read.
4. Give mental drill.
   $10 \times 57 \quad 100 \times 83 \quad 30 \times 9$
   $50 \times 6 \quad 40 \times 7$
   $20 + 5 \quad 40 + 6 \quad 30 - 2$
   $20 - 3 \quad 46 - 4$
   $8 + 9 - 2 \div 5 \times 8 + 6 - 2 \ (28)$
   $4 \times 8 + 3 \div 7 \times 9 - 3 \ (42)$
   $7 \times 6 - 2 \div 5 - 4 \times 7 + 3 \ (31)$
   $5 + 7 - 3 \times 7 + 1 \div 8 \ (8)$
   $9 \div 3 + 8 - 1 \times 3 \div 6 - 5 \ (0)$
   $4 \times 5 - 2 \div 3 \times 9 - 4 \ (50)$

Speed Drill

Give speed Drill 72 (converting measures).

T–157   Chapter 8   Long Division

Teaching Guide

1. *The long division process, and checking by multiplication.*
   a. Work through a problem or two on the board, with pupils telling you the next step as you go along.
   b. Check at least one problem with multiplication to refresh the pupils' memory of that process.
   c. Have the pupils practice solving and checking division problems on the board.

   $4)\overline{56}\ (14)$ $2)\overline{36}\ (18)$ $4)\overline{192}\ (48)$

   $3)\overline{171}\ (57)$ $2)\overline{130}\ (65)$ $5)\overline{365}\ (73)$

2. *Practice with fractions.*
   Give a variety of exercises involving fractions. The following drills are suitable for board practice. Items *e, f,* and *g* are the most important.
   a. **Write the fraction that means 2 parts out of 3.**
   b. **Write a fraction that is equivalent to 2/3.**
   c. **Write a pair of like fractions.**
   d. **Write the fraction that means 8 parts out of 12. Then reduce it to an equivalent fraction.** Encourage pupils to reduce to lowest terms; divide by the largest number possible.
   e. **Reduce these fractions.**
      $\frac{3}{6}$ $\frac{4}{8}$ $\frac{6}{8}$ $\frac{8}{12}$ $\frac{2}{12}$ $\frac{3}{9}$ $\frac{4}{10}$
   f. **Find the missing number in each pair.** Do not tell pupils whether to multiply or divide unless they seem confused.
      $\frac{1}{3} = \frac{4}{?}$ (12) $\frac{3}{6} = \frac{1}{?}$ (2) $\frac{2}{8} = \frac{?}{4}$ (1)
      $\frac{6}{16} = \frac{?}{8}$ (3) $\frac{1}{4} = \frac{?}{12}$ (3) $\frac{8}{10} = \frac{4}{?}$ (5)

   g. Change these measures involving fractions.
      6 in. = (1/2) ft.
      7 ft. = (2 1/3) yd.
      7 cups = (3 1/2) pt.
      1/4 lb. = (4) oz.
      5 qt. = (1 1/4) gal.
      12 days = (1 5/7) wk.

Supplementary Drill
Drill 102*

8. Write by fourths to 3 as you would count on a ruler.
$\frac{1}{4}, \frac{1}{2}, \frac{3}{4}, 1, 1\frac{1}{4}, 1\frac{1}{2}, 1\frac{3}{4}, 2, 2\frac{1}{4}, 2\frac{1}{2}, 2\frac{3}{4}, 3$

9. Write by eighths to 2 as you would count on a ruler.
$\frac{1}{8}, \frac{1}{4}, \frac{3}{8}, \frac{1}{2}, \frac{5}{8}, \frac{3}{4}, \frac{7}{8}, 1, 1\frac{1}{8}, 1\frac{1}{4}, 1\frac{3}{8}, 1\frac{1}{2}, 1\frac{5}{8}, 1\frac{3}{4}, 1\frac{7}{8}, 2$

10. Measure these lines with your ruler.
    a. ———————————————— 4 in.
    b. ——————————— $2\frac{3}{4}$ in.
    c. ————————————— $3\frac{1}{8}$ in.
    d. ————————————————— $4\frac{5}{8}$ in.

11. a. 1 is what part of 4? $\frac{1}{4}$ b. 3 is what part of 5? $\frac{3}{5}$

12. Write a fraction with a numerator of 2 and a denominator of 9. $\frac{2}{9}$

13. Reduce these fractions to equivalent fractions by dividing.
    a. $\frac{2}{16}$ $\frac{1}{8}$ b. $\frac{4}{6}$ $\frac{2}{3}$ c. $\frac{8}{12}$ $\frac{2}{3}$ d. $\frac{2}{8}$ $\frac{1}{4}$ e. $\frac{3}{6}$ $\frac{1}{2}$ f. $\frac{5}{15}$ $\frac{1}{3}$ g. $\frac{6}{10}$ $\frac{3}{5}$

14. Which pairs are equivalent fractions? Write the letters.
    a. $\frac{1}{2}$ $\frac{3}{5}$ (b.) $\frac{2}{3}$ $\frac{8}{12}$ (c.) $\frac{4}{8}$ $\frac{1}{2}$ d. $\frac{2}{3}$ $\frac{6}{4}$ e. $\frac{3}{4}$ $\frac{5}{8}$

15. Write the letter of each piece of money on your paper. After each letter, write the name and the value of that piece.

    a. quarter 25¢
    b. penny 1¢
    c. dime 10¢
    d. nickel 5¢
    e. ten-dollar bill $10
    f. one-dollar bill $1
    g. five-dollar bill $5
    h. twenty-dollar bill $20

73. Two-Step Reading Problems

Some reading problems have a hidden step that you must take before you can find the answer. The hidden step is a problem that you must solve before you can answer the question in the reading problem. Below is an example of such a two-step problem.

> Mother bought fabric for $9.45, thread for $0.99, and a zipper for $1.25. What was Mother's change from $15.00?
>
> 1. Read and think: What do I need to find?
> 2. Think: Which of the four arithmetic processes do I need to use?
> 3. Read the problem again. Think: Does it give all the information needed to answer the question?
> 4. Find the missing information.
> 5. Use the answer you found to get the final answer.
> 6. Ask: **Does my answer make sense? Always** ask yourself this question.
>
> *I must find Mother's change...* *Change? Subtract!* *I don't know what Mother spent.*
>
> Total bill
> $9.45
> 0.99
> + 1.25
> $11.69
>
> Change
> $15.00
> − 11.69
> $ 3.31

A. *Solve these problems. Each one has a hidden step.*

1. Ben spent $16.95 for a Bible dictionary and $0.59 for a bookmark. What was his change from $20.00? $2.46

2. Mother bought elastic for $1.45 and 2 cards of snap fasteners at $0.69 each. What was Mother's total bill? $2.83

3. Grandma gave Esther $5.00 for her birthday. How much will Esther have left if she buys 3 handkerchiefs for $0.85 each? $2.45

4. In order to read through the Bible in a year, Rachel reads 3 chapters every day of the week except Sunday. On Sunday she reads 5 chapters. How many chapters does Rachel read in one week? 23 chapters

5. Each day Alma spends 10 minutes studying her arithmetic facts and 35 minutes doing her assignment. How many minutes does Alma spend on arithmetic in 5 days? 225 minutes

LESSON 73

Objective
♦ To introduce *simple two-step reading problems.

Preparation
1. Division flash cards
2. A variety of coins and bills (optional)

Oral Drill
1. Drill the division facts.
2. Review the terms *numerator, denominator,* and *like fractions*.
3. Review key words in reading problems. **What process do we use to answer each question?**
   How much more? (s)
   What is the total? (a *or* m)
   How many in all? (a *or* m)
   How many in each group? (d)
   How much less? (s)
   How many in 5 equal groups? (m)
   How many are left? (s)
   How many in both groups? (a *or* m)
4. **Give the value of each group.**
   3 ten-dollar bills, 1 five-dollar bill ($35)
   2 twenty-dollar bills, 1 ten-dollar bill ($50)
   3 tens, 2 fives, 4 ones ($44)
   1 twenty, 3 tens, 2 ones ($52)
   3 twenties, 1 five, 6 ones ($71)
   6 tens, 3 fives, 5 ones ($80)
   4 twenties, 10 ones ($90)
   5 twenties ($100)
   3 quarters, 2 dimes, 1 nickel ($1.00)
   4 quarters, 4 dimes ($1.40)
   2 quarters, 6 dimes ($1.10)
   1 quarter, 3 dimes, 4 nickels (75¢)

T–159   Chapter 8   Long Division

Teaching Guide

Two-step reading problems.

a. Use the box in the pupil's lesson to introduce two-step problems. For each step listed, have pupils give the answer to the "think" question as follows: (1) Amount of change; (2) subtraction; (3) no—total bill is not given; (4) add to find total bill; (5) subtract total bill from $15.00; (6) yes—$3.31 is sensible for this problem.

b. Give some two-step problems that involve simple calculations. Have the pupils put their thinking into words as they find the answers. (The following problems are similar to the ones in the lesson.) Give individual help to pupils who need it.
 • Mae bought a small book for $2.00 and two bookmarks for $0.25 each. How much did she spend in all? ($2.50)
 • Father bought milk for $2.00, a loaf of bread for $1.00, and crackers for $1.00. What was his change from $5.00? ($1.00)
 • Daniel works in the barn 4 hours each weekday and 2 hours each Sunday. How many hours does Daniel work in the barn each week? (26 hr.)
 • For five days one week, Judith spent 40 minutes each day doing arithmetic and 40 minutes each day doing English. How many minutes did she spend doing arithmetic and English that week? (400 min.)
 • I had a ten-dollar bill. I bought a flashlight for $5.00 and batteries for $2.00. How much money did I have left? ($3.00)

Extra Review

Review long division.

$3 \overline{)147}$ (49) $4 \overline{)316}$ (79) $3 \overline{)222}$ (74)

$5 \overline{)185}$ (37) $2 \overline{)74}$ (37) $4 \overline{)96}$ (24)

Supplementary Drill

Drill 16 ×

Lesson 73   159

Review Exercises

B. *Copy, divide, and check.*

6. a. 2)96 quotient 48; 48 × 2 = 96
   b. 5)80 quotient 16; 16 × 5 = 80
   c. 4)64 quotient 16; 16 × 4 = 64

7. a. 5)345 quotient 69; 69 × 5 = 345
   b. 4)236 quotient 59; 59 × 4 = 236
   c. 3)237 quotient 79; 79 × 3 = 237

8. a. 2)172 quotient 86; 86 × 2 = 172
   b. 5)265 quotient 53; 53 × 5 = 265
   c. 2)116 quotient 58; 58 × 2 = 116

9. a. 4)192 quotient 48; 48 × 4 = 192
   b. 5)180 quotient 36; 36 × 5 = 180
   c. 3)147 quotient 49; 49 × 3 = 147

C. *Write the answers.*

10. What is the largest remainder you can have when you are dividing by 5? **4**
    when you are dividing by 3? **2**

11. Write these fractions in order, from largest to smallest.

    $\frac{1}{3}$ $\frac{1}{5}$ $\frac{1}{2}$ $\frac{1}{8}$ $\frac{1}{4}$ $\frac{1}{6}$ **$\frac{1}{2}, \frac{1}{3}, \frac{1}{4}, \frac{1}{5}, \frac{1}{6}, \frac{1}{8}$**

12. Count by halves from $\frac{1}{2}$ to 5.   **$\frac{1}{2}$, 1, $1\frac{1}{2}$, 2, $2\frac{1}{2}$, 3, $3\frac{1}{2}$, 4, $4\frac{1}{2}$, 5**

13. Tell what measurements the arrows above the ruler point to.
    a. $1\frac{1}{4}$ in.   b. $1\frac{7}{8}$ in.   c. $2\frac{1}{2}$ in.   d. $3\frac{3}{8}$ in.   e. $4\frac{3}{4}$ in.

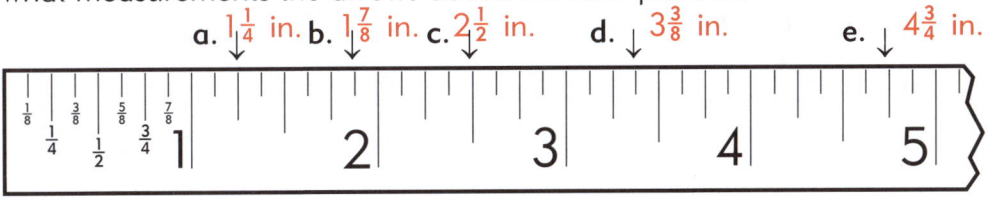

14. From 8:00 A.M. to 1:00 P.M. is how many hours? **5**

15. 5 dozen eggs = __60__ eggs   3 min. = __180__ sec.

16. 1 ton = __2,000__ lb.   2 lb. = __32__ oz.

17. $\frac{1}{3}$ yd. = __12__ in. $\frac{1}{4}$ yr. = __3__ mo.

18. How many half inches are in 4 inches? **8**

19. How many sixths are in 2 pies? **12**

20. Find the missing numbers in these pairs of equivalent fractions. You will need to multiply.
    a. $\frac{1}{3} = \frac{4}{?}$ **12**
    b. $\frac{2}{8} = \frac{?}{16}$ **4**
    c. $\frac{3}{5} = \frac{6}{?}$ **10**
    d. $\frac{1}{6} = \frac{?}{18}$ **3**
    e. $\frac{3}{5} = \frac{?}{25}$ **15**

74. Long Division With Remainders in the Quotient

In this lesson you will go one step further in division. The problems are just like those in Lesson 72 except that now the answers have remainders. Do not forget to write remainders where they belong.

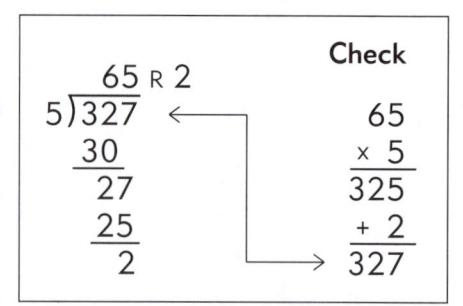

```
        65 R 2          Check
    5)327                 65
       30                × 5
       27                325
       25                + 2
        2                327
```

A. *Copy and divide.*

1. 3)46 **15 R 1**   4)71 **17 R 3**   2)53 **26 R 1**   3)74 **24 R 2**

2. 3)221 **73 R 2**   5)263 **52 R 3**   4)302 **75 R 2**   2)115 **57 R 1**

B. *Copy and divide. Check by multiplying and adding on the remainder.*

3. a. 5)291 **58 R 1**   b. 2)155 **77 R 1**   c. 4)67 **16 R 3**

```
  58          77          16
 x 5         x 2         x 4
 290         154          64
 + 1         + 1         + 3
 291         155          67
```

4. a. 3)56 **18 R 2**   b. 3)136 **45 R 1**   c. 5)222 **44 R 2**

```
  18          45          44
 x 3         x 3         x 5
  54         135         220
 + 2         + 1         + 2
  56         136         222
```

Review Exercises

C. *Write the answers to these facts. Watch the signs!*

5. 6 + 8 **14**   4 × 7 **28**   10 − 8 **2**   9 + 4 **13**   5 × 9 **45**

6. 12 × 6 **72**   11 − 5 **6**   9 + 6 **15**   24 ÷ 4 **6**   36 ÷ 6 **6**

7. 9 × 7 **63**   5 + 9 **14**   11 × 5 **55**   13 − 8 **5**   42 ÷ 6 **7**

8. 64 ÷ 8 **8**   8 × 7 **56**   5 + 7 **12**   9 + 8 **17**   8 × 9 **72**

9. 10 × 6 **60**   12 × 8 **96**   13 − 6 **7**   3 + 7 **10**   49 ÷ 7 **7**

D. *Copy and solve. Follow the signs.*

10.
```
  $12.35       $25.00       $5.08       $7.48             321 R 1
   40.26      − 17.49        ×  6        ×  5         3)964
 + 75.48       ──────       ──────      ──────
  ──────       $7.51        $30.48      $37.40
 $128.09
```

LESSON 74

Objective

♦ To introduce long division *with remainders in quotients.

Preparation

1. Addition flash cards
2. Speed Drill 74
3. Chalkboard:

    $\frac{1}{3}$ $\frac{3}{4}$ $\frac{4}{8}$ $\frac{6}{10}$ $\frac{2}{12}$

    $\frac{1}{5}$ $\frac{3}{8}$ $\frac{8}{16}$ $\frac{9}{12}$

Oral Drill

1. Drill the addition facts.
2. **Which fractions on the board are reduced to lowest terms?** Reduce those that are not already reduced.
3. Give mental drill.

    10×82 100×40 100×53
    40×6 80×5 30×9
    12×5 12×6 12×7
    12×8 12×9
    $7 \times 3 + 4 \div 5 \times 7 - 3 \div 8$ (4)
    $6 + 5 - 4 \times 8 + 4 \div 6 - 2$ (8)
    $8 \div 4 \times 8 + 2 \div 6 \times 9 + 3$ (30)
    $3 + 6 \times 9 - 1 \div 8 - 6 \times 7$ (28)
    $13 - 7 \times 7 + 3 \div 5 \times 8$ (72)
    $8 \times 5 - 4 \div 6 \times 9 + 1 \div 5$ (11)

4. Give the four facts in the 4, 7, 28 multiplication–division family; in the 5, 7, 12 addition–subtraction family.

Speed Drill

Give Speed Drill 74 (finding fractional parts).

T-161   Chapter 8   Long Division

Teaching Guide

Long division with remainders.

a. Review the long division process. Give some board practice.

$$3\overline{)42}^{(14)} \quad 5\overline{)120}^{(24)} \quad 4\overline{)144}^{(36)} \quad 2\overline{)132}^{(66)}$$

b. Work through a division problem with a remainder. This is the new part of today's lesson. Use the following problems for practice at the board or on paper. If the groundwork has been well laid, pupils should not experience difficulty.

$$3\overline{)14}^{(4\,R\,2)} \quad 4\overline{)246}^{(61\,R\,2)} \quad 5\overline{)231}^{(46\,R\,1)}$$

$$2\overline{)165}^{(82\,R\,1)} \quad 4\overline{)302}^{(75\,R\,2)} \quad 3\overline{)79}^{(26\,R\,1)}$$

c. Review checking a division problem with a remainder. Have pupils check one or several of the problems they just did. They must remember to add on the remainder.

Extra Review

Review reading problems. As the pupils solve the following problems, encourage them to think: **Does my answer make sense?**

1. *Simple one-step problems to be computed mentally.*
   • Jack had 13 butterflies. Jane had 3 more. How many did Jane have? (16 butterflies)
   • Three boys share 24 marbles. How many marbles can each boy have? (8 marbles)
   • Three girls share a candy bar. How much candy can each girl have? (1/3 bar)
   • Eight girls is how many more children than 6 boys? (2 children)
   • If you can walk 3 miles in one hour, how many miles could you walk in 2 hours? (6 miles)
   • You have $7.00 and spend $2.00. How much is left? ($5.00)

2. *Two-step problems.*
   • Last year 47 pupils attended the Dover Christian School. This year there are 24 pupils in Room 1, 17 pupils in Room 2, and 21 pupils in Room 3. How many more pupils attend the school this year? (15 pupils)
   • Mother bought 3 cans of soup at 50¢ a can, and a box of crackers for $1.00. What was the total cost? ($2.50)
   • You have $1.00. How much will you have left after you buy two 25-cent pens? (50¢)

Supplementary Drill

Drill 103*

Lesson 74   161

E. Solve these reading problems.

11. Mr. Grove bought 5 pounds of meat for $1.49 a pound. "That will be $7.35," said the butcher.

"I believe you made a mistake," Mr. Grove said. How much should Mr. Grove pay the butcher?   **$7.45**

12. In 1850, the average American farmer produced enough food for 4 people. How many farmers did it take to feed the people in a village of 260 people?   **65 farmers**

13. By 1910, one farmer produced enough food for 7 people. How many people could 65 farmers feed in 1910?   **455 people**

14. The average American farmer of 1994 produced enough food for 100 people. One farmer in 1994 could feed how many times as many people as a farmer in 1850? (See number 12.)   **25 times**

F. Do these exercises.

15. Are these fractions reduced to lowest terms? Write **yes** or **no**.

a. $\frac{2}{3}$ **yes**   b. $\frac{8}{10}$ **no**   c. $\frac{1}{2}$ **yes**   d. $\frac{4}{12}$ **no**   e. $\frac{5}{8}$ **yes**   f. $\frac{2}{4}$ **no**   g. $\frac{6}{9}$ **no**

16. Which of these numbers can be divided evenly by 2?

15   (40)   (56)   (178)   (390)   (532)   467   243

17. Which of these numbers can be divided evenly by 5?

(15)   32   (40)   (200)   (365)   559   306   (180)

18. Write these Roman numerals with Arabic numerals.

a. VIII **8**   b. LXII **62**   c. XIX **19**   d. XLVI **46**   e. LXXXIV **84**

19. Figure out the answer to the number puzzle.

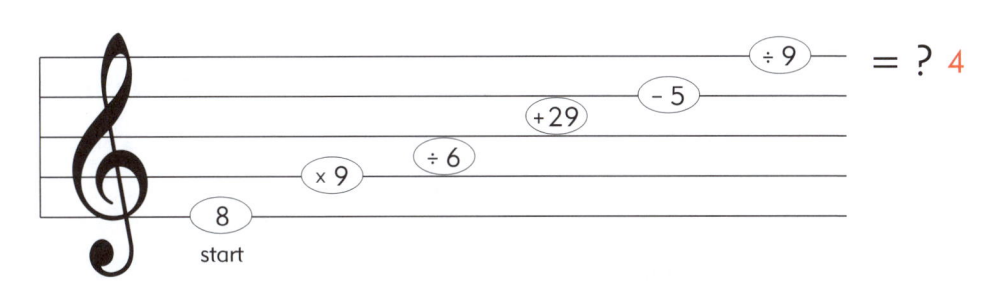

8 start → ×9 → ÷6 → +29 → −5 → ÷9 = ? **4**

75. Reducing Fractions to Lowest Terms

To "reduce a fraction" means to find an equivalent fraction by dividing. To **reduce a fraction to lowest terms** means to divide both **terms** (numerator and denominator) by the largest number possible. After a fraction is reduced to lowest terms, both terms (numerator and denominator) cannot be divided evenly by the same number.

$$\frac{12 \div 2 = 6}{16 \div 2 = 8}$$ (reduced, but not in lowest terms)

$$\frac{12 \div 4 = 3}{16 \div 4 = 4}$$ (in lowest terms) $$\frac{6 \div 2 = 3}{8 \div 2 = 4}$$ (in lowest terms)

A. *Write the answers.*

1. Are these fractions in lowest terms? Write **yes** or **no**.
   a. $\frac{1}{3}$ yes   b. $\frac{3}{6}$ no   c. $\frac{2}{7}$ yes   d. $\frac{4}{10}$ no   e. $\frac{8}{12}$ no   f. $\frac{2}{8}$ no   g. $\frac{3}{5}$ yes

2. Reduce these fractions to lowest terms.
   a. $\frac{4}{8}$ $\frac{1}{2}$ b. $\frac{6}{9}$ $\frac{2}{3}$ c. $\frac{2}{10}$ $\frac{1}{5}$ d. $\frac{4}{12}$ $\frac{1}{3}$ e. $\frac{10}{12}$ $\frac{5}{6}$ f. $\frac{5}{20}$ $\frac{1}{4}$ g. $\frac{4}{16}$ $\frac{1}{4}$

Look at the problem in the box. It is the same as the problem in the box in Lesson 74, except that the remainder is expressed as a fraction. The remainder is the numerator of the fraction, and the divisor is the denominator.

```
      65 2/5
  5)327
     30
     ‾‾
     27
     25
     ‾‾
      2
```

B. *Copy and divide. Write the remainders as fractions. (Not all the answers have remainders.)*

3. $5)\overline{88}$ = $17\frac{3}{5}$ $5)\overline{75}$ = 15 $2)\overline{99}$ = $49\frac{1}{2}$ $4)\overline{375}$ = $93\frac{3}{4}$ $3)\overline{198}$ = 66

4. $2)\overline{138}$ = 69 $4)\overline{340}$ = 85 $5)\overline{464}$ = $92\frac{4}{5}$ $2)\overline{111}$ = $55\frac{1}{2}$ $5)\overline{375}$ = 75

LESSON 75

Objectives

♦ To teach *reducing fractions to lowest terms.

♦ To review long division with remainders written as fractions.

Preparation

1. Division flash cards
2. Chalkboard:

   a. 390,400   23,006
       802,705   400,059

   b. $\underset{5\overline{)68}}{(13 \text{ R } 3)}$ $\underset{3\overline{)73}}{(24 \text{ R } 1)}$

       $\underset{4\overline{)347}}{(86 \text{ R } 3)}$ $\underset{3\overline{)167}}{(55 \text{ R } 2)}$

Oral Drill

1. Drill the division facts.
2. Count by fourths as you would read a ruler.
3. **How much is 3 ÷ 4? 1 ÷ 3? 2 ÷ 5? 4 ÷ 5?**
   1 is what part of 6? 2 is what part of 3?
4. **How many halves are in 4? How many thirds are in 3?**
5. Review the parts of number problems: addend, sum, minuend, subtrahend, difference, factor, product, divisor, dividend, quotient, remainder.
6. **Name two pairs of factors for 24.** It has been quite a while since the term *factor* was reviewed.
7. Have pupils read the numbers *(a)* on the board. Review place names.

Teaching Guide

1. *Reducing fractions to lowest terms.*

   a. Review finding equivalent fractions by dividing. Both the numerator and the denominator are divided by the same number. This process is called reducing the fraction.

      $\frac{3}{12}$ ($\frac{1}{4}$) $\frac{2}{8}$ ($\frac{1}{4}$) $\frac{5}{10}$ ($\frac{1}{2}$) $\frac{8}{16}$ ($\frac{1}{2}$)

      $\frac{6}{8}$ ($\frac{3}{4}$) $\frac{4}{10}$ ($\frac{2}{5}$) $\frac{2}{6}$ ($\frac{1}{3}$)

   b. **Reducing a fraction means changing it to smaller numbers. But even though the numbers are smaller, the size of the fraction itself is the same.** Use drawings or actual objects to reinforce this concept if necessary.

   c. **Sometimes the terms of a fraction can be divided by several different numbers.** Write 8/16 on the board. **By what numbers can we divide 8 and 16?** (2, 4, 8) **If we divide by 8, the largest number, 8/16 will be reduced to *lowest terms*. The fraction 1/2 cannot be reduced any further.**

   d. **After reducing a fraction, always check it to make sure it is really in lowest terms. If it is not, the new fraction must be reduced again.** Illustrate with the example in the lesson.

   e. Have pupils reduce the following fractions that are not already in lowest terms. Point out that if a fraction has a numerator of 1, it is always in lowest terms.

      $\frac{1}{4}$ $\frac{4}{6}$ ($\frac{2}{3}$) $\frac{5}{10}$ ($\frac{1}{2}$) $\frac{2}{3}$ $\frac{1}{5}$ $\frac{2}{4}$ ($\frac{1}{2}$)

      $\frac{3}{9}$ ($\frac{1}{3}$) $\frac{2}{5}$ $\frac{1}{8}$ $\frac{6}{10}$ ($\frac{3}{5}$) $\frac{2}{6}$ ($\frac{1}{3}$)

T–163   Chapter 8   Long Division

2. *Long division with remainders as fractions.*
   a. Work through the divisions *(b)* on the board, and write remainders with *R*.
   b. Review changing remainders to fractions. The *remainder* becomes the *numerator* of the fraction, and the *divisor* becomes the *denominator*. Have pupils tell how to express the remainders on the board as fractions.
   c. Use these problems for further practice.

   $2\overline{)125}$ (62 1/2) $5\overline{)164}$ (32 4/5) $3\overline{)168}$ (56)

   $5\overline{)328}$ (65 3/5) $3\overline{)225}$ (75) $4\overline{)263}$ (65 3/4)

Extra Review

Review reading problems.
   a. Have pupils tell how to solve each problem.
   • You know how old two people are. You want to find how much older the one is than the other. (subtract)
   • You know how many children there are and how many cookies are on the plate. You want to find the number of cookies each child can have. (divide)
   • Father bought several different items, and you know the price of each one. You want to find the total bill. (add)
   • You know the price of one item. You want to find the total price of 6 items like that. (multiply)
   • You know how many brothers and how many sisters Alma has. You want to find how many more brothers she has than sisters. (subtract)
   • You know how many verses are in one memory passage. You want to find how many verses are in 5 memory passages that size. (multiply)
   • You know the price of one candy bar. You know how much money you have. You want to find the number of candy bars you could buy. (divide)
   b. These are two-step problems. Ask the pupils for ideas as you work through each one step by step on the board.
   • How much for 2 gallons of vinegar at 45¢ a quart? (2 × 4 qt. = 8 qt.; 8 × 45¢ =$3.60)
   • Raymond weighs 75 pounds, and Michael weighs 10 pounds less. How much do the two boys weigh together? (75 lb. − 10 lb. = 65 lb.; 75 lb. + 65 lb. = 140 lb.)
   • One kind of car weighs 2,500 pounds. Does an elephant that weighs 5 tons weigh as much as 4 such cars? (4 × 2,500 lb. = 10,000 lb.; 5 × 2,000 = 10,000 lb.; yes)
   • There are 34 children in a class. All but 15 of them are boys. All but 5 of the boys live on farms. How many boys live on farms? (34 − 15 = 19 boys; 19 − 5 = 14 boys)

Note: The last several lessons have had a considerable number of review exercises, and so does this lesson. The purpose is to prepare the students for the midyear test at the end of this chapter. Note any areas where pupils have trouble, and give help as needed.

Supplementary Drills

Drill 112*

Drill 2 +

Review Exercises

C. *Divide, and write any remainders with R. Check your work.*

5. a. 4)56 14   ×4 / 56
   b. 4)74 18 R 2   ×4 / 72 +2 / 74
   c. 2)178 89   ×2 / 178

6. a. 5)78 15 R 3   ×5 / 75 +3 / 78
   b. 3)225 75   ×3 / 225 ... 75
   c. 4)293 73 R 1   ×4 / 292 +1 / 293

7. a. 3)76 25 R 1   ×3 / 75 +1 / 76
   b. 3)256 85 R 1   ×3 / 255 +1 / 256
   c. 4)347 86 R 3   ×4 / 344 +3 / 347

D. *Solve these reading problems.*

8. One school bus can hold 45 children. How many children will 4 buses hold?   **180 children**

9. Mother had $40.00. She bought groceries for a family whose father was hurt. Her bill was $37.78. How much did Mother have left?   **$2.22**

10. Gary feeds the chickens in the morning before he goes to school. Altogether he uses 8 scoops of feed to fill the 4 feeders. How many scoops of feed does Gary put in each feeder?   **2 scoops**

11. Bossie the cow gives 2 gallons of milk each milking. If she is milked twice a day, how much milk does Bossie give in a week?   **28 gallons**

E. *Give the value of the following sets of money.*

12. a. 2 one-dollar bills, 3 quarters, 2 dimes **$2.95**
    b. 4 ten-dollar bills, 2 five-dollar bills, 3 one-dollar bills **$53.00**
    c. 3 twenty-dollar bills, 2 ten-dollar bills, 1 five-dollar bill **$85.00**
    d. 1 twenty-dollar bill, 3 ten-dollar bills, 2 five-dollar bills, 1 dime **$60.10**
    e. 2 twenty-dollar bills, 7 one-dollar bills, 2 quarters, 4 nickels **$47.70**

F. *Answer the questions.*

13. What number is 10,000 more than 635,184? **645,184**

14. What number is 5,000 less than 27,052? **22,052**

15. Write each number with digits.
    a. two hundred eighty-nine thousand, four hundred sixty **289,460**
    b. one hundred two thousand, seventy-five **102,075**

76. Remainders as Fractions in Lowest Terms

When a remainder is written as a fraction, the fraction should be reduced to lowest terms. Remember, fractions are simpler to use when they are reduced. In the division at the right, the remainder is 2 and the fraction would be $\frac{2}{4}$. But $\frac{2}{4}$ is reduced to $\frac{1}{2}$ in the answer.

$$\begin{array}{r} 53\frac{1}{2} \\ 4\overline{)214} \\ \underline{20} \\ 14 \\ \underline{12} \\ 2 \end{array}$$

Check
$$\begin{array}{r} 53 \\ \times\ 4 \\ \hline 212 \\ +\ 2 \\ \hline 214 \end{array}$$

Look at the check for the problem above. Notice that the remainder is added on as it was **before** being changed to a fraction.

A. *Copy each answer, but write the remainder as a fraction. If the fraction is not reduced, reduce it to lowest terms.*

1. $3\overline{)47}$ 15 R 2 $15\frac{2}{3}$ $\quad$ $5\overline{)87}$ 17 R 2 $17\frac{2}{5}$ $\quad$ $2\overline{)59}$ 29 R 1 $29\frac{1}{2}$ $\quad$ $5\overline{)213}$ 42 R 3 $42\frac{3}{5}$ $\quad$ $4\overline{)311}$ 77 R 3 $77\frac{3}{4}$

2. $2\overline{)73}$ 36 R 1 $36\frac{1}{2}$ $\quad$ $4\overline{)222}$ 55 R 2 $55\frac{1}{2}$ $\quad$ $5\overline{)324}$ 64 R 4 $64\frac{4}{5}$ $\quad$ $4\overline{)173}$ 43 R 1 $43\frac{1}{4}$ $\quad$ $4\overline{)274}$ 68 R 2 $68\frac{1}{2}$

B. *Copy and divide. Write remainders as fractions in lowest terms.*

3. $4\overline{)275}$ $68\frac{3}{4}$ $\quad$ $5\overline{)430}$ 86 $\quad$ $2\overline{)134}$ 67 $\quad$ $4\overline{)250}$ $62\frac{1}{2}$ $\quad$ $5\overline{)104}$ $20\frac{4}{5}$

C. *Write remainders as fractions in lowest terms. Check as shown in the lesson.*

4. a. $2\overline{)114}$ 57 $\quad$ $\begin{array}{r}57\\ \times\ 2\\ \hline 114\end{array}$ $\quad$ b. $4\overline{)126}$ $31\frac{1}{2}$ $\quad$ $\begin{array}{r}31\\ \times\ 4\\ \hline 124\\ +\ 2\\ \hline 126\end{array}$ $\quad$ c. $3\overline{)275}$ $91\frac{2}{3}$ $\quad$ $\begin{array}{r}91\\ \times\ 3\\ \hline 273\\ +\ 2\\ \hline 275\end{array}$

5. a. $5\overline{)465}$ 93 $\quad$ $\begin{array}{r}93\\ \times\ 5\\ \hline 465\end{array}$ $\quad$ b. $4\overline{)344}$ 86 $\quad$ $\begin{array}{r}86\\ \times\ 4\\ \hline 344\end{array}$ $\quad$ c. $3\overline{)258}$ 86 $\quad$ $\begin{array}{r}86\\ \times\ 3\\ \hline 258\end{array}$

D. *Write the answers.*

6. Are these fractions reduced to lowest term? Write **yes** or **no**.
    a. $\frac{1}{4}$ yes b. $\frac{3}{5}$ yes c. $\frac{4}{8}$ no d. $\frac{1}{2}$ yes e. $\frac{2}{3}$ yes f. $\frac{6}{10}$ no g. $\frac{2}{6}$ no

7. Reduce these fractions to lowest terms.
    a. $\frac{3}{6}$ $\frac{1}{2}$ b. $\frac{6}{8}$ $\frac{3}{4}$ c. $\frac{4}{12}$ $\frac{1}{3}$ d. $\frac{2}{8}$ $\frac{1}{4}$ e. $\frac{4}{10}$ $\frac{2}{5}$ f. $\frac{8}{16}$ $\frac{1}{2}$ g. $\frac{6}{18}$ $\frac{1}{3}$

LESSON 76

Objectives

- To teach *reducing fractional remainders to lowest terms.
- To teach that *some remainders in reading problems should be expressed as fractions, and some should not.

Preparation

1. Multiplication flash cards
2. Speed Drill 76
3. Chalkboard:

    $\frac{1}{3}$ $\frac{4}{5}$ $\frac{2}{4}$ $\frac{3}{6}$ $\frac{1}{6}$

    $\frac{6}{16}$ $\frac{8}{12}$ $\frac{5}{8}$ $\frac{2}{20}$

Oral Drill

1. Drill the multiplication facts.
2. Count by halves, by fourths, and by eighths.
3. **Tell whether you would add, subtract, multiply, or divide to answer questions with these words.**
    how many more (s)
    how much less (s)
    the product (m)
    the difference (s)
    how many left (s)
    how many in each group (d)
    the sum (a)
    how many altogether (a *or* m)
    4 times as many (m)
    how many for each if 3 share (d)
    how much change (s)
    how much at 25¢ each (m)
    the total (a *or* m)
    a part of a number (d)
4. Review units of measure. **How many ounces are in a pound? How many days in a year? How many weeks in a year? . . .**

Speed Drill

Give Speed Drill 76 (comparing numbers).

T-165   Chapter 8   Long Division

Teaching Guide

1. *Reducing fractional remainders to lowest terms.*
   a. Review reducing fractions. Ask pupils which fractions on the board are in lowest terms. Reduce the ones that are not.
   b. **Divide these small numbers by larger ones, and reduce the fractions to lowest terms.**

2 ÷ 4 (1/2)	4 ÷ 6 (2/3)
4 ÷ 16 (1/4)	8 ÷ 16 (1/2)
2 ÷ 16 (1/8)	6 ÷ 15 (2/5)
6 ÷ 12 (1/2)	10 ÷ 12 (5/6)
4 ÷ 12 (1/3)	3 ÷ 12 (1/4)
9 ÷ 12 (3/4)	9 ÷ 15 (3/5)

   c. Review the long division process, and demonstrate changing remainders to fractions in lowest terms.

   $$4\overline{)98}\ (24\ 1/2) \qquad 3\overline{)163}\ (54\ 1/3)$$

   $$5\overline{)316}\ (63\ 1/5) \qquad 3\overline{)291}\ (97)$$

   $$4\overline{)174}\ (43\ 1/2)$$

   d. Show how to check this kind of division. **After multiplying, we add on the remainder as it was *before* being changed to a fraction.**

   Note: The largest divisor used in today's lesson is 5. Therefore, the only fractional remainder that needs to be reduced is 2/4.

2. *Deciding when remainders in reading problems should be divided.*
   a. Discuss the two problems in the pupil's book. **Both of these problems have the same numbers, and both use the word *share*. Are both answers the same?**
   b. Five puppies *cannot* be divided equally between two boys. John and Robert could each have 2 puppies. Then there would be one puppy left over. The answer to this problem is *2 puppies for each boy, and 1 puppy left over.*
   c. Cookies *can* be divided. John and Robert can each have 2 whole cookies, and the leftover cookie can be divided. The answer to this problem is *2 1/2 cookies for each boy*.
   d. **In reading problems solved by division, you must think whether it is sensible to change the remainder to a fraction or whether you should leave it as a remainder.**
   e. **Which of the following remainders would be sensible to change to fractions?**
   girls   pounds   gallons   doughnuts
   dozens   dimes   kittens   years
   buses   minutes   mice   pencils
   (Measures can be divided.)
   f. Give practice with more problems, changing the remainder to a fraction if it is sensible to do so.
   • Three boys shared 5 doughnuts. How many doughnuts can each boy have? (1 2/3 doughnuts)
   • Three boys shared 5 bunnies. How many bunnies can each boy have? (1 bunny, 2 left over)
   • Debbie has 63 pennies. She wants to put her pennies in 4 equal stacks. How many pennies will be in each stack? (15 pennies, 3¢ left over)
   • Twelve pencils are to be shared by 5 girls. How many pencils can each girl have? (2 pencils, 2 left over)
   • How much is 1/3 of 100 minutes? (33 1/3 minutes)
   • How many days are in half a week? (3 1/2 days)

Supplementary Drills

Drill 17 ×

Drill 113

Study the two problems below. Do they both have the same answer?

Problem 1: John and Robert's dog had five puppies. Each boy wants half of them. How many puppies can each boy have?

Problem 2: John and Robert have five cookies. Each boy wants half of them. How many cookies can each boy have?

The two answers are **not** the same. Puppies cannot be divided. Each boy can have 2 puppies, with 1 left over. The answer is 2 R 1.

Cookies **can** be divided. Each boy can have 2 whole cookies and half of the leftover cookie. The answer is $2\frac{1}{2}$ cookies.

> When you have a remainder in a reading problem, think: **Is it sensible to divide the leftover thing?** If so, change the remainder to a fraction. If not, leave it as a remainder.

E. Solve each problem. Write the remainder as a fraction if that is sensible.

8. Four boys share 6 sandwiches. How many sandwiches can each boy have? $1\frac{1}{2}$ sandwiches

9. On Saturday morning Janice worked for 185 minutes. She spent $\frac{1}{4}$ of that time doing her Sunday school lesson. How many minutes did Janice spend on her Sunday school lesson? $46\frac{1}{4}$ minutes

10. A mother rabbit has 8 bunnies. Henry, Scott, and Barry want to share them. How many bunnies can each boy have?   2 bunnies, 2 left over

11. Brother Metzler preached for 35 minutes. The devotional by Brother Smith was half as long. How long was the devotional? $17\frac{1}{2}$ minutes

12. Marilyn had 4 quarts of milk. She used $\frac{1}{3}$ of it to make pudding. How much milk did she use? $1\frac{1}{3}$ quarts

13. Aunt Beth has 212 pennies. She wants to give the pennies to her five nieces and nephews. How many pennies will each one get?   42 pennies, 2 left over

14. Two teams are needed to play prisoners' base. If 27 children play prisoners' base, can they be divided into equal teams?   no

166   Chapter 8   Long Division

77. Learning About Multiples

When you count by 2's from 2 to 24, you say the following numbers.

2, 4, 6, 8, 10, 12, 14, 16, 18, 20, 22, 24

The numbers above are **multiples** of 2. They are the products you get when you multiply 2 × 1, 2 × 2, 2 × 3, 2 × 4, and so on. The multiples of 2 are called even numbers.

> **A multiple of a number is a product of that number.**
> The multiples of 4 are 4, 8, 12, 16, 20, 24 . . .
> (The three dots mean that the numbers continue in the same way.)

A. *Write the answers.*

1. Write the multiples of 6 from 6 to 72.   6, 12, 18, 24, 30, 36, 42, 48, 54, 60, 66, 72

2. Write the multiples of 9 from 9 to 108.   9, 18, 27, 36, 45, 54, 63, 72, 81, 90, 99, 108

3. Which of these numbers are multiples of 5?
   12   (25)   (50)   (95)   103   (120)   (385)   257   (430)

4. Which of these numbers are multiples of 8?
   (8)   18   (24)   28   30   (32)   (40)   42   (48)   54

When you solve a long division problem, always bring down all the digits in the dividend. Each time you bring a digit down, you **must** write a digit in the quotient. In the division problems of this lesson, some problems have three digits in the quotient.

$$\begin{array}{r} 189 \\ 5\overline{)945} \\ \underline{5} \\ 44 \\ \underline{40} \\ 45 \\ \underline{45} \end{array}$$

B. *Copy, divide, and check. Some of the quotients have three digits. There are no remainders.*

5. a. $4\overline{)192}$ 48 $\begin{array}{r}48\\ \times 4\\ \hline 192\end{array}$ b. $2\overline{)356}$ 178 $\begin{array}{r}178\\ \times 2\\ \hline 356\end{array}$ c. $3\overline{)552}$ 184 $\begin{array}{r}184\\ \times 3\\ \hline 552\end{array}$ d. $5\overline{)730}$ 146 $\begin{array}{r}146\\ \times 5\\ \hline 730\end{array}$

6. a. $4\overline{)988}$ 247 $\begin{array}{r}247\\ \times 4\\ \hline 988\end{array}$ b. $5\overline{)265}$ 53 $\begin{array}{r}53\\ \times 5\\ \hline 265\end{array}$ c. $2\overline{)764}$ 382 $\begin{array}{r}382\\ \times 2\\ \hline 764\end{array}$ d. $3\overline{)144}$ 48 $\begin{array}{r}48\\ \times 3\\ \hline 144\end{array}$

LESSON 77

Objectives

- To introduce *the term *multiple*. (The concept is not new.)
- To teach long division *with three-digit quotients.

Preparation

1. Multiplication and division flash cards
2. Chalkboard:

    a. 17,038   302,500   400,009   287,060

    b. $\quad\underline{(282)}\quad\quad\underline{(42)}\quad\quad\underline{(133)}$
        $3\overline{)846}\quad\;\;5\overline{)210}\quad\;\;4\overline{)532}$

        $\quad\underline{(149)}\quad\quad\underline{(67)}\quad\quad\underline{(158)}$
        $5\overline{)745}\quad\;\;2\overline{)134}\quad\;\;2\overline{)316}$

Oral Drill

1. Drill the multiplication and division facts as time permits.
2. Count by 3's, by 4's, by 6's, by 7's, by 8's, and by 9's.
3. a. **Which of these numbers divide evenly by 2?**

    32   56   89   100   205
    386   467   712   450

    b. **Which of these divide evenly by 5?**

    15   70   235   110   456

    c. **Which of these divide evenly by 9?**

    18   24   27   32   36   90   75
    72   42   56   54   63   64   81

4. Read the large numbers *(a)* on the board. **What is 100 more than 17,038? 2,000 less? ...**

5. Give mental drill.

    10 × 65   100 × 70
    40 × 3   50 × 9
    60 × 8   20 + 8
    90 + 7   30 − 2
    41 − 3   20 − 3
    6 + 7 − 3 ÷ 2 × 7 − 3 ÷ 8 (4)
    4 × 9 ÷ 6 + 8 − 2 ÷ 6 (2)

T–167 Chapter 8 Long Division

Teaching Guide

1. *Multiples.*
   a. **A *multiple* is a product of any number. The multiples of 5 are 5, 10, 15, 20, and so on.** If you counted as suggested in part 2 of Oral Drill, you were saying the multiples of various numbers.
   b. **What are some multiples of 4? of 6? of 9?** Continue until you are sure pupils understand the idea of multiples.
   c. Which of these are multiples of 8?
      42 48 54 56 63 64
      72 76 81 80 8   18
      28 24 30 32 36 40
   d. (Optional) **Common multiples** are multiples that are shared by two or more numbers. **What is a common multiple of 2 and 4?** Write the multiples of 2. Below them write the multiples of 4. What are some common multiples? (4, 8, 12, 16 . . .) **What is a common multiple of 3 and 4?** (12) **of 3 and 5?** (15) **of 4 and 8?** (8) **of 3 and 6?** (6) **of 3 and 8?** (24) **of 6 and 8?** (24)

2. *Three-digit quotients in long division.*
   a. Point to the first division problem *(b)* on the board. Write the first quotient figure above the correct digit in the dividend. Then have pupils tell how many digits will be in the quotient.
   b. Work through the problem together. Remind the pupils: **Whenever you bring a digit down from the dividend, you *must* put a digit up in the quotient.**
   c. Have the pupils look at the remaining division problems on the board. Ask how many digits will be in the quotient of each one.
   d. Have pupils solve the remaining problems, and check their answers by multiplication.

Note: If pupils have many of the reading problems wrong in this lesson, try to find out why. Did they make computation mistakes, or did they fail to understand the problems? Here are a few more that are similar.

• If a jet is traveling 650 miles an hour, how much faster is it going than a train traveling at 90 miles an hour? (560 m.p.h.)

• A jet travels 650 miles an hour, and a train travels 90 miles an hour. How much farther will the jet go in *1 hour* than the train will go in *6 hours*? (110 mi.)

• Two buses were carrying 57 children. If the children were divided as equally as possible, how many children were on each bus? (57 ÷ 2 = 28 R 1; 28 on one bus, 29 on the other)

Supplementary Drills

Drill 105*

Drill 29 ÷

Lesson 77   167

Review Exercises

C. *Solve these reading problems.*

7. Mark bought milk for $2.15 and 3 loaves of bread for $1.19 each. What was his total bill? $5.72

8. Martha and Louise shared 7 pieces of paper. What was each girl's share? $3\frac{1}{2}$ pieces

9. A plane flies 530 miles an hour, and a car travels 65 miles an hour. How much faster is the plane traveling than the car? 465 miles per hour

10. A plane flies 530 miles an hour, and a car travels 65 miles an hour. How much farther does the plane travel in **1 hour** than the car travels in **5 hours**? 205 miles

11. There are 427 passengers on a jet. If each of them has 3 pieces of luggage, how many pieces of luggage are on the jet? 1,281 pieces

D. *Write the answer to each problem as a fraction reduced to lowest terms.*

12. $2 \div 4$ $\frac{1}{2}$ $4 \div 6$ $\frac{2}{3}$ $6 \div 12$ $\frac{1}{2}$ $8 \div 10$ $\frac{4}{5}$ $4 \div 12$ $\frac{1}{3}$

E. *Write the answers quickly. By now you should know them very well.*

13.
3	5	8	4	2	7	4	2	1
×4	×5	×3	×5	×7	×3	×7	×8	×5
12	25	24	20	14	21	28	16	5

14.
5	12	10	0	4	6	3	5	3
×6	×4	×2	×3	×4	×6	×3	×3	×6
30	48	20	0	16	36	9	15	18

15.
6	4	3	11	6	7	9	0	12
×7	×8	×8	×8	×2	×5	×4	×7	×1
42	32	24	88	12	35	36	0	12

16.
8	9	7	6	9	8	8	9	7
×6	×7	×7	×9	×9	×7	×8	×8	×9
48	63	49	54	81	56	64	72	63

17.
9	5	12	8	12	0	12	12	12
×6	×8	×7	×9	×6	×8	×3	×9	×8
54	40	84	72	72	0	36	108	96

78. Learning More About Factors

> 1. **A pair of factors** is multiplied to form a **product.** One factor is the **multiplicand,** and the other factor is the **multiplier.**
> Pairs of factors for 12:   1 × 12   2 × 6   3 × 4
>
> 2. The **factors** of a number are all the different numbers by which it is divisible.
> All the factors of 12: 1, 2, 3, 4, 6, and 12
>
> 3. A number is a **multiple** of each of its **factors.**
> 12 is a multiple of the factors 1, 2, 3, 4, 6, and 12.

A. *Follow the directions.*

1. Write the pairs of factors for these numbers.

a. 6	b. 8	c. 9	d. 15	e. 18	f. 24
1 × 6	1 × ? 8	1 × ? 9	1 × ? 15	1 × ? 18	1 × 24
2 × ? 3	2 × ? 4	3 × ? 3	3 × ? 5	2 × ? 9	2 × ? 12
				3 × ? 6	3 × ? 8
					4 × ? 6

2. Now write **all** the factors in order for these numbers. The factor pairs in number 1 can help you.

   a. 6: __1__ , __2__ , __3__ , __6__
   b. 8: __1__ , __2__ , __4__ , __8__
   c. 9: __1__ , __3__ , __9__
   d. 15: __1__ , __3__ , __5__ , __15__
   e. 18: __1__ , __2__ , __3__ , __6__ , __9__ , __18__
   f. 24: __1__ , __2__ , __3__ , __4__ , __6__ , __8__ , __12__ , __24__

3. Write the numbers that have 3 as a factor (the multiples of 3).

   (3)   5   (6)   (9)   (12)   13
   23   (24)   26   (30)   (33)   35

4. Write the numbers that have 7 as a factor (the multiples of 7).

   5   (7)   12   (14)   18   24
   27   (28)   (35)   40   (42)   (49)

LESSON 78

Objective

♦ To introduce *finding the factors of numbers.

Preparation

1. Multiplication and division flash cards
2. Speed Drill 78
3. Chalkboard:

   a. $\frac{1}{3}$ $\frac{3}{4}$ $\frac{2}{4}$ $\frac{4}{8}$ $\frac{3}{4}$ $\frac{5}{8}$ $\frac{2}{3}$ $\frac{6}{18}$

   b.   7   multiplicand (factor)
     ×4   multiplier (factor)
     28   product

Oral Drill

1. Drill the multiplication and division facts.
2. **Which of the following numbers are multiples of 6?**
   (6)   14   16   21   (24)
   (30)   (36)   40   (42)   45

   Which of the following numbers are multiples of 9?
   6   (9)   12   (18)   (27)
   35   42   (45)   (72)   (90)

3. Review the parts of addition, subtraction, multiplication, and division problems.

4. a. Have pupils identify the pair of equivalent fractions in *a* on the board.
   b. Have them find some like fractions on the board.

5. **Tell which fraction in each pair is larger.**

   $\frac{1}{3}$ or $\frac{1}{5}$ $\frac{2}{4}$ or $\frac{2}{6}$ $\frac{3}{5}$ or $\frac{4}{5}$ $\frac{2}{8}$ or $\frac{5}{8}$

6. **1 is what part of 4? 2 is what part of 7? What is 3 ÷ 8?**

7. Review units of measure.
   1 lb. = (16) oz.   1 ton = (2,000) lb.
   1 yr. = (365) days   1 yr. = (52) wk.
   6 mo. = (1/2) yr.   8 mo. = (2/3) yr.
   6 oz. = (3/8) lb.   8 oz. = (1/2) lb.

Speed Drill

Give Speed Drill 78 (place value).

T-169 Chapter 8 Long Division

Teaching Guide

Finding the factors of numbers.

a. **Do you remember what a factor is?** (one of two numbers multiplied to make a product)

b. **The two factors have special names. One is the *multiplier* and one is the *multiplicand*. The multiplicand is the number that is multiplied. The multiplier is the number by which the multiplicand is multiplied.** Point to the problem *(b)* on the board to illustrate.

c. **Factors go in pairs because two numbers are multiplied to make a product. What pairs of factors equal 12?** Write the pairs of numbers on the board like this: 1 × 12, 2 × 6, 3 × 4.

d. **Now let's list all the factors of 12 in numerical order (counting order). What is the smallest factor of 12?** (1) **the next?** (2) Continue until all the factors are listed: 1, 2, 3, 4, 6, 12.

e. **Factors are usually listed in the order of size** (numerical order).

f. Give more practice in finding pairs of factors and in listing the factors in numerical order. Use 9, 26, 20, and 21 for practice.

Extra Review

Review long division with remainders as fractions.

$2\overline{)198}$ (99) $2\overline{)573}$ (286 1/2) $5\overline{)815}$ (163)

$4\overline{)354}$ (88 1/2) $3\overline{)721}$ (240 1/3) $4\overline{)660}$ (165)

Supplementary Drill

Drill 30 ÷

326

Review Exercises

B. *Copy, divide, and check.*

5. a. 2)948 quotient 474; check: 474 × 2 = 948
   b. 5)230 quotient 46; check: 46 × 5 = 230
   c. 4)338 quotient 84 R 2; check: 84 × 4 = 336, + 2 = 338

6. a. 5)735 quotient 147; check: 147 × 5 = 735
   b. 3)134 quotient 44 R 2; check: 44 × 3 = 132, + 2 = 134
   c. 3)846 quotient 282; check: 282 × 3 = 846

7. a. 4)780 quotient 195; check: 195 × 4 = 780
   b. 5)442 quotient 88 R 2; check: 88 × 5 = 440, + 2 = 442
   c. 5)965 quotient 193; check: 193 × 5 = 965

C. *Write the answers quickly.*

8. 6)72 = 12   5)45 = 9   8)80 = 10   9)108 = 12   7)56 = 8   8)48 = 6

9. 8)96 = 12   7)84 = 12   9)72 = 8   4)36 = 9   5)60 = 12   7)77 = 11

10. 8 × 9 = 72   12 × 9 = 108   6 × 9 = 54   7 × 8 = 56   9 × 7 = 63   4 × 8 = 32   12 × 8 = 96   12 × 7 = 84   6 × 7 = 42

D. *Do these exercises.*

11. Copy and add.

4,593	2,091	4,896	$19.47	$26.03
1,834	3,727	254	63.50	8.29
3,579	6,845	7,485	24.68	17.50
+ 4,462	+ 753	+ 2,647	+ 32.28	+ 84.62
14,468	13,416	15,282	$139.93	$136.44

12. Reduce these fractions to lowest terms.
    a. $\frac{3}{9}$ = $\frac{1}{3}$ b. $\frac{2}{10}$ = $\frac{1}{5}$ c. $\frac{4}{8}$ = $\frac{1}{2}$ d. $\frac{8}{12}$ = $\frac{2}{3}$ e. $\frac{12}{18}$ = $\frac{2}{3}$ f. $\frac{6}{15}$ = $\frac{2}{5}$ g. $\frac{10}{16}$ = $\frac{5}{8}$

E. *Solve these reading problems.*

13. The Miller family has 48 cows. Father and Philip do the milking. How many cows does each milk if they share the milking evenly? **24 cows**

14. How many cows are in each row if the 48 cows are in 3 rows? **16 cows**

15. One day Father, Jeffrey, and Philip baled 8 loads of hay with 155 bales on each load. How many bales was that altogether? **1,240 bales**

16. Jeffrey drove the tractor over 9 acres of hayfield. Philip drove the tractor over 5 acres. How many fewer acres did Philip bale than Jeffrey? **4 acres**

79. Midyear Review

A. *Say the answers as quickly as you can.*

1.
4	8	5	3	9	2	5	6	7
+8	+9	+6	+7	+6	+7	+8	+7	+9
12	17	11	10	15	9	13	13	16

2.
10	12	8	14	9	11	13	18	10
−6	−7	−5	−8	−4	−9	−4	−9	−5
4	5	3	6	5	2	9	9	5

3.
6	7	9	4	8	6	5	7	9
×7	×9	×8	×9	×8	×9	×7	×8	×9
42	63	72	36	64	54	35	56	81

4. 4)28̄ = 7   8)72̄ = 9   3)27̄ = 9   5)40̄ = 8   6)48̄ = 8   7)21̄ = 3

5. 7)56̄ = 8   9)63̄ = 7   4)32̄ = 8   6)36̄ = 6   5)60̄ = 12   6)18̄ = 3

B. *Write a number from the problems for each word.*

6.
- a. addend 24 or 36
- b. difference 39
- c. dividend 75
- d. divisor 5
- e. factor 45 or 7
- f. minuend 58
- g. product 315
- h. quotient 15
- i. subtrahend 19
- j. sum 60

$$24 + 36 \atop 60 \qquad 45 \times 7 \atop 315 \qquad 58 - 19 \atop 39 \qquad 5)\overline{75} = 15$$

C. *Write the four facts in these number families.*

7. a. 5, 7, 12 $5+7=12$ $7+5=12$ $12-5=7$ $12-7=5$

   b. 8, 3, 24 $8\times 3=24$ $3\times 8=24$ $24\div 8=3$ $24\div 3=8$

D. *Give the answers only.*

8. $10 + 7$ 17 $20 + 4$ 24 $17 + 2$ 19
9. $12 + 14$ 26 $15 + 6$ 21 $27 + 7$ 34
10. $17 - 2$ 15 $25 - 3$ 22 10×32 320
11. 100×14 1,400 20×8 160 40×5 200
12. $\frac{1}{3}$ of 24 8 $\frac{1}{4}$ of 16 4 $\frac{1}{7}$ of 42 6
13. $1 \div 4$ $\frac{1}{4}$ $2 \div 3$ $\frac{2}{3}$ 3 is what part of 5? $\frac{3}{5}$
14. 1 yd. = __36__ in.   1 ton = __2,000__ lb.   1 yr. = __52__ wk.
15. 1 hr. = __60__ min.   1 qt. = __2__ pt.   June = __30__ days

LESSON 79

Objective

♦ To give a cumulative review of the things taught in the first eight chapters (listed below).

Concepts taught in Chapter 8:
- Long division with up to three quotient figures and with or without remainders
- Checking division by multiplication
- Reducing fractions to lowest terms
- Two-step reading problems
- Dividing the remainder in reading problems
- Multiples and factors (not included on the test)

Other material included in the review and the test:
- Number facts and families
- Terminology of the four processes (such as addend)
- Computation in the four processes
- Horizontal addition and multiplication
- Telling time; A.M. and P.M.
- Money
- Roman numerals
- Large numbers and place value
- Symbols < and >
- Measuring to the nearest 1/8 inch
- Units of measure
- Changing units of measure
- Finding a part of a number
- Finding equivalent fractions by multiplying or dividing
- Reducing fractions

Preparation

1. Look over the teacher's guide for this lesson and decide which areas your pupils need the most help with. You will not be able to review everything in one class period.
2. Optional materials: flash cards, money for counting, clock with movable hands

Teaching Guide

1. You may want to do the first two pages of the pupil's lesson along with, or instead of, the items in this section. This will provide a variety of drill in preparation for the test. Give extra drill in areas where the pupils are weak.
   a. Review the number facts.
   b. Review fractions.
      (1) Numerator and denominator; like fractions
      (2) Counting by fourths and by eighths
      (3) Comparing the size of fractions
      (4) Dividing a smaller number by a larger one
      (5) Changing the remainder in a division problem to a fraction
   c. Here are some areas that have not been reviewed recently and may need extra drill.
      (1) Terminology of the four processes
      (2) Roman numerals
      Write these as Arabic numerals.
      XI (11)   IX (9)   IV (4)   VI (6)
      XXXVIII (38)   XL (40)   L (50)
      LXIV (64)   LXXII (72)
      Write these as Roman numerals.
      29 (XXIX)   43 (XLIII)   55 (LV)
      80 (LXXX)   69 (LXIX)
      74 (LXXIV)   18 (XVIII)
      (3) Place value; reading and writing large numbers
      130,800   40,001
      308,070   487,591
      (4) Time, including A.M. and P.M. Review telling time and writing times.
      (5) Units of measure
      (6) Multiplying numbers by 10 and by 100
      10 × 70   100 × 82
      40 × 3   50 × 6   70 × 8
      (7) Money concepts
      (8) Divisibility rules for 2 and 5

T–171   Chapter 8   Long Division

2. Review computation.
   a. Review the four basic processes. Use some of the problems in the former review lessons (9, 20, 30, 40, 50, 59, 69) for practice as needed.
   b. Review division problems from Chapter 8.

   $5\overline{)80}$ (16) $4\overline{)316}$ (79) $5\overline{)425}$ (85)

   $3\overline{)135}$ (45) $2\overline{)139}$ (69 1/2) $4\overline{)532}$ (133)

   c. Review changing fractions to equivalent fractions by multiplying or dividing. Review the reducing of fractions to lowest terms.
   d. Review changing from one unit of measure to another, using these lessons: 34, 35, 45, 66. For changing by division, include numbers that do not divide evenly, and have pupils express remainders as fractions.
   e. Review measuring with a ruler.

3. Review reading problems.
   a. The following pupil's lessons give help with reading problems: 4, 8, 13, 19, 25, 36, 46, 49, 55, 68, 73, 76.
   b. In the teacher's guide, extra practice is given in these lessons: 20, 30, 39, 49, 59, 68, 69, 74, 75.

4. Tell students that they will have a major test in the next class.

Note: If you have done the first two pages of the pupil's lesson in class, assign only the last two pages as written work.

E. Do these exercises.

16. Copy the numbers, and place commas correctly.

469201   469,201   39264   39,264   810052   810,052

17. Write numerals for these number words.
- a. four hundred two thousand, six hundred ten   402,610
- b. two hundred fifteen thousand, forty-eight   215,048
- c. seventeen thousand, four   17,004

18. Copy each pair of numbers, and write < or > between them.
- a. $\frac{1}{4}$ < $\frac{1}{3}$
- b. 17,000 < 17,998
- c. 24,001 > 23,999

19. Change these Arabic numerals to Roman numerals.
- a. 47 XLVII
- b. 19 XIX
- c. 85 LXXXV
- d. 28 XXVIII
- e. 54 LIV

20. Change these Roman numerals to Arabic numerals.
- a. XVII 17
- b. XXXIV 34
- c. LVI 56
- d. XLV 45
- e. LXXXIX 89

21. Write each price in two ways: a. 15 cents   b. 4 dollars
    15¢ $0.15 $4 $4.00

22. Write with numerals and symbols: twelve dollars and thirty cents $12.30

23. Is time in the afternoon A.M. or P.M. ?

24. Tell what time each clock shows, or what part is shaded.
- a. 1:50
- b. 7:15
- c. $\frac{5}{8}$
- d. $\frac{2}{5}$

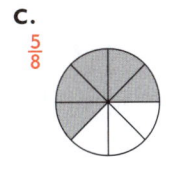

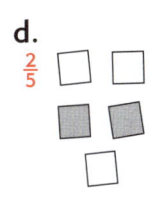

25. Count by eighths to 3 as you would count on a ruler.
$\frac{1}{8}, \frac{1}{4}, \frac{3}{8}, \frac{1}{2}, \frac{5}{8}, \frac{3}{4}, \frac{7}{8}, 1, 1\frac{1}{8}, 1\frac{1}{4}, 1\frac{3}{8}, 1\frac{1}{2}, 1\frac{5}{8}, 1\frac{3}{4}, 1\frac{7}{8}, 2, 2\frac{1}{8}, 2\frac{1}{4}, 2\frac{3}{8}, 2\frac{1}{2}, 2\frac{5}{8}, 2\frac{3}{4}, 2\frac{7}{8}, 3$

26. Which numbers divide evenly by 2?   25   (78)   (150)   (374)   461

27. Which numbers divide evenly by 5?   (30)   (105)   253   (325)   (400)

28. What fraction has a numerator of 4 and a denominator of 7? $\frac{4}{7}$

29. Is this a pair of like fractions? $\frac{1}{4}$ $\frac{3}{4}$ yes

(continued on next page)

172   Chapter 8   Long Division

F. *Copy and solve. Follow the signs.*

30.
$$\begin{array}{r} 5 \\ 4 \\ 7 \\ +8 \\ \hline 24 \end{array} \qquad \begin{array}{r} 7 \\ 6 \\ 3 \\ +4 \\ \hline 20 \end{array} \qquad \begin{array}{r} 8 \\ 3 \\ 5 \\ +9 \\ \hline 25 \end{array} \qquad \begin{array}{r} 2 \\ 8 \\ 8 \\ 5 \\ +6 \\ \hline 29 \end{array} \qquad \begin{array}{r} 4 \\ 9 \\ 5 \\ 6 \\ +7 \\ \hline 31 \end{array} \qquad \begin{array}{r} 12 \\ 55 \\ 36 \\ +74 \\ \hline 177 \end{array} \qquad \begin{array}{r} 49 \\ 26 \\ 74 \\ +38 \\ \hline 187 \end{array}$$

31.
$$\begin{array}{r} 494 \\ 267 \\ +354 \\ \hline 1,115 \end{array} \qquad \begin{array}{r} 972 \\ 157 \\ 346 \\ +257 \\ \hline 1,732 \end{array} \qquad \begin{array}{r} 8,046 \\ 6,832 \\ +4,837 \\ \hline 19,715 \end{array} \qquad \begin{array}{r} \$20.48 \\ 14.57 \\ +35.24 \\ \hline \$70.29 \end{array} \qquad \begin{array}{r} \$36.50 \\ 25.38 \\ +27.85 \\ \hline \$89.73 \end{array}$$

32.
$$\begin{array}{r} 501 \\ -278 \\ \hline 223 \end{array} \qquad \begin{array}{r} 7,302 \\ -3,545 \\ \hline 3,757 \end{array} \qquad \begin{array}{r} 6,000 \\ -4,193 \\ \hline 1,807 \end{array} \qquad \begin{array}{r} \$90.50 \\ -17.23 \\ \hline \$73.27 \end{array} \qquad \begin{array}{r} \$50.00 \\ -28.95 \\ \hline \$21.05 \end{array}$$

33.
$$\begin{array}{r} 378 \\ \times 4 \\ \hline 1,512 \end{array} \qquad \begin{array}{r} 986 \\ \times 6 \\ \hline 5,916 \end{array} \qquad \begin{array}{r} 873 \\ \times 8 \\ \hline 6,984 \end{array} \qquad \begin{array}{r} 568 \\ \times 5 \\ \hline 2,840 \end{array} \qquad \begin{array}{r} 609 \\ \times 7 \\ \hline 4,263 \end{array}$$

G. *Do these exercises.*

34. Divide, and write remainders as fractions.

   $3\overline{)25}$ → $8\frac{1}{3}$ $5\overline{)257}$ → $51\frac{2}{5}$ $2\overline{)154}$ → 77 $3\overline{)226}$ → $75\frac{1}{3}$ $4\overline{)660}$ → 165

35. Copy in columns. Check by addition.

   a. $7 - \$2.59$ $\$4.41$ $\begin{array}{r} \$4.41 \\ +2.59 \\ \hline \$7.00 \end{array}$ b. $\$15.25 - \$8.50$ $\$6.75$ $\begin{array}{r} \$6.75 \\ +8.50 \\ \hline \$15.25 \end{array}$

36. Copy and divide. Check by multiplication.

   a. $4\overline{)76}$ → 19 $\begin{array}{r} 19 \\ \times 4 \\ \hline 76 \end{array}$ b. $5\overline{)367}$ → 73 R 2 $\begin{array}{r} 73 \\ \times 5 \\ \hline 365 \\ +2 \\ \hline 367 \end{array}$ c. $4\overline{)512}$ → 128 $\begin{array}{r} 128 \\ \times 4 \\ \hline 512 \end{array}$

37. Change to equivalent fractions by multiplying.

   a. $\frac{1}{2} = \frac{4}{8}$ b. $\frac{2}{3} = \frac{6}{9}$ c. $\frac{3}{5} = \frac{6}{10}$

38. Reduce these fractions to lowest terms by dividing.

   a. $\frac{4}{16} = \frac{1}{4}$ b. $\frac{3}{12} = \frac{1}{4}$ c. $\frac{6}{8} = \frac{3}{4}$ d. $\frac{8}{16} = \frac{1}{2}$

H. *Find the missing numbers by multiplying or dividing.*

39. 3 lb. = __48__ oz.   5 doz. = __60__ things   12 qt. = __3__ gal.

40. $\frac{1}{3}$ yr. = __4__ mo.   5 cups = __$2\frac{1}{2}$__ pt.   10 ft. = __$3\frac{1}{3}$__ yd.

T–173 Chapter 8 Long Division

LESSON 80

Objective

- To test the pupils' mastery of the concepts taught in the first half of this course.

Teaching Guide

1. Give Speed Drill 80 (multiplication practice). Be sure pupils understand what they are to do.

   Note: Speed Drills are optional on test days.

2. Give any last-minute review that you feel is necessary.

3. Administer the test.

   Note: Chapter 8 Test is found in the test section in the back of this manual.

I. *Follow the directions.*

41. Measure these lines with your ruler.
    a. ———————————————— $3\frac{1}{2}$ in.
    b. —————————————————— $4\frac{1}{8}$ in.

42. Count the money, and give its value. $10.85

43. Tell the value of the following coins and bills.
    a. 3 ten-dollar bills, 2 five-dollar bills, 3 quarters $40.75
    b. 2 twenty-dollar bills, 4 ones, 2 quarters, 3 dimes, 2 pennies $44.82
    c. 3 twenty-dollar bills, 1 five-dollar bill, 1 quarter, 3 nickels $65.40

44. Write **add, subtract, multiply,** or **divide** for each question.
    a. How many left?   subtract   e. How much at 27¢ each?   multiply
    b. How many more?   subtract   f. What is the total?   add
    c. How many in all?   add   g. What is $\frac{1}{3}$ of a number?   divide
    d. How many in each group?   divide   h. How many in 4 groups of 6?   multiply

J. *Solve these reading problems.*

45. Rosanna is embroidering patches for a quilt. She needs 7 rows of patches with 6 patches in each row. How many patches does she need?
    42 patches

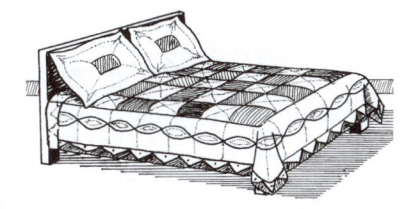

46. For the quilt border, Rosanna needs 258 triangle-shaped pieces and half as many square pieces. How many square pieces does Rosanna need?
    129 squares

47. If 3 girls share 7 kittens, how many kittens can each girl have?   2 kittens, R 1

48. The items on Aunt Ruth's grocery bill cost $1.27, $0.89, and $2.53. What was her change from $5.00? $0.31

49. Mother bought meat for $1.99 and 3 pounds of apples at $0.45 a pound. What was her bill? $3.34

50. Sarah lived 90 years before her son Isaac was born and 37 years afterward. How old was Sarah when she died?   127 years

80. Chapter 8 Test

Puzzle Page 2

Stair-step Numbers

The blocks on this page are arranged like stairsteps. Each row of blocks has one more block than the row above it. These blocks can help you to learn about "stair-step numbers."

The top row of blocks has **one** block, so **1** is a stair-step number. The next stair-step number is 1 + 2, or **3**. The next stair-step number is 1 + 2 + 3, or **6**. Other stair-step numbers are found by adding the other rows in order.

1										1 = **1**
1	2									1 + 2 = **3**
1	2	3								1 + 2 + 3 = **6**
1	2	3	4							1 + 2 + 3 + 4 = **10**
1	2	3	4	5						1 + 2 + 3 + 4 + 5 = **15**
1	2	3	4	5	6	21				
1	2	3	4	5	6	7	28			
1	2	3	4	5	6	7	8	36		
1	2	3	4	5	6	7	8	9	45	
1	2	3	4	5	6	7	8	9	10	55

Can you do this?

1. List the first five stair-step numbers (shown on this page).

2. Find the next five stair-step numbers. Add the numbers in each row as shown in the problems above.

PUZZLE PAGE 2

To the Teacher

This page is the second of four optional puzzle pages in the book. See notes to the teacher with Puzzle Page 1 at the end of Chapter 4.

"Stair-step numbers" are found by adding whole numbers in numerical order. The blocks on the page illustrate why these numbers can be called stair-step numbers.

Stair-step numbers are also called triangle numbers. These numbers are interesting in that the sum of any two adjacent stair-step numbers is a perfect square. For example, 1 + 3 = 4, 3 + 6 = 9, 6 + 10 = 16, and 10 + 15 = 25.

Finding the larger stair-step numbers by addition is tedious work. The process can be greatly simplified by using multiplication. For example, the fifth stair-step number is the sum of the numbers from 1 to 5. This number can be found as follows: Multiply the last number in the series (5) times the next higher number (6), and divide the product in half. Thus, the fifth stair-step number is 5 × 6 ÷ 2, or 15. The tenth stair-step number is 10 × 11 ÷ 2, or 55. And the *fiftieth* stair-step number is 50 × 51 ÷ 2, or 1,275.

Chapters 9–17

are covered in

Teacher's Manual

Part 2

Supplementary Drills

	Multiplication Tables	360
	Division Tables	361
Set I	Fact Drills	362
Set II	Mixed Computation Drills	395
Set III	Addition Drills	398
Set IV	Subtraction Drills	403
Set V	Multiplication Drills	407
Set VI	Division Drills	412
Set VII	Fraction Drills	415
Set VIII	Secondary Skills Drills	422

Multiplication Tables

0	1	2	3	4	5	6	7	8	9	10	11	12
×1	×1	×1	×1	×1	×1	×1	×1	×1	×1	×1	×1	×1
0	1	2	3	4	5	6	7	8	9	10	11	12

0	1	2	3	4	5	6	7	8	9	10	11	12
×2	×2	×2	×2	×2	×2	×2	×2	×2	×2	×2	×2	×2
0	2	4	6	8	10	12	14	16	18	20	22	24

0	1	2	3	4	5	6	7	8	9	10	11	12
×3	×3	×3	×3	×3	×3	×3	×3	×3	×3	×3	×3	×3
0	3	6	9	12	15	18	21	24	27	30	33	36

0	1	2	3	4	5	6	7	8	9	10	11	12
×4	×4	×4	×4	×4	×4	×4	×4	×4	×4	×4	×4	×4
0	4	8	12	16	20	24	28	32	36	40	44	48

0	1	2	3	4	5	6	7	8	9	10	11	12
×5	×5	×5	×5	×5	×5	×5	×5	×5	×5	×5	×5	×5
0	5	10	15	20	25	30	35	40	45	50	55	60

0	1	2	3	4	5	6	7	8	9	10	11	12
×6	×6	×6	×6	×6	×6	×6	×6	×6	×6	×6	×6	×6
0	6	12	18	24	30	36	42	48	54	60	66	72

0	1	2	3	4	5	6	7	8	9	10	11	12
×7	×7	×7	×7	×7	×7	×7	×7	×7	×7	×7	×7	×7
0	7	14	21	28	35	42	49	56	63	70	77	84

0	1	2	3	4	5	6	7	8	9	10	11	12
×8	×8	×8	×8	×8	×8	×8	×8	×8	×8	×8	×8	×8
0	8	16	24	32	40	48	56	64	72	80	88	96

0	1	2	3	4	5	6	7	8	9	10	11	12
×9	×9	×9	×9	×9	×9	×9	×9	×9	×9	×9	×9	×9
0	9	18	27	36	45	54	63	72	81	90	99	108

0	1	2	3	4	5	6	7	8	9	10	11	12
×10	×10	×10	×10	×10	×10	×10	×10	×10	×10	×10	×10	×10
0	10	20	30	40	50	60	70	80	90	100	110	120

0	1	2	3	4	5	6	7	8	9	10	11	12
×11	×11	×11	×11	×11	×11	×11	×11	×11	×11	×11	×11	×11
0	11	22	33	44	55	66	77	88	99	110	121	132

0	1	2	3	4	5	6	7	8	9	10	11	12
×12	×12	×12	×12	×12	×12	×12	×12	×12	×12	×12	×12	×12
0	12	24	36	48	60	72	84	96	108	120	132	144

Division Tables

	$\dfrac{1}{1\overline{)1}}$	$\dfrac{2}{1\overline{)2}}$	$\dfrac{3}{1\overline{)3}}$	$\dfrac{4}{1\overline{)4}}$	$\dfrac{5}{1\overline{)5}}$	$\dfrac{6}{1\overline{)6}}$	$\dfrac{7}{1\overline{)7}}$	$\dfrac{8}{1\overline{)8}}$	$\dfrac{9}{1\overline{)9}}$	$\dfrac{10}{1\overline{)10}}$	$\dfrac{11}{1\overline{)11}}$	$\dfrac{12}{1\overline{)12}}$
$\dfrac{0}{1\overline{)0}}$												
$\dfrac{0}{2\overline{)0}}$	$\dfrac{1}{2\overline{)2}}$	$\dfrac{2}{2\overline{)4}}$	$\dfrac{3}{2\overline{)6}}$	$\dfrac{4}{2\overline{)8}}$	$\dfrac{5}{2\overline{)10}}$	$\dfrac{6}{2\overline{)12}}$	$\dfrac{7}{2\overline{)14}}$	$\dfrac{8}{2\overline{)16}}$	$\dfrac{9}{2\overline{)18}}$	$\dfrac{10}{2\overline{)20}}$	$\dfrac{11}{2\overline{)22}}$	$\dfrac{12}{2\overline{)24}}$
$\dfrac{0}{3\overline{)0}}$	$\dfrac{1}{3\overline{)3}}$	$\dfrac{2}{3\overline{)6}}$	$\dfrac{3}{3\overline{)9}}$	$\dfrac{4}{3\overline{)12}}$	$\dfrac{5}{3\overline{)15}}$	$\dfrac{6}{3\overline{)18}}$	$\dfrac{7}{3\overline{)21}}$	$\dfrac{8}{3\overline{)24}}$	$\dfrac{9}{3\overline{)27}}$	$\dfrac{10}{3\overline{)30}}$	$\dfrac{11}{3\overline{)33}}$	$\dfrac{12}{3\overline{)36}}$
$\dfrac{0}{4\overline{)0}}$	$\dfrac{1}{4\overline{)4}}$	$\dfrac{2}{4\overline{)8}}$	$\dfrac{3}{4\overline{)12}}$	$\dfrac{4}{4\overline{)16}}$	$\dfrac{5}{4\overline{)20}}$	$\dfrac{6}{4\overline{)24}}$	$\dfrac{7}{4\overline{)28}}$	$\dfrac{8}{4\overline{)32}}$	$\dfrac{9}{4\overline{)36}}$	$\dfrac{10}{4\overline{)40}}$	$\dfrac{11}{4\overline{)44}}$	$\dfrac{12}{4\overline{)48}}$
$\dfrac{0}{5\overline{)0}}$	$\dfrac{1}{5\overline{)5}}$	$\dfrac{2}{5\overline{)10}}$	$\dfrac{3}{5\overline{)15}}$	$\dfrac{4}{5\overline{)20}}$	$\dfrac{5}{5\overline{)25}}$	$\dfrac{6}{5\overline{)30}}$	$\dfrac{7}{5\overline{)35}}$	$\dfrac{8}{5\overline{)40}}$	$\dfrac{9}{5\overline{)45}}$	$\dfrac{10}{5\overline{)50}}$	$\dfrac{11}{5\overline{)55}}$	$\dfrac{12}{5\overline{)60}}$
$\dfrac{0}{6\overline{)0}}$	$\dfrac{1}{6\overline{)6}}$	$\dfrac{2}{6\overline{)12}}$	$\dfrac{3}{6\overline{)18}}$	$\dfrac{4}{6\overline{)24}}$	$\dfrac{5}{6\overline{)30}}$	$\dfrac{6}{6\overline{)36}}$	$\dfrac{7}{6\overline{)42}}$	$\dfrac{8}{6\overline{)48}}$	$\dfrac{9}{6\overline{)54}}$	$\dfrac{10}{6\overline{)60}}$	$\dfrac{11}{6\overline{)66}}$	$\dfrac{12}{6\overline{)72}}$
$\dfrac{0}{7\overline{)0}}$	$\dfrac{1}{7\overline{)7}}$	$\dfrac{2}{7\overline{)14}}$	$\dfrac{3}{7\overline{)21}}$	$\dfrac{4}{7\overline{)28}}$	$\dfrac{5}{7\overline{)35}}$	$\dfrac{6}{7\overline{)42}}$	$\dfrac{7}{7\overline{)49}}$	$\dfrac{8}{7\overline{)56}}$	$\dfrac{9}{7\overline{)63}}$	$\dfrac{10}{7\overline{)70}}$	$\dfrac{11}{7\overline{)77}}$	$\dfrac{12}{7\overline{)84}}$
$\dfrac{0}{8\overline{)0}}$	$\dfrac{1}{8\overline{)8}}$	$\dfrac{2}{8\overline{)16}}$	$\dfrac{3}{8\overline{)24}}$	$\dfrac{4}{8\overline{)32}}$	$\dfrac{5}{8\overline{)40}}$	$\dfrac{6}{8\overline{)48}}$	$\dfrac{7}{8\overline{)56}}$	$\dfrac{8}{8\overline{)64}}$	$\dfrac{9}{8\overline{)72}}$	$\dfrac{10}{8\overline{)80}}$	$\dfrac{11}{8\overline{)88}}$	$\dfrac{12}{8\overline{)96}}$
$\dfrac{0}{9\overline{)0}}$	$\dfrac{1}{9\overline{)9}}$	$\dfrac{2}{9\overline{)18}}$	$\dfrac{3}{9\overline{)27}}$	$\dfrac{4}{9\overline{)36}}$	$\dfrac{5}{9\overline{)45}}$	$\dfrac{6}{9\overline{)54}}$	$\dfrac{7}{9\overline{)63}}$	$\dfrac{8}{9\overline{)72}}$	$\dfrac{9}{9\overline{)81}}$	$\dfrac{10}{9\overline{)90}}$	$\dfrac{11}{9\overline{)99}}$	$\dfrac{12}{9\overline{)108}}$
$\dfrac{0}{10\overline{)0}}$	$\dfrac{1}{10\overline{)10}}$	$\dfrac{2}{10\overline{)20}}$	$\dfrac{3}{10\overline{)30}}$	$\dfrac{4}{10\overline{)40}}$	$\dfrac{5}{10\overline{)50}}$	$\dfrac{6}{10\overline{)60}}$	$\dfrac{7}{10\overline{)70}}$	$\dfrac{8}{10\overline{)80}}$	$\dfrac{9}{10\overline{)90}}$	$\dfrac{10}{10\overline{)100}}$	$\dfrac{11}{10\overline{)110}}$	$\dfrac{12}{10\overline{)120}}$
$\dfrac{0}{11\overline{)0}}$	$\dfrac{1}{11\overline{)11}}$	$\dfrac{2}{11\overline{)22}}$	$\dfrac{3}{11\overline{)33}}$	$\dfrac{4}{11\overline{)44}}$	$\dfrac{5}{11\overline{)55}}$	$\dfrac{6}{11\overline{)66}}$	$\dfrac{7}{11\overline{)77}}$	$\dfrac{8}{11\overline{)88}}$	$\dfrac{9}{11\overline{)99}}$	$\dfrac{10}{11\overline{)110}}$	$\dfrac{11}{11\overline{)121}}$	$\dfrac{12}{11\overline{)132}}$
$\dfrac{0}{12\overline{)0}}$	$\dfrac{1}{12\overline{)12}}$	$\dfrac{2}{12\overline{)24}}$	$\dfrac{3}{12\overline{)36}}$	$\dfrac{4}{12\overline{)48}}$	$\dfrac{5}{12\overline{)60}}$	$\dfrac{6}{12\overline{)72}}$	$\dfrac{7}{12\overline{)84}}$	$\dfrac{8}{12\overline{)96}}$	$\dfrac{9}{12\overline{)108}}$	$\dfrac{10}{12\overline{)120}}$	$\dfrac{11}{12\overline{)132}}$	$\dfrac{12}{12\overline{)144}}$

Set 1: Fact Drills

Drill 1   *100 Addition Facts*

It is important to know the addition facts well. You should be able to write the answers to the 100 basic addition facts in 4 minutes or less.

	a.	b.	c.	d.	e.	f.	g.	h.	i.	j.
1.	1 + 1 = 2	4 + 0 = 4	7 + 3 = 10	9 + 1 = 10	0 + 0 = 0	1 + 2 = 3	2 + 3 = 5	3 + 1 = 4	1 + 0 = 1	0 + 9 = 9
2.	0 + 1 = 1	3 + 3 = 6	8 + 4 = 12	0 + 3 = 3	1 + 5 = 6	2 + 2 = 4	3 + 0 = 3	7 + 0 = 7	5 + 5 = 10	6 + 2 = 8
3.	2 + 0 = 2	1 + 3 = 4	0 + 5 = 5	8 + 1 = 9	5 + 0 = 5	4 + 4 = 8	0 + 6 = 6	0 + 2 = 2	1 + 7 = 8	5 + 3 = 8
4.	0 + 4 = 4	1 + 6 = 7	6 + 6 = 12	9 + 0 = 9	0 + 8 = 8	3 + 2 = 5	3 + 4 = 7	2 + 1 = 3	0 + 7 = 7	1 + 8 = 9
5.	1 + 4 = 5	7 + 2 = 9	9 + 9 = 18	2 + 4 = 6	5 + 1 = 6	4 + 5 = 9	8 + 0 = 8	7 + 1 = 8	6 + 0 = 6	5 + 4 = 9
6.	3 + 5 = 8	1 + 9 = 10	8 + 2 = 10	5 + 2 = 7	2 + 6 = 8	5 + 6 = 11	4 + 1 = 5	9 + 2 = 11	4 + 3 = 7	6 + 4 = 10
7.	2 + 5 = 7	6 + 1 = 7	6 + 3 = 9	4 + 2 = 6	2 + 8 = 10	2 + 7 = 9	8 + 8 = 16	4 + 6 = 10	5 + 7 = 12	3 + 8 = 11
8.	3 + 6 = 9	2 + 9 = 11	5 + 8 = 13	9 + 3 = 12	3 + 7 = 10	4 + 8 = 12	7 + 7 = 14	6 + 5 = 11	9 + 4 = 13	4 + 7 = 11
9.	7 + 4 = 11	7 + 8 = 15	9 + 5 = 14	6 + 7 = 13	3 + 9 = 12	5 + 9 = 14	6 + 8 = 14	4 + 9 = 13	8 + 9 = 17	9 + 6 = 15
10.	7 + 5 = 12	7 + 9 = 16	8 + 7 = 15	9 + 8 = 17	8 + 6 = 14	6 + 9 = 15	9 + 7 = 16	8 + 3 = 11	8 + 5 = 13	7 + 6 = 13

Drill 2 — *100 Addition Facts*

Can you write these answers in four minutes or less?

	a.	b.	c.	d.	e.	f.	g.	h.	i.	j.
1.	0 + 0 = 0	1 + 5 = 6	5 + 0 = 5	0 + 8 = 8	5 + 1 = 6	2 + 6 = 8	2 + 8 = 10	3 + 7 = 10	3 + 9 = 12	8 + 6 = 14
2.	1 + 1 = 2	7 + 4 = 11	0 + 1 = 1	2 + 0 = 2	0 + 4 = 4	1 + 4 = 5	3 + 5 = 8	2 + 5 = 7	3 + 6 = 9	7 + 5 = 12
3.	9 + 8 = 17	4 + 2 = 6	6 + 7 = 13	9 + 3 = 12	5 + 2 = 7	2 + 4 = 6	9 + 0 = 9	8 + 1 = 9	0 + 3 = 3	9 + 1 = 10
4.	1 + 2 = 3	2 + 2 = 4	4 + 4 = 8	5 + 9 = 14	3 + 2 = 5	4 + 5 = 9	5 + 6 = 11	2 + 7 = 9	4 + 8 = 12	6 + 9 = 15
5.	7 + 3 = 10	8 + 4 = 12	0 + 5 = 5	6 + 6 = 12	9 + 9 = 18	8 + 2 = 10	6 + 3 = 9	5 + 8 = 13	9 + 5 = 14	8 + 7 = 15
6.	1 + 6 = 7	4 + 0 = 4	3 + 3 = 6	1 + 3 = 4	7 + 8 = 15	1 + 9 = 10	6 + 1 = 7	2 + 9 = 11	7 + 2 = 9	7 + 9 = 16
7.	0 + 9 = 9	6 + 2 = 8	5 + 3 = 8	1 + 8 = 9	5 + 4 = 9	3 + 8 = 11	6 + 4 = 10	4 + 7 = 11	9 + 6 = 15	7 + 6 = 13
8.	8 + 3 = 11	4 + 9 = 13	6 + 5 = 11	4 + 6 = 10	9 + 2 = 11	7 + 1 = 8	2 + 1 = 3	0 + 2 = 2	7 + 0 = 7	3 + 1 = 4
9.	1 + 0 = 1	5 + 5 = 10	1 + 7 = 8	0 + 7 = 7	6 + 0 = 6	4 + 3 = 7	5 + 7 = 12	9 + 4 = 13	8 + 9 = 17	8 + 5 = 13
10.	3 + 0 = 3	2 + 3 = 5	0 + 6 = 6	3 + 4 = 7	8 + 0 = 8	8 + 8 = 16	7 + 7 = 14	4 + 1 = 5	6 + 8 = 14	9 + 7 = 16

Drill 3 — 100 Subtraction Facts

It is important to know the subtraction facts well. You should be able to write the answers to the 100 basic subtraction facts in 4 minutes or less.

	a.	b.	c.	d.	e.	f.	g.	h.	i.	j.
1.	1 − 1 = 0	8 − 0 = 8	4 − 3 = 1	3 − 3 = 0	0 − 0 = 0	2 − 1 = 1	3 − 0 = 3	9 − 2 = 7	5 − 1 = 4	6 − 3 = 3
2.	6 − 1 = 5	9 − 0 = 9	2 − 2 = 0	1 − 0 = 1	8 − 1 = 7	5 − 5 = 0	4 − 4 = 0	8 − 3 = 5	7 − 2 = 5	3 − 2 = 1
3.	2 − 0 = 2	6 − 5 = 1	8 − 4 = 4	4 − 2 = 2	9 − 1 = 8	7 − 0 = 7	3 − 1 = 2	4 − 0 = 4	6 − 2 = 4	5 − 0 = 5
4.	4 − 1 = 3	8 − 8 = 0	7 − 1 = 6	9 − 3 = 6	9 − 5 = 4	10 − 1 = 9	8 − 7 = 1	6 − 0 = 6	5 − 2 = 3	9 − 9 = 0
5.	5 − 3 = 2	10 − 5 = 5	8 − 2 = 6	6 − 4 = 2	7 − 7 = 0	8 − 5 = 3	7 − 4 = 3	5 − 4 = 1	11 − 3 = 8	9 − 8 = 1
6.	10 − 9 = 1	6 − 6 = 0	7 − 5 = 2	9 − 4 = 5	10 − 2 = 8	13 − 4 = 9	11 − 2 = 9	7 − 3 = 4	10 − 4 = 6	9 − 7 = 2
7.	7 − 6 = 1	9 − 6 = 3	11 − 5 = 6	12 − 3 = 9	14 − 7 = 7	8 − 6 = 2	12 − 6 = 6	10 − 3 = 7	16 − 8 = 8	14 − 5 = 9
8.	10 − 8 = 2	12 − 5 = 7	14 − 6 = 8	13 − 7 = 6	18 − 9 = 9	17 − 9 = 8	10 − 6 = 4	11 − 9 = 2	15 − 6 = 9	12 − 4 = 8
9.	15 − 8 = 7	17 − 8 = 9	10 − 7 = 3	12 − 9 = 3	14 − 9 = 5	13 − 5 = 8	11 − 8 = 3	16 − 7 = 9	13 − 9 = 4	11 − 6 = 5
10.	11 − 7 = 4	15 − 9 = 6	12 − 8 = 4	11 − 4 = 7	14 − 8 = 6	13 − 6 = 7	16 − 7 = 9	12 − 7 = 5	13 − 8 = 5	15 − 7 = 8

Drill 4 — 100 Subtraction Facts

Can you write the answers to these facts in 4 minutes or less?

	a.	b.	c.	d.	e.	f.	g.	h.	i.	j.
1.	8 − 0 = 8	9 − 0 = 9	6 − 5 = 1	8 − 8 = 0	10 − 5 = 5	6 − 6 = 0	9 − 6 = 3	12 − 5 = 7	17 − 8 = 9	15 − 9 = 6
2.	3 − 3 = 0	1 − 0 = 1	4 − 2 = 2	9 − 3 = 6	6 − 4 = 2	9 − 4 = 5	12 − 3 = 9	13 − 7 = 6	12 − 9 = 3	11 − 4 = 7
3.	2 − 1 = 1	5 − 5 = 0	7 − 0 = 7	10 − 1 = 9	8 − 5 = 3	13 − 4 = 9	8 − 6 = 2	17 − 9 = 8	13 − 5 = 8	13 − 6 = 7
4.	9 − 2 = 7	8 − 3 = 5	4 − 0 = 4	6 − 0 = 6	5 − 4 = 1	7 − 3 = 4	10 − 3 = 7	11 − 9 = 2	16 − 7 = 9	12 − 7 = 5
5.	6 − 3 = 3	3 − 2 = 1	5 − 0 = 5	9 − 9 = 0	9 − 7 = 2	14 − 5 = 9	9 − 8 = 1	12 − 4 = 8	11 − 6 = 5	15 − 7 = 8
6.	11 − 7 = 4	10 − 8 = 2	10 − 9 = 1	4 − 1 = 3	6 − 1 = 5	15 − 8 = 7	7 − 6 = 1	5 − 3 = 2	2 − 0 = 2	1 − 1 = 0
7.	4 − 3 = 1	2 − 2 = 0	8 − 4 = 4	7 − 1 = 6	8 − 2 = 6	7 − 5 = 2	11 − 5 = 6	14 − 6 = 8	10 − 7 = 3	12 − 8 = 4
8.	0 − 0 = 0	8 − 1 = 7	14 − 8 = 6	9 − 5 = 4	7 − 7 = 0	10 − 2 = 8	14 − 7 = 7	18 − 9 = 9	14 − 9 = 5	9 − 1 = 8
9.	16 − 7 = 9	11 − 8 = 3	10 − 6 = 4	12 − 6 = 6	11 − 2 = 9	7 − 4 = 3	8 − 7 = 1	3 − 1 = 2	4 − 4 = 0	3 − 0 = 3
10.	5 − 1 = 4	7 − 2 = 5	6 − 2 = 4	11 − 3 = 8	5 − 2 = 3	10 − 4 = 6	16 − 8 = 8	13 − 8 = 5	15 − 6 = 9	13 − 9 = 4

Drill 5 — Multiplication Facts: 1's–3's

	a.	b.	c.	d.	e.	f.	g.	h.	i.	j.
1.	2 × 3 = 6	9 × 0 = 0	1 × 2 = 2	11 × 3 = 33	8 × 2 = 16	11 × 0 = 0	5 × 3 = 15	7 × 1 = 7	12 × 2 = 24	6 × 3 = 18
2.	4 × 3 = 12	10 × 1 = 10	12 × 2 = 24	9 × 3 = 27	10 × 2 = 20	4 × 2 = 8	9 × 1 = 9	7 × 3 = 21	4 × 0 = 0	7 × 2 = 14
3.	11 × 2 = 22	12 × 3 = 36	12 × 1 = 12	6 × 3 = 18	6 × 2 = 12	3 × 3 = 9	5 × 1 = 5	8 × 0 = 0	5 × 3 = 15	9 × 2 = 18
4.	9 × 3 = 27	0 × 1 = 0	6 × 2 = 12	1 × 1 = 1	8 × 3 = 24	3 × 2 = 6	9 × 2 = 18	10 × 3 = 30	4 × 1 = 4	4 × 3 = 12
5.	2 × 2 = 4	11 × 3 = 33	10 × 2 = 20	8 × 2 = 16	7 × 2 = 14	8 × 1 = 8	8 × 3 = 24	4 × 0 = 0	5 × 3 = 15	5 × 2 = 10

Drill 6 — Multiplication Facts: 1's–5's

	a.	b.	c.	d.	e.	f.	g.	h.	i.	j.
1.	5 × 5 = 25	0 × 2 = 0	6 × 3 = 18	10 × 1 = 10	6 × 4 = 24	9 × 4 = 36	2 × 3 = 6	5 × 3 = 15	6 × 2 = 12	12 × 2 = 24
2.	8 × 3 = 24	4 × 4 = 16	7 × 4 = 28	12 × 5 = 60	10 × 2 = 20	11 × 1 = 11	3 × 4 = 12	7 × 5 = 35	8 × 4 = 32	2 × 5 = 10
3.	8 × 2 = 16	10 × 5 = 50	9 × 2 = 18	3 × 5 = 15	0 × 5 = 0	11 × 4 = 44	1 × 3 = 3	2 × 4 = 8	12 × 4 = 48	3 × 2 = 6
4.	10 × 3 = 30	11 × 5 = 55	1 × 1 = 1	7 × 2 = 14	4 × 3 = 12	9 × 5 = 45	12 × 3 = 36	4 × 5 = 20	2 × 2 = 4	8 × 5 = 40
5.	6 × 5 = 30	12 × 5 = 60	7 × 3 = 21	4 × 2 = 8	11 × 3 = 33	5 × 4 = 20	3 × 3 = 9	2 × 5 = 10	8 × 4 = 32	9 × 3 = 27

Drill 7   *Multiplication Facts: 1's–6's*

	a.	b.	c.	d.	e.	f.	g.	h.	i.	j.
1.	0 × 4 = 0	3 × 1 = 3	6 × 2 = 12	0 × 1 = 0	0 × 5 = 0	2 × 4 = 8	4 × 4 = 16	5 × 1 = 5	3 × 4 = 12	1 × 1 = 1
2.	3 × 3 = 9	5 × 3 = 15	4 × 0 = 0	1 × 2 = 2	6 × 0 = 0	0 × 0 = 0	2 × 5 = 10	3 × 6 = 18	6 × 4 = 24	2 × 2 = 4
3.	7 × 0 = 0	9 × 0 = 0	5 × 4 = 20	1 × 3 = 3	5 × 5 = 25	2 × 3 = 6	0 × 1 = 0	6 × 1 = 6	4 × 3 = 12	7 × 3 = 21
4.	1 × 4 = 4	2 × 1 = 2	0 × 2 = 0	3 × 5 = 15	5 × 2 = 10	4 × 1 = 4	8 × 0 = 0	7 × 1 = 7	7 × 4 = 28	6 × 3 = 18
5.	3 × 2 = 6	10 × 0 = 0	1 × 5 = 5	0 × 3 = 0	2 × 6 = 12	4 × 5 = 20	5 × 0 = 0	8 × 2 = 16	9 × 3 = 27	1 × 6 = 6
6.	2 × 0 = 0	0 × 6 = 0	9 × 1 = 9	6 × 5 = 30	8 × 3 = 24	7 × 2 = 14	11 × 0 = 0	10 × 1 = 10	4 × 2 = 8	7 × 5 = 35
7.	12 × 0 = 0	11 × 1 = 11	8 × 4 = 32	7 × 6 = 42	3 × 0 = 0	10 × 2 = 20	8 × 1 = 8	9 × 5 = 45	11 × 4 = 44	10 × 6 = 60
8.	12 × 3 = 36	8 × 6 = 48	9 × 4 = 36	11 × 5 = 55	12 × 2 = 24	9 × 2 = 18	5 × 6 = 30	10 × 3 = 30	12 × 5 = 60	9 × 6 = 54
9.	6 × 6 = 36	12 × 1 = 12	11 × 2 = 22	12 × 4 = 48	11 × 6 = 66	10 × 5 = 50	11 × 3 = 33	4 × 6 = 24	12 × 6 = 72	10 × 4 = 40
10.	8 × 5 = 40	8 × 6 = 48	9 × 4 = 36	3 × 3 = 9	9 × 2 = 18	9 × 6 = 54	7 × 5 = 35	3 × 6 = 18	4 × 4 = 16	6 × 6 = 36

Drill 8 — Multiplication Facts: 2's–6's

	a.	b.	c.	d.	e.	f.	g.	h.	i.	j.
1.	2 × 2 = 4	4 × 0 = 0	1 × 6 = 6	4 × 3 = 12	1 × 2 = 2	3 × 3 = 9	8 × 4 = 32	9 × 5 = 45	6 × 6 = 36	8 × 2 = 16
2.	4 × 4 = 16	8 × 6 = 48	3 × 2 = 6	7 × 2 = 14	0 × 6 = 0	5 × 4 = 20	8 × 3 = 24	0 × 3 = 0	5 × 5 = 25	1 × 4 = 4
3.	0 × 2 = 0	3 × 5 = 15	8 × 5 = 40	12 × 4 = 48	2 × 6 = 12	9 × 6 = 54	7 × 4 = 28	10 × 5 = 50	11 × 3 = 33	6 × 4 = 24
4.	7 × 5 = 35	12 × 2 = 24	10 × 3 = 30	9 × 4 = 36	6 × 3 = 18	4 × 2 = 8	2 × 3 = 6	1 × 5 = 5	3 × 4 = 12	4 × 5 = 20
5.	1 × 3 = 3	6 × 5 = 30	2 × 4 = 8	11 × 5 = 55	4 × 6 = 24	9 × 3 = 27	7 × 6 = 42	12 × 6 = 72	5 × 0 = 0	10 × 4 = 40
6.	10 × 6 = 60	9 × 2 = 18	5 × 2 = 10	12 × 3 = 36	11 × 2 = 22	5 × 6 = 30	10 × 2 = 20	11 × 6 = 66	11 × 4 = 44	5 × 3 = 15
7.	12 × 5 = 60	2 × 5 = 10	7 × 3 = 21	6 × 2 = 12	3 × 6 = 18	6 × 6 = 36	4 × 4 = 16	5 × 5 = 25	7 × 4 = 28	8 × 3 = 24
8.	3 × 3 = 9	7 × 6 = 42	10 × 5 = 50	12 × 4 = 48	8 × 2 = 16	8 × 4 = 32	4 × 5 = 20	12 × 6 = 72	7 × 3 = 21	12 × 2 = 24
9.	5 × 6 = 30	10 × 4 = 40	2 × 3 = 6	8 × 6 = 48	9 × 3 = 27	0 × 4 = 0	2 × 2 = 4	1 × 5 = 5	9 × 6 = 54	8 × 5 = 40
10.	7 × 2 = 14	5 × 3 = 15	4 × 6 = 24	3 × 6 = 18	12 × 6 = 72	12 × 3 = 36	1 × 2 = 2	6 × 5 = 30	7 × 5 = 35	4 × 5 = 20

Drill 9 Multiplication Facts: 6's and 7's

	a.	b.	c.	d.	e.	f.	g.	h.	i.	j.
1.	4 × 6 = 24	8 × 6 = 48	2 × 6 = 12	0 × 6 = 0	9 × 6 = 54	6 × 6 = 36	7 × 6 = 42	5 × 6 = 30	1 × 6 = 6	10 × 6 = 60
2.	3 × 6 = 18	12 × 6 = 72	11 × 6 = 66	6 × 6 = 36	9 × 6 = 54	4 × 6 = 24	8 × 6 = 48	3 × 6 = 18	7 × 6 = 42	12 × 6 = 72
3.	3 × 7 = 21	0 × 7 = 0	5 × 7 = 35	7 × 7 = 49	9 × 7 = 63	10 × 7 = 70	4 × 7 = 28	6 × 7 = 42	2 × 7 = 14	8 × 7 = 56
4.	11 × 7 = 77	8 × 7 = 56	1 × 7 = 7	3 × 7 = 21	7 × 7 = 49	12 × 7 = 84	5 × 7 = 35	9 × 7 = 63	4 × 7 = 28	12 × 7 = 84
5.	4 × 7 = 28	8 × 7 = 56	9 × 6 = 54	7 × 7 = 49	6 × 6 = 36	11 × 6 = 66	3 × 7 = 21	2 × 6 = 12	5 × 7 = 35	9 × 7 = 63
6.	8 × 6 = 48	2 × 7 = 14	5 × 6 = 30	10 × 6 = 60	3 × 6 = 18	6 × 7 = 42	12 × 6 = 72	11 × 7 = 77	0 × 7 = 0	4 × 6 = 24

	a.	b.	c.	d.
7.	6 × 5 = 30	7 × 6 = 42	7 × 4 = 28	6 × 3 = 18
8.	7 × 2 = 14	7 × 12 = 84	6 × 6 = 36	7 × 10 = 70
9.	6 × 4 = 24	7 × 7 = 49	6 × 1 = 6	6 × 12 = 72
10.	7 × 5 = 35	7 × 8 = 56	6 × 5 = 30	7 × 11 = 77
11.	6 × 8 = 48	6 × 9 = 54	7 × 9 = 63	7 × 3 = 21
12.	6 × 0 = 0	7 × 10 = 70	6 × 12 = 72	6 × 9 = 54
13.	6 × 3 = 18	6 × 6 = 36	7 × 12 = 84	7 × 5 = 35
14.	7 × 1 = 7	6 × 11 = 66	6 × 8 = 48	7 × 9 = 63

Drill 10   **Multiplication Facts: 2's–7's**

	a.	b.	c.	d.	e.	f.	g.	h.	i.	j.
1.	4 × 2 = 8	3 × 2 = 6	0 × 2 = 0	7 × 3 = 21	5 × 5 = 25	6 × 3 = 18	2 × 2 = 4	1 × 4 = 4	3 × 4 = 12	7 × 5 = 35
2.	1 × 7 = 7	0 × 3 = 0	1 × 2 = 2	6 × 7 = 42	4 × 4 = 16	8 × 5 = 40	9 × 3 = 27	2 × 6 = 12	5 × 4 = 20	4 × 7 = 28
3.	0 × 6 = 0	2 × 5 = 10	8 × 7 = 56	12 × 4 = 48	1 × 5 = 5	11 × 3 = 33	10 × 7 = 70	4 × 3 = 12	9 × 2 = 18	3 × 5 = 15
4.	2 × 3 = 6	1 × 6 = 6	10 × 3 = 30	7 × 4 = 28	8 × 4 = 32	5 × 6 = 30	10 × 2 = 20	0 × 4 = 0	8 × 3 = 24	6 × 6 = 36
5.	11 × 7 = 77	4 × 5 = 20	8 × 6 = 48	1 × 3 = 3	5 × 7 = 35	12 × 2 = 24	9 × 6 = 54	7 × 7 = 49	2 × 4 = 8	3 × 3 = 9
6.	10 × 5 = 50	9 × 7 = 63	8 × 2 = 16	4 × 6 = 24	6 × 2 = 12	3 × 7 = 21	0 × 7 = 0	2 × 7 = 14	12 × 5 = 60	11 × 4 = 44
7.	9 × 4 = 36	0 × 5 = 0	11 × 2 = 22	6 × 4 = 24	12 × 7 = 84	9 × 5 = 45	10 × 6 = 60	10 × 4 = 40	12 × 3 = 36	6 × 5 = 30
8.	3 × 6 = 18	5 × 2 = 10	11 × 5 = 55	12 × 6 = 72	7 × 2 = 14	5 × 3 = 15	11 × 6 = 66	7 × 6 = 42	4 × 7 = 28	6 × 4 = 24
9.	7 × 5 = 35	8 × 5 = 40	9 × 4 = 36	2 × 6 = 12	9 × 6 = 54	8 × 4 = 32	7 × 7 = 49	6 × 6 = 36	9 × 5 = 45	8 × 3 = 24
10.	4 × 4 = 16	8 × 7 = 56	0 × 2 = 0	6 × 7 = 42	1 × 4 = 4	12 × 5 = 60	9 × 3 = 27	8 × 6 = 48	3 × 7 = 21	9 × 7 = 63

Drill 11 **Multiplication Facts: 7's and 8's**

	a.	b.	c.	d.	e.	f.	g.	h.	i.	j.
1.	5 × 7 = 35	7 × 7 = 49	0 × 7 = 0	3 × 7 = 21	11 × 7 = 77	8 × 7 = 56	6 × 7 = 42	4 × 7 = 28	12 × 7 = 84	2 × 7 = 14
2.	1 × 7 = 7	9 × 7 = 63	10 × 7 = 70	4 × 7 = 28	7 × 7 = 49	9 × 7 = 63	12 × 7 = 84	8 × 7 = 56	3 × 7 = 21	6 × 7 = 42
3.	3 × 8 = 24	5 × 8 = 40	2 × 8 = 16	10 × 8 = 80	8 × 8 = 64	12 × 8 = 96	4 × 8 = 32	0 × 8 = 0	8 × 8 = 64	6 × 8 = 48
4.	7 × 8 = 56	1 × 8 = 8	9 × 8 = 72	11 × 8 = 88	5 × 8 = 40	6 × 8 = 48	9 × 8 = 72	4 × 8 = 32	12 × 8 = 96	3 × 8 = 24
5.	7 × 7 = 49	8 × 8 = 64	7 × 8 = 56	6 × 8 = 48	4 × 8 = 32	3 × 7 = 21	2 × 8 = 16	12 × 7 = 84	5 × 7 = 35	9 × 8 = 72
6.	5 × 8 = 40	8 × 7 = 56	2 × 7 = 14	10 × 7 = 70	3 × 8 = 24	6 × 7 = 42	4 × 7 = 28	12 × 8 = 96	11 × 8 = 88	9 × 7 = 63

	a.	b.	c.	d.
7.	8 × 4 = 32	7 × 3 = 21	8 × 10 = 80	8 × 6 = 48
8.	7 × 5 = 35	7 × 12 = 84	7 × 6 = 42	8 × 3 = 24
9.	7 × 1 = 7	8 × 11 = 88	7 × 7 = 49	8 × 5 = 40
10.	8 × 9 = 72	7 × 9 = 63	8 × 8 = 64	8 × 12 = 96
11.	8 × 3 = 24	8 × 0 = 0	7 × 8 = 56	7 × 4 = 28
12.	8 × 7 = 56	8 × 2 = 16	7 × 11 = 77	7 × 9 = 63
13.	7 × 2 = 14	7 × 10 = 70	7 × 12 = 84	8 × 8 = 64
14.	8 × 6 = 48	8 × 4 = 32	8 × 12 = 96	8 × 9 = 72

Drill 12   **Multiplication Facts: 3's–8's**

	a.	b.	c.	d.	e.	f.	g.	h.	i.	j.
1.	4 × 6 = 24	8 × 3 = 24	1 × 5 = 5	3 × 4 = 12	2 × 5 = 10	8 × 5 = 40	7 × 3 = 21	3 × 8 = 24	6 × 6 = 36	5 × 4 = 20
2.	7 × 5 = 35	3 × 3 = 9	6 × 5 = 30	8 × 8 = 64	9 × 4 = 36	6 × 3 = 18	7 × 7 = 49	8 × 6 = 48	4 × 4 = 16	2 × 3 = 6
3.	8 × 4 = 32	5 × 5 = 25	7 × 6 = 42	3 × 5 = 15	8 × 7 = 56	9 × 5 = 45	6 × 4 = 24	9 × 3 = 27	5 × 7 = 35	4 × 7 = 28
4.	2 × 4 = 8	8 × 3 = 24	9 × 6 = 54	3 × 7 = 21	9 × 8 = 72	7 × 7 = 49	7 × 5 = 35	5 × 6 = 30	4 × 8 = 32	6 × 7 = 42
5.	6 × 6 = 36	10 × 3 = 30	2 × 8 = 16	12 × 5 = 60	11 × 7 = 77	8 × 8 = 64	6 × 3 = 18	12 × 4 = 48	11 × 3 = 33	9 × 4 = 36
6.	2 × 7 = 14	4 × 6 = 24	10 × 5 = 50	11 × 8 = 88	12 × 6 = 72	9 × 7 = 63	3 × 7 = 21	8 × 7 = 56	5 × 8 = 40	10 × 6 = 60
7.	9 × 5 = 45	12 × 8 = 96	11 × 3 = 33	9 × 8 = 72	6 × 7 = 42	11 × 5 = 55	10 × 4 = 40	12 × 7 = 84	6 × 8 = 48	3 × 4 = 12
8.	9 × 6 = 54	11 × 7 = 77	4 × 8 = 32	5 × 5 = 25	12 × 3 = 36	9 × 8 = 72	9 × 7 = 63	10 × 3 = 30	8 × 8 = 64	4 × 6 = 24
9.	9 × 3 = 27	10 × 8 = 80	12 × 5 = 60	7 × 8 = 56	11 × 4 = 44	12 × 6 = 72	8 × 7 = 56	3 × 5 = 15	2 × 7 = 14	8 × 6 = 48
10.	9 × 6 = 54	5 × 7 = 35	10 × 7 = 70	9 × 3 = 27	4 × 7 = 28	7 × 7 = 49	8 × 5 = 40	6 × 7 = 42	12 × 3 = 36	8 × 8 = 64

Drill 13   **Multiplication Facts: 8's and 9's**

	a.	b.	c.	d.	e.	f.	g.	h.	i.	j.
1.	4 × 8 = 32	8 × 8 = 64	1 × 8 = 8	11 × 8 = 88	5 × 8 = 40	3 × 8 = 24	0 × 8 = 0	9 × 8 = 72	12 × 8 = 96	6 × 8 = 48
2.	2 × 8 = 16	7 × 8 = 56	10 × 8 = 80	8 × 8 = 64	9 × 8 = 72	12 × 8 = 96	4 × 8 = 32	7 × 8 = 56	6 × 8 = 48	5 × 8 = 40
3.	5 × 9 = 45	9 × 9 = 81	0 × 9 = 0	10 × 9 = 90	7 × 9 = 63	8 × 9 = 72	3 × 9 = 27	6 × 9 = 54	12 × 9 = 108	9 × 9 = 81
4.	7 × 9 = 63	1 × 9 = 9	11 × 9 = 99	2 × 9 = 18	6 × 9 = 54	4 × 9 = 36	12 × 9 = 108	3 × 9 = 27	4 × 9 = 36	5 × 9 = 45
5.	6 × 8 = 48	7 × 9 = 63	3 × 9 = 27	8 × 8 = 64	7 × 8 = 56	9 × 9 = 81	12 × 8 = 96	4 × 9 = 36	5 × 8 = 40	3 × 8 = 24
6.	5 × 9 = 45	11 × 8 = 88	9 × 8 = 72	4 × 8 = 32	8 × 8 = 64	12 × 9 = 108	4 × 9 = 36	2 × 8 = 16	6 × 9 = 54	10 × 9 = 90

	a.	b.	c.	d.
7.	9 × 2 = 18	8 × 3 = 24	9 × 11 = 99	8 × 6 = 48
8.	9 × 4 = 36	9 × 12 = 108	9 × 7 = 63	8 × 8 = 64
9.	8 × 7 = 56	9 × 9 = 81	8 × 1 = 8	8 × 5 = 40
10.	9 × 3 = 27	8 × 10 = 80	9 × 0 = 0	9 × 8 = 72
11.	9 × 6 = 54	8 × 12 = 96	8 × 8 = 64	9 × 10 = 90
12.	8 × 4 = 32	8 × 2 = 16	9 × 5 = 45	9 × 6 = 54
13.	9 × 7 = 63	9 × 8 = 72	9 × 8 = 72	8 × 3 = 24
14.	8 × 5 = 40	8 × 11 = 88	8 × 12 = 96	9 × 4 = 36

Drill 14 Multiplication Facts: 1's–9's

	a.	b.	c.	d.	e.	f.	g.	h.	i.	j.
1.	7 × 1 = 7	2 × 9 = 18	2 × 5 = 10	2 × 8 = 16	4 × 4 = 16	4 × 1 = 4	3 × 1 = 3	1 × 8 = 8	9 × 9 = 81	6 × 5 = 30
2.	7 × 7 = 49	6 × 1 = 6	5 × 4 = 20	3 × 3 = 9	1 × 1 = 1	9 × 2 = 18	8 × 8 = 64	0 × 3 = 0	12 × 4 = 48	10 × 8 = 80
3.	1 × 7 = 7	11 × 2 = 22	5 × 5 = 25	2 × 2 = 4	7 × 2 = 14	0 × 9 = 0	8 × 1 = 8	6 × 2 = 12	3 × 6 = 18	12 × 5 = 60
4.	2 × 4 = 8	4 × 5 = 20	8 × 3 = 24	10 × 3 = 30	8 × 2 = 16	6 × 4 = 24	1 × 4 = 4	11 × 9 = 99	6 × 6 = 36	3 × 2 = 6
5.	4 × 3 = 12	1 × 5 = 5	2 × 6 = 12	9 × 3 = 27	6 × 5 = 30	3 × 8 = 24	3 × 4 = 12	12 × 3 = 36	3 × 9 = 27	2 × 3 = 6
6.	3 × 5 = 15	6 × 3 = 18	7 × 3 = 21	2 × 7 = 14	8 × 4 = 32	11 × 8 = 88	4 × 2 = 8	5 × 2 = 10	4 × 8 = 32	1 × 2 = 2
7.	10 × 7 = 70	5 × 1 = 5	8 × 5 = 40	7 × 9 = 63	5 × 8 = 40	6 × 8 = 48	9 × 7 = 63	5 × 7 = 35	12 × 6 = 72	8 × 7 = 56
8.	6 × 9 = 54	7 × 8 = 56	5 × 9 = 45	9 × 6 = 54	8 × 9 = 72	4 × 7 = 28	12 × 8 = 96	7 × 5 = 35	4 × 9 = 36	7 × 6 = 42
9.	9 × 5 = 45	9 × 4 = 36	6 × 7 = 42	5 × 6 = 30	4 × 6 = 24	7 × 4 = 28	9 × 8 = 72	3 × 7 = 21	8 × 6 = 48	12 × 9 = 108
10.	11 × 6 = 66	3 × 7 = 21	12 × 7 = 84	9 × 9 = 81	6 × 3 = 18	10 × 4 = 40	8 × 0 = 0	6 × 9 = 54	9 × 7 = 63	12 × 2 = 24

Drill 15 **Multiplication Facts: 1's–9's**

	a.	b.	c.	d.	e.	f.	g.	h.	i.	j.
1.	0 × 5 = 0	8 × 3 = 24	4 × 4 = 16	2 × 1 = 2	1 × 7 = 7	8 × 2 = 16	6 × 4 = 24	0 × 0 = 0	5 × 1 = 5	3 × 2 = 6
2.	4 × 2 = 8	9 × 1 = 9	3 × 3 = 9	2 × 2 = 4	7 × 3 = 21	5 × 2 = 10	3 × 4 = 12	2 × 7 = 14	8 × 1 = 8	0 × 9 = 0
3.	5 × 3 = 15	3 × 0 = 0	2 × 6 = 12	9 × 2 = 18	1 × 1 = 1	0 × 4 = 0	7 × 4 = 28	4 × 6 = 24	6 × 5 = 30	3 × 6 = 18
4.	2 × 3 = 6	8 × 4 = 32	1 × 5 = 5	0 × 8 = 0	9 × 5 = 45	4 × 7 = 28	3 × 5 = 15	7 × 0 = 0	5 × 4 = 20	9 × 3 = 27
5.	3 × 7 = 21	5 × 5 = 25	10 × 2 = 20	9 × 4 = 36	7 × 2 = 14	11 × 4 = 44	6 × 6 = 36	2 × 4 = 8	8 × 5 = 40	12 × 1 = 12
6.	4 × 3 = 12	12 × 2 = 24	10 × 8 = 80	5 × 7 = 35	3 × 9 = 27	7 × 7 = 49	11 × 9 = 99	5 × 8 = 40	2 × 9 = 18	6 × 7 = 42
7.	6 × 3 = 18	5 × 6 = 30	9 × 6 = 54	2 × 8 = 16	12 × 4 = 48	6 × 2 = 12	1 × 6 = 6	11 × 0 = 0	8 × 6 = 48	7 × 8 = 56
8.	12 × 3 = 36	10 × 6 = 60	9 × 7 = 63	2 × 5 = 10	12 × 5 = 60	8 × 8 = 64	7 × 6 = 42	4 × 9 = 36	3 × 8 = 24	6 × 1 = 6
9.	4 × 5 = 20	8 × 9 = 72	10 × 9 = 90	6 × 8 = 48	11 × 3 = 33	5 × 9 = 45	7 × 5 = 35	7 × 9 = 63	11 × 2 = 22	10 × 3 = 30
10.	4 × 8 = 32	12 × 7 = 84	9 × 9 = 81	12 × 9 = 108	8 × 7 = 56	11 × 7 = 77	12 × 6 = 72	12 × 8 = 96	9 × 8 = 72	6 × 9 = 54

Drill 16 **Multiplication Facts: 3's–9's**

	a.	b.	c.	d.	e.	f.	g.	h.	i.	j.
1.	8 ×7 = 56	5 ×4 = 20	3 ×3 = 9	9 ×6 = 54	6 ×4 = 24	2 ×7 = 14	8 ×8 = 64	5 ×5 = 25	2 ×4 = 8	4 ×7 = 28
2.	9 ×9 = 81	4 ×4 = 16	7 ×7 = 49	3 ×6 = 18	5 ×9 = 45	8 ×4 = 32	6 ×6 = 36	9 ×5 = 45	3 ×5 = 15	6 ×8 = 48
3.	0 ×7 = 0	12 ×3 = 36	10 ×5 = 50	9 ×3 = 27	8 ×7 = 56	6 ×9 = 54	3 ×7 = 21	2 ×5 = 10	1 ×8 = 8	4 ×9 = 36
4.	5 ×6 = 30	11 ×9 = 99	4 ×8 = 32	6 ×3 = 18	2 ×9 = 18	5 ×7 = 35	7 ×8 = 56	8 ×3 = 24	3 ×4 = 12	7 ×4 = 28
5.	2 ×3 = 6	10 ×8 = 80	4 ×6 = 24	6 ×7 = 42	12 ×7 = 84	9 ×8 = 72	3 ×9 = 27	5 ×8 = 40	2 ×6 = 12	8 ×6 = 48
6.	9 ×7 = 63	12 ×5 = 60	10 ×3 = 30	9 ×4 = 36	12 ×4 = 48	7 ×3 = 21	8 ×9 = 72	0 ×6 = 0	7 ×5 = 35	4 ×5 = 20
7.	12 ×8 = 96	4 ×3 = 12	1 ×5 = 5	6 ×5 = 30	10 ×9 = 90	7 ×6 = 42	2 ×8 = 16	3 ×8 = 24	12 ×6 = 72	7 ×9 = 63
8.	5 ×3 = 15	8 ×5 = 40	12 ×9 = 108	11 ×3 = 33	10 ×4 = 40	8 ×8 = 64	11 ×6 = 66	10 ×7 = 70	7 ×7 = 49	4 ×0 = 0
9.	7 ×6 = 42	4 ×8 = 32	8 ×9 = 72	3 ×7 = 21	9 ×7 = 63	5 ×5 = 25	6 ×8 = 48	4 ×4 = 16	8 ×7 = 56	3 ×9 = 27
10.	5 ×6 = 30	8 ×3 = 24	3 ×6 = 18	9 ×9 = 81	4 ×7 = 28	7 ×8 = 56	6 ×9 = 54	9 ×5 = 45	12 ×3 = 36	7 ×5 = 35

Drill 17 Multiplication Facts: 6's–9's

	a.	b.	c.	d.	e.	f.	g.	h.	i.	j.
1.	4 × 6 = 24	12 × 6 = 72	8 × 6 = 48	6 × 6 = 36	9 × 6 = 54	3 × 6 = 18	7 × 6 = 42	10 × 6 = 60	2 × 6 = 12	5 × 6 = 30
2.	8 × 7 = 56	6 × 7 = 42	3 × 7 = 21	9 × 7 = 63	12 × 7 = 84	0 × 7 = 0	4 × 7 = 28	2 × 7 = 14	7 × 7 = 49	5 × 7 = 35
3.	5 × 8 = 40	3 × 8 = 24	8 × 8 = 64	2 × 8 = 16	4 × 8 = 32	11 × 8 = 88	6 × 8 = 48	9 × 8 = 72	12 × 8 = 96	7 × 8 = 56
4.	4 × 9 = 36	9 × 9 = 81	1 × 9 = 9	7 × 9 = 63	3 × 9 = 27	6 × 9 = 54	12 × 9 = 108	8 × 9 = 72	5 × 9 = 45	2 × 9 = 18
5.	10 × 7 = 70	6 × 7 = 42	9 × 9 = 81	8 × 8 = 64	7 × 7 = 49	4 × 9 = 36	7 × 8 = 56	12 × 6 = 72	5 × 8 = 40	8 × 9 = 72
6.	8 × 6 = 48	7 × 9 = 63	9 × 6 = 54	6 × 6 = 36	3 × 6 = 18	12 × 8 = 96	4 × 7 = 28	5 × 9 = 45	11 × 9 = 99	6 × 9 = 54

Drill 18 Multiplication Facts: 10's–12's

	a.	b.	c.	d.	e.	f.	g.	h.	i.	j.
1.	10 × 3 = 30	11 × 4 = 44	11 × 11 = 121	12 × 4 = 48	10 × 1 = 10	11 × 9 = 99	11 × 6 = 66	12 × 12 = 144	10 × 4 = 40	12 × 3 = 36
2.	12 × 6 = 72	12 × 2 = 24	10 × 5 = 50	11 × 7 = 77	12 × 7 = 84	11 × 3 = 33	12 × 9 = 108	10 × 6 = 60	12 × 5 = 60	11 × 10 = 110
3.	10 × 10 = 100	11 × 11 = 121	12 × 11 = 132	12 × 8 = 96	11 × 5 = 55	10 × 12 = 120	12 × 12 = 144	11 × 12 = 132	10 × 11 = 110	12 × 10 = 120

	a.	b.	c.	d.
4.	4 × 12 = 48	8 × 12 = 96	11 × 10 = 110	10 × 10 = 100
5.	12 × 12 = 144	9 × 12 = 108	11 × 11 = 121	7 × 12 = 84

Drill 19 — Multiplication Facts: 9's–12's

	a.	b.	c.	d.	e.	f.	g.	h.	i.	j.
1.	3 × 9 = 27	10 × 5 = 50	12 × 6 = 72	9 × 9 = 81	11 × 11 = 121	12 × 8 = 96	10 × 9 = 90	8 × 9 = 72	12 × 12 = 144	11 × 10 = 110
2.	11 × 5 = 55	12 × 3 = 36	7 × 9 = 63	10 × 10 = 100	6 × 9 = 54	12 × 5 = 60	11 × 4 = 44	10 × 6 = 60	5 × 9 = 45	12 × 4 = 48
3.	10 × 11 = 110	12 × 9 = 108	12 × 11 = 132	11 × 11 = 121	12 × 2 = 24	4 × 9 = 36	1 × 9 = 9	11 × 0 = 0	10 × 12 = 120	12 × 7 = 84
4.	11 × 12 = 132	10 × 10 = 100	12 × 12 = 144	2 × 9 = 18	12 × 9 = 108	10 × 11 = 110	11 × 9 = 99	11 × 7 = 77	12 × 10 = 120	10 × 3 = 30

Drill 20 — Multiplication Facts: 7's–12's

	a.	b.	c.	d.	e.	f.	g.	h.	i.	j.
1.	3 × 7 = 21	8 × 7 = 56	7 × 7 = 49	4 × 7 = 28	9 × 7 = 63	12 × 7 = 84	2 × 7 = 14	6 × 7 = 42	5 × 7 = 35	10 × 7 = 70
2.	6 × 8 = 48	5 × 8 = 40	9 × 8 = 72	8 × 8 = 64	11 × 8 = 88	4 × 8 = 32	3 × 8 = 24	12 × 8 = 96	2 × 8 = 16	7 × 8 = 56
3.	4 × 9 = 36	9 × 9 = 81	2 × 9 = 18	8 × 9 = 72	12 × 9 = 108	7 × 9 = 63	3 × 9 = 27	6 × 9 = 54	7 × 9 = 63	11 × 9 = 99
4.	10 × 9 = 90	10 × 10 = 100	10 × 6 = 60	10 × 5 = 50	10 × 11 = 110	10 × 4 = 40	10 × 0 = 0	10 × 12 = 120	10 × 8 = 80	10 × 10 = 100
5.	11 × 11 = 121	11 × 5 = 55	11 × 10 = 110	11 × 3 = 33	11 × 1 = 11	11 × 12 = 132	11 × 7 = 77	11 × 6 = 66	11 × 11 = 121	11 × 2 = 22
6.	12 × 10 = 120	12 × 2 = 24	12 × 6 = 72	12 × 11 = 132	12 × 12 = 144	12 × 5 = 60	12 × 4 = 48	12 × 3 = 36	12 × 12 = 144	12 × 9 = 108

Drill 21 Multiplication Facts: 5's–12's

	a.	b.	c.	d.	e.	f.	g.	h.	i.	j.
1.	3 ×8 = 24	5 ×5 = 25	12 ×7 = 84	10 ×4 = 40	7 ×9 = 63	9 ×8 = 72	4 ×5 = 20	4 ×8 = 32	11 ×11 = 121	12 ×12 = 144
2.	6 ×8 = 48	8 ×5 = 40	11 ×10 = 110	7 ×6 = 42	5 ×9 = 45	9 ×9 = 81	12 ×3 = 36	4 ×6 = 24	10 ×5 = 50	7 ×7 = 49
3.	5 ×6 = 30	10 ×10 = 100	12 ×8 = 96	3 ×9 = 27	11 ×6 = 66	6 ×7 = 42	8 ×8 = 64	4 ×7 = 28	9 ×7 = 63	12 ×2 = 24
4.	3 ×7 = 21	12 ×9 = 108	10 ×12 = 120	8 ×6 = 48	2 ×5 = 10	4 ×9 = 36	6 ×6 = 36	3 ×6 = 18	9 ×6 = 54	11 ×12 = 132
5.	3 ×5 = 15	12 ×5 = 60	6 ×9 = 54	2 ×9 = 18	10 ×2 = 20	8 ×7 = 56	5 ×7 = 35	11 ×9 = 99	12 ×10 = 120	7 ×8 = 56
6.	9 ×5 = 45	5 ×8 = 40	12 ×4 = 48	2 ×7 = 14	8 ×9 = 72	6 ×5 = 30	10 ×0 = 0	11 ×1 = 11	7 ×5 = 35	10 ×11 = 110
7.	8 ×8 = 64	2 ×6 = 12	11 ×11 = 121	12 ×6 = 72	12 ×12 = 144	12 ×7 = 84	12 ×5 = 60	9 ×9 = 81	4 ×9 = 36	10 ×7 = 70
8.	7 ×7 = 49	0 ×9 = 0	4 ×5 = 20	10 ×8 = 80	12 ×11 = 132	12 ×8 = 96	12 ×6 = 72	11 ×3 = 33	12 ×4 = 48	10 ×6 = 60
9.	10 ×12 = 120	8 ×6 = 48	6 ×9 = 54	5 ×5 = 25	11 ×4 = 44	12 ×7 = 84	7 ×9 = 63	12 ×9 = 108	12 ×5 = 60	4 ×7 = 28
10.	5 ×8 = 40	12 ×1 = 12	11 ×8 = 88	10 ×10 = 100	9 ×6 = 54	4 ×6 = 24	8 ×7 = 56	11 ×7 = 77	10 ×11 = 110	2 ×8 = 16

Drill 22 Multiplication Facts: 3's–12's

	a.	b.	c.	d.	e.	f.	g.	h.	i.	j.
1.	8 × 4 = 32	3 × 3 = 9	9 × 8 = 72	4 × 6 = 24	5 × 5 = 25	2 × 8 = 16	12 × 3 = 36	10 × 5 = 50	6 × 8 = 48	7 × 9 = 63
2.	9 × 3 = 27	5 × 6 = 30	2 × 3 = 6	9 × 9 = 81	12 × 6 = 72	11 × 6 = 66	8 × 7 = 56	7 × 3 = 21	4 × 4 = 16	12 × 12 = 144
3.	7 × 4 = 28	2 × 4 = 8	1 × 9 = 9	10 × 10 = 100	5 × 7 = 35	8 × 8 = 64	6 × 6 = 36	11 × 11 = 121	12 × 5 = 60	3 × 5 = 15
4.	6 × 3 = 18	12 × 8 = 96	7 × 8 = 56	3 × 8 = 24	9 × 5 = 45	8 × 6 = 48	5 × 4 = 20	11 × 4 = 44	11 × 10 = 110	6 × 9 = 54
5.	3 × 7 = 21	8 × 9 = 72	2 × 9 = 18	4 × 7 = 28	6 × 7 = 42	8 × 5 = 40	6 × 0 = 0	12 × 4 = 48	11 × 1 = 11	10 × 4 = 40
6.	5 × 3 = 15	1 × 8 = 8	9 × 6 = 54	4 × 3 = 12	3 × 9 = 27	2 × 7 = 14	12 × 8 = 96	9 × 7 = 63	12 × 6 = 72	6 × 5 = 30
7.	4 × 8 = 32	5 × 9 = 45	3 × 6 = 18	2 × 6 = 12	10 × 2 = 20	12 × 9 = 108	7 × 7 = 49	7 × 5 = 35	9 × 0 = 0	4 × 5 = 20
8.	2 × 5 = 10	10 × 12 = 120	11 × 12 = 132	12 × 7 = 84	5 × 8 = 40	6 × 4 = 24	12 × 3 = 36	4 × 9 = 36	11 × 9 = 99	12 × 2 = 24
9.	3 × 4 = 12	7 × 6 = 42	10 × 11 = 110	12 × 10 = 120	9 × 4 = 36	11 × 2 = 22	11 × 4 = 44	8 × 3 = 24	12 × 4 = 48	12 × 5 = 60
10.	12 × 11 = 132	12 × 7 = 84	12 × 9 = 108	12 × 12 = 144	10 × 3 = 30	10 × 4 = 40	11 × 11 = 121	8 × 8 = 64	11 × 6 = 66	9 × 9 = 81

Drill 23 **Multiplication Facts: 1's–12's**

	a.	b.	c.	d.	e.	f.	g.	h.	i.	j.
1.	7 × 1 = 7	8 × 2 = 16	4 × 0 = 0	2 × 2 = 4	9 × 2 = 18	1 × 1 = 1	0 × 8 = 0	6 × 2 = 12	5 × 1 = 5	0 × 3 = 0
2.	4 × 3 = 12	9 × 3 = 27	12 × 3 = 36	5 × 3 = 15	3 × 3 = 9	8 × 3 = 24	6 × 3 = 18	2 × 3 = 6	7 × 3 = 21	10 × 3 = 30
3.	8 × 4 = 32	11 × 4 = 44	4 × 4 = 16	9 × 4 = 36	3 × 4 = 12	7 × 4 = 28	2 × 4 = 8	6 × 4 = 24	12 × 4 = 48	5 × 4 = 20
4.	6 × 5 = 30	12 × 5 = 60	2 × 5 = 10	8 × 5 = 40	7 × 5 = 35	3 × 5 = 15	9 × 5 = 45	0 × 5 = 0	4 × 5 = 20	5 × 5 = 25
5.	7 × 6 = 42	2 × 6 = 12	9 × 6 = 54	3 × 6 = 18	6 × 6 = 36	12 × 6 = 72	10 × 6 = 60	8 × 6 = 48	4 × 6 = 24	5 × 6 = 30
6.	4 × 7 = 28	12 × 7 = 84	11 × 7 = 77	6 × 7 = 42	9 × 7 = 63	7 × 7 = 49	3 × 7 = 21	8 × 7 = 56	5 × 7 = 35	2 × 7 = 14
7.	5 × 8 = 40	9 × 8 = 72	3 × 8 = 24	8 × 8 = 64	4 × 8 = 32	2 × 8 = 16	6 × 8 = 48	12 × 8 = 96	1 × 8 = 8	7 × 8 = 56
8.	3 × 9 = 27	9 × 9 = 81	5 × 9 = 45	7 × 9 = 63	4 × 9 = 36	12 × 9 = 108	6 × 9 = 54	2 × 9 = 18	10 × 9 = 90	8 × 9 = 72
9.	10 × 10 = 100	11 × 11 = 121	11 × 2 = 22	10 × 7 = 70	10 × 12 = 120	11 × 12 = 132	10 × 4 = 40	11 × 10 = 110	11 × 8 = 88	10 × 11 = 110
10.	12 × 5 = 60	12 × 2 = 24	12 × 8 = 96	12 × 9 = 108	12 × 10 = 120	12 × 12 = 144	12 × 4 = 48	12 × 7 = 84	12 × 11 = 132	12 × 6 = 72

Drill 24   *Multiplication Facts: 1's–12's*

	a.	b.	c.	d.	e.	f.	g.	h.	i.	j.
1.	7 × 4 = 28	3 × 5 = 15	9 × 7 = 63	11 × 7 = 77	3 × 8 = 24	7 × 9 = 63	6 × 5 = 30	12 × 4 = 48	6 × 1 = 6	8 × 6 = 48
2.	5 × 5 = 25	8 × 8 = 64	2 × 2 = 4	0 × 0 = 0	9 × 9 = 81	10 × 10 = 100	12 × 12 = 144	4 × 4 = 16	7 × 7 = 49	6 × 6 = 36
3.	1 × 1 = 1	11 × 11 = 121	3 × 3 = 9	7 × 8 = 56	5 × 4 = 20	4 × 2 = 8	6 × 2 = 12	9 × 3 = 27	8 × 9 = 72	12 × 6 = 72
4.	2 × 9 = 18	0 × 7 = 0	2 × 5 = 10	8 × 4 = 32	4 × 6 = 24	12 × 7 = 84	10 × 11 = 110	12 × 8 = 96	2 × 3 = 6	1 × 8 = 8
5.	9 × 4 = 36	3 × 4 = 12	4 × 7 = 28	12 × 3 = 36	5 × 9 = 45	8 × 2 = 16	7 × 1 = 7	11 × 0 = 0	2 × 7 = 14	6 × 9 = 54
6.	8 × 3 = 24	4 × 8 = 32	3 × 9 = 27	10 × 12 = 120	12 × 5 = 60	9 × 8 = 72	5 × 3 = 15	12 × 6 = 72	7 × 5 = 35	6 × 7 = 42
7.	10 × 5 = 50	5 × 2 = 10	0 × 3 = 0	12 × 9 = 108	9 × 5 = 45	6 × 3 = 18	3 × 2 = 6	9 × 1 = 9	5 × 6 = 30	11 × 12 = 132
8.	5 × 7 = 35	3 × 6 = 18	2 × 4 = 8	1 × 4 = 4	8 × 7 = 56	7 × 3 = 21	4 × 9 = 36	12 × 2 = 24	11 × 10 = 110	6 × 8 = 48
9.	11 × 2 = 22	9 × 6 = 54	12 × 3 = 36	5 × 8 = 40	4 × 3 = 12	7 × 6 = 42	12 × 7 = 84	10 × 1 = 10	12 × 5 = 60	3 × 7 = 21
10.	12 × 10 = 120	2 × 6 = 12	12 × 4 = 48	2 × 8 = 16	6 × 4 = 24	8 × 5 = 40	12 × 9 = 108	12 × 8 = 96	12 × 11 = 132	12 × 2 = 24

Drill 25   *Division Facts: 1's–3's*

	a.	b.	c.	d.	e.	f.
1.	1)9 = 9	3)9 = 3	2)14 = 7	2)10 = 5	1)4 = 4	2)4 = 2
2.	3)15 = 5	1)2 = 2	3)27 = 9	2)12 = 6	1)0 = 0	3)3 = 1
3.	2)8 = 4	3)21 = 7	2)18 = 9	1)3 = 3	1)10 = 10	3)12 = 4
4.	3)30 = 10	2)16 = 8	1)6 = 6	2)6 = 3	3)18 = 6	2)22 = 11
5.	3)6 = 2	2)20 = 10	1)12 = 12	3)24 = 8	2)2 = 1	3)36 = 12
6.	2)24 = 12	3)33 = 11	1)5 = 5	2)0 = 0	3)27 = 9	3)18 = 6

Drill 26   *Division Facts: 1's–5's*

	a.	b.	c.	d.	e.	f.
1.	4)8 = 2	3)15 = 5	2)10 = 5	1)7 = 7	2)16 = 8	5)25 = 5
2.	3)12 = 4	4)20 = 5	5)30 = 6	3)24 = 8	2)12 = 6	4)12 = 3
3.	5)40 = 8	3)27 = 9	2)14 = 7	4)16 = 4	5)35 = 7	5)10 = 2
4.	2)8 = 4	3)9 = 3	1)4 = 4	5)0 = 0	4)24 = 6	3)18 = 6
5.	1)1 = 1	3)6 = 2	4)36 = 9	5)15 = 3	4)4 = 1	4)28 = 7
6.	3)21 = 7	2)20 = 10	1)8 = 8	5)45 = 9	3)33 = 11	2)2 = 1
7.	2)6 = 3	4)40 = 10	2)24 = 12	5)20 = 4	2)18 = 9	4)32 = 8
8.	2)4 = 2	3)36 = 12	3)24 = 8	5)50 = 10	4)0 = 0	4)44 = 11
9.	4)48 = 12	5)55 = 11	4)28 = 7	5)60 = 12	2)22 = 11	3)30 = 10

Drill 27   Division Facts: 3's–6's

	a.	b.	c.	d.	e.	f.
1.	3)12̄ = 4	5)15̄ = 3	3)3̄ = 1	4)20̄ = 5	6)0̄ = 0	6)18̄ = 3
2.	4)16̄ = 4	3)24̄ = 8	6)24̄ = 4	4)24̄ = 6	5)25̄ = 5	6)12̄ = 2
3.	5)35̄ = 7	4)8̄ = 2	6)42̄ = 7	3)33̄ = 11	4)28̄ = 7	3)21̄ = 7
4.	5)5̄ = 1	3)0̄ = 0	3)9̄ = 3	6)36̄ = 6	4)48̄ = 12	5)20̄ = 4
5.	5)40̄ = 8	6)48̄ = 8	5)10̄ = 2	3)15̄ = 5	3)36̄ = 12	6)60̄ = 10
6.	5)30̄ = 6	4)36̄ = 9	3)18̄ = 6	5)60̄ = 12	6)54̄ = 9	4)12̄ = 3
7.	6)66̄ = 11	3)6̄ = 2	4)32̄ = 8	5)50̄ = 10	6)30̄ = 5	6)72̄ = 12
8.	5)45̄ = 9	3)30̄ = 10	3)27̄ = 9	6)6̄ = 1	4)40̄ = 10	5)55̄ = 11

Drill 28   Division Facts: 6's and 7's

	a.	b.	c.	d.	e.	f.
1.	6)12̄ = 2	6)36̄ = 6	6)6̄ = 1	6)60̄ = 10	6)24̄ = 4	6)42̄ = 7
2.	6)72̄ = 12	6)18̄ = 3	6)48̄ = 8	6)66̄ = 11	6)30̄ = 5	6)54̄ = 9
3.	7)0̄ = 0	7)42̄ = 6	7)21̄ = 3	7)56̄ = 8	7)14̄ = 2	7)77̄ = 11
4.	7)49̄ = 7	7)70̄ = 10	7)28̄ = 4	7)84̄ = 12	7)35̄ = 5	7)63̄ = 9

	a.	b.	c.	d.
5.	24 ÷ 6 = 4	48 ÷ 6 = 8	18 ÷ 6 = 3	0 ÷ 6 = 0
6.	30 ÷ 6 = 5	42 ÷ 6 = 7	72 ÷ 9 = 8	36 ÷ 6 = 6
7.	60 ÷ 6 = 10	12 ÷ 6 = 2	54 ÷ 6 = 9	66 ÷ 6 = 11
8.	21 ÷ 7 = 3	35 ÷ 7 = 5	7 ÷ 7 = 1	49 ÷ 7 = 7
9.	14 ÷ 7 = 2	77 ÷ 7 = 11	42 ÷ 7 = 6	63 ÷ 7 = 9
10.	84 ÷ 7 = 12	28 ÷ 7 = 4	70 ÷ 7 = 10	56 ÷ 7 = 8

Drill 29   **Division Facts: 2's–7's**

	a.	b.	c.	d.	e.	f.
1.	4)20 = 5	3)6 = 2	7)49 = 7	5)35 = 7	6)72 = 12	4)32 = 8
2.	6)42 = 7	3)21 = 7	3)9 = 3	5)40 = 8	2)16 = 8	2)4 = 2
3.	7)56 = 8	3)36 = 12	4)36 = 9	6)24 = 4	2)24 = 12	3)18 = 6
4.	6)36 = 6	2)10 = 5	4)16 = 4	7)63 = 9	4)48 = 12	2)20 = 10
5.	4)12 = 3	5)25 = 5	7)7 = 1	7)28 = 4	3)18 = 6	5)45 = 9
6.	6)30 = 5	2)18 = 9	6)66 = 11	7)35 = 5	2)8 = 4	4)0 = 0
7.	2)12 = 6	7)21 = 3	6)54 = 9	4)28 = 7	5)15 = 3	6)48 = 8
8.	5)60 = 12	5)20 = 4	3)24 = 8	7)42 = 6	7)84 = 12	3)27 = 9

Drill 30   **Division Facts: 7's and 8's**

	a.	b.	c.	d.	e.	f.
1.	7)35 = 5	8)8 = 1	8)56 = 7	8)64 = 8	7)21 = 3	7)0 = 0
2.	8)16 = 2	7)63 = 9	7)28 = 4	8)40 = 5	7)56 = 8	8)32 = 4
3.	7)49 = 7	8)24 = 3	8)48 = 6	7)84 = 12	8)80 = 10	7)14 = 2
4.	7)77 = 11	8)96 = 12	7)70 = 10	7)42 = 6	8)72 = 9	8)88 = 11

	a.	b.	c.	d.
5.	42 ÷ 7 = 6	21 ÷ 7 = 3	56 ÷ 8 = 7	24 ÷ 8 = 3
6.	72 ÷ 8 = 9	32 ÷ 8 = 4	80 ÷ 8 = 10	28 ÷ 7 = 4
7.	16 ÷ 8 = 2	0 ÷ 8 = 0	84 ÷ 7 = 12	77 ÷ 7 = 11
8.	40 ÷ 8 = 5	49 ÷ 7 = 7	35 ÷ 7 = 5	96 ÷ 8 = 12
9.	56 ÷ 7 = 8	14 ÷ 7 = 2	64 ÷ 8 = 8	7 ÷ 7 = 1
10.	32 ÷ 8 = 4	63 ÷ 7 = 9	48 ÷ 8 = 6	64 ÷ 8 = 8

Drill 31 — Division Facts: 6's–8's

	a.	b.	c.	d.	e.	f.
1.	6)36 = 6	8)24 = 3	8)64 = 8	7)35 = 5	6)12 = 2	7)7 = 1
2.	8)56 = 7	6)18 = 3	7)49 = 7	7)84 = 12	6)24 = 4	7)56 = 8
3.	8)0 = 0	7)70 = 10	6)30 = 5	8)48 = 6	6)72 = 12	8)32 = 4
4.	7)21 = 3	8)40 = 5	6)66 = 11	7)14 = 2	7)28 = 4	7)35 = 5
5.	8)64 = 8	8)96 = 12	8)16 = 2	6)36 = 6	7)42 = 6	6)54 = 9
6.	8)72 = 9	6)6 = 1	6)48 = 8	7)63 = 9	8)80 = 10	7)84 = 12
7.	6)42 = 7	7)63 = 9	6)54 = 9	7)49 = 7	8)72 = 9	8)96 = 12

Drill 32 — Division Facts: 8's and 9's

	a.	b.	c.	d.	e.	f.
1.	8)64 = 8	8)24 = 3	8)32 = 4	8)8 = 1	8)88 = 11	8)56 = 7
2.	8)96 = 12	8)16 = 2	8)40 = 5	8)80 = 10	8)48 = 6	8)72 = 9
3.	9)18 = 2	9)81 = 9	9)27 = 3	9)72 = 8	9)36 = 4	9)63 = 7
4.	9)0 = 0	9)90 = 10	9)45 = 5	9)54 = 6	9)99 = 11	9)108 = 12

	a.	b.	c.	d.
5.	72 ÷ 8 = 9	64 ÷ 8 = 8	32 ÷ 8 = 4	63 ÷ 9 = 7
6.	24 ÷ 8 = 3	108 ÷ 9 = 12	88 ÷ 8 = 11	27 ÷ 9 = 3
7.	48 ÷ 8 = 6	45 ÷ 9 = 5	90 ÷ 9 = 10	54 ÷ 9 = 6
8.	18 ÷ 9 = 2	72 ÷ 9 = 8	81 ÷ 9 = 9	96 ÷ 8 = 12
9.	56 ÷ 8 = 7	16 ÷ 8 = 2	36 ÷ 9 = 4	40 ÷ 8 = 5
10.	54 ÷ 9 = 6	96 ÷ 8 = 12	64 ÷ 8 = 8	63 ÷ 9 = 7

Drill 33   **Division Facts: 6's–9's**

	a.	b.	c.	d.	e.	f.
1.	6)54 = 9	8)64 = 8	7)21 = 3	9)36 = 4	7)49 = 7	6)12 = 2
2.	8)72 = 9	6)36 = 6	9)27 = 3	8)16 = 2	7)42 = 6	9)81 = 9
3.	7)28 = 4	9)45 = 5	6)24 = 4	6)18 = 3	9)72 = 8	6)72 = 12
4.	9)63 = 7	9)0 = 0	8)32 = 4	7)35 = 5	6)48 = 8	9)54 = 6
5.	7)7 = 1	7)70 = 10	9)108 = 12	8)88 = 11	8)40 = 5	9)18 = 2
6.	6)42 = 7	8)48 = 6	9)81 = 9	7)63 = 9	8)24 = 3	7)84 = 12
7.	8)56 = 7	6)30 = 5	7)14 = 2	8)96 = 12	7)56 = 8	8)64 = 8

Drill 34   **Division Facts: 3's–9's**

	a.	b.	c.	d.	e.	f.
1.	7)28 = 4	7)49 = 7	4)20 = 5	5)40 = 8	8)56 = 7	9)18 = 2
2.	7)42 = 6	3)24 = 8	4)16 = 4	3)27 = 9	9)36 = 4	7)56 = 8
3.	8)0 = 0	7)84 = 12	6)66 = 11	5)45 = 9	8)48 = 6	5)30 = 6
4.	7)35 = 5	5)15 = 3	9)81 = 9	6)24 = 4	8)32 = 4	6)36 = 6
5.	9)72 = 8	4)28 = 7	3)18 = 6	5)5 = 1	8)72 = 9	8)64 = 8
6.	6)72 = 12	4)12 = 3	4)36 = 9	6)48 = 8	7)63 = 9	5)50 = 10
7.	5)25 = 5	8)40 = 5	3)9 = 3	4)32 = 8	9)54 = 6	6)12 = 2
8.	3)6 = 2	4)24 = 6	6)30 = 5	9)63 = 7	6)42 = 7	8)96 = 12
9.	4)48 = 12	3)21 = 7	5)35 = 7	9)45 = 5	9)108 = 12	6)54 = 9

Drill 35 Division Facts: 1's–9's

	a.	b.	c.	d.	e.	f.
1.	8)24 = 3	4)16 = 4	1)7 = 7	7)42 = 6	3)36 = 12	5)40 = 8
2.	9)27 = 3	3)18 = 6	2)16 = 8	8)64 = 8	4)40 = 10	6)18 = 3
3.	6)54 = 9	9)63 = 7	5)25 = 5	7)28 = 4	3)27 = 9	1)11 = 11
4.	4)20 = 5	8)40 = 5	8)72 = 9	4)48 = 12	2)10 = 5	2)6 = 3
5.	9)81 = 9	5)35 = 7	3)12 = 4	9)9 = 1	7)63 = 9	8)48 = 6
6.	4)28 = 7	7)70 = 10	8)96 = 12	5)15 = 3	1)5 = 5	3)24 = 8
7.	6)36 = 6	6)72 = 12	9)45 = 5	7)56 = 8	2)14 = 7	5)60 = 12
8.	5)55 = 11	8)16 = 2	6)0 = 0	8)56 = 7	5)30 = 6	6)48 = 8
9.	9)54 = 6	5)20 = 4	7)35 = 5	3)21 = 7	2)18 = 9	2)24 = 12
10.	7)49 = 7	6)30 = 5	8)32 = 4	9)72 = 8	2)20 = 10	4)12 = 3
11.	3)9 = 3	6)24 = 4	9)36 = 4	9)108 = 12	7)21 = 3	2)22 = 11
12.	4)32 = 8	2)8 = 4	6)42 = 7	7)14 = 2	2)12 = 6	4)36 = 9
13.	3)15 = 5	7)84 = 12	1)8 = 8	4)24 = 6	3)6 = 2	5)45 = 9
14.	9)90 = 10	4)8 = 2	6)12 = 2	9)81 = 9	5)25 = 5	9)99 = 11
15.	5)60 = 12	2)4 = 2	7)63 = 9	8)56 = 7	9)54 = 6	5)10 = 2

Drill 36 — Division Facts: 10's–12's

	a.	b.	c.	d.	e.	f.
1.	10)80 = 8	10)60 = 6	10)20 = 2	10)10 = 1	10)100 = 10	10)120 = 12
2.	10)30 = 3	10)90 = 9	10)70 = 7	10)40 = 4	10)110 = 11	10)50 = 5
3.	11)55 = 5	11)99 = 9	11)44 = 4	11)66 = 6	11)121 = 11	11)0 = 0
4.	11)33 = 3	11)77 = 7	11)110 = 10	11)22 = 2	11)132 = 12	11)88 = 8
5.	12)48 = 4	12)84 = 7	12)24 = 2	12)96 = 8	12)120 = 10	12)108 = 9
6.	12)12 = 1	12)60 = 5	12)36 = 3	12)144 = 12	12)72 = 6	12)132 = 11
7.	10)100 = 10	12)120 = 10	11)132 = 12	10)110 = 11	12)108 = 9	11)121 = 11
8.	12)132 = 11	11)110 = 10	12)144 = 12	11)121 = 11	10)120 = 12	10)100 = 10

Drill 37 — Division Facts: 8's–12's

	a.	b.	c.	d.	e.	f.
1.	8)64 = 8	10)70 = 7	9)63 = 7	12)48 = 4	11)77 = 7	10)100 = 10
2.	9)27 = 3	11)22 = 2	12)84 = 7	8)56 = 7	10)40 = 4	12)108 = 9
3.	12)36 = 3	8)32 = 4	9)45 = 5	10)30 = 3	9)81 = 9	11)132 = 12
4.	9)18 = 2	10)20 = 2	8)48 = 6	9)72 = 8	12)72 = 6	10)110 = 11
5.	8)24 = 3	12)96 = 8	9)36 = 4	10)60 = 6	11)55 = 5	12)144 = 12
6.	9)54 = 6	12)12 = 1	11)0 = 0	12)60 = 5	8)40 = 5	11)121 = 11
7.	8)72 = 9	9)108 = 12	8)16 = 2	12)24 = 2	8)96 = 12	10)120 = 12
8.	10)50 = 5	12)144 = 12	11)121 = 11	12)132 = 11	10)100 = 10	11)110 = 10

Drill 38 — Division Facts: 5's–12's

	a.	b.	c.	d.	e.	f.
1.	5)40 = 8	7)35 = 5	9)18 = 2	10)30 = 3	12)48 = 4	11)110 = 10
2.	8)48 = 6	6)42 = 7	12)24 = 2	6)24 = 4	11)88 = 8	12)144 = 12
3.	7)28 = 4	9)54 = 6	5)25 = 5	8)64 = 8	7)63 = 9	10)100 = 10
4.	6)36 = 6	8)32 = 4	10)70 = 7	9)72 = 8	6)48 = 8	12)132 = 11
5.	12)60 = 5	5)15 = 3	7)49 = 7	10)10 = 1	8)40 = 5	11)121 = 11
6.	6)30 = 5	5)45 = 9	8)56 = 7	9)27 = 3	11)22 = 2	10)110 = 11
7.	7)14 = 2	6)72 = 12	9)36 = 4	8)24 = 3	12)84 = 7	10)120 = 12
8.	5)30 = 6	9)81 = 9	8)16 = 2	5)35 = 7	11)66 = 6	11)132 = 12
9.	9)45 = 5	7)84 = 12	7)42 = 6	5)20 = 4	9)63 = 7	12)120 = 10
10.	5)50 = 10	6)54 = 9	12)36 = 3	8)96 = 12	8)72 = 9	9)108 = 12
11.	5)60 = 12	7)56 = 8	11)44 = 4	6)18 = 3	10)20 = 2	12)72 = 6
12.	6)12 = 2	7)21 = 3	10)40 = 4	12)96 = 8	5)10 = 2	12)144 = 12
13.	6)54 = 9	8)64 = 8	7)63 = 9	9)81 = 9	12)108 = 9	11)132 = 12
14.	8)48 = 6	5)45 = 9	7)70 = 10	7)56 = 8	9)81 = 9	10)100 = 10
15.	9)72 = 8	6)0 = 0	10)90 = 9	6)66 = 11	7)49 = 7	11)121 = 11

Drill 39 **Division Facts: 3's–12's**

	a.	b.	c.	d.	e.	f.
1.	3)21 = 7	6)30 = 5	4)12 = 3	8)40 = 5	8)64 = 8	9)63 = 7
2.	5)35 = 7	8)48 = 6	9)18 = 2	3)9 = 3	7)42 = 6	4)24 = 6
3.	8)56 = 7	5)60 = 12	6)6 = 1	10)20 = 2	11)55 = 5	12)48 = 4
4.	5)20 = 4	8)24 = 3	3)15 = 5	6)72 = 12	9)72 = 8	6)54 = 9
5.	4)32 = 8	10)10 = 1	5)45 = 9	6)60 = 10	7)28 = 4	8)16 = 2
6.	7)14 = 2	12)24 = 2	8)96 = 12	4)44 = 11	8)0 = 0	3)6 = 2
7.	9)36 = 4	3)12 = 4	4)20 = 5	12)84 = 7	7)49 = 7	5)30 = 6
8.	3)18 = 6	12)60 = 5	9)54 = 6	6)48 = 8	3)27 = 9	5)25 = 5
9.	6)24 = 4	10)70 = 7	7)56 = 8	11)88 = 8	12)96 = 8	4)16 = 4
10.	6)42 = 7	9)45 = 5	7)35 = 5	3)24 = 8	4)36 = 9	9)81 = 9
11.	6)18 = 3	6)36 = 6	9)0 = 0	9)108 = 12	7)63 = 9	4)28 = 7
12.	5)40 = 8	8)88 = 11	6)12 = 2	7)21 = 3	4)8 = 2	7)84 = 12
13.	8)32 = 4	12)72 = 6	4)48 = 12	8)72 = 9	9)27 = 3	12)36 = 3
14.	5)15 = 3	12)108 = 9	12)120 = 10	11)132 = 12	12)144 = 12	10)100 = 10
15.	5)10 = 2	12)132 = 11	11)121 = 11	10)110 = 11	11)110 = 10	10)120 = 12

Drill 40 **Division Facts: 3's–12's**

	a.	b.	c.	d.
1.	18 ÷ 6 = 3	27 ÷ 9 = 3	48 ÷ 6 = 8	121 ÷ 11 = 11
2.	24 ÷ 3 = 8	24 ÷ 12 = 2	24 ÷ 6 = 4	24 ÷ 8 = 3
3.	36 ÷ 9 = 4	36 ÷ 6 = 6	36 ÷ 12 = 3	30 ÷ 5 = 6
4.	16 ÷ 4 = 4	72 ÷ 9 = 8	21 ÷ 7 = 3	120 ÷ 12 = 10
5.	16 ÷ 8 = 2	15 ÷ 3 = 5	100 ÷ 10 = 10	24 ÷ 12 = 2
6.	18 ÷ 3 = 6	32 ÷ 8 = 4	42 ÷ 6 = 7	63 ÷ 7 = 9
7.	4 ÷ 4 = 1	49 ÷ 7 = 7	50 ÷ 10 = 5	144 ÷ 12 = 12
8.	30 ÷ 3 = 10	60 ÷ 5 = 12	32 ÷ 4 = 8	28 ÷ 4 = 7
9.	56 ÷ 8 = 7	54 ÷ 9 = 6	25 ÷ 5 = 5	36 ÷ 4 = 9
10.	90 ÷ 9 = 10	48 ÷ 8 = 6	24 ÷ 4 = 6	77 ÷ 11 = 7
11.	48 ÷ 4 = 12	84 ÷ 12 = 7	9 ÷ 3 = 3	110 ÷ 10 = 11
12.	12 ÷ 3 = 4	20 ÷ 5 = 4	40 ÷ 8 = 5	63 ÷ 9 = 7
13.	81 ÷ 9 = 9	108 ÷ 9 = 12	35 ÷ 7 = 5	15 ÷ 5 = 3
14.	42 ÷ 7 = 6	45 ÷ 9 = 5	21 ÷ 3 = 7	96 ÷ 8 = 12
15.	40 ÷ 10 = 4	56 ÷ 7 = 8	35 ÷ 5 = 7	12 ÷ 4 = 3
16.	27 ÷ 3 = 9	18 ÷ 9 = 2	132 ÷ 11 = 12	28 ÷ 7 = 4
17.	66 ÷ 11 = 6	64 ÷ 8 = 8	72 ÷ 12 = 6	108 ÷ 12 = 9
18.	27 ÷ 3 = 9	60 ÷ 12 = 5	84 ÷ 7 = 12	110 ÷ 11 = 10
19.	120 ÷ 12 = 10	30 ÷ 6 = 5	45 ÷ 5 = 9	132 ÷ 12 = 11
20.	14 ÷ 7 = 2	0 ÷ 4 = 0	20 ÷ 4 = 5	54 ÷ 6 = 9
21.	40 ÷ 5 = 8	96 ÷ 12 = 8	80 ÷ 10 = 8	70 ÷ 7 = 10
22.	4 ÷ 2 = 2	48 ÷ 12 = 4	72 ÷ 6 = 12	72 ÷ 8 = 9
23.	33 ÷ 11 = 3	120 ÷ 10 = 12	77 ÷ 7 = 11	12 ÷ 6 = 2
24.	36 ÷ 3 = 12	6 ÷ 3 = 2	54 ÷ 6 = 9	33 ÷ 3 = 11

Drill 41 **Division Facts: 1's–12's**

	a.	b.	c.	d.	e.	f.
1.	6)12 = 2	7)42 = 6	9)81 = 9	3)36 = 12	2)18 = 9	8)64 = 8
2.	5)40 = 8	3)27 = 9	12)48 = 4	10)60 = 6	7)21 = 3	3)15 = 5
3.	7)35 = 5	4)12 = 3	4)4 = 1	2)14 = 7	5)30 = 6	9)72 = 8
4.	6)24 = 4	8)48 = 6	11)55 = 5	2)24 = 12	8)56 = 7	6)54 = 9
5.	8)32 = 4	3)24 = 8	7)63 = 9	5)20 = 4	12)96 = 8	5)25 = 5
6.	4)16 = 4	1)5 = 5	2)20 = 10	7)84 = 12	3)18 = 6	12)132 = 11
7.	8)40 = 5	2)12 = 6	10)40 = 4	4)32 = 8	6)36 = 6	12)108 = 9
8.	6)30 = 5	4)28 = 7	8)72 = 9	6)72 = 12	5)15 = 3	11)110 = 10
9.	1)10 = 10	9)27 = 3	12)60 = 5	7)49 = 7	9)45 = 5	10)100 = 10
10.	5)10 = 2	1)0 = 0	2)4 = 2	6)48 = 8	8)96 = 12	12)72 = 6
11.	3)21 = 7	9)54 = 6	4)24 = 6	12)36 = 3	3)12 = 4	3)33 = 11
12.	4)36 = 9	9)63 = 7	5)35 = 7	11)22 = 2	6)42 = 7	9)18 = 2
13.	3)6 = 2	2)16 = 8	1)8 = 8	9)36 = 4	12)84 = 7	5)60 = 12
14.	5)45 = 9	7)14 = 2	6)66 = 11	7)56 = 8	8)24 = 3	3)9 = 3
15.	4)20 = 5	12)144 = 12	6)18 = 3	7)28 = 4	7)70 = 10	9)108 = 12
16.	9)0 = 0	12)24 = 2	8)16 = 2	11)121 = 11	10)120 = 12	2)10 = 5
17.	4)8 = 2	11)132 = 12	2)6 = 3	12)120 = 10	4)48 = 12	10)110 = 11

Drill 42 Division Facts: 1's–12's

	a.	b.	c.	d.
1.	16 ÷ 2 = 8	54 ÷ 6 = 9	35 ÷ 5 = 7	12 ÷ 3 = 4
2.	48 ÷ 8 = 6	72 ÷ 12 = 6	14 ÷ 7 = 2	22 ÷ 2 = 11
3.	63 ÷ 9 = 7	40 ÷ 8 = 5	40 ÷ 10 = 4	36 ÷ 4 = 9
4.	56 ÷ 7 = 8	21 ÷ 3 = 7	6 ÷ 1 = 6	18 ÷ 6 = 3
5.	48 ÷ 12 = 4	60 ÷ 5 = 12	72 ÷ 8 = 9	0 ÷ 3 = 0
6.	1 ÷ 1 = 1	9 ÷ 3 = 3	3 ÷ 3 = 1	25 ÷ 5 = 5
7.	12 ÷ 6 = 2	42 ÷ 7 = 6	36 ÷ 9 = 4	96 ÷ 12 = 8
8.	27 ÷ 3 = 9	18 ÷ 3 = 6	49 ÷ 7 = 7	110 ÷ 10 = 11
9.	45 ÷ 9 = 5	30 ÷ 6 = 5	44 ÷ 4 = 11	11 ÷ 1 = 11
10.	24 ÷ 6 = 4	144 ÷ 12 = 12	120 ÷ 12 = 10	72 ÷ 9 = 8
11.	48 ÷ 6 = 8	24 ÷ 8 = 3	84 ÷ 12 = 7	12 ÷ 2 = 6
12.	56 ÷ 8 = 7	121 ÷ 11 = 11	20 ÷ 4 = 5	32 ÷ 4 = 8
13.	40 ÷ 5 = 8	20 ÷ 2 = 10	28 ÷ 4 = 7	42 ÷ 6 = 7
14.	22 ÷ 11 = 2	120 ÷ 10 = 12	30 ÷ 5 = 6	64 ÷ 8 = 8
15.	54 ÷ 9 = 6	14 ÷ 2 = 7	35 ÷ 7 = 5	27 ÷ 9 = 3
16.	132 ÷ 12 = 11	63 ÷ 7 = 9	24 ÷ 4 = 6	5 ÷ 1 = 5
17.	48 ÷ 4 = 12	8 ÷ 2 = 4	70 ÷ 7 = 10	108 ÷ 9 = 12
18.	28 ÷ 7 = 4	132 ÷ 11 = 12	21 ÷ 7 = 3	60 ÷ 12 = 5
19.	18 ÷ 2 = 9	24 ÷ 12 = 2	32 ÷ 8 = 4	100 ÷ 10 = 10
20.	15 ÷ 3 = 5	16 ÷ 8 = 2	81 ÷ 9 = 9	45 ÷ 5 = 9
21.	72 ÷ 6 = 12	24 ÷ 3 = 8	16 ÷ 4 = 4	36 ÷ 3 = 12
22.	15 ÷ 5 = 3	108 ÷ 12 = 9	18 ÷ 9 = 2	36 ÷ 6 = 6
23.	20 ÷ 5 = 4	36 ÷ 12 = 3	55 ÷ 11 = 5	10 ÷ 2 = 5
24.	24 ÷ 2 = 12	12 ÷ 4 = 3	84 ÷ 7 = 12	6 ÷ 2 = 3
25.	20 ÷ 10 = 2	96 ÷ 8 = 12	8 ÷ 4 = 2	110 ÷ 10 = 11

Set II: Mixed Computation Drills

Drill 43 Mixed Computation

	a.	b.	c.	d.
1.	9 + 4 – 3 10	6 + 5 – 4 7	7 + 8 – 5 10	4 + 6 – 7 3
2.	8 + 3 – 6 5	7 + 7 – 5 9	3 + 5 – 2 6	7 + 9 – 3 13
3.	9 + 5 – 7 7	4 + 7 – 3 8	5 + 7 – 8 4	9 + 6 – 4 11
4.	7 + 6 – 5 8	9 + 9 – 5 13	7 + 3 – 5 5	8 + 8 – 4 12
5.	6 + 8 – 4 10	9 + 8 – 3 14	8 + 5 – 4 9	6 + 6 – 7 5

Drill 44 Mixed Computation

	a.	b.	c.	d.
1.	17 – 8 + 4 13	15 – 7 + 6 14	13 – 4 + 7 16	11 – 5 + 4 10
2.	16 – 7 + 5 14	12 – 4 + 3 11	14 – 7 + 8 15	18 – 9 + 7 16
3.	10 – 6 + 8 12	13 – 6 + 5 12	11 – 8 + 4 7	15 – 6 + 5 14
4.	14 – 9 + 5 10	11 – 7 + 8 12	17 – 9 + 7 15	12 – 6 + 4 10
5.	11 – 9 + 6 8	14 – 6 + 8 16	10 – 7 + 6 9	13 – 8 + 6 11

Drill 45 Mixed Computation

	a.	b.	c.
1.	8 + 3 – 6 + 4 9	7 + 2 + 6 – 5 10	8 – 2 + 7 + 4 17
2.	7 + 8 – 2 + 5 18	6 + 4 – 5 + 9 14	8 + 2 + 6 – 8 8
3.	9 – 4 + 6 – 3 8	7 – 3 – 4 + 8 8	9 + 5 – 4 – 6 4
4.	6 + 7 + 3 – 8 8	9 – 6 + 9 + 4 16	7 – 5 + 4 – 6 0

Drill 46 — Mixed Computation

	a.	b.	c.
1.	8 + 7 + 3 − 9 9	6 + 5 − 7 + 4 8	6 − 5 + 4 + 9 14
2.	3 + 4 + 8 + 6 21	7 + 5 − 6 − 3 3	8 + 9 − 6 − 4 7
3.	3 + 2 + 9 − 6 8	4 + 6 + 5 + 5 20	8 + 2 − 7 + 5 8
4.	9 + 9 − 4 − 5 9	5 + 4 − 3 + 9 15	9 − 3 + 8 − 7 7

Drill 47 — Mixed Computation With Multiplication

	a.	b.	c.	d.
1.	8 × 7 + 2 58	6 × 4 + 4 28	3 × 7 + 5 26	8 × 0 + 6 6
2.	4 × 8 + 3 35	7 × 5 + 2 37	4 × 5 + 3 23	5 × 8 + 4 44
3.	7 × 6 + 2 44	5 × 0 + 3 3	6 × 6 + 4 40	3 × 6 + 3 21
4.	8 × 6 + 1 49	7 × 7 + 2 51	4 × 3 + 2 14	9 × 8 + 4 76

Drill 48 — Mixed Computation With Multiplication

	a.	b.	c.	d.
1.	6 × 5 + 4 34	3 × 7 + 2 23	9 × 4 + 3 39	8 × 7 + 4 60
2.	7 × 0 + 5 5	4 × 6 + 1 25	2 × 7 + 2 37	6 × 8 + 2 50
3.	6 × 3 + 3 21	7 × 7 + 4 53	8 × 5 + 3 43	5 × 5 + 4 29
4.	8 × 3 + 2 26	3 × 9 + 4 31	8 × 8 + 1 65	6 × 0 + 4 4

Drill 49 — Mixed Computation With Multiplication

	a.	b.	c.	d.
1.	4 × 7 + 3 31	9 × 3 + 5 32	4 × 4 + 3 19	2 × 9 + 4 22
2.	7 × 1 + 5 12	8 × 4 + 3 35	2 × 8 + 4 20	7 × 8 + 2 58
3.	5 × 0 + 4 4	9 × 6 + 1 55	8 × 6 + 3 51	6 × 6 + 2 38
4.	4 × 5 + 3 23	5 × 9 + 0 45	6 × 7 + 4 46	7 × 5 + 5 40

Drill 50   Mixed Computation: Four Processes

Do each step in the order given.

	a.	b.	c.	d.
1.	7 × 4 − 1 ÷ 9 3	8 + 6 − 7 × 8 56	4 × 8 + 3 ÷ 5 7	4 + 5 ÷ 3 × 7 21
2.	6 ÷ 3 × 9 ÷ 6 3	8 − 4 × 9 ÷ 3 12	7 + 2 × 6 − 4 50	8 × 3 ÷ 4 + 9 15
3.	5 + 7 ÷ 3 − 4 0	6 × 7 − 2 ÷ 5 8	9 − 3 × 6 + 3 39	8 + 7 − 4 × 3 33

Drill 51   Mixed Computation: Four Processes

Do each step in the order given.

	a.	b.	c.	d.
1.	6 + 5 + 3 ÷ 7 2	5 × 5 − 4 ÷ 3 7	7 − 6 × 4 ÷ 2 2	4 + 8 ÷ 3 × 8 32
2.	8 − 3 × 7 + 5 40	9 × 4 − 4 ÷ 4 8	9 ÷ 3 × 8 ÷ 6 4	7 × 5 + 1 ÷ 6 6
3.	8 × 6 − 3 ÷ 5 9	5 + 9 ÷ 2 × 9 63	7 × 4 − 6 ÷ 2 11	9 + 9 ÷ 3 × 9 54

Drill 52   Mixed Computation: Four Processes

Do each step in the order given.

	a.	b.
1.	8 × 4 − 2 ÷ 5 × 7 42	9 ÷ 3 × 7 + 4 ÷ 5 5
2.	7 − 5 × 6 × 6 ÷ 8 9	6 + 5 × 6 − 2 ÷ 8 8
3.	6 × 7 + 3 ÷ 5 − 4 5	8 × 2 ÷ 4 + 7 × 11 121
4.	5 × 6 − 2 ÷ 4 × 7 49	9 − 4 × 8 + 2 ÷ 6 7
5.	7 + 3 × 10 − 1 ÷ 9 11	8 ÷ 2 × 5 + 1 ÷ 7 3

Drill 53   Mixed Computation: Four Processes

Do each step in the order given.

	a.	b.
1.	8 × 6 + 1 ÷ 7 + 2 × 9 81	4 + 4 × 8 − 1 ÷ 9 + 6 13
2.	7 + 8 ÷ 5 × 9 + 3 ÷ 5 6	9 − 7 × 2 × 7 − 1 ÷ 3 9
3.	8 + 4 × 5 ÷ 6 − 7 − 3 0	4 × 5 − 2 ÷ 3 × 2 × 12 144
4.	9 × 6 + 2 ÷ 7 × 6 − 8 40	9 × 8 ÷ 6 ÷ 4 + 8 × 10 110
5.	6 ÷ 3 + 5 × 8 − 1 ÷ 11 5	7 + 4 + 5 ÷ 2 × 8 − 3 61

Set III: Addition Drills

Drill 54 *Horizontal Addition*

	a.	b.	c.	d.	e.
1.	11 + 5 16	14 + 4 18	12 + 6 18	13 + 5 18	10 + 7 17
2.	12 + 3 15	10 + 5 15	15 + 4 19	12 + 7 19	15 + 3 18
3.	14 + 7 21	13 + 9 22	16 + 4 20	17 + 5 22	15 + 5 20
4.	16 + 6 22	18 + 7 25	11 + 9 20	13 + 7 20	18 + 4 22
5.	19 + 5 24	15 + 6 21	12 + 7 19	14 + 9 23	17 + 7 24

Drill 55 *Column Addition*

	a.	b.	c.	d.	e.	f.	g.	h.
1.	6 3 +4 13	4 4 +8 16	2 3 +7 12	3 4 +8 15	5 1 +7 13	1 7 +9 17	0 5 +8 13	3 5 +4 12
2.	6 6 +4 16	8 2 +7 17	4 4 +6 14	0 7 +9 16	7 6 +5 18	3 5 +7 15	2 5 +7 14	8 3 +4 15

Drill 56 *Column Addition*

	a.	b.	c.	d.	e.	f.	g.	h.
1.	5 2 3 +6 16	2 4 4 +3 13	1 9 7 +2 19	8 3 4 +2 17	6 4 5 +3 18	3 4 6 +1 14	5 1 6 +5 17	4 5 9 +1 19
2.	4 2 6 +5 17	7 1 7 +5 20	2 3 5 +9 19	9 3 4 +1 17	3 7 5 +5 20	0 4 8 +6 18	5 4 3 +7 19	2 6 6 +4 18

Drill 57 *Horizontal Addition*

	a.	b.	c.	d.
1.	5 + 3 + 8 16	4 + 2 + 4 10	3 + 4 + 8 15	6 + 3 + 6 15
2.	4 + 5 + 9 18	3 + 2 + 9 14	1 + 7 + 8 16	5 + 2 + 7 14
3.	7 + 3 + 8 18	2 + 8 + 5 15	4 + 6 + 7 17	1 + 9 + 4 14
4.	6 + 5 + 7 18	9 + 4 + 3 16	8 + 3 + 5 16	7 + 7 + 4 18
5.	2 + 9 + 6 17	7 + 8 + 1 16	6 + 7 + 6 19	4 + 8 + 6 18

Drill 58 *Column and Horizontal Addition*

	a.	b.	c.	d.	e.	f.	g.	h.
1.	7	5	3	8	6	5	8	9
	2	6	7	5	4	9	3	1
	8	6	7	4	9	4	2	4
	+6	+4	+5	+7	+3	+8	+7	+7
	23	21	22	24	22	26	20	21

2. a. 8 + 5 + 3 + 4   20   b. 5 + 2 + 3 + 8   18   c. 4 + 7 + 3 + 8   22

3. a. 3 + 7 + 5 + 6   21   b. 7 + 1 + 9 + 5   22   c. 9 + 3 + 4 + 7   23

Drill 59 *Column Addition With Regrouping*

	a.	b.	c.	d.	e.	f.	g.	h.
1.	8	3	3	2	7	1	5	6
	4	5	2	8	6	5	4	4
	5	2	5	4	1	9	2	3
	3	5	0	5	6	3	5	7
	+4	+9	+8	+4	+2	+6	+7	+2
	24	24	18	23	22	24	23	22
2.	4	1	8	5	2	9	3	2
	7	4	5	3	8	4	3	6
	4	3	5	8	7	8	6	8
	6	7	6	0	1	3	8	4
	+3	+8	+4	+4	+5	+5	+3	+6
	24	23	28	20	23	29	23	26

Drill 60 — Carrying

	a.	b.	c.	d.	e.	f.
1.	27 + 78 105	85 + 96 181	49 + 47 96	38 + 36 74	76 + 79 155	95 + 15 110
2.	843 + 759 1,602	927 + 447 1,374	186 + 527 713	742 + 885 1,627	398 + 464 862	375 + 726 1,101
3.	$9.85 + 4.86 $14.71	$7.36 + 2.97 $10.33	$2.93 + 4.49 $7.42	$8.87 + 9.89 $18.76	$9.96 + 4.96 $14.92	$7.98 + 4.56 $12.54

Drill 61 — Carrying With Large Numbers

	a.	b.	c.	d.	e.	f.
1.	5,692 + 3,786 9,478	9,487 + 2,354 11,841	2,950 + 1,158 4,108	5,381 + 7,559 12,940	1,547 + 4,267 5,814	3,428 + 9,855 13,283
2.	46,705 + 71,926 118,631	83,157 + 18,739 101,896	92,784 + 36,825 129,609	37,926 + 72,074 110,000	50,781 + 94,593 145,374	29,593 + 53,697 83,290

Drill 62 — Carrying in Columns

	a.	b.	c.	d.	e.	f.
1.	73 47 + 17 137	58 16 + 24 98	46 72 + 77 195	93 24 + 14 131	17 35 + 42 94	82 38 + 25 145
2.	25 17 + 42 84	44 83 + 37 164	87 26 + 45 158	31 74 + 52 157	94 25 + 49 168	56 52 + 77 185

Drill 63 — Carrying in Columns

	a.	b.	c.	d.	e.	f.
1.	72 64 20 + 57 **213**	91 38 16 + 25 **170**	35 66 42 + 13 **156**	84 85 31 + 52 **252**	29 71 53 + 45 **198**	55 35 26 + 80 **196**
2.	63 27 17 + 24 **131**	70 68 44 + 14 **196**	58 12 37 + 45 **152**	16 75 72 + 36 **199**	54 83 49 + 56 **242**	39 25 60 + 13 **137**

Drill 64 — Carrying in Columns

	a.	b.	c.	d.	e.
1.	893 594 + 272 **1,759**	574 278 + 309 **1,161**	731 825 + 465 **2,021**	469 976 + 344 **1,789**	126 364 + 718 **1,208**
2.	515 450 + 628 **1,593**	189 363 + 425 **977**	538 228 + 192 **958**	394 755 + 659 **1,808**	900 753 + 849 **2,502**

Drill 65 — Carrying in Columns

	a.	b.	c.	d.	e.
1.	5,834 5,625 + 7,146 **18,605**	4,790 8,563 + 2,145 **15,498**	2,917 6,623 + 6,466 **16,006**	7,395 3,406 + 9,541 **20,342**	6,480 1,567 + 6,053 **14,100**
2.	18,594 24,387 + 43,211 **86,192**	86,239 17,412 + 55,364 **159,015**	53,187 79,620 + 70,299 **203,106**	24,986 86,365 + 34,164 **145,515**	63,509 18,453 + 72,814 **154,776**

Drill 66 — Columns With Money

	a.	b.	c.	d.	e.
1.	$3.45 6.19 + 0.49 $10.13	$6.50 3.42 + 7.65 $17.57	$4.18 7.28 + 1.24 $12.70	$5.89 2.43 + 3.50 $11.82	$6.70 0.65 + 5.37 $12.72
2.	$23.85 70.00 + 49.99 $143.84	$49.19 31.56 + 25.17 $105.92	$15.68 44.20 + 40.59 $100.47	$37.80 6.25 + 55.45 $99.50	$60.45 17.38 + 32.17 $110.00
3.	$8.10 6.55 0.27 + 2.67 $17.59	$4.97 3.62 3.10 + 2.48 $14.17	$2.39 7.41 4.00 + 7.32 $21.12	$5.70 2.15 5.69 + 0.42 $13.96	$8.00 0.79 3.85 + 4.26 $16.90

Drill 67 — Large Additions

	a.	b.	c.	d.	e.
1.	482 727 319 + 965 2,493	975 445 763 + 327 2,510	166 786 255 + 442 1,649	954 916 329 + 790 2,989	883 274 118 + 723 1,998
2.	8,392 4,918 4,832 + 2,628 20,770	5,481 5,567 6,108 + 5,716 22,872	3,962 8,216<
5,443 + 4,637 22,258	4,219 7,573 7,529 + 3,640 22,961	5,306 4,825 1,477 + 8,085 19,693
3.	23,045 16,737 74,174 + 28,725 142,681	81,726 64,383 32,640 + 39,134 217,883	35,902 71,346 46,259 + 26,380 179,887	75,000 26,974 13,587 + 12,596 128,157	62,416 28,553 41,600 + 72,458 205,027

Set IV: Subtraction Drills

Drill 68 *Subtraction*

	a.	b.	c.	d.	e.	f.
1.	85 − 53 32	96 − 72 24	78 − 37 41	63 − 43 20	49 − 16 33	88 − 36 52
2.	956 − 145 811	748 − 244 504	999 − 184 815	720 − 410 310	683 − 620 63	875 − 552 323
3.	785 − 484 301	690 − 270 420	536 − 120 416	749 − 236 513	827 − 617 210	358 − 135 223

Drill 69 *Borrowing*

	a.	b.	c.	d.	e.	f.
1.	64 − 27 37	93 − 48 45	70 − 15 55	51 − 36 15	82 − 44 38	60 − 38 22
2.	81 − 38 43	42 − 26 16	95 − 59 36	78 − 49 29	66 − 18 48	73 − 24 49

Drill 70 *Borrowing*

	a.	b.	c.	d.	e.	f.
1.	850 − 366 484	365 − 147 218	713 − 516 197	439 − 267 172	580 − 127 453	421 − 372 49
2.	542 − 429 113	618 − 377 241	720 − 535 185	973 − 688 285	351 − 199 152	924 − 636 288

Drill 71 — *Horizontal Subtraction*

Write answers only.

	a.	b.	c.	d.	e.
1.	19 – 3 16	17 – 5 12	14 – 3 11	15 – 5 10	18 – 4 14
2.	38 – 2 36	26 – 5 21	48 – 6 42	39 – 5 34	25 – 4 21
3.	95 – 3 92	86 – 4 82	37 – 2 35	44 – 3 41	54 – 4 50
4.	67 – 5 62	48 – 6 42	59 – 4 55	18 – 4 14	75 – 3 72
5.	18 – 7 11	24 – 2 22	66 – 6 60	37 – 4 33	39 – 9 30

Drill 72 — *Borrowing From Zero*

	a.	b.	c.	d.	e.	f.
1.	500 − 285 = 215	700 − 380 = 320	800 − 477 = 323	600 − 206 = 394	400 − 389 = 11	900 − 112 = 788
2.	703 − 348 = 355	802 − 603 = 199	601 − 214 = 387	804 − 598 = 206	902 − 576 = 326	705 − 627 = 78

Drill 73 — *Subtracting Money*

	a.	b.	c.	d.	e.
1.	$5.00 − 2.97 = $2.03	$8.00 − 4.79 = $3.21	$9.00 − 6.20 = $2.80	$4.00 − 1.35 = $2.65	$7.00 − 3.48 = $3.52
2.	$9.27 − 3.39 = $5.88	$3.64 − 0.75 = $2.89	$5.03 − 1.89 = $3.14	$8.10 − 3.45 = $4.65	$6.00 − 5.71 = $0.29
3.	$6.19 − 1.25 = $4.94	$4.50 − 3.68 = $0.82	$9.22 − 7.27 = $1.95	$8.95 − 3.48 = $5.47	$7.05 − 2.39 = $4.66

Drill 74 *Borrowing Practice*

	a.	b.	c.	d.	e.
1.	4,810 − 4,528 282	6,362 − 3,535 2,827	8,419 − 2,712 5,707	5,473 − 4,944 529	7,111 − 3,725 3,386
2.	7,522 − 1,685 5,837	9,400 − 3,406 5,994	4,120 − 2,834 1,286	6,248 − 5,629 619	8,341 − 5,999 2,342

Drill 75 *Borrowing From Zero*

	a.	b.	c.	d.	e.
1.	5,000 − 2,984 2,016	7,000 − 1,999 5,001	9,000 − 3,528 5,472	8,000 − 2,465 5,535	6,000 − 5,376 624
2.	6,001 − 3,679 2,322	8,004 − 1,248 6,756	7,206 − 6,748 458	5,002 − 3,595 1,407	9,303 − 3,688 5,615

Drill 76 *Borrowing From Zero*

	a.	b.	c.	d.	e.
1.	7,020 − 3,459 3,561	4,015 − 2,628 1,387	8,200 − 4,375 3,825	9,010 − 7,482 1,528	9,040 − 1,777 7,263
2.	5,022 − 4,378 644	6,300 − 2,499 3,801	7,031 − 5,862 1,169	8,020 − 5,046 2,974	9,004 − 6,307 2,697

Drill 77 — Borrowing From Zero

	a.	b.	c.	d.	e.
1.	6,290 − 3,854 **2,436**	3,821 − 2,555 **1,266**	7,030 − 5,280 **1,750**	8,206 − 4,392 **3,814**	4,005 − 3,408 **597**
2.	5,803 − 3,245 **2,558**	7,062 − 2,548 **4,514**	9,540 − 1,548 **7,992**	7,021 − 4,763 **2,258**	6,800 − 4,279 **2,521**
3.	7,000 − 3,902 **3,098**	3,040 − 1,063 **1,977**	5,308 − 4,719 **589**	8,000 − 2,465 **5,535**	9,408 − 2,725 **6,683**

Drill 78 — Subtracting Money

	a.	b.	c.	d.	e.
1.	$28.00 − 17.24 **$10.76**	$35.00 − 8.07 **$26.93**	$80.00 − 29.98 **$50.02**	$60.00 − 32.50 **$27.50**	$76.00 − 45.35 **$30.65**
2.	$42.70 − 18.36 **$24.34**	$75.12 − 27.06 **$48.06**	$36.05 − 14.87 **$21.18**	$55.00 − 27.13 **$27.87**	$40.10 − 34.72 **$5.38**

Drill 79 — Subtracting Money

	a.	b.	c.	d.	e.
1.	$70.50 − 52.58 **$17.92**	$43.05 − 24.34 **$18.71**	$95.00 − 38.06 **$56.94**	$60.00 − 52.89 **$7.11**	$50.03 − 25.20 **$24.83**
2.	$64.02 − 26.54 **$37.48**	$89.46 − 47.38 **$42.08**	$83.92 − 62.95 **$20.97**	$47.00 − 35.50 **$11.50**	$90.40 − 79.00 **$11.40**

Set V: Multiplication Drills

Drill 80 *Multiplication*

	a.	b.	c.	d.	e.	f.
1.	42 × 2 = 84	21 × 5 = 105	53 × 3 = 159	14 × 2 = 28	71 × 4 = 284	62 × 3 = 186
2.	312 × 3 = 936	143 × 2 = 286	221 × 4 = 884	103 × 3 = 309	320 × 2 = 640	433 × 2 = 866
3.	623 × 3 = 1,869	502 × 4 = 2,008	410 × 6 = 2,460	311 × 8 = 2,488	712 × 3 = 2,136	820 × 2 = 1,640

Drill 81 *Multiplication With Carrying*

	a.	b.	c.	d.	e.	f.
1.	73 × 5 = 365	52 × 6 = 312	48 × 3 = 144	16 × 3 = 48	35 × 5 = 175	64 × 4 = 256
2.	18 × 2 = 36	29 × 3 = 87	54 × 5 = 270	32 × 7 = 224	19 × 2 = 38	27 × 4 = 108

Drill 82 *Multiplication With Carrying*

	a.	b.	c.	d.	e.	f.
1.	14 × 4 = 56	53 × 7 = 371	92 × 5 = 460	36 × 4 = 144	65 × 2 = 130	26 × 3 = 78
2.	27 × 4 = 108	44 × 8 = 352	19 × 4 = 76	35 × 6 = 210	54 × 5 = 270	25 × 7 = 175

Drill 83 — Multiplication With Carrying

	a.	b.	c.	d.	e.	f.
1.	528 × 3 = 1,584	219 × 2 = 438	473 × 3 = 1,419	540 × 4 = 2,160	976 × 4 = 3,904	731 × 6 = 4,386
2.	278 × 2 = 556	345 × 3 = 1,035	520 × 9 = 4,680	286 × 3 = 858	149 × 3 = 447	636 × 2 = 1,272

Drill 84 — Multiplying Money

	a.	b.	c.	d.	e.	f.
1.	$7.54 × 5 = $37.70	$3.18 × 4 = $12.72	$6.30 × 5 = $31.50	$2.89 × 3 = $8.67	$4.62 × 6 = $27.72	$3.41 × 7 = $23.87
2.	$2.34 × 9 = $21.06	$8.60 × 5 = $43.00	$7.26 × 6 = $43.56	$9.25 × 7 = $64.75	$3.18 × 4 = $12.72	$5.76 × 5 = $28.80

Drill 85 — Multiplication With Carrying

	a.	b.	c.	d.	e.	f.
1.	47 × 7 = 329	28 × 4 = 112	16 × 6 = 96	36 × 7 = 252	15 × 8 = 120	24 × 5 = 120
2.	18 × 6 = 108	43 × 9 = 387	37 × 3 = 111	29 × 5 = 145	54 × 6 = 324	65 × 7 = 455

Drill 86 — Multiplication With Carrying

	a.	b.	c.	d.	e.	f.
1.	72 × 8 = 576	26 × 7 = 182	34 × 8 = 272	17 × 7 = 119	45 × 6 = 270	38 × 5 = 190
2.	64 × 9 = 576	83 × 6 = 498	16 × 9 = 144	25 × 7 = 175	39 × 3 = 117	47 × 4 = 188

Drill 87 — Multiplication With Carrying

	a.	b.	c.	d.	e.	f.
1.	657 × 5 = 3,285	348 × 6 = 2,088	926 × 7 = 6,482	475 × 6 = 2,850	184 × 5 = 920	269 × 4 = 1,076
2.	970 × 7 = 6,790	523 × 9 = 4,707	764 × 6 = 4,584	391 × 5 = 1,955	648 × 4 = 2,592	875 × 5 = 4,375

Drill 88 — Multiplication With Zero

	a.	b.	c.	d.	e.	f.
1.	703 × 3 = 2,109	805 × 6 = 4,830	409 × 5 = 2,045	208 × 7 = 1,456	607 × 4 = 2,428	502 × 9 = 4,518
2.	804 × 4 = 3,216	307 × 7 = 2,149	902 × 9 = 8,118	109 × 4 = 436	506 × 7 = 3,542	700 × 8 = 5,600

Drill 89 — Multiplication With Carrying

	a.	b.	c.	d.	e.
1.	4,503 × 6 = 27,018	8,276 × 4 = 33,104	1,935 × 5 = 9,675	6,280 × 6 = 37,680	3,748 × 3 = 11,244
2.	1,624 × 7 = 11,368	4,079 × 4 = 16,316	5,602 × 9 = 50,418	9,265 × 3 = 27,795	4,350 × 8 = 34,800

Drill 90 — Multiplying Money

	a.	b.	c.	d.	e.
1.	$63.92 × 5 = $319.60	$81.40 × 8 = $651.20	$65.07 × 7 = $455.49	$36.18 × 3 = $108.54	$14.53 × 8 = $116.24
2.	$46.90 × 4 = $187.60	$30.75 × 5 = $153.75	$27.43 × 6 = $164.58	$18.09 × 5 = $90.45	$67.92 × 3 = $203.76

Drill 91 — Multiplying by Multiples of Ten

	a.	b.	c.	d.	e.	f.
1.	45 × 60 = 2,700	27 × 30 = 810	19 × 40 = 760	36 × 60 = 2,160	80 × 60 = 4,800	74 × 40 = 2,960
2.	73 × 70 = 5,110	65 × 40 = 2,600	90 × 30 = 2,700	55 × 70 = 3,850	28 × 40 = 1,120	39 × 50 = 1,950

Drill 92 — Two-Digit Multipliers

	a.	b.	c.	d.	e.
1.	84 × 23 = 1,932	79 × 14 = 1,106	45 × 25 = 1,125	60 × 74 = 4,440	27 × 43 = 1,161
2.	76 × 15 = 1,140	32 × 48 = 1,536	18 × 26 = 468	63 × 93 = 5,859	90 × 34 = 3,060

Drill 93 — Two-Digit Multipliers

	a.	b.	c.	d.	e.
1.	$0.24 × 36 = $8.64	$0.63 × 38 = $23.94	$0.17 × 70 = $11.90	$0.58 × 34 = $19.72	$0.92 × 51 = $46.92
2.	$0.87 × 24 = $20.88	$0.29 × 53 = $15.37	$0.45 × 56 = $25.20	$0.60 × 97 = $58.20	$0.36 × 16 = $5.76

Drill 94 — Two-Digit Multipliers

	a.	b.	c.	d.	e.
1.	735 × 26 = 19,110	620 × 78 = 48,360	409 × 64 = 26,176	143 × 79 = 11,297	824 × 35 = 28,840
2.	246 × 76 = 18,696	905 × 54 = 48,870	367 × 70 = 25,690	480 × 53 = 25,440	398 × 43 = 17,114

Drill 95 — Two-Digit Multipliers

	a.	b.	c.	d.	e.
1.	627 × 17 = 10,659	345 × 56 = 19,320	876 × 37 = 32,412	159 × 42 = 6,678	708 × 64 = 45,312
2.	2,685 × 25 = 67,125	4,906 × 64 = 313,984	8,964 × 40 = 358,560	3,719 × 52 = 193,388	5,273 × 38 = 200,374

Drill 96 — Two-Digit Multipliers

	a.	b.	c.	d.	e.
1.	4,690 × 35 = 164,150	5,086 × 62 = 315,332	3,462 × 74 = 256,188	9,768 × 43 = 420,024	1,453 × 69 = 100,257
2.	$17.20 × 58 = $997.60	$45.00 × 39 = $1,755.00	$28.76 × 16 = $460.16	$31.98 × 40 = $1,279.20	$56.05 × 97 = $5,436.85

Drill 97 — Multiplication by Multiples of One Hundred

a.	b.	c.	d.	e.
845 × 600 = 507,000	923 × 300 = 276,900	178 × 400 = 71,200	904 × 800 = 723,200	537 × 500 = 268,500

Drill 98 — Three-Digit Multipliers

a.	b.	c.	d.	e.
398 × 124 = 49,352	127 × 362 = 45,974	760 × 426 = 323,760	534 × 514 = 274,476	295 × 432 = 127,440

Set VI: Division Drills

Drill 99   *Division With Remainders*

	a.	b.	c.	d.	e.	f.
1.	4)15 3 R 3	3)19 6 R 1	2)11 5 R 1	5)17 3 R 2	4)26 6 R 2	5)34 6 R 4
2.	3)28 9 R 1	5)12 2 R 2	4)31 7 R 3	3)25 8 R 1	2)15 7 R 1	5)28 5 R 3

Drill 100   *Division With Remainders*

	a.	b.	c.	d.	e.	f.
1.	4)27 6 R 3	6)32 5 R 2	5)43 8 R 3	7)22 3 R 1	3)20 6 R 2	6)39 6 R 3
2.	2)13 6 R 1	7)47 6 R 5	6)50 8 R 2	4)22 5 R 2	3)14 4 R 2	7)37 5 R 2

Drill 101   *Two-Step Division*

	a.	b.	c.	d.	e.	f.
1.	4)64 16	3)42 14	5)65 13	3)72 24	2)70 35	5)80 16
2.	2)38 19	4)76 19	3)45 15	5)90 18	4)56 14	3)84 28

Drill 102   *Two-Step Division*

	a.	b.	c.	d.	e.
1.	5)125 25	4)232 58	2)116 58	3)222 74	2)154 77
2.	4)140 35	5)270 54	3)171 57	5)145 29	4)216 54

Drill 103   *Two-Step Division With Remainders*

	a.	b.	c.	d.	e.
1.	2)35 17 R 1	5)384 76 R 4	3)202 67 R 1	4)139 34 R 3	5)69 13 R 4
2.	4)315 78 R 3	3)134 44 R 2	4)187 46 R 3	3)80 26 R 2	5)98 19 R 3

Drill 104 — Division Practice

	a.	b.	c.	d.	e.
1.	$45\frac{3}{4}$ 4)183	$68\frac{1}{2}$ 2)137	14 4)56	$68\frac{1}{3}$ 3)205	$65\frac{3}{5}$ 5)328
2.	$15\frac{2}{5}$ 5)77	76 3)228	$56\frac{1}{2}$ 4)226	$19\frac{2}{3}$ 3)59	65 5)325

Drill 105 — Three-Step Division

	a.	b.	c.	d.	e.
1.	188 4)752	169 5)845	265 2)530	175 3)525	139 5)695
2.	153 4)612	138 3)414	144 5)720	235 4)940	268 3)804

Drill 106 — Division Practice

	a.	b.	c.	d.	e.
1.	$88\frac{1}{2}$ 4)354	257 2)514	$166\frac{2}{5}$ 5)832	$156\frac{2}{3}$ 3)470	168 4)672
2.	$39\frac{2}{5}$ 5)197	$159\frac{1}{2}$ 2)319	156 4)624	$253\frac{1}{3}$ 3)760	$137\frac{4}{5}$ 5)689

Drill 107 — Dividing Money

	a.	b.	c.	d.
1.	$1.27 6)$7.62	$1.84 3)$5.52	$1.60 5)$8.00	$0.59 4)$2.36
2.	$1.15 7)$8.05	$3.59 2)$7.18	$2.74 3)$8.22	$0.85 5)$4.25
3.	$1.18 8)$9.44	$0.25 9)$2.25	$2.55 3)$7.65	$1.35 7)$9.45

Drill 108 — Dividing Large Numbers

	a.	b.	c.	d.
1.	1,745 5)8,725	2,467 3)7,401	223 8)1,784	863 4)3,452
2.	540 9)4,860	1,374 6)8,244	1,228 5)6,140	969 7)6,783
3.	1,857 4)7,428	2,718 2)5,436	675 6)4,050	1,125 8)9,000

Drill 109 — Dividing Large Numbers

	a.	b.	c.	d.
1.	3)5,189 = 1,729 R 2	8)7,305 = 913 R 1	4)7,144 = 1,786	7)3,251 = 464 R 3
2.	5)8,640 = 1,728	2)7,813 = 3,906 R 1	9)4,275 = 475	6)9,260 = 1,543 R 2
3.	7)4,621 = 660 R 1	3)7,125 = 2,375	4)9,129 = 2,282 R 1	8)6,826 = 853 R 2

Drill 110 — Dividing With Zero

	a.	b.	c.	d.
1.	4)5,000 = 1,250	3)6,104 = 2,034 R 2	5)8,500 = 1,700	8)8,200 = 1,025
2.	6)7,206 = 1,201	4)9,020 = 2,255	3)8,112 = 2,704	7)9,660 = 1,380
3.	5)6,030 = 1,206	8)1,450 = 181 R 2	6)6,024 = 1,004	9)4,554 = 506
4.	2)6,016 = 3,008	4)7,030 = 1,757 R 2	9)9,150 = 1,016 R 6	7)2,137 = 305 R 2

Drill 111 — Dividing Money

	a.	b.	c.	d.
1.	5)$12.35 = $2.47	8)$82.40 = $10.30	4)$72.00 = $18.00	6)$38.52 = $6.42
2.	3)$17.31 = $5.77	7)$84.42 = $12.06	5)$83.00 = $16.60	9)$69.12 = $7.68
3.	2)$21.00 = $10.50	6)$72.36 = $12.06	3)$62.10 = $20.70	4)$33.00 = $8.25

Set VII: Fraction Drills

Drill 112 — Reducing Fractions

Reduce these fractions to simplest form.

	a.	b.	c.	d.	e.	f.
1.	$\frac{2}{10} = \frac{1}{5}$	$\frac{5}{20} = \frac{1}{4}$	$\frac{10}{15} = \frac{2}{3}$	$\frac{8}{12} = \frac{2}{3}$	$\frac{9}{24} = \frac{3}{8}$	$\frac{6}{8} = \frac{3}{4}$
2.	$\frac{4}{6} = \frac{2}{3}$	$\frac{12}{24} = \frac{1}{2}$	$\frac{5}{15} = \frac{1}{3}$	$\frac{12}{18} = \frac{2}{3}$	$\frac{18}{21} = \frac{6}{7}$	$\frac{6}{18} = \frac{1}{3}$
3.	$\frac{15}{40} = \frac{3}{8}$	$\frac{16}{24} = \frac{2}{3}$	$\frac{9}{12} = \frac{3}{4}$	$\frac{16}{36} = \frac{4}{9}$	$\frac{10}{16} = \frac{5}{8}$	$\frac{15}{25} = \frac{3}{5}$

Drill 113 — Reducing Fractions

Reduce these fractions to simplest form.

	a.	b.	c.	d.	e.	f.
1.	$\frac{3}{12} = \frac{1}{4}$	$\frac{12}{16} = \frac{3}{4}$	$\frac{14}{21} = \frac{2}{3}$	$\frac{16}{24} = \frac{2}{3}$	$\frac{9}{27} = \frac{1}{3}$	$\frac{7}{14} = \frac{1}{2}$
2.	$\frac{10}{25} = \frac{2}{5}$	$\frac{6}{30} = \frac{1}{5}$	$\frac{12}{20} = \frac{3}{5}$	$\frac{11}{22} = \frac{1}{2}$	$\frac{8}{24} = \frac{1}{3}$	$\frac{10}{30} = \frac{1}{3}$
3.	$\frac{9}{15} = \frac{3}{5}$	$\frac{30}{40} = \frac{3}{4}$	$\frac{10}{18} = \frac{5}{9}$	$\frac{8}{16} = \frac{1}{2}$	$\frac{4}{24} = \frac{1}{6}$	$\frac{5}{25} = \frac{1}{5}$

Drill 114 — Improper Fractions

Change these improper fractions to whole or mixed numbers.

	a.	b.	c.	d.	e.	f.
1.	$\frac{10}{5} = 2$	$\frac{7}{6} = 1\frac{1}{6}$	$\frac{11}{4} = 2\frac{3}{4}$	$\frac{12}{7} = 1\frac{5}{7}$	$\frac{6}{5} = 1\frac{1}{5}$	$\frac{15}{3} = 5$
2.	$\frac{21}{7} = 3$	$\frac{14}{3} = 4\frac{2}{3}$	$\frac{7}{2} = 3\frac{1}{2}$	$\frac{4}{3} = 1\frac{1}{3}$	$\frac{20}{4} = 5$	$\frac{19}{9} = 2\frac{1}{9}$
3.	$\frac{8}{4} = 2$	$\frac{17}{5} = 3\frac{2}{5}$	$\frac{30}{10} = 3$	$\frac{17}{6} = 2\frac{5}{6}$	$\frac{25}{5} = 5$	$\frac{13}{2} = 6\frac{1}{2}$

Drill 115 — Improper Fractions

Change these improper fractions to whole or mixed numbers.

	a.	b.	c.	d.	e.	f.
1.	$\frac{11}{9} = 1\frac{2}{9}$	$\frac{16}{4} = 4$	$\frac{14}{4} = 3\frac{1}{2}$	$\frac{21}{6} = 3\frac{1}{2}$	$\frac{15}{9} = 1\frac{2}{3}$	$\frac{4}{2} = 2$
2.	$\frac{16}{6} = 2\frac{2}{3}$	$\frac{13}{5} = 2\frac{3}{5}$	$\frac{17}{8} = 2\frac{1}{8}$	$\frac{10}{4} = 2\frac{1}{2}$	$\frac{28}{5} = 5\frac{3}{5}$	$\frac{16}{8} = 2$
3.	$\frac{18}{3} = 6$	$\frac{24}{4} = 6$	$\frac{18}{4} = 4\frac{1}{2}$	$\frac{5}{3} = 1\frac{2}{3}$	$\frac{12}{7} = 1\frac{5}{7}$	$\frac{12}{8} = 1\frac{1}{2}$

Drill 116 — Adding Like Fractions

	a.	b.	c.	d.	e.
1.	$\frac{2}{3} + \frac{2}{3} = 1\frac{1}{3}$	$\frac{7}{8} + \frac{3}{8} = 1\frac{1}{4}$	$\frac{5}{12} + \frac{7}{12} = 1$	$\frac{4}{9} + \frac{7}{9} = 1\frac{2}{9}$	$\frac{4}{11} + \frac{5}{11} = \frac{9}{11}$
2.	$\frac{1}{8} + \frac{5}{8} = \frac{3}{4}$	$\frac{1}{2} + \frac{1}{2} = 1$	$\frac{3}{4} + \frac{1}{4} = 1$	$\frac{3}{5} + \frac{4}{5} = 1\frac{2}{5}$	$\frac{3}{10} + \frac{8}{10} = 1\frac{1}{10}$
3.	$\frac{1}{6} + \frac{1}{6} = \frac{1}{3}$	$\frac{5}{8} + \frac{7}{8} = 1\frac{1}{2}$	$\frac{1}{3} + \frac{2}{3} = 1$	$\frac{5}{9} + \frac{2}{9} = \frac{7}{9}$	$\frac{3}{7} + \frac{6}{7} = 1\frac{2}{7}$

Drill 117 — Subtracting Like Fractions

	a.	b.	c.	d.	e.
1.	$\frac{3}{7} - \frac{1}{7} = \frac{2}{7}$	$\frac{11}{12} - \frac{1}{12} = \frac{5}{6}$	$\frac{3}{4} - \frac{1}{4} = \frac{1}{2}$	$\frac{7}{8} - \frac{3}{8} = \frac{1}{2}$	$\frac{2}{3} - \frac{1}{3} = \frac{1}{3}$
2.	$\frac{4}{5} - \frac{3}{5} = \frac{1}{5}$	$\frac{9}{10} - \frac{3}{10} = \frac{3}{5}$	$\frac{5}{6} - \frac{1}{6} = \frac{2}{3}$	$\frac{11}{12} - \frac{5}{12} = \frac{1}{2}$	$\frac{7}{8} - \frac{1}{8} = \frac{3}{4}$
3.	$\frac{7}{9} - \frac{4}{9} = \frac{1}{3}$	$\frac{3}{8} - \frac{1}{8} = \frac{1}{4}$	$\frac{6}{7} - \frac{2}{7} = \frac{4}{7}$	$\frac{8}{11} - \frac{6}{11} = \frac{2}{11}$	$\frac{7}{12} - \frac{5}{12} = \frac{1}{6}$

Drill 118 — Adding and Subtracting Like Fractions

	a.	b.	c.	d.	e.
1.	$\frac{2}{3} + \frac{1}{3} = 1$	$\frac{7}{12} + \frac{1}{12} = \frac{2}{3}$	$\frac{11}{16} - \frac{3}{16} = \frac{1}{2}$	$\frac{3}{5} - \frac{2}{5} = \frac{1}{5}$	$\frac{9}{10} + \frac{3}{10} = 1\frac{1}{5}$
2.	$\frac{8}{9} - \frac{2}{9} = \frac{2}{3}$	$\frac{6}{7} + \frac{4}{7} = 1\frac{3}{7}$	$\frac{7}{8} - \frac{5}{8} = \frac{1}{4}$	$\frac{1}{4} + \frac{3}{4} = 1$	$\frac{5}{6} + \frac{5}{6} = 1\frac{2}{3}$
3.	$\frac{3}{8} + \frac{7}{8} = 1\frac{1}{4}$	$\frac{11}{16} - \frac{7}{16} = \frac{1}{4}$	$\frac{11}{12} - \frac{5}{12} = \frac{1}{2}$	$\frac{7}{10} + \frac{3}{10} = 1$	$\frac{7}{16} + \frac{5}{16} = \frac{3}{4}$

Drill 119   Adding and Subtracting Mixed Numbers

	a.	b.	c.	d.	e.
1.	$4\frac{1}{3}$ $+1\frac{1}{3}$ $5\frac{2}{3}$	$6\frac{2}{11}$ $+3\frac{8}{11}$ $9\frac{10}{11}$	$2\frac{5}{7}$ $+3\frac{1}{7}$ $5\frac{6}{7}$	$2\frac{3}{8}$ $+2\frac{1}{8}$ $4\frac{1}{2}$	$5\frac{3}{10}$ $+2\frac{5}{10}$ $7\frac{4}{5}$
2.	$6\frac{2}{3}$ $-3\frac{1}{3}$ $3\frac{1}{3}$	$6\frac{9}{10}$ $-5\frac{3}{10}$ $1\frac{3}{5}$	$7\frac{4}{5}$ $-4\frac{3}{5}$ $3\frac{1}{5}$	$9\frac{3}{4}$ $-4\frac{1}{4}$ $5\frac{1}{2}$	$5\frac{11}{12}$ $-2\frac{7}{12}$ $3\frac{1}{3}$
3.	$5\frac{1}{7}$ $+4\frac{3}{7}$ $9\frac{4}{7}$	$3\frac{5}{9}$ $+3\frac{1}{9}$ $6\frac{2}{3}$	$2\frac{1}{5}$ $+1\frac{2}{5}$ $3\frac{3}{5}$	$1\frac{5}{12}$ $+1\frac{1}{12}$ $2\frac{1}{2}$	$2\frac{5}{8}$ $+4\frac{1}{8}$ $6\frac{3}{4}$

Drill 120   Lowest Common Denominator

Find and write the lowest common denominator for each pair of fractions.

	a.	b.	c.	d.	e.	f.
1.	$\frac{2}{3}$ $\frac{5}{12}$ 12	$\frac{4}{5}$ $\frac{3}{4}$ 20	$\frac{7}{8}$ $\frac{1}{3}$ 24	$\frac{5}{6}$ $\frac{4}{9}$ 18	$\frac{1}{3}$ $\frac{4}{7}$ 21	$\frac{3}{5}$ $\frac{7}{15}$ 15
2.	$\frac{5}{7}$ $\frac{1}{2}$ 14	$\frac{1}{4}$ $\frac{1}{6}$ 12	$\frac{1}{2}$ $\frac{2}{3}$ 6	$\frac{3}{4}$ $\frac{5}{8}$ 8	$\frac{2}{5}$ $\frac{1}{2}$ 10	$\frac{4}{9}$ $\frac{5}{18}$ 18

Drill 121   Lowest Common Denominator

Find the lowest common denominator for each pair of fractions. Then change the fractions to equivalent fractions having that denominator.

	a.	b.	c.	d.
1.	$\frac{1}{5}$ $\frac{3}{10}$ $\frac{2}{10}$ $\frac{3}{10}$	$\frac{4}{9}$ $\frac{5}{6}$ $\frac{8}{18}$ $\frac{15}{18}$	$\frac{1}{4}$ $\frac{2}{3}$ $\frac{3}{12}$ $\frac{8}{12}$	$\frac{1}{2}$ $\frac{5}{16}$ $\frac{8}{16}$ $\frac{5}{16}$
2.	$\frac{3}{8}$ $\frac{1}{3}$ $\frac{9}{24}$ $\frac{8}{24}$	$\frac{2}{5}$ $\frac{2}{3}$ $\frac{6}{15}$ $\frac{10}{15}$	$\frac{7}{12}$ $\frac{1}{6}$ $\frac{7}{12}$ $\frac{2}{12}$	$\frac{1}{2}$ $\frac{3}{4}$ $\frac{2}{4}$ $\frac{3}{4}$
3.	$\frac{4}{9}$ $\frac{1}{2}$ $\frac{8}{18}$ $\frac{9}{18}$	$\frac{3}{8}$ $\frac{1}{4}$ $\frac{3}{8}$ $\frac{2}{8}$	$\frac{3}{8}$ $\frac{5}{6}$ $\frac{9}{24}$ $\frac{20}{24}$	$\frac{7}{10}$ $\frac{9}{20}$ $\frac{14}{20}$ $\frac{9}{20}$

Drill 122 — Adding Unlike Fractions

	a.	b.	c.	d.	e.
1.	$\frac{1}{4} + \frac{1}{2} = \frac{3}{4}$	$\frac{3}{8} + \frac{7}{16} = \frac{13}{16}$	$\frac{1}{4} + \frac{1}{6} = \frac{5}{12}$	$\frac{1}{2} + \frac{2}{3} = 1\frac{1}{6}$	$\frac{1}{3} + \frac{5}{12} = \frac{3}{4}$
2.	$\frac{7}{8} + \frac{3}{4} = 5\frac{5}{8}$	$\frac{1}{4} + \frac{2}{3} = \frac{11}{12}$	$\frac{2}{3} + \frac{5}{6} = 1\frac{1}{2}$	$\frac{3}{5} + \frac{1}{3} = \frac{14}{15}$	$\frac{1}{3} + \frac{5}{9} = \frac{8}{9}$

Drill 123 — Adding Unlike Fractions

	a.	b.	c.	d.	e.
1.	$\frac{1}{6} + \frac{3}{4} = \frac{11}{12}$	$\frac{1}{2} + \frac{5}{6} = 1\frac{1}{3}$	$\frac{7}{12} + \frac{3}{4} = 1\frac{1}{3}$	$\frac{1}{2} + \frac{7}{10} = 1\frac{1}{5}$	$\frac{1}{5} + \frac{3}{4} = \frac{19}{20}$
2.	$\frac{3}{8} + \frac{3}{4} = 1\frac{1}{8}$	$\frac{1}{14} + \frac{6}{7} = \frac{13}{14}$	$\frac{2}{9} + \frac{1}{6} = \frac{7}{18}$	$\frac{1}{3} + \frac{3}{4} = 1\frac{1}{12}$	$\frac{3}{16} + \frac{1}{4} = \frac{7}{16}$

Drill 124 — Subtracting Unlike Fractions

	a.	b.	c.	d.	e.
1.	$\frac{3}{4} - \frac{1}{2} = \frac{1}{4}$	$\frac{4}{5} - \frac{1}{3} = \frac{7}{15}$	$\frac{7}{8} - \frac{1}{2} = \frac{3}{8}$	$\frac{5}{6} - \frac{1}{4} = \frac{7}{12}$	$\frac{13}{16} - \frac{3}{4} = \frac{1}{16}$
2.	$\frac{7}{9} - \frac{1}{6} = \frac{11}{18}$	$\frac{5}{8} - \frac{7}{16} = \frac{3}{16}$	$\frac{7}{12} - \frac{1}{3} = \frac{1}{4}$	$\frac{7}{10} - \frac{2}{5} = \frac{3}{10}$	$\frac{8}{9} - \frac{1}{3} = \frac{5}{9}$

Drill 125 — Subtracting Unlike Fractions

	a.	b.	c.	d.	e.
1.	$\frac{3}{8} - \frac{1}{4} = \frac{1}{8}$	$\frac{1}{2} - \frac{1}{3} = \frac{1}{6}$	$\frac{5}{6} - \frac{2}{3} = \frac{1}{6}$	$\frac{5}{6} - \frac{1}{9} = \frac{13}{18}$	$\frac{3}{4} - \frac{1}{3} = \frac{5}{12}$
2.	$\frac{5}{6} - \frac{1}{4} = \frac{7}{12}$	$\frac{3}{8} - \frac{3}{16} = \frac{3}{16}$	$\frac{3}{5} - \frac{1}{2} = \frac{1}{10}$	$\frac{3}{8} - \frac{1}{3} = \frac{1}{24}$	$\frac{11}{16} - \frac{1}{2} = \frac{3}{16}$

Drill 126 — Adding Mixed Numbers With Unlike Fractions

	a.	b.	c.	d.	e.
1.	$4\frac{2}{3} + 5\frac{1}{6} = 9\frac{5}{6}$	$7\frac{3}{8} + 1\frac{1}{2} = 8\frac{7}{8}$	$3\frac{1}{4} + 4\frac{2}{5} = 7\frac{13}{20}$	$3\frac{3}{10} + 2\frac{3}{5} = 5\frac{9}{10}$	$2\frac{2}{3} + 6\frac{1}{12} = 8\frac{3}{4}$
2.	$6\frac{1}{2} + 3\frac{1}{3} = 9\frac{5}{6}$	$2\frac{3}{5} + 2\frac{1}{3} = 4\frac{14}{15}$	$4\frac{2}{3} + 4\frac{1}{4} = 8\frac{11}{12}$	$1\frac{1}{8} + 2\frac{1}{2} = 3\frac{5}{8}$	$2\frac{1}{9} + 5\frac{2}{3} = 7\frac{7}{9}$

Drill 127 — Adding Mixed Numbers With Unlike Fractions

	a.	b.	c.	d.	e.
1.	$4\frac{1}{4} + 4\frac{1}{2} = 8\frac{3}{4}$	$6\frac{1}{6} + 1\frac{1}{3} = 7\frac{1}{2}$	$1\frac{2}{5} + 3\frac{1}{10} = 4\frac{1}{2}$	$2\frac{4}{9} + 3\frac{1}{3} = 5\frac{7}{9}$	$3\frac{1}{4} + 5\frac{3}{8} = 8\frac{5}{8}$
2.	$3\frac{2}{3} + 3\frac{1}{8} = 6\frac{19}{24}$	$1\frac{3}{16} + 1\frac{1}{2} = 2\frac{11}{16}$	$5\frac{2}{5} + 1\frac{1}{4} = 6\frac{13}{20}$	$2\frac{1}{4} + 6\frac{1}{6} = 8\frac{5}{12}$	$8\frac{3}{4} + 2\frac{3}{16} = 10\frac{3}{4}$

Drill 128   Subtracting Mixed Numbers With Unlike Fractions

	a.	b.	c.	d.	e.
1.	$5\frac{1}{2}$ $-3\frac{3}{8}$ $2\frac{1}{8}$	$6\frac{11}{12}$ $-2\frac{3}{4}$ $4\frac{1}{6}$	$4\frac{13}{16}$ $-3\frac{1}{2}$ $1\frac{5}{16}$	$3\frac{5}{6}$ $-1\frac{1}{4}$ $2\frac{7}{12}$	$6\frac{7}{10}$ $-4\frac{2}{5}$ $2\frac{3}{10}$
2.	$8\frac{2}{3}$ $+4\frac{5}{12}$ $4\frac{1}{4}$	$7\frac{3}{5}$ $-2\frac{1}{3}$ $5\frac{4}{15}$	$5\frac{5}{6}$ $-4\frac{1}{2}$ $1\frac{1}{3}$	$9\frac{3}{4}$ $-3\frac{2}{3}$ $6\frac{1}{12}$	$4\frac{1}{4}$ $-1\frac{1}{16}$ $3\frac{3}{16}$

Drill 129   Subtracting Mixed Numbers With Unlike Fractions

	a.	b.	c.	d.	e.
1.	$3\frac{1}{2}$ $-2\frac{3}{10}$ $1\frac{1}{5}$	$9\frac{3}{4}$ $-4\frac{2}{5}$ $5\frac{7}{20}$	$5\frac{7}{12}$ $-\frac{1}{3}$ $5\frac{1}{4}$	$6\frac{8}{9}$ $-3\frac{1}{2}$ $3\frac{7}{18}$	$10\frac{2}{3}$ $-6\frac{1}{5}$ $4\frac{7}{15}$
2.	$4\frac{1}{3}$ $-2\frac{1}{4}$ $2\frac{1}{12}$	$8\frac{5}{8}$ $-3\frac{1}{3}$ $5\frac{7}{24}$	$7\frac{7}{8}$ $-3\frac{5}{16}$ $4\frac{9}{16}$	$5\frac{2}{3}$ $-2\frac{1}{9}$ $3\frac{5}{9}$	$6\frac{3}{4}$ $-\frac{1}{12}$ $6\frac{2}{3}$

Drill 130   Adding and Subtracting Mixed Numbers

	a.	b.	c.	d.	e.
1.	$8\frac{1}{2}$ $-6\frac{3}{16}$ $2\frac{5}{16}$	$3\frac{1}{4}$ $+2\frac{5}{12}$ $5\frac{2}{3}$	$4\frac{1}{3}$ $+3\frac{1}{2}$ $7\frac{5}{6}$	$6\frac{3}{4}$ $-\frac{1}{5}$ $6\frac{11}{20}$	$7\frac{5}{8}$ $-2\frac{1}{4}$ $5\frac{3}{8}$
2.	$1\frac{1}{2}$ $+5\frac{3}{10}$ $6\frac{4}{5}$	$9\frac{4}{5}$ $-4\frac{1}{2}$ $5\frac{3}{10}$	$3\frac{1}{6}$ $+3\frac{2}{5}$ $6\frac{17}{30}$	$5\frac{1}{4}$ $-1\frac{1}{6}$ $4\frac{1}{12}$	$7\frac{5}{16}$ $+\frac{3}{8}$ $7\frac{11}{16}$

Set VIII: Secondary Skills Drills

Drill 131 — Changing Measures to Smaller Units
Find the missing numbers.

	a.	b.	c.
1.	6 quarts = __24__ cups	6 quarts = __12__ pints	3 gallons = __12__ quarts
2.	4 feet = __48__ inches	5 yards = __15__ feet	3 weeks = __21__ days
3.	2 pints = __4__ cups	3 years = __36__ months	5 quarts = __10__ pints
4.	6 yards = __18__ feet	4 gallons = __16__ quarts	5 weeks = __35__ days

Drill 132 — Changing Measures to Larger Units
Find the missing numbers.

	a.	b.	c.
1.	8 quarts = __2__ gallons	28 days = __4__ weeks	36 months = __3__ years
2.	15 feet = __5__ yards	12 cups = __3__ quarts	12 cups = __6__ pints
3.	48 inches = __4__ feet	10 pints = __5__ quarts	14 days = __2__ weeks
4.	4 cups = __1__ quart	24 inches = __2__ feet	8 cups = __4__ pints

Drill 133 — Changing Measures
Find the missing numbers. You will need to decide whether to multiply or divide.

	a.	b.	c.
1.	12 months = __1__ year	12 quarts = __3__ gallons	12 cups = __6__ pints
2.	8 gallons = __32__ quarts	8 quarts = __16__ pints	8 cups = __2__ quarts
3.	3 hours = __180__ minutes	2 pounds = __32__ ounces	21 days = __3__ weeks
4.	3 yards = __9__ feet	3 feet = __1__ yard	3 yards = __108__ inches

Drill 134 — Changing Measures
Find the missing numbers. You will need to decide whether to multiply or divide. A few answers have fractions.

	a.	b.	c.
1.	4 tons = __8,000__ pounds	2 minutes = __120__ seconds	9 feet = __3__ yards
2.	8 quarts = __32__ cups	8 cups = __4__ pints	8 gallons = __32__ quarts
3.	6 weeks = __42__ days	11 pints = __5½__ quarts	3 yards = __108__ inches
4.	10 cups = __2½__ quarts	2 days = __48__ hours	6 pints = __3__ quarts

Drill 135 — Changing Measures

Find the missing numbers. You will need to decide whether to multiply or divide. A few answers have fractions.

	a.	b.	c.
1.	3 pounds = __48__ ounces	24 months = __2__ years	10 cups = __2½__ quarts
2.	6 feet = __72__ inches	8 quarts = __2__ gallons	5 feet = __1⅔__ yards
3.	10 quarts = __20__ pints	4 hours = __240__ minutes	28 days = __4__ weeks
4.	2 years = __104__ weeks	12 hours = __½__ day	4 pints = __8__ cups

Drill 136 — Understanding Numbers

A. Copy the pairs of numbers and write < or > between them.

	a.	b.	c.
1.	673 _>_ 637	9,206 _>_ 9,160	4,329 _<_ 4,429
2.	8,901 _>_ 8,899	7,098 _<_ 7,100	6,499 _<_ 6,500
3.	3,040 _>_ 3,004	5,299 _>_ 5,200	1,000 _<_ 9,999

B. Write these number words with digits.

4. six thousand, ten   6,010
5. four thousand, nine hundred five   4,905
6. seven thousand, four hundred twelve   7,412
7. two thousand, twenty-nine   2,029
8. eight thousand, five hundred fifty-seven   8,557
9. one thousand, one   1,001

C. Write words for these numbers.

10. 8,030   eight thousand, thirty
11. 1,265   one thousand, two hundred sixty-five
12. 7,002   seven thousand, two
13. 2,948   two thousand, nine hundred forty-eight

Drill 137 — Understanding Numbers

A. Copy these pairs of numbers and write < or > between them.

	a.	b.	c.
1.	67,897 < 68,000	41,000 > 14,000	18,620 > 17,699
2.	42,009 < 42,090	70,302 > 70,032	23,999 < 25,010
3.	264,000 < 264,100	339,998 > 338,998	999,999 > 100,000
4.	399,000 < 400,000	128,046 > 127,064	529,046 < 530,000

B. Write these numbers with digits.

5. one hundred one thousand   101,000
6. three hundred sixteen thousand, eight hundred five   316,805
7. forty-five thousand, eleven   45,011
8. nine hundred thousand, two hundred fifty-four   900,254
9. thirty-one thousand, one   31,001
10. four hundred twelve thousand, three hundred three   412,303

Drill 138 — Understanding Numbers

A. Study this number, and answer the questions about it.   185,923,640

1. Which digit is in hundred thousands' place?   9
2. Which digit stands for a number of ten millions?   8
3. What is the **place value** of the 5 in this number?   millions
4. What is the **combined** value of the 2?   2 ten thousands (Accept 20,000.)
5. What number is 1,000,000 more than 185,923,640?   186,923,640
6. What number is 10,000 less than 185,923,640?   185,913,640

B. Write these numbers with digits.

7. three million, three thousand, three hundred three   3,003,303
8. fifteen million, two hundred thousand   15,200,000
9. seven hundred twenty-eight million   728,000,000
10. four hundred million, thirty-five thousand, sixty-nine   400,035,069
11. eight million, seven hundred forty-two   8,000,742
12. two hundred sixty-one million, eight hundred five thousand, nine hundred fourteen   261,805,914
13. eighteen million, three hundred thirteen thousand, four hundred fifty-five   18,313,455

Drill 139 — Understanding Numbers

A. Copy the numbers and write < or > between them.

a.
1. 4,765,000 __>__ 4,756,000
2. 3,050,505 __<__ 3,505,050
3. 17,098,900 __<__ 17,100,999
4. 259,273,416 __<__ 260,273,416

b.
1. 8,003,000 __>__ 8,000,300
2. 5,600,000 __>__ 5,090,600
3. 93,000,000 __<__ 93,000,020
4. 304,001,999 __>__ 300,999,999

B. Write the answers only.

5. What number is 100,000 more than 64,379,142?   64,479,142
6. What number is 10,000,000 more than 64,379,142?   74,379,142
7. What number is 10,000 less than 64,379,142?   64,369,142
8. What number is 1,000,000 less than 64,379,142?   63,379,142

C. Write these numbers with digits.

9. seventy-eight million, seventy-eight thousand, seventy eight   78,078,078
10. one hundred one million, one hundred ten thousand, ten   101,110,010
11. three hundred sixty-five million   365,000,000
12. eighteen million, two thousand, eleven   18,002,011
13. five hundred nine million, seven hundred thousand   509,700,000
14. four million, forty thousand, four hundred four   4,040,404

Drill 140 — Understanding Numbers

Match the number words with the correct digits.

- __c__ 1. 50,005
- __d__ 2. 50,500
- __a__ 3. 500,005
- __h__ 4. 500,050
- __f__ 5. 5,000,050
- __j__ 6. 5,050,000
- __k__ 7. 50,005,000
- __b__ 8. 50,500,000
- __e__ 9. 500,000,050
- __i__ 10. 500,005,000

a. five hundred thousand, five
b. fifty million, five hundred thousand
c. fifty thousand, five
d. fifty thousand, five hundred
e. five hundred million, fifty
f. five million, fifty
g. fifty million, five hundred
h. five hundred thousand, fifty
i. five hundred million, five thousand
j. five million fifty thousand
k. fifty million, five thousand

Drill 141 — Rounding Numbers

A. Round these numbers to the nearest 10.

	a.	b.	c.	d.	e.
1.	28 30	63 60	147 150	319 320	784 780
2.	591 590	226 230	7,802 7,800	4,177 4,180	5,238 5,240

B. Round these numbers to the nearest 100.

3.	591 600	226 200	4,783 4,800	2,865 2,900	9,348 9,300
4.	6,207 6,200	8,535 8,500	75,192 75,200	13,426 13,400	84,777 84,800

Drill 142 — Rounding Numbers

1. Round to the nearest 10.
   - a. 82 *80*
   - b. 478 *480*
   - c. 193 *190*
   - d. 2,507 *2,510*
   - e. 6,946 *6,950*

2. Round to the nearest 100.
   - a. 478 *500*
   - b. 2,507 *2,500*
   - c. 6,946 *6,900*
   - d. 31,267 *31,300*
   - e. 84,315 *84,300*

3. Round to the nearest 1,000.
   - a. 6,946 *7,000*
   - b. 3,551 *4,000*
   - c. 31,267 *31,000*
   - d. 84,315 *84,000*

4. Round to the nearest 1,000.
   - a. 75,625 *76,000*
   - b. 329,160 *329,000*
   - c. 541,459 *541,000*
   - d. 198,086 *198,000*

5. Round to the nearest $1.00.
   - a. $4.29 *$4.00*
   - b. $8.56 *$9.00*
   - c. $13.70 *$14.00*
   - d. $27.38 *$27.00*

Drill 143 — Roman Numerals

Write these Arabic numerals as Roman numerals.

	a.	b.	c.	d.	e.	f.
1.	14 XIV	27 XXVIII	45 XLV	30 XXX	19 XIX	52 LII
2.	68 LXVIII	88 LXXXVIII	16 XVI	47 XLVII	64 LXIV	70 LXX
3.	29 XXIX	35 XXXV	73 LXXIII	81 LXXXI	56 LVI	49 XLIX

Drill 144 Roman Numerals

Write these Roman numerals as Arabic numerals.

	a.	b.	c.	d.	e.	f.
1.	XLVII 47	LXXXIII 83	IX 9	XIII 13	LIV 54	LX 60
2.	XXXVI 36	XXIV 24	LXXVII 77	XLIII 43	XXXVIII 38	
3.	XV 15	LXIX 69	LXXXII 82	LXXIV 74	XLIX 49	

Drill 145 Roman Numerals

Write these Arabic numerals as Roman numerals.

	a.	b.	c.	d.	e.	f.
1.	84 LXXXIV	95 XCV	31 XXXI	46 XLVI	67 LXVII	53 LIII
2.	98 XCVIII	29 XXIX	80 LXXX	17 XVII	72 LXXII	94 XCIV
3.	136 CXXXVI	350 CCCL	285 CCLXXXV	144 CXLIV	299 CCXCIX	318 CCCXVIII

Drill 146 Roman Numerals

Write these Roman numerals as Arabic numerals.

	a.	b.	c.	d.	e.	f.
1.	LXVIII 68	VII 7	XLIV 44	LXXXI 81	XXIX 29	XC 90
2.	CCLXX 270	CXXVI 126	CXCIX 199	LXXIII 73	CCCLV 355	
3.	CLVII 157	XCVIII 98	CCCXIV 314	XLV 45	CCXCII 292	

Drill 147 Decimals

Write as decimals.

1. three and seven tenths   3.7
2. fourteen and eighty hundredths   14.80
3. sixty-nine and five hundredths   69.05
4. thirty-five hundredths   0.35
5. twenty and four tenths   20.4
6. five hundred twelve and three hundredths   512.03
7. a. $8\frac{1}{10}$ 8.1   b. $\frac{48}{100}$ 0.48   c. $25\frac{6}{100}$ 25.06   d. $\frac{8}{10}$ 0.8   e. $16\frac{27}{100}$ 16.27   f. $59\frac{8}{100}$ 59.08

Drill 148 — Decimals

A. Write these number words as decimals.

1. seventeen and five hundredths   17.05
2. forty-three and six tenths   43.6
3. eight hundredths   0.08
4. ninety-nine and nine tenths   99.9
5. two hundred twenty-eight and eleven hundredths   228.11
6. eight hundred six and seventy-two hundredths   806.72

B. Copy. Write <, >, or = between the numbers in each pair.

	a.	b.	c.
7.	3 = 3.0	4.5 < 4.58	1.07 < 1.7
8.	8.29 < 8.92	6.8 > 6.08	9.3 = 9.30
9.	0.1 > 0.08	5.6 > 5.46	2.15 < 2.2

Drill 149 — Decimals

A. Write as decimals.

1. twenty-five hundredths   0.25
2. six tenths   0.6
3. seven and nine hundredths   7.09
4. fifty-five and two tenths   55.2
5. seven hundred three and thirteen hundredths   703.13
6. one hundred ninety-six and three hundredths   196.03

B. Write each set of numbers in order from smallest to largest.

7. **a.** 3.1   3.2   3.11   3.1, 3.11, 3.2   **b.** 7.85   7.8   7.5   7.5, 7.8, 7.85
8. **a.** 0.3   0.03   0.33   0.03, 0.3, 0.33   **b.** 4.4   4.04   4   4, 4.04, 4.4
9. **a.** 0.18   0.21   0.2   0.18, 0.2, 0.21   **b.** 1.9   2.3   3.1   1.9, 2.3, 3.1
10. **a.** 9.6   9.4   9.05   9.05, 9.4, 9.6   **b.** 6.2   6.02   6.15   6.02, 6.15, 6.2

Drill 150 — Decimals

A. Copy and follow the signs.

	a.	b.	c.	d.	e.
1.	8.3 7.5 4.5 + 3.4 — 23.7	4.2 8.6 3.7 + 7.5 — 24.0	94.5 13.7 + 54.8 — 163.0	7.28 6.50 3.62 + 1.53 — 18.93	17.06 54.86 + 26.45 — 98.37
2.	9.2 − 1.7 — 7.5	60.4 − 26.5 — 33.9	7.18 − 4.55 — 2.63	53.05 − 27.96 — 25.09	842.1 − 376.5 — 465.6

B. Copy in columns with the decimal points in a straight column. Add zeroes to make the right side straight. Then follow the signs.

3. a. 89.4 + 7.95 + 16 + 5.2   118.55   b. 734 + 26.5 + 6.97 + 0.4   767.87
4. a. 652.18 + 48.6 + 295.3   996.08   b. 38.25 + 944.7 + 7.1 + 0.39   990.44
5. a. 93.7 − 35.65   58.05   b. 720 − 35.7   684.3   c. 83.21 − 16.5   66.71
6. a. 57 − 13.8   43.2   b. 9.3 − 2.68   6.62   c. 74.39 − 46   28.39

Speed Drills

Speed Drill 2

1.
0	3	8	0	1	2	3	7	5	6
+1	+3	+4	+3	+5	+2	+0	+0	+5	+2
1	6	12	3	6	4	3	7	10	8

2.
2	6	6	4	2	2	8	4	5	3
+5	+1	+3	+2	+8	+7	+8	+6	+7	+8
7	7	9	6	10	9	16	10	12	11

3.
0	1	6	9	0	3	3	2	0	1
+4	+6	+6	+0	+8	+2	+4	+1	+7	+8
4	7	12	9	8	5	7	3	7	9

4.
3	2	5	9	3	4	7	6	9	4
+6	+9	+8	+3	+7	+8	+7	+5	+4	+7
9	11	13	12	10	12	14	11	13	11

5.
7	7	8	9	8	6	9	8	8	7
+5	+9	+7	+8	+6	+9	+7	+3	+5	+6
12	16	15	17	14	15	16	11	13	13

2 pt. each

Speed Drill 4

1.
1	7	0	2	0	1	3	2	3	7
+1	+4	+1	+0	+4	+4	+5	+5	+6	+5
2	11	1	2	4	5	8	7	9	12

2.
1	2	4	5	3	4	5	2	4	6
+2	+2	+4	+9	+2	+5	+6	+7	+8	+9
3	4	8	14	5	9	11	9	12	15

3.
1	5	1	0	6	4	5	9	8	8
+0	+5	+7	+7	+0	+3	+7	+4	+9	+5
1	10	8	7	6	7	12	13	17	13

4.
8	4	6	4	9	7	2	0	7	3
+3	+9	+5	+6	+2	+1	+1	+2	+0	+1
11	13	11	10	11	8	3	2	7	4

5.
1	4	3	1	7	1	6	2	7	7
+6	+0	+3	+3	+8	+9	+1	+9	+2	+9
7	4	6	4	15	10	7	11	9	16

2 pt. each

Speed Drill 6

1.
$$\begin{array}{r}35\\+62\\\hline 97\end{array}\qquad\begin{array}{r}28\\+44\\\hline 72\end{array}\qquad\begin{array}{r}41\\+97\\\hline 138\end{array}\qquad\begin{array}{r}75\\+85\\\hline 160\end{array}$$

2.
$$\begin{array}{r}85\\+28\\\hline 113\end{array}\qquad\begin{array}{r}39\\+18\\\hline 57\end{array}\qquad\begin{array}{r}17\\+56\\\hline 73\end{array}\qquad\begin{array}{r}56\\+34\\\hline 90\end{array}$$

3.
$$\begin{array}{r}470\\+358\\\hline 828\end{array}\qquad\begin{array}{r}823\\+89\\\hline 912\end{array}\qquad\begin{array}{r}696\\+578\\\hline 1{,}274\end{array}$$

6 pt. each

Speed Drill 8

1.
$$\begin{array}{r}3\\6\\+8\\\hline 17\end{array}\quad\begin{array}{r}5\\4\\+6\\\hline 15\end{array}\quad\begin{array}{r}2\\3\\+7\\\hline 12\end{array}\quad\begin{array}{r}8\\1\\+5\\\hline 14\end{array}\quad\begin{array}{r}4\\3\\+6\\\hline 13\end{array}\quad\begin{array}{r}5\\3\\+7\\\hline 15\end{array}\quad\begin{array}{r}3\\3\\+5\\\hline 11\end{array}$$

2.
$$\begin{array}{r}2\\7\\+9\\\hline 18\end{array}\quad\begin{array}{r}6\\4\\+6\\\hline 16\end{array}\quad\begin{array}{r}5\\2\\+9\\\hline 16\end{array}\quad\begin{array}{r}8\\4\\+5\\\hline 17\end{array}\quad\begin{array}{r}4\\7\\+7\\\hline 18\end{array}\quad\begin{array}{r}4\\2\\+8\\\hline 14\end{array}\quad\begin{array}{r}7\\3\\+5\\\hline 15\end{array}$$

5 pt. each

Speed Drills

Speed Drill 10

1.
    5 + 9 = 14
    8 + 7 = 15
    4 + 8 = 12
    9 + 6 = 15
    7 + 5 = 12
    6 + 8 = 14

2.
    5 + 4 + 8 = 17
    7 + 4 + 6 = 17
    36 + 23 + 24 = 83
    52 + 14 + 63 = 129
    74 + 35 + 25 = 134

3.
    463 + 351 + 146 = 960
    715 + 745 + 67 = 1,527
    826 + 360 + 477 = 1,663

1: 4 pt. each
2–3: 6 pt. each

Speed Drill 12

1. 2−1=1; 5−5=0; 7−0=7; 10−1=9; 8−5=3; 13−4=9; 8−6=2; 17−9=8; 13−5=8; 13−6=7

2. 16−7=9; 11−8=3; 10−6=4; 12−6=6; 11−2=9; 7−4=3; 8−7=1; 3−1=2; 4−4=0; 3−0=3

3. 6−3=3; 3−2=1; 5−0=5; 9−9=0; 9−7=2; 14−5=9; 9−8=1; 12−4=8; 11−6=5; 15−7=8

4. 8−0=8; 9−0=9; 6−5=1; 8−8=0; 10−5=5; 6−6=0; 9−6=3; 12−5=7; 17−8=9; 15−9=6

5. 4−3=1; 2−2=0; 8−4=4; 7−1=6; 8−2=6; 7−5=2; 11−5=6; 14−6=8; 10−7=3; 12−8=4

2 pt. each

Speed Drills

Speed Drill 14

1.
| 3 − 3 = 0 | 1 − 0 = 1 | 4 − 2 = 2 | 9 − 3 = 6 | 6 − 4 = 2 | 9 − 4 = 5 | 12 − 3 = 9 | 13 − 7 = 6 | 12 − 9 = 3 | 11 − 4 = 7 |

2.
| 5 − 1 = 4 | 7 − 2 = 5 | 6 − 2 = 4 | 11 − 3 = 8 | 5 − 2 = 3 | 10 − 4 = 6 | 16 − 8 = 8 | 13 − 8 = 5 | 15 − 6 = 9 | 13 − 9 = 4 |

3.
| 11 − 7 = 4 | 10 − 8 = 2 | 10 − 9 = 1 | 4 − 1 = 3 | 6 − 1 = 5 | 15 − 8 = 7 | 7 − 6 = 1 | 5 − 3 = 2 | 2 − 0 = 2 | 1 − 1 = 0 |

4.
| 0 − 0 = 0 | 8 − 1 = 7 | 14 − 8 = 6 | 9 − 5 = 4 | 7 − 7 = 0 | 10 − 2 = 8 | 14 − 7 = 7 | 18 − 9 = 9 | 14 − 9 = 5 | 9 − 1 = 8 |

5.
| 9 − 2 = 7 | 8 − 3 = 5 | 4 − 0 = 4 | 6 − 0 = 6 | 5 − 4 = 1 | 7 − 3 = 4 | 10 − 3 = 7 | 11 − 9 = 2 | 16 − 7 = 9 | 12 − 7 = 5 |

2 pt. each

Speed Drill 16

1. Place commas correctly.
   a. 39,026   b. 592,741   c. 9,308   d. 469,175

2. Write numbers to match. You will not use all the numbers.

   __3__ a. thirty thousand, two hundred twelve   (1) 32,012
   __1__ b. thirty-two thousand, twelve   (2) 302,120
   __7__ c. thirty-two thousand, one hundred twenty (3) 30,212
   __6__ d. three hundred two thousand, twelve   (4) 320,012
   __4__ e. three hundred twenty thousand, twelve   (5) 302,312
   __2__ f. three hundred two thousand, one hundred twenty (6) 302,012
                                                    (7) 32,120

3. Write two addition and two subtraction facts for each number family.

   a. 8, 5, 3
   5 + 3 = 8; 3 + 5 = 8; 8 − 5 = 3; 8 − 3 = 5

   b. 11, 7, 4
   7 + 4 = 11; 4 + 7 = 11; 11 − 7 = 4; 11 − 4 = 7

   4 pt. each

Speed Drills

Speed Drill 18

1.
11	18	10	13	15	12
−7	−9	−8	−6	−9	−5
4	9	2	7	6	7

2.
70	53	95	64	82
−46	−38	−24	−37	−52
24	15	71	27	30

3.
632	500	748	913
−428	−245	−675	−624
204	255	73	289

1: 4 pt. each
2–3: 6 pt. each

Speed Drill 20

Follow the signs.

1.
10	8	9	17	8	6
−7	+8	+6	−8	−5	+7
3	16	15	9	3	13

2.
65	41	37		682
24	76	25	579	137
+17	+38	+42	+849	+155
106	155	104	1,428	974

3.
90	53	725	806
−43	−25	−163	−428
47	28	562	378

1: 4 pt. each
2–3: 6 pt. each

Speed Drill 22

1.
| 7 − 6 = 1 | 9 − 6 = 3 | 11 − 5 = 6 | 12 − 3 = 9 | 14 − 8 = 6 | 8 − 3 = 5 | 12 − 7 = 5 | 16 − 7 = 9 |

2.
| 5 + 2 + 7 = 14 | 4 + 8 + 4 = 16 | 9 + 5 + 3 = 17 | 7 + 3 + 6 = 16 | 2 + 4 + 7 = 13 | 6 + 8 + 4 = 18 |

3.
| 73 + 24 + 34 = 131 | 91 + 37 + 29 = 157 | 562 + 346 + 71 = 979 | 480 + 145 + 926 = 1,551 |

1: 3 pt. each
2–3: 5 pt. each

first page

Speed Drill 24

1.
| 2 + 0 = 2 | 1 + 3 = 4 | 0 + 5 = 5 | 8 + 1 = 9 | 5 + 0 = 5 | 4 + 4 = 8 | 0 + 6 = 6 | 0 + 2 = 2 | 1 + 7 = 8 | 5 + 3 = 8 |

second page

2.
| 1 + 1 = 2 | 4 + 0 = 4 | 7 + 3 = 10 | 9 + 1 = 10 | 0 + 0 = 0 | 1 + 2 = 3 | 2 + 3 = 5 | 3 + 1 = 4 | 1 + 0 = 1 | 0 + 9 = 9 |

3.
| 1 + 4 = 5 | 7 + 2 = 9 | 9 + 9 = 18 | 2 + 4 = 6 | 5 + 1 = 6 | 4 + 5 = 9 | 8 + 0 = 8 | 7 + 1 = 8 | 6 + 0 = 6 | 5 + 4 = 9 |

4.
| 7 + 4 = 11 | 7 + 8 = 15 | 9 + 5 = 14 | 6 + 7 = 13 | 3 + 9 = 12 | 5 + 9 = 14 | 6 + 8 = 14 | 4 + 9 = 13 | 8 + 9 = 17 | 9 + 6 = 15 |

5.
| 3 + 5 = 8 | 1 + 9 = 10 | 8 + 2 = 10 | 5 + 2 = 7 | 2 + 6 = 8 | 5 + 6 = 11 | 4 + 1 = 5 | 9 + 2 = 11 | 4 + 3 = 7 | 6 + 4 = 10 |

6.
| 3 + 3 = 6 | 5 + 5 = 10 | 9 + 0 = 9 | 8 + 3 = 11 | 6 + 3 = 9 | 8 + 8 = 16 | 5 + 8 = 13 | 9 + 4 = 13 | 7 + 9 = 16 | 8 + 7 = 15 |

2 pt. each

Speed Drills

Speed Drill 26

Write the values. Use the cent mark (¢).

1. 1 dime = __10¢__   1 quarter = __25¢__

2. 1 half dollar = __50¢__   1 nickel = __5¢__

3. 1 dollar = __100¢__   4 nickels = __20¢__

4. 6 dimes = __60¢__   8 pennies = __8¢__

5. 7 nickels = __35¢__   4 quarters = __100¢__

6. 3 half dollars = __150¢__ 5 dimes = __50¢__

7. 23 pennies = __23¢__   3 quarters = __75¢__

8. 4 dimes + 7 pennies = __47¢__   1 quarter + 2 nickels = __35¢__

6 pt. each

first page

Speed Drill 28

1. $\begin{array}{r}6\\-1\\\hline 5\end{array}$ $\begin{array}{r}9\\-0\\\hline 9\end{array}$ $\begin{array}{r}2\\-2\\\hline 0\end{array}$ $\begin{array}{r}1\\-0\\\hline 1\end{array}$ $\begin{array}{r}8\\-1\\\hline 7\end{array}$ $\begin{array}{r}5\\-5\\\hline 0\end{array}$ $\begin{array}{r}4\\-4\\\hline 0\end{array}$ $\begin{array}{r}8\\-3\\\hline 5\end{array}$ $\begin{array}{r}7\\-2\\\hline 5\end{array}$ $\begin{array}{r}3\\-2\\\hline 1\end{array}$

second page

2. $\begin{array}{r}2\\-0\\\hline 2\end{array}$ $\begin{array}{r}6\\-5\\\hline 1\end{array}$ $\begin{array}{r}8\\-4\\\hline 4\end{array}$ $\begin{array}{r}4\\-2\\\hline 2\end{array}$ $\begin{array}{r}9\\-1\\\hline 8\end{array}$ $\begin{array}{r}7\\-0\\\hline 7\end{array}$ $\begin{array}{r}3\\-1\\\hline 2\end{array}$ $\begin{array}{r}4\\-0\\\hline 4\end{array}$ $\begin{array}{r}6\\-2\\\hline 4\end{array}$ $\begin{array}{r}5\\-0\\\hline 5\end{array}$

3. $\begin{array}{r}5\\-3\\\hline 2\end{array}$ $\begin{array}{r}10\\-5\\\hline 5\end{array}$ $\begin{array}{r}8\\-2\\\hline 6\end{array}$ $\begin{array}{r}6\\-4\\\hline 2\end{array}$ $\begin{array}{r}7\\-7\\\hline 0\end{array}$ $\begin{array}{r}8\\-5\\\hline 3\end{array}$ $\begin{array}{r}7\\-4\\\hline 3\end{array}$ $\begin{array}{r}5\\-4\\\hline 1\end{array}$ $\begin{array}{r}11\\-3\\\hline 8\end{array}$ $\begin{array}{r}9\\-8\\\hline 1\end{array}$

4. $\begin{array}{r}7\\-6\\\hline 1\end{array}$ $\begin{array}{r}9\\-6\\\hline 3\end{array}$ $\begin{array}{r}11\\-5\\\hline 6\end{array}$ $\begin{array}{r}12\\-3\\\hline 9\end{array}$ $\begin{array}{r}14\\-7\\\hline 7\end{array}$ $\begin{array}{r}8\\-6\\\hline 2\end{array}$ $\begin{array}{r}12\\-6\\\hline 6\end{array}$ $\begin{array}{r}10\\-3\\\hline 7\end{array}$ $\begin{array}{r}16\\-8\\\hline 8\end{array}$ $\begin{array}{r}14\\-5\\\hline 9\end{array}$

5. $\begin{array}{r}11\\-7\\\hline 4\end{array}$ $\begin{array}{r}15\\-9\\\hline 6\end{array}$ $\begin{array}{r}12\\-8\\\hline 4\end{array}$ $\begin{array}{r}11\\-4\\\hline 7\end{array}$ $\begin{array}{r}14\\-8\\\hline 6\end{array}$ $\begin{array}{r}13\\-6\\\hline 7\end{array}$ $\begin{array}{r}16\\-7\\\hline 9\end{array}$ $\begin{array}{r}12\\-7\\\hline 5\end{array}$ $\begin{array}{r}13\\-8\\\hline 5\end{array}$ $\begin{array}{r}15\\-7\\\hline 8\end{array}$

6. $\begin{array}{r}10\\-8\\\hline 2\end{array}$ $\begin{array}{r}12\\-5\\\hline 7\end{array}$ $\begin{array}{r}14\\-6\\\hline 8\end{array}$ $\begin{array}{r}13\\-7\\\hline 6\end{array}$ $\begin{array}{r}18\\-9\\\hline 9\end{array}$ $\begin{array}{r}17\\-9\\\hline 8\end{array}$ $\begin{array}{r}10\\-6\\\hline 4\end{array}$ $\begin{array}{r}11\\-9\\\hline 2\end{array}$ $\begin{array}{r}15\\-6\\\hline 9\end{array}$ $\begin{array}{r}12\\-4\\\hline 8\end{array}$

2 pt. each

Speed Drill 30

Watch the signs!

1.
   - 8 − 6 = 2
   - 7 + 0 = 7
   - 9 + 2 = 11
   - 13 − 4 = 9
   - 10 − 3 = 7
   - 7 − 4 = 3
   - 11 − 5 = 6
   - 8 + 8 = 16
   - 4 + 7 = 11

2.
   - 5 + 8 = 13
   - 14 − 7 = 7
   - 3 + 6 = 9
   - 6 + 9 = 15
   - 12 − 8 = 4
   - 16 − 7 = 9
   - 9 + 5 = 14
   - 6 − 5 = 1
   - 8 − 4 = 4

3.
   - 6 + 8 = 14
   - 2 + 3 = 5
   - 10 − 8 = 2
   - 11 − 7 = 4
   - 9 − 2 = 7
   - 3 + 8 = 11
   - 6 + 6 = 12
   - 8 − 5 = 3
   - 10 − 6 = 4

4.
   - 15 − 7 = 8
   - 17 − 8 = 9
   - 2 + 7 = 9
   - 6 + 5 = 11
   - 7 − 7 = 0
   - 13 − 6 = 7
   - 8 + 4 = 12
   - 12 − 9 = 3
   - 4 + 9 = 13

2 pt. each

Speed Drill 32

1.
   - 7 × 3 = 21
   - 0 × 1 = 0
   - 7 × 2 = 14
   - 9 × 1 = 9
   - 3 × 2 = 6
   - 10 × 0 = 0
   - 6 × 2 = 12
   - 12 × 1 = 12
   - 5 × 0 = 0
   - 12 × 3 = 36

2.
   - 5 × 3 = 15
   - 8 × 1 = 8
   - 6 × 0 = 0
   - 1 × 1 = 1
   - 5 × 2 = 10
   - 8 × 3 = 24
   - 4 × 2 = 8
   - 3 × 0 = 0
   - 10 × 2 = 20
   - 0 × 3 = 0

3.
   - 7 × 0 = 0
   - 3 × 4 = 12
   - 1 × 5 = 5
   - 0 × 0 = 0
   - 3 × 3 = 9
   - 2 × 1 = 2
   - 9 × 2 = 18
   - 1 × 6 = 6
   - 8 × 0 = 0
   - 0 × 4 = 0

4.
   - 2 × 2 = 4
   - 10 × 1 = 10
   - 12 × 0 = 0
   - 9 × 3 = 27
   - 7 × 2 = 14
   - 1 × 4 = 4
   - 1 × 0 = 0
   - 0 × 2 = 0
   - 10 × 3 = 30
   - 11 × 2 = 22

5.
   - 2 × 3 = 6
   - 9 × 0 = 0
   - 1 × 2 = 2
   - 11 × 3 = 33
   - 8 × 2 = 16
   - 11 × 1 = 11
   - 1 × 3 = 3
   - 7 × 1 = 7
   - 12 × 2 = 24
   - 6 × 3 = 18

2 pt. each

Speed Drills

Speed Drill 34

1. $\begin{array}{r}4\\ \times 4\\ \hline 16\end{array}$ $\begin{array}{r}11\\ \times 2\\ \hline 22\end{array}$ $\begin{array}{r}7\\ \times 1\\ \hline 7\end{array}$ $\begin{array}{r}3\\ \times 0\\ \hline 0\end{array}$ $\begin{array}{r}4\\ \times 3\\ \hline 12\end{array}$ $\begin{array}{r}8\\ \times 1\\ \hline 8\end{array}$ $\begin{array}{r}2\\ \times 2\\ \hline 4\end{array}$ $\begin{array}{r}7\\ \times 3\\ \hline 21\end{array}$ $\begin{array}{r}3\\ \times 6\\ \hline 18\end{array}$

2. $\begin{array}{r}10\\ \times 1\\ \hline 10\end{array}$ $\begin{array}{r}4\\ \times 6\\ \hline 24\end{array}$ $\begin{array}{r}9\\ \times 4\\ \hline 36\end{array}$ $\begin{array}{r}2\\ \times 3\\ \hline 6\end{array}$ $\begin{array}{r}3\\ \times 1\\ \hline 3\end{array}$ $\begin{array}{r}12\\ \times 2\\ \hline 24\end{array}$ $\begin{array}{r}8\\ \times 3\\ \hline 24\end{array}$ $\begin{array}{r}2\\ \times 5\\ \hline 10\end{array}$ $\begin{array}{r}7\\ \times 4\\ \hline 28\end{array}$

3. $\begin{array}{r}1\\ \times 6\\ \hline 6\end{array}$ $\begin{array}{r}3\\ \times 3\\ \hline 9\end{array}$ $\begin{array}{r}9\\ \times 2\\ \hline 18\end{array}$ $\begin{array}{r}10\\ \times 4\\ \hline 40\end{array}$ $\begin{array}{r}1\\ \times 0\\ \hline 0\end{array}$ $\begin{array}{r}4\\ \times 1\\ \hline 4\end{array}$ $\begin{array}{r}2\\ \times 6\\ \hline 12\end{array}$ $\begin{array}{r}9\\ \times 3\\ \hline 27\end{array}$ $\begin{array}{r}8\\ \times 2\\ \hline 16\end{array}$

4. $\begin{array}{r}9\\ \times 1\\ \hline 9\end{array}$ $\begin{array}{r}3\\ \times 5\\ \hline 15\end{array}$ $\begin{array}{r}11\\ \times 4\\ \hline 44\end{array}$ $\begin{array}{r}1\\ \times 3\\ \hline 3\end{array}$ $\begin{array}{r}2\\ \times 4\\ \hline 8\end{array}$ $\begin{array}{r}12\\ \times 4\\ \hline 48\end{array}$ $\begin{array}{r}3\\ \times 2\\ \hline 6\end{array}$ $\begin{array}{r}10\\ \times 3\\ \hline 30\end{array}$ $\begin{array}{r}1\\ \times 1\\ \hline 1\end{array}$

5. $\begin{array}{r}7\\ \times 2\\ \hline 14\end{array}$ $\begin{array}{r}4\\ \times 0\\ \hline 0\end{array}$ $\begin{array}{r}12\\ \times 3\\ \hline 36\end{array}$ $\begin{array}{r}4\\ \times 5\\ \hline 20\end{array}$ $\begin{array}{r}2\\ \times 1\\ \hline 2\end{array}$ $\begin{array}{r}4\\ \times 2\\ \hline 8\end{array}$ $\begin{array}{r}11\\ \times 3\\ \hline 33\end{array}$ $\begin{array}{r}3\\ \times 4\\ \hline 12\end{array}$ $\begin{array}{r}4\\ \times 8\\ \hline 32\end{array}$

2 pt. each

Speed Drill 36

1. $\begin{array}{r}1\\ \times 6\\ \hline 6\end{array}$ $\begin{array}{r}8\\ \times 5\\ \hline 40\end{array}$ $\begin{array}{r}3\\ \times 3\\ \hline 9\end{array}$ $\begin{array}{r}9\\ \times 2\\ \hline 18\end{array}$ $\begin{array}{r}10\\ \times 4\\ \hline 40\end{array}$ $\begin{array}{r}5\\ \times 4\\ \hline 20\end{array}$ $\begin{array}{r}8\\ \times 4\\ \hline 32\end{array}$ $\begin{array}{r}2\\ \times 6\\ \hline 12\end{array}$ $\begin{array}{r}9\\ \times 3\\ \hline 27\end{array}$

2. $\begin{array}{r}4\\ \times 4\\ \hline 16\end{array}$ $\begin{array}{r}11\\ \times 2\\ \hline 22\end{array}$ $\begin{array}{r}5\\ \times 6\\ \hline 30\end{array}$ $\begin{array}{r}7\\ \times 2\\ \hline 14\end{array}$ $\begin{array}{r}3\\ \times 0\\ \hline 0\end{array}$ $\begin{array}{r}4\\ \times 3\\ \hline 12\end{array}$ $\begin{array}{r}8\\ \times 1\\ \hline 8\end{array}$ $\begin{array}{r}2\\ \times 2\\ \hline 4\end{array}$ $\begin{array}{r}7\\ \times 3\\ \hline 21\end{array}$

3. $\begin{array}{r}5\\ \times 5\\ \hline 25\end{array}$ $\begin{array}{r}2\\ \times 0\\ \hline 0\end{array}$ $\begin{array}{r}3\\ \times 6\\ \hline 18\end{array}$ $\begin{array}{r}10\\ \times 2\\ \hline 20\end{array}$ $\begin{array}{r}4\\ \times 6\\ \hline 24\end{array}$ $\begin{array}{r}9\\ \times 4\\ \hline 36\end{array}$ $\begin{array}{r}2\\ \times 3\\ \hline 6\end{array}$ $\begin{array}{r}5\\ \times 3\\ \hline 15\end{array}$ $\begin{array}{r}12\\ \times 2\\ \hline 24\end{array}$

4. $\begin{array}{r}8\\ \times 3\\ \hline 24\end{array}$ $\begin{array}{r}1\\ \times 4\\ \hline 4\end{array}$ $\begin{array}{r}7\\ \times 4\\ \hline 28\end{array}$ $\begin{array}{r}12\\ \times 5\\ \hline 60\end{array}$ $\begin{array}{r}11\\ \times 4\\ \hline 44\end{array}$ $\begin{array}{r}3\\ \times 4\\ \hline 12\end{array}$ $\begin{array}{r}7\\ \times 5\\ \hline 35\end{array}$ $\begin{array}{r}8\\ \times 4\\ \hline 32\end{array}$ $\begin{array}{r}2\\ \times 5\\ \hline 10\end{array}$

5. $\begin{array}{r}8\\ \times 2\\ \hline 16\end{array}$ $\begin{array}{r}10\\ \times 5\\ \hline 50\end{array}$ $\begin{array}{r}1\\ \times 1\\ \hline 1\end{array}$ $\begin{array}{r}7\\ \times 3\\ \hline 21\end{array}$ $\begin{array}{r}9\\ \times 5\\ \hline 45\end{array}$ $\begin{array}{r}1\\ \times 0\\ \hline 0\end{array}$ $\begin{array}{r}2\\ \times 4\\ \hline 8\end{array}$ $\begin{array}{r}12\\ \times 4\\ \hline 48\end{array}$ $\begin{array}{r}12\\ \times 3\\ \hline 36\end{array}$

2 pt. each

Speed Drill 38

1.
11	8	14	10	12	15	7	16	11
−7	−5	−9	−5	−3	−8	−6	−7	−9
4	3	5	5	9	7	1	9	2

2.
8	4	9	5	6	3	7	8	6
+6	+9	+9	+6	+9	+7	+5	+9	+7
14	13	18	11	15	10	12	17	13

3.
3	5	5	3	4	3	5	4	4
×8	×6	×5	×4	×8	×7	×9	×7	×9
24	30	25	12	32	21	45	28	36

3 pt. each

Speed Drill 40

1.
34	50	27	83	45	82
× 2	× 4	× 2	× 3	× 3	× 5
68	200	54	249	135	410

2.
97	15	67	312	846	956
× 4	× 7	× 3	× 9	× 4	× 5
388	105	201	2,808	3,384	4,780

6 pt. each

Speed Drills

Speed Drill 42

1.
```
   8
   4
   7
 + 5
 ---
  24
```
```
  457
− 264
 ----
  193
```
```
  67
×  4
 ---
 268
```
```
  84
  25
 +57
 ---
 166
```

2.
```
  700
− 382
 ----
  318
```
```
  5,698
 +7,849
 ------
 13,547
```
```
  53
×  9
 ---
 477
```
```
  389
×   4
 ----
 1,556
```

3.
```
  852
− 736
 ----
  116
```
```
  612
×   8
 ----
 4,896
```
```
  6,810
 −1,576
 ------
  5,234
```
```
  483
  674
 +736
 ----
 1,893
```

6 pt. each

Speed Drill 44

1. a. 7 + 4 − 6 + 7 + 3 = __15__ b. 5 − 1 + 5 + 6 − 7 = __8__

2. a. 3 + 5 − 7 + 2 + 8 = __11__ b. 8 + 9 − 3 − 7 + 6 = __13__

3. a. 8 − 5 − 3 + 6 + 8 = __14__ b. 5 + 4 + 5 − 9 + 7 = __12__

4. a. 6 + 5 − 8 + 9 − 4 = __8__   b. 6 − 5 + 7 + 8 − 4 = __12__

5. a. 4 + 6 + 6 − 8 − 6 = __2__   b. 7 + 8 − 5 − 6 − 4 = __0__

7 pt. each

Speed Drill 46

1. 1 foot = __12__ inches   1 quart = __2__ pints
2. 1 yard = __3__ feet   1 minute = __60__ seconds
3. 1 hour = __60__ minutes   1 year = __12__ months
4. 1 week = __7__ days   1 quarter = __25__ cents
5. 1 gallon = __4__ quarts   1 dime = __10__ cents
6. 1 pint = __2__ cups   1 dollar = __100__ cents
7. 1 day = __24__ hours   1 yard = __36__ inches
8. 1 quart = __4__ cups   6:00 A.M = 6:00 in the __morning__

6 pt. each

Speed Drill 48

1. 3)9̄ = 3   2)18̄ = 9   1)8̄ = 8   4)16̄ = 4   3)12̄ = 4   2)10̄ = 5   4)0̄ = 0
2. 4)20̄ = 5   4)12̄ = 3   1)1̄ = 1   2)8̄ = 4   2)14̄ = 7   4)24̄ = 6   1)5̄ = 5
3. 3)0̄ = 0   1)0̄ = 0   4)28̄ = 7   3)18̄ = 6   2)10̄ = 5   2)6̄ = 3   4)36̄ = 9
4. 4)8̄ = 2   4)32̄ = 8   5)0̄ = 0   3)21̄ = 7   2)16̄ = 8   2)2̄ = 1   3)15̄ = 5
5. 3)27̄ = 9   2)4̄ = 2   1)4̄ = 4   4)4̄ = 1   2)12̄ = 6   3)24̄ = 8   3)6̄ = 2
6. 1)3̄ = 3   1)9̄ = 9   3)3̄ = 1   3)21̄ = 7   4)24̄ = 6   2)0̄ = 0   4)32̄ = 8

2 pt. each

Speed Drills

Speed Drill 50

1. $5\overline{)5}=1$ $3\overline{)6}=2$ $2\overline{)6}=3$ $4\overline{)0}=0$ $1\overline{)7}=7$ $3\overline{)15}=5$ $5\overline{)10}=2$

2. $3\overline{)12}=4$ $4\overline{)20}=5$ $3\overline{)3}=1$ $1\overline{)5}=5$ $2\overline{)14}=7$ $2\overline{)10}=5$ $4\overline{)16}=4$

3. $5\overline{)25}=5$ $3\overline{)9}=3$ $3\overline{)0}=0$ $4\overline{)36}=9$ $3\overline{)21}=7$ $2\overline{)18}=9$ $3\overline{)18}=6$

4. $5\overline{)40}=8$ $4\overline{)12}=3$ $3\overline{)27}=9$ $4\overline{)28}=7$ $2\overline{)12}=6$ $5\overline{)30}=6$ $3\overline{)24}=8$

5. $2\overline{)8}=4$ $4\overline{)32}=8$ $5\overline{)15}=3$ $5\overline{)45}=9$ $5\overline{)35}=7$ $4\overline{)4}=1$ $1\overline{)8}=8$

6. $4\overline{)8}=2$ $5\overline{)20}=4$ $4\overline{)24}=6$ $2\overline{)2}=1$ $2\overline{)4}=2$ $2\overline{)16}=8$ $5\overline{)40}=8$

2 pt. each

Speed Drill 52

1. $3 \times 8 = 24$ $5 \times 7 = 35$ $3 \times 4 = 12$ $2 \times 6 = 12$ $6 \times 8 = 48$ $4 \times 9 = 36$ $1 \times 6 = 6$ $10 \times 5 = 50$ $6 \times 4 = 24$

2. $4 \times 5 = 20$ $1 \times 8 = 8$ $2 \times 9 = 18$ $5 \times 5 = 25$ $3 \times 9 = 27$ $6 \times 2 = 12$ $4 \times 4 = 16$ $5 \times 3 = 15$ $3 \times 2 = 6$

3. $5 \times 6 = 30$ $2 \times 7 = 14$ $3 \times 6 = 18$ $4 \times 8 = 32$ $6 \times 7 = 42$ $1 \times 9 = 9$ $6 \times 6 = 36$ $4 \times 2 = 8$ $5 \times 9 = 45$

4. $6 \times 9 = 54$ $4 \times 7 = 28$ $2 \times 8 = 16$ $1 \times 5 = 5$ $0 \times 3 = 0$ $4 \times 9 = 36$ $11 \times 3 = 33$ $6 \times 3 = 18$ $4 \times 6 = 24$

5. $5 \times 4 = 20$ $3 \times 3 = 9$ $10 \times 4 = 40$ $11 \times 6 = 66$ $2 \times 9 = 18$ $5 \times 8 = 40$ $5 \times 7 = 35$ $3 \times 7 = 21$ $6 \times 5 = 30$

2 pt. each

Speed Drill 54

1. $10 \times 78 = \underline{780}$ $10 \times 62 = \underline{620}$ $10 \times 17 = \underline{170}$

2. $100 \times 6 = \underline{600}$ $100 \times 49 = \underline{4{,}900}$ $100 \times 31 = \underline{3{,}100}$

3. $20 \times 7 = \underline{140}$ $40 \times 8 = \underline{320}$ $60 \times 5 = \underline{300}$

4. $4 \times 6 + 5 = \underline{29}$ $7 \times 4 + 3 = \underline{31}$ $8 \times 3 + 4 = \underline{28}$

5. $5 \times 5 + 2 = \underline{27}$ $6 \times 7 + 4 = \underline{46}$ $6 \times 6 + 3 = \underline{39}$

6. $15 - 5 - 4 = \underline{6}$ $11 - 6 - 3 = \underline{2}$ $14 - 6 - 4 = \underline{4}$

7. $7 + 8 + 4 = \underline{19}$ $5 + 7 + 6 = \underline{18}$ $4 + 9 + 7 = \underline{20}$

5 pt. each

Speed Drill 56

Match the letters to the words in the list. Two words will have two letters before them.

$\underline{i}$ 1. product

$\underline{f}$ 2. difference $837 \leftarrow a$ $751 \leftarrow d$

$\underline{m}$ 3. dividend $\underline{+\,498} \leftarrow b$ $\underline{-\,265} \leftarrow e$

$\underline{l}$ 4. divisor $1{,}335 \leftarrow c$ $486 \leftarrow f$

$\underline{g, h}$ 5. factor (2)

$\underline{d}$ 6. minuend   j   k

$\underline{a, b}$ 7. addend (2) $76 \leftarrow g$ ↓   ↓

$\underline{j}$ 8. quotient $\underline{\times\,4} \leftarrow h$ 6 R 2

$\underline{k}$ 9. remainder $304 \leftarrow i$ $5\overline{)32}$

$\underline{e}$ 10. subtrahend   ↑   ↑

$\underline{c}$ 11. sum   l   m

7 pt. each

Speed Drills

Speed Drill 58

1. a. 4 × 7 + 5 − 3 = __30__   b. 8 + 5 − 6 × 8 + 4 = __60__

2. a. 9 − 6 × 7 + 4 = __25__   b. 6 × 6 − 4 − 2 + 5 = __35__

3. a. 9 + 7 − 6 × 4 = __40__   b. 8 − 4 + 7 × 5 + 5 = __60__

4. a. 6 + 7 − 4 × 6 = __54__   b. 3 + 8 − 5 × 7 + 3 = __45__

5. a. 3 × 2 × 4 + 5 = __29__   b. 4 × 5 − 2 − 9 × 3 = __27__

7 pt. each

Speed Drill 60

Write remainders as fractions.

1. $5\overline{)27} = 5\frac{2}{5}$ $4\overline{)19} = 4\frac{3}{4}$ $2\overline{)13} = 6\frac{1}{2}$ $3\overline{)25} = 8\frac{1}{3}$

2. $5\overline{)350} = 70$ $4\overline{)845} = 211\frac{1}{4}$ $3\overline{)188} = 62\frac{2}{3}$ $2\overline{)685} = 342\frac{1}{2}$

10 pt. each

Speed Drills

Speed Drill 62

first page
1. 0+4=4   1+6=7   6+6=12   9+0=9   0+8=8   3+2=5   3+4=7   2+1=3   0+7=7   1+8=9

second page
2. 1+4=5   7+2=9   9+9=18   2+4=6   5+1=6   4+5=9   8+0=8   7+1=8   6+0=6   5+4=9

3. 3+5=8   1+9=10   8+2=10   5+2=7   2+6=8   5+6=11   4+1=5   9+2=11   4+3=7   6+4=10

4. 7+3=10   8+4=12   0+5=5   6+6=12   9+9=18   8+2=10   6+3=9   5+8=13   9+5=14   8+7=15

5. 7+4=11   7+8=15   9+5=14   6+7=13   3+9=12   5+9=14   6+8=14   4+9=13   8+9=17   9+6=15

6. 3+6=9   2+9=11   5+8=13   9+3=12   3+7=10   4+8=12   7+7=14   6+5=11   9+4=13   4+7=11

2 pt. each

Speed Drill 64

1. 8+4+9+1=22   5+6+3+6=20   4+6+5+4=19   8+5+5+3=21   7+7+5+9=28   3+8+7+8=26

2. 9+4+5+9=27   4+8+7+7=26   8+9+4+2=23   2+6+8+5=21   6+7+7+3=23   9+6+5+6=26

7 pt. each

425

Speed Drills

Speed Drill 66

Fill in the missing Roman numerals.

I   II   III   IV   V   VI   VII   VIII   IX   X

XI   XII   XIII   XIV   XV   XVI   XVII   XVIII   XIX   XX

XXI   XXII   XXIII   XXIV   XXV   XXVI   XXVII   XXVIII   XXIX   XXX

XXXI   XXXII   XXXIII   XXXIV   XXXV   XXXVI   XXXVII   XXXVIII   XXXIX   XL

4 pt. each

Speed Drill 68

first page
1. $\begin{array}{r}1\\-1\\\hline 0\end{array}$ $\begin{array}{r}8\\-0\\\hline 8\end{array}$ $\begin{array}{r}4\\-3\\\hline 1\end{array}$ $\begin{array}{r}3\\-3\\\hline 0\end{array}$ $\begin{array}{r}0\\-0\\\hline 0\end{array}$ $\begin{array}{r}2\\-1\\\hline 1\end{array}$ $\begin{array}{r}3\\-0\\\hline 3\end{array}$ $\begin{array}{r}9\\-2\\\hline 7\end{array}$ $\begin{array}{r}5\\-1\\\hline 4\end{array}$ $\begin{array}{r}6\\-3\\\hline 3\end{array}$

second page
2. $\begin{array}{r}4\\-1\\\hline 3\end{array}$ $\begin{array}{r}8\\-8\\\hline 0\end{array}$ $\begin{array}{r}7\\-1\\\hline 6\end{array}$ $\begin{array}{r}9\\-3\\\hline 6\end{array}$ $\begin{array}{r}9\\-5\\\hline 4\end{array}$ $\begin{array}{r}10\\-1\\\hline 9\end{array}$ $\begin{array}{r}8\\-7\\\hline 1\end{array}$ $\begin{array}{r}6\\-0\\\hline 6\end{array}$ $\begin{array}{r}5\\-2\\\hline 3\end{array}$ $\begin{array}{r}9\\-9\\\hline 0\end{array}$

3. $\begin{array}{r}7\\-6\\\hline 1\end{array}$ $\begin{array}{r}9\\-6\\\hline 3\end{array}$ $\begin{array}{r}11\\-5\\\hline 6\end{array}$ $\begin{array}{r}12\\-3\\\hline 9\end{array}$ $\begin{array}{r}14\\-7\\\hline 7\end{array}$ $\begin{array}{r}8\\-6\\\hline 2\end{array}$ $\begin{array}{r}12\\-6\\\hline 6\end{array}$ $\begin{array}{r}10\\-3\\\hline 7\end{array}$ $\begin{array}{r}16\\-8\\\hline 8\end{array}$ $\begin{array}{r}14\\-5\\\hline 9\end{array}$

4. $\begin{array}{r}2\\-0\\\hline 2\end{array}$ $\begin{array}{r}6\\-5\\\hline 1\end{array}$ $\begin{array}{r}8\\-4\\\hline 4\end{array}$ $\begin{array}{r}4\\-2\\\hline 2\end{array}$ $\begin{array}{r}9\\-1\\\hline 8\end{array}$ $\begin{array}{r}7\\-0\\\hline 7\end{array}$ $\begin{array}{r}3\\-1\\\hline 2\end{array}$ $\begin{array}{r}4\\-0\\\hline 4\end{array}$ $\begin{array}{r}6\\-2\\\hline 4\end{array}$ $\begin{array}{r}5\\-0\\\hline 5\end{array}$

5. $\begin{array}{r}10\\-8\\\hline 2\end{array}$ $\begin{array}{r}12\\-5\\\hline 7\end{array}$ $\begin{array}{r}14\\-6\\\hline 8\end{array}$ $\begin{array}{r}13\\-7\\\hline 6\end{array}$ $\begin{array}{r}18\\-9\\\hline 9\end{array}$ $\begin{array}{r}17\\-9\\\hline 8\end{array}$ $\begin{array}{r}10\\-6\\\hline 4\end{array}$ $\begin{array}{r}11\\-9\\\hline 2\end{array}$ $\begin{array}{r}15\\-6\\\hline 9\end{array}$ $\begin{array}{r}12\\-4\\\hline 8\end{array}$

6. $\begin{array}{r}11\\-7\\\hline 4\end{array}$ $\begin{array}{r}15\\-9\\\hline 6\end{array}$ $\begin{array}{r}12\\-8\\\hline 4\end{array}$ $\begin{array}{r}11\\-4\\\hline 7\end{array}$ $\begin{array}{r}14\\-8\\\hline 6\end{array}$ $\begin{array}{r}13\\-6\\\hline 7\end{array}$ $\begin{array}{r}16\\-7\\\hline 9\end{array}$ $\begin{array}{r}12\\-7\\\hline 5\end{array}$ $\begin{array}{r}13\\-8\\\hline 5\end{array}$ $\begin{array}{r}15\\-7\\\hline 8\end{array}$

2 pt. each

Speed Drill 70

Write numerals for these number words.

_____2,106_____	**1.**	two thousand, one hundred six
_____50,000_____	**2.**	fifty thousand
_____70,380_____	**3.**	seventy thousand, three hundred eighty
_____425,011_____	**4.**	four hundred twenty-five thousand, eleven
_____910,600_____	**5.**	nine hundred ten thousand, six hundred
_____48,002_____	**6.**	forty-eight thousand, two
_____137,091_____	**7.**	one hundred thirty-seven thousand, ninety-one
_____16,016_____	**8.**	sixteen thousand, sixteen

10 pt. each

Speed Drill 72

1. 1 quart = __2__ pints   1 gallon = __4__ quarts
2. 1 day = __24__ hours   1 minute = __60__ seconds
3. 1 pound = __16__ ounces   1 quart = __4__ cups
4. 1 dozen = __12__ things   1 pint = __2__ cups
5. 1 yard = __3__ feet   1 ton = __2,000__ pounds
6. 1 foot = __12__ inches   1 dollar = __100__ cents
7. 1 yard = __36__ inches   1 quarter = __25__ cents
8. 1 year = __12__ months   November = __30__ days
9. 1 year = __365__ days   July = __31__ days
10. 1 week = __7__ days   March = __31__ days

5 pt. each

Speed Drills

Speed Drill 74

Write the answers only.

1. $\frac{1}{3}$ of 24 = __8__ $\frac{1}{6}$ of 54 = __9__ $\frac{1}{2}$ of 24 = __12__
2. $\frac{1}{8}$ of 32 = __4__ $\frac{1}{4}$ of 12 = __3__ $\frac{1}{3}$ of 15 = __5__
3. $\frac{1}{2}$ of 18 = __9__ $\frac{1}{9}$ of 18 = __2__ $\frac{1}{8}$ of 40 = __5__
4. $\frac{1}{6}$ of 30 = __5__ $\frac{1}{6}$ of 18 = __3__ $\frac{1}{4}$ of 36 = __9__
5. $\frac{1}{4}$ of 28 = __7__ $\frac{1}{3}$ of 33 = __11__ $\frac{1}{5}$ of 50 = __10__
6. $\frac{1}{7}$ of 49 = __7__ $\frac{1}{8}$ of 64 = __8__ $\frac{1}{6}$ of 66 = __11__
7. $\frac{1}{2}$ of 20 = __10__ $\frac{1}{5}$ of 30 = __6__ $\frac{1}{9}$ of 27 = __3__
8. $\frac{1}{9}$ of 63 = __7__ $\frac{1}{7}$ of 42 = __6__ $\frac{1}{2}$ of 22 = __11__
9. $\frac{1}{5}$ of 20 = __4__ $\frac{1}{3}$ of 36 = __12__ $\frac{1}{7}$ of 21 = __3__
10. $\frac{1}{8}$ of 48 = __6__ $\frac{1}{4}$ of 16 = __4__ $\frac{1}{9}$ of 9 = __1__

3 pt. each

Speed Drill 76

Circle the larger number in each pair.

1. a. (½) ⅕   b. ¼ (⅓)
2. a. 3/7 (5/7)   b. (⅓) 1/7
3. a. 329 (392)   b. 699 (701)
4. a. 4,010 (4,100)   b. (6,000) 5,899
5. a. 3,899 (3,999)   b. (8,888) 7,888
6. a. 7,257 (7,267)   b. 4,033 (4,303)
7. a. (5,505) 5,499   b. (3,010) 3,000
8. a. 16,456 (17,456) b. 25,000 (25,003)
9. a. (32,000) 31,000 b. (48,859) 48,850

5 pt. each

Speed Drill 78

Write the six place names for the digits in this number.

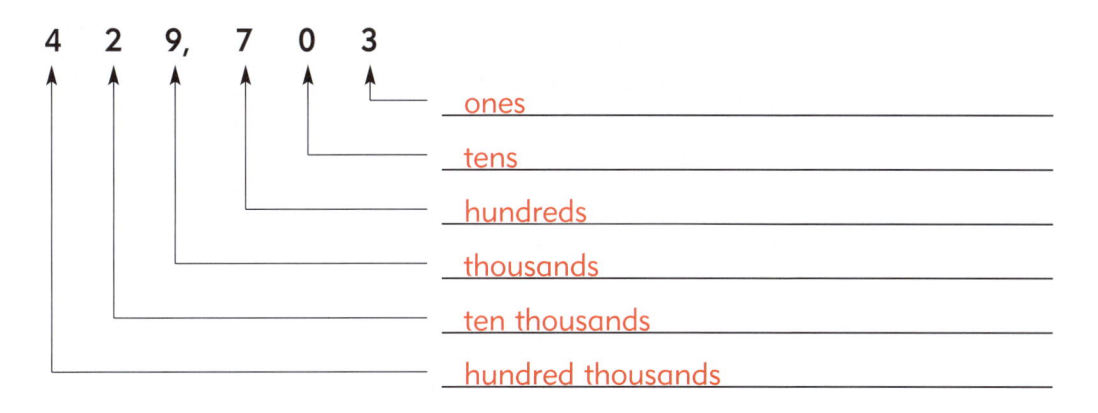

4 2 9, 7 0 3

- ones
- tens
- hundreds
- thousands
- ten thousands
- hundred thousands

Write the number with words.

four hundred twenty-nine thousand, seven hundred three

10 pt. each

Speed Drill 80

1. Multiply each number by 7.

   7 _49_   5 _35_   3 _21_   8 _56_   4 _28_   9 _63_   12 _84_

2. Multiply each number by 4.

   8 _32_   4 _16_   11 _44_   6 _24_   12 _48_   7 _28_   5 _20_

3. Multiply each number by 9.

   9 _81_   10 _90_   2 _18_   4 _36_   8 _72_   6 _54_   3 _27_

4. Add 7 to each number.

   8 _15_   3 _10_   9 _16_   7 _14_   8 _15_   1 _8_   6 _13_

5. Add 5 to each number.

   6 _11_   4 _9_   8 _13_   12 _17_   20 _25_   9 _14_   17 _22_

3 pt. each

Speed Drills

Speed Drill 82

1. $1 \times 8 = 8$ $6 \times 7 = 42$ $8 \times 4 = 32$ $4 \times 6 = 24$ $3 \times 5 = 15$ $6 \times 8 = 48$ $2 \times 9 = 18$ $0 \times 5 = 0$ $7 \times 3 = 21$

2. $8 \times 5 = 40$ $4 \times 4 = 16$ $3 \times 2 = 6$ $2 \times 7 = 14$ $7 \times 7 = 49$ $5 \times 6 = 30$ $1 \times 7 = 7$ $8 \times 8 = 64$ $5 \times 9 = 45$

3. $4 \times 9 = 36$ $8 \times 7 = 56$ $3 \times 8 = 24$ $7 \times 9 = 63$ $6 \times 6 = 36$ $4 \times 5 = 20$ $2 \times 5 = 10$ $6 \times 3 = 18$ $5 \times 7 = 35$

4. $7 \times 4 = 28$ $6 \times 2 = 12$ $4 \times 3 = 12$ $3 \times 3 = 9$ $7 \times 8 = 56$ $11 \times 6 = 66$ $12 \times 7 = 84$ $1 \times 6 = 6$ $10 \times 5 = 50$

5. $12 \times 6 = 72$ $12 \times 4 = 48$ $12 \times 3 = 36$ $12 \times 8 = 96$ $10 \times 7 = 70$ $12 \times 5 = 60$ $3 \times 9 = 27$ $8 \times 9 = 72$ $11 \times 7 = 77$

2 pt. each

Speed Drill 84

1. $3 \times 8 = 24$ $8 \times 9 = 72$ $5 \times 7 = 35$ $4 \times 4 = 16$ $2 \times 8 = 16$ $8 \times 8 = 64$ $9 \times 6 = 54$ $7 \times 3 = 21$ $9 \times 4 = 36$

2. $8 \times 6 = 48$ $5 \times 4 = 20$ $11 \times 1 = 11$ $12 \times 2 = 24$ $8 \times 7 = 56$ $9 \times 7 = 63$ $4 \times 7 = 28$ $3 \times 5 = 15$ $6 \times 5 = 30$

3. $6 \times 6 = 36$ $9 \times 5 = 45$ $5 \times 5 = 25$ $3 \times 4 = 12$ $4 \times 8 = 32$ $7 \times 7 = 49$ $9 \times 9 = 81$ $12 \times 5 = 60$ $10 \times 8 = 80$

4. $11 \times 8 = 88$ $5 \times 8 = 40$ $12 \times 9 = 108$ $4 \times 6 = 24$ $2 \times 2 = 4$ $12 \times 3 = 36$ $0 \times 6 = 0$ $6 \times 7 = 42$ $7 \times 9 = 63$

5. $12 \times 7 = 84$ $9 \times 8 = 72$ $12 \times 4 = 48$ $3 \times 6 = 18$ $12 \times 6 = 72$ $12 \times 8 = 96$ $10 \times 9 = 90$ $10 \times 1 = 10$ $9 \times 3 = 27$

2 pt. each

Speed Drill 86

1. $5\overline{)15}=3$ $4\overline{)32}=8$ $6\overline{)6}=1$ $6\overline{)12}=2$ $3\overline{)9}=3$ $4\overline{)20}=5$ $5\overline{)35}=7$

2. $2\overline{)8}=4$ $2\overline{)18}=9$ $5\overline{)45}=9$ $4\overline{)28}=7$ $2\overline{)10}=5$ $6\overline{)36}=6$ $4\overline{)12}=3$

3. $5\overline{)20}=4$ $2\overline{)4}=2$ $6\overline{)30}=5$ $4\overline{)36}=9$ $3\overline{)27}=9$ $6\overline{)48}=8$ $3\overline{)18}=6$

4. $6\overline{)54}=9$ $2\overline{)14}=7$ $3\overline{)24}=8$ $1\overline{)4}=4$ $3\overline{)21}=7$ $6\overline{)42}=7$ $4\overline{)8}=2$

5. $5\overline{)30}=6$ $3\overline{)3}=1$ $6\overline{)18}=3$ $6\overline{)60}=10$ $5\overline{)55}=11$ $4\overline{)48}=12$ $3\overline{)12}=4$

6. $5\overline{)40}=8$ $4\overline{)24}=6$ $4\overline{)16}=4$ $3\overline{)6}=2$ $3\overline{)36}=12$ $5\overline{)25}=5$ $4\overline{)40}=10$

2 pt. each

Speed Drill 88

1. $5\overline{)35}=7$ $6\overline{)18}=3$ $9\overline{)9}=1$ $5\overline{)30}=6$ $4\overline{)12}=3$ $7\overline{)49}=7$ $3\overline{)3}=1$

2. $6\overline{)36}=6$ $4\overline{)24}=6$ $3\overline{)15}=5$ $7\overline{)42}=6$ $7\overline{)28}=4$ $3\overline{)21}=7$ $8\overline{)24}=3$

3. $7\overline{)14}=2$ $6\overline{)54}=9$ $8\overline{)64}=8$ $7\overline{)21}=3$ $8\overline{)48}=6$ $4\overline{)32}=8$ $3\overline{)27}=9$

4. $2\overline{)16}=8$ $8\overline{)72}=9$ $7\overline{)42}=6$ $5\overline{)40}=8$ $3\overline{)24}=8$ $3\overline{)9}=3$ $2\overline{)24}=12$

5. $1\overline{)5}=5$ $8\overline{)8}=1$ $8\overline{)64}=8$ $4\overline{)16}=4$ $6\overline{)48}=8$ $7\overline{)35}=5$ $8\overline{)56}=7$

6. $2\overline{)6}=3$ $4\overline{)36}=9$ $7\overline{)56}=8$ $7\overline{)14}=2$ $8\overline{)32}=4$ $5\overline{)25}=5$ $8\overline{)40}=5$

2 pt. each

Speed Drills

Speed Drill 90

1. 7)14̄ = 2   5)30̄ = 6   4)8̄ = 2   2)6̄ = 3   8)64̄ = 8   9)18̄ = 2   4)24̄ = 6

2. 9)27̄ = 3   4)36̄ = 9   5)25̄ = 5   4)40̄ = 10   7)49̄ = 7   3)21̄ = 7   6)18̄ = 3

3. 7)56̄ = 8   9)72̄ = 8   5)20̄ = 4   3)36̄ = 12   9)81̄ = 9   7)28̄ = 4   2)18̄ = 9

4. 6)36̄ = 6   5)50̄ = 10   7)42̄ = 6   8)72̄ = 9   8)56̄ = 7   6)54̄ = 9   3)3̄ = 1

5. 7)35̄ = 5   5)40̄ = 8   2)10̄ = 5   2)20̄ = 10   9)63̄ = 7   6)42̄ = 7   5)45̄ = 9

6. 9)99̄ = 11   6)48̄ = 8   9)54̄ = 6   9)45̄ = 5   7)63̄ = 9   8)48̄ = 6   8)24̄ = 3

2 pt. each

Speed Drill 92

Write A *for add,* S *for subtract,* M *for multiply, or* D *for divide. Do not solve the problems.*

__S__ 1. Jay has more stamps than John. How many more?

__M__ 2. What is the cost of 4 at 16¢ each?

__D__ 3. What is $\frac{1}{3}$ of a number?

__S__ 4. How much younger is Sylvia than Shirley?

__A__ 5. What is the total of all the items on Mother's list?

__D__ 6. How many 3's are in 9?

__S__ 7. Mother had $40.00. She spent some. How much does she have left?

__M__ 8. There are three groups of 6 each. How many are there altogether?

10 pt. each

Speed Drill 94

Speed Drill 94

Name _____

Count the money and write the value.   Score _____

1. a. = <u>60¢</u>   b. = <u>75¢</u>

2. a. = <u>12¢</u>   b. = <u>5¢</u>

3. a. = <u>$1.30</u>   b. = <u>$10.05</u>

4. = <u>60¢</u>

5. = <u>91¢</u>

6. = <u>69¢</u>

10 pt. each

Speed Drill 96

Write each price in two ways.

1. a. sixteen cents 16¢ $0.16
   b. nine cents 9¢ $0.09
2. a. three dollars $3 $3.00
   b. ten dollars $10 $10.00

Write each price with a dollar sign and a decimal point.

3. five dollars and seventy-nine cents $5.79
4. eighteen dollars and five cents $18.05

Fill in the blanks.

5. a. 1 dollar = 10 dimes
   b. 1 half dollar = 5 dimes
6. a. 6 nickels = 3 dimes
   b. 6 nickels = 30 pennies
7. a. 2 quarters = 50 pennies
   b. 1 dollar = 4 quarters
8. a. 2 dollars = 4 half dollars
   b. 1 quarter = 5 nickels

1–2: 4 pt. each blank
3–8: 6 pt. each blank

Speed Drill 98

1.
```
   34      63      89
   77      86      42     437     925
 + 83      74      35     629     756
 ----    + 58    + 36   + 561   + 487
  194     ---     ---   -----   -----
          281     202   1,627   2,168
```

2.
```
                              482
         5,480   2,597        354
 6,853   3,786   1,645        718
+8,976  +1,534  +8,633       +293
------  ------  ------      -----
15,829  10,800  12,875      1,847
```

8 pt. each

Speed Drill 100

1.
```
   560        703        827        641
 − 385      − 268      − 423      − 281
   175        435        404        360
```

2.
```
  9,000      7,010      5,393      8,700
− 6,549    − 4,825    − 1,649    − 7,410
  2,451      2,185      3,744      1,290
```

8 pt. each

Speed Drill 102

1.
```
   17         25         43         96         87
 ×  4       ×  6       ×  4       ×  3       ×  2
   68        150        172        288        174
```

2.
```
   74         81         60         58         63
 ×  5       ×  8       ×  9       ×  5       ×  7
  370        648        540        290        441
```

8 pt. each

Speed Drills

Speed Drill 104

1. $4\overline{)15}$ = 3 R 3 $3\overline{)22}$ = 7 R 1 $5\overline{)33}$ = 6 R 3 $2\overline{)17}$ = 8 R 1

2. $4\overline{)9}$ = 2 R 1 $6\overline{)19}$ = 3 R 1 $4\overline{)34}$ = 8 R 2 $3\overline{)17}$ = 5 R 2

3. $2\overline{)11}$ = 5 R 1 $5\overline{)19}$ = 3 R 4 $6\overline{)38}$ = 6 R 2 $5\overline{)27}$ = 5 R 2

8 pt. each

Speed Drills 106–168

are found in Teacher's Manual, book 2

10. Chapter 1 Test

Score _____

Name _____ Date _____

A. *Write the answers. (1 pt. each; 24 total)*

1.
8	5	10	4	14	15	6	9
+5	+6	−6	+7	−5	−8	+9	−4
13	11	4	11	9	7	15	5

2.
7	12	16	9	18	8	10	13
−6	−7	−8	+5	−9	+6	−3	−9
1	5	8	14	9	14	7	4

3. Add 4 to each number.

   8 _12_   12 _16_   19 _23_   15 _19_

4. Add. Remember to use the basic facts.

   13 + 5 = _18_   14 + 8 = _22_   11 + 9 = _20_   16 + 3 = _19_

B. *Follow the directions. (1 pt. each; 9 total)*

5. Write the addition and subtraction facts that belong in this number family: 17, 9, 8.

   _9 + 8 = 17_   _8 + 9 = 17_   _17 − 9 = 8_   _17 − 8 = 9_

6. Label the parts of these problems.

85	>	_addends_		854	_minuend_
+ 64				− 253	_subtrahend_
149		_sum_		601	_difference_

4   Chapter 1 Test

C. *Follow the signs, and work carefully.* (2 pt. each; 58 total)

7.
```
   9      4      7      7      2      6      8      6
   6      4      6      3      4      8      9      6
 + 5    + 6    + 3    + 8    + 9    + 4    + 6    + 9
  ──     ──     ──     ──     ──     ──     ──     ──
  20     14     16     18     15     18     23     21
```

8.
```
                                        53     468     829
  57     36     172    546     26     342     754
 + 18   + 79   + 37   + 594   + 47   + 153   + 603
  ──     ──     ───    ────    ──     ───    ─────
  75    115    209   1,140    126     963   2,186
```

9.
```
  73     89    149    981    105    264    879
 - 43   - 7   - 72   - 670  - 73   - 54   - 435
  ──    ──    ──    ───    ──    ───    ───
  30    82    77    311    32    210    444
```

10.
```
                                         85    377    398
 128    649    137    859     19    298    621
 - 34   - 28   - 55   + 491   + 25   + 125   + 345
  ──    ───    ──    ────    ───    ───    ─────
  94    621    82   1,350   129    800   1,364
```

D. *Solve these reading problems. Do your work in the space at the right.* (3 pt. each; 9 total)

11. One week it rained and rained. It rained 2 inches on Monday, 1 inch on Wednesday, and 4 inches on Thursday. How many inches of rain fell that week?   _____7 in._____

12. Aunt Lena brought 36 cupcakes. We ate 12 of them at the first meal. How many were left?   _____24 cupcakes_____

13. Gerald is collecting stamps. He has 241 stamps in one book and 179 stamps in another book. How many stamps does Gerald have in both books?   _____420 stamps_____

Subtract points wrong from 100% for score.

Progressing With Arithmetic   Chapter 2 Test   5

21. Chapter 2 Test

Score _____

Name _____ Date _____

A. *Write the answers to these facts.* (1 pt. each; 18 total)

1.
8	11	12	16	6	9	10	14	7
+4	−6	−9	−7	+8	+4	−7	−5	+8
12	5	3	9	14	13	3	9	15

2.
5	13	9	4	11	6	17	12	9
+8	−4	−6	+6	−9	+2	−9	−6	+3
13	9	3	10	2	8	8	6	12

B. *Write the answers.* (1 pt. each blank; 10 total)

3. Write numerals for these number words.
   a. two thousand, six hundred eleven   2,611
   b. nineteen thousand, forty-seven   19,047
   c. one hundred fifty thousand, five   150,005
   d. four hundred thirty-one thousand, two hundred   431,200

4. Write the combined value of each underlined digit.
   a. 1<u>5</u>,980   5 thousands   b. <u>9</u>73,064   9 hundred thousands

5. Write each price in two ways.
   a. 75 cents   75¢ $0.75   b. 6 dollars $6 $6.00

C. *Write the value of each set of money.* (2 pt. each; 4 total)

6. a.   22¢   b.   65¢

6   Chapter 2 Test

D. *Add carefully.* (2 pt. each; 16 total)

7.
```
  4     8     3     5     4     9     7     6
  6     3     5     7     3     2     3     8
  6     3     5     7     5     3     5     6
 +7    +8    +7    +9    +7    +8    +9    +8
 ──    ──    ──    ──    ──    ──    ──    ──
 17    19    15    21    19    22    24    28
```

E. *Subtract. Remember to borrow only when necessary.* (2 pt. each; 24 total)

8.
```
  82     50     838    723    714    602
 -15    - 8    -745   - 37   -129   -398
 ──     ──     ───    ───    ───    ───
 67     42      93    686    585    204
```

9.
```
 711    800    128    827    930    700
-699   -325   - 58   -615   -829   -347
 ──    ───    ──     ───    ───    ───
 12    475    70     212    101    353
```

F. *Subtract. Check by addition.* (2 pt. each; 12 total)

10.
```
 900    655    $5.70   $2.01   $7.05   $1.66
-245   +245   - 3.69  + 3.69  - 5.39  + 5.39
 ───   ───   ──────  ──────  ──────  ──────
 655   900    $2.01   $5.70   $1.66   $7.05
```

G. *Solve these reading problems. Do your work in the space at the right.*
(3 pt. each; 15 total)

11. Ellen is 9 and her brother is 15. Ellen is how much younger than her brother?
    6 years

12. If you have $6.50 and spend $2.35, how much will you have left?
    $4.15

13. Lamar bought a devotional booklet for $2.95 and a bookmark for $0.39. How much did he spend in all?
    $3.34

14. Lucy gave the clerk a $5.00 bill to pay for $3.27. How much change should she receive?
    $1.73

15. Lisa lives 25 miles from her Grandpa Birky's house. After her family moves next week, they will be 250 miles from Grandpa Birky's. Lisa's family will be how much farther from Grandpa's than they were before?
    225 mi.

Subtract points wrong from 100% for score.

Progressing With Arithmetic Chapter 3 Test 7

31. Chapter 3 Test

Name _____ Date _____

Score _____

A. *Write the answers.* (1 pt. each; 30 total)

1. 3 × 4 = __12__   8 × 3 = __24__   11 × 4 = __44__   5 × 5 = __25__
2. 7 × 5 = __35__   7 × 4 = __28__   10 × 3 = __30__   8 × 6 = __48__

3.
6	5	3	7	7	4	5	8	0
×6	×4	×3	×1	×6	×6	×3	×4	×5
36	20	9	7	42	24	15	32	0

4.
12	7	8	9	9	2	2	6	10
×4	×3	×2	×6	×5	×6	×3	×3	×6
48	21	16	54	45	12	6	18	60

5. 10 + 7 = __17__   11 + 14 = __25__   10 + 12 = __22__   15 + 13 = __28__

B. *Circle the correct answers.* (1 pt. each; 3 total)

6. P.M. means (before, (after)) noon.
7. School starts at 8:30 ((A.M.), P.M.).
8. 12:00 in the day is 12:00 ((noon), midnight).

C. *Write the time each clock shows.* (1 pt. each; 3 total)

9. __6:45__   __6:10__   __3:55__

D. *Write A, S, or M for add, subtract, or multiply.* (1 pt. each; 7 total)

10. __S__ a. How many are left?
    __A__ b. What is the cost of both?
    __S__ c. How much younger was Isaac?
    __M__ d. How much at 15¢ each?
    __A__ e. What was the total bill?
    __M__ f. How many in 4 groups that size?
    __S__ g. What was the change?

E. *Fill in the blanks.* *(1 pt. each; 6 total)*

11. 1 day = __24__ hr.   1 gal. = __4__ qt.   1 qt. = __2__ pt.
12. 3 qt. = __12__ cups   4 hr. = __240__ min.   8 pt. = __16__ cups

F. *Add carefully. Regroup if you can.* *(2 pt. each; 16 total)*

13.
```
   8      4      8      3             94             843
   5      6      4      5     25      51     276     215
   3      6      7      4     17      28      35     726
  +7     +9     +7     +9    +54     +35    +475    +382
  ──     ──     ──     ──    ───     ───    ────   ─────
  23     25     26     21     96     208     786   2,166
```

G. *Multiply carefully. Check by going over your work.* *(2 pt. each; 26 total)*

14.
```
   90     82     46     75     49     63     76
   ×3     ×4     ×6     ×5     ×4     ×7     ×4
  ───    ───    ───    ───    ───    ───    ───
  270    328    276    375    196    441    304
```

15.
```
  512    526    256    143    523    832
   ×4     ×3     ×5     ×3     ×7     ×6
 ─────  ─────  ─────  ─────  ─────  ─────
 2,048  1,578  1,280    429  3,661  4,992
```

H. *Solve these reading problems. Do your work in the space at the right.*
(3 pt. each; 9 total)

16. If the price of soup is $0.53 a can, how much would you pay for 5 cans?

    __$2.65__

17. Several families went to sing for blind Mrs. Sanders. David carried 5 song books into the house, Merlin carried 4, Gary carried 6, and Carl carried 6. How many song books did the boys carry altogether?

    __21 songbooks__

18. If each of the four boys had carried 5 books, how many books would they have carried?

    __20 songbooks__

Subtract points wrong from 100% for score.

Progressing With Arithmetic   Chapter 4 Test   9

41. Chapter 4 Test (First Quarter)

Score _____

Name _____   Date _____

A. *Write the answers to these facts.* (1 pt. each; 28 total)

1.
3 6 10 12 5 9 15 8
$+9$ $+5$ -7 -5 $+9$ -4 -7 $+9$
12 11 3 7 14 5 8 17

2.
7 8 4 12 9 7 5 9
$\times 6$ $\times 5$ $\times 6$ $\times 2$ $\times 6$ $\times 1$ $\times 6$ $\times 4$
42 40 24 24 54 7 30 36

3. $4\overline{)16} = 4$ $2\overline{)14} = 7$ $5\overline{)35} = 7$ $3\overline{)27} = 9$ $4\overline{)28} = 7$ $5\overline{)15} = 3$

4. $3\overline{)21} = 7$ $4\overline{)40} = 10$ $6\overline{)48} = 8$ $5\overline{)5} = 1$ $6\overline{)36} = 6$ $3\overline{)24} = 8$

B. *Write the answers.* (1 pt. each blank; 30 total)

5. $\frac{1}{3}$ of 15 = __5__ $\frac{1}{4}$ of 32 = __8__ $\frac{1}{2}$ of 16 = __8__

6. Write the four facts in this addition–subtraction family.
7, 4, 11   __7 + 4 = 11__   __4 + 7 = 11__   __11 – 7 = 4__   __11 – 4 = 7__

7. Write the four facts in this multiplication–division family.
3, 9, 27   __3 × 9 = 27__   __9 × 3 = 27__   __27 ÷ 3 = 9__   __27 ÷ 9 = 3__

8. Fill in the missing numbers. You will need to multiply.
1 qt. = __4__ cups   1 yd. = __36__ in.   1 day = __24__ hr.
3 yd. = __9__ ft.   4 gal. = __16__ qt.   5 ft. = __60__ in.

9. Write the Arabic numerals for these Roman numerals.
XVII __17__   LX __60__   XXXIV __34__   XLII __42__   XXIX __29__

10. Write the Roman numerals for these Arabic numerals.
12 __XII__   80 __LXXX__   59 __LIX__   44 __XLIV__

11. Write each price in two ways.
four cents __4¢__ __$0.04__   three dollars __$3__ __$3.00__

12. Circle the digit in the thousands' place. 44④,444

13. Write this number in words: 250,008.
__two hundred fifty thousand, eight__

10 Chapter 4 Test

14. Write < or > in each blank.   1,400 _>_ 1,399   5,106 _<_ 5,601

15. a. What time is shown?   b. What part is shaded?

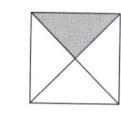

    _2:45_   _6:25_   _2/3_   _1/4_

16. Write the value. _53¢_

C. *Follow the signs. Work carefully.* (2 pt. each; 36 total)

17.
```
    8        27                      925
    6        16       364            127       $1.45       $5.60
    5        43       285            381        3.08        0.46
   +7       +35      +256           +204       +5.37       +6.24
   ──       ───      ────           ────       ─────       ─────
   26       121      905           1,637       $9.90      $12.30
```

18.
```
   50       305       117            800       $9.00       $6.72
  -28      -267       -45           -389       -0.65       -3.58
   ──      ────       ───           ────       ─────       ─────
   22        38        72            411       $8.35       $3.14
```

19.
```
   65        50       943            715        452         830
   ×7        ×9        ×3             ×4         ×6          ×6
   ──       ───     ─────          ─────      ─────       ─────
  455       450     2,829          2,860      2,712       4,980
```

D. *Solve these reading problems. Do your work in the space at the right.* (2 pt. each; 6 total)

20. If 4 boys share 12 cookies equally, how many will each boy get?   _3 cookies_

21. 18 boys each carry 3 chairs. How many chairs can they carry in all?   _54 chairs_

22. Gary is 14 and Randy is 20. Randy is how many years older than Gary?   _6 yr. older_

Subtract points wrong from 100% for score.

Progressing With Arithmetic   Chapter 5 Test   11

51. Chapter 5 Test

Score _____

Name _____   Date _____

A. *Write the answers only.* (1 pt. each; 25 total)

1.
  8 × 5 = 40   7 × 8 = 56   9 × 5 = 45   12 × 7 = 84   8 × 4 = 32   6 × 3 = 18

2.
  9 × 9 = 81   7 × 7 = 49   9 × 7 = 63   6 × 8 = 48   12 × 8 = 96   8 × 9 = 72

3. 9)36 = 4   8)64 = 8   8)8 = 1   9)72 = 8   9)27 = 3

4. 9)18 = 2   8)24 = 3   7)35 = 5   7)42 = 6   9)54 = 6

5. $\frac{1}{8}$ of 64 = __8__ $\frac{1}{9}$ of 63 = __7__ $\frac{1}{7}$ of 28 = __4__

B. *Write the answers.* (1 pt. each blank; 23 total)

6. 10 × 90 = __900__   10 × 45 = __450__   50 × 8 = __400__

7. 100 × 25 = __2,500__   100 × 6 = __600__   60 × 7 = __420__

8. How many days are in April? __30__   in August? __31__

9. Write the value of the underlined digit in this number: 55<u>5</u>,555.   __5 thousands__

10. Write the number that is
    a. 100 more than 37,450   __37,550__
    b. 10,000 less than 492,358   __482,358__

11. Write the correct numbers in the blanks.
    a. 1 yr. = __12__ mo.   d. 4 wk. = __28__ days   g. 8 qt. = __2__ gal.
    b. 3 ft. = __1__ yd.   e. 10 cups = __5__ pt.   h. 5 yd. = __15__ ft.
    c. 1 day = __24__ hr.   f. 21 days = __3__ wk.   i. 2 yd. = __72__ in.

12. Write **add, subtract, multiply,** or **divide.**

    a. How many groups of 4 are in 24? __divide__

    b. 18 is how many more than 9? __subtract__

    c. What is the cost of 6 at 12¢ each? __multiply__

C. Follow the signs. Work carefully. *(2 pt. each; 40 total)*

13.

7,513	8,541	9,462	$4.17	$6.52
− 4,259	− 629	− 3,785	× 3	× 9
3,254	7,912	5,677	$12.51	$58.68

14.

876	957	970	602	804
× 6	× 7	× 8	× 3	× 8
5,256	6,699	7,760	1,806	6,432

15. 4)17 = 4 R 1   3)23 = 7 R 2   5)42 = 8 R 2   8)20 = 2 R 4   7)32 = 4 R 4

16. 8)45 = 5 R 5   6)25 = 4 R 1   4)30 = 7 R 2   7)51 = 7 R 2   3)11 = 3 R 2

D. Solve these reading problems. Do your work in the space at the right.
(3 pt. each; 12 total)

17. Four boys share 16 pencils. How many pencils will each boy have?
    __4 pencils__

18. Laura is learning Psalm 27, which has 14 verses. If she learns two verses each week, how many weeks will it take to learn the psalm?
    __7 weeks__

19. Aunt Grace bought milk for $2.09, bread for $1.19, and oranges for $1.98. What was her total bill?
    __$5.26__

20. Father bought 3 pounds of roofing nails for $1.75 a pound. What was the cost of the nails?
    __$5.25__

Subtract points wrong from 100% for score.

60. Chapter 6 Test

Name _____ Date _____

Score _____

A. *Write the answers.* (1 pt. each; 28 total)

1. 9 × 8 = 72   8 × 7 = 56   12 × 5 = 60   4 × 9 = 36   7 × 9 = 63   12 × 9 = 108   6 × 9 = 54   8 × 8 = 64   7 × 6 = 42

2. 6)48 = 8   8)72 = 9   9)81 = 9   9)54 = 6   8)96 = 12   7)28 = 4

3. a. $\frac{1}{7}$ of 49 = __7__   b. $\frac{1}{3}$ of 36 = __12__   c. $\frac{1}{4}$ of 32 = __8__

4. a. 3 ÷ 4 = __$\frac{3}{4}$__   b. 1 ÷ 5 = __$\frac{1}{5}$__   c. 2 is what part of 3? __$\frac{2}{3}$__

5. a. 10 × 53 = __530__   b. 100 × 14 = __1,400__   c. 30 × 9 = __270__

6. Write **A, S, M,** or **D** for **add, subtract, multiply,** or **divide**. You may use a letter more than once.

    __S__ a. How many more?   __M__ c. Four times as many

    __D__ b. Three boys share   __D__ d. How many 4's in 40?

B. *Follow the directions.* (8 points total)

7. Circle the numbers that divide evenly by 5.

    (30)   47   (85)   (200)   153   (275)   508

8. Circle the numbers that divide evenly by 2.

    (20)   47   (98)   35   61   (84)   (56)   13

C. *Solve and check each problem.* (1 pt. each; 14 total)

9. a. 6,050 − 2,378 = 3,672   3,672 + 2,378 = 6,050   b. 7,000 − 2,859 = 4,141   4,141 + 2,859 = 7,000   c. 8,004 − 7,628 = 376   376 + 7,628 = 8,004

10. 4)368 = 92   92 × 4 = 368   7)289 = 41 R 2   41 × 7 = 287 + 2 = 289   6)21 = 3 R 3   3 × 6 = 18 + 3 = 21   2)845 = 422 R 1   422 × 2 = 844 + 1 = 845

D. *Find the answers.* (2 pt. each; 34 total)

11. Divide. Write any remainders with R.

    2)87 = 43 R 1   3)639 = 213   4)248 = 62   2)146 = 73   7)359 = 51 R 2   5)258 = 51 R 3

12. Divide. Write the remainders as fractions.

    3)14 = $4\frac{2}{3}$ 2)15 = $7\frac{1}{2}$ 5)22 = $4\frac{2}{5}$ 4)247 = $61\frac{3}{4}$ 3)214 = $71\frac{1}{3}$

13. Follow the signs. Work carefully.

    $3.29 + 5.86 + 7.65 = $16.80

    $8.05 − 2.98 = $5.07

    $20.00 − 7.45 = $12.55

    $7.58 × 6 = $45.48

    $8.09 × 7 = $56.63

    5)$3.05 = $0.61

E. *Solve these reading problems. Do your work in the space at the right.* (3 pt. each; 12 total)

14. If 3 boys share 2 candy bars, what part of a candy bar will each boy have?

    $\frac{2}{3}$ candy bar

15. Grandpa Witmer has plenty of time to read. He wants to read through the *Martyrs Mirror*, a book with 1,141 pages. Already Grandpa has read 655 pages. How many pages does he still have to read?

    486 pages

16. A service station ordered 30 spark plugs. How many cars could they service if each car takes 4 spark plugs? How many would be left over?

    7 cars, 2 spark plugs left

17. What is the cost of 6 spark plugs at $1.87 each?

    $11.22

Subtract points wrong from 100% for score.

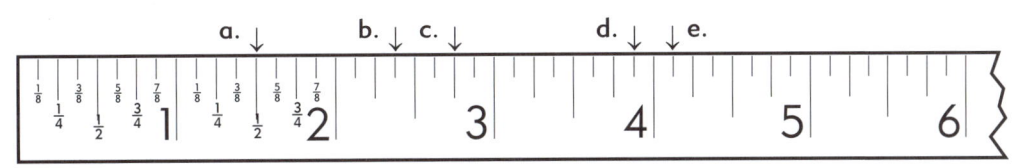

70. Chapter 7 Test

A. *Write the answers.* (1 pt. each blank; 29 total)

1. Count by fourths from $\frac{1}{4}$ to 2 as you would on a ruler.

   $\frac{1}{4}$ $\frac{1}{2}$ $\frac{3}{4}$ 1 $1\frac{1}{4}$ $1\frac{1}{2}$ $1\frac{3}{4}$ 2

2. a. 1 whole = __3__ thirds   b. 4 wholes = __8__ halves   c. 3 = __12__ fourths

3. a. $1\frac{1}{2}$ = __3__ halves   b. $3\frac{1}{2}$ = __7__ halves   c. $1\frac{1}{4}$ = __5__ fourths

4. Write with numbers. a. five and three-fourths __$5\frac{3}{4}$__   b. two and five-eighths __$2\frac{5}{8}$__

5. Write **denominator** or **numerator** in each blank.

   a. $\frac{3}{5}$ → __numerator__

          → __denominator__

   b. The __denominator__ tells how many parts are in the whole thing.

6. Write < or > between each pair of fractions.

   a. $\frac{1}{3}$ __<__ $\frac{2}{3}$ b. $\frac{1}{2}$ __>__ $\frac{1}{3}$ c. $\frac{4}{5}$ __>__ $\frac{3}{5}$ d. $\frac{3}{5}$ __<__ $\frac{3}{4}$

7. Which two pairs of fractions in number 6 are **like fractions**? Write the letters. __a__ __c__

8. Fill in the blanks.
   a. 1 lb. = __16__ oz.   c. 1 yr. = __52__ wk.   e. 1 ton = __2,000__ lb.
   b. 1 yr. = __365__ days   d. $\frac{1}{2}$ lb. = __8__ oz.   f. $\frac{1}{4}$ ft. = __3__ in.

B. *Follow the directions.* (2 pt. each; 26 total)

9. Fill in the blanks.
   a. 4 lb. = __64__ oz.   c. 2 tons = __4,000__ lb.   e. 10 days = __$1\frac{3}{7}$__ wk.
   b. 9 ft. = __3__ yd.   d. 8 qt. = __2__ gal.   f. 7 pt. = __$3\frac{1}{2}$__ qt.

10. Write what measurement on the ruler each arrow points to.
    a. __$1\frac{1}{2}$__ in.   b. __$2\frac{3}{8}$__ in.   c. __$2\frac{3}{4}$__ in.   d. __$3\frac{7}{8}$__ in.   e. __$4\frac{1}{8}$__ in.

16   Chapter 7 Test

11. Measure the line after each letter, and write its length in the blank.

$1\frac{5}{8}$ in.   a. ─────────

$3\frac{1}{2}$ in.   b. ──────────────────────

(Lines shown here are reduced copy of pupil's test.)

C. Find the answers. *(2 pt. each; 30 total)*

12. Multiply to find the missing numbers in these pairs of equivalent fractions.

   a. $\frac{2}{3} = \frac{6}{9}$ b. $\frac{1}{2} = \frac{6}{12}$ c. $\frac{3}{4} = \frac{6}{8}$ d. $\frac{1}{4} = \frac{4}{16}$ e. $\frac{2}{3} = \frac{4}{6}$

13. Divide to change these fractions to equivalent fractions.

   a. $\frac{3}{12} = \frac{1}{4}$ b. $\frac{2}{6} = \frac{1}{3}$ c. $\frac{4}{8} = \frac{1}{2}$ d. $\frac{2}{16} = \frac{1}{8}$ e. $\frac{6}{10} = \frac{3}{5}$

14. Divide. Express the remainders as fractions.

$7\overline{)30}$ = $4\frac{2}{7}$ $5\overline{)258}$ = $51\frac{3}{5}$ $3\overline{)187}$ = $62\frac{1}{3}$ $2\overline{)849}$ = $424\frac{1}{2}$ $6\overline{)427}$ = $71\frac{1}{6}$

D. Solve these reading problems. Do your work in the space at the right. *(3 pt. each; 12 total)*

15. The Shank family was traveling to Iowa for the yearly Bible conference. They drove 502 miles on the first day and 487 miles on the second day. How much farther did they drive on the first day than on the second day?   **15 mi.**

16. If Father drove 50 miles each hour, how far did the family travel in 5 hours?   **250 mi.**

17. How many 5-pound bags of potatoes can be filled from a 60-pound bushel?   **12 bags**

18. The four Gospels (Matthew, Mark, Luke, and John) have 28, 16, 24, and 21 chapters. How many chapters are in the four Gospels altogether?   **89 chapters**

Subtract points wrong from 100% for score.

Progressing With Arithmetic   Chapter 8 Test   17

80. Chapter 8 Test (Second Quarter)

Score _____

Name _____   Date _____

A. *Write the answers only.* (1 pt. each; 36 total)

1.
10	8	9	15	13	3	11	5
− 8	+ 7	+ 5	− 6	− 9	+ 9	− 7	+ 8
2	15	14	9	4	12	4	13

2.
8	7	9	5	12	9	6	8
× 7	× 6	× 8	× 7	× 7	× 7	× 9	× 6
56	42	72	35	84	63	54	48

3. $4\overline{)28} = 7 \quad 7\overline{)35} = 5 \quad 9\overline{)81} = 9 \quad 6\overline{)72} = 12 \quad 8\overline{)64} = 8$

4. 10 × 85 = __850__   100 × 43 = __4,300__   30 × 5 = __150__

5. 80 × 8 = __640__   20 + 4 = __24__   15 + 13 = __28__

6. 16 + 8 = __24__   18 − 3 = __15__ $\frac{1}{5}$ of 25 = __5__

7. $\frac{1}{3}$ of 27 = __9__   3 ÷ 4 = __$\frac{3}{4}$__   1 ÷ 5 = __$\frac{1}{5}$__

8. 1 lb. = __16__ oz.   1 yr. = __365__ days   1 qt. = __4__ cups

B. *Solve and check each problem.* (3 pt. each; 9 total)
(Count 2 pt. for each division and 1 pt. for each check.)

9. a. $5\overline{)70} = 14$ 14 × 5 = 70

b. $3\overline{)257} = 85 \text{ R } 2$ 85 × 3 = 255; 255 + 2 = 257

c. $6\overline{)624} = 104$ 104 × 6 = 624

18   Chapter 8 Test

C. *Follow the directions.* (1 pt. each blank; 21 total)

10. Place commas correctly. Then write the numbers with words.

   a. 14,005   fourteen thousand, five

   b. 209,078   two hundred nine thousand, seventy-eight

11. a. Write Arabic numerals: XIV = 14   XLVII = 47

   b. Write Roman numerals: 25 = XXV   69 = LXIX

12. Write < or > between each pair.

   a. 13,099 < 14,100   b. $\frac{1}{4}$ < $\frac{1}{2}$ c. $15 > $0.15

13. Write **A.M.** or **P.M.** in the blank.

   Eight o'clock in the morning is 8:00   A.M.

14. Measure the line after each letter, and write its length in the blank.

   $1\frac{3}{4}$ in.   a. _____

   $4\frac{3}{8}$ in.   b. _____

   (Lines shown here are reduced copy of pupil's test.)

15. a. Reduce to lowest terms: $\frac{4}{12} = \frac{1}{3}$ $\frac{12}{16} = \frac{3}{4}$ $\frac{4}{20} = \frac{1}{5}$

   b. Find the missing numbers: $\frac{1}{3} = \frac{3}{9}$ $\frac{3}{4} = \frac{6}{8}$ $\frac{2}{4} = \frac{6}{12}$

16. Fill in the missing numbers.

   a. 3 tons = 6,000 lb.   b. 8 qt. = 2 gal.   c. 5 ft. = $1\frac{2}{3}$ yd.

17. Write the value of the bills and coins below. (2 pt.) $30.90

   1 twenty-dollar bill, 2 five-dollar bills, 3 quarters, 1 nickel, 1 dime

Progressing With Arithmetic   Chapter 8 Test   19

D. *Solve the problems. (2 pt. each; 24 total)*

18. a. 6 + 5 + 3 + 2 + 7 = __23__

  b. ▽6 — ☐×5 — ⬡÷3 — ◇−6 — ☐×9 — ◯+3 = __39__

19.
9,174	$21.08	7,000	5,080	$42.73
2,806	17.75	− 1,378	− 1,496	− 15.65
285	+ 34.62	5,622	3,584	$27.08
+ 3,564	$73.45			
15,829				

20.
736	498	$5.16	88	242½
× 9	× 4	× 7	4)352	2)485
6,624	1,992	$36.12		

E. *Solve these reading problems. Do your work in the space at the right.*
(2 pt. each; 10 total)

21. Delmar bought a hammer for $7.79 and 2 pounds of nails for $0.69 a pound. What was his total bill?
  __$9.17__

22. If Wanda's bill is $8.37, how much change should she get from $10.00?
  __$1.63__

23. If 4 girls share 26 marbles, how many marbles will each girl have?
  __6 marbles, 2 left__

24. Abraham lived to be 175 years old. His son Isaac lived to be five years older. How old was Isaac?
  __180 yr.__

25. Blue Mountain Church has 18 benches. If 7 people sit on each bench, how many people can be seated on the benches?
  __126 people__

Subtract points wrong from 100% for score.

Handbook
of Terms and Rules

Page numbers in parentheses tell where additional information is found.

Addition (14)
1. The answer to an addition problem is the **sum**.
2. An **addend** is one of the numbers added together to make a sum.

A.M. (46)
Before noon (from Latin *ante meridiem*).

Arabic numerals (66)
Numerals written the way we usually write them, using the figures 0, 1, 2, 3, 4, 5, 6, 7, 8, and 9.

Area (310, See also *Geometry*.)
The measure of surface space. To find the area of a square or rectangle, multiply the length times the width. The answer is given in square units.

Average (270)
A balance between smallest and greatest in a group of numbers.
To find the average of a group of numbers
1. Add all the numbers;
2. Then divide the sum by the number of addends.

Common factor (241)
A number that is a factor of two or more numbers.
      Example: 3 is a **common factor** of 6 and 9.

Change (49, 290)
To find change, subtract the cost of an item from the amount you would give the clerk, or "count it out" as you lay out the coins.

```
    $2.00    money given
  - 1.38    cost of purchase
    $0.62    change
```

$1.38, (penny)—$1.39, (penny)—$1.40, (dime)—$1.50, (quarter)—$1.75, (quarter)—$2.00

Decimals (286, 288)
1. A **decimal** is a number with a decimal point and digits on both sides of the decimal point. The first two places after the decimal point are **tenths** and **hundredths**.
    Examples: 7.5 18.26 0.3
2. The **decimal point** is the dot between the whole number and the first decimal place.
3. A **decimal fraction** is a decimal less than one.
    Examples: 0.7 0.18
4. When adding or subtracting decimals, the decimal points must all be lined up one under the other.

Denominator (76, See also *Fractions*.)
The bottom number of a fraction. It tells into how many parts a whole thing is divided.

Digit (24)
One of the characters used to write numerals. The digits used in our number system are 0, 1, 2, 3, 4, 5, 6, 7, 8, and 9.

Digital Value (24, 48)
The value of a digit regardless of its position in a numeral.

Distance, Rate, Time (232)
1. To find the distance, multiply the rate and the time.
    distance = rate × time
    Example: 60 miles per hour × 3 hours = 180 miles
2. To find the rate, divide the distance by the time.
    rate = distance ÷ time
    Example: 110 miles ÷ 2 hours = 55 miles per hour

Division
1. Parts of a division problem. (84, 86)
    a. The answer to a division problem is called the **quotient**.
    b. The **dividend** is the number that is divided into parts. *Six* is the dividend in both of these examples: 2)6   6 ÷ 3
    c. The **divisor** tells into how many parts the dividend is divided. *Four* is the divisor in both of these examples: 4)12   8 ÷ 4
    d. A **remainder** is the part of a division answer that shows how many are left after the dividend is divided into groups.
2. The steps for solving division problems are Divide, Multiply, Compare, Subtract, Compare, Bring down. (86, 116)

3. To check the answer to a division problem, multiply the quotient by the divisor. If there is a remainder, add it on. The answer is the dividend. (117, 124)

$$3 \overline{)68}^{\,22\ R\ 2} \qquad \begin{array}{r} 22 \\ \times\ 3 \\ \hline 66 \\ +\ 2 \\ \hline 68 \end{array}$$

Divisibility rules (121, 318)
    a. If a number ends with 0, 2, 4, 6, or 8, it is divisible by 2.
    b. If a number ends with 5 or 0, it is divisible by 5.
    c. If a number ends with 0, it is divisible by 10.

Estimate (292)
    An answer that is not exact, but gives us an idea of what the exact answer is.

Factor (56, 168, See also *Multiplication*.)
    A number that is multiplied to form a product. The multiplier and the multiplicand are both factors.
    Examples: $3 \times 7 = 21$ 3 and 7 are factors of 21
                          2, 3, 4, and 6 are all factors of 12

Fractions

Fraction words

1. The **denominator** is the bottom number of a fraction. It tells into how many parts a whole thing is divided. The **numerator** is the top part of a fraction. It tells how many of the parts are included. (76)

$$\frac{3}{4} \begin{array}{l} \text{— numerator} \\ \text{— denominator} \end{array}$$

2. **Like fractions** have the same denominator. (134)
    Example: $\frac{3}{5}$ and $\frac{1}{5}$ are like fractions.

3. **Equivalent fractions** are equal in value. The fraction with smaller numbers is in **lower terms**. (137, 162)
    Example: $\frac{6}{12}, \frac{2}{4}$, and $\frac{1}{2}$ are all equivalent fractions.
               $\frac{2}{4}$ is in lower terms.
               $\frac{1}{2}$ is in lowest terms.

4. A **proper fraction** is less than one whole unit. The numerator is less than the denominator. (238)
    Example: $\frac{4}{7}$

5. An **improper fraction** has enough parts to make one whole unit or more. The numerator is equal to or greater than the denominator. (238)
    Examples: $\frac{5}{5}$ $\frac{4}{3}$

6. A **mixed number** is the combination of a whole number and a fraction. (136)
   Example: $5\frac{1}{2}$

Working with fractions

1. To find a fractional part of a number, divide by the denominator of the fraction. If the numerator is more than one, also multiply by the numerator. (78, 262)
   Example: $\frac{1}{3}$ of 24 = 24 ÷ 3 = 8
   $\frac{2}{3}$ of 24 = 24 ÷ 3 = 8, then 2 × 8 = 16

2. To find an equivalent fraction, multiply or divide the numerator and the denominator by the same number. (138, 144)
   Examples: $\frac{3 \times 2}{4 \times 2} = \frac{6}{8}$ $\frac{12 \div 6}{18 \div 6} = \frac{2}{3}$

3. To **reduce** a fraction to lower terms, divide the numerator and the denominator by the same number. (144)
   Example: $\frac{5 \div 5}{10 \div 5} = \frac{1}{2}$

4. To find how many fractional parts are in a whole number, multiply the number by the number of parts in one whole. (139)
   Example: How many sixths are in 4? 4 × 6 = 24

5. To add or subtract fractions, the denominators must be the same. Add or subtract the numerators and keep the same denominator. (240, 248)

   $$\frac{1}{5} + \frac{3}{5} = \frac{4}{5} \qquad \frac{1}{4} = \frac{2}{8}, \; +\frac{1}{8} = \frac{1}{8}, \; = \frac{3}{8}$$

6. To change an improper fraction to a whole number or mixed number, divide the numerator by the denominator. (242)
   Examples: $\frac{8}{4}$ 8 ÷ 4 = 2 $\frac{12}{5}$ 12 ÷ 5 = $2\frac{2}{5}$

Geometry

1. A **rectangle** has four straight sides and four square corners. Opposite sides are equal. (299)

2. A **square** has four **equal** sides and four square corners. (299)

3. A **triangle** has three straight sides and three corners. (299)

4. The circle. (303)
   a. A **circle** is formed by an even curve with no corners.
   b. A **diameter** is the distance across a circle, going through the center.
   c. A **radius** is the distance from any point on the circle to the center.

5. The **perimeter** is the distance around a straight-sided figure. To find the perimeter of a shape, add the lengths of all the sides. (306)

6. **Area** is the measure of surface space.
   To find the area of a square or rectangle, multiply the length times the width. The answer is given in square units. (310)

Indefinite units

Units of measure that are not all exactly the same because they vary from person to person. The span and the cubit are indefinite units. (298)

Measures

Working with measures

1. Know your **key numbers**. When a measure is stated like this: 1 yard = 3 feet, 3 is the key number for yards and feet.
   Because 1 hour = 60 minutes, 60 is the key number for hours and minutes. (60)
2. To change larger units of measure to smaller units, **multiply** by the key number. (60)
   Example: 4 hours × 60 = 240 minutes
3. To change smaller units of measure to larger units, **divide** by the key number. (80)
   Example: 60 inches ÷ 12 = 5 feet
4. When adding measures, keep the sum in simplest form. In the following example, 7 inches + 8 inches = 15 inches. Since that is larger than 1 foot, change 12 of the inches to 1 foot. (204)

$$\begin{array}{r} 3 \text{ feet } 7 \text{ inches} \\ + 2 \text{ feet } 8 \text{ inches} \\ \hline 5 \text{ feet } 15 \text{ inches} = 6 \text{ feet } 3 \text{ inches} \end{array}$$

5. When subtraction of measures requires borrowing from a larger unit, reduce the larger unit by one, and increase the smaller unit by the amount of the key number. (210)

$$\begin{array}{rcl} 4 \text{ weeks } 3 \text{ days} & = & 3 \text{ weeks } 10 \text{ days} \\ - 1 \text{ week } 6 \text{ days} & & - 1 \text{ week } 6 \text{ days} \\ \hline & & 2 \text{ weeks } 4 \text{ days} \end{array}$$

Mixed number (136, See also *Fractions*.)
The combination of a whole number and a fraction.

Multiple (166)

A number that is the product of another one.
Examples: 10 is a multiple of 2 and of 5.
6, 12, 18, 24, and 30 are all multiples of 3.

Multiplication

Parts of a multiplication problem.
1. The answer to a multiplication problem is the **product**. (56)
2. A **factor** is one of the numbers multiplied to make a product. (56)
3. The **multiplicand** is the factor that tells the value of one group. (168)
   Five is the multiplicand in both of these examples: 2 × 5 $\begin{array}{r} 5 \\ \times\ 4 \\ \hline \end{array}$
4. The **multiplier** is the factor that tells how many times a group is repeated. (168)
   Three is the multiplier in both of these examples: 3 × 7 $\begin{array}{r} 6 \\ \times\ 3 \\ \hline \end{array}$
5. A **partial product** is the answer from multiplying by one digit in a problem that has more than one digit in the multiplier. (226)

$$\begin{array}{r} 285 \\ \times\ 47 \\ \hline 1995 \\ 1140 \end{array}$$ partial products

Multiplication short cuts (106, 177)
   To multiply a number by 10, write 0 after it.
   To multiply a number by 100, write 00 after it.
   To multiply a number by 1,000, write 000 after it.

Number family (22, 74)

The related facts that are made with the same numbers.
This is a number family of addition and subtraction facts:
   2 + 7 = 9   7 + 2 = 9   9 − 7 = 2   9 − 2 = 7
This is a number family of multiplication and division facts:
   3 × 5 = 15   5 × 3 = 15   15 ÷ 5 = 3   15 ÷ 3 = 5

Numerator (76, See also *Fractions*.)

The top number of a fraction. It tells how many of the parts are included.

Perimeter (306, See also *Geometry*.)

The distance around a straight-sided figure. To find the perimeter of a shape, add the lengths of all the sides.

Period (176)

A group of three digits for ones, tens, and hundreds. A period can represent units, thousands, or millions. Periods are separated by commas.

Place value (24, 48)

The position of a digit, which indicates its value as ones, tens, hundreds, thousands, and so on.

P.M. (46)

After noon (from Latin *post meridiem*).

Roman numerals (66, 68, 280)

A number system used by the Romans of long ago. In this system, I, V, X, and other letters are used to represent numbers.

$$I = 1 \quad V = 5 \quad X = 10 \quad L = 50 \quad C = 100$$

These rules will help you to read Roman numerals:
1. If a letter is followed by an equal or smaller value, add the two values.
$$XVII = X + V + I + I = 17$$
2. If a smaller letter comes before a larger letter, subtract the smaller value from the larger. $IX = 10 - 1 = 9$
3. If a smaller letter comes between two larger letters, first subtract the small value from the one after it. Then add.
$$XIV \quad 5 - 1 = 4 \quad 10 + 4 = 14$$

Round numbers (178, 180)

Numbers that are not exact and usually end with one or more zeroes.
Follow these rules to round numbers correctly.
1. To round to the nearest ten—round up if the ones' digit is greater than 5; round down if it is less than 5.
2. To round to the nearest hundred—round up if the tens' digit is greater than 5; round down if it is less than 5.
3. To the nearest thousand—round up if the hundreds' digit is greater than 5; round down if it is less than 5.

Scale drawing (308)

A drawing in which a small measure represents a larger unit of measure.

Subtraction (20)

1. The answer to a subtraction problem is the **difference**.
2. The **minuend** is the top, or larger, number.
3. The **subtrahend** is the bottom, or smaller, number.

Unit

1. The number *one*, as in "units, tens, hundreds."
2. One whole thing, such as "a whole unit has three thirds."
3. One of a type of measure. Feet, minutes, quarts, and pounds are all units of measure.

Whole number (140)

A number that does not include a fraction.

Index

addends 12
addition 12
   basic facts 17
   carrying 14
   carrying twice 16
   checking 13, 124
   column 13
   unlike fractions 248, 250, 252
   mixed numbers 244, 250
   number family 22
   reading problems 19
   regrouping addends 54
   units of measure 202, 204, 206
Arabic numerals 66
area 310, 312
average 270
bar graphs 200
Bible measures 298
change 49
   counting 290
   finding 49
checking
   addition 13, 124
   division 117, 124, 164
   multiplication 125, 344
   subtraction 23, 125
circle 303
column addition 13
common denominator 246
common factors 241
common multiples 246

cubit 298
decimal point 282
decimal fractions 286
denominator 76
diameter 303
difference 20
digital value 48
dividend 84
divisibility rules
   for 2 and 5 121
   for 10 318
division 74
   checking 117, 124, 164
   long division 116, 154, 160
   of money 129
   reading problems 83, 105, 110
   steps 116
   to form a fraction 120
   two-digit divisors 326, 328, 338, 340
divisor 84
English measure 298
estimating 292
even numbers 58, 84
factors 56, 241
fractions 76
   by dividing 120
   comparing 134, 135
   decimal 286
   division remainders 122, 164
   equivalent 137, 138, 144

Index

finding part of a number 77, 78, 262
like fractions 134
lowest terms 162
mixed numbers 136, 140, 242
on rulers 140, 142
proper, improper 238, 242
reducing 144, 162
simplest form 244
unlike fractions 248, 250

fraction terms
denominator 76
numerator 76

gram 304

graphs
bar 200
picture 198

greater than, symbol 26

improper fractions 238, 242

kilogram 304

less than, symbol 26

lowest common denominator 246

liquid measure 57

liter 304

measures
Bible 298
changing 60, 80
English 298
metric 300, 304
regrouping 204, 210

measure equivalents
liquid measure 57
time 46, 97, 149
length 80, 298
weight 147

metric measure 300, 304

minuend 20

mixed numbers 136, 140, 238
adding and subtracting 244
from improper fractions 242
multiplying 264

money
coins 40
dividing 129
dollar sign and
  decimal point 42, 282
finding change 49, 290

multiple 166

multiplicand 168

multiplication 56
by 10 or 100 106
by 1,000 177
carrying in 62
checking 125, 344
mixed numbers 264
reading problems 61
two- and three-digit 58, 322, 332

multiplier 168

number family 22, 74

number systems
Arabic 66
Roman 66, 68

numerator 76

odd numbers 58, 84

partial product 226

picture graphs 198

perimeter 306

period 176

place value 48, 176
ones, tens, hundreds 14
to ten thousands 24
millions 176
period 176

process terms
  addends 12
  difference 20
  dividend 84
  divisor 84
  factor 56
  minuend 20
  partial product 226
  product 56
  quotient 84
  remainder 86
  subtrahend 20
  sum 12

product 56

proper fractions 238

puzzle page 94, 174, 258, 358

quotient 84

radius 303

reading problems
  addition key words 19
  distance, rate, time 232
  dividing 83, 105, 110
  estimating 292
  steps in solving 148
  subtraction key words 27, 37
  two-step 158
  multiplying 61
  sketches 284
  without numbers 192

rectangle 94

reducing fractions 144, 162
  lowest terms 162
  simplest form 244

remainder 86

right angle 299

Roman numerals 66, 68, 280

rounding numbers 178, 180
  money 186

rulers 140, 142

scale drawing 308

span 298

square 94

square measure 310, 312

subtraction 20
  borrowing in 32
  borrowing twice 36
  checking 23, 125
  from zero 38, 126
  mixed numbers 244, 250
  number family 22
  reading problems 27, 37
  units of measure 202, 210, 212
  unlike fractions 250, 252

subtrahend 20

sum 12

symbols
  < and > 26
  ' and " 298

telling time 44
  A.M., P.M. 46
  equivalents 46, 97

"times-and" problems 60

triangle 94

units of measure
  adding 202, 204
  changing units 60, 80, 102, 146
  length 80
  subtracting 202, 210, 212
  time 46, 206, 212

whole numbers 140

zero
  in division 272
  in multiplication 108, 110
  in subtraction 38, 126